Writers for Young Adults

Writers for Young Adults

Ted Hipple
Editor

VOLUME 3

CHARLES SCRIBNER'S SONS
Macmillan Reference USA
Simon & Schuster Macmillan
New York

Simon & Schuster and Prentice Hall International
London   Mexico City   New Delhi   Singapore
Sydney   Toronto

Library of Congress Cataloging-in-Publication Data
Writers for young adults / Ted Hipple, editor.
     p.   cm.
    Summary: Contains articles on writers whose works are popular with
young adults, including contemporary authors, such as Francesca Lia
Block and Maya Angelou, and classic authors, such as Sir Arthur
Conan Doyle and Louisa May Alcott.
    ISBN 0-684-80475-1 (v. 1 : hardcover). — ISBN 0-684-80476-X (v. 2
: hardcover). — ISBN 0-684-80477-8 (v. 3 : hardcover). — ISBN
0-684-80474-3 (set : hardcover)
    1. Young adult literature, American—Bio-bibliography—
Dictionaries.   2. Young adult literature, English—Bio-
bibliography—Dictionaries.   3. Authors, American—Biography—
Dictionaries.   4. Authors, English—Biography—Dictionaries.
[1. Authors, American.   2. Authors, English.   3. Young adult
literature.]   I. Hipple, Theodore W.
PS490.W75   1997
810.9'9283'03   97-6890
[B]—DC21   CIP
                                         AC

5 7 9 11 13 15 17 19 20 18 16 14 12 10 8 4

Printed in the United States of America. The paper used in this publication meets the
minimum requirements of the American National Standard for Information Sciences—
Permanence of Paper for Printed Library Materials, ANSI Z39.48–1984.

Contents

Writers for Young Adults

Richard Peck

(1934-)

by Donald R. Gallo

In a short story called "I Go Along," Richard Peck's teenage narrator, Gene, attends a poetry reading and sees a living poet for the first time in his life. One of the many things that surprise Gene is that the poet is "not dressed like a poet." The guy is wearing Levi's, boots, and a "heavy-duty belt buckle," looking pretty much like Gene and his buddies (p. 188).

If you ever get to meet Richard Peck, even though he has written poems, do not expect him to dress like the poet or Gene in that story. Envision just the opposite: carefully fitted sports jacket, sharply creased slacks, starched dress shirt, perfectly knotted tie, polished shoes—all very neat. Standing tall, trim, and straight—like an obedient son remembering his mother's admonitions—he speaks the way he looks: crisply and somewhat formally.

If you get to speak with him, you'll probably find him to be charming, witty, personable, considerate, and thought-

All quotations not attributed to a specific publication were made by Richard Peck during interviews in New York City in June and December 1987 and appear by permission of Richard Peck.

> *"Love may be eternal, but romance has a time limit.*

There is an article about S. E. Hinton in volume 2 and an article about Paul Zindel later in this volume.

provoking. You will surely hear him proclaim one or more of his one-sentence bits of witty wisdom (some people call them Peck-isms), such as "[L]ove may be eternal, but romance has a time limit" ("The Invention of Adolescence," p. 188). Or "Watching television is what you do with your life when you don't want to live it." And he has said to many teenagers and their teachers: "Nobody but a reader ever became a writer." He'll certainly make you think.

Richard Peck is one of the most highly regarded authors who write for young people. In a survey of leaders from the Assembly on Literature for Adolescents of the National Council of Teachers of English (ALAN) conducted in 1988 (Gallo, "Who Are the Most Important YA Authors?"), Peck is noted as the third most important individual in the field of writing for young adults. (Only S. E. Hinton and Paul Zindel received more votes.) Nine of his nineteen novels for teenagers have been designated as Best Books for Young Adults by the American Library Association, with *Are You in the House Alone?* being listed by that same organization as one of the 100 "Best of the Best" books published between 1967 and 1992. Then, in 1990, the School Library Journal and the Young Adult Services Division of the American Library Association named Richard Peck the recipient of their Margaret A. Edwards Award. Peck was only the second person to receive this prestigious award (S. E. Hinton was the first) that is given to authors "whose book or books have provided young adults with a window through which they can view the world and which will help them to grow and understand themselves and their role in society." He has also received other awards for his work, including the 1990 ALAN Award for his "outstanding contributions to young adult literature."

Beginnings

Although Richard Peck says he always wanted to be a writer, he did not write his first novel until he was 37 years old. He had been born in the Midwestern town of Decatur in Central Illinois, surrounded by a supportive, hard-working, extended family, including his grandparents and four great aunts. Decatur later provided Peck with the model for the town of Dunthrope in *Dreamland Lake* and *Representing Super Doll* as well as Bluff City in the turn-of-the-century Blossom Culp novels.

His mother, trained as a dietician, cooked wonderful meals and passed on to Richard a love of books and reading. His father, raised on a farm and then injured in France during World War I, ran a gas station on the edge of town that was a gathering place for "old truckers and farmers and railroaders" who "hung out, telling tales," Peck says in *Something About the Author Autobiography Series* (p. 177). On his grandparents Walnut Grove Farm, Richard listened to stories of his relatives' Victorian pasts, which may account for his views that life in the past was much more interesting than life today. And if you have read several of Peck's novels, you will notice that many of them contain an older person, usually somebody a little eccentric and quite spunky, whose wise advice provides guidance to the confused teenage characters. Among the most memorable are Uncle Miles (named after his own great-uncle) who appears in *The Ghost Belonged to Me* (the first of the Blossom Culp books), and Kate's great-grandmother, Polly Prior, in *Remembering the Good Times*.

In school, like at home, he grew up with a clear set of values about proper behavior. In his autobiography *Anonymously Yours*, Peck credits his dancing teacher. Miss Van Dyke, with teaching him proper social behavior (p. 37). Proper grammar and careful writing were taught by all his teachers, he asserts in "The Invention of Adolescence and Other Thoughts on Youth": "the format of grammar . . . the symmetry of sentences, the shapes of paragraphs. The sense of words and their sounds" (p. 183). His most influential teacher seems to have been Miss Franklin. As a senior in the college-bound English class at Decatur High School, he was assured by Miss Frankling that she alone possessed the power to get him into the college of his choice. And if he intended to succeed in her class, he had to write about something more interesting than himself. In fact, he says she wrote on his first paper: "NEVER EXPRESS YOURSELF AGAIN ON MY TIME. FIND A MORE INTERESTING TOPIC." The shock of that response sent him to the library and set in motion a lifetime of research that has provided Peck with a load of advice for young writers to whom he speaks at schools and libraries around the country. It was Miss Franklin who taught him that "writing is not self-expression. Writing is communication . . . "And "the only real writing is rewrit-

dietician person trained in food and nutrition

Victorian referring to the period during the reign of Queen Victoria of England (1837–1901)

The United States fought a war in **Korea** from 1950 to 1953 to defend South Korea against Communist North Korea. The war took over 54,000 American lives and ended in a draw.

ing." "She also taught us how to gather material more interesting than ourselves and to pin it to a page," Peck says in *Something about the Author Autobiography Series* (p. 181).

With a scholarship at DePauw University and the threat of being drafted and sent to Korea in the early 1950s, Richard studied hard. Aiming to be a teacher he graduated in 1956.

Journeys

Having grown up in the atmosphere of central Illinois which the local residents thought was the center of the universe, young Richard could only imagine what life was like elsewhere. Three experiences brought him a wider view of the world that changed his life significantly. His first was a summer vacation visit with a relative in New York City when he was sixteen. He knew immediately that "this was the place I'd been homesick for all along . . . ." (*Something About the Author Series,* p. 180). Then, for his junior year in college, he received permission to study abroad. His adventure began with passage on the luxury liner *Ile de France* and continued with the study of British history and literature at Exeter University, with side trips through the British countryside. Peck's experiences later allowed him to set parts of one of his adult novels and three of his young adult novels in England. A variety of more recent sea voyages on cruise ships provided Peck with settings for *Those Summer Girls I Never Met* and *Unfinished Portrait of Jessica.*

As journeys were important to Richard Peck's personal growth, so too are journeys important to the growth of major characters in almost all of his novels. In "An Interview with Richard Peck," he told Paul Janeczko: "In all of my novels, the main character takes a trip, a geographic trip. They all slip the bonds of peer group and family for an independent look at the world" (p. 97). Although that is not the case in *Remembering the Good Times* or *The Last Safe Place on Earth,* it certainly is in *Father Figure, Representing Super Doll, Those Summer Girls I Never Met, Unfinished Portrait of Jessica,* and all the Blossom Culp books.

Richard, who worked at a variety of jobs to earn the money for his first two trips, received free transportation for the third significant trip of his life: he joined the army immediately after college and was sent to Germany. Two years in the military, he says in *Anonymously Yours,* taught him more than an equal amount of time in college did (p. 79). In addition to polishing his writing skills by ghost writing letters for his fellow soldiers and making up sermons for the post's chaplains, Peck expanded his view of the world by traveling widely throughout Europe.

Lessons

After returning to the States and earning a master's degree at Southern Illinois University, Richard Peck had his first taste of high school teaching at Glenbrook North High School in a suburb of Chicago, a place that later became the setting for *Close Enough to Touch*. He lasted there for two years, after which he worked as a textbook editor in Chicago for two more years, then landed a job at Hunter College and Hunter College High School in New York City in 1965. Except for very brief periods of time living elsewhere, Richard Peck has made New York City his home since then.

His teaching experiences in Illinois and in New York City left him with significant impressions about schools, teenagers, and parents that continue to influence him today. He felt that academic standards were crumbling, students were more concerned about conforming than about achieving, parents were too permissive—beliefs that show themselves clearly in many of his novels, especially *Princess Ashley* and *Remembering the Good Times*. By seeing how students reacted to literature, Peck also learned, he says in *Speaking for Ourselves,* "that a novel must entertain first before it can do anything else" (p. 166). But novels have the potential for teaching that neither teachers nor parents have. In *Love and Death at the Mall* (1994), Peck says that "novels rush in where parents fear to tread" (p. 121). And from the day he quit teaching in 1972 in order to begin a career as a writer, Peck has created characters that contemporary teenagers can recognize, if not always identify with, by their clothing, their language, their problems, and their behaviors.

> *Peck says that "novels rush in where parents fear to tread."*
>
>

Writing

Since his first forays into publishing, Richard Peck has always shown his versatility as a writer. He has edited two collections of essays and three anthologies of poetry for teenagers; written three novels for adults, along with several newspaper pieces, dozens of magazine essays, and numerous book reviews; published several poems, a picture book for children, and several "prayers" such as "A Teenager's Prayer" that includes the line "Give me the understanding that nobody ever grows up in a group so that I can find my own way"; written four short stories, including "Priscilla and the Wimps," which has become one of the most popular short stories ever written for teenagers; and published an autobiography, a book of essays about his writing, chapters in several books for teachers, and, so far, nineteen novels for young people, with a twentieth in production as this is being written (to be titled *Lost in Cyberspace*). Not one of his young adult novels has ever been out of print.

His novels show significant versatility in both form and content: he's written about deadly serious problems of teenage pregnancy (*Don't Look and It Won't Hurt*), rape (*Are You in the House Alone?*), death (*Close Enough to Touch*), and suicide (*Remembering the Good Times*), but he is also a master of satire, as he proves in *Secrets of the Shopping Mall* and *Bel-Air Bambi and the Mall Rats,* as well as the four novels that feature Blossom Culp. He has also written time-travel novels (though they are not technically science fiction) in *Voices After Midnight* as well as the Blossom Culp books, *Ghosts I Have Been, The Dreadful Future of Blossom Culp,* and *Blossom Culp and the Sleep of Death.*

satire a method of writing that uses humor and parody to mock or criticize

The Blossom novels are also extremely funny, as is *Bel-Air Bambo and the Mall Rats* along with parts of almost all of Peck's other novels. "I like satire. I like wordplay. I like whole comic scenes. I like humor to serious intent," he says in *Presenting Richard Peck* (p. 116). He seems to have the most fun with characters' names in *Bel-Air Bambi and the Mall Rats,* where you will find not only the Babcocks—Bambi, Buffie, Brick, Beth, and Bill—but also Jess Neverwood, Justin Thyme, Bob Wire, Gene Poole, Coach "Bear" Bottoms, and the female leader of the Mall Rats, Tanya Hyde.

In fact, if you enjoy wordplay, you'll find numerous examples of it throughout Peck's writing. In *The Ghost Belonged to Me,* for example, Alexander says: "I knew she had not eaten anything since Friday noon in order to get into her coming out dress" (p. 56). And in *Bel-Air Bambi,* knowing that Bambi and Buffie have come to their little town from Los Angeles where there are gangs, Tanya asks what their sign and their colors are. Bambi replies: "Sagittarius" and says she looks best in beige. Tanyas, of course, wants to know, if there are no gangs, who runs the school (pp. 46–47).

Aphorisms abound in Peck's novels as well as his nonfiction. He uses them to comment on the foibles of people and society, especially of teachers, school curricula, and administrators, even though, as Gallo points out in *Presenting Richard Peck,* those statements "are sometimes a bit more erudite that the maturity of the teenager speaking them would warrant" (p. 117). Chelsea, in *Princess Ashley,* for example, says: "In tenth grade you like rumors better than the truth anyway" (p. 24). Or in *Remembering the Good Times,* Buck remarks a little too insightfully: "It's funny how much you want to work before you're old enough to hold a job" (p. 8). Peck obviously wants to convey thought-provoking messages throughout his books for teenagers.

In Peck's novels you will find messages about father-son relationships, mother-daughter relationships, relationships with peers, parental responsibility, teachers' roles, and nostalgia for the past. But probably the most important message Richard Peck conveys in every one of his books is the need for decision-making. He said it most succinctly in a speech at the Children's Literature Festival at the University of Southern Mississippi in 1981 and has repeated it in numerous ways ever since: "YOU WILL NEVER BEGIN TO GROW UP UNTIL YOU START TO ACT AND THINK INDEPENDENTLY OF YOUR PEERS." That theme is evident in Peck's first novel *Dreamland Lake* published in 1973; it is central to the story in *Princess Ashley* published in 1987, and it is the essence of the story in Peck's most recent novel *The Last Safe Place on Earth,* where religious fanaticism threatens to overpower individual rights and independent thinking.

Making readers think is what Richard Peck does best. In the most recent publicity release from Bantam Doubleday Dell about Peck's work, he states: "I want to write novels that ask honest questions about serious issues. A novel is never an answer; it's always a question."

Selected Bibliography

WORKS BY RICHARD PECK

Novels for Young Adults

Don't Look and It Won't Hurt (1972)

Dreamland Lake (1973)

Through a Brief Darkness (1973)

aphorism short saying

foible flaw or shortcoming

erudite scholarly or intellectual

succinct brief and to the point

fanaticism extreme or narrow-minded enthusiasm and devotion

If you like the works of Richard Peck, you might also like the works of other popular writers, such as S.E. Hinton and Paul Zindel..

Representing Superdoll (1974)
The Ghost Belonged to Me (1975)
Are You in the House Alone? (1976)
Ghosts I Have Been (1977)
Father Figure (1978)
Secrets of the Shopping Mall (1979)
Close Enough to Touch (1981)
The Dreadful Future of Blossom Culp (1983)
Remembering the Good Times (1985)
Blossom Culp and the Sleep of Death (1986)
Princess Ashley (1987)
Those Summer Girls I Never Met (1988)
Voices After Midnight (1989)
Unfinished Portrait of Jessica (1991)
Bel-Air Bambi and the Mall Rats (1993)
The Last Safe Place on Earth (1995)

Novels for Adults
Amanda/Miranda (1980)
This Family of Women (1983)
New York Time (1981)

Children's Picture Books
Monster Night at Grandma's House, illustrated by Don Freeman (1977)
Whatever Happened to Thanksgiving? Unpublished manuscript.

Edited Essay Collections
Edge of Awareness: Twenty-five Contemporary Essays, with Ned E. Hoopes (1966)
Leap into Reality: Essays for Now (1973)

Edited Poetry Collections
Mindscapes: Poems for the Real World (1971)
Pictures that Storm Inside My Head: Poems for the Inner You (1976)
Sounds and Silences: Poetry for Now (1970)

Educational Books
A Consumer's Guide to Educational Innovations, with Mortimer Smith and George Weber (1972)

The Creative Word 2, with Stephen N. Judy (1973)

Open Court Correlated Language Arts Program (1967)

Transitions: A Literary Paper Casebook, compiled by Richard Peck (1974)

Urban Studies: A Research Paper Casebook, compiled by Richard Peck (1973)

Self-Published Book

Old Town: A Complete Guide: Strolling, Shopping, Supping, Sipping, 2d edition, with Norman Strasma (1965)

Autobiography

Anonymously Yours (1991)

Love and Death at the Mall: Teaching and Writing for the Literate Young (1994)

Short Stories

"I Go Along." In *Connections: Short Stories by Outstanding Writers for Young Adults.* Edited by Donald R. Gallo. New York: Delacorte, 1989, pp. 184–191.

"Priscilla and the Wimps." In *Sixteen: Short Stories by Outstanding Writers for Young Adults.* Edited by Donald R. Gallo. New York: Delacorte, 1984, pp. 42–45.

"Shadows." In *Visions: Nineteen Short Stories by Outstanding Writers for Young Adults.* Edited by Donald R. Gallo. New York: Delacorte, 1987, pp. 2–9.

"The Size of the Universe." *Southwest Review,* Autumn 1986, pp. 493–509.

Poems

"Early Admission." In *Presenting Richard Peck* by Donald R. Gallo. Boston: Twayne Publishers, 1989, p. 48.

"The Geese." In *Sounds and Silences: Poetry for Now.* Edited by Richard Peck. New York: Delacorte, 1970, p. 9.

"Irish Child." *Chicago Tribune Magazine,* 17 September 1972.

"Jump Shot." In *Mindscapes: Poems for the Real World.* Edited by Richard Peck. New York: Delacorte, 1971, p. 8.

"Lesson in History." *Chicago Tribune Magazine,* 7 July 1974.

"Mission Uncontrolled." In *Mindscapes: Poems for the Real World.* Edited by Richard Peck. New York: Delacorte, 1971, pp. 86–87.

"Nancy." In "Phoenix Nest." Edited by Martin Levin, *Saturday Review,* vol. 52, 21 June 1969, p. 6.

"Street Trio." In "Phoenix Nest." Edited by Martin Levin, *Saturday Review,* vol. 54, 4 September 1971, p. 6.

"TKO." In *Sports Poems.* Edited by R. R. Knudson and P. K. Ebert. New York: Dell Publishing Company, 1971, p. 142.

Chapters in Books

"Nobody but a Reader Ever Became a Writer." In *Authors' Insights: Turning Teenagers into Readers and Writers.* Edited by Donald R. Gallo. Portsmouth, N.H.: Boynton/Cook-Heinemann, 1992, pp. 77–89.

"Problem Novels for Readers Without Any." *In Reading Their World: The Young Adult Novel in the English Classroom.* Edited by Virginia R. Monseau and Gary M. Salvner. Portsmouth, N.H.: Boynton/Cook-Heinemann, 1992, pp. 71–76.

Essays

"Art Deco: The Newest 'Antique.'" *House Beautiful,* August 1973, pp.61–63.

"Can Students Evaluate Their Education?" *The PTA Magazine,* February 1971, pp. 4–7.

"Care and Feeding of the Visiting Author." *Top of the News,* spring 1982, pp. 251–255.

"Coming Full Circle: From Lesson Plans to Young Adult Novels." *Horn Book,* April 1985, pp. 208–215.

"Consciousness-Raising." *American Libraries,* February 1974, pp. 75–76.

"A Conversation with Richard Peck." Dell Publishing Company publicity brochure, n.d.

"Delivering the Goods." *American Libraries,* October 1974, pp. 492–494.

"An Exclusive Interview with Blossom Culp." Dell Publishing Company publicity brochure, 1987.

"From Realism to Melodrama." *American Libraries,* February 1975, pp. 106–108.

"The Genteel Unshelving of a Book." *School Library Journal.* May 1986, pp. 37–39.

"The Great Library-Shelf Witch Hunt." *Booklist,* 1 January 1992, pp. 816–817.

"Growing up Suburban: 'We Don't Use Slang, We're Gifted.'" In "In the YA Corner," *School Library Journal,* October 1985, pp. 118–119.

"In the Country of Teenage Fiction." *American Libraries,* April 1973, pp. 204–207.

"The Invention of Adolescence and Other Thoughts on Youth." *Top of the News,* winter 1983, pp. 182–190.

"It's a World Away and Yet So Close." *New York Times,* 7 October 1972, pp. 4, 12.

"I Was the First Writer I Ever Met." *Voices of Youth Advocates,* October 1981.

"Love Is Not Enough." *School Library Journal,* September 1990, pp. 153–154. Printed also in *Journal of Youth Services in Libraries,* Fall 1990, pp. 35–39.

"Of Rabbits and Roadsters." *American Libraries,* July/August 1974, pp. 360–361.

"People of the World: A Look at Today's Young Adults and Their Needs." *School Library Media Quarterly,* fall 1981, pp. 16–21.

"A Personal Letter from Blossom Culp to Whom It May Concern." Dell Publishing Company publicity brochure, n.d.

"Rape and the Teenage Victim." *Top of the News,* winter 1978, pp. 175–176.

"Richard Peck Discusses Adolescent Rape." Dell Publishing Company publicity release, n.d.

"Richard Peck Responds to National Book Week with 7 Do's and 7 Don'ts for Parents." Avon Books publicity release.

"Some Thoughts on Adolescent Lit." *News from ALAN,* September/October 1975, pp. 4–7.

"St. Charles Is the Last Trolley Left." *New York Times,* 28 January 1973, pp. 3, 17.

"Suicide as a Solution?" Dell Publishing Company publicity brochure, n.d.

"Teenagers' Tastes." *American Libraries,* May 1974, pp. 235–236.

"Ten Questions to Ask About a Novel. *ALAN Newsletter,* spring 1978, pp. 1, 7.

"Traveling in Time." *The ALAN Review,* Winter 1990, pp. 1–3.

"We Can Save Our Schools." *Parents' Magazine & Better Family Living,* September 1971, pp. 51–52, 98–101.

"A Writer from Illinois." *Illinois Libraries,* June 1986, pp. 392–394.

"YA Books in the Decade of the Vanishing Adult." *Top of the News,* winter 1986, pp. 129–131.

"Young Adult Books." *Horn Book,* September/October 1986, p. 619.

Prayers and Credos

"I Read." From acceptance speech for Margaret A. Edwards Award, American Library Association Conference. Chicago, June 1990. Published in *School Library Journal,* September 1990, p. 154, and *Journal of Youth Services in Libraries,* Fall 1990, pp. 38–39.

"A Teenager's Prayer." In "Young Adult Books," *Horn Book,* September/October 1968 p. 621.

"The Fervent Prayer of a Teenager's Parent." *The ALAN Review,* Winter 1987, p. 51.

"A Teacher's Prayer." News from Dell Books, n.d. Reprinted in *The ALAN Review,* Winter 1989, p. 35.

Unpublished Speeches

Speech at Central Connecticut State University, 9 April 1975.

Speech at the Children's Book Council/American Booksellers Association, New Orleans, 24 May 1986.

Speech at the Children's Literature Festival, University of Southern Mississippi, Hattiesburg, 19 March 1981.

WORKS ABOUT RICHARD PECK

Books and Parts of Books

Commire, Anne, ed. *Something About the Author,* 18. Detroit: Gale Research, 1980, pp. 242–244.

Donelson, Kenneth L. and Nilsen Alleen Pace, *Literature for Today's Young Adults.* Glenview, Ill., Scott, Foresman and Company, 1980.

Gallo, Donald R., ed. *Speaking for Ourselves: Autobiographical Sketches by Notable Authors of Books for Young Adults,* Urbana, Ill.: National Council for Teachers of English, 1990, pp. 165–167.

Gunton, Sharon R., ed. *Contemporary Literary Criticism,* 21. Detroit: Gale Research, 1982, pp. 295–301.

Locher, Frances Carol, ed. *Contemporary Authors,* 85–88. Detroit: Gale Research, 1980, pp. 458–459.

Nilsen, Alleen Pace, and Kenneth L. Donelson, *Literature for Today's Young Adults,* 2d ed. Glenview, Ill.: Scott, Foresman and Company, 1985.

Sarkassian, Adele, ed. *Something About the Author Autobiography Series,* Detroit: Gale Research, 1985, vol. 2, pp. 175–186.

Schwartz, Sheila. *Teaching Adolescent Literature: A Humanistic Approach.* Rochelle Park, N.J.: Hayden Book Company, 1979.

Tovey, Janice K. "Writing for the Young Adult Reader: An Analysis of Audience in the Novels of Richard Peck." Master's thesis, Illinois State University, 1988.

Articles

Crew, Hilary. "Blossom Culp and Her Ilk: The Independent Female in Richard Peck's Fiction." *Top of the News,* Spring 1987, pp. 297–301.

Gallo, Donald R. "Who Are the Most Important YA Authors?" *The ALAN Review,* vol. 16, no., 3 Spring 1989, pp. 18–20.

Scheler, Curt. "Peck Is the Author Whose Dreams Came True." *Grand Rapids Press,* 25 July 1982.

Interviews

"An Interview with Richard Peck." *Scholastic Voice,* 6 September 1985, 12–13.

Janeczko, Paul. "An Interview with Richard Peck." *English Journal,* February 1976, pp. 97–99.

Mercier, Jean F. "PW Interviews Richard Peck." *Publishers Weekly,* 14 March 1980, pp. 6–7.

"Questions & Answers." Bantam Doubleday Dell publicity flyer, November 1984.

Ross, Jean W. "CA Interview." *Contemporary Authors, New Revision Series,* 19 Edited by Linda Metzger. Detroit: Gale Research, 1987, pp. 367–370.

Stanek, Lou Willet. "Just Listening: Interviews with Six Adolescent Novelists: Patricia McKillip, Robert Cormier, Norma Klein, Richard Peck, S. E. Hinton, Judy Blume." *Arizona English Bulletin,* April 1976, pp. 23–38.

How to Write to the Author
Richard Peck
c/o Puffin Books
375 Hudson Street
New York, NY 10014

Sutton, Roger. "A Conversation with Richard Peck." *School Library Journal,* June 1990, pp. 36–40.

Speeches

Workshop at Montclair (New Jersey) Public Library, 8 December 1987. Audiocassette recording.

Robert Newton Peck

(1928-   )

by John S. Simmons

All works of imaginative literature—poems, novels, short stories, plays, and so on—offer a unique way of looking at the world. Novels, however, give us the big picture, providing enough detail about people, places, events, and problems for us to look closely at a broad landscape of life. While novelists may deal with facts or even real people, they go beyond these facts to look at the inner significance of people's lives and the events they encounter. Like all fiction writers, novelists use their imagination to make a new world because the facts alone do not satisfy their need for self-expression. They weave real-life incidents and characters into a tapestry that is uniquely their own, a creation of their imagination.

When you read novels, how much of the material is based on the authors' own experiences and how much is created from their imaginations? Some novelists use larger doses of imagination than others. It is doubtful, for example, that Robert Cormier was ever a son of a man being pursued by an organized crime group while being "protected" by the CIA. Jack London, on the other hand, lived very close to the reality he describes in his novels. In fact, when one of his stories was criticized as too brutal and violent, the author allegedly responded, "I saw it happen, in a joint in Singapore." In short, novelists run the gamut in the degree to which they have actually *lived* their stories. In creating his novels, Robert Newton Peck has remained close to the events and people of his own life.

Peck was born on 17 February 1928 in a rural area of Vermont. His family lived on a farm which they owned, but they were close to poverty. Their two greatest commitments were to each other and to the Shaker faith which, the novelist feels, not only held them together but gave them the pride in themselves and a love for the natural surroundings God had provided them. That faith certainly influences Peck to create stories that reflect relevant life values: willingness to do hard physical labor, dependence on family for support, total respect for father and mother, love for neighbors, and an unswerving belief that God would provide both the wherewithal to survive and the spiritual inspiration to find meaning and value in life—despite material limits and hardships.

Peck's father was a hard-working man: devout, but somewhat crude and truly illiterate. He worked on his farm until the day he died and did so uncomplainingly. Such fathers are to be found frequently in Peck's novels, especially in his best-known work, *A Day No Pigs Would Die* (1972). Peck's father also wanted the best for his children. He sent his beloved son to a run-down, ill-equipped, one-room schoolhouse down a dirt road in rural Vermont. There young Robert learned the two skills that would shape his life unalterably: he learned to read and he learned to write.

His teacher, Miss Kelly, taught all six grades in that school. She was a strict disciplinarian and set high standards. She also urged her students to read the well-worn books of the school's small library, contained on a three-foot-long shelf. Without question, the reading Peck did in that school would fuel his imagination. He was to use this imagination to write forty-six novels (probably more as of this writing), more than one hundred poems, the words and music to thirty-five songs, and three television specials. Unlike a writer such as London, the world traveler, Peck did not need a large environment in which to shape his stories; he utilized the surroundings in which he lived, the people with whom he interacted, and his imagination, which received a big boost from that shelf in the one-room schoolhouse.

Outside his immediate family, one of the people whom Peck came to know was a schoolmate named Luther Wesley Vinson. Luther's nickname was "Soup," and he became the author's closest friend during those grade-school years. Together, they got into and out of childhood scrapes. More than once, their teacher, Miss Kelly, used her trusty ruler on their backsides as punishment for their wrongdoings. Their Tom Sawyer–Huckleberry Finn relationship endured through school and beyond. The author's devotion to his friend Soup is clearly reflected in the books he wrote. From 1974 to 1988, Peck wrote eleven "Soup" novels, each one celebrating imaginatively the adventures, misfortunes, and characters of the boy with whom he grew up. All the novels are set in their Vermont homeland. Most are quite episodic; that is, they seem to jump from adventure to adventure as experienced by Soup and his narrator/friend Rob without too much unity. They are laced with lots of humorous dialogue and detail and with a significant dose of sentimentality. The author leaves no doubt as to his admiration for and commitment to his lifelong friend.

To enjoy the works of Robert Newton Peck, you have to accept his deep-seated love for and loyalty to family and close friends. These strong feelings often lead to incidents in many novels that are quite sentimentalized. This is true of all the "Soup" novels, as has been stated previously. It is also found in *Hang for Treason* (1976), a story of friendship and conflict between two adolescent boys; one is an American patriot and the other is a Tory loyalist during the era of the American Revolution. The same is true of *Banjo* (1982), a story that brings together a boy from a privileged home and an impoverished classmate who has been shunned by all the students in his school until now. The boys start out to write a report on a local hermit but get themselves into Tom-and-Huck misadventures along the way. The emerging friendship, plus the heart of gold revealed by the outwardly mean, unfriendly hermit, are a bit schmaltzy even if the story is exciting. A third noteworthy example is *Millie's Boy* (1973), a rather complex tale that involves the illegitimate son of a murdered prostitute. Tit Smith, the teenage protagonist, is

To enjoy the works of Robert Newton Peck, you have to accept his deep-seated love for and loyalty to family and close friends.

The Adventures of Tom Sawyer and Adventures of Huckleberry Finn were written by Mark Twain. There is an article about him later in this volume.

A **Tory loyalist** was an American who supported the British rather than colonial independence during the American Revolution.

schmaltzy sentimental

helped out of one predicament after another by kindly adults who appear just in the nick of time. Tit finally gets his retribution when his cruel father is killed by a dog while attempting an act of child molestation. Many profound emotions emerge in this story, particularly loyalty and love.

There is, however, another side of Peck, the novelist, which is unquestionably the biggest reason his work has been taken seriously for the past twenty-plus years. Relying on his childhood and adolescent life experiences, this author, in the idiom of the day, "tells it like it is." His description of farm and country life is nothing like that extolled by the pastoral poetry often assigned for study in literature courses (Wordsworth, Shelley, Keats, Longfellow, and other poets). Instead, Peck portrays in vivid and often uncomfortable detail the rough, smelly, dirt-caked life on the farm that characterized rural families who lived and toiled during the first half of this century. There were real people who were poor and uneducated, who were at the mercy of Mother Nature, who were usually isolated from urban assistance, and who did not have the advantages or the money to purchase fancy John Deere or International Harvester farming machinery. Furthermore, the author is precise and unrelenting in spelling out the details of that life. Family members, young and old, suffer serious injuries, animals scream and shriek as they are being slaughtered (usually with a knife), blood and gore decorate the landscape, and deodorant products are never available. Peck is at his best describing pain, both physical and emotional. He treats human suffering in a patient, almost clinical manner, and he doesn't spare the detail. Those who switch channels during the torture and suffering scenes probably will not appreciate Peck's novels. The pain, hardship, and bloodshed are never included at random, however, nor is the main purpose of these descriptions to provide the reader with feelings of discomfort or revulsion. Through these stressful experiences, the author's central characters maintain their sense of self-respect, grow closer to friends and family members, and grow in determination and awareness. This is especially true of teenage main characters, most of whom come through an initiation into adulthood the hard way. They are, however, more self-possessed and better able to discern the road ahead because of these difficult rites of passage. For Peck, the hard life to be endured in a crude, rural environment—often buffeted by the impassive forces

pastoral poetry poetry about shepherds or rural life that tends to portray nature as sweet and beautiful

of nature—provides the appropriate crucible for character growth. Be forewarned, however, that those who have weak stomachs better choose another novelist.

Readers of Peck's books won't have any trouble visualizing his settings, interpreting his characters, or getting his messages. There is a great deal of outdoor action, and much of it is fast-paced and physical. His scenery is never over-described but is clearly perceived. The story lines move along steadily with few interruptions in time. Most of his characters speak their minds in a forthright, often blunt, manner. Peck does not seem to be very partial to overly sensitive, self-absorbed head cases. He is for readers who like their male characters up-front and usually hard-nosed. In fact, he does much better with male than with female characters. The man's man motif runs uncompromisingly through his stories. In addition, his language is appropriately straightforward, but profanity and obscene allusions are nowhere to be found. If your folks are worried about the presence of cuss words in your personal reading, you will never have to hide a Peck novel under the pillow.

Peck's Masterpiece

Without question, the novel for which Peck is best remembered is his first one, *A Day No Pigs Would Die* (1972). In this work, we see several of the features that make Peck the unique writer he is. It is the story of Rob, a Shaker boy growing up on a poor Vermont farm. Rob is twelve when the story begins. While he is on his way to school, he encounters a cow having great difficulty giving birth to a calf. He delivers the calf, saves the cow's life, and is seriously injured in the process. His father finds him and his family nurses him back to health. As a reward, Rob is given a piglet by his neighbor who is the owner of the cow. Since Rob's father butchers pigs as a side job, Rob is well aware of what goes into the care and feeding of such animals.

In the opening chapter, a number of dominant Peck themes emerge: the life of a struggling farm family; a boy in his early teens who knows the meaning of hard farm work; the blood and pain, as well as the danger, associated with farm life of that era; the cooperative attitudes of neighbors; the stern role model offered by the father, Mr. Haven Peck;

Be forewarned, however, that those who have weak stomachs better choose another novelist.

motif situation or theme

themes central messages about life in a literary work

the close-knit family life of that place and time; and a boy coveting his first real possession. As Pinky, the female pig, becomes more mature, Rob learns that she is sterile and cannot become the breeder he hoped she would be. He also becomes aware that his father, who has been impoverished all his life, and who is illiterate but deeply religious and intensely proud of his role as family head and provider, is dying of tuberculosis. The latter fact makes Rob increasingly aware that, when his father passes away, it will be up to him, by then thirteen, to assume the duties of household head—a far cry from Holden Caulfield's pathetic goal of becoming a New York City "catcher in the rye."

As Haven Peck's condition worsens, the family faces a grim winter, made more threatening by a food shortage on the farm. They, Haven and Rob, reach the inevitable decision: Pinky, Rob's beloved pig, must be slaughtered. Pinky has become a favorite of the Peck family. She is loving, spirited, and well-behaved, all of which makes her impending death more difficult for all to bear, especially for Rob, who has come to love the animal as he might another human being. He is, however, his father's son and when the time comes, assists in the butchering of the terrified, pathetically squealing Pinky. When the act has been completed, Rob cries, apparently for the first time in the presence of his father. Then Haven Peck sheds tears, reflecting the loving, understanding father who exists beneath the stern exterior he shows the rest of the world. For that moment, he and his son are one in the commission of a violent, tragic action done not out of anger or cruelty but for the good of a family in need. While the details of Pinky's death are related in typically inexorable detail, the true impact of the death and its meaning come across with great intensity. Rob wails:

> "Oh, Papa. My heart's broke."
> "So is mine," said Papa. "But I'm thankful you're a man . . . That's what being a man is all about boy. It's doing what's got to be done." (P. 129)

And through that scene, we see more of the main Peck themes reflected: the hard choices in a life in which survival is the name of the game; the closeness of father and son intensified by a tragic event; and the passage by Rob of a mile-

Holden Caulfield is the main character in *The Catcher in the Rye*, which was written by J. D. Salinger. There is an article about Salinger later in this volume.

post on the way to adulthood. The author has never since cast them more vividly than he did in Pinky's death scene.

Soon after the pig's slaughter, Haven Peck dies. Because he is his father's son, thirteen-year-old Rob takes charge. He arranges the funeral, digs the grave, presses his father's burial clothes, conducts the funeral, and then leads his aunt and mother to the grave site. In short, he assumes the role of the man toward whom he had been moving from the novel's opening chapter.

All the neighbors attend Haven Peck's funeral. With the passing of the respected friend and neighbor, they observe that burial day as a day when no pigs would die. Haven Peck's job of slaughtering pigs would be taken up by the new head of the Peck household—and the struggle for survival in that remote, cold corner of New England will resume. It is a struggle marked by honest labor, family love, neighborly cooperation, and adherence to the letter and spirit of a stern religious creed. Above all, it is a struggle carried on with dignity, and that is the theme which is at the core of Robert Newton Peck's tales of life and hard times.

In 1994, some twenty-three years after writing *A Day No Pigs Would Die,* Peck published *A Part of the Sky,* a true sequel to the novel just discussed. It picks up the life of Rob Peck immediately after his father's death. At age thirteen, Rob willingly accepts the burden of managing the family farm. His mother and Aunt Carrie are not strong enough to offer more than marginal assistance in the completion of outdoor tasks well-taught by his father. Determined to maintain the farm, Rob exerts every effort to keep the family together and the land productive. His total preoccupation with that operation leaves him little time for school (which he is quite willing to sacrifice) and for a budding romance with a classmate named Becky Lee Tate. Although Becky's home situation is luxurious compared to Rob's, she is strongly attracted to him, pursues him aggressively, and temporarily wins his favor by helping him pass English. Their relationship does not rival those shown on afternoon TV soap operas, but the affection they share, built on mutual respect, trust, and admiration, represents one of the few optimistic notes sounded in this book.

Rob's road to successful management of his farm is a rocky one from the outset. The Vermont weather is characteristically harsh and unforgiving. He loses his two animal

The **Great Depression** was a severe recession that began when the stock market crashed in 1929 and that lasted almost ten years. By the winter of 1932–1933, 14 to 16 million Americans were unemployed. Many died from a lack of food and inadequate living conditions.

mainstays, Solomon, the ox, and Daisy, a cow gone barren. Solomon dies in harness, and Rob must sell Daisy to a slaughterhouse. As he did with his beloved Pinky, Rob watches the killing of the cow while inner emotions wrack him. He is also plagued by a mortgage he cannot maintain, and the farm is ultimately repossessed by the bank. This loss of property has become a common occurrence in the novel, which is set in the early, numbing years of the Great Depression. Rob's herculean struggles to meet payments are no less futile than those of a number of neighbors—as was indeed true of thousands of American landowners during the 1930s. John Steinbeck's epic work, *The Grapes of Wrath,* traces the struggles of the Joad family dispossessed of their Oklahoma land, but at least the Joads have able-bodied adults to carry on the struggle. In *A Part of the Sky,* Rob Peck is a boy doing a man's job. His efforts can be compared to that of Travis in Fred Gipson's *Old Yeller,* Buck Callaway in Paul Annixter's *Swiftwater,* Rudi Matt in James R. Ullman's *Banner in the Sky,* and Esther Forbes' title character in *Johnny Tremaine.* All of these earlier young adult novels portray huge undertakings but, unlike Rob, the main characters have succeeded by the story's end. When the Peck family finally abandons their home and moves into the town to accept the charity of the local merchant, Porter Ferguson, darkness seems to take over.

> As the wagons got loaded, I felt grateful there was so much to do. Possessions, even the few we had, have a way of owning you, body and brain. With a door constant open, the house becomes so icy cold. No pulse.
> It was like our home was nearing death.
> The more it emptied, the sadder it seemed to fill with sorrow. Mama and Aunt Carrie shuffled around inside touching places. Not with gloves. Their fingers were bare, as though searching the wood and stone for something lost. (P. 155)

There is an article about John Steinbeck later in this volume.

As the novel ends, there is not much for Rob, his mother, and his aunt to cheer about. They have lost their home. They are living in a small attic apartment, the temporary guests of Mr. Ferguson. They have no savings, and Rob has no job prospects. Yet they do not wallow in despair and self-pity. What they haven't lost is their dignity, their Shaker faith and hope, their happy memories—and each other. These treasures, as they celebrate a cold Christmas Eve, seem to be enough to hold them together.

After dropping out of high school, Peck fought in World War II in Europe as a common foot soldier. After the war, he went back to school, finished college, and even tried law school. The desire to write about his own experiences and code, as seen through the prism of his imagination, however, finally won out. He has become a writer of renown and a person who remains true to the lifestyle he feels is the "right one." In 1995, he was in his mid-sixties, and he lived in Central Florida where he continued to write. Part of this writing was in the form of letters; Peck estimates that he's written to 100,000 young readers over the years. As he describes himself in Donald R. Gallo's *Speaking for Ourselves*, "RNP is a cornball, flag-waving, redneck patriot who loves America and respects the thinking of Americans who do hard physical work. He writes about them, folks who stand in dirt and look up at rainbows" (p. 69).

In that sense, the man and his books are one.

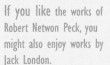

Peck estimates that he's written to 100,000 young readers over the years.

If you like the works of Robert Netwon Peck, you might also enjoy works by Jack London.

Selected Bibliography

WORKS BY ROBERT NEWTON PECK

Novels for Young Adults

A Day No Pigs Would Die (1972; 1994)

Millie's Boy (1973)

Path of Hunters (1973)

Soup (1974)

Soup and Me (1975)

Wild Cat (1975)

Hamilton (1976)

Hang for Treason (1976)

Rabbits and Redcoats (1976)

Last Sunday (1977)

Patooie (1977)

Trig (1977)

Soup for President (1978)

Trig Sees Red (1978)
Basket Case (1979)
Clunie (1979)
Hub (1979)
Soup's Drum (1980)
Trig Goes Ape (1980)
Justice Lion (1981)
Kirk's Law (1981)
Soup On Wheels (1981)
Banjo (1982)
Trig or Treat (1982)
Soup in the Saddle (1983)
Dukes (1984)
Soup's Goat (1984)
Jo Silver (1985)
Spanish Hoof (1985)
Soup on Ice (1985)
Soup on Fire (1987)
Soup's Uncle (1988)
Arly (1989)
Soup's Hoop (1989; 1992)
Higbee's Halloween (1990)
Arly's Run (1991)
Little Soup's Birthday (1991)
Little Soup's Hayride (1991)
Little Soup's Turkey (1992)
Soup in Love (1992)
Little Soup's Bunny (1993)
A Part of the Sky (1994)
Soup Ahoy (1994)

Fiction for Adult Readers
The Happy Sadist (1962)
The King's Iron (1972)
Fawn (1975)
Eagle Fur (1978)
The Seminole Seed (1983)
The Horse Hunters (1988)

Nonfiction for Adult Readers
Path of Hunters: Animal Struggle in a Meadow (1973)
Secrets of Successful Fiction (1980)
Fiction Is Folks (1983)
My Vermont (1985)
Novels of Initiation: A Guidebook for Teaching Literature to Adolescents (1989)

Autobiography
"Robert Newton Peck." In *Something About the Author Autobiography Series.* Detroit: Gale Research, 1986, vol. 1.

Musicals
King of Kazoo

WORKS ABOUT ROBERT NEWTON PECK

Books and Parts of Books
Donelson, Kenneth R., and Aileen Pace Nilsen. *Literature for Today's Young Adults.* Glenview, Ill.: Scott, Foresman & Co., 1989.

Gallo, Donald R., ed. *Speaking for Ourselves: Autobiographical Sketches by Notable Authors for Young Adults.* Urbana, Ill.: National Council of Teachers of English, 1990, pp. 168–170.

Articles
Hartvigsen, M. Kip, and Christen Hartvigsen. "Haven Peck's Legacy in *A Day No Pigs Would Die.*" *English Journal,* April 1985.

Hipps, G. Melvin. "Male Initiation Rites in *A Day No Pigs Would Die.*" *Arizona English Bulletin,* spring 1976.

Milner, Joseph O., and Frederick Carter. "All My Sorrows: Pain in Adolescent Fiction." *ALAN Review,* winter 1980.

Morrell, Judy. "Pinky's Tale: An Appreciative Response to *A Day No Pigs Would Die.*" *Virginia English Bulletin,* winter 1986.

Peck, David. *Novels of Initiation: A Guidebook for Teaching Literature to Adolescents.* New York: Teachers College, 1989.

Sarkissian, Adele, ed. *Something About the Author Autobiography Series.* Detroit: Gale Research, 1986.

How to Write to the Author
Robert Newton Peck
c/o Alfred A. Knopf, Inc.
201 East 50th Street
New York, NY 10022

Simmons, John, and Edward Deluzian. *Teaching Literature in Middle and Secondary Grades.* Boston: Allyn & Bacon, 1992.

Spencer, Lois R. "A Sea Change: Positive Family Relationships in Young Adult Literature." *Books for the Junior High Years,* spring 1989.

Stella Pevsner

by Michaeline Chance-Reay

S tella Pevsner adores cats. She collects antique dolls. She likes to read, travel, and go to art fairs; and she really loves to write. Growing up, she wanted to be a tap dancer, a singer, or an actress, and, with a name that means "star," maybe some type of fame was inevitable for her. As a writer, Pevsner gets to play even more parts than she could as an actress; she can be young or old, male or female. As Louise Rosenblatt suggested in *Literature as Exploration,* we can try on roles, attitudes, and adventures vicariously in reading; and so it is with writing. When a person composes fiction, there is an unending supply of people, places, and excitement to imagine.

vicariously through the experiences of another person

In *Speaking for Ourselves,* Pevsner says she was the baby of her family, having three brothers and two sisters who pushed her around and spoiled her but who always encouraged her interests in art and performing. In high school she wrote a humor column for the school newspaper. In college she took courses in art, education, and advertising, and she eventually wrote copy for various advertising agencies in Chicago. She continued freelance writing after she married and had four children, and it was at their request that she began writing children's books.

Beginnings

Pevsner's career as a writer for young adults started in 1967 with a one-act play, *The Young Brontës,* and a book titled *Break a Leg!* in 1969. This book, reissued as *New Girl* in 1983, was about young Fran, who overcame being shy and began to appreciate her uniqueness when she acted in a play. In *Footsteps on the Stairs,* which followed in 1970, the topics are Fran's brother and a fear he overcame.

In *Contemporary Authors*, Pevsner compares her writing to the art of collage because, she thinks, "In each . . . a collage or a novel . . . the artist/author takes bits of this and that, scraps and dreams and memories, and weaves them into a design which is new and strange and yet somehow familiar" (Colburn, p. 452). For example, in *Something About the Author* (1994), Pevsner explains that in one of her first stories, *Call Me Heller, That's My Name,* which won the Chicago Women in Publishing first annual award for children's literature in 1973, she drew on her experiences with her older sisters and their boyfriends, a distinct historical period known as the Roaring Twenties, and a real railroad tragedy she had read about in a newspaper, using an imaginary town for the setting.

The **Roaring Twenties** is a nickname for the decade of the 1920s in America. World War I had jusy ended, and it was an exciting time of renewal and prosperity, during which new music, literature, dance, and fashion developed.

Solidifying Her Career

Pevsner's fourth book, *A Smart Kid Like You* (1975), was very well received. It is about a junior high student whose parents divorce and her subsequent relationship with her mother and stepmother. It won the Dorothy Canfield Fisher award and the Vermont Congress of Parents and Teachers' award in 1977. It also won recognition as the Junior Literary Guild outstanding book and was made into an ABC "After School Special" television movie starring Kristy McNichol.

subsequent following, later

The real town of Galena in Pevsner's home state of Illinois is the setting for *Keep Stompin' Till the Music Stops*

(1977), where the idea of each person's affinity for a place is explored. This tender portrayal of the struggle of a learning-disabled seventh grader to help his grandfather continue living independently was selected as the Notable Children's Trade Book in the field of Social Studies in 1977.

Immediately following in 1978, *And You Give Me a Pain, Elaine* describes the frustration of sibling rivalry. It won the Society of Children's Book Writers Golden Kite Award, the Society of Midland Authors Clara Ingram Judson award, and the Omar Award.

Pevsner in the 1980s

Popularity and the shallow, manipulative individuals a young girl meets in her quest for it are the topics of *Cute Is a Four-Letter-Word* (1980). This book received the Friends of the Chicago Public Library's Carl Sandburg Award in 1980. The topic of first romance, which is touched upon in *Cute Is a Four-Letter Word*, is fully developed in *I'll Always Remember You . . . Maybe* (1981). Darien, a high school senior, experiences the pain and confusion of breaking up with her long-time boyfriend. She then begins a new relationship with a more mature outlook because of what she has learned. In November 1981, *School Library Journal* praised the author for her respectful treatment of young love and heartbreak and classified the book as above average romance fiction.

First love, the heartbreak of its ending, and the maturation that can follow from a female point of view is also the topic of *Lindsay, Lindsay, Fly Away Home* (1983). Sent home from India to live with an aunt, Lindsay suffers from a sense of isolation and can only write to the Indian boyfriend she left behind. In its 15 September 1983 issue, *Booklist* was impressed with this portrayal of a young woman's development into a more content and secure person as a result of going through some difficult experiences.

Although humor is found in all Pevsner's books, *Me, My Goat, and My Sister's Wedding* (1985) is unmistakably a comedy. The title gives a clue to the culmination of what starts out as an attempt by Doug, Frank, and Woody to help a friend going on a camping trip.

In *Something About the Author Autobiography Series*, Pevsner explained that reading a story about multiple births

affinity feeling of preference or connection

> *Although humor is found in all Pevsner's books,* Me, My Goat, and My Sister's Wedding *(1985) is unmistakably a comedy.*

culmination end, climax

quintuplets five siblings born during the same birth

and wondering about their sibling relationships gave her the idea for two of her subsequent stories. *Sister of the Quints* (1987) is about Natalie, the older sister of quintuplets, and her desire to move to Colorado, where she can be with her biological mother and escape the complications of her new family situation. In the sequel *I'm Emma, I'm a Quint* (1993), readers learn what it is like to be one of the quintuplets. Emma has many of the same struggles as any teenager, in addition to those that accompany being part of such an unusual family group. The book also includes a follow-up on Natalie, who is planning her wedding.

In *How Could You Do It, Diane?* (1989), the horror of a teen's suicide and its aftermath are seen though the eyes of the sad and bewildered family, who try to make sense of this senseless act. This look at every parent's worst fear was recognized in 1989 by the American Library Association on its Best Books for Young Adults list. Zena Sutherland, writing for the *Bulletin of the Center for Children's Books*, was impressed by the book's degree of sympathy and insight.

Pevsner in the 1990s

trauma overwhelming event that may later haunt or trouble a person

The lack of long-term friendships and other traumas of a teen who has moved often because of his parent's lifestyle is the subject of *The Night the Whole Class Slept Over* (1991). It also explores the role of grandparents in a young person's life.

Pevsner's novel *Jon, Flora, and the Odd-Eyed Cat* (1994) has received mixed responses. Chris Sherman, writing for *Booklist*'s 1 November 1994 issue, says, "Readers looking for an unusual story will find it in this story about true friends" (p. 492). In another and more detailed review, Carolyn Noah, in the *School Library Journal* (October, 1994), calls the book disappointing. She says the themes of the effects of prejudice, a young person's right to decide with whom to live, and the use of fantasy to survive stressful situations are touched on but not really developed; the characters are unengaging, and the plot is sluggish. The story is about fourteen-year-old Jon, who is recuperating from rheumatic fever and must move to a small town in the Carolinas with his family. He makes friends with twelve-year-old Flora, who says she is a Druid, and her odd-eyed cat. The plot then revolves around their plans to hold a ceremony on the night of the summer solstice. The story is unusual, but the elements that make it appealing to young readers are not. These elements, which have appeared in all Pevsner's works over the last three decades, have made her stories popular and have won her many awards.

summer solstice the day of the year, about 22 June, with the longest period of daylight

What Makes the Books Tick?

A person of any age who has gone to browse at a local bookstore or library cannot help but want to find out what lies behind such whimsical and provocative titles as *Me, My Goat and My Sister's Wedding, I'll Always Remember You . . . Maybe,* and *Jon, Flora, and the Odd-Eyed Cat.* These titles bait not only reluctant readers but anyone with a healthy curiosity, which children and adolescents certainly have. Odd-eyed cats, goats, and the youngsters who cherish, befriend, and have fun with them are the characters we meet. Although most of Pevsner's protagonists are female, she creates realistic and enjoyable characters of both sexes. Their prototypes can be found in all schools. Some of them we either know already or would like to know. We can also learn from them in a number of ways.

whimsical oddly humorous or fanciful

protagonist main character of a literary work

prototype early or original model

We learn from what is said by characters like Heller, Lindsay, and Jon. The dialogue is funny and real, and there is plenty of it. It is often almost theatrical, reflecting Pevsner's early acting interests and the ongoing drama that adolescents not only often cause but also endure. Pevsner's style is conversational. She uses words that make readers chuckle. Most beginning readers, and a number of adults, prefer books that are filled with repartee and are short on the detailed descriptions. Pevsner's dialogue is one of her greatest strengths as a writer.

repartee witty conversation

Plots and subplots, or what the characters do, are many and varied. Although some readers may find a number of the subplots distracting, others relish the complexity of Pevsner's story lines. How these stories play out is somewhat predictable, but even this can be appealing to young readers. Adolescents, who live in a tentative world, can find comfort in the expected. Even experienced, sophisticated, and avid readers, according to Victor Nell in *Lost in a Book,* choose to read the predictable. Pevsner's topics range from light to se-

avid very eager

rious, and each book reflects her engaging sense of humor and her ability to entertain through story.

Pevsner's themes, or the messages she attempts to transmit, revolve around our ability to use what we can—often humor—to balance what is threatening, unjust, or just plain incomprehensible. Her stories present adolescence as a stage, a time like any other in life, from which we eventually move, taking with us lessons learned.

Pevsner's conclusions are positive and may be labeled as pat. They often promise a light at the end of what may seem like a dark tunnel on a young person's journey; however, most children are aware that not all conflicts in real life can be resolved. Pevsner's happy endings may simply strengthen and enlighten the readers by encouraging them to see positive alternatives and to strive for as much understanding and happiness as possible in their own lives. They must know what is ideal before they can strive for it.

Readers who have enjoyed Pevsner's style may like the books of Judy Blume, Paula Danziger, Susan Beth Pfeffer, and Phyllis Reynolds Naylor. Like Pevsner, Blume wanted to be an actress early in her life. These writers also have a penchant for enticing titles and offbeat characters. They all write about growing up, growing wiser, and developing insight. They tell entertaining stories, using humor and lively dialogue to address the serious and not-so-serious concerns of adolescents.

Selected Bibliography

WORKS BY STELLA PEVSNER

Novels for Young Adults

Break A Leg (1969), reprinted as *New Girl* (1983)

Footsteps on the Stairs (1970)

Call Me Heller, That's My Name (1973)

A Smart Kid Like You (1975)

Keep Stompin' Till the Music Stops (1977)

And You Give Me a Pain, Elaine (1978)

Cute Is a Four-Letter Word (1980)

I'll Always Remember You . . . Maybe (1981)

Lindsay, Lindsay, Fly Away Home (1983)

Me, My Goat, and My Sister's Wedding (1985)

Sister of the Quints (1987)

How Could You Do It, Diane? (1989)

The Night the Whole Class Slept Over (1991)

I'm Emma, I'm a Quint (1993)

Jon, Flora, and the Odd-Eyed Cat (1994)

Plays

The Young Brontës (1967)

WORKS ABOUT STELLA PEVSNER

Codell, Cindy Darling. Review of *I'm Emma, I'm a Quint.* In *School Library Journal,* December 1993, p. 116.

Colburn, Candy. *What Do Children Read Next?* Detroit: Gale Research, 1994.

Commire, Anne, ed. *Something About the Author.* Detroit: Gale Research, 1976, vol. 8, pp. 154–155.

Gallo, Donald R., ed. *Speaking for Ourselves.* Urbana, Ill.: National Council of Teachers of English, 1990, pp. 171–172.

Hile, Kevin S., and Diane Telgen, eds. *Something About the Author.* Detroit: Gale Research, 1994, vol. 77, pp. 156–159.

Holtze, Sally H., ed. *Fifth Book of Junior Authors and Illustrators.* New York: H. W. Wilson, 1983, pp. 245–246.

Locher, Frances C., and Ann Evory, eds. *Contemporary Authors.* Detroit: Gale Research, 1976, vols. 57–60, p. 452.

McCarthy, Carol. Review of *How Could You Do It, Diane?* In *School Library Journal,* October 1989, p. 145.

Nell, Victor. *Lost in a Book.* New Haven, Conn.: Yale University Press, 1988.

Phelan, Carolyn. Review of *The Night the Whole Class Slept Over.* In *Booklist,* October 1991, p. 331.

Review of *I'll Always Remember You . . . Maybe.* In *Booklist,* 1 October 1981, p. 188.

Review of *I'll Always Remember You . . . Maybe.* In *School Library Journal,* November 1981, p. 109.

Review of *Lindsay, Lindsay, Fly Away Home.* In *Booklist,* 15 September 1983, p. 160.

Review of *Lindsay, Lindsay, Fly Away Home.* In *School Library Journal,* November 1983, p. 96.

Review of *Me, My Goat, and My Sister's Wedding.* In *Booklist,* 15 April 1985, p. 1199.

Review of *The Night the Whole Class Slept Over.* In *School Library Journal,* November 1991, p. 124.

Rosenblatt, Louise. *Literature as Exploration.* New York: Appleton-Century, 1938.

Sherman, Chris. Review of *Jon, Flora, and the Odd-Eyed Cat.* In *Booklist,* 1 November 1994, p. 492.

How to Write to the Author
Stella Pevsner
c/o Clarion Books
215 Park Avenue South
New York, NY 10003

Something About the Author Autobiography Series. Detroit: Gale Research, 1992, pp. 183–193.

Sutherland, Zena. Review of *How Could You Do It, Diane?* In *Bulletin of the Center for Children's Books,* September 1989, p. 14.

K. M. Peyton

(1929-)

by Jeanne Marcum Gerlach

K. M. Peyton is the well-known author of many distinguished books for young people, published both in the United States and abroad. Born in Birmingham, England, Peyton spent four years as a student at the Manchester School of Art and then, in 1952, became an art instructor at the Northhampton High School. She is married to an artist and they live with their two young daughters in Essex, England. When she is not riding or sailing with her family or writing a book, Peyton likes to go for long walks, listen to music, read history, or do gardening (Peyton, 1964).

Adventures in Writing

You might assume that since Peyton is an active adventurer, her books are inspired by some of her adventures. You might also assume that since she read history, the chances are good that her fiction is historically sound. Both of your assumptions would be correct.

Describing how she decided to become a writer, Peyton begins by talking about horses. In *Something About the Author Autobiography Series* she says, "Because of the dearth of real-life ponies in my childhood career, I had to make do with imaginary ones, and this, I realize in retrospect, is what started my writing career" (p. 243). She talks about her desire to own a horse; her love affair with Titch, a chestnut pony who grazed in a field near her home; the long stories she wrote about invented ponies; and her make-believe pony, Talisman (really her bicycle).

Not only did Peyton dream about and write about ponies, she read about them too. "I browsed in the children's section and borrowed pony books. Some I had out so many times I knew them by heart," she says in *Something About the Author Autobiography Series* (p. 244). Eventually, one of Peyton's teachers offered her a pony if her parents promised to pay to have it transported to their property, but her parents refused the offer because they did not have a place to keep it. One of Peyton's friends got the pony and Peyton was able to see it every day after school. All this time, Peyton was writing books. When she finished writing a book she would send the manuscript to a publisher, but it always came back with a rejection slip. Then one day, at the suggestion of her teacher, Peyton's parents gave one of her stories to a neighbor who, in turn, gave it to a publisher friend. The manuscript was published as a book, *Sabre, the Horse from the Sea* (1947). Thus, at sixteen, Peyton became a published author.

Sabre, the Horse from the Sea is about a young girl who was evacuated to the seaside from London after the World War II bombings. There she finds a gray thoroughbred on the beach. The story follows the young girl's adventures with the beautiful horse and her relationship with a pilot who is stationed at a nearby aerodrome (airfield). In this way, Peyton combined her fantasies about horses with her love of adventure and romance to create her first novel.

Peyton continued writing, and by the time *Sabre, the Horse from the Sea* was published, she had already completed her second book and had it accepted for publication. She was excited about being a published author but was determined to go to art school to pursue another passion. Eventually she moved to Manchester to attend the Manchester Art School, where she specialized in painting and met her husband to be, Mike.

During the bombing of London and other British cities by Germany during World War II, many parents **evacuated,** or moved out of danger, their children. The children were often sent to the countryside or another country, living with friends or relatives until the war was over.

The couple was soon married, and they set off on a honeymoon that lasted four months. Peyton describes their adventures in *Something About the Author Autobiography Series:*

> We hitchhiked through France; lived in a cave outside Cannes with several other "travelers"; walked across Switzerland through the mountains, living out or in hay barns; and went down into Italy and stayed in Rome, Florence, and Venice—free, in monasteries and convents as it was the Holy Year and one was invited in! If not, we stayed in youth hostels when in a town. Then we traveled back over the Brenner Pass into Austria. (P. 248)

Later, the newlyweds hitchhiked back to Paris where they worked collecting and selling wastepaper until they earned enough for their fares back home to Manchester. You might think that those adventures would become great material for Peyton's future writings. She admits in her reflections: "I have always felt that my marriage to Mike was very good for my development as a writer, for life has never been dull with him, and some of our adventures have given me great material" (*Something About the Author Autobiography Series,* p. 248).

Soon after their honeymoon adventure, Peyton returned to school to obtain a teaching degree and later took a job teaching in a girls' school. Mike became a cartoonist. During Peyton's school holidays, they continued their travel adventures hitchhiking around Europe, Canada, and New York City. They made their home in Essex and five years later began their family—two daughters.

During this time, Peyton had been writing, using the material from her travels for the basis of her works. From the canoeing and sailing adventures, she wrote *The Hard Way Home* (1962), *Stormcock Meets Trouble* (1961), *Sea Fever* (1963), *The Maplin Bird* (1965), and *The Plan for Birdsmarsh* (1965). *The Maplin Bird* and *Sea Fever,* set in the nineteenth century, are a collection of adventure stories about young boys who make a living from fishing.

Another book based on Peyton's sailing adventures is *Thunder in the Sky* (1966). In this novel, Peyton uses her knowledge of the history of World War I, stories that she

"I have always felt that my marriage to Mike was very good for my development as a writer, for life has never been dull with him, and some of our adventures have given me great material."

zeppelins cigar-shaped airships, like blimps, but having a rigid frame

plot the deliberate sequence of events in a literary work

heard in a local pub from World War I skippers about the danger from zeppelins and aircraft fire, and her own sailing experiences, to create the adventures of three young brothers who, in 1914, were faced with the decision of whether or not to enlist in the army and go to war. Peyton uses her research for the flying sequence in this book, and her lifelong love of airplanes helped her develop the plot.

The Flambards Trilogy

trilogy a series of three literary works that are closely related and share a single theme

Flambards (1967), *The Edge of the Cloud* (1969), and *Flambards in Summer* (1969) make up the Flambards trilogy, for which Peyton won the Carnegie Medal in 1969. Four other critically acclaimed books by Peyton are *Froggett's Revenge* (1985), *A Midsummer Night's Death* (1979), *Prove Yourself a Hero* (1977), and *Who, Sir? Me, Sir?* (1983).

The Edge of the Cloud, the second book in the trilogy, opens with these intriguing words:

befuddled confused, as if with alcohol

> "We've eloped," Christina said to Aunt Grace. She had not meant to use the silly word, but it had got stuck in her head, and she was too befuddled with cold to catch it before it slipped out. (P. 7)

As a reader, I was hooked. I guessed that Christina must have married Will, and I assumed that the novel was going to focus heavily on romance. Continuing my read, however, I learned that I was only half right. Christina and Will have not really eloped, but they are indeed thinking about marriage. Christina quickly explains to Aunt Grace, "Oh, we know it will be a year yet. Will has to work things out" (p. 7). Soon I learned that Will not only has a passion for Christina, but also a passion for flying—an extremely risky activity in the early part of the twentieth century. I wondered if Will's flying toward his dreams to design, make, and fly planes would take him away from Christina.

Because it offers both romance and adventure, *The Edge of the Cloud* will appeal to young adults of both genders. The elements of adventure and romance, coupled with well-developed characters and a believable plot will keep readers interested in the story. An added bonus is the chance to learn about life in England in the early 1900s.

The first book of the trilogy, *Flambards,* and the third book, *Flambards in Summer,* are based on Peyton's research on World War I, as well as on her knowledge of horses and Edwardian country life. This award-winning trilogy enjoyed great success among young adult readers. Several years after the Flambards books were published, their success enticed Yorkshire Television to make them into a thirteen-part television series. Because of the series' great success, both as books and as a television production, Peyton decided to write a fourth book, *Flambards Divided* (1982). Although the book sold well, Yorkshire Television did not make it into a film.

Edwardian characteristic of the time of King Edward VII of England (1901–1910)

The Pennington Books and Beyond

After the success of the Flambards trilogy, Peyton decided to write the story of an antisocial young man. She invented Patrick Pennington and wrote three novels about him and his girlfriend. *Pennington's Seventeenth Summer* (1970), *The Beethoven Medal* (1971), and *Pennington's Heir* (1973) became Peyton's second successful trilogy. She based Pennington's character on a boy she had seen on a train. The time was the 1960s, and he was returning home from school and wore a Beatles' haircut. Peyton remarks about young Pennington: "In my book I gave him an overload of talent—at swimming, football, playing the piano, sailing" (*Something About the Author Autobiography Series,* p. 251). She admits that he is an overdrawn hero but confesses that she loved writing the Pennington books more than any of her others.

Peyton's books are realistic, honest, and aesthetically, artistically, and thematically pleasing. The works deal with issues that young readers are likely to be confronting, providing students with situations that help them find meaning in their own worlds. As we have learned from the English educator Louise Rosenblatt, the key concept that links learning and reading and responding to literature is meaningfulness. She says:

> There is an even broader need that literature fills, particularly for the adolescent reader. Much that in life itself might seem disorganized and meaningless takes on

order and significance when it comes under the organizing and vitalizing influence of the artist. The youth senses in himself new and unsuspected emotional impulses. He sees the adults about him acting in inexplicable ways. In literature he meets emotions, situations, people presented in significant patterns. He is shown a causal relationship between actions, he finds approval given to certain kinds of personalities and behavior rather than to others, he finds molds into which to pour his own nebulous emotions. In short, he often finds meaning attached to what otherwise would be for him merely brute facts. (1968, p. 42)

Peyton's writing for young adults awakens the readers to worlds of adventure, mystery, and romance. It provides them with the experiences that they might compare with and relate to their own. It helps them to learn.

If you like the works of K. M. Peyton, you might also enjoy the works of L. M. Montgomery.

Selected Bibliography

WORKS BY K. M. PEYTON AS KATHLEEN HERALD

Sabre: The Horse from the Sea (1947)
The Mandrake (1949)
Crab the Roan (1953)

WORKS BY K. M. PEYTON

Novels

North to Adventure (1959)
Stormcock Meets Trouble (1961)
The Hard Way Home (1962)
Sea Fever (1963)
Brownsea Silver (1964)
The Maplin Bird (1965)
The Plan for Birdmarsh (1965)
Thunder in the Sky (1966)
Fly-by-Night (1968)
Pennington's Seventeenth Summer (1970), also published

as *Pennington's Last Term* (1971)
The Beethoven Medal (1971)
The Pattern of Roses (1972)
Pennington's Heir (1973)
The Team (1975)
The Right-Hand Man (1976)
Prove Yourself a Hero (1977)
A Midsummer Night's Death (1979)
Marion's Angels (1979)
Dear Fred (1981)
Flambards Divided (1982)
Going Home (1982)
Free Rein (1983)
Who, Sir? Me, Sir? (1983)
The Last Ditch (1984)
Froggett's Revenge (1985)
Plain Jack (1988)
Downhill All the Way (1988)
Skylark (1989)
Darkling (1989)
Poor Badger (1990)
Apple Won't Jump (1992)
The Boy Who Wasn't There (1992)

The Flambards Trilogy
Flambards (1967)
The Edge of the Cloud (1969)
Flambards in Summer (1969)

Autobiography
Peyton, K. M. "K. M. Peyton." In *Speaking for Ourselves, Too: More Autobiographical Sketches by Notable Authors of Books for Young Adults.* Edited by Donald R. Gallo. Urbana, Ill.: National Council of Teachers of English, 1993, pp.158–159.

Sarkissian, Adele, ed. "K. M. Peyton." In *Something About the Author Autobiography Series.* Detroit: Gale Research, 1994, vol. 17, pp. 243–257.

How to Write to the Author
K. M. Peyton
c/o Peter Smith Publisher Inc.
5 Lexington Avenue
Magnolia, MA 01930

WORKS ABOUT K. M. PEYTON

Bowden, Jane A., ed. "K. M. Peyton." In *Contemporary Authors*. Detroit: Gale Research, 1978, vol. 69–72, pp. 469–470.

Commire, Anne, ed. "K. M. Peyton." In *Something About the Author*. Detroit: Gale Research, 1990, vol. 62, pp. 144–148.

Chevalier, Tracy, ed. "K. M. Peyton." In *Twentieth-Century Children's Writers*. Chicago: St. James, 1989, pp. 775–776.

Susan Beth Pfeffer

(1948-   )

by Kylene Beers

I n Susan Beth Pfeffer's *Family of Strangers* (1992), sixteen-year-old Abby is in therapy with Dr. Leibowitz, learning how to put her life back together. Dr. Leibowitz tells Abby:

> I have a friend who believes in resolutions. She thinks everything can be resolved, that there don't have to be any loose ends, that life's a book with chapters and The End printed neatly on the last page. I keep telling her she's wrong (not that she asks), that there isn't a neat resolution for everything, that some feelings always stay unresolved, that life is filled with murky waters. (Pp. 157–158)

Those words not only offer Abby insight into life but also offer readers insight into Susan Beth Pfeffer, the highly acclaimed author for young adults.

Quotations from Susan Beth Pfeffer that are not attributed to a published source are from a personal interview conducted by the author of this article on 24 April 1995 and are published here by permission of Susan Beth Pfeffer.

The Writer

Pfeffer was born on 17 February 1948 to Leo Pfeffer, a lawyer and a professor, and Freda Plotkin Pfeffer. She has one brother, who is named Alan. The author of more than forty-seven books for children and young adults, she has received much acclaim for her young adult books, which for the most part end without definite resolutions. Pfeffer explains that "what interests me the most are aftermaths. How people respond *after* an event. I see a tragedy—say a kidnapping or a death—and I don't focus on that event per se; instead, I wonder about the aftermath, the consequences of what happened. I've always been intrigued with what happens next." That is what Pfeffer explores in her books for young adults: what happens next. She dives straight into life's murky waters, not looking for neat answers but exploring the emotions and reactions of normal people in horrific situations.

per se by itself

About David (1980), *The Year Without Michael* (1987), *Family of Strangers,* and *Twice Taken* (1994) all thrust ordinary teenagers into extraordinary situations. "I'm most interested in how kids react. You know *Twice Taken* is a very different story if the main character is twenty-five years old." *Twice Taken* chronicles sixteen-year-old Brooke's discovery that her father abducted her years ago from her mother, and her return to a mother who is at best a hazy memory and at worst an unwanted, intrusive stranger. *About David* follows Lynn's struggle to understand how her best friend could murder his parents and then commit suicide. Left with only David's private journals to offer insight, Lynn relives his life through the words in his journals as she tries to comprehend David's senseless killings and as she attempts to create a life for herself in the wake of this disaster.

In a similar way, Jody struggles to create a new life for her family and herself in the year following her brother's disappearance in *The Year Without Michael*. Never knowing whether Michael was kidnapped, had run away, or was murdered, Jody, her parents, and her sister live in the quagmire of uncertainty, always waiting for Michael's return. As her parents become increasingly unable to cope with their son's disappearance, Jody becomes more determined to accept the loss and to keep her remaining family intact. *Family of Strangers* also thrusts an unsuspecting teenager, Abby, into an incredible situation as her parents' unresolved anger and

quagmire swamp or situation that is difficult to get out of

despair over their young son's death finally lead Abby to attempt suicide.

Commenting about her work, Pfeffer notes:

> In all of those books, I was interested in family, but more interested in consequences. In *About David,* I wanted to describe how you get over a catastrophe. In *The Year Without Michael,* I wanted to explore the aftermath of a missing child. In *Twice Taken,* I wanted to show what happens after a missing child is found. Also, in all of them I wanted to focus on family. That is the thing that all kids have—family. Family may look different for different kids, but still, they all have one.

A Look at Four Novels

About David, The Year Without Michael, and *Family of Strangers* share other interesting similarities. All have teenage female protagonists dealing with death or loss. These books all show a sixteen year old reacting to the loss of a male sibling or friend. In *Family of Strangers* loss occurs through the death of a brother. In *The Year Without Michael* loss comes through disappearance. And just as Jody's family does not know where Michael is, neither does the reader. In fact, Pfeffer does not know either. "I don't know if Michael is dead or not. I didn't want an advantage over Jody and her family or over the reader. So, I never worked out what happened to him—I just had him disappear."

In *About David,* the loss is the death of Lynn's best friend, David. *Twice Taken* approaches loss a little differently: Brooke has been lost to her mother for eleven years. Abducted from her mother by her father when she was five, Brooke lived with her father for eleven years, at first believing that her mother was dead but later being told that she was not wanted by her mother. While *The Year Without Michael* gives readers a glimpse of life when a family member is missing, *Twice Taken* shows the impact that an absent member's return has on a family.

All four books deal with family life; but more importantly, they all address endurance and survival, a recurrent theme in Pfeffer's books. "I like to take normal kids and put them into peculiar—sometimes very peculiar—situations and then see what happens," she says. "I like to see how they endure, how they survive."

One way in which all Pfeffer's characters survive is by learning about control: what happens when they lose control, what happens when others attempt to control them, what happens when they take control of their own destinies. Dr. Leibowitz, Abby's therapist in *Family of Strangers,* tells Abby that "you can have some control over friends and lovers and husbands, but almost none over parents and siblings and children" (p. 158). Control has long been an issue for Pfeffer. She says that she does not "like structure imposed upon me. I never responded positively to imposed structure. It's not that I'm not a structured person. I'm very structured—but it's *my* structure, not something imposed upon me." Pfeffer's dislike of imposed control shows up in her characters. Lynn, Jody, Abby, and Brooke share Pfeffer's streak of independence, and they all find that it is when they are willing to focus on controlling only their own lives that they are free to grow and accept others as they are.

In *About David,* Lynn agonizes that she could have stopped David from murdering his parents and committing suicide. Only after she comes to believe that she could not control David's actions does she begin to accept what has happened. In *Family of Strangers*, Abby finally reaches the heartbreaking understanding that her father will probably never be able to reach out to her the way she would want, that if there is to be any reaching out, she would have to do it, and that she would have to be pleased with her actions and not count on his reactions. Recognizing that she has no control over his feelings or actions frees her to be responsible for her own feelings and actions.

A similar breakthrough comes for Jody in *The Year Without Michael.* Soon after Michael's disappearance, Jody sees how her absent brother is now controlling all her thoughts and actions:

> I'll start eating more sensibly later, Jody said. When Michael comes home, she thought to herself, the way she always did now. I'll concentrate on my schoolwork when Michael comes home. I'll straighten out

> *Dr. Leibowitz, Abby's therapist in* Family of Strangers, *tells Abby that "you can have some control over friends and lovers and husbands, but almost none over parents and siblings and children."*

my room when Michael comes home. I'll eat more sensibly, brush my teeth more regularly, jog every day, watch less TV, stop biting my nails, my lips, my tongue, when Michael comes home. I'll start sleeping again, and breathing again, and laughing again, when Michael comes home. I'll be Jody Chapman again when Michael comes home. I'll be alive again when Michael comes home. (P. 142)

But Michael does not come home, and the longer Jody and her family let this absent person continue to control what they do—and do not do—the longer they will have less and less of a life. After Jody goes to New York on a quest to find her brother, she realizes that looking for him is hopeless, and her father realizes what it would mean to lose all his children. At that moment they understand that they can continue to love Michael but must find a way to get on with their own lives, to stop letting him control their thoughts, and words, and actions.

In *Twice Taken,* Brooke sees a picture of herself as a young child on a television program about missing children. After calling the 800 number listed on the screen to report herself as that missing child, Brooke is quickly rushed away from the parent she now learns was her abductor. She is told that her real name is Amy, and she is sent to live with a mother, stepfather, and siblings she knew nothing about. She is forbidden to talk to the people who had been a part of her life for eleven years. Feeling as if she has lost all control, Brooke struggles to hold onto her former life and simultaneously become happy with her new one. Her mother, still in mourning for five-year-old Amy, works hard to turn Brooke into the five-year-old child she once knew. Only after Brooke and her mom realize that they cannot force themselves to love or like the other, that those feelings must occur naturally, do they begin to forge a true relationship.

forge   to form

Other Novels

Other novels for young adults by Pfeffer also deal with relationships and loss. *The Ring of Truth* (1993), *A Matter of Principle* (1982), and *Most Precious Blood* (1991) differ from

Pfeffer's other young adult books in that they do not involve a main character directly confronting the loss of a loved one. Yet the three books are similar in that they all focus on relationships that are threatened because of the main character's loss of innocence.

Most Precious Blood tells the story of Val Castaldi, the daughter of a suspected Mafia giant, and her discovery that she was bought by her father as an infant after her parents discovered they could not have their own children. As Val faces the truth about her own heritage, she also faces the truth about her father. Although her life has been filled with privileges, she now understands that those privileges have come at a high cost to others. Fearful of her father's retribution, she is nevertheless determined not to follow in his ways. Val knows that the truth, as painful as it may be, keeps her from becoming like her father, even though she was happier when she did not know the truth about him or about her heritage.

A Matter of Principle shows what happens when Becca and her friends publish an underground newspaper filled with stories that the sponsor of the sanctioned school newspaper refuses to print. Once the principal reads their paper, he suspends the group until they agree to apologize for what they have done. Becca refuses to apologize, believing that all she has done is to exercise her freedom of speech. Some of her fellow writers, however, discover that standing up for their principles is too difficult, and they opt to apologize. As Becca's relationships with her friends change over this incident, she learns what can be lost when one takes a stand on principles.

In *The Ring of Truth,* sixteen-year-old Sloan also takes a stand on principles, when she finds herself in the middle of a political scandal. Sloan becomes frightened and confused after a very powerful, and somewhat drunk, politician makes a pass at her during a party. The granddaughter of an enormously rich, powerful, political woman, Sloan thinks she is doing the right thing when she confirms a rumor that the lieutenant governor made a pass at her. What she fails to understand is that her best friend has lied about her involvement with the same man, in order to give Sloan's accusations credibility. Sloan feels surrounded by lies when she learns that her grandmother has lied to her for years about her younger brother's death. After living a sheltered life for years,

retribution here, punishment

underground unofficial, created outside the establishment

Sloan learns that life is not made of absolutes but is full of half-truths and compromises, and that knowing these can make it much more difficult.

All seven of these books for young adults have more in common beyond similar themes. All their protagonists are sixteen-year-old females. Two books, *About David* and *Family of Strangers,* use therapists to help these young girls understand their predicaments. *The Year Without Michael* ends with the family deciding to call a therapist. Another two books, *Ring of Truth* and *A Matter of Principle,* have the protagonists' boyfriends working at a restaurant called Burger Bliss. ("Any time I need a fast-food restaurant, I call it Burger Bliss," says Pfeffer.) And in almost all the books, school is a place where bad things happen.

In *About David,* Mr. Glick, the English teacher, decides to discuss the suicidal tendencies of Chatterton, a British poet, after David's suicide. His lack of sensitivity on the issue of suicide pushes David's close friend Jeffrey to the breaking point. He begins screaming and is later institutionalized. In *The Year Without Michael,* Jody acts in a similar manner when she falls apart after a history teacher pushes her for an answer. In *A Matter of Principle,* Becca finds herself in trouble, partly because of an unsupportive teacher and principal. Likewise, in *The Ring of Truth,* at the first hint of scandal, the school administrators remind Sloan that "this is not a school for scandal" (p. 95) and request that she "stay away from school for the next few days" (p. 96). In *Most Precious Blood,* school does not seem too positive a place as the nuns in charge appear to turn their backs on Mr. Castaldi's mobster connections so that he will continue to make sizable donations to the school.

In these books, the cafeteria is often the place in which the teenage characters meet to sort through problems; but when teachers or administrators come on the scene, problems grow or new ones arise. Why? Perhaps because, as Pfeffer explains, she "always disliked school. There were teachers I loved and teachers I liked and classes I loved, but the whole thing called school, I disliked."

Many teenagers dislike school, and Pfeffer's own dislike of the institution comes through realistically. Other parts of her novels are also very realistic. Whether showing characters who are dealing with suicide, murder, natural death, abandonment, or abduction, Pfeffer's novels seem so realistic

> *As Pfeffer explains, she "always disliked school. There were teachers I loved and teachers I liked and classes I loved, but the whole thing called school, I disliked."*

that they appear to be based on much research. "Not true," says Pfeffer:

> I don't do much research, maybe no research for my novels. But I did have a librarian write me recently and point out a mistake I made in *Twice Taken* that a little research would have avoided. In that book, the mom accuses her recently returned-home teenage daughter of being an alcoholic and attending an Alateen meeting. The librarian wrote to tell me that Alateen is for teenagers of alcoholics. If you are an alcoholic, you go to AA [Alcoholics Anonymous] no matter what your age is. That time my lack of research resulted in a mistake. Sometimes I ask someone a question. For *About David,* I asked someone about guns so I'd know what kind to say he used, that was all. I write my books in about one month, six weeks at the max, and write them one time through and then I'm done. I just don't do the research.

The Storyteller

Survival, endurance, control, independence, aftermath, and consequences: all these issues make their way into Pfeffer's novels. For her characters, who face seemingly insurmountable obstacles, Pfeffer creates plausible, realistic scenarios. How does she do that?

plausible appearing worthy of belief

> I can do it because I have lots of empathy. I don't see this as a positive or negative trait. It's just something I have. And it's a handy thing to have if you are writing about people who don't exist. As a kid, I didn't develop strong friendship abilities. I certainly wasn't a social kid. So I spent time watching others. That was what intrigued me—how others interacted. And I knew from third grade that I was a very good storyteller. I was an imaginative kid—perhaps more than others; perhaps that was just the part of me I chose to develop.

How people interact, how they react, how they face life's cruelest blows and live on: Susan Beth Pfeffer gives us glimpses of survivors. In doing so, she encourages readers to look for the survivor within themselves.

Selected Bibliography

WORKS BY SUSAN BETH PFEFFER

Books for Young Adults

Just Morgan (1970)

Better Than All Right (1972)

Rainbows and Fireworks (1973)

The Beauty Queen (1974)

Whatever Words You Want to Hear (1974)

Marly the Kid (1975)

Starring Peter and Leigh (1979)

About David (1980)

A Matter of Principle (1982)

Starting with Melodie (1983)

Fantasy Summer (1984)

Getting Even (1986)

The Year Without Michael (1987)

Most Precious Blood (1991)

Family of Strangers (1992)

The Ring of Truth (1993)

Twice Taken (1994)

Series

Make Me a Star (1985–1986)

The Sebastian Sisters (1988–1990)

Books for Upper Elementary Readers

Kid Power (1977)

Just Between Us (1980)

What Do You Do When Your Mouth Won't Open? (1981)

Courage, Dana (1983)

Kid Power Strikes Back (1984)

The Friendship Pact (1986)

Rewind to Yesterday (1988)

If you like the works of Susan Beth Pfeffer, you might also enjoy the works of Chris Crutcher and Cynthia Voigt.

Turning Thirteen (1988)

Future Forward (1989)

Dear Dad, Love Laurie (1989)

Make Believe (1993)

Nobody's Daughter (1995)

WORKS ABOUT SUSAN BETH PFEFFER

Commire, Anne, ed. "Susan Beth Pfeffer." In *Something About the Author*. Detroit: Gale Research, 1973, vol. 4.

Holtze, Sally Holmes, ed. "Susan Beth Pfeffer." In *The Sixth Book of Junior Authors and Illustrators*. New York: H. W. Wilson & Co., 1989.

Locher, Frances C., and Ann Evory, eds. "Susan Beth Pfeffer." In *Contemporary Authors*. Detroit: Gale Research, 1978, vols. 29–31.

Rinn, Miriam. "Author Profile." Book Report, January 1994, pp. 29–30.

How to Write to the Author
Susan Beth Pfeffer
c/o Henry Holt & Co., Inc.
115 West 18th Street
New York, NY 10011

Kin Platt

(1911-)

by M. Jerry Weiss

Kin Platt, born in New York City, is a perceptive, multitalented author of books for children, young adults, and adults. In addition to being a writer, he is a cartoonist, a painter, and a sculptor.

Early Dreams

As a child Platt had several dreams: to be the greatest runner in the world, to be an outstanding baseball pitcher, to be a writer as well as an artist whose artwork would be displayed in museums throughout the world, and to be a famous composer whose music would be played in great concert halls. He was an avid reader who enjoyed pulp (cheaply produced) books that featured exciting sports, adventure, and western heroes in action. In his childhood days he did lots of swapping of books with others. Discovering the library was a great event in his life. He read almost everything, including

Kin Platt himself drew the above portrait.

53

There is an article about Jack London in volume 2.

Edward Lear
(1812–1888),
François Rabelais
(1483–1553), and
Miguel de Cervantes (1547–1616)
are all famous writers
of humor and satire.
Charles Lamb
(1775–1834) was an
English essayist and
critic, and **Thomas
De Quincey**
(1785–1859) was an
English author most
famous for his description of his addiction to opium.

Joseph McCarthy
(1908–1957) was a
Republican senator
from Wisconsin who
attracted much attention in the 1950s. He
charged that Communists had infiltrated the U.S. government. Many of his
claims were unfounded, and after
televised hearings of
his charges against
the U.S. Army, he
lost much of his support.

fairy tales, myths, legends, and other kinds of stories about good fighting evil. Writers such as Charles Lamb, Edward Lear, François Rabelais, Miguel de Cervantes, and Thomas De Quincey were among his favorites. Jack London also influenced him with his exciting stories of struggle for survival.

Through his reading, especially of Joyce Cary's *The Horse's Mouth,* Platt learned that to be a genuine artist one must live only for one's art and learn how to survive. There is nothing easy about choosing to be an artist. Platt acknowledges the many sacrifices that he made, even sleeping on a bare floor or in a railroad station, being hungry, and living among beggars to pursue his dream.

Platt drew funny cartoons in school. In the 1930s, he was a successful cartoonist and caricaturist for newspapers, and a radio comedy writer as well, working for some of the biggest stars in broadcasting. His comic strip "Mr. and Mrs." had a lengthy run of seventeen years. Later he started another strip, "The Duke and the Duchess," which ran on Sundays and was a comic reflection on some of the political events of the day, including the hearings held by Senator Joseph McCarthy. The paper's publisher soon reminded Platt that if he had been hired for his political ideas, he would have been published on the editorial page. In 1954 this Sunday comic strip was discontinued. "The Duke and the Duchess" foreshadowed Platt's concerns about political and social issues, which would appear in several of his books for young adults. He had written hundreds of radio scripts, hundreds of animated cartoons for films and television, and thousands of comic-book stories. Now he wanted to concentrate on one good thing, and that turned out to be *The Blue Man.*

Becoming a Novelist

Susan Hirschman, who was assisting Ursula Nordstrom at the publishing company Harper, was the person responsible for convincing the company to publish *The Blue Man* in 1961. It tells the story of a dangerous, pathological crusader determined to cleanse the world according to his own fantasies.

Miriam S. Mathies, writing in the November 1961 *School Library Journal,* concluded her review of *The Blue Man* by stating, "The vernacular is so exaggerated and details of the plot so fantastic that even with the final more or less plausible explanation, the book cannot be recommended for purchase." She also commented on Platt's short, choppy, ungrammatical sentences. Of course, this style draws young readers to the book, making it fast-paced and realistic. Other reviewers did credit the book with being exciting. Platt's unusual plot and writing style made an enjoyable fantasy story.

Censorship affected several of Platt's books. When *Mystery of the Witch Who Wouldn't* was published in 1969, for example, the book was burned in Michigan because the author was accused of encouraging witchcraft. It is important to note that other popular authors for children and young adults, including R. L. Stine, Caroline Cooney, Christopher Pike, Joan Lowery Nixon, Lois Duncan, and John Bellairs have created "chiller thrillers," and such books are among the most popular in bookstores and libraries. Later reviewers objected to Platt's use of strong street language in his books for young adults. He was not trying to be sensational; he told his stories as he saw them. However, the fact that this language added to the realism and was natural for the characters made no difference to librarians and teachers who could, and did, ban his works.

Some editors did not support Platt's efforts either, although in 1965 Susan Hirschman was instrumental in the publication of *Big Max,* his first mystery for beginning readers. In 1966 Harper Brothers turned down Platt's *Sinbad and Me,* a full-length mystery for young readers. In this book Steve, a precocious twelve year old, and Sinbad, his bulldog, go through a series of adventures to solve the mysterious disappearance of Big Nick Murdock and his boat. Some editors said it was too long and needed to be cut, but Platt refused this advice. The book appealed to John Francis Marion, a new editor at the Chilton Company in Philadelphia. When it was published, it won the prestigious Mystery Writers of America Edgar Award as the best juvenile mystery in 1967.

Phyllis Cohen, in her review of *Sinbad and Me* in the October 1966 *Young Readers Review,* said, "This is a funny book. So few mysteries are genuinely funny, that this one stands out like a beacon! . . . The dialogue may be breezy, but the plot is solid—certainly one of the cleverest mysteries for youngsters I've ever read."

Platt has had his ups and downs with publishers. In a personal letter to me, dated 4 February 1995, he writes, "Editors have decided to get into the act more and try to direct

Censorship affected several of Platt's books.

There are articles about Caroline Cooney and Lois Duncan in volume 1. There is an article about Joan Lowery Nixon in volume 2.

Reviewers objected to Platt's use of strong street language in his books for young adults. He was not trying to be sensational; he told stories as he saw them.

For fast and breezy reading see Jay Bennett's books such as *The Executioner* and *Sing Me a Death Song.*

their own agendas. For better and worse." Platt acknowledges that listening to editors, whether they are right or wrong, is a requirement for getting published, but one needs to keep in mind the quantity and quality of this successful writer in so many fields to realize that in many cases he really does seem to know best. He has often been ahead of his time, and fortunately several editors and publishers have recognized his talents and kept publishing his books.

In that same letter, he says he has "always been interested in how rotten parents influence kids, and also environment and social pressures on the underprivileged." Such concerns led him to write *The Boy Who Could Make Himself Disappear* (1968). This is one of several of Platt's books that made a major impact on readers. It is extremely relevant today, for it deals with divorce and with a single parent who is more concerned with herself than with her son, Roger. This young protagonist, who is emotionally confused by the divorce and has a serious speech impediment, feels embarrassment, which affects his very being, both in and out of school. He is on the verge of schizophrenia. Who has the time to help? Zena Sutherland, in a review in the September 1968 *Bulletin of the Center for Children's Books,* stated, "[Roger's] sad musings on incidents of the past, his efforts to cope with his mother's hostility, and his valiant efforts to cooperate with the speech therapist are brilliantly told."

Another of Platt's emotionally strong books, *Hey, Dummy,* was published in 1971. Betsy Byars reviewed it in the 12 March 1978 *New York Times Book Review,* and her comments are worth quoting at length:

> Bringing the tragedy of mental retardation to the printed page is difficult. Only the simplest truth is needed, and yet nothing that is said ever seems quite enough. Through the wry, sensitive Neil Comstock, Kin Platt says more than anybody so far, and he says it with gentleness and guts.

[*Hey, Dummy*] begins with a three-man football game in which the Dummy becomes unwittingly involved when he picks up the stray ball. Boyish violence ensues, leaving Neil disturbed. "Thinking about that Dummy just lying there and saying 'Aaaah' after I hit him, ruined my game."

impediment something that interferes or slows the progress of; a **speech impediment** is often stammering or a lisp

schizophrenia a psychotic disorder in which one loses contact with one's environment, displays deteriorating levels of function within everyday life, and exhibits a disintegration of personality

Betsy Byars also writes for young adults. There is an article about her in volume 1.

Neil's involvement with the Dummy increases. . . . [Soon Neil] is attempting to look at the world as the Dummy does. He tries to put himself into Alan's skin. . . .

The build-up to the final tragedy is slow and sure. A young girl is attacked in the park, and the Dummy becomes the target of mob actions. Neil, totally committed now, helps him escape. His evaluation of the situation is one of the most poignant moments of the novel. "I'm in big trouble. . . . I'm sure I had to do what I did but it just didn't work out the way things are supposed to when you feel you're doing right." And then he agonized, "if only he wasn't such a Dummy!"

poignant deeply affecting; touching

Despite an occasional jarring note, the book has a realistic feel to it. This is largely due to the dimension of the characters. The Dummy and Neil dominate, but Neil's kooky sister could be a book in herself. And Mr. Alvarado, a Mexican-American teacher, in three appearances comes off as a complex and wholly believable character. There are flashes of humor in this compelling novel, but the nature of mental retardation does not lend itself to a happy ending. And the last word, uttered by Neil, is the same sound with which the Dummy tries to communicate throughout the book, the confused, helpless, "Aaaah." (p. 8)

Chloris and the Creeps (1973) won the Distinguished Book of the Year award from the Southern California Council on Literature for Children and Young People. Platt then wrote two books, *Chloris and the Freaks* (1975) and *The Terrible Love Life of Dudley Cornflower* (1976), which were published by Dick Jackson, an editor at Bradbury Press.

Kids in Gangs

Platt's first editor, Susan Hirschman, left Harper and became the publisher of Greenwillow Books at Morrow. She accepted *Headman* (1975), a book about gangs, which won an American Library Association Notable Book award. This strong story is about a young teenager, Owen Kirby, who has been committed for a two-year sentence to Camp Sawyer, a youth correctional center in northern California. Owen had been attacked by a gang and had defended himself with a weapon. Although Owen knows how to play the game of getting along in camp, he is constantly reminded of his home environment and of the fact that he has to join a gang there in order to survive.

replete fully filled

Home is the back streets of Los Angeles, replete with filth, noise, and violence. When Owen is released to go home because his mother is sick, he is attacked several times and becomes the headman of his own gang. Then he sees the boy who attacked him and is sure he can beat him. When Owen confronts the boy and challenges him, the boy shoots him. One wonders whether any lessons can be learned in any correctional institution to help young people survive in such an environment. The strong language and action make this a popular book with young adult readers.

Another book about gangs, *The Doomsday Gang* (1977) concerns five boys who, rejected by other gangs in their Los Angeles neighborhood, form their own, the Doomsday Gang. There is one major problem: how mentally competent are these young men? There is much violence, destruction, and harsh street language. Reviews condemned the book for one or more of these three elements. Yet Platt wanted to point out that gang members function in worlds that are different from courts, schools, and social agencies.

Run for Your Life (1977), *Dracula, Go Home* (1979), and *Frank and Stein and Me* (1982) have mystery, action, suspense, and humor, as does *Flames Going Out* (1980). *The Ape Inside of Me* (1980) is another strong book by Platt that shows the quick personality changes possible within a young person. Fifteen-year-old Eddie seems unable to control his temper; he is frustrated and often lacks self-confidence. For these reasons he invents Kong, a macho alter ego whom he blames for his temper tantrums and fights. Eddie gradually gains control of his temper and succeeds. This book is a genuine winner in showing the growing pains of young people.

Sports and Beyond

For other novels about sports, see Robert Lipsyte, Walter Dean Myers, Todd Strasser, and Cynthia Voigt.

If running is a reader's game, then *Brogg's Brain* (1981) is most noteworthy. Fifteen-year-old Monty Davis runs the mile for the school track team because he enjoys running, not because he is competitive or feels he has to win. His coach and his father both think Monty is not putting all he can into his running efforts. Monty is very disturbed by all of this. He just wants to have fun running. Then he dates Cindy, a Japanese American marathon runner, and takes her to a movie, *Brogg's Brain,* in which a talking brain dominates various characters. The two discuss the possibilities of someone sending personal messages to himself in to order to achieve certain goals.

Monty's father does not let up on him; he urges Monty to work harder to succeed as a champion runner. In an angry moment, Monty stalks out of the house to run in the park, where he meets Julie, who happens to be a champion marathon runner and who can outrun him every time. They talk, and she offers him some tips. They begin running together.

Then the day arrives for a major track meet with a rival school. The coach instructs Monty in how to run to wear out a rival school runner, Ellison, so that Monty's two teammates can go on to win first and second place in the track meet. Monty gets the feeling he can run better than he has ever run before. He cannot wear out Ellison, but he goes on to beat him, winning the race. Monty discovers the joys of competitive running.

Kin Platt says he appreciates the fact that he has reached many young people through his books and caused them to think. "Girl readers were most responsive, with their own problems at home or school which I tried to solve," Platt wrote in a 1995 letter to me. "Boys were responsive also and several claimed they had read their first book. That's a plus." Platt's advice to would-be writers is, "Know your subject and characters. Fight on." His concluding remarks in the letter are revealing: "As you may have guessed, I don't like to talk much about writing. It's a magical process for me and hopefully for a reader."

Selected Bibliography

WORKS BY KIN PLATT

The Blue Man (1961)

Big Max, with illustrations by Robert Lopshire (1965)

Sinbad and Me (1966)

The Boy Who Could Make Himself Disappear (1968)

Mystery of the Witch Who Wouldn't (1969)

Hey, Dummy (1971)

Chloris and the Creeps (1973)

Chloris and the Freaks (1975)

For stories about the emotional stresses that young people face, you may want to read novels by Bruce Brooks, Robert Cormier, Chris Crutcher, and Paul Zindel.

Platt's advice to would-be writers is, "Know your subject and characters. Fight on."

Readers who enjoy Kin Platt's work might also enjoy reading Jack London, Caroline B. Cooney, Joan Lowery Nixon, and Lois Duncan. For fast and breezy reading see Jay Bennett's books, such as *The Executioner* and *Sing Me a Death Song.* For stories about the emotional stresses that young people face, you may want to read novels by Bruce Brooks, Robert Cormier, Chris Crutcher, and Paul Zindel. For other novels about sports, see Robert Lipsyte, Walter Dean Myers, Todd Strasser, and Cynthia Voigt.

Headman (1975)

The Terrible Love Life of Dudley Cornflower (1976)

The Doomsday Gang (1977)

The Mystery of the Missing Moose, with illustrations by Robert Lopshire (1977)

Run for Your Life, with photographs by Chuck Freedman (1977)

Dracula, Go Home, with illustrations by Frank Mayo (1979)

The Ape Inside of Me (1980)

Chloris and the Weirdos (1980)

Flames Going Out (1980)

The Ghost of Hellsfire Street (1980)

Brogg's Brain (1981)

Frank and Stein and Me (1982)

Crocker (1983)

Darwin and the Great Beasts (1992)

WORKS ABOUT KIN PLATT

Gallo, Donald R., ed. *Speaking for Ourselves: Autobiographical Sketches by Notable Authors of Books for Young Adults.* Urbana: National Council of Teachers of English, 1990, pp. 176–177.

How to Write to the Author
Kin Platt
c/o Greenwillow Books
1350 Avenue of the Americas
New York, NY 10019

Edgar Allan Poe

(1809–1849)

by Alan M. McLeod

In Edgar Allan Poe's "The Imp of the Perverse," a short essay and story defining what causes us to do what we know is not in our best interest—what will present to us the direst of consequences—the narrator speaks the following words:

> I am safe—I am safe—yes—if I be not fool enough to make open confession! . . . And now my own casual self-suggestion, that I might possibly be fool enough to confess the murder of which I had been guilty, confronted me, as if the very ghost of him whom I had murdered—and beckoned me on to death.

Earlier in the same essay, Poe wrote:

> There lives no man who at some period has not been tormented, for example, by an earnest desire to tanta-

Although he wrote more than 150 years ago, Poe still manages to stir our emotions through his poetry and prose.

circumlocution using an unneccesarily large number of words

involutions wordy entanglements

lize a listener by circumlocution. The speaker is aware that he displeases; he has every intention to please . . . yet, the thought strikes him, that by certain involutions and parentheses, this anger may be engendered. That single thought is enough. The impulse increases to a wish, the wish to a desire, the desire to an uncontrollable longing, and the longing, (to the deep regret and mortification of the speaker, and in defiance of all consequences,) is indulged.

Few stories better illustrate the complexity of Poe as a writer: his masterful use of language, his cunning turns of phrase, and his fascination with terror. With a few exceptions, his stories are told by a first-person narrator; sometimes that narrator is an observer of, but more often a participant in, the story.

Who Was Edgar Allan Poe?

Some have called Poe the "master of the macabre." Certainly his tales of horror include macabre, or ghastly, details. But he is also known as the inventor of the detective story, a writer of science fiction, a major contributor to the short story as a type of literature, an imaginative poet striving for perfection, and an effective critic.

convention accepted literary method or technique

dynamic changing and in motion

Although he wrote more than 150 years ago, Poe still manages to stir our emotions through his poetry and prose. One may, in reading Poe's work, notice some differences in punctuation, particularly in the use of commas, from accepted convention (see, for example, the commas around the parenthetical expression in the preceding long quotation), or occasional variations in the spelling used in twentieth-century English. Language is dynamic, and some of its conventions and vocabulary change over time.

A Thumbnail Sketch of Poe's Life

Edgar Poe, a writer of tremendous imagination and true originality, and one of the most influential writers produced in the United States, was born in Boston, Massachusetts, on 19

January 1809. His parents, David Poe, Jr., and Elizabeth Arnold Poe, were professional actors, and they performed in plays staged anywhere from New England to the South. While on tour when Edgar, called Eddy, was two years old, his mother died in Richmond, Virginia. At that time, Mr. Poe had already abandoned the family, which also included Eddy's older brother and younger sister.

Mrs. Poe is buried in the churchyard at St. John's Church in Richmond. It is the same church where, less than forty years before, Patrick Henry made his impassioned "Give me liberty or give me death" speech to inhabitants of the American colonies then deliberating whether to declare independence from England.

Poe was taken in as a foster child by John Allan, a successful businessman in Richmond, and his wife, Frances. Although he never adopted Poe, Allan raised him, and Poe eventually took the Allan name as his middle name. Except for a five-year period when the family was in England, Poe lived in Richmond until his late teens. An excellent student, he spent one term at the University of Virginia, leaving when he could not stay ahead of his creditors—a circumstance that happened over and over again in his life, and one that led to permanent estrangement from his foster father.

Although he lived at various times in Baltimore, Philadelphia, and New York, Poe spent much of his life in Richmond. The Poe Museum is situated in the oldest stone house there, reputedly located in the same block as one of the Allan family residences.

Poe began writing poetry when in his teens (he published *Tamerlane and Other Poems* when he was eighteen), and he apparently wrote throughout his time in the military as an enlisted man (rising to the rank of sergeant major) and later as a cadet at West Point. He had a fascination with the military, but he could not, or would not, submit to the long-term commitment; he resigned from West Point in March 1831.

After West Point, Poe filled a number of short-term positions to support his writing, and he became an effective critic and editor. In late 1835 he returned to Richmond and became the editor of the *Southern Literary Messenger*. The next year, in Baltimore, he married his cousin, Virginia Clemm, who was then only thirteen years old. That Virginia was so young, probably too young to be marrying, concerned Poe. We know this because there are accounts: first,

deliberating debating or considering

creditor person to whom one owes money

estrangement separation and hostility

that he misrepresented her age, saying she was fifteen, for example; second, that he held a more public, probably second, wedding in Richmond when Virginia was fourteen; and third, that she appears on their marriage bond as twenty-one.

Later, Poe served at various times as the editor of *Burton's Gentleman's Magazine, Graham's Magazine,* and *Broadway Journal,* and he wrote as well for numerous periodicals, including the *New York Mirror.* His caustic manner and frequent disagreements with publishers made his editing positions generally of short duration; he was often fired. He also gave lectures and readings, and he sought various ways to support Virginia and her mother. Because Poe was paid very little for his publications and his editing, he was dependent on various sponsors to make ends meet. He battled poverty throughout his adulthood.

caustic harsh; biting like an acid

After Virginia died of tuberculosis in 1847, Poe had a series of romantic attachments or sentimental relationships with at least four women, most of them married or widowed, including briefly Jane Locke and Nancy Richmond. He was for a short time engaged to Sarah Helen Whitman and later to Elmira Royster Shelton of Richmond. While returning to New York to straighten out his financial affairs prior to marrying the widow Shelton, Poe became quite ill in Baltimore and died there on 7 October 1849.

opium a bitter and brownish addictive drug made from the dried juice of the opium poppy

Myths still abound that Poe smoked opium, which allegedly enabled him to write imaginative tales, and that he died in a drunken stupor. Such rumors are misleading because Poe's constitution could not tolerate alcohol and he became ill if he took a drink: therefore, although the facts are unknown, it is not likely that drunkenness caused his death. Furthermore, his imagination was so vivid that he needed no drug-induced stimulus. These rumors undoubtedly arose from the petty jealousies of Poe's contemporaries, individuals who could not accept Poe's greatness and the fact that he excelled in many areas of literature.

The Tales and Stories

In his stories, Poe masterfully details imagined terror, he skillfully evokes mystery and horror, and he presents bizarre characters and events. Look, for example, at "Hop-Frog."

Hop-Frog is the court jester (fool) to the king. Poe tells us, "His value was trebled [tripled] in the eyes of the king, by the fact of his being also a dwarf and a cripple." He is the butt of many jokes and subject to much cruelty. Hop-Frog, abetted by another captive, the beautiful Trippeta, plots revenge. When the king plans a masquerade ball but despairs of how to disguise himself, Hop-Frog suggests that the king and his seven ministers come as the "Eight Chained Ourang-Outangs." Through a series of steps, Hop-Frog eventually succeeds in hooking the masked king and ministers, chained together, to a lowered chandelier. Then he quickly causes them to be hoisted high in the air above the ballroom. He scrambles over them, setting them on fire before scampering up the chain to the skylight and shouting:

abetted helped

> "I now see distinctly," he said, "what manner of people these maskers are. They are a great king and his seven privy-councillors—a king who does not scruple to strike a defenseless girl, and his seven councillors who abet him in the outrage. As for myself, I am simply Hop-Frog, the jester—and *this is my last jest.*"

In "The Oval Portrait," Poe's narrator, a wounded man, has stopped at a temporarily abandoned chalet. When he cannot sleep, he decides to study the portraits in his bedroom and a book that describes them. He is fascinated by the portrait of a beautiful young woman (some critics speculate that this is a manifestation of Poe reflecting on his child bride). The portrait is of the artist's wife, and the artist is so consumed with capturing her essence on canvas that he cannot see she is dying as he paints her:

chalet a remote herdsman's hut in the Alps, or a cottage or house in that style

manifestation appearance or demonstration

> And he would not see that the tints which he spread upon the canvas were drawn from the cheeks of her who sat beside him. And when many weeks had passed, and but little remained to do, save one brush upon the mouth and one tint upon the eye, the spirit of the lady again flickered up as a flame within the socket of the lamp. . . . the painter stood entranced before the work which he had wrought . . . and crying with a loud voice, "This is indeed Life itself!"

"The Tell-Tale Heart" is one of Poe's most popular tales, revealing as it does the madness of the narrator, his irrational behavior, and his compulsion to incriminate himself. Few writers can convey a sense of horror as effectively as Poe. Look at the following passage from the story: it is near midnight, and the narrator has been standing in pitch blackness looking at an old man sleeping. A noise has wakened the old man, who lies in his bed not knowing what is there but sensing an evil presence. The narrator recalls:

> Meantime the hellish tattoo [drumming] of the heart increased. It grew quicker and quicker, and louder and louder every instant. The old man's terror *must* have been extreme! It grew louder, I say, louder every moment!—do you mark me well? I have told you that I am nervous: so I am. And now at the dead hour of the night, amid the dreadful silence of that old house, so strange a noise as this excited me to uncontrollable terror.

"The Fall of the House of Usher" was made into popular movies in 1949, 1960, and 1979.

Another form of terror is conveyed in "The Fall of the House of Usher." The narrator, a boyhood friend of Roderick Usher, has come to visit at Usher's invitation. He can tell that Usher is mentally disturbed, and he sees the crumbling condition of the mansion as reflecting Usher's own state. Usher's twin sister, Madeline, is cataleptic (she can fall into a deathlike sleep). One night Roderick comes to the narrator to say that Madeline is dead. They place her body in a coffin and carry it to a vault where Roderick wishes to preserve it for a fortnight (fourteen days) before burial. Some days later, the narrator finds Usher murmuring:

> Not hear it?—yes, I hear it, and *have* heard it. Long—long—long—many minutes, many hours, many days have I heard it—yet I dared not—oh, pity me, miserable wretch that I am!—I dared not—I *dared* not speak! *We have put her living in the tomb!* Said I not that my senses were acute? I *now* tell you that I heard her first feeble movements in the hollow coffin. . . . MADMAN! I TELL YOU THAT SHE NOW STANDS WITHOUT THE DOOR!

Revenge combined with terror is the subject of "The Cask of Amontillado." Montressor, the narrator, has previously been insulted by Fortunato. Fortunato fancies himself a connoisseur of fine wines, and amontillado is such a wine. Montressor craftily employs this knowledge to gain his revenge.

connoisseur expert; one who knows

Poe examined terror from other vantage points. "The Masque of the Red Death" explores efforts to secure safety for oneself and friends. In order to escape a quick-killing plague, Prince Prospero takes a thousand healthy friends to a well-protected, well-provisioned castle far in the country. Once they are inside the castle, they seal the doors and windows and proceed to enjoy life. In the sixth month of their seclusion, Prospero holds a masquerade ball. Everyone is having a wonderful time until the appearance of a hideous, unknown masquerader (mummer), who struts from room to room. Prospero attacks him and is killed.

"The Masque of the Red Death" was made into popular movies in 1964 and 1989.

> Then, summoning the wild courage of despair, a throng of the revelers at once threw themselves into the black apartment, and, seizing the mummer, whose tall figure stood erect and motionless within the shadow of the ebony clock, gasped in unutterable horror at finding the grave-cerements [shrouds] and corpse-like mask which they handled with so violent a rudeness, untenanted by any tangible form.

untenanted by empty of

These are representative of Poe's horror and science fiction tales. Examples of others worth reading include "The Pit and the Pendulum" (set during the Spanish Inquisition) and "Ligeia" (with its themes of reincarnation and preserving beauty).

reincarnation belief that when a human or animal dies, the soul returns in another body, possibly as another species

Detective Fiction

Poe is credited with inventing the story of detection, or mystery story, typically including an unofficial detective with powerful deductive ability, a reluctant police officer, scientific data, and seemingly insignificant details employed to solve the riddle and prevent unjust punishment. The Mystery Writers of America honor Poe by presenting the Edgar Allan Poe Award each year to the writer of the best detective story.

deductive using logic and reason

> *Another good detective story by Poe is "The Gold Bug."*

Sherlock Holmes and his assistant **Dr. Watson** are characters in the detective stories of Sir Arthur Conan Doyle. There is an article about Doyle in volume 1.

Poe's detective stories, designed on the basis of ratiocination (the use of logical reasoning and the imagination) include "The Murders in the Rue Morgue" and "The Purloined Letter," two stories revealing the reasoning powers of Poe's detective, C. Auguste Dupin. In many respects, Dupin is the forerunner of Sherlock Holmes, and his narrator colleague is the approximate equivalent of Dr. Watson. Another good detective story by Poe is "The Gold Bug."

Poetry and Philosophy

Poe loved poetry, but it was his tales that sold. It is interesting to note that at least three poems appear among the tales: "The Haunted Palace" in "The Fall of the House of Usher," "The Conqueror Worm" in "Ligeia," and "To One in Paradise" in "The Assignation."

Poe gives one of his important definitions for stories and poetry in his critical review of Nathaniel Hawthorne's "Twice-Told Tales":

> The tale proper, in our opinion, affords unquestionably the fairest field for the exercise of the loftiest talent, which can be afforded by the wide domains of mere prose. Were we bidden to say how the highest genius could be most advantageously employed for the best display of its own powers, we should answer, without hesitation—in the composition of a rhymed poem, not to exceed in length what might be perused in an hour. . . . We need only here say, upon this topic, that in almost all classes of composition, the unity of effect or impression is a point of the greatest importance. It is clear, moreover, that this unity cannot be thoroughly preserved in productions whose perusal cannot be completed at one sitting.

perused examined

This unity of effect is achieved by Poe in a number of ways, whether that effect is terror, melancholy sadness, ideal love, or fate. In "Letter to B_____," he writes "Poetry, above all things, is a beautiful painting whose tints, to minute inspection, are confusion worse confounded, but start boldly

confounded complicated or obscured

out to the cursory glance of the connoisseur." Later in the letter he adds:

> A poem, in my opinion, is opposed to a work of science by having for its immediate object, pleasure, not truth . . . to which end music is an essential, since the comprehension of sweet sound is our most indefinite conception. Music, when combined with a pleasurable idea, is poetry; music without the idea is simply music; the idea without the music is prose from its very definitiveness.

Thus in his poem "To Helen," Poe is so struck with the classic beauty of this idealized person that it causes him to compare her "To the glory that was Greece/And the grandeur that was Rome."

His poem "The Bells" magnificently combines sound and melody, through the careful use of internal and end rhyme, tonal effects, and onomatopoeia (words whose sounds approximate their meaning, such as "clanging," "jingling," "clash," and "tinkle") he creates a musical, rhythmical verse that resonates variously with bells of merriment, happiness, turbulence, and melancholy:

tonal effects here, the arrangement of sounds and rhythms in words or music

> Keeping time, time, time
> In a sort of Runic rhyme,
> To the throbbing of the bells—
> Of the bells, bells, bells

rune ancient mark or writing thought to have magical or symbolic power

One of Poe's most popular poems, "The Raven," is also a major part of the subject of his "The Philosophy of Composition." In this essay, Poe further describes his theories about art, especially poetry, and he draws upon his experience in writing this poem to illustrate those theories. He writes:

"The Raven" was made into popular movies in 1935 and 1963.

> I had now gone so far as the conception of a Raven—the bird of ill omen—monotonously repeating the one word, "Nevermore" at the conclusion of each stanza, in a poem of melancholy tone. . . . I asked myself—"Of all melancholy topics, what, according to the *universal* understanding of mankind, is the most melan-

choly?" "Death"—was the obvious reply. "And when," I said, "is this most melancholy of topics most poetical?". . ."When it most closely allies itself to Beauty." The death, then, of a beautiful woman is, unquestionably, the most poetical topic in the world . . . .

I had now to combine the two ideas, of a lover lamenting his deceased mistress, and a Raven continuously repeating the word "Nevermore." I had to combine these, bearing in mind my design of varying, at every turn, the *application* of the word repeated; but the only intelligible mode of such combination is that of imagining the Raven employing the word in answer to the queries of the lover.

intelligible clear and understandable

Reading the poem reveals how Poe employs the technique of a bereaved lover posing questions to a raven perched on a bust of Pallas Athena, the Greek goddess of wisdom, above the door to his room:

bereaved suffering from a loss

But the raven, sitting lonely on the placid bust, spoke only
That one word, as if his soul in that one word he did outpour.
Nothing farther then he uttered—not a feather then he fluttered—
Till I scarcely more than muttered, "Other friends have flown
before—
On the morrow he will leave as my hopes have flown before."
Then the bird said, "Nevermore."
. . .
Prophet!" said I, "thing of evil!—prophet still, if bird or devil!—
Whether Tempter sent, or whether tempest tossed thee here ashore,
Desolate, yet all undaunted, on this desert land enchanted—
On this home by Horror haunted,—tell me truly, I implore—

Is there—is there balm in Gilead?—tell me—tell
me, I implore!"
Quoth the raven, "Nevermore."

And to each question asked by the narrator, the bird provides only the one answer. This poem joins "Lenore,"
"Annabel Lee," and others in celebrating doomed women. In
that respect, it echoes tragic heroines in Poe's tales, from
Ligeia in "Ligeia" to Madeline Usher in "The Fall of the House
of Usher."

Conclusion

Poe wrote to create effect; he did not write to teach a lesson
or a moral value, but to achieve artistic perfection. He pursued beauty and the imagination, seeing the purpose of literature as producing pleasure or an effect, and as simultaneously appealing to the reader's reason and emotion. Rarely
has a writer so effectively accomplished his or her goals. And
it would be difficult to find an author who excelled as did
Poe in three distinct areas—poetry, short stories, and literary
criticism. Poe remains one of this country's finest and most
influential writers.

Selected Bibliography

MODERN EDITIONS OF INDIVIDUAL WORKS BY EDGAR ALLAN POE

The Narrative of Arthur Gordon Pym of Nantucket (1960)
The Fall of the House of Usher (1971)
The Raven (1972)
Eureka: A Prose Poem (1973)
The Narrative of Arthur Gordon Pym (1973)
A Chapter on Autography (1974)
The Narrative of Arthur Gordon Pym (1975)
The Cask of Amontillado (1980)
The Imaginary Voyages (1981)
Marginalia (1981)
The Black Cat (1984)

If you like the works of Edgar Allan Poe, you might also enjoy the works of Jay Bennett, Stephen Crane, Sir Arthur Conan Doyle.

The Raven (1984; 1986)

Eureka: A Prose Poem: An Essay on the Material and Spiritual Universe (1991)

MODERN EDITIONS OF COLLECTED WORKS BY EDGAR ALLAN POE

Tales (1952)

Poe's Poems and Essays (1955)

Poems and Essays (1958)

Poe's Tales of Mystery and Imagination (1962)

Short Stories (1964)

Tales of Mystery and Imagination (1964)

Poems (1965)

The Purloined Letter, and The Murders in the Rue Morgue (1966)

The Fall of the House of Usher and Other Writings: Poems, Tales, Essays, and Reviews (1967; 1986)

The Complete Poetry and Selected Criticism of Edgar Allan Poe (1968; 1981)

The Gold Bug and Other Tales of Mystery (1969)

The Raven and Other Poems (1969)

Great Short Works of Edgar Allan Poe (1970)

Seven Tales (1971)

The Illustrated Edgar Allan Poe (1976)

The Science Fiction of Edgar Allan Poe (1976)

The Short Fiction of Edgar Allan Poe (1976)

Collected Poems, Essays on Poetry (1977)

The Complete Works of Edgar Allan Poe (1965; 1979)

Selected Tales (1980)

The Unknown Poe: An Anthology of Fugitive Writing by Edgar Allan Poe (1980)

The Annotated Tales of Edgar Allan Poe (1981)

Selections from the Critical Writings of Edgar Allan Poe (1981)

The Unabridged Edgar Allan Poe (1983)

Essays and Reviews (1984)

Poetry and Tales (1984)

You can see Poe's New York home as it might have looked when he wrote many of his works. It is located in a small park near the corner of the Grand Concourse and East Kingsbridge Road in the Bronx. For information write to:
The Bronx County Historical Society
3309 Bainbridge Avenue
Bronx, NY 10467

Many of Poe's belongings, as well as various documents, tributes, and exhibits, are on display at the Poe Museum in Virginia. You can write or visit:
The Edgar Allan Poe Museum
1914 East Main Street
Richmond, VA 23223

The Brevities: Pinakidia, Marginalia, Fifty Suggestions, and Other Works (1985)

The Annotated Tales of Edgar Allan Poe (1986)

Writing in the Broadway Journal: Nonfictional Prose (1986)

The Essential Poe (1991)

The Collected Tales and Poems of Edgar Allan Poe (1992)

Edgar Allan Poe Reader (1993)

WORKS ABOUT EDGAR ALLAN POE

Budd, Louis J., and Edwin H. Cady, eds. *On Poe.* Durham, N.C.: Duke University Press, 1993.

Dameron, J. Lasley. *Edgar Allan Poe: A Bibliography of Criticism, 1827–1967.* Charlottesville, Va.: University Press of Virginia, 1974.

Dayan, Joan. *Fable of Mind: An Inquiry into Poe's Fiction.* New York: Oxford University Press, 1987.

Fisher, Benjamin Franklin IV, ed. *Poe and His Times: The Artist and His Milieu.* Baltimore: Edgar Allan Poe Society, 1990.

Halliburton, David. *Edgar Allan Poe: A Phenomenological View.* Princeton, N.J.: Princeton University Press, 1973.

Kennady, J. Gerald. *Poe, Death, and the Life of Writing.* New Haven: Yale University Press, 1987.

Meyers, Jeffrey. *Edgar Allan Poe: His Life and Legacy.* New York: Scribners, 1992.

Miller, John Carl. *Building Poe Biography.* Baton Rouge: Louisiana State University Press, 1977.

Quinn, Patrick F. *Poe and France: The Last Twenty Years.* Baltimore: Edgar Allan Poe Society, 1970.

Reilly, John E. *John Henry Ingram's Poe Collection at the University of Virginia.* Charlottesville, Va.: University of Virginia Library, 1994.

Silverman, Kenneth. *Edgar A. Poe: Mournful and Never-ending Remembrance.* New York: HarperCollins, 1991.

Another Poe site is in Baltimore. You can write or visit:
The Edgar Allan Poe House and Museum
203 North Amity Street
Baltimore, MD 21223

Ann Rinaldi

(1934-)

by Joy H. McGregor

History lives for Ann Rinaldi, although it did not always excite her. In an interview with me, Rinaldi admitted that at one time she found history boring. She knew the stories and myths but cared nothing about them. In 1976, the bicentennial year of the United Stated of America, while she was writing for the *Trentonian* in Trenton, New Jersey, her editor asked her to interview St. John Terrill, the originator of a reenactment of the crossing of the Delaware and the man playing the part of George Washington. Though not the least bit intrigued by the assignment, Rinaldi did her job. Talking to this man, she became enthusiastic. She learned from Terrill that the group needed young people to take part. She encouraged her fourteen-year-old son, Ron, to try out, which he agreed to do. Thus began a new way of life for the Rinaldi family.

Quotations from Ann Rinaldi that are not attributed to a published source are from a telephone interview conducted by the author of this article on 21 April 1995 and are published here by permission of Ann Rinaldi.

A Love of History

Ron Rinaldi's interest in history grew, as did his self-confidence, and he began guiding tours at historical sites in Trenton and across the Delaware River in Pennsylvania. Both he and his sister, Marcella, became involved with more and more reenactments, and Rinaldi did what many parents do—she joined in. She cooked food, made costumes, and traveled to all the sites. For eight years, Rinaldi, her husband Ron, and the two children lived the eighteenth-century life. She saw history firsthand and loved it.

Ron Rinaldi collected artifacts and a vast library of history and eventually obtained a master's degree in military history. As his interest in history grew even more, so did his parents' involvement. Through Ann Rinaldi's attending the reenactments, traveling to historic sites and monuments, and typing her son's papers throughout his college years, everything came together for her. Although she had been writing contemporary novels, she realized she wanted to write a story about the surrender of the British at Trenton during the Revolutionary War. This story became *Time Enough for Drums* (1986).

Unfortunately, publishers were not yet ready to accept historical fiction for young adults. Ten publishers turned down *Time Enough for Drums,* claiming that history would not sell to this age group. But watching children growing up in the world of historical reenactment, Rinaldi saw their fascination when history became real to them. She knew that historical fiction could accomplish the same purpose. After two years, Holiday House contacted Rinaldi, offering to publish her historical novel. Rinaldi attributes the change of heart to the increasing attention placed on literature-based reading programs, which emphasize learning to read through reading literature rather than basal readers. Suddenly a need for historical fiction existed. Happy to fill the niche, Rinaldi drew on her involvement with history for ideas.

basal something used for teaching beginners

Rinaldi's son and daughter appear in the cover illustration of *Time Enough for Drums* as John Reid and Jemima Emerson. The illustrator needed models in Revolutionary War period costume. Having access to appropriate costumes, Ron and Marcella agreed to pose for the jacket art.

Rinaldi credits two influences for her success. The first is her son, for "taking my hand and leading me through the world of history." Ron is now in the field of law enforcement, which Rinaldi sees as highly compatible with his education. She describes him as a person whose belief in family developed through his experiences with history and who believes strongly in this country and in justice. He emulates some of his heroes—George Washington, Thomas Paine, and Benjamin Franklin—in his desire to help "make things right."

Rinaldi recognizes the field of journalism, where she learned to write, as a second influence on her work. Though she wrote stories from age ten on, she sold none to a publisher. After becoming a journalist for the *Trentonian,* she rapidly learned the newspaper business and wrote features, news, and columns. At the same time, she turned a previously written short story into a novel, which sold immediately and became her first book, *Term Paper* (1980).

Rinaldi sees a connection between her son's value system, her own childhood goals, her favorite writers, and her own writing. She admires Eudora Welty, William Faulkner, Truman Capote, Harper Lee, and Olive Ann Burns. She shares a sense of family and a sense of loss with these southern novelists, though she herself is from New York and New Jersey. As a child, Rinaldi wanted to escape an unhappy family situation, get married and have a "normal" family. She has lived with a sense of loss because her mother died right after Rinaldi was born on 27 August 1934. Raised by a domineering father and an emotionally destructive stepmother, she grew up thinking she was worthless and could never amount to anything. She recognized the damaging effects of this upbringing and strove to break the cycle by marrying a "normal guy" and instilling in her own children a belief in themselves, a feeling of being loved and supported.

The Contemporary Novels

Rinaldi's works reflect the themes of the writers she admires. Whether contemporary or historical, most of her novels explore family relationships and loss. Her first two books, *Term Paper* and *Promises Are for Keeping* (1982), are about the rebellious Nicki, who is being raised by older brothers. In *Term Paper,* Nicki must come to terms with her father's death; in the sequel, *Promises Are for Keeping,* she loses her brothers' trust through a series of questionable actions. Most

Rinaldi recognizes the field of journalism, where she learned to write, as a second influence on her work.

There is an article about Harper Lee in volume 2.

theme central message about life in a literary work

characterization
method by which a
writer creates and
develops the appear-
ance an personality
of a character

plot the deliberate
sequence of events
in a literary work

melodrama drama
or scenes character-
ized by exaggerated
sentimentality or in-
flated emotion

reviewers commended Rinaldi's portrayal of a realistic, typical kid and lifelike emotional confrontations. Both books
were praised for strong, consistent characterization and well-
paced plots.

The second pair of contemporary novels, *But in the Fall
I'm Leaving* (1985) and *The Good Side of My Heart* (1987),
also explore family relationships and loss. In these books
Brianna ("Brie"), abandoned by her mother, is raised by her
father and an older brother, a priest. Often alienated from her
father, Brie misses the mother she never knew. Her affinity
for trouble leads her into complex, involved relationships
and situations in both stories.

Neither of these titles fared as well with reviewers as did
Rinaldi's first two books. Although the willful main character
was again described as realistic and many-sided, other characters were considered poorly developed. Rinaldi's flair for
melodrama drew both criticism and acclaim, with plots described as "numbingly convoluted" in *Publishers Weekly*
(June 1985) and "engrossing" and "refreshing" by reviewer
Diane C. Donovan in *Best Sellers*. In the *Bulletin of the Center for Children's Books* (June 1987), the reviewer Zena
Sutherland criticized Rinaldi's inconsistent use of distracting
phonetic spellings such as "gonna," "wanna," and "hadda" in
The Good Side of My Heart. Similar criticism emerged again in
reviews of later books over portrayal of southern accents or
use of slang or historically correct pronunciations.

Historical Novels

The Revolutionary War

While successfully writing contemporary young adult novels,
Rinaldi tried to get a story published about fifteen-year-old
Jemima Emerson, who is living in Trenton, New Jersey, during the Revolutionary War. Jem's story revolves around her
family's involvement on both sides of the conflict. The research for *Time Enough for Drums* began in 1981, but the
novel did not see publication until 1986. Some reviewers objected to Jem's lack of substance in her romantic involvement. Usually feisty, she eventually defers to her tutor, John
Reid, in a decidedly nonfeminist manner; she is manipulated
and tamed by him while falling in love with him. Therese
Bigelow, in *School Library Journal* (May 1986), commented

that the desire among reviews for Jem to show more spirit may spring from their own twentieth-century prejudices.

Rinaldi continued to write historical fiction after the success of *Time Enough for Drums*. She explored several historical periods, but none as much as the Revolutionary War. Four more novels deal with this period: *A Ride into Morning: The Story of Tempe Wick* (1991), *The Fifth of March: A Story of the Boston Massacre* (1993), *Finishing Becca: The Story of Peggy Shippen and Benedict Arnold* (1994), and *The Secret of Sarah Revere* (1995).

Mary Cooper, a fourteen-year-old cousin of the legendary Tempe Wick, is the heroine of *A Ride into Morning*. Mary tells the unproven legend of the woman who hid her horse in the house to keep British troops from stealing it, and in Mary's telling, the legend comes to life. Although actual details of Tempe Wick's involvement are unavailable, some historical characters, such as General Anthony Wayne, are accurately portrayed. Again Rinaldi emphasizes family relationships, this time the tension between the cousins and Mary's sense of loss over separation from her family. *A Ride into Morning* was criticized by Marian Rafal in *VOYA* (June 1991) because Tempe Wick herself is portrayed as unsympathetic. Zena Sutherland, in the *Bulletin of the Center for Children's Books* (May 1991), credited Rinaldi with successfully meshing fiction and history. Rinaldi's excellent historical documentation, differentiating between historically accurate elements and those created by the author, was praised by most reviewers.

The Fifth of March: A Story of the Boston Massacre includes several historically accurate figures: John and Abigail Adams, John Hancock, Paul Revere, Henry Knox, and Crispus Attucks. Fourteen-year-old Rachel Marsh, the protagonist, was actually an indentured servant in the Adams household. Rinaldi compares the story's drama with the Los Angeles riots that were taking place as this book was in its finishing stages. Chris Sherman points out in *Booklist* (January 1994) that many issues raised in the book are relevant today: "The role of peacekeeping forces, the use of violence to achieve political goals, and the courage required to take a stand" (p. 925). Alongside the political implications, Rinaldi deals with family life and loss again. Rachel's only living relative is cruel Uncle Eb, whose influence she wants to banish. She longs for the things Abigail Adams gained from her family: love, an education, and self-respect.

indentured servant a person who signs a contract to work for someone for a specified length of time in exchange for maintenance and travel expenses (such as the cost of traveling by boat from Europe to the United States)

evocation the calling to mind of

foil a character who, by contrast, makes clear the qualities of another character

Separation from family recurs in *Finishing Becca: The Story of Peggy Shippen and Benedict Arnold,* in which fictional Becca Syng becomes lady's maid to real-life character Peggy Shippen. Janice del Negro, writing in *Booklist* (15 November 1994), applauded "Rinaldi's evocation of the rip-roaring life and devil-be-damned personality of Peggy Shippen" (p. 590). While Becca is the foil for displaying the flamboyance of Peggy Shippen, Becca's enforced isolation from her family provides another story thread.

Rinaldi's choice of obtrusive terminology (this time the word "nigra"), while historically legitimate, was considered distracting by del Negro. Though Rinaldi consistently uses this term through all her historical works, its use might divert the reader's attention from other story elements since the term is not typically encountered in similar works.

Another novel dealing with the Revolutionary War, *The Secret of Sarah Revere* (1995), tells Paul Revere's story through the perspective of his fourteen-year-old daughter, Sarah. Betty Carter, in *ALAN Review* (spring 1996), and Susan Dove Lempke, in *School Library Journal* (November 1995), praise the realistic portrayal of the Boston setting, while Kay Vandergrift, in *School Library Journal* (November 1995), commends Rinaldi for the real and believable characters and the female viewpoint of what has typically been "an all-male story of American history and politics" (p. 122).

The Civil War

Civil War events provide the setting for the novels *The Last Silk Dress* (1988) and *In My Father's House* (1993). *The Last Silk Dress* dramatizes family relationships, with teenager Susan struggling to cope with an abusive, unstable mother and an awful truth about her beloved father. Political and social ills are portrayed through the family's involvement with slaves and an absent brother's secrets. Though the Civil War background is accurate, most major characters are fictitious.

Zena Sutherland, writing in the *New York Times Book Review* (10 April 1988), pointed out the uneven phonetic spelling of southern dialogue while praising the structure and characterization in Rinaldi's writing. Elizabeth M. Reardon, in *School Library Journal* (May 1988), commended the realism of this unromanticized portrayal of the South.

In My Father's House, chosen as one of the American Library Association's Best Books for Young Adults of 1994, builds upon the actual coincidence that both the beginning and the end of the Civil War took place on properties belonging to Wilmer McLean, on sites hundreds of miles apart. The immediate story revolves around McLean's stepdaughter, Osceola Mason. Family relationships and loss again are important, with Oscie desperately missing her deceased father but learning to accept, respect, and finally love her stepfather.

The characters were variously critiqued by reviewers. Lucinda Snyder Whitehurst, commenting in *School Library Journal* (March 1993), suggested that their acceptance of the futility of the Civil War is too modern to be realistic. Roger Sutton, in *The Bulletin of the Center for Children's Books* (March 1993), described the characters as lacking personality; but Deborah L. Dubois suggested in *VOYA* (June 1993) that readers would identify with these characters and their attempts to assert their independence. Carol Jean Pingel, reviewing the novel in *Book Report* (September/October 1993), described the historical figures as accurately portrayed and interesting, and Carolyn Phelan (*Booklist,* 15 February 1993), described Oscie's growing maturity as convincing.

Other Historical Events

Five historical novels deal with events other than wars. *Wolf by the Ears* (1991) is based on the story of Harriet Hemings, a servant in Thomas Jefferson's household who might have been Jefferson's daughter. The Salem witch trials provide the drama for *A Break with Charity* (1992). A trilogy encompassing three generations in several geographic settings consists of *A Stitch in Time* (1994), *Broken Days* (1995), and *The Blue Door* (1995).

trilogy a series of three literary works that are closely related and share a single theme

Both *Wolf by the Ears* and *A Break with Charity* were selected as ALA Best Books for Young Adults. *Wolf by the Ears* was also chosen as one of the Best of the Best in Young Adult Literature, a 1994 American Library Association (ALA) listing of the best books for young adults written over the past twenty-five years. The title *Wolf by the Ears* comes from Thomas Jefferson's statement that slavery is like holding a "wolf by the ears, and we can neither hold him, nor safely let him go." The story of Harriet's decision to leave Monticello and pass as white is told through Harriet's journal.

In dealing with whether or not Harriet Hemings' father was Thomas Jefferson, Rinaldi was criticized in *Kirkus Reviews* (1 March 1991) for not emphasizing that her source of information is speculative theory, not proven fact. The historical notes in this novel are scanty compared to those in Rinaldi's other novels, providing little information about which characters and situations are fictional and which are not. Zena Sutherland, however, commended Rinaldi in the *Bulletin of the Center for Children's Books* (June 1991) for presenting the issue so candidly and capably. The story itself is described by reviewers as absorbing, realistic, and insightful.

In *A Break with Charity,* Rinaldi portrays through the eyes of an outsider the horror and malice of events leading to the Salem witch trials. Fourteen-year-old Susanna English is a historical figure, but her involvement with the accusers is the authors invention. She is forced to keep an awful secret to protect her family from false accusation. Skillfully blending fact with fiction, Rinaldi creates a believable, suspenseful, and enthralling scenario. Although Carolyn Noah, writing in *School Library Journal* (September 1992), criticized the characters as rigid and the speech as overly formal, other reviewers commended Rinaldi for her storytelling and for contrasting the simple, unembellished style with the dramatic and terrible subject matter.

The Quilt trilogy, beginning with *A Stitch in Time,* is constructed around a quilt in progress. A quilt section is taken by each of three Chelmsford sisters, who are choosing different paths for their future. The themes of alienation and loss emerge again in a family with a cruel, uncaring father and a dead mother. This book received more negative reviews than most of Rinaldi's novels; it was called melodramatic, too detailed, and boring. Some reviewers, however, commended Rinaldi for building in details so skillfully that readers could keep them straight throughout the novel.

This first book of the trilogy uses fictional characters to introduce the reader to the early textile industry through one sister's story. The three stories are linked through the daughter of another sister in the second book, *Broken Days,* and through the granddaughter of the third sister in the third book, *The Blue Door.* The parts of the quilt play a symbolic role in reuniting the family, with alienation from family play-

scanty less than enough

symbolic standing for or representative of something else, for example, "the dove is symbolic of peace"

ing a major role in the lives of the main characters in each book in the trilogy.

Keep Smiling Through (1996) moves to recent history, a different war, and a younger heroine, with ten-year-old Kay growing up in New Jersey during World War II. This book is a fictionalized autobiography of Rinaldi's childhood, dealing with the fears and suspicions of the time. Based on Rinaldi's home and neighborhood, it is her way of coping with her own childhood memories.

Conclusion

The most consistently praised elements of all Rinaldi's historical novels are the quality of the historical research and the clear delineation between fact and fiction. Rinaldi is recognized as a skilled storyteller, capable of weaving many intricate threads together, blending fact and fiction, making historical characters and situations real. The fabric she creates is as unifying as the Chelmsford quilt.

Selected Bibliography

WORKS BY ANN RINALDI

Contemporary Novels
> *Term Paper* (1980)
> *Promises Are for Keeping* (1982)
> *But in the Fall I'm Leaving* (1985)
> *The Good Side of My Heart* (1987)

Historical Novels
> *Time Enough for Drums* (1986)
> *The Last Silk Dress* (1988)
> *A Ride into Morning: The Story of Tempe Wick* (1991)
> *Wolf by the Ears* (1991)
> *A Break with Charity: A Story About the Salem Witch Trials* (1992)
> *The Fifth of March: A Story of the Boston Massacre* (1993)
> *In My Father's House* (1993)
> *Finishing Becca: The Story of Peggy Shippen and Benedict Arnold* (1994)

If you like the works of Ann Rinaldi, you might also enjoy other historical fiction written by James Lincoln Collier and Christopher Collier, Bette Greene, Avi, or Rosemary Sutcliff.

A Stitch in Time (1994)

Broken Days (1995)

The Secret of Sarah Revere (1995)

The Blue Door (1996)

Keep Smiling Through (1996)

The Second Bend in the River (1997)

Autobiography

"Term Paper." *Library Journal,* 1 October 1980, vol. 105, p. 2122.

"Ann Rinaldi." In *Speaking for Ourselves, Too.* Edited by Donald R. Gallo. Urbana, Ill.: National Council of Teachers of English, 1993, pp. 164–165.

WORKS ABOUT ANN RINALDI

Bigelow, Therese. Review of *Time Enough for Drums. School Library Journal,* May 1986, pp. 108–109.

Carter, Betty. Review of *The Secret of Sarah Revere. ALAN Review,* spring 1996, p. 32.

Commire, Anne, ed. *Something About the Author.* Detroit: Gale Research, 1988, vol. 50, p. 167.

———. *Something About the Author.* Detroit: Gale Research, 1988, vol. 51, pp. 149–151.

Contemporary Authors. Detroit: Gale Research, 1984, vol. 111, pp. 391–392.

Del Negro, Janice. Review of *Finishing Becca. Booklist,* 15 November 1994, p. 590.

Donovan, Diane C. Review of *But in the Fall I'm Leaving. Best Sellers,* September 1985, p. 240.

Dubois, Deborah L. Review of *In My Father's House. VOYA,* June 1993, p. 94.

Hile, Kevin S., ed. *Something About the Author.* Detroit: Gale Research, 1994, vol. 78, pp. 169–173.

Lempke, Susan Dove. Review of *The Secret of Sarah Revere. Booklist,* 15 November 1995, pp. 548–549.

Noah, Carolyn. Review of *A Break with Charity. School Library Journal,* September 1992, p. 279.

Phelan, Carolyn. Review of *In My Father's House. Booklist,* 15 February 1993, p. 1054.

Pingel, Carol Jean. Review of *In My Father's House*. *Book Report*, September/October 1993, p. 48.

Rafal, Marian. Review of *A Ride Into Morning*. *VOYA*, June 1991, p. 101.

Reardon, Elizabeth M. Review of *The Last Silk Dress*. *School Library Journal*, May 1988, p. 112.

Review of *But in the Fall I'm Leaving*. *Publishers Weekly*, 7 June 1985, p. 81.

Review of *Wolf by the Ears*. In *Kirkus Reviews*, 1 March 1991, p. 321–322.

Sherman, Chris. Review of *The Fifth of March*. *Booklist*, 15 January 1994, p. 925.

Sutherland, Zena. Review of *The Good Side of My Heart*. *Bulletin of the Center for Children's Books*, June 1987, p. 195.

———. Review of *The Last Silk Dress*. *New York Times Book Review*, 10 April 1988, p. 38.

———. Review of *A Ride into Morning*. *Bulletin of the Center for Children's Books*, May 1991, p. 225.

———. Review of *Wolf by the Ears*. *Bulletin of the Center for Children's Books, June 1991, p. 247.*

Sutton, Roger. Review of *In My Father's House*. *Bulletin of the Center for Children's Books*, March 1993, p. 223.

Vandergrift, Kay. Review of *The Secret of Sarah Revere*. *School Library Journal*, November 1995, p. 122.

Whitehurst, Lucinda Snyder. Review of *In My Father's House*. *School Library Journal*, March 1993, p. 224.

How to Write to the Author
Ann Rinaldi
c/o Scholastic, Inc.
555 Broadway
New York, NY 10012

Colby Rodowsky

(1932-   )

by Melissa Comer

The so-called terrible twos are often forgotten by parents as their children enter the stage characterized by the question, "Mom, can I use the car tonight?" Parents take a deep breath and pray that the end is in sight, while their sons and daughters ride the roller coaster of adolescence, facing the problems associated with alcoholism and other addictions, divorce, abandonment, sex, disabilities, peer pressure, and disillusionment, just to name a few. Colby Rodowsky, the author of several novels for young adults, addresses all these issues and more in her books. She presents them in a way with which young adults can identify.

After reading Rodowsky's books, you will probably find yourself wondering why you never thought of the solutions that some of her characters do. You may also come to realize that you are not the only person in the world who has, or has had, the headache of dealing with a mother or father who is controlled by liquor or has left you to pursue another life. Rodowsky's characters know too well that life is not al-

Quotations from Colby Rodowsky not attributed to a published source are from a telephone interview conducted by the author of this article on 9 May 1995 and are published by permission of Colby Rodowsky.

87

She stores away everything that has happened in her life and uses it in her writing.

premise something assumed or taken for granted

ways a bed of roses. They learn, however, that if life gives you lemons, you make lemonade.

A Writer's Life

If you could pick up the telephone and call Colby Rodowsky in Baltimore, Maryland, where she was born to Frank M. Fossett and Mary C. Fitz Townsend and where she lives now, you would realize that you were talking to someone who knows about teenagers. She married Lawrence Rodowsky, an appeals court judge, and she gave birth to six children, whom she saw through the difficult teen years. As an English major in college, Rodowsky edited her school's literary magazine and was always interested in writing. Yet, according to an interview conducted by Jean W. Ross for *Contemporary Authors,* Rodowsky did not actually begin writing until she was forty. She attributes her late start to the years she spent rearing her children. In her own words, she first "learned to make cupcakes and Halloween costumes and peanut-butter-and-jelly sandwiches." Although she found time to read during those years, there was one thing missing, one thing that kept haunting her: the books that she had not written. So, when her children were old enough to fend for themselves, she embarked on a career that she had placed "on a back burner" and began, at last, to write.

We have all heard that anything that happens to us happens for a reason. Rodowsky uses this premise to her advantage. She stores away everything that has happened in her life and uses it in her writing. She writes about what she knows. She draws on various sources for her writing. People in a crowd or a painting may inspire her to take pen in hand or to formulate ideas and put them into the recesses of her mind to use later. Rodowsky has stated that she spends a couple of months just thinking about a novel and then six to eight months writing it. "I know where I'm going, but not how I'm going to get there," she says.

If you were to pay Rodowsky a visit during the time she was actively writing a book, you would find her starting to work around nine-thirty in the morning, not stopping until lunch time, finishing the day around three or four o'clock in the afternoon, and beginning all over again the next day, following the same pattern. When asked to select which book of hers she likes the best, she laughs and admits that choosing a favorite would be like picking one of her children over the other. Rodowsky will say, however, that *Julie's Daughter* (1985) was perhaps the most difficult to write, but not because of the hard subject matter. When it was published, there were questions about whether it was targeted for an audience of adults or adolescents. She says that she did not write the book for any particular age group; she just wrote it. She also notes that the Sydney books—*Sydney, Herself* (1989) and *Sydney, Invincible* (1995)—were possibly the easiest.

Themes and Characters

The themes of Rodowsky's books are universal, and her characters seem like real people. They remind us of a brother or sister, a mom or dad, a friend, or ourselves. We simultaneously like and dislike them. Family plays an important role in these books. It is portrayed in different lights, not all of which are positive. In *Hannah in Between* (1994) the family unit is an extended one, including not only Mom and Dad but also Grandpa, Grandma, and various aunts and uncles. For the most part it is viewed in a good light, but Hannah's mother has a "problem" that Hannah finds embarrassing, even though she loves her mom.

theme central message about life in a literary work

The father in *Lucy Peale* (1992) is a preacher who shows little or no love for his children and wife. He is continually telling Lucy how to act, dress, and think. When she encounters a tough problem, instead of supporting her, he turns his back on her. He is a man who concentrates more on his church and what people will think than on his own flesh and blood. Julie, in *Julie's Daughter,* leaves her infant child, Slug, in a red wagon at a bus station. She is found and raised by Julie's mother. Drew Wakeman's dad in *Keeping Time* (1983) does not know how to communicate with his children and does not want to learn. Drew has no idea how to talk to his dad. The Wakemans are a good illustration of a generation gap.

Reading Rodowsky's books, one might think that she had experienced an unhappy childhood, but that does not appear to be the case. For the most part she enjoyed growing up in Baltimore, New York City, and Washington, D.C., and spending summers with her grandmother on the eastern shore of Virginia, which she refers to again and again in her novels as Ocean City. (Lucy's father in *Lucy Peale* calls it Sin City.) The unfavorable parental images just seem to happen, much as they do in real life.

Rodowsky's characters, like real people, want an escape from day-to-day living. In *Keeping Time,* Drew Wakeman leaves his world when family life gets to be too much for him. He travels back in time to sixteenth-century London, where he does not have to face the sadness caused by his sister's leaving or a father who is unable to act like one. Tanner, in *P.S. Write Soon* (1978), flees in a different way. She wears a leg brace (named Fenhagen) and is unable to do things like ride a skateboard or play softball. But in her letters to her pen pal, Jessie Lee, she presents herself as whole, escaping into a world in which there is no disability. Lying becomes her reality and her means of appearing to be someone she is not.

Julie's Daughter deals with teenage pregnancy. The identity of Slug's father is anyone's guess; her mother, Julie, has no idea. And until she is seventeen, Slug does not know Julie. Having a child is too much for Julie to handle. Unlike Julie, Lucy, in *Lucy Peale,* is an innocent. She becomes pregnant the first time she has sex. She believes that she will be a good, nurturing, and loving mother, even though she did not experience much love as a child. But neither Julie nor Lucy is prepared to have children. Lucy is, in a sense, more equipped emotionally for a baby than Julie is, but even she is not aware that she needs prenatal care. Luckily, she meets Jake, who is her savior and her voice of reason. Neither pregnancy, however, is a very positive experience for the young mothers in these stories.

prenatal occurring or performing before birth

Although divorce is as common to us in today's world as a covered wagon was to the pioneers of previous centuries, it still is not easy for teenagers whose parents are going through it. Sydney Downie, in Rodowsky's novel *Sydney, Invincible,* knows this only too well. She wants to help Wally Martin, her boyfriend, survive and make sense of his parents' splitting up, but she feels inadequate to do so. In the end, like most people who have gone through a family breakup, Wally and his younger brother, Porter, endure the drastic changes in their lives; and Sydney is able to offer both of the Martin boys a friendship that gives them back some of the stability they have lost.

An illusion is a false impression or perception. To become disillusioned means to lose such an impression, to see someone for who he or she actually is. No one in our society is exempt from becoming disillusioned, and characters in Colby Rodowsky's books also fall prey to disillusionment. Hannah's mother, in *Hannah in Between,* shatters Hannah's image of her as understanding, caring, and loving, someone who always has time for her daughter. All of that changes as alcohol begins to control her mother. Hannah starts to see that life is full of misconceptions, and things are rarely what they appear to be.

Zephyr Kennealy, Sydney Downie's creative-writing teacher in *Sydney, Invincible,* is certainly not who she pretends to be. Sydney believes Zephyr when she says that together they will turn words into pearls. In Sydney's eyes, Zephyr is a free spirit who has really lived life, and Sydney wants to be like Zephyr one day. She places Zephyr on a pedestal, only to have her fall from it. Zephyr misleads Sydney when she allows and encourages Sydney and her fellow classmates to pursue a news story that will land them in trouble. She then deserts them when they need her to stand up for them. Sydney is disillusioned by the experience and realizes that people can be deceiving.

Real-Life Characters

Whatever the theme may be in one of Colby Rodowsky's stories, it is as real to life as her characters. She has stated that her characters often take over and develop a life of their own. In an article in *Writer,* she recalls attending a great aunt's funeral, and while she was at the cemetery, characters she had portrayed in *The Gathering Room* (1981) seemed to her to be present:

> I started to look around, casting quick **surreptitious** glances behind this angel, that vault or marble lamb. I knew, somehow, that they were all there. Mudge and his friends. . . . And, of course, Aunt Ernestus. That's how real they are to me. How real I try to make them to my readers.

surreptitious done secretly, with the intention of not being observed

In *Something About the Author* Rodowsky reveals that her characters and their personalities do not come from her own children but are rather more likely to resemble the child she was or the ones whom she observes. She also admits that her characters and their problems are a combination of reality and imagination; they are thus the best of both worlds.

Rodowksy's research gives her subject matter realism. One gets the feeling while reading *Keeping Time* that Elizabethan England was exactly as Drew experiences it. Tanner's disability in *P.S. Write Soon* is so vivid that you imagine what her stay in the hospital was like, and you can actually feel the awkwardness of her leg brace. You know the pain and resentment that Dorrie in *What About Me?* (1976) feels toward her brother "Fredlet," who has Down's syndrome, because of Rodowsky's descriptions and story line. Her research allows the reader a glimpse of what it means to live in a family that has to deal with a disability.

The adolescents portrayed in her books are attempting to make sense of their world. They are trying to understand their parents, their teachers, and what is happening to them. They have dreams and goals like most teenagers. They want to live life and experience what it has to offer. They cry and laugh. They worry and wonder about what the future holds for them. Once you finish reading one of Rodowsky's novels, you want to know what happens to the people you have read about. You make up lives for them and hope that they are happy, forgetting, if only for an instant, that they are fictional characters—and wishing they were not.

Rodowsky has said that she hopes to keep writing for a long time. An only child and often alone, she was an avid reader and has said that she read almost anything, almost everywhere, using books for companionship. Her novels are able to offer readers the same escape that books offered her, solitude without loneliness.

If you like works by Colby Rodowsky, you might also like the books of Judy Blume and Sue Ellen Bridgers.

Selected Bibliography

WORKS BY COLBY RODOWSKY

Novels for Young Adults

P.S. Write Soon (1978)

Evy-Ivy-Over (1978)

A Summer's Worth of Shame (1980)

The Gathering Room (1981)

H, My Name Is Henley (1982)

Keeping Time (1983)

Julie's Daughter (1985)

Fitchett's Folly (1987)

Sydney, Herself (1989)

Dog Days (1990)

Lucy Peale (1992)

Hannah in Between (1994)

Sydney, Invincible (1995)

Articles

"Where Characters Come From." *Writer,* July 1985, vol. 98, p. 12.

WORKS ABOUT COLBY RODOWSKY

Commire, Anna, ed. *Something About the Author.* Detroit: Gale Research, 1980, vol. 21, p. 126.

Ross, Jean W. "Colby Rodowsky." In *Contemporary Authors*. Edited by Thomas Wiloch. Detroit: Gale Research, 1988, vol. 23, pp. 340–344.

How to Write to the Author
Colby Rodowsky
c/o Farrar, Straus & Giroux Inc.
19 Union Square West
New York, NY 10003

Marilyn Sachs

(1927-   )

by Marilyn H. Karrenbrock Stauffer

Until about forty years ago, books for young people were "safe." Children were well behaved (or at least *tried* to be). Families were usually white, middle-class people living in suburbs. No one was very ill or died or was divorced. All this changed in the mid-1960s with the "new realism." Marilyn Sachs helped bring about this change.

When she wrote her first book, *Amy Moves In,* in 1954, everything about it was wrong. Amy was a crybaby and a liar. Her family was Jewish and poor and lived in the Bronx. Halfway through the book, her mother was struck by a car and hospitalized. When the manuscript was rejected, Sachs put it away for ten years.

> *One of the reasons Sachs's books are so realistic is that they are often based on incidents in her life.*
>
>

Did That Really Happen?

One of the reasons Sachs's books are so realistic is that they are often based on incidents in her life. Her early books were set in a neighborhood like the one where she grew up. In the first three books, Amy and her older sister Laura closely resemble Marilyn Stickle (the author's birth name) and her sister Jeannie. Sachs admired her sister, just as Amy admires Laura. She was often the victim of neighborhood bullies, and her sister fought her bullies as Laura did for Amy. When Sachs wrote *Veronica Ganz* (1968), a story about a bully, she intended to get revenge by killing Veronica off at the end. But, the author reports in *Something About the Author Autobiography Series,* her daughter Anne told her, "If you kill Veronica Ganz, I will never speak to you again as long as I live" (p. 209). The author got a more subtle revenge in *The Truth about Mary Rose* (1973), when she made a grown-up Veronica into a dentist, whom some people consider a bully.

Sachs was born on 18 December 1927 in New York City. Her family lived on Jennings Street in the Bronx, a vibrant community with many children who played on the sidewalks, on the school playground, and even in the street. *Amy Moves In,* which was published in 1964, tells of playing ball, jumping rope, and throwing snowballs from behind snow forts, activities obviously based upon the author's fond memories.

Sachs started kindergarten at age four. In *Something About the Author Autobiography Series,* she says, "My mother said I was five. Either she thought I was amazingly mature for my age or she wanted to get rid of me. I prefer the former reason" (p. 198). One humiliating incident of this early schooling is described in *Class Pictures* (1980):

> Richie Kronberg was pointing at Lolly. She was standing in the circle just like everybody else. Her mouth was even shaped in a circle as if she had been singing. But we knew right away that Lolly had been doing something else because down on the ground a long, dark, narrow stream moved quickly out from between Lolly's legs. (P. 6)

Sachs's age was also misrepresented when she and her sister were sent to camp. The minimum age was eight, but she was only six. This experience is recreated with a minor character in *Laura's Luck* (1965). One lasting effect of that summer is Sachs's fear of the dark, caused by terrifying stories of ghosts and vampires told in the bunks at night.

When Sachs was in the third grade, her mother was hospitalized for many months after an accident and thereafter walked with a limp. Amy and Laura's mother suffers a similar fate. The author's mother died when she was twelve. Sachs says, "She brought order and stability to our lives that we never regained after her death" (*Something About the Author Autobiography Series,* p. 203).

A Born Writer

Sachs always wanted to write. In "About the Author," in *Amy Moves In,* she says:

> **In Junior High School I was elected Class Writer (nobody ran against me) and in High School I also became Class Writer, again running uncontested. Nobody else seemed to want that distinction. I wrote continuously in High School as editor of the school paper and contributor to the school magazine. My first big moment came when I won a literary contest with a short story entitled "The Icicle and The Leaf." (Pp. 190–191)**

Gloria, the main character of *A Summer's Lease* (1979), writes a story with this title. This book contains several autobiographical incidents. Sachs's father wanted her to go to work rather than to college; Gloria's mother feels the same. Like Gloria, Sachs was invited by a favorite teacher to spend the summer in the country caring for children. The death of the youngest girl also became part of the plot.

One of the most surprising parallels in Sachs's life and her books is the existence of the Bears' House. This delightful little dollhouse really did belong to her teacher, and Sachs really did receive it unexpectedly on the last day of school, just as Fran Ellen does in *The Bears' House* (1971).

Two of Sachs's enduring interests have been boys and social causes. While she was growing up, one of her closest

Whether or not Sachs finds boys hard to understand, almost all her books are about girls.

left-wing movement a political movement that is considered more radical than conservative (in the 1940s, the left-wing movement would have been socialism or communism)

bookmobile a truck used as a traveling library

friends was a boy, which may explain why girls in her books often have friends who are boys. As Sachs grew older, her interest in boys became romantic. She once met a boy on a bus, but he was interested in one of her friends, a situation Judy faces in *Bus Ride* (1980). While attending Hunter College, Sachs became a member of a left-wing movement in which she met Morris Sachs. They were married on 26 January 1947. Morris Sachs is a sculptor.

After finishing college in 1949, Sachs knew that she wanted to write but did not know what she wanted to write. She became a children's librarian at the Brooklyn Public Library, serving in several branches and on a bookmobile, visiting hospitals, and telling stories. She received a master's degree in library science from Columbia University in 1953. Her work convinced Sachs that she wanted to write for young people. In 1954, she took six months off to write *Amy Moves In,* but when it was rejected, she went back to work. Her daughter, Anne, was born in 1957; a son, Paul, was born in 1960. In 1961 the Sachs family moved to San Francisco, where they have lived ever since. For a few years, Marilyn Sachs worked part-time at the library there. In 1963, a friend with whom she had worked in Brooklyn, who had become an editor, called her and asked to see the manuscript she had written a decade earlier. It was accepted at once, and Sachs has published approximately a book a year since.

What Are the Books About?

Most of Sachs's books are set in the real world, but a couple, *Matt's Mitt* (1975) and *Fleet-Footed Florence* (1981), are tall-tale picture books. These books were written for her son, who was interested only in baseball. In *Fourteen* (1983), Rebecca's mother, a children's book writer, tries to write a baseball story about her son, saying, "You remember, Rebecca, it was such a boring story nobody wanted to buy it. And besides, it's hard for me to understand boys. Arthur was very patient and answered all my questions, but I never could get into how he thinks" (p. 5). Whether or not Sachs finds boys hard to understand, almost all her books are about girls.

The Great Depression

Sachs's earliest books are set in the Great Depression years, but readers feel they are contemporary. Joan McGrath reports in *Twentieth-Century Children's Writers* that when a grown-up Veronica Ganz appears in *The Truth about Mary Rose* (1973), readers say, "but she's *my* age" (p. 848). Two of Sachs's books are definitely historical. *A Pocket Full of Seeds* (1973), a Holocaust story set in France, is based on the experiences of a woman whose family was arrested by the Gestapo while she was visiting friends. The mother in *Call Me Ruth* (1982) is based on Sachs's maternal grandmother, Sarah Smith. In *Authors and Artists for Young Adults,* the author says, "I explored the question of what it meant for my grandparents' generation—largely a generation of immigrants—to be American" (p. 181). Ruth looks down upon her mother, Fanny, as a "greenhorn" who does not adjust easily to American life. Fanny becomes involved in the labor movement and takes part in the Shirtwaist Makers' Strike of 1909, during which she is arrested and sent to a workhouse.

The **Holocaust** was the mass murder of at least 11 million people, especially Jews, by the Nazis during World War II. The word "holocaust" means "thorough destruction by fire." The **Gestapo** were the secret police force of Nazi Germany.

Jealousy

Sachs's early books were primarily for children, but several, such as *The Bears' House* and *A Pocket Full of Seeds,* tell such strong stories that they are read by many young adults. With *A Summer's Lease* in 1979, the author turned primarily to young adult books. She writes about characters who are very real but not necessarily admirable or likable. Jealously is a major theme. Gloria, in *A Summer's Lease,* is fiercely jealous of Jerry, her rival in writing class. Although she recognizes this failing, she is unable to control it. Pat, in *Class Pictures,* masters her jealousy of pretty, popular Lolly, her best friend since kindergarten. This book shows the difficulties friends face as they grow apart, but its hopeful acceptance of the future is satisfying. *What My Sister Remembered* (1992) is a powerful portrayal of two sisters, adopted by different families, who are each jealous of the other's circumstances.

Jealousy can turn into a struggle for power and control. In *The Fat Girl* (1983), Jeff, after making fun of Ellen's size, feels remorse and befriends her. Gradually he takes over her life, remaking her into the image he wants. Jeff tells the story, giving readers a clear contrast between what he thinks he is doing and what is actually happening to Ellen and to himself. Intelligent, unconventional Cass, in *Baby Sister* (1986), tries hard to make her younger sister Penny into her own image. Penny, though, knows she must be her own person and gradually learns to stand up to Cass.

Other Subjects

Mothers are often portrayed unsympathetically. They may be mildly abusive, shouting and slapping, or overprotective. Fathers are usually supportive but weak, unable to stand up to the mothers. However, the teenagers often do not appreciate their parents. In *Just Like a Friend* (1989), Patti and her mother Vi act more like friends than mother and daughter, and Patti's father babies both of them. When he has a heart attack, Vi goes to pieces, leaving Patti and her grandmother to deal with the situation. Patti blames each of the family members in turn for her mother's childishness, forgetting the love she has received.

Sachs wrote four light romances for Dutton's "Skinny Book" series: *Bus Ride, Hello . . . Wrong Number* (1981), *Beach Towels* (1982), and *Thunderbird* (1985). The books are almost entirely conversation, sounding just like teenagers talk. This makes them easy to read, although sometimes it is hard to tell who is talking. Humor is important in these books and many others by Sachs. Even the most serious ones usually have touches of humor. *Dorrie's Book* (1975) is laugh-out-loud funny. Eleven-year-old Dorrie, a pampered only child, suddenly finds herself one of six: her mother has triplets, and two neglected children move in. The book is illustrated with childlike drawings by Anne Sachs. In *Circles* (1991), everyone thinks Beebe and Mark would be perfect for each other if they could only meet. *Fourteen* combines humor, romance, and mystery. In the book, Rebecca feels that her mother has used her as a model in each of her books. It is too much to bear when her mother begins a book about first love, since Rebecca has not had one. Then she meets the new boy next door, whose father has mysteriously disappeared.

Sachs includes social problems in all her books. In *The Bears' House,* a family of neglected children struggles to survive, and *Underdog* (1985) tells of an unwanted orphan girl and a neglected dog. Parents are often dead, divorced, or absent. Prejudice of various kinds is shown. *At the Sound of the Beep* (1990) explores homelessness. In this story, twins Mathew and Mathilda will be separated when their parents divorce. In desperation, they run away and join the homeless in Golden Gate Park. But is the park safe when a murderer is loose? This is Sachs's most exciting book. Her most ambitious social project is *The Big Book for Peace* (1990), which she conceived and edited with Ann Durrell. Numerous children's authors and illustrators contributed to the book.

> *"Read for pleasure and without realizing it, you will learn the craft of writing."*
>

How Does She Write?

Sachs says that her writing always begins with research, which may take about a month. Then, she says in *Authors and Artists for Young Adults,* "I start with a character, or a group of characters and in the first few chapters try to figure out why they belong in a book together. I have a vague plan in my head, and after drafting several chapters I can do a 'general outline' of the whole book" (p. 178).

Sachs usually writes a half chapter each day, although sometimes she can write a whole chapter. Her daughter Anne is her best critic, reading all her drafts. First drafts usually take about three months, although a few have taken only a few weeks. The corrected draft goes to her editor, who suggests revisions, which take about a month. One problem Sachs has is keeping her mind on the book she is currently writing rather than on the one she intends to do next. She often seems to alternate between serious books and lighter ones.

> *About writing, Sachs says, "I start with a character, or a group of characters and in the first few chapters try to figure out why they belong in a book together."*
>

Her advice to young writers is to read all they can: "Read for pleasure and without realizing it, you will learn the craft of writing. You will absorb from those writers you admire the ability to put words together, to tell a story, to pace, to highlight, to beguile" (*Something About the Author Autobiography Series,* p. 204). She also thinks that daydreaming is essential for a writer. The stories told by her family members were other important influences.

What Do the Readers Say?

Reviewers have been lavish with praise for Sachs. They use phrases like "sympathy and realism," "vitality," "natural conversations and a lively pace," and "rich and perceptive picture." *The Bears' House* was a finalist for the National Book Award in 1972, and *Call Me Ruth* won the Association of Jewish Libraries Award in 1983. *The Fat Girl* was named to the Best Books for Young Adults list of the American Library Association in 1984. These three books are considered Sachs's best. Miriam Lang Budin, who reviewed *Baby Sister* for *School Library Journal,* said that the book "may especially appeal to girls not much taken with mainstream high-school life" (p. 106). This statement sums up Sachs's writing, which deals with the losers, the misfits, the kids who fall through the cracks.

Young readers get passionate about Sachs's writing. "I just hated Amy and Laura's father," said one such reader whom I know. "He was always taking them out on the stoop and lecturing them about being good. He laid such a guilt trip on them." Another said, "*Class Pictures* is the realest book I know." One commented about *Baby Sister,* "I think it was written about my cousin. She fell in love with her sister's boyfriend and married him just like Penny did. And she sews real well, too!" The *Publishers Weekly* review of *Fran Ellen's House* (1987) said that "the book's one drawback is that to be fully appreciated, it must be read in conjunction with the first heartbreaking story." One student agreed: "It was confusing. They kept telling you that something had happened but they didn't say when or just exactly what it was." Sachs's popularity was shown when *A Summer's Lease* won the South Carolina Young Adult Book Award, given by students in 1985.

If you like Marilyn Sachs, you might also like Eve Bunting, Hila Colman, Paula Danziger, and Lois Lowry.

Selected Bibliography

WORKS BY MARILYN SACHS

Amy Moves In (1964)

Laura's Luck (1965)

Amy and Laura (1966)

Veronica Ganz (1968)

Peter and Veronica (1969)

Mary (1970)

The Bears' House (1971)

Reading Between the Lines, play (1971)

A Pocket Full of Seeds (1973)

The Truth About Mary Rose (1973)

Dorrie's Book (1975)

Matt's Mitt (1975)

A December Tale (1976)

A Secret Friend (1978)

A Summer's Lease (1979)

Bus Ride (1980)

Class Pictures (1980)

Fleet-Footed Florence (1981)

Hello . . . Wrong Number (1981)

Beach Towels (1982)

Call Me Ruth (1982)

The Fat Girl (1983)

Fourteen (1983)

Thunderbird (1985)

Underdog (1985)

Baby Sister (1986)

Almost Fifteen (1987)

Fran Ellen's House (1987)

Just Like a Friend (1989)

At the Sound of the Beep (1990)

The Big Book for Peace, edited by Ann Durrell and Marilyn Sachs (1990)

Circles (1991)

What My Sister Remembered (1992)

Thirteen Going on Seven (1993)

WORKS ABOUT MARILYN SACHS

Berger, Laura Stanley, ed. *Twentieth-Century Young Adult Writers*. Detroit: St. James, 1994.

Budin, Miriam Lang. Review of *Baby Sister. School Library Journal,* August 1986, p. 106.

Commire, Anne, ed. "Marilyn Sachs." In *Something About the Author*. Detroit: Gale Research, vol. 3, 1972, pp. 180-182.

———. "Marilyn Sachs." In *Something About the Author.* Detroit: Gale Research, vol. 52, 1988, pp. 141-146.

De Montreville, Doris, and Elizabeth D. Crawford, eds. *Fourth Book of Junior Authors and Illustrators.* New York: H. W. Wilson, 1978.

Garrett, Agnes, and Helga P. McCue, eds. *Authors and Artists for Young Adults.* Detroit: Gale Research, 1989, vol. 2.

Gallo, Donald R., ed. *Speaking for Ourselves: Autobiographical Sketches by Notable Authors of Books for Young Adults.* Urbana, Ill.: National Council of Teachers of English, 1990, pp. 179–181.

McGrath, Joan. "Sachs, Marilyn (nee Stickle)." In *Twentieth-Century Children's Writers.* 3d ed. Edited by Tracy Chevalier. Chicago: St. James, 1989.

Marowski, Daniel G., ed. *Contemporary Literary Criticism.* Detroit: Gale Research, 1985, vol. 35.

Olendorf, Donna, ed. *Something About the Author.* Detroit: Gale Research, 1992, vol. 68.

"Review of *Fran Ellen's House.*" *Publishers Weekly,* 11 September 1987, p. 96.

Riley, Carolyn, ed. *Children's Literature Review.* Detroit: Gale Research, 1976, vol. 2.

Sarkissian, Adele, ed. *Something About the Author Autobiography Series.* Detroit: Gale Research, 1986, vol. 2.

How to Write to the Author
Marilyn Sachs
c/o Peter Smith Publisher, Inc.
5 Lexington Avenue
Magnolia, MA 01930

J. D. Salinger

(1919-)

by Warren French

J erome David (J. D.) Salinger, born on 1 January 1919, has published nothing since 1965. In a telephone interview, one of the few he has granted, he described publication as "a terrible invasion" of his privacy (*New York Times,* 3 November 1974). Yet while thousands of other books published between 1951 and 1963 have been forgotten, Salinger's four thin books with plain dust jackets, which are all he has authorized to remain in print, continue to sell briskly all over the world—and to win the affection of new generations of young readers. These books also keep alive what the critic George Steiner called in 1959 "The Salinger Industry," speculations about this mysterious writer who lives in isolation on a remote New England mountain and his often quoted, sometimes inscrutable stories.

Salinger's works were not always puzzling. His early stories, which he refuses to allow to be reprinted, were quite conventional anecdotes in the fashionably colloquial language of "the young folks" of the time, as he called them in

inscrutable not easily understood or interpreted

> *Holden Caulfield is a confused and insecure teenager. He makes crushing judgments about "phonies" whom he meets, in order to mask his inability to develop a satisfying identity.*

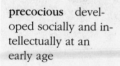

precocious developed socially and intellectually at an early age

his first published story. The extraordinary reputation that Salinger has since developed is based almost entirely upon his creation of two memorable, controversial characters: Holden Caulfield and Seymour Glass. They have almost nothing in common except growing up in luxurious apartments on New York's fashionable East Side where Salinger himself grew up. Rather, Holden and Seymour are polar opposites.

Holden Caulfield is a confused and insecure teenager. He makes crushing judgments about the "phonies" whom he meets, in order to mask his inability to develop a satisfying identity. Seymour Glass is an abnormally precocious and single-minded individual. He seeks to manage other people's lives and often makes outrageous demands upon them. Holden is a survivor who finally achieves peace of mind, so that several generations of other young people, bewildered by the reckless pace of modern life, have been able to identify with him and share his dreams. Seymour, on the other hand, is Salinger's vision of an incorruptible artist. He kills himself rather than compromise with a phony world. Seymour entered Salinger's life just as Holden was leaving it, when the writer himself was withdrawing from society.

Early Writings

Salinger began writing stories at school in the mid-1930s, but none of those written before 1939 are known to exist now. He was not a good student. He was dismissed from the fashionable McBurney School in New York and sent to Valley Forge Military Academy, the model for Pencey Prep in *The Catcher in the Rye* (1951). His father, a prosperous importer, sent Salinger to Austria and Poland to learn the business in 1937, before the German annexation of Austria and invasion of Poland. Salinger returned in 1938 to Ursinus College in Pennsylvania, but he spent only one semester there, writing a slangy column that featured movie reviews for the campus newspaper. He never graduated from college. His talents were first recognized when he took a short-story writing course at Columbia University in 1939. His teacher was Whit Burnett, editor of *Story* magazine. Many of the important mid-century writers were discovered by Burnett for his influential magazine. He published "The Young Folks" and three more stories by Salinger, who also contributed to popular family magazines such as *Collier's, The Saturday Evening Post,* and *Cosmopolitan* until 1948.

William Jameson Junior, the principal character in "The Young Folks," has a different name from Holden Caulfield. He is also a bit more sophisticated and less sympathetically depicted, but he is the prototype of Salinger's more famous tormented teenager, tough on the surface but sentimental under the skin. All Salinger's early stories were moving toward *The Catcher in the Rye.* As early as 1941 he sold to the *New Yorker* a story about Holden Morrisey Caulfield (the middle name never appears again). Yet when the United States entered World War II, the magazine decided that the story was too downbeat. It was a time when the national morale needed boosting. The story did not appear until 1945, when Salinger updated "Slight Rebellion off Madison" (as he did again when he used the material in his novel). Holden was also mentioned in several stories that Salinger wrote while serving during the war in the U.S. Army in England and Europe. In one of these stories Holden is mentioned as missing in action by a brother who does not appear in the novel.

Salinger even had a shorter version of *The Catcher in the Rye* accepted for publication in 1945, but he withdrew it and spent another five years reworking it. After it was published in 1951, he never wrote about Holden Caulfield again. During the period in which Salinger was rewriting his only novel, he had a traumatic experience that greatly affected his career. The biographer Ian Hamilton has established that Salinger married a French doctor in September 1945 while he was still in Europe. Little is known about her, however, except that her first name was Sylvia and that after following him to the United States, she returned to Europe and divorced him. The marriage broke up in July 1946 during a vacation trip to Daytona Beach, Florida, in a popular hotel much like the one in Salinger's story "A Perfect Day for Bananafish."

Critics have been puzzled by the startling difference between "The Inverted Forest" (*Cosmopolitan,* December 1947), the longest of the early short stories (which Salinger now refuses to allow to be reprinted), and "Bananafish," his first story about Seymour Glass (*New Yorker,* 31 January 1948), because they appeared so soon after each other. "The Inverted Forest" is an obscure, rambling tale about a poet with little self-confidence who leaves his own wife for another man's. His new wife is a dominating woman who insists that he give up writing for a limited audience and instead make money writing popular works. "A Perfect Day for Bananafish" is the hard-hitting account of Seymour Glass's odd behavior before he kills himself in the hotel room where his wife, whom he has called "Miss Spiritual Tramp of 1948," is sleeping.

Although Salinger never wrote about Holden Caulfield as an adult, his character Raymond Ford could pass for a grown-up Holden, especially as Holden behaves in the short story "I'm Crazy" (*Collier's,* 22 December 1945). It appeared at the time the first version of Salinger's novel was to have been published. This story, which contains some episodes that were rewritten for *The Catcher in the Rye,* ends with Holden's dejected recognition that he is "never going to be one of those successful guys." Like "The Inverted Forest," it is the story of a loser who cannot escape from humiliating situations. "A Perfect Day for Bananafish," on the other hand, is the story of an egoist who feels he must liberate himself from a squalid society by committing suicide, regardless of the effects of this decision upon others. Clearly, some profound change occurred in the perspective from which Salinger viewed the United States after he returned from World War II and while he was recovering from the breakup of his first marriage.

The change is evident in the dramatic difference between two versions of the climactic scene in *The Catcher in the Rye* in which Holden tells his little sister, Phoebe, what he really cares about. In "I'm Crazy" all Holden can come up with is the lame explanation that he likes girls he has not met yet. But in the conversation that provides the novel's title, Holden explains that he would like to be a "catcher in the rye," someone who would prevent carefree little kids from falling over "some crazy cliff." Some commentators have argued that Holden maintains an unrealistic and escapist attitude to the end of the novel; but by that time, Holden has abandoned his wistful dream. He observes that if kids fall off the carousel grabbing for golden rings, "they fall off, but it's bad if you say anything to them." The novel is not about a new Peter Pan who will never grow up. Rather, it is about a maturing person who comes to terms with the world in a way that Seymour Glass never could.

squalid filthy, vile

wistful yearning or longing in a sad state of mind

Peter Pan (1906), by J. M. Barrie, is a classic fantasy story for children.

Why did Salinger abandon a half-grown Holden to resurrect a departed Seymour? He is not likely to explain, but perhaps we can develop a thesis from the new direction his storytelling took. It is likely that the work on *The Catcher in the Rye* was pretty well finished before Salinger wrote "Bananafish." Just about this time, a new influence was beginning to manifest itself in his lifestyle and in his works. Salinger (and Seymour, among other characters) became interested in the doctrines of Advaita Vedanta, a form of the Hindu religion, which stresses a rejection of materialism and the gradual advancement, through reincarnations, of the human soul toward spiritual perfection. After this he refused all requests to reprint his earlier stories, which he regarded as an apprentice's work, and followed up his novel with a group of nine stories, all but two of which first appeared in the *New Yorker* before being collected in 1953 as *Nine Stories*.

materialism love of wealth and material possessions; belief that physical matter is the only reality

The Seymour Glass Story

Beginning with "A Perfect Day for Bananafish," the startling tale of Seymour Glass's violent escape from a world he considers devoid of spiritual values, the collection portrays other ways of dealing with a world that, as suggested by the title of one of Salinger's most praised stories, "For Esmé—with Love and Squalor," has sunk into dishonesty and vulgarity because of a lack of love.

In "Uncle Wiggily in Connecticut," Eloise, who lost her lover (one of the Glass family) to a freak accident during World War II, is now trapped in a loveless marriage in suburbia. She finds tearful relief only in remembering that once she was a "nice girl." In "Just Before the War with the Eskimos," Ginnie, a teenage girl, realizes that she is going to have to make the best of a world like Eloise's. In "The Laughing Man," an ambitious law student finds his romantic relationship falling to pieces and realizes that he cannot escape into fantasy. In "Down at the Dinghy" another of the Glasses, Boo Boo, protects her four-year-old son from anti-Semitism, for the moment, by a stratagem that can only be a stopgap. In "For Esmé," Salinger portrays a remarkable girl making the best of a situation and pulling others through crises. It is noteworthy, however, that Esmé is an English aristocrat and

stratagem trick

stopgap a temporary means of achieving something

squalor dirtiness and degradation, often associated with extreme poverty

enigmatic puzzling, mysterious

that her sensitive behavior obviously contrasts with that of the German and American women described in the story. In "Pretty Mouth and Green My Eyes," one of Salinger's few stories involving only adult characters, we are plunged into the greatest squalor of all: a revelation of adulterated business and marital relations.

Finally in two of his most enigmatic stories, Salinger depicts characters who have managed to transcend this squalid world. In "De Daumier-Smith's Blue Period" a once pretentious young artist carries out Holden Caulfield's vision of putting aside personal ambitions and leaving people to shape their own futures. In "Teddy," another precocious young genius—like Seymour—finds spiritual relief in escaping the world without taking his own life by submitting to a predestined fate.

About the time *Nine Stories* appeared, Salinger himself escaped at least some squalid aspects of society by making his final move to a mountaintop home in remote Cornish, New Hampshire. He married his second wife, Claire Douglas, a Radcliffe college student, in 1953. They have two children—Margaret Ann (born 1955) and Matthew (born 1960). In 1967 the marriage disintegrated. Salinger's wife could no longer endure the lonely isolation of their situation.

The first story to emerge from this private world, "Franny," is about a college student, Franny, who is undergoing a spiritual crisis that her self-centered and arrogant boyfriend does not understand. There is no mention in the original story that she is another of the Glass children, but she was assimilated into the family in a later story, "Zooey," in which her breakdown is finally cured by an inspiring message from her brother, the title character. The two stories were later published together in Salinger's third book, *Franny and Zooey* (1961).

In the meantime, Seymour Glass had reappeared in "Raise High the Roof Beam, Carpenters." In it, the curious story of his wedding day is recounted in minute detail by his brother Buddy, making heavy use of Seymour's diaries, which are laced with Advaita teachings. A number of years later, Buddy finally gets around in the story "Seymour: An Introduction" (which was later combined with "Roof Beam" in Salinger's last book) to disclosing a principal clue for understanding the Glass family saga. This clue is to the motive for Seymour's suicide: "The true artist-seer . . . is mainly dazzled to death by his own scruples, the blinding shapes and colors of his own sacred human conscience" (p. 123). There is no way of resolving the critical debate about whether this was what Salinger had in mind when he wrote the first Seymour story; but we do learn in this book that Buddy Glass was the author of Salinger's own stories.

When this last of Salinger's four books appeared in 1963, it seemed that this might be the end of the Glass family history; however, in 1965, "Hapworth 16, 1924," provided most of the material in one weekly issue of the *New Yorker*. This story purports to consist of a seemingly interminable letter that seven-year-old Seymour wrote to his parents from summer camp. It explains in detail his astonishingly precocious sexual activity and other feats and concludes with a long list of the books that he wishes sent to camp, along with the reasons for his recommending these classics. Even Salinger's associates at the *New Yorker* found this composition disastrous. Since then, there has been only silence from Cornish, except for a few outbursts from Salinger protesting, and taking legal action against, the pirated publication of his uncollected stories and a biography making unauthorized use of some of his letters.

purports claims

Selected Bibliography

WORKS BY J. D. SALINGER

The Catcher in the Rye (1951, 1953, 1958, 1964)

Nine Stories (1953, 1954, 1964)

Franny and Zooey (1961, 1964)

Raise High the Roof Beam, Carpenters and *Seymour: an Introduction* (1963, 1965)

"Hapworth 16, 1924." In *The New Yorker*, 19 June 1965, pp. 32–40.

WORKS ABOUT J. D. SALINGER

Alsen, Eberhard. *Salinger's Glass Stories as a Composite Novel*. Troy, N.Y.: Whitson, 1983.

Bloom, Harold, ed. *J. D. Salinger: Modern Critical Views*. New York: Chelsea House, 1987.

Eppes, Betty. "What I Did Last Summer." In *Paris Review*, 24 July 1981, pp. 221–239. (Some unusual interviews.)

If you like the work of J. D. Salinger, you might also like works by F. Scott Fitzgerald, William Goldman, Jack Kerouac, Carson McCullers, and Guy Owen.

French, Warren. *J. D. Salinger, Revisited*. Boston: Twayne, 1988.

Grunwald, Henry Anatole. *Salinger: A Critical and Personal Portrait*. New York: Harper, 1962.

Gwynn, Frederick L., and Joseph L. Blotner. *The Fiction of J. D. Salinger*. Pittsburgh: University of Pittsburgh Press, 1958.

Hamilton, Ian. *In Search of J. D. Salinger*. New York: Random House, 1988.

Kurian, Elizabeth N. *A Religious Response to the Existential Dilemma in the Fiction of J. D. Salinger*. New Delhi: India Intellectual Publishing House, 1992. This most useful and profound study of Salinger's fiction is unfortunately not available in an American edition. Dr. Kurian explains the three religious traditions influencing Salinger's fiction—Hindu, Buddhist, and Judeo-Christian—and shows how they are interwoven in arriving principally in the Glass family stories at his answers to complex problems of a confused and troubled society.

Maxwell, William. "J. D. Salinger." In *Book-of-the-Month Club News,* Midsummer 1951, pp. 5–6.

Miller, James E., Jr. *J. D. Salinger*. Minneapolis: University of Minnesota Press, 1965.

Ohmann, Carol, and Richard Ohmann. "Reviewers, Critics, and *The Catcher in the Rye*." In *Critical Inquiry,* vol. 3, Autumn 1976, pp. 15–37.

Salzberg, Joel. *Critical Essays on Salinger's "The Catcher in the Rye."* Boston: G. K. Hall, 1990.

Salzman, Jack. *New Essays on "The Catcher in the Rye."* New York and London: Cambridge University, 1991.

Stashower, Daniel M. "On First Looking into Chapman's Holden: Speculations on a Murder." *American Scholar,* vol. 52, 1983, pp. 373–377.

Steiner, George. "The Salinger Industry." In *Nation,* 14 November 1959, pp. 360–363.

Sublette, Jack R. *J. D. Salinger: An Annotated Bibliography: 1938–1981*. New York: Garland, 1984.

Wenke, John. *J. D. Salinger: A Study of the Short Fiction*. Boston: Twayne, 1991.

Graham Salisbury

(1944-   )

by Chris Crowe

Graham Salisbury (nicknamed Sandy) is the kind of guy you would love to have for an older brother. He is softspoken and gentle, considerate and polite, intelligent and funny. And he really cares about people, especially young people. You could talk to him about important things and know he would listen without preaching or condemning. He would be there when you needed him and say exactly what you needed to hear. He could take you deep-sea fishing or snorkeling or surfing. Maybe—if you were interested—he could also teach you how to write a song or, even better, a short story.

If you were tired or bored, you could just kick back on the beach and ask him to tell you about his childhood in Hawaii, to fill your head with incredibly vivid details of life on one of the world's most beautiful islands. Just imagine: You stretch out on your beach towel and say, "Sandy, tell me about the Big Island."

He drops alongside you in the sand, pulls his knees up,

Quotations by Graham Salisbury that are not attributed to a published source are from personal interviews conducted by the author of this article on 10 August 1994 and 3 April 1995 and are published here by permission of Graham Salisbury.

The state of Hawaii consists of 132 islands, of which Hawaii is the largest. Hawaii is often referred to as the **Big Island.**

113

and is quiet for a moment, looking out into the surf, gathering his thoughts, searching his recollections. Then he begins, his gentle voice barely audible above the waves.

> In the sleepy flea-sized Big Island town of Holualoa, there was an old man I liked: a Filipino barber. His shop was in his house just off Mamalahoa, a twisty old patched-over road that circles the island of Hawaii. I was twelve years old. I just moved to Kona from the island of Oahu—Mom, me, and my three sisters freshly married to a deep-sea fisherman named John.

> I liked Holualoa, fifteen hundred feet up from sea level and as quiet as a junkyard. The smell of sun-warmed mangos and guavas and cow manure surrounded you wherever you went, sweet and rich and earthy.

> I walked alone up the quiet old road to get my hair cut. Hardly ever even saw a car pass, and when one did the driver would wave, every time. People I'd never even seen before.

> But those haircuts are embedded in my memory forever, because that singular, slow, easy, luxurious experience was filled with sensorial gifts: the sweet smell of guavas rotting in the jungle; the incredibly awesome sight of the ocean from that altitude; combs submerged in jars of blue water; the sound of scissors snipping around my ears; the echo of roosters crowing in the distance; the feel of freshly cut stubble on the back of my neck; and the smooth porcelain arms of the chair under my hands.

> And the taste of time creeping by, slow as a bug.

Salisbury has more stories to tell, stories about the lives of boys in the Islands, boys like him. If you're not lucky enough to have him around in person, you can pick up *Blue Skin of the Sea* (1992) or *Under The Blood-Red Sun* (1994) and be transported to Hawaii and into the lives of the boys and their families who live there. It is almost as good as lying on the beach, listening to him with the surf pounding in the background.

Mangos and **guavas** are tropical fruits common to Hawaii.

Salisbury's Life

The Early Years

Graham Salisbury was born in 1944 on a naval base in Philadelphia. His father, Lieutenant Commander Henry "Hank" Graham, was a naval academy graduate and a fighter pilot. Salisbury's mother, Barbara Twigg-Smith, a sixth- generation descendant of Congregational missionaries to Hawaii, was an artist. When Salisbury was two months old, his father was assigned to an aircraft carrier in the Pacific, so Salisbury and his mother returned to Hawaii, where her family had lived since 1820.

On Salisbury's first birthday, 11 April 1945, his father was shot down and killed while flying a combat mission over southern Japan. "I have no memory of him," Salisbury says. "In my mind he has always been a man of immense courage."

When Salisbury was two, his mother married again. Guy Salisbury, another navy man, adopted Sandy and fathered three daughters before dying of cancer when Sandy was ten, again leaving him without a father or a memory of one.

When Salisbury was thirteen, his mother was married for the third time, to a deep-sea charter-boat fisherman named John. Salisbury recalls John in "Ice," which appears in *Going Where I'm Coming From* (1995): "He had thick, wavy hair and muscles like Sylvester Stallone. He could surf, he could water-ski on bare feet, he could free dive to eighty feet and stay down for close to three minutes .   .   . he was everything I, at thirteen, wanted to be" (pp. 19–20). The family moved from Oahu to Kailua-Kona on the Big Island, and Salisbury was enrolled in a boys' boarding school, Hawaii Preparatory School, where he completed junior high and high school.

During his teenage years, two men had a profound influence on Salisbury: his stepfather (John) and James Monroe Taylor, the headmaster of the preparatory school. Taylor drilled into Salisbury the concepts of discipline, hard work, moral character, compassion, excellence, and leadership. "This roundish, happy, committed man was one of the great influences of my life," Salisbury recalls. "'Hitch your wagon to a star,' was a phrase he used. Aim high. I liked the sound of it then. But later, after I'd developed a brain, I liked the truth of it. To this great man, I owe the foundation of what-ever 'character' I can lay claim to."

Salisbury's stepfather had an almost opposite effect. "All the good things [Mr. Taylor] poured into me, it seemed, my stepfather drained out," Salisbury says. His brief memoir, "Ice," describes one of the hard lessons he learned from his stepfather, a "crusher of self-esteem" (p. 20). Salisbury's rela-tionship with his stepfather during his twelfth and thirteenth years is the basis for his third book, a memoir tentatively ti-tled *Lord of the Deep.*

After High School

After graduation from prep school, Salisbury enrolled at the University of Vermont, where he "played around, had a great time, and pretty much flunked out." He left school in his sec-ond semester and returned to Hawaii. The following fall, he enrolled at Santa Barbara City College and once again did poorly. After that, he decided to give up school for a while and joined a rock band as a bass player. His quartet played in Arizona, California, and Idaho. "We were pretty good," says Salisbury. "Red-faced beer drinkers loved us."

When Salisbury was twenty-one and the Vietnam War was raging, the United States Army drafted him. He quit his band and prepared to go to Los Angeles to report for induc-tion, but just before he left, he received notice that as a sole survivor he was exempt from the draft. "That letter from my draft board surely saved my sanity, if not my life," he says. "I felt guilty that my father had to die in a war so I could get out of one. Like I said, I've always thought of him as the one with the guts."

Salisbury went to Los Angeles anyway and joined Millen-nium, a seven-man studio band, as a singer and songwriter. The band recorded an album with Columbia Records, and a song Salisbury wrote, "Five A.M.," became a number-one hit in the Philippines. Despite his modest success with Millen-nium, he realized that the music business was not for him, so he returned to school, first to Los Angeles City College and then to California State University, Northridge, where he studied to become an elementary school teacher. His time away from school had improved him as a student; he was graduated in 1974, magna cum laude.

After graduation, Salisbury went to Bergamo, Italy, to study the Montessori teaching method. He earned his Montessori certificate, returned to the United States, and got a job teaching at a small Montessori school in Utah. When the school closed, he worked as a production manager at BYU (Brigham Young University) Graphics in Provo, Utah, a job he held until he moved in 1984 to Portland, Oregon, where he still lives with his wife, Robyn, and six children.

Writing Career

Salisbury never expected to become a writer. "That I have found this way of expression is truly amazing to me," he says. "Me, the one who flunked English. Twice. The one who never read as a boy. Me, a *writer.*" He credits his discovery of writing to two things: a man and a fear. Those two things plus his "big break" combined to bring *Blue Skin of the Sea* into print.

The man was Alex Haley. When Salisbury used to sit up at nights feeding his first son, he started reading Haley's *Roots,* a novel about American slavery. The force with which Haley portrayed the characters and their lives stunned Salisbury, moved him, woke him up to the power of words and the wonder of books.

The fear was public speaking. In his freshman year at Vermont, Salisbury embarrassed himself badly on the first day of speech class. "I could hardly stand up and give my name in *any* group situation thereafter," he remembers. He remained silent for the rest of the semester and vowed he would never speak in public again. Several years later, he decided to try to overcome his fear. He enrolled in a Dale Carnegie public speaking course and found that writing the required five-minute speeches was easy for him. He also discovered that he could stretch the truth from his memories to create fiction, fiction that interested others.

By then, Salisbury was hooked and continued to write, teaching himself to craft short stories and sending some of the better ones to magazines. Eventually, he realized that he needed more formal training in writing, so he enrolled in the Master of Fine Arts writing program at Vermont College of Norwich University. After two years of study and writing, he was graduated in 1990 with his master's degree and a draft of *Blue Skin of the Sea.*

The **Montessori method** is an educational system developed in the early 1900s. The method is designed to help children develop their independence and intelligence through the use of special lessons for specified age groups.

> *Salisbury never expected to become a writer. "That I have found this way of expression is truly amazing to me. Me, the one who flunked English. Twice. The one who never read as a boy. Me, a writer."*

> *"I want my readers to see what I see. So I write, then rewrite and rewrite and rewrite, until it's as clear as a diamond. This is the real secret to writing well. . . . Rewrite, rewrite, rewrite, until it sings."*

A few of Salisbury's short stories (including some that eventually found their way, in slightly different form, into *Blue Skin of the Sea*) were published in literary magazines, but he had not yet found a publisher for his book-length manuscript. His big break came at his MFA reading in Vermont.

As a part of his final project, Salisbury read "The Old Man." C. Michael Curtis, fiction editor of the *Atlantic Monthly* magazine, was in the audience and later asked for a copy of the entire manuscript to show a friend of his at a major publishing house. Nothing ever came of that request, but a few months later it led to a chance conversation with Wendy Lamb, an editor at Bantam Doubleday Dell. She also asked to see Salisbury's manuscript. Soon after receiving it, she called to tell him that Delacorte wanted to publish *Blue Skin of the Sea*. The book was published in 1992 and won many awards, including the prestigious PEN/Norma Klein Award for a promising new writer for young adults.

In 1994, Salisbury's second book, *Under the Blood-Red Sun,* was also published by Delacorte. This book also received much positive recognition and many awards, including the 1994 Scott O'Dell Award for Historical Fiction.

Style, Themes, and Ideas

Once you have heard Salisbury speak or read his books, stories, or essays, you know imagery and detail are important in his writing. "I want my readers to see what I see. So I write, then rewrite and rewrite and rewrite, until it's as clear as a diamond. This is the real secret to writing well. Writing is rewriting. That's it. Look no further. Buy no more books on writing. Rewrite, rewrite, rewrite, until it sings." When he is rewriting, he is constantly on the lookout for better visual words to make his imagery more effective.

There is an article about Chris Crutcher in volume 1 and an article about Will Hobbs in volume 2. Articles about Richard Peck and Gary Soto appear in this volume.

Salisbury admires the work of several other writers, especially young adult authors Richard Peck, Gary Soto, Chris Crutcher, and Will Hobbs. "I like these particular writers because they tell good stories and write in well-crafted, visual English. They also make me *feel* things—love, anger, joy, sadness, hope—things that make me human."

Salisbury's own stories make people feel human, but they also cause readers to think about themselves and their lives. That ability, he says in his 1992 speech "Being a Boy Can Be Dangerous," is one of the great gifts of fiction. "It expands our vision and uncovers possibilities. It gives us hope where in our real lives hope is often invisible, especially to young people" (p. 262). Although it is clear that Salisbury wants his stories to have a positive influence on his readers, he writes to explore, not to preach or lecture. As he says in "A Leaf on the Sea," his fall 1994 *ALAN Review* article, "If my stories show boys choosing certain life options, and the possible consequences of having chosen those options, then maybe I will have finally done something worthwhile" (p. 14).

Nearly all of Salisbury's writing comes from the "confused, meandering, brainless time in my life I now call my boyhood," he says in "A Leaf on the Sea." "I have never forgotten the almost unendurable heartaches of my lost teenage loves, or the fear and tension that gripped me when I knew some kind of fight was imminent. It's all still there, deep inside me" (p. 11). His fiction has many parallels with his life, but it is not autobiographical. Its subject is broader than just the life of one individual: it is about fathers and sons, love and fear, and boyhood in Hawaii.

Salisbury's own essentially fatherless childhood affected him deeply. Family, or the lack of it, has always been an important issue with him. "It's no surprise that I write a lot about relationships, especially family relationships," he says in *Something About the Author Autobiography Series* (p. 201). In *Blue Skin of the Sea* Sonny aches for his mother, despite the nurturing he receives from Aunty Pearl. At the same time, he is both afraid of and curious about his father, a mysterious man he hardly knows. Tomi, in *Under the Blood-Red Sun*, also depends on family relationships—and the memory of those relationships—to sustain him in the extremely difficult times after the attack on Pearl Harbor.

Perhaps because of his own experience with the struggles boys have growing up (which he discusses in his autobiographical essays "A Leaf on the Sea," "Being a Boy Can Be Dangerous," and "Ice"), Salisbury is especially interested in how boys become good men, in how their characters are shaped, and in the things that turn boys into bad men. Both Sonny and Tomi endure a variety of hardships in the novels, but these difficulties ultimately shape them into good young men. When you read Salisbury's novels and stories, you will

> *"I have never forgotten the almost unendurable heartaches of my lost teenage loves, or the fear and tension that gripped me when I knew some kind of fight was imminent. It's all still there, deep inside me."*

notice that parents, bullies, fear of various things, father-son relationships, and the nurturing love of family play important roles in the development of the main characters. These helps and hardships bring the characters to maturity and prepare them for more adult roles in society.

Salisbury also uses realistic local Hawaiian characters, settings, and language (especially dialogue and Hawaiian pidgin) in ways that please readers and critics. Although his main characters, so far, have been ethnic minorities, their struggles and concerns reflect the universality of adolescence. Readers in Boston or Salt Lake City or Dallas might be heartened to see that even teenagers on the island paradise of Hawaii deal with the same problems they do.

Salisbury's writing is marked by his desire to help young people, especially boys, find their way in life and to help them avoid the fear, hate, neglect, and machismo that can damage them and turn them into careless and abusive adults. He remains committed to writing good books for teenagers: "For me, writing is more a way of making a contribution than a living . . . it's more important to give back what Mr. Taylor gave me: a few good things to think about."

Readers who enjoy Graham Salisbury's works might also enjoy the works of Will Hobbs.

Selected Bibliography

WORKS BY GRAHAM SALISBURY

Novels

> *Blue Skin of the Sea* (1992)
> *Under the Blood-Red Sun* (1994)

Selected Short Fiction

> "The Dropping Stone." *Chaminade Literary Review,* spring 1988, pp. 76–92.
> "Jewels." *Hawaii Pacific Review,* spring 1989, pp. 51–60.
> "You Would Cry to See Waiakea Town." *Bamboo Ridge,* fall 1989, pp. 112–129.
> "The Old Man." *Manoa: A Journal of Pacific and International Writing,* spring 1990, pp. 81–91.
> "Shark Bait." In *Ultimate Sports: Short Stories by Outstanding Writers for Young Adults.* Edited by Donald R. Gallo. New York: Delacorte, 1995, pp. 118–143.

Nonfiction

"Being a Boy Can Be Dangerous," *Journal of Youth Services in Libraries,* spring 1993, pp. 259–262.

"Bellows Field: A Writer's Metaphor," *Hawaii Library Association Journal,* June 1994, pp. 15–20.

"A Leaf on the Sea," *ALAN Review,* fall 1994, pp. 11–14."Ice." In *Going Where I'm Coming From.* Edited by Ann Mazer. New York: Persea Books, 1995, pp. 18–26.

"Word of Mouth." *Library Journal,* 15 September 1992, p. 120.

WORKS ABOUT GRAHAM SALISBURY

Bradburn, Frances. Review of *Under the Blood-Red Sun. Booklist,* 15 October 1994, p. 425.

Corsaro, Julie. Review of *Blue Skin of the Sea. Booklist,* 15 June 1992, p. 1835.

Crowe, Chris. "Graham Salisbury." In *Writers of Multicultural Fiction for Young Adults: A Bio-Critical Sourcebook.* Edited by M. Daphne Kutzner. Westport, Conn.: Greenwood, 1995.

Lord, John R. Review of *Under the Blood-Red Sun.* In *Voice of Youth Advocates,* October 1994, p. 216.

Meeker, Amy. "Flying Starts." *Publishers Weekly,* 13 July 1992, pp. 22–24.

Review of *Blue Skin of the Sea. Kirkus Reviews,* 15 June 1992, p. 785.

Review of *Blue Skin of the Sea. Publishers Weekly,* 15 June 1992, p. 104.

Richmond, Gale. Review of *Blue Skin of the Sea. School Library Journal,* June 1992, p. 140.

Salisbury, Graham. "Graham Salisbury." In *Something About the Author Autobiography Series.* Edited by Diane Telgen. Detroit: Gale Research, 1994, pp. 200–201.

How to Write to the Author
Graham Salisbury
c/o Bantam Doubleday Dell
Books for Young Readers
1540 Broadway
New York, NY 10036

Carl Sandburg

(1878–1967)

by Mike Angelotti

Carl Sandburg wrote much of himself into the six lines and twenty-one words of "Fog," one of his most quoted poems.

> The fog comes
> on little cat feet.
> It sits looking
> over harbor and city
> on silent haunches
> and then moves on.

As a man and literary artist, Sandburg was restless, unpredictable, searching, moving from place to place, from job to job, from poet to reporter to biographer to social activist, from poetry to prose to poetry to prose, stopping for a moment, looking it over, then moving on. He was not one to waste time. He often wrote snatches of poetry while on news-reporting assignments. He was able to use his reporter's eye for detail, and his reporter's ability to compress information, to compose vivid poetry in concise language.

"Fog" is an example of Sandburg the reporter writing poetry. He composed it one day in 1913 while waiting impatiently to interview a juvenile court judge for *The Day Book,* a Chicago newspaper. He had noticed the fog on Chicago Harbor during the walk from his office to meet the judge. Sandburg the reporter captured the details of fog and cat, and the uncluttered language to express them. Sandburg the poet brought the fog and the cat into a single impression, a metaphor, as though creating a wondrous, spiritual creature: part animal, part mist.

But a good deal of Sandburg's poetry, particularly during his early years in Chicago, was not as metaphoric or imagistic as "Fog." Often, his poetry expressed his observations and thoughts literally, as though written off the top of his head. He was a working reporter, mainly for the *Chicago Daily News,* until age fifty-four, and that work allowed him close contact with the people and events of the day. Many of those events were tragic and violent. Frequently, the stories that Sandburg covered provided the subject matter of his poems, which plainly conveyed both his passion and his rage. About social injustice, in the poem "The Right to Grief," he wrote, "I shall cry over the dead child of a stockyards hunky." About World War I, in the poem "Killers," he wrote, "And a red juice soaks the dark soil./ And the sixteen million are killing . . . and killing and killing."

These lines reflect Sandburg's antiwar sentiment, his passion for social justice, and his deep respect for the lives of individual human beings, particularly the exploited. His poems defined him as a man and provoked controversy among many established literary critics and poets. They objected to his use of the free-verse form, his conversational speech rhythms, his strong voice, and his literal treatment of realistic subject matter. These made his poems different from the traditional forms, rhythms, and romantic subject matter of the day. In 1916, the question from Sandburg's critics was simple: Is this poetry? The answer was equally simple: by the rules of tradition, no; but by the new rules being created by Amy Lowell, Ezra Pound, Wallace Stevens, Theodore Dreiser, and others of the revolutionary group of new writers, yes. Thereafter, not much of Sandburg's literary work, neither prose nor poetry, would escape controversy.

And Sandburg's literary productivity was substantial. During his lifetime, he published more than 1,000 poems, winning the Pulitzer Prize for poetry in 1951. He also wrote a 1.5-million-word, six-volume biography of Abraham Lincoln that won a Pulitzer Prize for history in 1940. He was poet, journalist, biographer, political activist, historian, musician, entertainer, novelist, screenwriter, writer of children's books. He won most major literary awards available to him, was named the Poet of the People and the Poet Laureate of the United States, was awarded honorary doctoral degrees by at least thirteen universities, including Harvard and Yale, and had schools, streets, and buildings named after him. He wrote countless journalistic pieces and occasional papers, and by his count he wrote twenty-three books, most of which challenged established literary tradition and social institutions. Yet his place in American letters, even of the twentieth century, remains in question.

When you look at Carl Sandburg's life as a writer, three distinct periods emerge: the pre-Chicago period (1878–1912), the Chicago years (1912–1945), and the post-Chicago period (1945–1967). Scholars generally agree that his most productive writing occurred during his Chicago years; that he was unorthodox, radical, a revolutionary from start to finish; that he was a passionate crusader for social justice, both as journalist and as poet; and that his work was distinctly Sandburg and uniquely American. They do not agree on the quality or the definition of his work or on whether that work is strong enough to place him among great American writers.

The Pre-Chicago Period (1878–1912)

Carl August Sandburg was born 6 January 1878 in Galesburg, Illinois. He was the oldest son of seven children born into a Swedish immigrant family. His father, August, was a semiliterate blacksmith's helper for the Chicago, Burlington, and Quincy Railroad. His mother, Clara, a former hotel maid, dedicated her life to the care and education of her family. Carl Sandburg educated himself through extensive reading after he left school following the eighth grade to supplement the meager family income.

In 1897, at nineteen, Sandburg took to the road as a hobo, riding in boxcars. He worked his way west to Denver as a farmhand, railroad laborer, and dishwasher, then back again in 1898 to Galesburg. There he enlisted in the Sixth Illinois Regiment to serve a six-month tour during the Spanish-American War, after which he enrolled as a special student at Lombard College in Galesburg. In 1899 he was appointed to West Point but failed the mathematics and grammar entrance exams. He returned to Lombard, where he edited the college literary magazine and yearbook and excelled at literature, writing, and athletics. But he left Lombard in 1902 during his senior year, without graduating, to hit the road again. This time he worked his way to the east coast, often as a door-to-door salesman, before returning in 1904 to Galesburg, where he wrote for the *Galesburg Evening Mail.*

In 1905, Sandburg decided that his future was in Chicago. He worked there as an editor-journalist for *Tomorrow Magazine* and *The Lyceumite* before moving to Wisconsin in 1908 to work as a journalist—and as an organizer, political writer, and lecturer for the Social Democratic party. While in Wisconsin he was a reporter-editor for several publications, including the *Milwaukee Journal* and *La Follette's Weekly Magazine.* It was there that he married Lillian (Paula) Steichen, sister of the famous photographer Edward Steichen. A remarkable scholar and teacher in her own right, Paula gave birth to their first child, Margaret, in 1911. Carl Sandburg returned to Chicago in 1912 to take a job with the *Chicago Evening World,* a socialist newspaper.

Sandburg's life up to 1912 laid the groundwork for the philosophy, talent, and emotionalism that were to drive his Chicago years. He lived the struggle of a working-class immigrant family. He experienced firsthand the long hours and dangerous working conditions of the blue-collar worker. He was a hobo and wanderer who walked the streets and country roads of the United States, met the poorest of its people, and suffered their pain, hunger, hard times, and exploitation. Out of all this, he developed his passion for the country and its people, his sense of the soul of the American people, and his rage against injustice to anyone.

Sandburg took note of the details of life around him, sharpened his talent for writing, and deepened his taste for poetic expression. He wrote what he observed and felt. As his *Chicago Poems* (1916) would reveal, sometimes he attacked viciously, as he did Billy Sunday, a popular evangelist of the time: "You slimy bunkshooter. . . Jesus wouldn't stand for the stuff you're handing out."

Sometimes Sandburg appealed softly, as he did in his poignant portraits of working women and immigrant laborers. At other times he simply responded to the beauty that he saw as he did with "Fog." In sum, he worked his material from two sides, soft and hard, always—consciously and unconsciously—from a poetic base, even in his prose. In fact, at the *Chicago Daily News* he was known as "the poet of the newsroom." In a very real sense, all Sandburg's writing was poetic. He shaped only part of it into verse forms. What emerges from a study of Carl Sandburg's lifework is a prodigious volume of work, reflecting a man of enormous energy who was as passionate about what he loved as he was about what enraged him. And he wrote about it. Bluntly.

> **evangelist** a passionate, devoted preacher

> *In a very real sense, all Sandburg's writing was poetic. He shaped only part of it into verse forms.*

The Chicago Years (1912–1945)

While in Chicago, Sandburg published widely as a poet, journalist, biographer, children's writer, novelist, musician, and collector of folksongs. He published journalistic pieces regularly for a number of publications, chiefly *The Day Book,* during his early Chicago years, but aside from a poem here and there he was unable to break through as a recognized poet until 1914. It was then that *Poetry: A Magazine of Verse* published nine of his poems, including "Chicago," which was to become Sandburg's signature poem. It begins:

> Hog Butcher for the World,
> Tool Maker, Stacker of Wheat,
> Player with Railroads and the Nation's Freight Handler;
> Stormy, husky, brawling,
> City of the Big Shoulders:
> They tell me you are wicked and I believe them.

Sandburg goes on to describe the city's "painted women," its "crooked" judicial system, its brutality "on the faces of women and children." But he also writes with as much passion about its vitality, strength, and soul, which he

believed came from the people, especially its immigrants and
working class:

Come and show me another city . . .
Bragging and laughing that under his wrist is the pulse, and
    under his ribs
the heart of the people,
Laughing!

> *Sandburg's passion for the people, the beauty, and the energy of the city was matched by his rage against its social injustice, particularly to women, children, minorities, and the working class.*

And that was the point. Sandburg's passion for the people, the beauty, and the energy of the city was matched by his rage against its social injustice, particularly to women, children, minorities, and the working class; and he chose to express his feelings in poetry, using the frank language and explicit detail he had learned as one of Chicago's most prolific journalists. He was poet, reporter, and social reformer all in one. That was Carl Sandburg's truth: to express the whole truth as he saw it, naked, at a literal level, in the language of the people; to be their champion. He pursued this purpose relentlessly, and some thought to a fault.

The publication of "Chicago" was followed by Sandburg's first and possibly best-known major book of poetry, *Chicago Poems* (1916). In the book, he often explores themes of social injustice by using vignettes of individual victims. "Anna Imroth," for example, is the story of a young working girl who dies jumping from a factory roof during a fire because there is no fire escape. Sandburg shows his anger at the exploitation of the working class and how he is moved by their loss of dreams in poems such as "The Harbor," in which "women/ Looked from their hunger-deep eyes," and "They Will Say," in which he suggests that the worst that men will say about his city is, "You took little children away from the sun . . . / To work . . . and die empty hearted." In "Skyscraper," he includes a tribute to the common people of the city, who "give the building a soul of dreams and thoughts and memories. / . . . men who sunk the pilings. . . . Smiles and tears of each office girl go into the soul of the building."

Predictably, *Chicago Poems* was controversial. Critical response to the book was a replay of that to the poem "Chicago" two years earlier. As they had then, Sandburg's fellow revolutionaries applauded his boldness and the power of his work. But his critics attacked his lack of discipline and his disregard for standard poetics. After the publication of *Chicago Poems,* there was little else that Carl Sandburg did that did not result in mixed reviews.

Between 1916 and 1945, Sandburg composed the bulk of his published poetry. Following *Chicago Poems,* he shifted his focus from the turbulent big-city setting to the more tranquil prairie of his youth in *Cornhuskers* (1918). The result was a more subdued poet's voice, more consistent with rural small-town life and the rhythms of nature. It still used the diction of the common person but was essentially lacking the violence and pathos of the struggle between the individual and the system that had characterized his portrayal of Chicago life.

Many thought that Sandburg's third book of poetry, *Smoke and Steel* (1920), was his best up to that time. But there is an unmistakable darkness, even a certain disillusionment and cynicism, that characterize this body of work. Carl Sandburg is there, more contemplative, more controlled, more poetic; but the loud-voiced, bold idealist of *Chicago Poems* is not. By the time he published his next three books of poetry, *Slabs of the Sunburnt West* (1922), *Good Morning, America* (1928), and *The People, Yes* (1936), he was acknowledged internationally as a significant figure in American letters, not only for his poetry but also for his children's literature, folk music, and various works of prose.

The most important of Sandburg's prose pieces was his massive biography of Abraham Lincoln, published as *Abraham Lincoln, The Prairie Years* (1926) and *Abraham Lincoln: The War Years* (1939). In biography, as in poetry, Sandburg the poet and storyteller adjusted the conventions of the literary form to accommodate his purpose and writing style, in order to compose what has been called a six-volume prose poem. He once again drew upon his poet's soul to embed the narrative in lyrical nuance and his reporter's eye to present layer upon layer of historical fact from multiple points of view. Most often, he did so with no authorial comment, leaving it to the reader to interpret from the body of facts and character sketches presented. Sandburg's biography of Lincoln was regarded by many historians, scholars, and critics as not only the most literary but also the most authentic Lincoln biography written to that time.

> *The most important of Sandburg's prose pieces was his massive biography of Abraham Lincoln.*

pathos   element in literature that evokes pity or compassion

cynicism   distrust, pessimism

The Post-Chicago Period (1945–1967)

In 1945, Carl Sandburg and his family fulfilled a long-held dream by moving to Connemara Farm near Flat Rock, North Carolina. But the hectic pace of his first sixty-seven years was taking its toll on Sandburg's legendary robust health and superhuman work schedule. He had to slow down. Although he and Paula had collected his earlier work into *Complete Poems* (1950), for which he won the 1951 Pulitzer Prize for poetry, he devoted much of his later life to writing prose, most notably the first volume of his autobiography, *Always the Young Strangers* (1953). It took the reader through his life to age twenty. The book was a critical success, applauded as much for the authentic picture it painted of the American Midwest of that period as for the literary art applied to his life story. Intent on completing a number of other projects but hampered by failing health, Sandburg never completed volume two. He died at age eighty-nine the morning of 22 July 1967.

Final Thoughts

> *Sandburg's simple lines reveal him as an honest battler for the common person, the downtrodden, the forgotten, who struggled to survive each day. His poetry was equally rough and tough, soft and sentimental. American.*

Carl Sandburg the poet was a tough Chicago newspaperman who rattled the poetry establishment in 1916 with the publication of *Chicago Poems,* his first major book. He was a different poet for his time. His simple lines reveal him as an honest battler for the common person, the downtrodden, the forgotten, who struggled to survive each day. Sandburg's poetry was equally rough and tough, soft and sentimental. American. Uniquely his. Whether he is remembered best for his poetry or for his prose is arguable. He won a Pulitzer Prize for each, although his well-received 1951 Pulitzer for *Complete Poems, 1950* was severely attacked in the September 1951 issue of *Poetry* magazine by William Carlos Williams, highly regarded American poet-critic and old friend of Sandburg. Williams questioned, among other things, the form and art of Sandburg's poems, as well as the stature of Sandburg as a poet. This attack hurt Sandburg personally and damages his standing as a poet to this day. Issues surrounding his poetry aside, most critics seem to agree that his Lincoln biography is his most noteworthy literary achievement. But even in that he was first a poet, then a reporter, and therefore the historical prose in his Lincoln work sings like an extended prose poem.

Penelope Niven, a biographer of Sandburg, has since 1978 worked through thousands of previously uncataloged Sandburg papers at Connemara and has interviewed many previously untapped people who personally knew the writer. She made this observation in the preface to her 1991 biography of Carl Sandburg:

> Sandburg's critics have called him a superficial, undisciplined poet and a careless biographer of Lincoln. His papers unveil a different Sandburg, however. They document his care and thought in crafting poetry and prose, his painstaking revisions, his thorough, sometimes groundbreaking scholarship, the punctual reporter's regard for deadlines and economy.

Hobo, poet, reporter, social critic, biographer, historian, novelist, writer for children, collector of folk songs, balladeer. Carl Sandburg was as restless as a cat, moving softly, tough enough to survive backstreet alley fights. He wanted to taste all of life and all of writing. It was said that he lived three lives before he reached forty and six more before he reached eighty-nine. On something like this subject he closed his "Notes for a Preface" to his *Complete Poems* (1950):

> I should like to think that as I go on writing there will be sentences truly alive, with verbs quivering, with nouns giving color and echoes. It could be, in the grace of God, I shall live to be eighty-nine, . . and speaking my farewell to earthly scenes, I might paraphrase: "If God had let me live five years longer I should have been a writer."

Selected Bibliography

WORKS BY CARL SANDBURG

Books on History, Biography, and Society

The Chicago Race Riots (1919)

Abraham Lincoln: The Prairie Years, two volumes (1926)

The American Songbag (1927)

Readers of Carl Sandburg might also enjoy works by Maya Angelou, another poet who writes about social issues; Christopher and James Lincoln Collier, who write biographies and historical fiction; Stephen Crane and Emily Dickinson, who wrote poetry in free verse; Charles Dickens, renowned for his social protest writings; Robert Frost, a contemporary literary rival; Jack London, a close friend of Sandburg's who wrote about social issues; and John Steinbeck, another contemporary.

Steichen the Photographer (1929)

Mary Lincoln, Wife and Widow (1932)

Lincoln and Whitman Miscellany, an essay (1938)

Abraham Lincoln: The War Years, four volumes (1939)

Storm Over the Land, excerpted from *Abraham Lincoln: The War Years* (1942)

Home Front Memo (1943)

The Photographs of Abraham Lincoln, with Frederick H. Meserve (1944)

Lincoln Collector: The Story of the Oliver R. Barrett Lincoln Collection (1949)

The New American Songbag (1950)

Always the Young Strangers (1953)

Abraham Lincoln: The Prairie Years and The War Years (1954)

The Sandburg Range (1957)

Ever the Winds of Chance (1983)

Novel

Remembrance Rock (1948)

Poetry

Chicago Poems (1916)

Cornhuskers (1918)

Smoke and Steel (1920)

Slabs of the Sunburnt West (1922)

Selected Poems, edited by Rebecca West (1926)

Good Morning, America (1928)

The People, Yes (1936)

Poems of the Midwest (1946)

Complete Poems (1950)

Harvest Poems: 1910–1960 (1960)

Honey and Salt (1963)

The Complete Poems of Carl Sandburg, rev. and expanded ed. (1970)

Books for Young Readers

Rootabaga Stories (1922)

Rootabaga Pigeons (1923)

Abe Lincoln Grows Up (1928)

Early Moon (1930)

Potato Face (1930)

Prairie Town Boy (1955)

Wind Song (1960)

The Wedding Procession of the Rag Doll and the Broom Handle and Who Was in It (1967)

WORKS ABOUT CARL SANDBURG

Callahan, North. *Carl Sandburg: His Life and Works.* University Park and London: Pennsylvania State University Press, 1987.

Crowder, Richard. *Carl Sandburg.* New York: Twayne, 1964.

Granger, Bill. "Carl Sandburg: Chicago's Poet." In *Chicago Tribune Magazine,* 18 December 1994.

Haas, Joseph, and Gene Lovitz, eds. *Carl Sandburg: A Pictorial Biography.* New York: G. P. Putnam's Sons, 1967.

Mitgang, Herbert, ed. *The Letters of Carl Sandburg.* New York: Harcourt, Brace & World, Inc., 1968.

Niven, Penelope. *Carl Sandburg: A Biography.* New York: Scribners, 1991.

Perkins, Agnes. "Carl Sandburg," *Writers for Children.* New York: Scribners, 1987.

Sandburg, Helga. *A Great and Glorious Romance: The Story of Carl Sandburg and Lillian Steichen.* New York: Harcourt Brace Jovanovich, 1978.

To learn more about Carl Sandburg, you can visit or write to:
The Carl Sandburg Home National Historic Site 1928 Little River Road Flat Rock, NC 28731

Sandra Scoppettone

(1936-)

by Allan O'Grady Cuseo

What does one say to a popular author of novels for young adults when she says she does not think that she will be writing any more books for this readership? That is exactly what Sandra Scoppettone is saying.

Scoppettone's writing career did not begin with novels for teenagers. When she was in her twenties she wrote four adult novels, and all were rejected by publishers. She decided to try writing novels for young adults and soon gained the national recognition that had previously eluded her. She has also written for movies, television, and the theater. Now the author of the very popular young adult novels *The Late Great Me* (1976), *Trying Hard to Hear You* (1974), and *Happy Endings Are All Alike* (1978) believes that her young-adult writing career is over. She is quick to state, "I have said all I had to say," although she laughingly cautions, "But then, I don't like to use the word *never.* . . . You never know." Scoppettone has also written *Long Time Between Kisses*

> *We cannot say that Scoppettone writes "pretty" books for young adults; rather, her novels deal with difficult subjects in an unsentimental and, at times, brutal manner.*
>
>

(1982) and *Playing Murder* (1985) for young adults, but these novels never achieved the readership of the others. Perhaps they were not as controversial and therefore did not attract the readership they might have deserved. We cannot say that Scoppettone writes "pretty" books for young adults; rather, her novels deal with difficult subjects in an unsentimental and, at times, brutal manner.

The Author's Background

Sandra Scoppettone grew up in South Orange, New Jersey, but has lived on Long Island for many years. She also enjoys her loft in SoHo, a section of New York City. Writing seems to be in her blood. Her father, Casimiso Scoppettone, wanted to be a writer but was unable to follow his dream because he had to provide for the needs of the family. Scoppettone was lucky that he and her mother, Helen Katherine Scoppettone, encouraged her. They believed in her and her talent and helped her financially when she moved to New York City to begin her life as a writer.

She shares her life with her partner of more than twenty years, the writer Linda Crawford. Two Persian cats, Nick and Nora Charles, also share their home. These fluffy felines were made famous in Scoppettone's Lauren Laurano adult mysteries. Although at one time she was fascinated by antiques and considered them to be her hobby, they no longer interest her. She now devotes her work hours to writing adult mysteries, and she spends personal time on her computer. She admits being caught up in the Internet and other on-line services and being fascinated with all the possibilities of computers.

Although Scoppettone said in the *Fifth Book of Junior Authors* (1983) that she had yet to write any autobiographical fiction, the award-winning *The Late Great Me,* which tells of a teenage alcoholic, seems to reflect much of her own experience. Careful readers might also discover that she used her partner's surname, Crawford, in *Trying Hard to Hear You.* Alcoholism is an important subject for Scoppettone. She has been a recovering alcoholic since 1975, and this recovery is one of her proudest achievements. She believes that her priorities in life include remaining sober and continuing to write.

Scoppettone had several plays produced Off-Off Broadway in the 1970s. She did not write for the theater for very long. She now believes that the 1970s were not particularly friendly to female playwrights. Writing for the theater did seem the right thing to do at the time as she had always been, and still is, an avid theatergoer (and moviegoer as well). Her fascination with the creation of imaginary characters can be traced to her youth, when she would eavesdrop on family conversations and create stories based on what she heard. Even though she originally believed her goal as a writer was to write plays, she says now that she does not have the interest to write for the theater. She will delightfully tell people, though, that this creative spirit remains hidden and still stirs every time she enters a theater.

Scoppettone's young adult novels feature characters who are dealing with alcoholism, rape, homosexuality (particularly lesbianism), homophobia, and death. These works have been controversial with parents, teachers, librarians, and reviewers from their first publication, and they have been banned from schools and libraries in several parts of the country. It is the rare teacher who will assign a Sandra Scoppettone novel for classroom discussion, with the possible exception of *The Late Great Me*.

homophobia hostility toward or discrimination against gay, lesbian, or bisexual people; also, fear of and hatred of homosexuals

This author has been accused by some of writing only about controversial or "hot" topics. Although her novels may have made some reviewers nervous with their honest approach to sexual orientation, they have won several awards. The accusation of sensationalism seems absurd when one examines Scoppettone's life, for it is clear that she is writing about what she knows. A primary interest of her life, evident in all her writings, has been the role of women in society and the manner in which they have been treated. She has been "out of the closet" as a lesbian since 1954, and her homosexuality, like her alcoholism, has greatly influenced her young adult novels.

sensationalism a style of writing that is shocking, intense, and disturbing (such emotional responses are often achieved by using gruesome details)

It Does Not Matter Whom You Love

During the summer of 1973 Scoppettone was asked to direct a summer stock musical using high school actors. She remembers that two boys in the cast were gay. She used her experience with the company that summer to write one of the first young adult novels to include gay males as major characters and possibly the first to discuss homophobia. In *Trying Hard to Hear You,* a haunting and emotional novel, the protagonist, Camilla Crawford, tells of her close-knit summer stock crowd's discovery that two of the teenagers, Jeff and Phil, are in love with each other. Besides dealing with homophobia and the internal conflicts that a homosexual may experience, Scoppettone shows the disastrous effects of gossip on individuals. The town gossip labels Phil a "faggot," which leads him to try to "prove" his manhood by asking out one of the girls, Penny. The two of them share a quart of tequila, go for a ride with Jeff, and are killed when their car hits a tree. Some reviewers have commented that the car crash and Phil's death could be interpreted as a punishment for his gayness, but this interpretation would not seem to be consistent with Scoppettone's beliefs.

The novel gives the young-adult reader a look at Camilla's transition from shock on learning of Jeff's homosexuality to gradual acceptance of him as a person no different from any other. It contains many positive images of the homosexual. The reader is educated along with Camilla as she realizes that she has known little of homosexuality but has accepted societal myths about sexual orientation. In her first young adult novel, Scoppettone introduces a theme that recurs in all her work: as long as people love instead of hate, it makes no difference whom they love.

It might seem surprising to some teenage readers to find such topics in a young adult novel, and with its honest look at teenage homosexuality, the book has caused some discomfort for readers of various ages. Some teenagers may even be apprehensive about discussing Scoppettone's novels about homosexuality with their friends or family, for fear that their own sexual orientation may be questioned. It cannot be denied, however, that Scoppettone is a trailblazer in writing about the topic for young adults. This novel was controversial at its publication and remained so well into the 1990s.

Scoppettone followed this novel of teenage gay male love with *Happy Endings Are All Alike.* It features two teenage girls, Jaret and Peggy, who are in love with each other. After their love is discovered, the woman-hating Richard "Mid" Summers beats and rapes Jaret. Mid violates Jaret both physically and emotionally, not only because she is a female but also because she is a lesbian. "I hate your

guts," he tells her. Mid carefully plans his rape, powerfully attacks Jaret with a knife, and beats her with his fists. This dramatic scene is one of the most violently written in literature
for young adults. Scoppettone writes furiously, "The sound
of flesh and bone connecting with flesh and bone magnified
inside her head to a deafening pitch. The intensity of noise
almost obliterated pain. Not quite. She had never felt anything
like it. . . . She was being pushed, pulled, scrambled."

Scoppettone creates a memorable character in Mid, the
rapist. She makes him even more frightening to the reader by
using a stream-of-consciousness writing style to develop his
character. Mid's antifemale thoughts are expressed in his diary, and for much of the story the reader is kept unaware of
his identity.

Early reviews of this uncompromising novel cautioned
readers that the rape scene was too brutal and violent for
teenagers. In the April 1980 issue of *VOYA,* one reviewer
wrote that the rape seemed superfluous, added "apparently
to pep up the proceedings [and which] wrenches the book
away from the more mundane concerns of young lesbians
coming out." We must remember, however, that rape is not a
sexual act but an act of violence and that a rape scene in a
work of fiction must be realistically brutal to be honest.

> **superfluous** more
> than is necessary; ex-
> cessive

In this novel, Scoppettone uses her characters to urge
women to speak out against rape and violence and to urge
families to support each other when it happens to one of
their members. One of the novel's strengths is its piercing examination of the bigotry and discrimination that lesbians encounter as women, rape victims, and lesbians. As in *Trying
Hard to Hear You,* Scoppettone uses *Happy Endings* to present society's negative treatment of gay and lesbian people.
Again, she has characters struggle internally with sexual orientation. It is the homophobia of the other characters, family
members and friends, that causes the protagonists to question themselves, their actions, and consequently their very
existence.

In a 1983 issue of *Top of the News,* Scoppettone stated
that the novel was attacked by reviewers because of the
openness with which she developed the characters' lesbianism as well as for the violence of the rape scene. She says
that her intent was to write about rape, not about lesbianism,
but she is confident that the reviewers' homophobia colored
their thoughts. "If I'd written a book about a heterosexual

woman who'd been raped," she says, "everyone could accept this as a matter of fact."

In *Happy Endings Are All Alike,* Scoppettone expresses some of her deepest concerns about the role of females in our society and the violence against them. This unsettling but honest novel may disturb some readers with its frank depiction of teenage sexual activity and explicit brutality. As her intent was to write about the brutality of rape, however, it is clear that she believes her readers are able to handle such difficult subjects.

Abuse of the Body—and of the Mind

Long Time Between Kisses is set in Scoppettone's area of New York City, SoHo, which is in lower Manhattan. This book is about individuality and first love. It may be the least known of Scoppettone's works and can be said to be her "punk" novel, with its references to drugs and its unconventional protagonist, who sports bright purple hair. The novel's sophisticated character, who lives in a loft, and the many sentences containing Yiddish phrases may put some readers off; but the story of a lonely young girl who discovers truths about herself and begins to realize that life has its high points, as well as its low ones, is consistent with other Scoppettone's novels for young adults.

The Late Great Me is told in the first person by Geri, a seventeen-year-old alcoholic. Although Scoppettone says that it is not actually her personal story, she believes that she was a teenage alcoholic. "I think I was an alcoholic the first time I picked up a drink," she says in *Authors & Artists for Young Adults.* Like the protagonists in Scoppettone's other novels, Geri Peters considers herself to be an outsider. Geri is introduced to drinking when she meets Dave Townsend, a good-looking newcomer to her school. Dave's mother, also an alcoholic, dies before the novel's end as a result of her drinking. When Geri is drinking, she is able to overcome her shyness and gain access to the popular crowd at school.

Sexual and physical violence against women figures in this novel too. Geri has a fight with her boyfriend, goes on a drinking binge, has a blackout, and wakes up in a rented room, where she is physically abused by a stranger who attempts to have sex with her. This is not the only blackout for Geri; they are frequent, and the vivid descriptions of them

protagonist the main character of a literary work

are terrifying to the reader. Scoppettone also writes of the vomiting, the hangovers, and the sexual looseness that often accompany excessive drinking. Geri's loss of control through alcohol is so realistically depicted that it may be difficult to read, but it is accurate and honest. A teacher who is a member of Alcoholics Anonymous reaches out to Geri and convinces her to attend her first meeting. Through AA meetings, Geri begins to gain control over her drinking. By the novel's end, she has been sober for ninety days and is attempting to gain more self-esteem. As in other Scoppettone novels, this central character learns to examine herself and begins to realize that others' opinions of her are not so important.

Murder, She Writes

During the mid-1990s, Scoppettone was mostly interested in writing mysteries, but this was not a new interest. She has said that she loves English mysteries, especially the works of Ruth Rendell. In 1985 she wrote her only young adult mystery, *Playing Murder.* This novel with many characters concerns murder and hidden identities. The family of the protagonist, Anna, moves to a resort island in Maine to run a family restaurant. Kirk, the good-looking son of the previous owner, is murdered, and it seems that many people had reasons to wish him dead. A unique twist is that Anna, imitating her mystery-writing mother's detective character, tries to solve the crime. This novel has never achieved the wide readership of Scoppettone's more controversial novels.

In the mystery genre, Scoppettone is best known for her adult mysteries, written under her own name and under the pseudonym Jack Early. In the latter books—*A Creative Kind of Killer* (1984), which received several awards; *Razzamatazz* (1985); and *Donato and Daughter* (1988)—Fortune Fanelli is the private eye. Among the adult mysteries that Scoppettone has written is *Everything You Have Is Mine* (1991), which introduces her most famous character, Lauren Laurano, the first lesbian private eye in a novel published by a mainstream publisher. Scoppettone has said that this is the first book she has ever written directly about herself. Rape occurs in this book also, and in *My Sweet Untraceable You* (1993), Lauren observes the deteriorating health of her partner's brother, who has AIDS.

Scoppettone has written for all ages, beginning with her picture books, *Suzuki Beane* (1961) and *Bang Bang You're Dead* (1969), both illustrated by Louise Fitzhugh, and including her plays, television scripts, screenplays, and novels for adult readers. Only time will tell whether she has indeed finished her work in young adult literature, the body of which has gained her national recognition.

Readers who enjoy Scoppettone's writing may also want to read the works of M. E. Kerr, another lesbian author who writes of the gay and lesbian experience in many of her novels for young adults. Rosa Guy, in whose novel there is a lesbian character, is another author of possible interest.

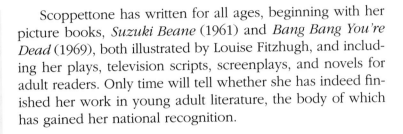

Selected Bibliography

WORKS BY SANDRA SCOPPETTONE

Picture Books

Suzuki Beane, illustrated by Louise Fitzhugh (1961)

Bang Bang You're Dead, illustrated by Louise Fitzhugh (1969)

Plays

Home Again, Home Again Jiggity Jig, produced at Cubiculo Theatre (1969)

Something for Kitty Genovese, performed by Valerie Bettis Repertory Company (1971)

Stuck, produced at Eugene O'Neill Memorial Theatre, Waterford, Conn. (1972), and Open Space Theatre, New York, New York (1976)

Screenplays

Scarecrow in a Garden of Cucumbers (1972)

The Inspector of Stairs (1975)

Plays and Movies for Television

Love of Life, CBS (1972)

A Little Bit Like Murder, ABC (1973)

The Late Great Me (1976)

Donato and Daughter (1993)

Young Adult Novels

Trying Hard to Hear You (1974)

Happy Endings Are All Alike (1978)

Long Time Between Kisses (1982)

Playing Murder (1985)

Adult Novels as Sandra Scoppettone

Some Unknown Person (1977)

Such Nice People (1980)

Innocent Bystanders (1983)

Everything You Have Is Mine (1991)

I'll Be Leaving You Always (1993)

My Sweet Untraceable You (1994)

Adult Novels as Jack Early

A Creative Kind of Killer (1984)

Razzamatazz (1985)

Donato and Daughter (1988)

WORKS ABOUT SANDRA SCOPPETTONE

Hile, K. S., ed. *Authors & Artists for Young Adults.* Detroit: Gale Research, 1983, vol. 11.

Holtze, S. H., ed. *Fifth Book of Junior Authors.* New York: H. W. Wilson, 1983.

Klein, N. "Some Thoughts on Censorship: An Author Symposium." In *Top of the News,* Winter 1983, pp. 137–153.

Olson, R. "Almost Grown and Gay." *VOYA,* April 1980, pp. 19–23.

MEMOIR AND INTERVIEW

Scoppettone, Sandra. *Happy Endings Are All Alike.* New York: Dell, 1978.

"Trying Hard to Reach Them: An Interview with Sandra Scoppettone." In *Top of the News,* Fall 1979, pp. 106–113.

How to Write to the Author
Sandra Scoppettone
c/o Little, Brown and Company, Inc.
34 Beacon Street
Boston, MA 02108

Ouida Sebestyen

(1924-   )

by Virginia R. Monseau

When Ouida Sebestyen was a child, she loved to spend her time writing plays. She and her friends would star in these productions, dressing up in old clothes, sometimes wrapping themselves in old blankets and bedspreads. Sebestyen calls these improvised plays "pretend memories," and she has used them in some of her books. Much of Sebestyen's writing, though fictional, is autobiographical, reflecting her gentle nature and love of life.

Family Relationships

Though Ouida Sebestyen lives alone and enjoys it, she values the closeness and love that exist in strong families. She has a very close relationship with her son, Corbin, and as an only child herself, she spent many happy times with her parents. In fact, her award-winning novel *Words by Heart*

In Words by Heart, *Lena feels a need to be independent and is sometimes torn between her desire to be protected by her father and her need to be her own person.*

(1979) is based on her years growing up in Vernon, Texas, where she was born on 13 February 1924; her aunt inspired the character of Lena Sills. "She took care of seven kids," Sebestyen tells us: "Saw them all through college and provided a very strong foundation" (Monseau, *Presenting Ouida Sebestyen,* p. 23). The entire book is actually a farewell to Sebestyen's father, who, though he did not live to see the book published, lives on in the character of Ben Sills.

The relationship of Ben Sills and his daughter, Lena, is at the center of *Words by Heart.* Lena desperately loves her father and tries hard to impress him with her "magic mind," as she memorizes Bible verses that he particularly likes. He, in turn, protects her, calling her his "baby girl" and encouraging her to "be somebody" when she grows up. But Lena also feels a need to be independent and is sometimes torn between her desire to be protected by her father and her need to be her own person. He is her role model, yet she cannot understand his refusal to fight back against the racial prejudice that he experiences. There is a point in the story, however, when Lena becomes her father's protector, when she sets out alone to find him, and, realizing that he is mortally wounded, when she must decide whether to honor his dying wish that she help his injured killer, Tater. So it is only through her father's death that Lena comes to understand who she wants to be. Her decision to be merciful and help Tater is her way of showing her father, even in death, how much she loves him.

In addition to Lena and her father, the family in *Words by Heart* also includes Lena's stepmother, Claudie, and Claudie's children, Roy and Armilla. At first, Claudie represents competition for Ben's attention, so Lena has a difficult time warming up to her. Also, Claudie's "no-nonsense" attitude makes Lena long even more for the warmth of her dead mother's love. Somewhere inside, though, Lena knows how much Claudie and her father love each other, and this helps her to put things into perspective. Even though Claudie is crushed by the loss after Ben dies, Lena's strength is bolstered by Claudie's proud demeanor and courageous behavior, and she realizes that both she and Claudie will see to it that Ben's memory lives on.

Not all the families in Ouida Sebestyen's books are traditional in nature. In *Far from Home* (1980) we see through the eyes of Salty Yeager an unusual family living together in a boarding house. Tom Buckley, his wife, Babe, Babe's nephew Hardy McCaslin, and Hardy's wife, Rose Ann, live at the Buckley Arms, where Salty and his eighty-four-year-old great-grandmother Mam also hope to find a home. Eventually they are all joined by Jo Miller, whom Salty finds wandering the streets in the final stages of her pregnancy. The bizarre and sometimes emotionally wrenching events that occur as Salty tries to learn whether Tom is his biological father draw this "family" together in strange ways.

Salty's mother's dying wish, that he go to Tom Buckley and ask to be taken in, is the catalyst that propels Salty into this confusing situation. He is hurt and angry at Tom's hostility toward him, not understanding the man's guilt at fathering a son with Salty's mother, Dovie, while separated from his wife, Babe. Since Tom and Babe have reconciled, Salty is a threat to family harmony should Babe learn the truth.

catalyst something that causes activity or a reaction

Though this book is primarily about Salty's search for a home and family, it is also about the adults who share his life. Each adult in the story has some particular influence on Salty as he makes his journey toward self-realization. Mam— whose character is based on Sebestyen's own mother, who died the day after the author finished *Far from Home*—is Salty's link to the past, to his responsibility. Though quirky and sometimes tiresome, she communicates her love and caring. Even Babe, though she hardly knows Salty, is kind and understanding, encouraging Tom to take him in. In fact it is Babe who inadvertently helps Salty understand that love between a man and a woman is different from love between a father and son. Hardy McCaslin, the childlike practical joker, brings laughter into Salty's life, conspiring with him to perform the kind of skits that Sebestyen wrote and performed in her own childhood days. Jo Miller's positive attitude toward life, even in the face of her estrangement from her husband, and her loving acceptance of her baby help Salty understand the importance of his name—Saul T.— which means "asked for." Finally, Tom Buckley gives to Salty the one thing he wants and needs the most: a father. Throughout the story, as Tom battles his inner demons, Salty senses the man's love for him. Gradually he begins to see the person that his mother loved, the man who named him "Saul T." Salty's growth is evident when he begins to under-

quirky full of peculiar actions, thoughts, and behavior

stand and accept that, though Tom loves him as a father, because of Babe he can never publicly acknowledge Salty as his own.

A different kind of family exists in *IOU's* (1982). As a single parent and an only child, Annie and Stowe Garrett are two against the world, determined to make it on their own in spite of little money and limited prospects. This touching mother-and-son relationship bears a striking resemblance to Ouida Sebestyen's own relationship with her son, Corbin. In fact, she admits to the similarity but quickly points out that the book is not her son's story, nor hers. Even so, the richness of her own experience lends to the book the kind of credibility that is Sebestyen's hallmark.

Like Lena Sills's feelings toward her father in *Words by Heart,* Stowe Garrett is ambivalent about his relationship with his mother. He is thirteen, on the cusp between childhood and young adulthood, and he struggles with the dilemma of wanting to break free of his mother's influence, yet needing to feel secure in her love. Sensing this, Annie tries to give him the freedom he needs, yet she still wants to keep him close. Stowe is protective of his mother, trying to make up for the hurt she experienced at being disinherited by her father and later deserted by her husband. Trying to assume responsibility as the "man in the family," he alternates—sometimes comically—between being the protector and the protected.

The bond between Stowe and Annie is tested when they travel in their old pickup truck, "Horseless," to Oklahoma, where Stowe has been summoned by his dying grandfather, Annie's father. Angry at the old man for what he has done to Annie emotionally, Stowe thinks about his own father, who deserted him in the same way. Worrying that the resentment he has been harboring toward his father might result in the same kind of useless alienation that occurred between Annie and her father, he asks Annie for his father's address. It is a difficult moment for both of them, but Annie summons the strength to say, "I understand." "It was beautiful when you belonged just to me," she tells Stowe, adding, "But I've got to warn you. I'm going to stay part of your life" (p. 184). Stowe accepts that easily, and we know that this mother and son are preparing themselves for the changes that will take place in their relationship over the years.

cusp turning point

Courage

All the protagonists in Ouida Sebestyen's books are courageous to some extent, but perhaps the most admirable is Jackie McGee in *The Girl in the Box* (1988). Alone in a dark cellar, where she has been thrown after being abducted by an unknown kidnapper whom she calls No Face, she keeps her sanity by typing letters to friends, family, and herself on a small portable typewriter she was carrying when abducted. Evident in all these letters is the conviction that life is too precious to give up easily and too promising to live carelessly, a belief shared by Ouida Sebestyen herself.

Jackie has only a jug of oily water and a pile of stale baked goods to keep her alive physically, yet she is somehow nourished spiritually by the strength that comes from her writing. With each letter she reflects on some aspect of her life, coming to understand others and herself a little better as a result. In writing to her parents, she discovers just how much they have done for her and how very much she loves them. In this time of crisis she even regrets that she never developed any deep religious convictions that might help see her through as she asks for help from God. Her notes to her friends April and Zack, with whom she had recently argued, reveal a more mature Jackie, who is beginning to understand that the dissolution of their friendship was as much her fault as it was theirs. Writing to her English teacher, Miss Flannery (a character named for the author Flannery O'Connor), prompts Jackie to compose a "story within a story," fictionalizing her relationship with April and Zack, thus helping her work out the sadness and confusion she feels as a result of their broken friendship. From her writing she draws the spiritual strength that keeps hope alive, and at the end of the novel we see a physically weak Jackie climbing the stairs toward the light, still hopeful that she will be found.

Like Jackie, Yankee Belew in *On Fire* (1985), a companion novel to *Words by Heart,* shows us an admirable strength of character: a combination of bravery, intelligence, and compassion that helps change the lives of Sammy and Tater Haney. Together the three of them form an unlikely triangle, a relationship that Sebestyen intentionally created. Of Yankee, the author says, "She was very important. She wanted to

Flannery O'Connor was an American short-story writer and novelist. Most of her stories are set in the South and often concern Roman Catholic themes such as redemption and salvation.

succeed, and she could do it, in her own way" (Monseau, *Presenting Ouida Sebestyen,* p. 74). Sensing that Sammy is on a destructive path, as he emulates and admires his older brother, Tater (who murdered Ben Sills in *Words by Heart*), Yankee takes Sammy in when he has no place to go. She does not think twice about assuming responsibility for her late sister's little boy, Charlie, and she braves the insults of others, refusing to listen to their insinuations about Nellie's questionable lifestyle. She even gives Sammy money to follow their brother to Pegler, Colorado, where Tater plans to work in the mines.

Yankee's good example is a source of confusion for Sammy, since her attitude and behavior are so different from what he has experienced. She is honest, refusing to eat food that has been stolen or bought with dishonest money. She is willing to work hard, sacrificing her own physical comfort to provide Charlie with the food and warmth he needs. She is also emotionally strong, standing against the mine bosses who caused her brother's death and the union members who want to evict her from her small living quarters. Through all her turmoil, however, she remains compassionate toward everyone. At the end of the novel we see her comforting Tater as he begins to regret his evil ways, and we get the feeling that she will have a positive influence on his future.

The Power of Love and Trust

Closely tied to the themes of family relationships and spiritual courage is Sebestyen's emphasis on the power of love and trust in her works. In *Out of Nowhere* (1994) she creates a cast of characters who defy our conventional sense of "family," yet who demonstrate through their interaction the meaning of the words *love* and *trust*. Both Harley Nunn, the book's protagonist, and May Woods, the sixty-eight-year-old woman who rescues him from abandonment, have been deserted by people they loved and trusted. Hurt and angry, both are cautious about forming new relationships. When Harley finds Ish, a pit bull who has also been abandoned, he begins a long journey toward self-realization.

When we first meet Harley and May, their spirits are as dry as the desert in which they have been abandoned. Fearful and frustrated, they are uncertain of what the future holds. Fresh from their misfortunes, they size each other up and consider the risks of trust. Ish, too, is leery, his animal instincts telling him to be careful. But when they reach May's home and encounter Singer, a freshness enters their lives. Though she too is alone, Singer communicates a zest for life that becomes contagious. When Harley is beset by self-doubt, she helps him see his potential and encourages him to take risks. When May resists her good-natured behavior, Singer responds by doing more chores around the house to ease the older woman's burden. When she senses that Ish needs more love and affection, she helps Harley find it within himself to give. These three people and a dog who come together from "out of nowhere" teach each other to believe again in human kindness. Like the characters in all Sebestyen's works, they remind us that, in a world so full of indifference and despair, we are our own best hope.

Of all Sebestyen's works, *Words by Heart* has received the most critical acclaim. Developed from a short story of the same name, which she wrote in 1968, the book received many awards and was televised by PBS as part of its "Wonderworks" series. Reviews of all Sebestyen's novels have been overwhelmingly favorable, though some controversy has been generated over *The Girl in the Box* because of its disturbing plot and painful ending. Some critics question the story's credibility, while other cite the devastating ending as too "dark" for young adult readers. Some teachers have been so stunned by the story that they hesitate to recommend it to their students. Other compare it favorably to *The Diary of Anne Frank*.

Ouida Sebestyen likes to think that she is "making magic" when she writes. She loves words—to talk about them, to experiment with them, to find just the right phrase or sentence to convey her thoughts and feelings. When she decided to write for a young audience, she made a commitment to help them see that life, though difficult, is beautiful and precious. Of her critics, she says, "I learn from them," and she tries hard to understand their points of view. She explained her feelings about being a writer in the spring 1984 *ALAN Review,* feelings that are perhaps best illustrated in the similarity she sees between writing and parenting:

> **Having children and writing books for them are both acts of faith and giving. Parents and writers make the**

leery suspicious

beset troubled; harassed

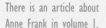

Like the characters in all Sebestyen's works, they remind us that, in a world so full of indifference and despair, we are our own best hope.

There is an article about Anne Frank in volume I.

first leap when they choose to love what doesn't yet exist but is coming and will someday be. . . . Writers and parents put a lot of energy and time into earning trust, being fair, and keeping a tolerant dialogue going between generations. . . . A book written for young readers has to come out of the child in the writer as well as the adult, from the same memory-place where parents find empathy (Pp. 2–3).

Conclusion

The child who wrote plays for herself and her friends has become the woman who believes in her readers and who writes so that they will believe in themselves. Like many artists, her desire to create comes from a need to express a deeply felt idea or truth, and she does so with honesty and affection. This is Ouida Sebestyen's gift to all the people, young and old, who read and enjoy her books.

Readers who enjoy the works of Ouida Sebestyen might also enjoy works by Mildred Delois Taylor, Sue Ellen Bridgers, Katherine Paterson, and Cynthia Voigt.

Selected Bibliography

WORKS BY OUIDA SEBESTYEN

Novels

Words by Heart (1979)

Far from Home (1980)

IOU's (1982)

On Fire (1985)

The Girl in the Box (1988)

Out of Nowhere (1994)

Short Stories

"Children Are a Blessing." In *Everywoman* (1950); published in England in *Mother and Home* (1951)

"Words by Heart." *Ingenue,* December 1968, pp. 54–55, 68–72

"Welcome." In *Sixteen Short Stories by Outstanding Writers for Young Adults.* Edited by Donald R. Gallo (1984)

"Playing God." In *Visions: Nineteen Short Stories by Outstanding Writers for Young Adults.* Edited by Donald Gallo (1987)

"After the Wedding." In *Connections: Short Stories by Outstanding Writers for Young Adults*. Edited by Donald R. Gallo (1989)

Play

Holding Out. In *Center Stage: One-Act Plays for Teenage Readers and Actors*. Edited by Donald R. Gallo (1990)

WORKS ABOUT OUIDA SEBESTYEN

Cline, Ruth. "A Visit with Ouida Sebestyen." *English Journal,* October 1980, pp. 52–53.

Monseau, Virginia R. *Presenting Ouida Sebestyen*. New York: Twayne, 1995.

Sebestyen, Ouida. "Balancing the Books." Speech given at the International Conference of the Children's Literature Association, San Diego, California, June 1990. Printed in conference proceedings, *Work and Play in Children's Literature*. Edited by Susan R. Gannon and Ruth Anne Thompson, Pleasantville, N.Y.: Pace University Press, pp. 39–44.

———. "Family Matters." In *ALAN Review,* spring 1984, pp. 1–3.

How to Write to the Author
Ouida Sebestyen
c/o Orchard Books
95 Madison Avenue
New York, NY 10016

aters were often closed, not only because of the threat of the plague but because the plays themselves were thought to be politically dangerous. At the time Shakespeare lived, the English public theater was not well established: English drama had its origins in church, where biblical scenes and events were enacted in what were known as mystery plays. As times had changed, however, these sacred church plays had died out, and nonsacred, or secular, theater had just begun to take its place. It was only in 1576 that the first public playhouse was built in London.

When Shakespeare moved to London after 1585, he therefore worked in an emerging art form and in an exciting time. And Shakespeare was successful: he acted and wrote, and he even owned a playhouse. He was respected and respectable. He was the first playwright to have his formal biography written and published with his works and, as we can tell from his financial records, he became prosperous.

By 1592 William Shakespeare was firmly established in the great city of London, the author of ten plays, and successful enough to inspire jealousy and be called "an upstart crow" by a fellow dramatist, Robert Greene. Shakespeare appears on the London tax rolls in 1595, and we know he was a member, at different times, of two or three acting companies. He acted in Ben Jonson's *Every Man in His Humor* in 1598 and in Jonson's *Sejanus* in 1603. In fact, Shakespeare was enough of an actor to play Adam in his own *As You Like It* and was also the ghost in *Hamlet*. He was a member of the Lord Chamberlain's Men, an acting troupe under the patronage of Queen Elizabeth I, and he made two court performances during the Christmas celebration of 1594; records show that he was paid twenty pounds. In 1596 the Chamberlain's troupe gave all six court performances for Elizabeth I during the Christmas season, a testament to their great popularity.

Shakespeare, of course, did more writing than acting. While he may have penned much of his drama in London, we also suspect that he went back to Stratford to write, especially during the frequent times that the London theaters were closed because of the plague. Public gathering spots were commonly shut down so that people could not gather in large groups and spread infection. Sadly, all of his visits to

Plague, an epidemic, contagious disease, killed about a fourth of the European population from 1347–1352. Also called the "Black Death," plague was feared at theaters because the close confines could easily spread the disease to everyone.

A **coat of arms** was a design, shaped like a shield, that officially symbolized a person or family; people would reproduce it on their clothes, armor, houses, coaches, and so on.

Stratford were not happy ones. William Shakespeare's only son, Hamnet, died at the age of eleven and was buried in 1596, leaving Shakespeare with two daughters.

Unlike many unrecognized and unappreciated artists, William Shakespeare enjoyed real success throughout much of his lifetime. He began to get wealthy around 1596, the year he bought his father a coat of arms, essentially establishing John Shakespeare's right to call himself a gentleman. We also know that William bought and restored New Place, a large house in Stratford into which his family moved in 1597. In 1602 he bought more than 100 acres in Stratford, as well as other land and houses.

Shakespeare's financial success also helped him amass enough money in 1599 to build, with others, the Globe, an open-air playhouse. He continued to write and perform not only for the public but for the current monarchy. Shakespeare's work was a great favorite of Elizabeth I and, when she died in 1603, his popularity continued with the new king, James I.

The Later Years (1603–1616)

With the accession in 1603 of James to the throne, William Shakespeare's popularity greatly intensified. He wrote and published plays (during this period he completed *Othello, King Lear, Macbeth,* and *The Tempest*), and the performances of his work were even more well received. Queen Elizabeth I's Chamberlain's Men became King James I's King's Men in 1603, and the troupe performed frequently. On the domestic scene, William Shakespeare's eldest daughter, Susanna, married in 1607 and presented her father with his first grandchild in 1608.

Around 1610, however, Shakespeare appears to have slowed his pace and, with the writing of *The Tempest* in 1611, he semiretired and appeared to write no more after 1613. The Globe burned in 1613 and, although no one was hurt, the loss was serious. The Globe was eventually rebuilt, but Shakespeare moved to the Blackfriars theater in 1609–1610 as it was a closed, not outdoor, theater, and therefore warmer. Shakespeare continued to spend time in Stratford and, when he returned to London, to work on publishing editions of his plays. In 1613 he bought a London house, Blackfriars Gatehouse.

Like many of his contemporaries, William Shakespeare was keenly aware of mortality. People in his era were not long lived, and Shakespeare made a will around 1615 and tried, in that document, to insure that the estate he had amassed would stay in the family. His bequest to his wife Anne of his "second best bed" has been debated by scholars for many years. What that gift actually means is open to interpretation, but it is not clear that Shakespeare meant to belittle Anne. Unfortunately, there were no male grandchildren from the marriages of either Susanna or Judith (Judith was married just months before her father's death), and Shakespeare's wealth, consisting at the time of his death of property and 350 pounds in cash, eventually went to strangers.

When William Shakespeare died on 23 April 1616, he was interred in Holy Trinity Church, the same church in which he had been baptized. Anne lived some years after him and died on 6 August 1623.

Challenges to Authorship

For some scholars, one of the most intriguing things about William Shakespeare is the controversy over his authorship of the many comic, historical, and tragic plays and sonnets attributed to him. One critic has estimated that more than 4,000 books have been written on the subject of Shakespeare's authorship. The source of the dispute swirls around the extent of Shakespeare's genius and originality. Some people have so overstated Shakespeare's talent that the natural reaction is to assume that no one person could have written all that is credited to William Shakespeare.

Candidates thought to have written work attributed to Shakespeare include: Francis Bacon, Christopher Marlowe, Edward de Vere (seventeenth Earl of Oxford), Henry Wriothesley (third Earl of Southampton), William Stanley (sixth Earl of Derby), Anne Hathaway, and even Queen Elizabeth I. Because of the fascination with William Shakespeare, the man and his work, and the fragmentary nature of the era's records, it is doubtful that this controversy will ever die. Many, however, believe that the poetry and plays attributed to Shakespeare were indeed written by him.

> *Some people have so overstated Shakespeare's talent that the natural reaction is to assume that no one person could have written all that is credited to William Shakespeare.*

The Tragedies

Shakespeare wrote a number of tragic plays, many of which are commonly taught in secondary schools. *Hamlet* is the tale of a young prince who, after a ghostly encounter with the spirit of his dead father, the former king, avenges what he believes is his father's murder. In *Romeo and Juliet,* two young people, members of feuding families, fall in love, secretly marry, and are separated. They are reunited in the end, but it is only in death. In *Julius Caesar,* set in ancient Rome, conspirators plot the death of the play's title character but, after assassinating him, must deal with the consequences. The main character in *King Lear* is an older monarch who divides his kingdom among his daughters with unexpected results. *Othello* is a complicated tale of interracial tension, deceit, and betrayal, in which a great general, tricked into believing that his bride is unfaithful, murders his innocent wife. In *Macbeth,* the main character is ambitious and impatient, and in order to advance his career murders those who rank above him.

The Comedies

Shakespeare's comedies all revolve around love: mistaken, misbegotten, frustrated, and star-crossed love. In *The Tempest, The Merchant of Venice, All's Well That Ends Well, A Midsummer Night's Dream, Much Ado About Nothing, As You Like It,* and *The Taming of the Shrew,* Shakespeare's characters meet, fall in love, wear disguises, use magic, argue, break up, make up, and marry. Some of Shakespeare's most lyrical writing is in *A Midsummer Night's Dream* and *The Tempest;* the war between the sexes operates in *The Taming of the Shrew,* and *The Merchant of Venice* mixes love and justice and features one of Shakespeare's most controversial characters, the Jewish moneylender Shylock.

A movie adaptation of ***Much Ado About Nothing***, directed by and starring Kenneth Branagh, was released in 1993.

The Histories

Richard II, Richard III, Henry IV, Part 1, Henry IV, Part 2, and *Henry V* are all tales of English kings and their battles, betrayals, deceits, and triumphs. The very hard-drinking, fun-loving character Falstaff, who appears in *Henry IV, Part 1* and *Part 2,* is one of Shakespeare's most beloved creations and, reportedly, was also a great favorite of Queen Elizabeth I.

The Sonnets

Shakespeare wrote 154 sonnets, and most of them detail themes of love. Again, controversy centers on the playwright: whether a woman or a man—or both—was the object of these sonnets is still a hotly debated issue. At any rate, in this demanding fourteen-line rhyming format, Shakespeare created some of the most famous poems ever written, and they endure as fine examples of the genre.

A **sonnet** is a fourteen-line poem with a specific, concise form. It has a set rhyme scheme (pattern in which the ends of lines rhyme with each other), and each line has the same rhythm (iambic pentameter, or five sections consisting of one unstressed and one stressed syllable each). It is certainly a difficult form to master.

Shakespeare's Language

Shakespeare is known and beloved as much for his word-smithing, his ability to craft a phrase, and his ability to create a picture as for anything else about his plays and poetry. Even after hundreds of years in which the English language itself has remarkably changed (as all living languages do), Shakespeare's lines are mimicked, reproduced, and widely quoted. There are countless often-noted images, metaphors, puns, aphorisms, and allusions in Shakespeare, and much that has been written about his work concentrates exclusively on the use of language. Shakespeare was, simply put, one of the best writers in English not only of his age but of all time.

Shakespeare wrote prose, and he also wrote poetry, employing pentameter couplets, blank verse, and the six-line (ababcc) stanza. Depending on the character speaking, the context of the situation, and the nuance of meaning he was trying to convey, Shakespeare could be vulgar as well as tender in his language; he could write equally convincing lines for characters who were going into battle as for those who were falling in love. Slang and elevated language are found in Shakespeare; his writing can be both formal and playful. Even today much of Shakespeare's humorous language is still funny, and his more tragic speeches convey an almost modern pathos. While some of his sentence constructions and vocabulary can be difficult for modern readers, Shakespeare is an effective and often breathtaking wordmaster, convincing and brilliant.

aphorism short saying

allusion a passing reference to fictional or historical characters, events, or places the writer assumes the reader will recognize

In *As You Like It,* Shakespeare characterizes human life in an extended metaphor:

> All the world's a stage,
>
> And all the men and women merely players.
>
> They have their exits and their entrances,
>
> And one man in his time plays many parts.
>
> (Act II, scene vii, ll. 138–141)

In *Macbeth,* the title character again returns to the theater metaphor, seeing a person's existence like a rather inept actor on a stage. It is a world-weary but apt characterization, and it contains a famous phrase that eventually became the title of one of the twentieth century's most important novels, William Faulkner's *The Sound and the Fury*:

> Life's but a walking shadow, a poor player
>
> That struts and frets his hour upon the stage
>
> And then is heard no more. It is a tale
>
> Told by an idiot, full of sound and fury,
>
> Signifying nothing.
>
> (Act V, scene v, ll. 24–28)

pragmatic practical and realistic, as opposed to idealistic

In 1996, the movie ***Romeo and Juliet***, starring Leonardo Di Caprio and Claire Danes, was released. While the dialogue is still Shakespearian English, the setting is a glitzy city of the 1990s. The 1968 adaptation, starring Michael York and Olivia Hussey, is a classic version of the play.

Shakespeare's language can also take us unawares. Lady Macbeth's question, after she has helped murder King Duncan, is pragmatic but provides a visual shock: "Yet who would have thought," she queries, "the old man to have had so much blood in him?" In *Romeo and Juliet,* when the sarcastic Mercutio, now dying of a sword wound, is asked how badly he is hurt, he jokes, but the jest is precise. His wound, he says, is "not so deep as a well, nor so wide as a church-door" but "'tis enough, 'twill serve," meaning that it will kill him very shortly.

Insult is also a large part of Shakespeare's writing, and scholars have found countless instances in which the characters skillfully attack each other verbally as well as physically.

In *King Lear,* a character notes that "You are not worth the dust which the rude wind / Blows in your face." And, in *Othello,* the wicked Iago turns not only on his hapless wife but upon all women in general. The insult Iago delivers clearly demonstrates Shakespeare's fine—and characteristic—use of parallelism:

> You are pictures out of doors,
>
> Bells in your parlours, wild-cats in your kitchens,
>
> Saints in your injuries, devils being offended,
>
> Players in your housewifery, and housewives in your beds.
>
> (Act II, scene I, ll. 109–112)

A recent film adaptation of **Othello**, starring Laurence Fishburne, was released in 1995.

Shakespeare is known by many as the writer of great romantic lines, and in *Romeo and Juliet* one finds the finest, most lyrical pieces of loving adulation. Waiting for evening and Romeo's visit, Juliet cries:

> Come, gentle night, come, loving, black-brow'd night,
>
> Give me my Romeo; and when he shall die,
>
> Take him and cut him out in little stars,
>
> And he will make the face of heaven so fine
>
> That all the world will be in love with night,
>
> And pay no worship to the garish sun.
>
> (Act III, scene ii, ll. 20–25)

Shakespeare also knew how to praise the dead. At the devastating conclusion of *Hamlet,* when many of the main characters are dead and dying, Horatio views Hamlet's body and says:

> Now cracks a noble heart. Good-night, sweet prince,
>
> And flights of angels sing thee to thy rest!
>
> (Act V, scene ii, ll. 361–362)

Hamlet has been made into several movies, the most notable starring Sir Laurence Olivier in 1948, Mel Gibson in 1990, and Kenneth Branagh in 1997.

Similarly, in *Julius Caesar* the dead Brutus is memorably memorialized:

> His life was gentle, and the elements
>
> So mix'd in him that Nature might stand up
>
> And say to all the world, "This was a man!"
>
> (Act V, scene v, ll. 73-75)

Readers of Shakespeare's plays and poetry find his language fresh, striking, and, even today, truly spectacular.

Conclusion

William Shakespeare is, as Ben Jonson called him (and many still agree), the "Soule of the Age," a writer who could put into words some of the most complicated and compelling ideas and human emotions. Shakespeare wrote lines that, in his own words from the play *Antony and Cleopatra,* "age cannot wither . . . nor custom stale," and all of us are the richer for the "infinite variety" of the literature he crafted.

If you like the works of William Shakespeare, you may enjoy reading Leon Garfield's abridgements of Shakespeare's plays.

Selected Bibliography

INDIVIDUAL WORKS BY WILLIAM SHAKESPEARE

Few exact dates for Shakespeare's works are known, yet we do know that his writing career spanned the years of 1585 to 1616. The dates given below are approximate, but they show the steady progress of Shakespeare's career. Modern editions are available in every library and bookstore.

Henry VI, Part 1 (1589–1590; revised 1594–1595)

Henry VI, Part 2 (1590–1591)

Henry VI, Part 3 (1590–1591)

Richard III (1592–1593)

Venus and Adonis (1592–1593)

The Comedy of Errors (1592–1594)

Sonnets (1593–1599)

The Rape of Lucrece (1593–1594)
Titus Andronicus (1593–1594)
The Taming of the Shrew (1593–1594)
The Two Gentlemen of Verona (1594)
Love's Labour's Lost (1594–1595; revised 1597)
King John (1594–1596)
Richard II (1595)
Romeo and Juliet (1595–1596)
A Midsummer Night's Dream (1595–1596)
The Merchant of Venice (1596–1597)
Henry IV, Part 1 (1596–1597)
The Merry Wives of Windsor (1597; revised probably 1600–1601)
Henry IV, Part 2 (1598)
Much Ado About Nothing (1598–1599)
Henry V (1599)
Julius Caesar (1599)
As You Like It (1599)
Hamlet (1600–1601)
The Phoenix and the Turtle (probably 1601)
Twelfth Night (1601–1602)
Troilus and Cressida (1601–1602)
All's Well That Ends Well (1602–1603)
Measure for Measure (1604)
Othello (1604)
King Lear (1605)
Macbeth (1606)
Antony and Cleopatra (1606–1607)
Coriolanus (1607–1608)
Timon of Athens (1607–1608)
Pericles (1607–1608)
Cymbeline (1609–1610)
The Winter's Tale (1610–1611)
The Tempest (1611)
Henry VIII (1612–1613)
Cardenio (1612–1613; the text of this play was lost)
The Two Noble Kinsmen (1613)

COLLECTED WORKS BY WILLIAM SHAKESPEARE

The Comedies and Tragedies of Shakespeare (1944)

The Play's the Thing: Seventeen of Shakespeare's Greatest Dramas (1963)

The Works of Mr. William Shakespeare (1967)

The Riverside Shakespeare (1974)

The Royal Shakespeare Theatre Edition of the Sonnets of William Shakespeare (1975)

Shakespeare's Sonnets (1978)

The Complete Works of Shakespeare (1980)

New Poems by Shakespeare: Order and Meaning Restored to the Sonnets (1981)

Shakespeare's Plays in Quarto: A Facsimile Edition (1981)

Shakespeare's Sonnets and A Lover's Complaint (1985)

William Shakespeare: The Complete Works (1986)

The Complete Oxford Shakespeare (1987)

An Oxford Anthology of Shakespeare (1987)

The Poems (1988)

The Poems: Venus and Adonis, The Rape of Lucrece, The Phoenix and the Turtle, The Passionate Pilgrim, A Lover's Complaint (1992)

The First Folio of Shakespeare: 1623 (1994)

WORKS ATTRIBUTED TO WILLIAM SHAKESPEARE

Spurious and Doubtful Works: Pseudo-Shakespearian Plays, edited by Karl Warnke and Ludwig Proescholdt (1973)

Disputed Plays of William Shakespeare, edited by William Kozlenko (1974)

WORKS ABOUT WILLIAM SHAKESPEARE

Andrews, John F., ed. *William Shakespeare: His World, His Work, His Influence.* New York: Scribners, 1985.

Barber, C. L. *The Whole Journey: Shakespeare's Power of Development.* Berkeley: University of California Press, 1986.

Bate, Jonathan. *Shakespearean Constitutions: Politics, Theatre, Criticism, 1730–1830.* Oxford: Clarendon Press; New York: Oxford University Press, 1989.

Bentley, Gerald Eades. *Shakespeare: A Biographical Handbook.* New Haven, Conn.: Yale University Press, 1961.

Bethell, Tom. "Looking for Shakespeare: The Case for Oxford." *Atlantic Monthly,* October 1991, pp. 45–63, 74–75.

Bradshaw, Graham. *Misrepresentations: Shakespeare and the Materialists.* Ithaca, N.Y.: Cornell University Press, 1993.

Boyce, Charles. *Shakespeare A to Z.* New York: Facts On File/Roundtable Press, 1990.

Campbell, Oscar, and Edward Quinn. *The Reader's Encyclopedia of Shakespeare.* New York: Thomas Y. Crowell Co., 1966.

Chambers, E. K. *William Shakespeare, Volumes I and II.* Oxford: Clarendon Press, 1930, 1951.

Chute, Marchette. *Shakespeare of London.* New York: E. P. Dutton, 1949.

Colie, Rosalie Littel. *Shakespeare's Living Art.* Princeton, N.J.: Princeton University Press, 1974.

Dawson, Giles E. *The Life of William Shakespeare.* New York: Cornell University Press, 1958, 1963.

Dobson, Michael. *The Making of the National Poet: Shakespeare, Adaptation and Authorship, 1660–1769.* Oxford: Clarendon Press; New York: Oxford University Press, 1992.

Eagleton, Terry. *William Shakespeare.* Oxford and New York: B. Blackwell, 1986.

Epstein, Norrie. *The Friendly Shakespeare.* New York: Viking Press, 1992.

Foakes, R. A. *Hamlet Versus Lear: Cultural Politics and Shakespeare's Art.* Cambridge and New York: Cambridge Univeristy Press, 1993.

Fraser, Russell. *Shakespeare: The Later Years.* New York: Columbia University Press, 1992.

———. *Young Shakespeare.* New York: Columbia University Press, 1988.

Gardner, Martin. "William Shakespeare: By Divers Hands." *Book World,* 19 January 1992, p. 5.

Girard, Rene. *A Theatre of Envy: William Shakespeare.* New York: Oxford University Press, 1991.

Giroux, Robert. *The Book Known As Q: A Consideration of Shakespeare's Sonnets.* New York: Atheneum, 1982.

Grady, Hugh. *The Modernist Shakespeare: Critical Texts in a Material World.* Oxford: Clarendon Press; New York: Oxford University Press, 1991.

Greenblatt, Stephen Jay. *Shakespearean Negotiations: The Circulation of Social Energy in Renaissance England.* Berkeley: University of California Press, 1988.

Halliday, F. E. *Shakespeare.* New York: Thames & Hudson Inc., 1986.

Hapgood, Robert. *Shakespeare the Theater-Poet.* Oxford: Clarendon Press; New York: Oxford University Press, 1988.

Hawkins, Harriet. *The Devil's Party: Critical Counter-Interpretations of Shakespearian Drama.* Oxford: Clarendon Press; New York: Oxford University Press, 1985.

Highfill, Philip H., Jr., ed. *Shakespeare's Craft: Eight Lectures.* Carbondale, Ill.: Southern Illinois University Press, 1982.

Ioppolo, Grace. *Revising Shakespeare.* Cambridge, Mass.: Harvard University Press, 1991.

Johnson, Samuel. *Selections from Johnson on Shakespeare.* New Haven, Conn.: Yale University Press, 1986.

Knapp, Robert S. *Shakespeare: The Theater and the Book.* Princeton, N.J.: Princeton University Press, 1989.

Lloyd Evans, Gareth. *The Shakespeare Companion.* New York: Scribners, 1978.

Matus, Irvin. "Looking For Shakespeare: The Case for Shakespeare." *Atlantic Monthly,* October 1991, pp. 64–73, 78–82.

McDonald, Russ. *Shakespeare and Jonson, Jonson and Shakespeare.* Lincoln, Nebr.: University of Nebraska Press, 1988.

———. *Shakespeare Reread: The Texts in New Contexts.* Ithaca, N.Y.: Cornell University Press, 1994.

McManaway, James G. *The Authorship of Shakespeare.* Charlottesville, Va.: University Press of Virginia, 1962, 1974.

Ridler, Anne. *Shakespeare Criticism, 1919–1935*. London: Oxford University Press, 1965.

———. *Shakespeare Criticism, 1935–1960*. London: Oxford University Press, 1970.

Rowse, A. L. *William Shakespeare: A Biography*. New York: Harper & Row, 1963.

Schoenbaum, S. *William Shakespeare: A Documentary Life*. New York: Oxford University Press, 1975.

———. *William Shakespeare: A Compact Documentary Life*. Oxford: Oxford University Press, 1977.

———. *Shakespeare: The Globe and the World*. New York: Folger Shakespeare Library and Oxford University Press, 1979.

———. *Shakespeare Survey*. Cambridge, New York: Cambridge University Press, 1948.

———. *Rebels and Lovers: Shakespeare's Young Heroes and Heroines: A New Approach to Acting and Teaching*. New York: New York University Press, 1976.

———. *Shakespeare in Performance: An Introduction Through Six Major Plays*. New York: Harcourt Brace Jovanovich, 1976.

Siegel, Paul N. *Shakespeare in His Time and Ours*. Notre Dame, Ind.: University of Notre Dame Press, 1968.

Smith, David Nichol. *Shakespeare Criticism: A Selection*. London and New York: Oxford University Press, 1946.

Sundelson, David. *Shakespeare's Restorations of the Father*. New Brunswick, N.J.: Rutgers University Press, 1983.

Swinburne, Charles. *Sacred and Shakespearian Affinities*. New York: Haskell House, 1971.

Taylor, Gary. *Reinventing Shakespeare: A Cultural History, From the Restoration to the Present*. New York: Oxford University Press, 1991.

———. *Shakespeare Reshaped, 1606–1623*. Oxford: Clarendon Press; New York: Oxford University Press, 1993.

Vickers, Brian. *Appropriating Shakespeare: Contemporary Critical Quarrels*. New Haven, Conn.: Yale University Press, 1993.

Viswanathan, S. *The Shakespeare Play as Poem: A Critical Tradition in Perspective*. Cambridge and New York: Cambridge University Press, 1980.

Many Shakespeare festivals are held all over the United States every year, many of them in open air theaters, like Shakespeare's Globe Theater. To find out more about a festival near you, read about it on the Internet at: http://www.yahoo.com/Arts/Performing_Arts/Drama/Plays/Playwrights/Shakespeare_William_1564_1616_/Festivals/ or search the Internet, using the keyword "Shakespeare."

Wells, Lawrence. "Shakespeare Slept Here: Or Did He?" *American Way,* 1 December 1992, pp. 59–66, 103–105.

Wells, Stanley W. *Re-editing Shakespeare for the Modern Reader.* Oxford: Clarendon Press; New York: Oxford University Press, 1984.

Wells, Stanley, ed. *The Cambridge Companion to Shakespeare Studies.* Cambridge and New York: Cambridge University Press, 1986.

Wilson, F. P. *Shakespeare and the New Bibliography.* Oxford: Clarendon Press, 1970.

William Sleator

(1945-   )

by Hazel K. Davis

W illiam Sleator often refers to himself as an oddball. He told several interesting stories about his child-hood in *Presenting William Sleator* (1992). How-ever, it was not until the publication of *Oddballs* in 1993 that readers were treated fully to the peculiarities of the Sleator family. In the essay "From Interstellar Pigs to Spirit Houses" (1992), Sleator says, "With *Oddballs* I have finally achieved realism. It's a collection of autobiographical stories about growing up in St. Louis in the 50's and 60's, stories that em-phasize the importance of non-conformity and independent thinking."

realism fidelity to real life

Some of the stories in *Oddballs* are quite funny from a child's or an adolescent's point of view. Some may make the reader envious, wishing that his or her parents were as easy-going. A few of the stories make parents and grandparents cringe. No wonder Sleator dedicated the book to his family with the caveat "Please forgive me!" He says on the inside back cover, "But as far as I'm concerned, it's all in all a pretty

caveat an explana-tion to prevent mis-interpretation; a warning

> *Sleator uses bits of biographical material in several of his works.*
>
>

accurate picture of what life was like. My mother, of course, might not entirely agree."

Sleator uses bits of biographical material in several of his works: His sister Vicky and her harsh treatment of dolls in *Among the Dolls* (1974); the tormenting of his young brother Tycho by the older siblings in *The Green Futures of Tycho* (1981); the musical background and touring from Sleator's work as a ballet pianist and more sibling rivalry in *Fingers* (1983); and an alien character in *Interstellar Pig* (1984) who looks like one of the drawings by Bill's friend Nicole in the mural on Bill's wall as he describes it in *Oddballs*. Probably every book by Sleator has a bit of his life in it.

Sleator's experiences in Thailand have greatly influenced two of his latest novels. In *The Spirit House* (1991), a young student from Thailand comes to live with a family in the United States. In the sequel, *Dangerous Wishes* (1995), the American family goes to Thailand where the mother will do research.

The Early Years

William Warner Sleator was born on 13 February 1945 in Havre de Grace, Maryland. Sleator's parents are both professionals. His mother is a pediatrician and his father is a psychologist. In *Oddballs,* Sleator relates that the children never had to go to the doctor; they received all their injections and medical treatment at home from their mother. Sleator and his sister Vicky, who was only a year and a half younger, were quite close. Because Bill was nine and Vicky was seven when Danny was born, they were not only old enough to help care for the baby but also old enough to think of all kinds of ways to torment him. When Mrs. Sleator was pregnant with Tycho, Bill and Vicky would tease Danny with pictures of babies and taunts about the coming baby. Naturally Danny resented the new baby, and as Sleator says in *Oddballs,* "The baby, who had a sweet and gentle nature, adored his older brother. Danny accepted this affection on good days, helping him build things with blocks and other toys. On bad days, he slapped him around" (pp. 6–7). This rivalry continued until Danny was eleven or twelve according to Sleator.

The parents would leave Bill and Vicky in charge of Danny and Tycho with some rather bizarre consequences. Bill and Vicky made up a song about parents who left their children one night and never returned. According to Sleator, the little boys would cry throughout the song and then demand to hear it again. Other rather sadistic games were played to frighten the little kids and any of the neighbor children who might be around.

The Sleators were very permissive parents. They allowed their children to read anything they wanted and to amuse themselves with little supervision. They encouraged them to be individuals and not part of the crowd. One activity involved the father taking Bill and Vicky blindfolded to a strange part of town and leaving them there with ten cents. The dime was to call home if they had not found their way back by dark. Bill and Vicky had to use the dime only once: when some friends went along on the adventure and panicked. The friends were not allowed to play with Bill and Vicky at their house again.

In high school Bill and Vicky did not try to fit in with the popular clique. In fact they called the popular kids *pituh*. "It was these slaves to peer pressure whom we considered the most pituh of all—somehow they did not seem to understand that we, as oddballs and deliberate nonconformists, were far superior to them in every way" (*Oddballs,* p. 72).

Sleator was accepted into Harvard despite his mediocre grades because of his creativity and his great scores on the SAT (Scholastic Aptitude Test) and college entrance exams. When Harvard took another look at his grades and decided not to admit him, Bill's father made a few phone calls and successfully got him readmitted. As he states in *Presenting William Sleator,* those four years at Harvard were the most miserable years of his life. Bill studied music and English, managed to compose some "music for student films and plays, served on the editorial board of the *Crimson,* and kept a journal that contained more than 1,000 typed pages" (p. 7). He still keeps a journal but now it is on his computer, where he does most of his writing.

Sleator has written several children's books. All but one have their grounding in the real world, but all have that fantastic element so apparent in his novels. Sleator explains in "From Interstellar Pigs to Spirit Houses" about his writing in general:

The strategies that worked for me were to ground the story firmly in the real world, a familiar world with

sadistic delighting in being cruel to others

clique an exclusive group

characters and situations the reader can identify with. And then to have one fantastic element, and to have it creep **in** in a way that seems very realistic at first. In this way, by the time something truly impossible happens, the readers have been prepared for it, and coaxed into a state of mind in which the specific impossible element seems logical, or even inevitable.

House of Stairs

M. C. Escher (1902–1972) was a graphic artist. His prints often contained illusions based on mathematical concepts.

His first financially and critically successful book was *House of Stairs,* published in 1974. Inspired by an M. C. Escher print titled *House of Stairs,* which depicted strange wormlike creatures climbing endless staircases, and also inspired by an interest in behavior modification, Sleator writes about five teenagers placed in a structure filled with stairs that do not lead anywhere. The only food source available is a machine with blinking lights that rewards certain behavior with food pellets. All five characters engage in what seems to be the appropriate behavior until the time comes when the machine will reward them with food only for uncivilized and cruel behavior toward each other. At that point Peter—a quiet, shy, sensitive boy—and Lola—a loud, outspoken, rough girl—decide they will not participate in such activities. They practically starve themselves before the government-sponsored experiment is stopped. Lola and Peter have failed, but the other three will now go on for further training, no doubt eventually to become prison officials or to run concentration camps.

Freedom of the individual is a major theme in Sleator's stories, one that is just as important today as it was in 1974. Although Peter and Lola are able to withstand the attempt to modify their behavior through peer pressure and thereby transform them into inhumane monsters, they almost die in the process, and in the eyes of the experimenters, they are failures. Many parallels to contemporary life, including the political world, can be drawn quite effectively.

Interstellar Pig

"*Interstellar Pig* [1984] is one of my fantastic—and most successful—books," says Sleator in the spring 1992 issue of *ALAN Review.* It is a favorite of many readers, including those in California who gave it the California Young Reader's Medal in 1989.

Sixteen-year-old Barney and his parents are on a beach vacation, living in an old house once owned by a sea captain. When three strange individuals move in next door, the fantastic element begins to creep in. Soon the quiet, shy, introverted Barney is caught up in the middle of a life-and-death game with aliens, all from different worlds.

introverted turned inward

Part of the enthusiasm that readers show for this book may be attributed to the game itself, which is similar to many of the computer games available today. Barney defeats the aliens, despite their neural whips and disguise selectors. Humor is apparent throughout the book, but some of the funniest material appears near the end of the book as Barney fights off the aliens. After defeating them, Barney, before his parents come home, calmly sweeps up the dead lichen aliens along with the sand. He thinks, "It was always that way at the beach—no way to keep the sand out."

The Spirit House

In *The Spirit House,* Sleator attempts to move away from the fantastic element that was so much a part of his other books. In "From Interstellar Pigs to Spirit Houses" he says, "I began to get tired of the 'genie in the bottle' format." Yet he does not quite succeed in removing the fantastic element, as he himself admits: "Even though I was very, very careful to make sure that everything in the book can be attributed to coincidence, the book is still not absolutely realistic. . . . I had not yet completely broken away from the same old formula—ambiguous as it may be, but the spirit of the house itself can still be seen as a device with fantastic but limited powers." Sleator sees *The Spirit House* as a bridge between science fiction and fantasy.

His interest in Thailand and his fascination with its people and their beliefs were strong influences on this book. The narrator is Julie, a fifteen-year-old girl. Her parents have arranged for Bia, a young Thai student, to come and live with the family for a year. When he arrives he is not at all like the young man they were expecting from his letters and picture. As a gesture of friendship Bia gives Julie a jade pendant. Julie's younger brother, Dominic, builds a spirit house in the hopes of making Bia feel more at home. Things quickly begin to go wrong for Julie. Her face breaks out in pimples, her hair is a mess, her friends avoid her. Nothing seems to help until she decides to give the spirit the jade pendant. Suddenly things begin to go right for her.

All the strange occurrences in the novel could be explained by coincidence; however, there is still room for doubt, as in the ominous ending when Julie on the flight to Thailand appears to lose the pendant she is returning to the Erewan Shrine, thus fulfilling her promise to the spirit. As she leaves the plane it does not look as if she is going to have a happy vacation in Thailand.

ominous foreboding or a feeling of future misfortune

Others See Us

The fantastic element in *Others See Us* (1993) is a swamp full of toxic waste that can give those who fall into it or accidentally ingest it the ability to read minds. The narrator, sixteen-year-old Jared, has been looking forward to the annual summer get-together of his extended family at the beach. When he falls off his bike into the swamp, he begins to read the minds of those around him. His grandmother, who has this mind-reading ability also, has used it to steal money from people's bank accounts and to blackmail the neighbors into selling their house. She also blackmails Jared and his cousin Annelise (a truly despicable character) to do her bidding. When Grandma and Jared bring about Annelise's downfall, the reader feels that they are using their unusual powers for good; however, there is no indication that Grandma has any regret for her earlier actions, and we are left feeling fairly sure that she will continue to use those special powers to benefit herself and her family.

None of the characters in *Others See Us* are particularly likable or admirable. Jared is content to go along with whatever Grandma wants him to do. Sleator uses spiders and spiderweb imagery throughout the novel. With a little effort of the imagination, we can see Grandma as a spider who successfully snares three of her grandchildren. She uses Annelise's own words to trap and destroy her; the other two become part of her network.

Good versus evil is one of the themes in the novel as is family loyalty. Reading it provokes interesting thoughts about

Jared's relationship with his female cousins and about the deviousness of Grandma.

Dangerous Wishes

Sleator's *Dangerous Wishes* is a sequel to *The Spirit House,* which ends with Julie's arrival in Thailand, just after having lost the jade pendant she was taking to the Erewan Temple. In this book Julie's parents and brother Dominic (Dom) come to Bangkok for a month so their mother can do first-hand research on the position of women in Thai society.

Sleator presents a great deal of material about life in Thailand through the adventures of Dom and his new Thai friend, Tek. The two boys journey from Bangkok to Tek's village near the Cambodian border. There they look for a pendant that had been found on a body from a plane crash three years earlier. Dom is a typical American teenager, not willing to follow Tek's advice on what to say and whom to talk to in the village. Still, the boys do find the pendant and even though they are being followed by a *khwan*—the evil spirit of one of the village's bad men—as soon as they place the pendant on the altar good things begin to happen.

Most of the occurrences in this novel could be attributed to coincidence, but as in *The Spirit House,* there are mysteries such as Tek's object—a computer that prints out "Thank you, Tek" in Thai letters when the pendant is removed from the skeleton. There is also the *khwan,* which follows the boys and can be seen and heard by everyone at the temple.

Dom's adventures in Tek's village and the subsequent chase by the *khwan* keep the reader turning pages. The change of luck that occurs the minute the pendant is placed on the spirit's altar can only be attributed to that fantastic element Sleator has tried so hard to get away from. The culture of the people of Thailand is much more apparent in this sequel. The description of the refuse-filled waterways is unappealing, and readers may wonder if Dom would gain any special powers as a result of his fall into the filthy water, but Sleator has already used that idea in *Others See Us.*

Friendship and learning to adjust to other cultures are major themes in this book. Parents (as always) are rather cardboard-like figures who generally go along with whatever their adolescent children want.

Conclusion

Over the years Sleator's works have been highly praised. A reviewer in *Library Journal* called *House of Stairs* "Topflight SF/suspense." Trev Jones in *School Library Journal* says *Interstellar Pig* is "compelling on the first reading—but stellar on the second." Not all reviews have been totally glowing, however. Some critics have spotted weak or exaggerated characterization in Sleator's books *Fingers* (1983), *Singularity* (1984), and *The Boy Who Reversed Himself* (1986). Orson Scott Card thinks that tomorrow's science fiction writers and readers will look back at Sleator's work with the same kind of affection we now have for Robert Heinlein.

Sleator is attempting to get away from the "genie in the bottle" and move toward more realistic fiction. *Oddballs* is realistic, maybe a bit exaggerated, but who remembers growing up exactly the way things really happened? No doubt every member of Sleator's family remembers the stories he tells in slightly different versions. He may choose to write more about the adventures of the Sleator children: Bill, Vicky, Danny, and Tycho. He will almost surely continue to write about Thailand. He is quite happy living there most of the time now, and the country offers a wealth of material on which to draw. Only Sleator himself can tell us what he will produce next, and he may be too busy living and writing it to tell us.

Robert Heinlein (1907–1988) was a controversial American science fiction writer who wrote *Starship Troopers* and *Stranger in a Strange Land.*

If you like the works of William Sleator, you might also enjoy the works of Madeleine L'Engle and Avi.

Selected Bibliography

WORKS BY WILLIAM SLEATOR

Novels

The Angry Moon (1970)

Blackbriar (1972)

Run (1973)

Among the Dolls (1974)

House of Stairs (1974)

Into the Dream (1979)

Once, Said Darlene (1979)

The Green Futures of Tycho (1981)

That's Silly (1981)

Fingers (1983)

Interstellar Pig (1984)

Singularity (1984)

The Boy Who Reversed Himself (1986)

The Duplicate (1988)

Strange Attractors (1990)

The Spirit House (1991)

Oddballs (1993)

Others See Us (1993)

Dangerous Wishes (1995)

Short Stories

"The Elevator." In *Things That Go Bump in the Night.* Edited by Jane Yolen and Martin H. Greenburg. New York: Harper & Row, 1989.

"In the Tunnels." In *Am I Blue? Coming Out from the Silence.* Edited by Marion Dane Bauer. New York: Harper-Collins, 1994.

Nonfiction

Take Charge: A Personal Guide to Behavior Modification, with William H. Redd (1976)

"What Is It About Science Fiction?" In *ALAN Review,* winter 1988, vol. 15, pp. 4–6.

"From Interstellar Pigs to Spirit Houses." In *ALAN Review,* spring 1992, vol. 19, pp. 10–15.

"Getting to Be a Writer." E. P. Dutton brochure, n.d.

WORKS ABOUT WILLIAM SLEATOR

Card, Orson Scott. "Books to Look For." *Science Fiction,* August 1988, p. 37.

Daggett, Margaret. "Recommended: William Sleator." *English Journal,* March 1987, pp. 93–94.

Davis, James E., and Hazel K. Davis. *Presenting William Sleator.* New York: Twayne, 1992.

———. "Nudging Readers over the Edge into Science Fiction and Fantasy: William Sleator's Works." *Western Ohio Journal,* 1989, pp. 97–101.

**How to Write to
the Author**
William Sleator
77 Worcester Street
Boston, MA 02118

Jones, Trev. Review of *Interstellar Pig. School Library Journal,* September 1984, p. 134.

Pollack, Pamela D. Review of *House of Stairs. Library Journal,* 15 March 1974, p. 904.

Review of *House of Stairs. Library Journal,* 15 May 1974, p. 1451.

Gary Soto

(1952-   )

by Ted Fabiano

" **I** had not been born to be scared out of my wits, but that is what happened," writes Gary Soto in *Living up the Street: Narrative Recollections* (1985, p. 141), one of several books in which the acclaimed author explores his years growing up in Fresno, California.

Soto may have felt more fear than humor as a boy, but the older Soto, who has written the popular books for young adults, such as *Baseball in April, and Other Stories* (1990), *Small Faces* (1986), *Taking Sides* (1991), and *Jesse* (1995), delights his readers by showing hope, promise, and laughter in even the toughest situations. After recognizing the prominence of fear in the line quoted above, he concludes that same short story in this way: "I laugh at the funny scenes that aren't funny, and I can't think of any better life" (p. 142).

Soto has examined his own life and those of others in the Fresno community through many forms of expression: he is a critically acclaimed poet, essayist, and filmmaker, as well as an award-winning author of fiction. Among his many awards are

Quotations from Gary Soto that are not attributed to a published source are from an unpublished telephone interview conducted on 5 May 1995 by the author of this article and are published here by permission of Gary Soto.

the Academy of American Poets prize in 1975; the American Book Award for *Living up the Street* in 1985; three awards, including a Best Books for Young Adults Citation from the American Library Association, for *Baseball in April, and Other Stories* in 1990; and the Carnegie Medal in 1993 for the video "The Pool Party," based on his short story of the same name.

Beginnings as a Writer

It might seem that someone who has been successful in many different forms of communication would have been interested in reading and writing from the beginning. Not so, says Soto. As he told me in an interview: "I didn't start becoming interested in literature until college." Picking up a poetry anthology while putting off a research paper, the twenty-year-old Soto leafed through the pages and became fascinated by the works of modern masters.

Unintimidated by the challenge of writing as well as the authors he was beginning to admire, Soto began to write poems of his own, and he soon enrolled in poetry writing classes at Fresno State University. In an interview published in *Contemporary Literary Criticism,* Soto recalls the "truly humbling experience" of Philip Levine's class, in which bad poems received harsh treatment. Soto says that he learned "craft" from his teacher. In his own words: "He taught us how to handle language with care" (p. 279).

Philip Levine (1928–) is an American poet whose major subjects include the Spanish Civil War and the American working classes.

"More Than Just a Good Ethnic Writer"

After earning a bachelor's degree at California State University, Fresno, in 1974 and a master's degree in fine arts from the University of California, Irvine, in 1976, Soto's emerging ability to "handle language" found an audience with the publication of *The Elements of San Joaquin* in 1977. This poetry collection met with critical acclaim: in *Western American Literature,* Jerry Bradley writes, "[Soto] is considerably more than just a good ethnic writer; he is a good poet" (p. 73); and Peter Cooley in *Parnassus: Poetry in Review,* writes, "his voice possesses the kind of unaffected honesty we experience only in conversations with friends" (p. 309). (Both of these reviews are reprinted in "Gary Soto" in *Contemporary Literary Criticism.*)

unaffected natural or sincere, not false

Soto's voice has been heard by readers of all ages; but, as he told me in an interview, he does not write with an audience in mind. *Living up the Street,* a collection of twenty-one autobiographical vignettes (or "prose recollections," in the words of the publisher) appeals to both adults and young readers. In that book, Soto begins with short pieces that show him as a five year old feeling a "general meanness," struggling to find experiences that match the images he sees on television. His life—as portrayed in "Looking for Work," in which Gary unsuccessfully attempts to get his brother and sister to dress up at meals—does not resemble those on the television series "Father Knows Best" or "Leave it to Beaver." Soto does not dwell on his status as an outsider or as a Mexican in a world of American dreams. But "The Beauty Contest," in which Gary has his younger brother compete against "blond and fair-skinned kids in good clothes," does reveal cultural barriers that Mexican-Americans face.

Soto does not simply tell about his experiences or despair about the plight of the poor. His power comes from showing, from painting pictures that allow the reader to feel the wonder, promise, and pain of everyday life. Interesting analogies allow the reader to experience the curiosity and innocence of a child without sounding childish. In "One Last Time," he writes, "After ten minutes of groping for grapes, my first pan brimmed with bunches. I poured them on a paper tray, which was bordered by a wooden frame that kept the grapes from rolling off, and they spilled like jewels from a pirate's chest" (p. 103). Such descriptions—"the night heat slowly descending upon us like a heavy jacket" (p. 146), from "Getting By," being another example—dot each recollection to startle and fascinate the reader.

Books for Young Readers

After Soto gathered critical praise for *Living up the Street,* he used the same format in *Baseball in April, and Other Stories* (1990), which found an audience among middle- and upper-level readers. These stories are written in much the same style as his previous recollections, except that Soto uses character names instead of the first person. His characters also find that their own experiences come up short of their expectations. In "The Karate Kid," Gilbert Sanchez, a fifth

autobiographical relating to the author's own life

vignette short episode or anecdote

Father Knows Best and ***Leave it to Beaver*** were popular American television comedies produced during the 1950s. Both shows depicted traditional ideals of white, middle-class, suburban American families.

plight difficult situation

analogy comparison

grader inspired by a popular movie about a boy who turns the tables on school bullies, signs up for karate lessons. To his dismay, he learns nothing from a lenient and uninterested instructor; he even fantasizes about sustaining an injury that would allow him to quit the boring lessons. No more immune to the schoolyard bully Pete the Heat than before, Gilbert stays home to read comic books when *Karate Kid, Part Two* comes to the theater.

lenient permissive, not strict

> "I woke up to poetry and went to bed with poetry."

Even the glamorous and perfect Barbie betrays Veronica Solis in "Barbie." Disgusted by her imitation Barbie doll, Veronica longs for and finally receives an authentic version from her Uncle Rudy. Unfortunately, Barbie loses her head following an argument between Veronica and Martha, who had tried to switch her doll with Veronica's. Barbie's head cannot be repaired, and Veronica must settle for the company of the headless doll and her imitation companion.

While continuing to publish poetry collections for adults, such as *Who Will Know Us?: New Poems* (1990) and *Home Course in Religion: New Poems* (1991), Soto delivered poetry for young readers with *A Fire in My Hands: A Book of Poems* in 1990 and *Neighborhood Odes* in 1992. In the foreword to *A Fire in My Hands,* Soto explains how he began a "single-minded" pursuit of poetry: "I woke up to poetry and went to bed with poetry. I memorized poems, read English poets because I was told they would help shape my poems, and read classical Chinese poetry because I was told that it would add clarity to my work. But I was most taken by Spanish and Latin American poets, particularly Pablo Neruda" (p. 5). Soto describes his own poetry as an attempt to "express [the] simple beauty" of common things. "I like to think of my poems as a 'working life,' by which I mean that my poems are about commonplace, everyday things—baseball, an evening walk, a boyhood friendship, first love, fatherhood, a tree, rock 'n' roll, the homeless, dancing. The poems keep alive the small moments which add up to a large moment: life itself" (p. 6).

Soto prefaces each of the twenty-three poems with an anecdote. Before "That Girl," he tells of how, as a seventh grader, his sudden interest in girls distracted him from his studies in the library. In the poem, he writes:

> My maps were half-colored,
> History a stab in the dark,
> And fractions the inside

> Of a pocket watch
> Spilled on my desk.
> I was no good. And who do I
> Blame? That girl. (P. 16)

However, the work, like the distraction, persists.

> A pencil rolled from the
> Table when she clicked open
> Her binder. I looked up,
> Gazed, looked back down:
> The Nile is the longest river . . . (P. 16)

A prime example of Soto's masterful handling of the language is seen in "Oranges." While walking around the block with a girl named Margie, he buys her a ten-cent chocolate with a nickel and an orange, one of those that he typically sold to earn spending money. While she eats her chocolate, he opens his orange:

> I peeled my orange
> That was so bright against
> The gray of December
> That, from some distance,
> Someone might have thought
> I was making a fire in my hands. (P. 124)

Neighborhood Odes presents twenty-one poems written in ode style. Soto says in the forword to *A Fire in My Hands* that he admired Neruda's odes, "short-line poems celebrating common things like tomatoes, socks, scissors, and artichokes" (p. 6). Similarly, Soto writes odes to his library, weightlifting, a goat, and weddings. In "Ode to the Sprinkler," he writes of the joy that the sprays of water provided for him as a child:

> There is no swimming
> Pool on
> Our street,
> Only sprinklers
> On lawns,
> The helicopter
> Of water
> slicing our legs.

We run through
The sprinkler,
Water on our
Lips, water
Dripping
From eyelashes,
Water like
fat raindrops
That fall from
Skinny trees when
You're not looking. (P. 6)

Soto published two novels during the same time period: *Taking Sides* and *Pacific Crossing* (1992). Both feature Lincoln Mendoza, a boy from the barrio whose family moves to the suburbs, and Tony Contreras, his best friend. In *Taking Sides,* Lincoln moves and begins to attend Columbus Junior High, whose basketball team is scheduled to play against his old school, Franklin. Worried that he will lose Tony, who plays for Franklin, as a best friend, Lincoln tries to straddle the lines between friendship, his own team, and personal pride.

barrio Hispanic neighborhood, usually urban

Pacific Crossing takes Lincoln and Tony across the ocean to Japan for the summer. Lincoln trains in the martial arts, but his stay is not entirely foreign to him; many of his experiences remind him of home. Although differences in Mexican, American, and Japanese cultures become clear through their conversations and activities, the friendship Lincoln forms with Mitsuo and the fun they have transcend cultural differences.

transcend rise above

The 1990s

The 1990s have revealed even more dimensions to Soto's artistry. He has published two books for young children: *Too Many Tamales* (1993), a picture book, and *The Pool Party* (1993), which became the subject for his award-winning video. He produced two other short films, *The Bike* (1991) and *Novio Boy* (1994).

Small Faces, a series of prose recollections originally published in 1986, was reissued in 1993. Readers of *Living up the Street* and *A Summer Life,* his 1990 autobiographical collection, will want to read about the author's life with his wife Carolyn and more reflections on his past. In "June," an essay in *A Summer Life,* he remembers a former girlfriend and thinks about time passing:

> June Barrett, June Flores, June Oda. They enter our lives like bright shadows and pass us up as they make their move for the good jobs and even better lives. They slip into business suits the color of money, and hurry-up steps, their hair bouncing from eagerness. They mother children. They host parties. They talk and make sense. Drinks are passed around from a serving tray, and their smiles, reflexes like springs, open up. (P. 87)

Local News (1993) is a collection of stories especially relevant for young adults. "Blackmail," the first of thirteen stories, shows young Angel's struggle to avoid the embarrassments and punishments meted out by his older brother, Javier, the "Little Weasel." "Trick-or-Treat" tells of a young girl named Alma, and of the Halloween on which she dresses up for candy only to discover her friend Sara throwing a more grown-up party to which she was not invited.

In 1995, the author published three books: *Jesse,* a novel about a seventeen year old who leaves his family and an unhappy home to join his brother at a junior college; *Summer on Wheels*; and *Boys at Work.* During his prolific writing career, Soto also taught as an assistant professor of English and Ethnic Studies, associate professor, and part-time senior lecturer in English at the University of California in Berkeley. In 1993, writing became his full-time occupation.

prolific producing a large amount

Soto, who lives with his wife and daughter in Berkeley, California, has always encouraged young poets and writers. In *A Fire in My Hands,* he advises young poets to "look to your own lives," which he says, "are at work, too" (p. 7). Fittingly, the author, who was inspired to write by a poetry anthology he picked up in the library, is one of the youngest poets ever to appear in *The Norton Anthology of Modern Poetry,* perhaps the most referred to collection of poetry in print.

If you like the works of Gary Soto, then you might also like Peter Dickinson.

Selected Bibliography

WORKS BY GARY SOTO

Books For Young Adults

Small Faces (1986; 1993)
Baseball in April, and Other Stories (1990)
A Fire in My Hands: A Book of Poems (1990)
Taking Sides (1991)
Neighborhood Odes (1992)
Pacific Crossing (1992)
Local News (1993)
Crazy Weekend (1994)
Boys at Work (1995)
Canto Familiar/Familiar Song, poetry (1995)
Jesse (1995)
Summer on Wheels (1995)

Books For Adults

The Elements of San Joaquin, poetry (1977)
The Tale of Sunlight, poetry (1978)
Where Sparrows Work Hard, poetry (1981)
Black Hair, poetry (1985)
Living Up the Street: Narrative Recollections (1985; 1992)
Lesser Evils: Ten Quartets, autobiography (1988)
A Summer Life (1990)
Who Will Know Us?: New Poems (1990)
Home Course in Religion: New Poems (1991)
New and Selected Poems (1995)

Books For Children

The Skirt (1992)
The Pool Party (1993)
Too Many Tamales, picture book (1993)
Chato's Kitchen (1995)
Ricky's Mustache (1995)

Films

The Bike (1991)
The Pool Party (1993)
Novio Boy (1994)

WORKS ABOUT GARY SOTO

Bradley, Jerry. "Review of *The Elements of San Joaquin.*" *Western American Literature,* spring 1979, pp. 73–74.

Cooley, Peter. "Review of *The Elements of San Joaquin.*" *Parnassus: Poetry in Review,* fall/winter 1979, vol. 8, no. 1, pp. 304–310.

"Gary Soto." In *Contemporary Literary Criticism.* Edited by James Draper. Detroit: Gale Research, 1985, vol. 32, pp. 401–402.

"Interview with Gary Soto." In *Contemporary Literary Criticism.* Edited by Jean C. Stine and Daniel G. Marowski. Detroit: Gale Research, 1994, vol. 80.

How to Write to the Author

Gary Soto
43 The Crescent
Berkeley, CA 94708

Jerry Spinelli

(1941-   )

by Robert C. Small, Jr.

" **I** said, what about school?"
Maniac turned to him, "What about it?"
"You gotta go. You're a kid. Ain't ya?"
"I'm not going."
"But gotta. Doncha? They'll make ya."
"Not if they don't find me." (*Maniac Magee,* pp. 85-86)

Why would anyone not want to go to school? Jerry Spinelli knows, though Maniac Magee's reason may not be a common one. Here's why Maniac doesn't want to go to school:

Maniac felt why more than he knew why. It had to do with homes and families and schools, and how a school seems sort of like a big home, but only a day home, because then it empties out; and you can't stay there at night because it's not really a home, and you could never use it as your address, because an address is where you stay at night, where you walk right in the front door without knocking, where everybody talks to each other and uses the same toaster. So all the other kids would be heading for their homes, their night homes, each of them, hundreds, flocking from school like birds from a tree, scattering across town, each breaking off to his or her own place, each knowing exactly where to land. School. Home. No, he was not going to have one without the other. (P. 86)

Jerry Spinelli wrote that. He understands what school is when you have a home and family: sometimes a pain, but usually all right. But he also understands what school is when you do not have a home and a family. A pain too big to have.

Let me tell you about Jerry Spinelli. I first met him through a funny book with a weird title: *Space Station Seventh Grade* (1982). Right from the start, I thought it was funny and strange. This is what I read at the beginning:

One by one my stepfather took the chicken bones out of the bag and laid them on the kitchen table. He laid them down real neat. In a row. Five of them. Two leg bones, two wing bones, one thigh bone.

And bones is all they were. There wasn't a speck of meat on them.

Was this really happening? Did my stepfather really drag me out of bed at seven o'clock in the morning on my summer vacation so I could stand in the kitchen in my underpants and stare down at a row of chicken bones?

"Look familiar?" I heard him say. (P. 3)

Of course, you have probably read this book. Most people have. It has become famous. Guess who had eaten the chicken and put the bones back?

longer hot, boring, or interesting, but safe—safe from the ninth graders who run the school and will pee on your sneaker if you're on their way to the urinal."

In his next book, *Who Put That Hair in My Toothbrush?* Jerry has twelve-year-old Megin and her older brother, Greg, tell about mostly the same things and events but in alternating chapters, first by Megin, then by Greg. Since, like most teenagers, they're usually battling with each other, what one has to say cuts down the other.

In *Maniac Magee,* Jerry decided to tell the story himself. At least, there is a narrator, who is not a character in the book, telling about Maniac—who he is, what he did, and why he is called Maniac when his name is really Jeffrey. The whole book is pretty much about the answer to that last question. This is how Jerry tells us about Maniac living in the zoo:

> If you were the baby buffalo at the Elmwood Park Zoo, maybe it would have gone something like this:
>
> You wake up. You have breakfast, compliments of mother's milk. You mosey on over to the lean-to. Surprise! A strange new animal in there. Bigger than you, but a lot smaller than Mom. Hair, but only on top of its head. Sitting in the straw, munching on a carrot, like Mom does. . . . You nuzzle the new, funny-smelling, hairy-headed animal. It nuzzles you back. Mom doesn't seem to mind. (P. 79)

lean-to sloped shack or shed supported by trees or posts at one end and pinned to the ground at the other

That "funny-smelling" animal is Maniac, of course. Maniac lives in the zoo for a good while.

The Real Jerry Spinelli

Jerry Spinelli writes those funny books that keep us laughing but also thinking about school, home, and life in general, whether we are twelve or twenty or fifty-two. He gets inside what it is like to be a boy or a girl; and, since we have all been one or the other, he gets inside each of us. Sometimes he shows us doing, saying, and thinking things that are not exactly polite, but many of us are not exactly polite all the time.

Who is Jerry Spinelli really? This is who he says he is ("Jerry Spinelli" flyer, 1994):

> I never became a cowboy or a baseball player, and now I'm beginning to wonder if I ever really became a writer. I find that I hesitate to put that label on myself, to define myself by what I do for a living. After all, I also pick berries and touch ponies and skim flat stones over water and marvel at the stars and breathe deeply and grin from ear to ear and save the best part for last. I've always done those things. Which is to say, I never had to become anything. Or anyone. I always, already, was.

> Call me a berrypicking, ponytouching star-marveler.

If you like Jerry Spinelli, you might also like Hadley Irwin and Gordon Korman.

Selected Bibliography

WORKS BY JERRY SPINELLI

Books

Space Station Seventh Grade (1982)

Who Put That Hair in My Toothbrush? (1984)

Night of the Whale (1985)

Jason and Marceline (1986)

Dump Days (1988)

The Bathwater Gang (1990)

Maniac Magee (1990)

Fourth Grade Rats (1991)

Report to the Principal's Office (1991)

There's a Girl in My Hammerlock (1991)

The Bathwater Gang Gets Down to Business (1992)

Do the Funky Pickle (1992)

Who Ran My Underwear Up the Flagpole? (1992)

Picklemania (1993)

Short Stories and Articles

"Before the Immaculate Cuticles." *SIGNAL,* fall 1989, pp. 3–5.

"School Spirit." In *Connections: Short Stories by Outstanding Writers for Young Adults,* Edited by Donald R. Gallo. New York: Delacorte Press, 1989. pp. 170–180.

"Jerry Spinelli." In *Speaking for Ourselves*. Edited by Donald R. Gallo. Urbana, Ill.: National Council of Teachers of English, 1990.

"Maniac Magee: Homer on George Street." *Horn Book*, January/February, 1991, no. 1, pp. 40–41.

"Newbery Acceptance Speech." *Journal of Youth Services in Libraries*, summer 1991, vol. 4, no. 4, pp. 335–389.

"Jerry Spinelli." Author publicity flyer. New York: Simon & Schuster, 1994.

WORKS ABOUT JERRY SPINELLI

Chance, Rosemary. "Spinelli, Jerry." In *Twentieth-Century Young Adult Authors*. Edited by Laura Standley Berger. Detroit: St. James Press, 1994, pp. 611–612.

Hal, May, ed. "Jerry Spinelli." In *Contemporary Authors*. Detroit: Gale Research, 1990, p.424.

Review of *Space Station Seventh Grade*. *Kirkus Reviews*, 1 November 1992, pp. 1196–1197.

Senick, Gerard J., ed. "Jerrry Spinelli." In *Children's Literature Review*. Detroit: Gale Research, 1992, pp. 201–207.

Telgen, Diane, ed. "Jerry Spinelli." In *Something About the Author*. Detroit: Gale Research, 1993, pp. 180–183.

How to Write to the Author
Jerry Spinelli
331 Melvin Road
Phoenixville, PA 19460

John Steinbeck

(1902–1968)

by Warren French

The development of the United States in the twentieth century was profoundly influenced by the disappearance of the frontier. Before the end of the nineteenth century, settlement had spread from the Atlantic to the Pacific and from Alaska to Mexico. When the physical limits of the land were reached, many of those who had led and who expected to lead the conquest of the frontier became frustrated and bitter; they sank into nostalgic reveries about the "good old days." The most powerful fictional account of the loss of the frontier would come from a shy, dreamy writer born almost with the twentieth century in a rural California trading post. There, memories of the perils and rewards of expanding a nation were still vivid and haunting. That writer's name was John Steinbeck.

nostalgic homesick or longing for a past way of life

reveries daydreams

Becoming a Writer

Steinbeck was born on 27 February 1902 in Salinas, California. His middle-class family descended from mid-nineteenth-century German and Irish immigrants. They wanted their only son (Steinbeck had three sisters) to become a respected lawyer. Encouraged by an English teacher, however, he decided when he was fifteen to become a writer. Later, his schoolmates would scarcely remember him, for he spent all the time he could sitting by his lonely bedroom window, turning out fantastic stories. He sometimes shared these with selected companions in a dimly lit cellar. They never became known beyond this narrow circle, for he was too reticent to include his name and address when he sent them to magazines. Little exists of Steinbeck's early work because in 1932 he burned a vast pile of his unpublished stories. Around this time he discovered in his native California valleys and mountains the settings and themes for his most celebrated novels. They would lift him from provincial obscurity to international fame.

reticent quiet and shy

provincial local

False Starts

Steinbeck's first published novel, *Cup of Gold* (1929), is almost unrecognizably different from his mature works of the Depression years. His favorite childhood reading was Sir Thomas Malory's *Morte D'Arthur,* the tragically heroic account of Britain's legendary king and his knights of the Round Table; and Steinbeck was at first interested in writing about remote times and exotic characters. (He tried for many years to perfect a modernized version of Malory's work.) *Cup of Gold* is a swashbuckling tale of the Spanish main, in which the pirate Henry Morgan betrays his crew and ends up a colonial governor. It provides, however, a key to understanding the point of view that dominates the first decade of Steinbeck's fiction in Morgan's explanation to his former cohorts, whom he is about to have hanged: "Civilization will split up a character, and he who refuses to split goes under" (pp. 254–255). This cynical pronouncement embodies young Steinbeck's attitude toward "the civilization" that the poet T. S. Eliot established as characteristic of the years between the two world wars with his influential epic poem *The Waste Land.* In *To a God Unknown* (1933), the second written but third published of Steinbeck's extant novels, he begins to

Sir Thomas Malory (?-1471?) is generally believed to be the author of *Morte D'Arthur,* completed around 1470. The title is French and means "The Death of Arthur."

extant existing

write about the California coast of his childhood but super-imposes upon it the frightening specter of Joseph Wayne. Wayne, a migrant from New England, has a mystical vision about making his own wasteland fruitful but finds he can ful-fill the vision only by sacrificing his life.

The Story Cycles

Such doomed figures are featured in Steinbeck's next three works of fiction that launched his wary quest for fame, be-ginning with his mastery of the "story cycle." Various names, including "story cycles," have been given to works like Sher-wood Anderson's *Winesburg, Ohio* (which Steinbeck listed late in his life in *America and Americans* [1966], with only five others as distinguished novels by his contemporaries). These fictional works are composed of a series of episodes that can be enjoyed individually as short stories but also can be read in sequence as a satisfying novel involving the same characters, settings, and themes.

Although Steinbeck's first three novels sold poorly before their publishers went bankrupt, two breakthroughs in the early 1930s paved the road out of his personal wasteland just about the time of his first marriage, to Carol Henning, who served during a trying period as his typist and most discern-ing critic.

In 1933, the prestigious *North American Review* pub-lished his first two short stories to reach a national audience, the first two parts of *The Red Pony* (1937). Then in 1934, the Chicago bookseller Ben Abramson pressed on a visiting pub-lisher, Pascal Covici, Steinbeck's first story cycle, *The Pas-tures of Heaven* (1932). Covici sat up all night reading it and then phoned Steinbeck's agents and offered to publish his new story cycle, *Tortilla Flat* (1935), which so many publish-ers had rejected that the author had given up hope for it.

Beyond their episodic form, these three story cycles have much in common that has made them especially appealing to those just beginning to read fiction—not only for enjoyment but also for insights into life. By 1945, when the four episodes of *The Red Pony* were published together as one novel, it had been widely acclaimed in the United States and abroad. The book is a universal portrayal of a young person's difficult tran-sition from dependent childhood to independent maturity.

superimpose place one layer on another so that both can be seen together as one

discerning having clear insight and un-derstanding

The story is set against the background of the vanishing frontier, which appealed to both young readers and adults. Young Jody Tiflin is, like Steinbeck, an early-twentieth-century California boy inspired by tales of medieval knights. His heroic dreams are temporarily shattered by the death of his red trick-show pony, unsuited to the rigors of life on the range, and later by the death of a beloved mare in giving birth to the pony's successor. Another disillusioning experience is the disappearance of an old Mexican who has come back to die on land that had been taken from his family. Most important to Jody's maturing is the story of the bitter frustration of his maternal grandfather, "The Leader of the People" of that story's title. He has spent most of his life guiding pioneers over the dangerous plains and mountains, but his career has been ended by the closing of the frontier. He is now one of a line of old men who gaze bitterly into the Pacific Ocean and lament younger generations' loss of the spirit of "Westering."

Like the characters in *The Red Pony,* those in the ironic *The Pastures of Heaven* are doomed to "split up" before the encroachment of "civilization" on their refuge. This encroachment takes the form of self-satisfied and insensitive family members who prove a curse to their neighbors by driving them out of their retreats into an increasingly materialistic and discontented world.

encroachment
gradual approach leading to domination

The Doomsday Novels

Tortilla Flat ends in an even worse catastrophe. Danny, the leader of a band of gypsy-like *paisanos* (fellow countrymen) who spend their days idly in the hills beyond Monterey, inherits two houses. He tries to establish a kind of commune for his buddies, but he cannot accept the responsibilities of civilization. He plunges to his death in a futile struggle with a mysterious "other," as the last of his house burns down, leaving his band of outsider friends homeless again. The cycle was popular escapist reading during the Depression and won Steinbeck his first award as the best California novel of the year, but some Mexican Americans have attacked the book for portraying the *paisanos* condescendingly.

Steinbeck returned again in his next two novels to other problems of young men who keep alive the frontier traditions of self-reliance. *In Dubious Battle* (1936) started out as the biography of an agricultural labor organizer whom Steinbeck met, but Steinbeck's agents thought it would be wiser to convert the work into a novel. Using as the background a mythical labor strike, Steinbeck tells the story of an idealistic youth, Jim Nolan, who joins a radical group supporting an apple pickers' strike. Steinbeck portrays with understated satire but deadly accuracy that good intentions are not enough to protect Nolan form being tricked into a death trap by the power brokers of organized society. Many readers are even more distressed by the unexplained death of an altruistic doctor, based on Steinbeck's friend Ed Ricketts, who provides medical aid for the strikers without committing himself to their political dogmas.

Steinbeck completed what might be called a trilogy of the oppressed with another experimental work that has become much more popular and highly honored than its predecessors, *Of Mice and Men* (1937). This is the first and most successful of three works that can be read as novels or performed as plays. In *Tortilla Flat,* Danny dies because he cannot cope with the demands of civilization. In *In Dubious Battle,* Jim Nolan and Doc Burton are eradicated because they will not sell out to the power brokers of organized society. In *Of Mice and Men,* however, two wandering ranch hands, George and Lennie, are victims of an imperfect nature that they cannot control. Lennie is enormously strong but slow-witted; he does not know how to control his own strength. As long as George controls Lennie's actions, the two men manage to survive, spurred on by a dream of owning a little farm of their own together. George, however, cannot watch Lennie's every move, and after the powerful Lennie accidentally kills a woman, George feels obliged to kill his friend to protect him from a lynch mob intent on torturing him.

All three novels are about the doomed efforts of the principal characters to realize the American dream of becoming an independent person.

The Grapes of Wrath

The success of *Of Mice and Men,* both as a book and as a prize-winning play, resulted in great changes in Steinbeck's life. He had been touring the camps where migrant workers, attracted to California from the Dust Bowl of Oklahoma and Texas, were struggling to survive. Steinbeck was appalled by

satire method of writing that uses humor and parody to mock or criticize

dogma strict, established opinion or position

Of Mice and Men was made into popular movies in 1939, 1981, and 1992.

The **Dust Bowl** was a region in America's southern Great Plains where dry weather and strong winds blew away farmers' soil, creating huge dust storms in the late 1930s and causing many farmers to pack up and leave.

the camp conditions he had seen. He wrote a series of articles about them for the *San Francisco News* in September 1936 and made plans for several novels about the migrants. In February 1938 he wrote the "L'Affaire Lettuceberg," which bitterly satirized the residents of his hometown of Salinas for the tactics they used to break a strike. We can only guess about the details, however, because in one of those flamboyant gestures that punctuated his career, he destroyed the completed manuscript. In a letter to his agents, Steinbeck justified his action with an eloquent statement about his work: "My whole work drive has been aimed at making people understand each other and then I deliberately write this book the aim of which is to cause hatred through partial understanding" (*Working Days,* p. xi). He then determined to replace the story with *The Grapes of Wrath,* his longest novel up to that time. He finished the book after five months of exhausting labor.

For *The Grapes of Wrath,* his most ambitious effort, Steinbeck devised his boldest innovation. Beginning with what he calls a "general chapter" describing the Dust Bowl of the 1930s, he follows with a second chapter that introduces the Joads. They are one of the many former sharecropping families being driven off their land during the Depression. For the rest of the book, general chapters about the national crisis alternate with accounts of the Joads' progress across the Dust Bowl in search of a new home, a little farm of their own. But the Joads are foiled in this effort by the landowners. They hate the migrants, thinking that they "had heard from their grandfathers how easy it was to steal land from a soft man" (pp. 256–257). The future of the Joad family is uncertain as the novel ends. But it is clear that they are going to carry on. They are down, but they are not going to split up. Beginning with this novel, hailed as a major achievement, Steinbeck ended his novels on a more optimistic note. He did not expect *The Grapes of Wrath* to sell well, but it became an enormous success, topping best-seller lists for two years and winning a Pulitzer Prize.

The **Great Depression** was a severe economic crisis that began with the stock market crashed in 1929 and that lasted almost ten years. By the winter of 1932–1933, 14 to 16 million Americans were unemployed. Many died from a lack of food and inadequate living conditions.

Troublesome Celebrity

Unfortunately, Steinbeck's life was not completely rosy thereafter. While many, including Eleanor Roosevelt, praised *The Grapes of Wrath* lavishly, it was bitterly attacked by outraged

Western landowners who threatened violent retribution. Steinbeck's marriage crumbled under the pressure of his celebrity; and although a second marriage, to Gwendolyn Conger, produced his only two sons in 1944 and 1946, it ended after five years because of their conflicting career demands. Then in 1948, his closest friend and adviser, Ed Ricketts, was accidentally killed.

Meanwhile, critics carped that his work was deteriorating because he replaced characters based on people he had known well in devastating and immediate conflicts with "universalized figures," two-dimensional types manipulated against stylized backgrounds, especially after he offered his services to the government during World War II. *The Moon Is Down* (1942), his second play and novelette, is about a mythical nation's resistance to Nazi-like invaders. It greatly heartened readers in occupied Europe, but American reviewers complained that it was too soft on the invaders. *Bombs Away* (1942), a story about training an Army Air Corps bomber team, was his first piece of patriotic propaganda written at the insistence of President Franklin D. Roosevelt, for whom Steinbeck also suggested ideas for campaign speeches. Finally, he temporarily abandoned fiction altogether, when he was permitted to visit the Mediterranean fighting front and send back dispatches to a newspaper syndicate.

Cannery Row

His observations of the war so demoralized Steinbeck that he retreated to his publisher's office to cap off his memorable depictions of the now-vanished world of the Monterey region in the 1930s with *Cannery Row* (1945), a very different novel from its predecessors. Seeking to avoid any mention of the war, Steinbeck cast his friend Ed Ricketts as the proprietor of a marine biological laboratory, known only as Doc to the outcasts who live on the wrong side of the railroad tracks and want to honor him for the way he has boosted their morale. After comically unsuccessful efforts, they throw a party that has been long remembered by readers as an upbeat glorification of a person who, though not materially successful, loves his work, his friends, and his self-determined lifestyle and who has succeeded in transcending the obstacles with which civilization seeks to split up a person.

retribution revenge

Cannery Row was the basis for a disappointing film that was released in 1981.

transcend rise above

Looking Backward

With *Cannery Row,* Steinbeck exhausted his best stock of personal memories. His fictional attempts to deal with post–World War II society were never as successful as his recollections of the days before he became a celebrity. He set off to Mexico to write and film (in English and Spanish) *The Pearl* (1947). It is based on a popular short Mexican fable about a poor fisherman who finds the greatest pearl of the world. He learns that the only way to escape the plots of greedy people, who kill his son, is to throw the priceless pearl back into the sea. The story has been widely commended for its upbeat moral, but its ornate language and melodramatic plot emphasize the story's unreality.

Steinbeck was less successful with *The Wayward Bus* (1947), an unlikely account of an agonizing journey of self-discovery. Steinbeck regarded his characters in this story as a representative cross section of post–World War II Californians. His third and last play and novelette, *Burning Bright* (1950), was a noble but misguided effort to preach that "every man is father to all children" (p. 108). Turning his back on a world that seemed to have moved past him, he set out again for Mexico to make a film about the revolutionary leader Emiliano Zapata with director Elia Kazan. While the film is an artistic success, the problems it engendered with both American and Mexican officials so enraged Steinbeck that he gave up his longtime enthusiasm for both Mexico and filmmaking.

He started, as his publishers had long hoped he would, *East of Eden* (1952), a story about the Salinas Valley during his childhood years. It proved to be his longest novel, for which he devised another innovation by alternating chapters about his mother's pioneering farming family with a luridly Gothic tale about the imaginary Trask family and its disastrous effects on the community. This time, however, as the biographer Jay Parini comments, Steinbeck did not "manage to pull off what he had attempted" (p. 439). The mixture did not jell. It is not clear why the alternating chapters are in the same book. Neither story provides a broad backdrop for the other, as the general chapters did for the Joads in *The Grapes of Wrath.* Steinbeck would not attempt anything on this large a scale again.

---

ornate complex and decorative

melodramatic sentimental or having inflated emotions

Emiliano Zapata (1879–1919) was a rebel leader of the Mexican Revolution of 1911. As a Mexican Indian, the welfare of his people were his main concern.

Elia Kazan (1909–) is an acclaimed American stage and film director whose movies included *A Streetcar Named Desire* and Steinbeck's *Viva Zapata!* and *East of Eden.*

East of Eden was made into a popular movie in 1955 and a television miniseries in 1982.

lurid horrific and sensational

Gothic relating to a style of fiction involving unnatural mystery and darkness.

Looking Forward

Steinbeck returned to contemporary subjects in the auto-biographical columns that he wrote in Paris in 1954 for the newspaper *Le Figaro.* He followed these with three final novels that illustrate his desperate attempt to adjust his vision to a changing world. *Sweet Thursday* (1954) is an attempt to update *Cannery Row* and provide a libretto for one of Rodgers and Hammerstein's few unsuccessful stage musicals, *Pipe Dream,* which fails to recapture the vision of the original. *The Short Reign of Pippin IV* (1957), a satire of French politics in the 1950s, is much more amusing but it has already dated badly. *The Winter of Our Discontent* (1961) is Steinbeck's only novel set on Long Island, where he had moved in 1955. It is a heavy-handed return to the moralizing tone of *The Pearl* and *Burning Bright.*

Travels with Charley

In 1962, Steinbeck enjoyed fresh success with one of his biggest sellers, *Travels with Charley: In Search of America.* This book is an account of his 1960 trip to get reacquainted with his native country accompanied by a great blue poodle—an unsettling journey that comes to a demoralizing conclusion when he encounters the Cheerleaders, a group of vulgar New Orleans white mothers protesting school desegregation. He followed this successful book with *America and Americans.* It is not so well known as many of his works, but it is essential for understanding Steinbeck's devotion to his country and its people. It was written as Steinbeck approached the end of his life and after he had won the Nobel Prize for literature in 1962.

Reading this "book of opinions, unashamed and individual," as Steinbeck prefaces it, we realize how much the author was like the grandfather in *The Red Pony.* Steinbeck, however, never gave up the quest for what he describes in his last book as "a new path and a new purpose to fulfill," even though he did admit that "the direction may be unthinkable to us now" (p. 142). Steinbeck died on 20 December 1968.

Segregation is the separation of a race, class, or ethnic group by discriminatory means, including separate schools. **School desegregation**, the process of undoing the separation of African Americans from the rest of society, began in the United States in the late 1950s.

Readers who enjoy the works of John Steinbeck might also enjoy the works of Stephen Crane, Emily Dickinson, Robert Frost, Harper Lee, and Robert Louis Stevenson.

Selected Bibliography

WORKS BY JOHN STEINBECK

Fiction

Cup of Gold (1929)

The Pastures of Heaven (1932)

To a God Unknown (1933)

Tortilla Flat (1935)

In Dubious Battle (1936)

Of Mice and Men (1937)

The Red Pony (1937; expanded 1945)

The Long Valley (1938)

The Grapes of Wrath (1939)

Bombs Away (1942)

The Moon is Down (1942)

Cannery Row (1945)

The Pearl (1947)

The Wayward Bus (1947)

Burning Bright (1950)

East of Eden (1952)

Sweet Thursday (1954)

The Short Reign of Pippin IV (1957)

The Winter of Our Discontent (1961)

The Acts of King Arthur and His Noble Knights, edited by Horton Chase (1976)

Plays

Of Mice and Men: A Play in Three Acts (1937)

The Moon is Down: A Play in Two Parts (1942)

Burning Bright (1951)

Film Scripts

The Forgotten Village (1941)

Viva Zapata!, edited by Robert Morsberger (1975)

Zapata: A Narrative in Dramatic Form of the Life of Emiliano Zapata, edited by Robert Morsberger (1993)

Autobiographical Nonfiction

Their Blood Is Strong (1938) (Reprinted in *A Companion to "The Grapes of Wrath,"* 1963, 1989)

Sea of Cortez, with Edward F. Ricketts (1941)

Once There Was a War (1943; 1958)

A Russian Journal (1948)

Speech Accepting the Nobel Prize for Literature (1962)

Travels with Charley: In Search of America (1962)

America and Americans (1966)

Journal of a Novel: The "East of Eden" Letters (1969)

Working Days: The Journals of "The Grapes of Wrath" (1989)

WORKS ABOUT JOHN STEINBECK

Biography

Benson, Jackson J. *Looking for Steinbeck's Ghost.* Norman: University of Oklahoma Press, 1988.

————.*The True Adventures of John Steinbeck, Writer.* New York: Viking, 1984.

DeMott, Robert J. *Steinbeck's Reading.* New York: Garland. 1984. A list of nearly 1,000 books that Steinbeck is known to have owned or borrowed, annotated with many of his comments about them and biographical information.

Enea, Sparky, as told to Audry Lynch. *With Steinbeck in the Sea of Cortez.* Los Osos, Calif.: Sand River Press, 1991.

Parini, Jay. *Steinbeck: A Biography.* London: Heinemann, 1994; New York: Holt, 1995.

Steinbeck, John, IV. *In Touch.* New York: Knopf, 1969.

Critical Studies

Astro, Richard. *John Steinbeck and Edward F. Ricketts: The Shaping of a Novelist.* Minneapolis: University of Minnesota Press, 1973.

Bloom, Harold, ed. *John Steinbeck: Modern Critical Views.* New York: Chelsea House, 1987.

Coers, Donald V., Paul D. Ruffin, and Robert J. DeMott, eds. *After "The Grapes of Wrath": Essays on John Steinbeck in Honor of Tetsumaro Hayashi.* Athens: Ohio University Press, 1995.

Ditsky, John, ed. *Critical Essays on Steinbeck's "The Grapes of Wrath."* Boston: G. K. Hall, 1989.

Fontenrose, Joseph. *John Steinbeck: An Introduction and an Interpretation.* New York: Barnes and Noble, 1963.

French, Warren, ed. *A Companion to "The Grapes of Wrath."* New York: Viking, 1963.

———. *John Steinbeck's Fiction Revisited.* New York: Twayne, 1994.

———.*John Steinbeck's Nonfiction.* New York: Twayne, 1996.

Hayashi, Tetsumaro, ed. *Steinbeck's Short Stories in "The Long Valley": Essays in Criticism.* Muncie, Ind.: Steinbeck Research Institute, 1991.

Hughes, R. S. *John Steinbeck: A Study of the Short Fiction.* Boston: Twayne, 1989.

Lisca, Peter. *The Wide World of John Steinbeck.* New Brunswick, N.J.: Rutgers University Press, 1958.

———.*John Steinbeck: Nature and Myth.* New York: Crowell, 1978. An introduction for young readers by the scholar who initiated serious study of the novelist.

Millichap, Joseph R. *Steinbeck and Film.* New York: Ungar, 1983.

Owens, Louis. *John Steinbeck's Re-vision of America.* Athens: University of Georgia Press, 1985.

Simmonds, Roy. *Steinbeck's Literary Achievement.* Muncie, Ind.: John Steinbeck Society of America, 1976.

———.*John Steinbeck: The War Years, 1939–1945.* Lewisburg, Pa.: Bucknell University Press, 1996.

Tedlock, Ernest W., Jr., and C. V. Wicker, eds. *Steinbeck and His Critics: A Record of Twenty-Five Years.* Albuquerque: University of New Mexico Press, 1957.

Wyatt, David, ed. *New Essays on "The Grapes of Wrath."* New York: Cambridge University Press, 1990.

You can learn more about the author by visiting:
The John Steinbeck Memorial Museum
222 Central Avenue
Pacific Grove, CA 93950
For information about the museum, write to:
The John Steinbeck Memorial Museum
470 Foam Street
Monterey, CA 93940

Robert Louis Stevenson

(1850–1894)

by Linda J. Wilson

If you've ever dreamed of running away from home, setting out on adventures to faraway places, skipping school or church, pursuing a career your parents would never approve of, or simply wearing the kind of hat that no one else wears, you might have a lot in common with Robert Louis Stevenson, the author of *Treasure Island, Kidnapped,* and many other novels, essays, plays, and poems. Even though he lived more than one hundred years ago in Scotland, the events of his life, and especially his reactions to these events, seem surprisingly modern. Because he recorded his observations and ideas in his journals and in letters to friends and relatives, we know a lot about his life and how he became a well-known author during his own short lifetime.

Growing Up

Robert Louis Stevenson was born in Edinburgh, Scotland, in 1850. We know some very important facts about his childhood which help to explain the content of his later books. He was a very sickly child, probably with tuberculosis, and was sometimes confined to bed for weeks and to his house for long winter months at a stretch. During this time, he spent many hours playing in bed with tin soldiers and telling and listening to stories. There were also much more active times spent with his cousins at the seashore, during which they played make-believe games of pirates, smugglers, and buried treasure. As one biographer, Calder, pointed out:

> Many children exist in a border territory between fantasy and reality. Stevenson was exceptional in relishing his fantasy to such an extent that he made every effort to preserve it for the whole of his life. As a child, fantasy helped him to cope with, to find happiness in, a lonely existence dominated by ill health. As a grown man it was still a prime source of pleasure, not so much as a means of escaping reality, which he knew well enough could not be done, but as a way of making life more colourful and more interesting. (P. 37)

When he was thirty five years old, he wrote a book of charming poems still widely read today, *A Child's Garden of Verses,* which combines a child's view with an adult's remembrance of many of these pastimes. One of the poems begins:

> When I was sick and lay a-bed,
> I had two pillows at my head,
> And all my toys beside me lay
> To keep me happy all the day.

We know he was spoiled by his parents and by a nurse, Alison Cunningham, whom he called "Cummy." It was a loving household, but also a strict religious environment, and the stories he heard from Cummy and his father about a stern God and the horrors of Christian martyrdom gave him nightmares. There were many other happier stories told as well, and it is

martyr person who suffers or dies for a cause or religion

evident very early in his life that he joined in the storytelling. One example is reported by Grover in a biography of Stevenson written for children. Once when he was very young, he was punished by having to stand in a corner. When his nurse told him his time was up, he whispered, "Hush, Cummy, hush! I'm telling myself a wonderful story." (p. 15)

Another activity in his childhood which influenced his later writing was the trips he took with his father who was a lighthouse engineer. This experience with the sea and the coast, and with ships and the men who sailed them, is evident in his adventure novels, *Treasure Island* and *Kidnapped,* stories clearly written by a person with a firsthand knowledge and love of the sea.

Breaking Away

Because of his prolonged bouts with illness, Stevenson did not attend school regularly as a child. These habits continued at the University of Edinburgh where he enrolled at the age of sixteen to study engineering. Later in life, as reported in *Yesterday's Authors of Books for Children,* he wrote about his university years, "No one ever played truant with more deliberate care and no one ever had more certificates for less education." (p. 318)

truant absent from school

From his father's point of view, worse than his son's truancy was his pronouncement that he was not interested in pursuing engineering, but rather wanted to be a writer. This decision was not easy for his father to accept, since his own father and grandfather had been lighthouse engineers. Thomas Stevenson, however, apparently came around, and father and son agreed to compromise: the younger Stevenson would pursue a degree in law which he actually completed but never practiced.

Stevenson's appearance and lifestyle during his university years also disturbed his conservative parents. He had shoulder length hair and consistently wore a wide-brimmed hat, a dark velvet jacket, a colored flannel shirt, and a tie that, as his biographer Calder quotes from a contemporary, "might be a strip torn from a cast-away carpet." (p. 17) Many people referred to him at this time in his life as "Velvet Coat." His excessive thinness was accentuated by his eccentric clothes. McLynn, a recent biographer, quoted one of Steven-

eccentric odd and quirky

son's friends who described him during his late teen-age years as "in body . . . assuredly badly set up. His limbs were long, lean and spidery, and his chest flat, so as almost to suggest some malnutrition, such sharp corners did his joints make under his clothes." (p. 27) His dark brown eyes were his most striking feature.

Apparently his unconventional dress habits continued throughout his life, and there were a number of times when he was denied entrance to a hotel, eating establishment, or bank because of his disheveled appearance. Several people remarked on his emaciated appearance as he grew older. McLynn reported that an American who met Stevenson toward the end of his life in Samoa described him unflatteringly at one meeting as "a bundle of sticks in a bag" (p. 384) and at another meeting as "an insane stork." (p. 388)

A far greater blow to his father than his dress or his choice of profession was Stevenson's confession that he had become an agnostic, that he no longer believed nor practiced Presbyterianism, his family's religion. He and several of his friends had established a club at Edinburgh University which they called the LJR Club (for Liberty, Justice, Reverence). Not so surprising nor so different from university students today, club meetings consisted of late night discussions of religion and values—and a good deal of drinking. The motto of the club was "Disregard everything our parents have taught us."

Stevenson's agnosticism, his father's reaction to it in the form of anger and self-blame, and his mother's hysterics severely strained their relationship for many years. It is a testament to the patience and depth of caring on both sides that they were able, after a time, to re-establish their ties.

Casting Off

From the time he was a teen-ager in the 1860s until his death in 1894, Stevenson spent his life "casting off" for ports unknown in search of adventure and a place where he could find some relief from his chronic illness. Ironically, the man who longed for adventure and wrote so convincingly about it, was truly an invalid a good deal of his life, and faced death many times.

His university years and those directly following them were spent in repeated trips to continental Europe, most no-

emaciated extremely skinny or gaunt

agnostic person who neither accepts nor rejects the existence of God

invalid person who is very ill or crippled and cannot be physically active

tably France and Belgium. During many of these trips he was deathly ill, spitting up blood and confined to bed. It was in France in 1876 that he met and fell in love with Mrs. Fanny Osbourne, a married American woman at least ten years older than he. She found it necessary to return to her husband and home near San Francisco in 1878. Despite his ill health and without telling his disapproving parents in advance, he pursued Fanny Osbourne across the Atlantic by ship, and then across the United States by train. He was not financially able to afford first-class accommodations, and the long, strenuous trip nearly killed him.

They were married in 1880 and returned to Scotland, but not for long. The harsh winters of Scotland forced them to look for a more agreeable climate, first in Europe, then in up-state New York (which was hardly more agreeable than Scotland!), and then to the South Pacific. They finally built a home in Samoa in 1890 where Stevenson died four years later at the age of forty four.

strenuous difficult and exhausting

"No Need of Psychology or Fine Writing"

It is difficult for us at this point in history to appreciate how radically Robert Louis Stevenson changed the face of literature written for young people. Until *Treasure Island,* written in 1881-1882, almost all authors of books for the young felt a duty to be "preachy," to include moral lessons in their stories. Stevenson felt no such need; in a letter to a friend quoted in the *Children's Literature Review,* he wrote, "It's awful fun, boys' stories. You just indulge the pleasure of your heart, that's all; no trouble, no pain." (p. 225) And in an essay he wrote about *Treasure Island,* he said, "It was to be a story for boys; no need of psychology or fine writing" (p. 194). We get the feeling that he was aware of his break with morality when he confessed, "It [*Treasure Island*] seemed to me as original as sin." (p. 194)

Stevenson's story of how *Treasure Island* came to be written is quoted in *Children's Literature Review.* He was passing an afternoon with his stepson Lloyd, making colored drawings. Looking at the map of an island he had drawn which he called "Treasure Island," "the future characters of the book began to appear there visibly among imaginary woods; and their brown faces and bright weapons peeped out upon me from unexpected quarters, as they passed to and fro, fighting and hunting treasure" (p. 194).

One critic, Robert Kiely, talks about "the exhilarating sense of *casting off*" that the characters in the book have and that we as readers have when we begin reading the story:

> I mean casting off both in the nautical sense of leaving port and in the conventional sense of throwing off encumbrances. It is the perennial thrill of the schoolboy tossing away his books on the last day of the term or the youth flinging off his sticky clothes for the first swim of the season. (Pp. 68-69)

In *Treasure Island,* Stevenson created a whole world of his own, leaving behind parents, Scotland, Presbyterianism, tuberculosis, and money troubles. We are caught up in the speed of the book——no matter how long it takes to read the book, the events in the book move so swiftly and are so exciting, we have the feeling that we have raced through it. Indeed, Stevenson himself raced through it, writing the first fifteen chapters in just two weeks, then setting it aside for six months, and completing the second half in two more weeks.

Stevenson wrote several more adventure novels "for boys" (although I suspect that more than a few girls have read and enjoyed these books through the years). In addition to *Treasure Island,* two of these books are still regularly read today: *Kidnapped,* which he wrote in 1886, and, to a much lesser extent, *The Black Arrow,* written in 1888. Like *Treasure Island,* they were serialized in the magazine *Young Folks* before being published as novels.

Finding the Treasure

Because Stevenson wrote his books more than a hundred years ago, enough time has elapsed so that many people have read and then written about his books, giving us clues for finding and appreciating the treasure that is buried in them. One observation many critics have made is the interesting fact that the young men, who are the main characters in his novels for young people, seem to be the least developed, and consequently the least interesting, characters in

exhilarating exciting and liberating

encumbrances things that weigh a person down

perennial always existing

Treasure Island was made into popular films in 1934, 1950, and 1972, and into a television movie in 1990. **Kidnapped** was also made into a movie in 1960.

his books. It is the morally ambiguous characters who are the most memorable. Long John Silver in *Treasure Island* is one good example; another is Alan Breck Stewart in *Kidnapped*. There is no doubt that Silver is a villain, but there is certainly something heroic about him as well. He lies, deceives, and manipulates both his fellow mutineers as well as the men he mutinies against, and yet he does have his own code of ethics. Similarly, Stewart, friend and mentor to David Balfour, the main character, has contradictory qualities——he is vain and cruel, but also brave, honest and a good friend.

The figures of Long John Silver and Alan Breck Stewart personify one of the themes that runs through Stevenson's works——the duality of human nature. Breaking away from his own narrow religious roots and the rigid morality present in children's books throughout the nineteenth century, Stevenson seems to be saying that all of us contain within us both good and evil. To him, black and white, good and evil, are not mutually exclusive. Probably his most famous story incorporating this theme is *The Strange Case of Dr. Jekyll and Mr. Hyde,* a story whose main character (characters?) has become synonymous with what we might call in our own time a "split personality."

Another clue to finding the treasure in Stevenson's books is to reflect upon the way he uses the element of chance or luck in his stories. One critic, Kiely, has studied Stevenson's fiction and nonfiction and concluded unequivocally that "Stevenson passionately believed that the greater part of life was chance" (p. 24). Certainly coincidence or luck plays an important role in his adventure stories. Time and again, Jim Hawkins, the young man who narrates most of *Treasure Island,* just happens to be in the right place at the right time—such as falling asleep hidden in the apple barrel and overhearing the plans for mutiny. At other times, forces beyond his control—such as the wind or the weather—work to his advantage. The unexpectedness of chance provides an excitement, a sense of letting go of responsibility, and a quirkiness to Stevenson's stories. These qualities are in direct contrast to the moralistic children's stories which preceded his, in which moral behavior always determines consequences.

Finding the treasures buried in Stevenson's stories requires us to consider what McLynn, writing about *Treasure Island,* calls a "lack of a moral centre" (p. 199). It is his viewpoint that greed is the governing motive for a country squire and doctor to leave their settled lives and search for buried

ambiguous capable of being understood in more than one way

mutually exclusive incapable of existing at the same time

The story of Doctor Jekyll and Mr. Hyde has been made into movies many times from 1920 to the present. It has also inspired or influenced many books and movies.

treasure. But other critics argue that the main reason for the search is the search itself. In other words, the reason why Jim Hawkins, Dr. Livesey and Squire Trelawny sail for a Caribbean Island in *Treasure Island* is not to get rich quick, but to experience the voyage and the search for treasure. Similarly, in *Kidnapped,* the hero, David Balfour, struggles to regain his birthright, but the importance of his inheritance pales alongside the actual perilous adventures Balfour experiences on sea and over land.

In the end, we are left, as we are with all enduring literature, to make our own decisions regarding the author's intentions. And in the process of digging for treasure, we can find a lot of fun in the digging itself.

If you like Robert Louis Stevenson, you might also like Jack London, Edgar Allan Poe, and Mark Twain.

Selected Bibliography

WORKS BY ROBERT LOUIS STEVENSON

First Editions

Treasure Island, Cassell (1883)

The Strange Case of Dr. Jekyll and Mr. Hyde, Scribner (1886)

Kidnapped, Scribner (1886)

The Black Arrow: A Tale of the Two Roses, Scribner (1888)

David Balfour, Scribner, 1893, published in England as *Catriona: A Sequel to Kidnapped,* Cassell (1893)

Notable Editions with Illustrations

Treasure Island, illustrated by N. C. Wyeth, Scribner (1911; reprinted, 1972)

Kidnapped, illustrated by N. C. Wyeth, Scribner (1913; reprinted, 1973)

The Black Arrow: A Tale of the Two Roses, illustrated by N. C. Wyeth, Scribner (1916)

David Balfour, illustrated by N. C. Wyeth, Scribner (1924; reprinted, 1961)

Modern Editions

Treasure Island, New York Graphic Society (1972)

The Strange Case of Dr. Jekyll and Mr. Hyde, illustrated by Rick Schreiter, Watts (1967)

Kidnapped, Penguin (1975)

The Black Arrow: A Tale of the Two Roses, illustrated by Don Irwin, Childrens Press (1970)

Selected Editions of Collected Works

Colvin, Sidney. *The Works of R. L. Stevenson,* Edinburgh edition, 18 volumes, Chatto & Windus, 1894–1898

The Works of R. S. Stevenson, Biographical edition, 31 volumes, Scribner, 1905–1939.

Selected Editions of Letters

Colvin, Sidney. *The Letters of Robert Louis Stevenson to His Family and Friends,* Scribner, 1899.

Booth, Bradford A. and Ernest Mehew, eds. *The Letters of Robert Louis Stevenson,* 2 vols. New Haven, Conn.: Yale University Press, 1994.

SELECTED BIOGRAPHICAL AND CRITICAL STUDIES

Beer, Patricia. "Kidnapped." *Children's Literature in Education* 14, no. 1 (Spring 1983): pp. 54–62.

Calder, Jenni. *Robert Louis Stevenson: A Life Study.* New York: Oxford University Press, 1980.

Children's Literature Review, vol. 10. Detroit: Gale Research, 1986, pp. 193–235.

Dictionary of Literary Biography: British Children's Writers, 1880–1914, vol. 141. Detroit, Mich.: Gale Research Inc., 1994, pp. 271–283.

Eigner, Edwin M. *Robert Louis Stevenson and Romantic Tradition.* Princeton, N.J.: Princeton University Press, 1966.

Grover, Eulalie Osgood. *Robert Louis Stevenson: Teller of Tales.* New York: Dodd Mead & Co., 1940, republished by Gale Research, Detroit, Mich., 1975.

Kiely, Robert. *Robert Louis Stevenson and the Fiction of Adventure.* Cambridge, Mass.: Harvard University Press, 1965.

Major Authors and Illustrators for Children and Young Adults, Detroit, Mich.: Gale Research, 1993, vol. 5., pp. 2219–2225.

McLynn, Frank. *Robert Louis Stevenson: A Biography.* London: Hutchinson, 1993.

Pickering, Sam. "Stevenson's 'Elementary Novel of Adventure.'" *Research Studies,* June 1981, pp. 99–106.

You can write or visit:
The Robert Louis Stevenson Memorial Cottage
11 Stevenson Lane
Saranac, NY 12983
You can also visit:
The Robert Louis Stevenson House
530 Houston Street
Monterey, CA 93940
For information about the House, write to:
The Robert Louis Stevenson House
20 Custom House Plaza
Monterey, CA 93940

Saposnik, Irving S. *Robert Louis Stevenson.* New York: Twayne, 1974.

Ward, Hayden W. "'The Pleasure of Your Heart': Treasure Island and the Appeal of Boys' Adventure Fiction." *Studies in the Novel,* Fall 1974, 304–317.

Yesterday's Authors of Books for Children, vol. 2. Detroit, Mich.: Gale Research, 1978, pp. 307–331.

Todd Strasser

(1950-   )

by Elaine Stephens

It took Todd Strasser six years of writing and rewriting to finish his first book, *Angel Dust Blues* (1979), and to get it published. Since then, he has become a popular and prolific author of young adult literature. His work falls into three main categories: realistic fiction for students in middle school and high school, humorous and historical fiction for younger readers, and novelizations of screenplays for a wide range of readers. Strasser has always loved to write and tell stories, although as a young person he never thought he would be an author. About writing, he says in *Scholastic Authors Online* (1995), "I love to lose myself in the story. It's sort of like being in a daydream all day long. It's like experiencing lives and places I've never been. It's like playing pretend when you were a kid."

Quotations from Todd Strasser that are not attributed to a published source are from personal interviews conducted by the author of this article in 1995 and are published here by permission of Todd Strasser.

Early Years

Todd Strasser grew up during the fifties and sixties on Long Island in a typical middle-class suburban home. Although he was a mediocre student who needed tutoring in reading during elementary school, he liked science and sports. In high school he was not a particularly good English student, but he found that he liked writing letters. In "Becoming a YA Novelist" (in *The VOYA Reader,* 1990), Strasser describes himself in this manner: "An average athlete, a somewhat obnoxious wise guy whose only unusual trait was a keen interest in lower echelon creatures from birds through reptiles and including amphibians, fish, and insects. In school they called me 'nature boy' and worse" (p. 236).

Although his mother did some writing and his grandfather wrote funny poems about the family, Strasser is uncertain what inspired him to start writing. But like so many other writers, something compelled him to try to put words on paper. As he explains in *Scholastic Authors Online,* "From somewhere inside came the desire, almost the need, to write." In college, Strasser enrolled in a premed program intending to become a doctor but found himself writing short stories and poetry instead of lab reports.

When the confusion over his life work increased and his grades dropped, Strasser left college. For the next two years, he traveled around the United States and Europe, working at odd jobs. He then returned to college determined to become a writer. During his last semester, he took a creative writing class and began writing *Angel Dust Blues,* but with little confidence that it would ever be published.

After graduation, Strasser worked in a public relations office, a newspaper office, and an advertising agency. He continued to write fiction, learning the craft of writing as he revised *Angel Dust Blues.* Even with its publication in 1978, he had to support himself through a variety of jobs. At one time he had his own fortune cookie company. Now a successful full-time writer, Strasser, his wife, and their two children live in a suburb of New York. He describes his hobbies by saying, "I like to fish, play tennis, ski, go to movies, read, do carpentry and other repairs around the house, and some low-level gardening. I also like to play with my kids and help and watch them grow."

> *"From somewhere inside came the desire, almost the need, to write."*

Sources for Strasser's Books

In writing for young adults, Strasser draws upon his own adolescence, including his interest in sports, knowledge of science, love of the sea, and desire to be a doctor. During high school he also experienced the death of a close friend due to drunk driving, and he had another friend who suffered for many years from a progressively debilitating disease. Yet some of Strasser's books go beyond his own personal experiences. About the rock and roll trilogy (*Rock 'n' Roll Nights,* 1982; *Turn It Up!,* 1984; and *Wildlife,* 1988), Strasser states, "I think a point came where I went from writing about what I'd experienced to what I wished I experienced, and, frankly, I wished I'd been a rock and roll star. I still love rock and roll. Writing three books about it was sort of like going into a daily eight-hour daydream for two years about being a rock and roll musician."

debilitating weakening

Strasser's realistic fiction focuses on entertaining stories that mirror adolescent conflicts. He says in *Scholastic Authors Online,* "My ideas come from things I've experienced, things I wish I'd experienced, or things that really bother me. I then create conflicts and see how they get resolved. Almost always, there's a person who needs or wants something and there's an obstacle in his or her way. The story is about how they overcome the obstacle."

Beyond the Reef (1989) serves as an example of how Strasser's stories often involve resolving both an external and an internal conflict. Chris and his parents move to Key West to search for sunken Spanish treasure. Although initially it seems like an adventurous way of life, their lives gradually deteriorate, and ultimately Chris must make some difficult decisions. In this story, Chris is not only seeking sunken treasures but is also searching for what is important in life, what he believes in, and who he will be as an adult. At the end of the story, Chris states, "I learned that when you find something you love, you've got to stick with it no matter what. You can't ever give up. And if you work hard enough and long enough, you may not find all the treasure, but you'll find enough to get by" (p. 237).

In looking for dramatic and interesting conflicts, Strasser believes that writing about teenagers offers rich possibilities. He explains, "After all, no group of characters can be more

tumultuous confusing and overwhelming

volatile, impassioned, and sensitive than teenagers. No time of life is more tumultuous, aggravating, and poignant than adolescence (especially to adolescents). To me they are the best subjects one could hope to find for a dramatic story" ("Becoming a YA Novelist," p. 235).

The People in the Books

Strasser's main characters are usually decent young men, likable and believable but with real problems and concerns. His young men may drink a beer, but they do not use drugs; they may lust after girls, but they do not use them; and they also have a sense of humor. In *Workin' for Peanuts* (1983), Jeff Mead, a recent high school graduate with no clear plans for his future, expresses his doubts and confusion about life with a wry observation about human behavior:

> Lately I've been thinking a lot about why people are the way they are. I mean, why does my father give me such a hard time sometimes? And why does Rick feel that he has to steal and cheat and join a gang like the Derelicts? And why do girls like Sandra and Emily feel that they have to act superior? Sometimes I think that so much of the way people act is unnecessary. I mean, after all, what are we? We're just human animals really, just creatures that basically go from one feeding to the next, like goldfish. How come we have to complicate life so much? (P. 64)

Scott Tauscher, seventeen and dealing with his raging male hormones in *A Very Touchy Subject* (1985), is frustrated by his girlfriend's "hands-off" approach to their relationship. Sex seems to be everywhere, but for him it is still elusive. When his fifteen-year-old neighbor makes herself available to him, Scott is sorely tempted, even though he knows she has serious personal problems. Scott's father attempts to express his concerns, but Scott responds to him with a mixture of frustration and humor:

> My father pauses and clears his throat. "You've got to be careful when you, uh, fool around with a girl like

her, Scott. I mean, I was once a teenager and I know what it's like. And I imagine that a girl like Paula can be quite a temptation. But you must keep in mind that just one mistake can have a devastating effect on your life."

All I can do is stare at him. I don't know whether to laugh or what. "You think the only reason I've shown any concern about Paula Finkel is because I'm trying to get into her shorts?"

My father looks uncomfortable. "Well, it just seems like a possible explanation. The girl has lived next door for two years and you've never shown any interest before. And I'm not blaming you, son. I know what being a teenager is like. All I'm saying is, please be careful."

God, I wish he'd stop telling me he knows what being a teenager is like, because if he really knew, he would understand this a hell of a lot better. (Pp. 134-135)

Strasser's main characters are searching to understand their values and to develop a moral code to live by, often receiving mixed or confusing messages from the adults around them. In *The Accident* (1988), Matt Thompson, by sheer luck, is not with four of his friends when they are killed in a drunk driving accident. Everyone blames Chris, a wild kid from a poor family, but Matt senses there is more to the story. As he seeks to discover what really happened and why the influential adults in town are trying to cover it up, he must confront difficult questions about truth and power and justice.

> *Strasser's main characters are searching to understand their values and to develop a moral code to live by, often receiving mixed or confusing messages from the adults around them.*
>
>

"But isn't it immoral *not* to tell the people the truth?" asked Matt.

Mr. Stewart leaned toward him. "I'm not sure I know how to explain this to you, Matt. You're a bright kid, but you're also young and idealistic. What I think you're going to learn someday is that politics is a game of favors. In its crudest terms, it's 'I'll scratch your back if you'll scratch mine.' If the scratching is done for personal gain, then it's called corruption. If it's done for the good of the people, it's called politics." (Pp. 164–165)

David Gilbert, in *Friends Till the End* (1981), wrestles with his decision to turn down a full-ride soccer scholarship for college in order to enroll in a premed program. His decision disappoints his friends and his father, who was fulfilling his own needs for athletic success and recognition through David's high school soccer career.

> It was a gut feeling: soccer—no, doctor—yes. I couldn't explain it. How does anyone know what they want to do—other than just feeling that it's right for them? If I lived my life and looked back at the end and saw that I'd been a soccer player, I'd feel it wasn't worthwhile. But I couldn't tell that to Chunk. Maybe he'd look back and see that it was worthwhile. (P. 168)

Strasser's realistic fiction frequently deals with issues of popularity and social class. His own junior high school experiences were unhappy. "Life appeared to be divided into two groups—the popular and the unpopular," Strasser explains. "Convinced of my unpopularity, I tried to learn the secret of being accepted by the other side. But that only made things worse, and finally I became convinced that popularity was strictly genetic. Somehow I'd missed out on those genes." ("Becoming a YA Novelist," pp. 236–237)

Strasser's characters struggle with these same issues. In *Friends Till the End,* for example, David describes his girlfriend, Rena:

> She was part of the "sophisticated" newspaper-yearbook crowd—pretty, smart (some would say snobby), always dressed well, the kind who went to the city to see a new movie instead of waiting for it to come to the local theatre. I was just a jock. That meant we had different friends, different classes, different ideas. A jock and a smarty dating was Cooper's Neck High's version of a mixed couple. (Pp. 17–18)

full-ride all expenses paid

In *Workin' for Peanuts,* Jeff, a stadium vendor from a struggling working-class family, falls for Melissa, a wealthy, upper-class girl whose family owns the stadium. Initially they enjoy each other's company, but soon the differences between them become too big to ignore.

> "I'm sorry, Jeff. I just—I just never knew."
>
> "Knew what, Melissa?"
>
> "That you knew that kind of people," Melissa says.
>
> That kind of people? Oh, yeah, I see what she's saying. People who live in Rivington. Gangs and thieves and guys whose mothers have to drive buses for a living. Suddenly I don't feel so hopeful. It's like, face it, kid, for the rest of your life you're going to be one of that kind of people. The people who, as far as Melissa Stotts is concerned, are on the other side. Her words really hit me hard because I see now that when you get right down to the bottom line, Melissa looks at it the same way the rest of them do. Our side and their side. Us against them. But it's not fair for her to include me as one of them. (P. 190)

Most of Strasser's main characters avoid using drugs, although some of their friends may. Alex Lazar, in *Angel Dust Blues,* however, not only uses drugs but also becomes a dealer and then must face the difficult consequences.

> Now Alex felt frightened. That whole year, that whole change in his life had gone out of his control. It was no longer just between him and his absentee parents or between him and his irrelevant teachers or even between him and some of the nerds he went to school with. These men were the police and their idea of punishment was considerably more than losing a week's allowance or being kept after school for detention. In the back seat Alex pushed his knees together so that the detective next to him wouldn't notice that they were shaking. (Pp. 8–9)

In the rock and roll trilogy, Gary Specter, leader of the band, watches as the drummer, Karl, increasingly abuses drugs and alcohol. After a near-fatal accident forces Karl into treatment, he talks to Gary:

> "I always thought that if I got to be rich and famous I'd become a different person," Karl continued. "A person I liked more. Then we got rich and famous. I got rid of my pimples and I got my mother nice clothes and a nice place to live. But I was still the same Karl. Everything outside had changed, but nothing had changed inside. I used to go to sleep at night wondering if—no, *hoping*—I'd wake up in the morning and magically be someone else. But every morning I woke up and I was still me. It was like there was no escape from Karl Roesch and there never would be. And that's when I really started to go nuts." (P. 163)

Like most adolescents, Strasser's characters crisscross over the line separating adolescence from adulthood, between typical teenage antics and getting into serious trouble. They struggle to sort out their experiences and to learn from them.

Like most adolescents, Strasser's characters crisscross over the line separating adolescence from adulthood, between typical teenage antics and getting into serious trouble. They struggle to sort out their experiences and to learn from them. David and his friends, in *Friends Till the End,* try to understand the implications of Howie's battle with leukemia:

> I guess for the first time in our lives we were understanding that things like disease and death could happen to us. You grow up thinking you're pretty much invulnerable and then one day you meet someone like Howie, someone your own age, and bang—it hits you. (P. 174)

After Alex is arrested in *Angel Dust Blues,* he tries to figure out where the line is set and why:

> Alex wondered if there was some kind of line you crossed, not in terms of age, but in terms of what you did, that separated you from that great mass of fun-loving young people known as "the kids." If you

smoked cigarettes in the bathroom at school, even if you smoked grass in the bathroom, you were still a kid. . . .

But if you sold grass you crossed the line. You were no longer a "kid," you were now a "dealer," as if it took some great sinister effort to sell a drug rather than simply take it. But it didn't. It was deceptively easy to sell a few joints of grass, and from there it wasn't much harder to sell a nickel bag, or an ounce or even a pound. (P. 11)

In *The Accident,* Matt tries to understand Chris's self-destructive behavior. Matt drives Chris to school when Chris tells him:

"Yeah, I'm still wasted." Chris tapped the side of his head with his hand. "Can't see straight." He went to the passenger side and got in. . . .

"Went to bed smashed, got up smashed," Chris groaned.

Matt could tell he was proud of that. It was part of that peculiar burnout creed: the more messed up you were, the cooler you were. (P. 30)

Many of Strasser's books for younger audiences combine humor, science, and a bit of the supernatural. In *The Complete Computer Popularity Program* (1984), *The Mall from Outer Space* (1987), *Help! I'm Trapped in My Teacher's Body* (1993), and *Please Don't Be Mine, Julie Valentine!* (1994), Strasser's own offbeat sense of humor is readily apparent. When asked where he gets such zany ideas, Strasser replies, "I get my ideas from thinking up weird situations and how normal kids would deal with them" (*Scholastic Authors Online,* 1995). His historical fiction, also for younger audiences, combines excitement and adventure within a historical context. In all of his books for younger readers, Strasser's main characters are basically good kids but independent-minded and prone to take risks that sometimes backfire on them.

Other Works

Strasser is well known for his novelization of screenplays such as *Free Willy, Home Alone,* and *Ferris Bueller's Day Off.* *The Wave* (1981) was published originally under the pseudonym of Morton Rhue but has been reissued in his real name. Strasser has written more than thirty novelizations. About them, he says, "I do a lot of novelizations because they're fun and they help me make money so that I can write my original books. I like books better. It takes about three weeks to write a novelization while it takes one to two years to write a book. I write the novelization from the screenplay while they're filming the movie. Someone else has already written the screenplay, however" (*Scholastic Authors Online,* 1995).

In the late 1980s and early 1990s Strasser wrote for several television shows, including *Tribes, Riviera,* and *Guiding Light.* He also adapted his book *The Accident* into the television movie *Over the Limit.*

Strasser starts writing every weekday morning around 8:30 in a room of his house that he uses as an office. He writes on a laptop computer, which he often takes with him when he travels to speak at schools and conferences. On most days, he writes until about 1:00 P.M., then takes a break to eat lunch, run errands, and walk his dog. Around 2:30 he returns to his office and writes until dinnertime. He also conducts writing workshops for young people and speaks at conferences, schools, and libraries about the craft of writing. About his life as an author, Strasser says, "I like to write and it seems to me to be a lot more fun than selling life insurance. I love producing books. I love laughing at my own dumb jokes, and I love not having a boss and not having to sit in boring meetings" (*Scholastic Authors Online,* 1995).

> *About his life as an author, Strasser says, "I like to write and it seems to me to be a lot more fun than selling life insurance."*
>
>

Readers who enjoy Todd Strasser's works might also enjoy the works of Leon Garfield and Gordon Korman.

Selected Bibliography

WORKS BY TODD STRASSER

Novels

Angel Dust Blues (1979)

Friends Till the End (1981)

Rock 'n' Roll Nights (1982)

Workin' for Peanuts (1983)

The Complete Computer Popularity Program (1984)
Turn It Up! (1984)
A Very Touchy Subject (1985)
The Mall from Outer Space (1987)
The Accident (1988)
Wildlife (1988)
Beyond the Reef (1989)
Moving Target, with Dennis Freeland (1989)
The Diving Bell (1992)
Help! I'm Trapped in My Teacher's Body (1993)
Summer's End (1993)
Summer's Promise (1993)
Abe Lincoln for Class President (1994)
Street Fighter (1994)
Help! I'm Trapped in the First Day of School (1994)
Please Don't Be Mine, Julie Valentine! (1994)
Help! I'm Trapped in Obedience School (1995)
Howl-A-Ween (1995)
How I Changed My Life (1995)
Who's That Guy? (In the All-Girl Band) (1995)
Wordsworth Series (1995)

Novels for Adults
The Family Man (1988)

Novelizations of Screenplays
The Wave (1981)
Ferris Bueller's Day Off (1985)
Cookie (1989)
Pink Cadillac (1989)
Home Alone (1990)
Walt Disney's "Peter Pan" (1990)
Home Alone 2: Lost in New York (1992)
Honey, I Blew Up the Kid (1992)
Addams Family Values (1993)
The Beverly Hillbillies (1993)
Disney's Villains Collection: Stories from the Film (1993)
Free Willy (1993)
The Good Son (1993)

Disney's It's Magic!: Stories from the Films (1994)
Walt Disney's "Lady and the Tramp" (1994)

How to Write to the Author

Todd Strasser
c/o HarperCollins Publishers
10 East 53rd Street
New York, NY 10022

WORKS ABOUT TODD STRASSER

"Becoming a YA Novelist." In *The VOYA Reader.* Edited by Dorothy M. Broderick. Metuchen, N.J.: Scarecrow, 1990, pp. 235–239.
Scholastic Authors Online, 1995.

Edward Stratemeyer

(1862-1930)

by Deidre A. Johnson

Edward Stratemeyer did not write most of the books that made him famous. Many were actually issued years after his death. Although he enjoyed writing, his most significant contributions to fiction for young adults occurred because he turned writing into a production process, resulting in books that were not only literary creations but also commodities. In fact, the names of some of his characters, like Nancy Drew and the Hardy Boys, are now trademarked, affording them the same legal protection as a product name. And, like commercial products, they are regularly revised and repackaged to appeal to the tastes of a new generation of consumers.

Edward Stratemeyer

Stratemeyer was born on 4 October 1862 in Elizabeth, New Jersey. He began his career by writing fiction for boys' story papers—inexpensive periodicals, resembling newspapers,

> *He quickly established himself in this market, selling more than seventy serials from 1889 through 1906, using his own name and at least a dozen pseudonyms.*

pseudonyms fictitious or pen names

Horatio Alger (1832–1899) was an American author of novels for boys. He became famous for his "rags to riches" tales of boys from poor backgrounds achieving fame and wealth through honest, hard work.

that published serialized stories—and magazines. He quickly established himself in this market, selling more than seventy serials from 1889 through 1906, using his own name and at least a dozen pseudonyms. Although he wrote several types of stories, including science fiction, school stories, and outdoor and travel adventures, many of his serials imitated the Horatio Alger success tale but with light mystery incorporated into the plot. They often traced an adolescent's efforts to unravel some mystery concerning his family or a lost inheritance, a forerunner of the type of problems that many of his series characters would face. A prolific writer, Stratemeyer also penned sixty-two dime novels—including thirty-three detective stories—from 1890 to 1898. From about 1893 to 1897, he gained additional experience in juvenile fiction by editing several story papers.

Stratemeyer's transition into clothbound series books, the field he later dominated, came in 1894 with *Richard Dare's Venture* and *Last Cruise of the Spitfire*. Both were revisions of story-paper serials. His first original book, *Under Dewey at Manila* (1898), capitalized on the then-current interest in the Spanish-American war and marked his entry into historical fiction. In 1899, he began the Rover Boys and developed the formula used successfully in many later series: several outgoing, assertive, upper-middle-class adolescents uncover adventure (and sometimes mystery) while traveling or attending school.

The Stratemeyer Syndicate and Its Series

An entrepreneur, Stratemeyer sought ways to increase book production, and, about 1904, he founded the Stratemeyer Literary Syndicate, his fiction factory. He created plots for series books, then hired competent writers to turn them into book-length manuscripts, which he purchased outright for a flat fee (usually about $125). He also occasionally bought rights to others' books or stories and arranged to publish them. Around 1906, Stratemeyer suggested that publishers reduce the price of his series books from one dollar to fifty cents, in order to promote additional sales.

With these arrangements in place, Stratemeyer concentrated on diversifying his series offerings. Between 1906 and

1930, he launched more than eighty series aimed at every possible interest. He created series about moviemaking (Motion Picture Chums, Moving Picture Girls), aviation (Air Service Boys, Ted Scott), athletics (Baseball Joe, Girls of Central High), transportation (Ralph of the Railroad, Motor Girls, Motor Boys), technology (Radio Boys, Radio Girls), science fiction (Great Marvel, Tom Swift), careers (Blythe Girls, Boys of Business), western and outdoor life (Saddle Boys, Outdoor Chums), schoolgirls (Billie Bradley, Betty Gordon), anthropomorphic toys and animals (Make-Believe, Kneetime Animal series), and young children (Bobbsey Twins, Six Little Bunkers). At one point, he had more than thirty pseudonymous series in progress.

Leslie McFarlane and the Early Hardy Boys

Stratemeyer's first mystery series, Nat Ridley, appeared in 1926, the same year in which he hired a Canadian journalist, Leslie McFarlane (1902–1977), to ghostwrite volumes in the Dave Fearless adventure series. As McFarlane states in *The Ghost of the Hardy Boys,* ghostwriting was hack work; the money enabled him to leave his newspaper job and to spend his mornings dashing off chapters of Dave Fearless' wildly implausible adventures and his afternoons lovingly crafting more serious pieces for literary magazines.

ghostwriting writing for and under someone else's name

After three Dave Fearless titles, Stratemeyer sent McFarlane outlines for a new series, the Hardy Boys, to be published under the pseudonym Franklin W. Dixon. The series featured two teenage brothers, sons of famous detective Fenton Hardy, who hope someday to become professional detectives like their father. The pair solve mysteries in and around their hometown of Bayport, frequently by assisting Fenton. McFarlane wrote in *Ghost of the Hardy Boys* that he found these a refreshing "change from Dave Fearless[.] No man-eating sharks. . . . No cannibals, polar bears or man-eating trees. Just the everyday doings of everyday lads in everyday surroundings" (p. 63). He thought that the series "deserved something better than slapdash treatment," that he could "contribute a little style, occasional words of more than two syllables, maybe a little sensory stimuli [and humor]" (pp. 63–64).

In "The Great Hardys," John Seebeck demonstrates how McFarlane's attitude shaped these early stories. The first eleven, all written by McFarlane from outlines primarily by Stratemeyer, show the greatest continuity, especially in the use of recurring secondary characters, many of whom later virtually disappear from the series. McFarlane placed the Hardy boys, fifteen-year-old Joe and sixteen-year-old Frank, in a boyish world with friends, outings, and practical jokes. He sometimes devoted entire chapters to escapades unconnected with the mystery and included "the things that boys like (caves, tunnels, spooky old houses, food . . .)" and "create[d] atmosphere [through] detailed descriptions" (p. 6).

Plots commonly dealt with only one or two mysteries rather than several. Although the Hardys were never average boys (what average teenager owned a motorcycle and a speedboat and received a $1,000 reward for solving a mystery in the 1920s?), McFarlane's use of realistic secondary characters, detailed settings, and minor incidents developed a more natural environment that was lacking in later volumes.

Mildred Wirt Benson and the Early Nancy Drew

In 1929, Stratemeyer created another mystery series to be published under a new pseudonym, Carolyn Keene, and assigned the outlines to Mildred Wirt Benson (1905–). A journalist like McFarlane, Wirt Benson had started with the Syndicate in 1926 and worked on an existing series, Ruth Fielding, before Stratemeyer entrusted her with his new offering. It featured a sixteen-year-old girl, Nancy Drew. Like the Hardys, she had a flair for finding and solving mysteries and a famous father, the attorney Carson Drew, who sometimes asked her assistance on difficult cases. In *Rediscovering Nancy Drew*, Deidre Johnson quotes Wirt Benson's statement that with Nancy she tried to create a character who was different from the "namby-pamby type of heroine that had been dominating series books for many, many years" (p. 36).

Stratemeyer was not pleased with the result. An old-fashioned man, he found Wirt Benson's Nancy "too flip . . . too vivacious," too radical a departure from traditional heroines. But despite his misgivings, he relayed the manuscript to the publisher, whose enthusiastic response convinced him to allow Wirt Benson's characterization to stand.

Harriet Adams and Edna Stratemeyer

Accepting Wirt Benson's characterization of Nancy and using her manuscript without significant alterations was one of Stratemeyer's last decisions for the Syndicate. He became ill and died on 10 May 1930. His two daughters, Harriet Stratemeyer Adams (1892–1982) and Edna Stratemeyer (later Edna Squier, 1895–1974), assumed control. Adams had edited manuscripts for her father in 1914 and 1915, before her marriage, but Stratemeyer had not permitted her to work for him after she wed. After his death, she again began editing manuscripts, as well as creating outlines and dealing with publishers. Her sister's role is less clear, although it is known that she too plotted manuscripts and handled some correspondence with ghostwriters until she left the Syndicate in 1942. The sisters soon dropped many existing series, but they also added several new mystery series. One, issued under the Carolyn Keene pseudonym, was the Dana Girls series about two schoolgirl sleuths at boarding school.

The Hardy Boys

McFarlane and Wirt Benson continued to write most of the Hardy Boys and Nancy Drew titles and some Dana Girls books, but a few changes occurred. Hardy Boys plots became more complex, incorporating anywhere from four to eight mysteries, all interconnected. The somewhat more "bizarre . . . and sometimes eerie" plots occasionally contained elements of science fiction and horror stories, as John Seebeck writes in "The Great Hardys." No longer merely greedy criminals, villains acquired macabre overtones, as with Pedro Vincenzo from *The Mark on the Door* (1934), "who liked to brand his personal insignia on the foreheads of his victims" (p. 15). Many of the longer descriptions disappeared. The latter may have been a result of Adams' tighter editing or of the sisters' use of increasingly more detailed outlines, which left writers less freedom to add their own material.

characterization method by which a writer creates and develops the appearance and personality of a character

> *Nancy Drew enjoys a dignity, freedom, and autonomy that, at the time, were accorded almost exclusively to males, an association strengthened by the object that characterizes her independence: her blue roadster.*

paradoxical nature of the nature of someone with contradictory qualities

The books also incorporated elements found in several earlier—and many subsequent—Hardy Boys tales. Many of the stories dealt with technology or scientific discoveries. Arthur Prager, in his *Rascals at Large,* finds that plots frequently followed a five-stage pattern: after accepting a case, the brothers receive a threat or warning to desist (stage one), but they continue undaunted, aided by a convenient coincidence that puts them on the trail of a suspect (stage two). They soon encounter trouble (stage three) but continue their pursuit until they are captured (stage four), ultimately escaping or being rescued, bringing the criminals to justice, and receiving a generous reward (stage five). Outdoor settings and trendy, fast transportation—key elements since volume one—remained essential to the series.

Nancy Drew

The Nancy Drew series also experienced some alterations. Adams took a particular interest in Nancy Drew, somewhat to Wirt Benson's discomfort, and began modifying her character. According to Johnson in *Rediscovering Nancy Drew,* Wirt Benson explained, "There was a beginning conflict in what is Nancy. Mrs. Adams . . . was more cultured and more refined [than I was]. . . . We just had two different types of Nancys" (pp. 36–37). Not only did Nancy become somewhat "more refined," she also gained two new best friends, series regulars Bess Marvin and George Fayne, and a boyfriend, Ned Nickerson. In keeping with her new character, Nancy treated the Drews' housekeeper Hannah Gruen more graciously, and Hannah evolved into more of a friend and maternal figure.

Books from this period firmly established the essential and paradoxical nature of the "classic" Nancy Drew. Nancy enjoys a dignity, freedom, and autonomy that, at the time, were accorded almost exclusively to males, an association strengthened by the object that characterizes her independence: her *blue* roadster. Yet Nancy is not masculine. While her character traits "counter every stereotype of 'feminine' weakness, including such standard fictional attributes as frivolity, vanity, squeamishness . . . irrationality . . . [and] incompetence," Nancy is also a lady, well-mannered, well-dressed, and modest, according to Anne MacLeod in "Nancy Drew and Her Rivals" (pp. 445, 449). She works amid settings that "are all feminine, domestic, aristocratic, slightly Gothic," writes Bobbie Ann Mason in *The Girl Sleuth* (p. 57). And, according to Patricia Craig and Mary Cadogan in *The Lady Investigates,* even the titles of books—and the objects central to the mysteries, "the old albums, stagecoaches, dancing puppets, scarlet slippers, and so on . . . [—are] objects with a traditional appeal for girls" (p. 155).

Changes in the Syndicate and Series

McFarlane stopped writing for the Syndicate in 1947. Wirt Benson left in 1948, the same year in which yet another journalist, Andrew Svenson (1910–1975) was hired as a writer and editor. During the next decade, although Adams continued to draft outlines for most of the books, various ghostwriters penned the manuscripts, some of which were then extensively revised by the Syndicate. From 1957 until 1980, Adams outlined and wrote most of the Nancy Drew books herself, and Syndicate staff edited them. An assortment of writers, including Adams and Svenson (who became a Syndicate partner in 1961), created outlines and manuscripts for the Hardy Boys.

These personnel shifts precipitated additional changes in the series. Prior to 1957, books had averaged 210 to 215 pages; after 1957, with a new and younger generation of readers, the Syndicate decreased the length by approximately 20 percent. Kathleen Chamberlain writes in "The Secrets of Nancy Drew" that the stories "move forward at breakneck pace." Along with this change, the Syndicate modified the writing style, deleting many extraneous scenes that had added atmosphere or developed character, simplifying the vocabulary and sentence structure, and adding educational material. Nancy and the Hardys also became two years older.

The streamlined versions successfully reached their target audience, but many of those familiar with the earlier versions criticized the bland writing and characterizations and the "substitution of empty action for prolonged drama and suspense," as John Seebeck relates in "The Great Hardys." In 1959, the Syndicate also began revising existing titles in both series. They removed ethnic stereotypes and dated material, and they adjusted the style to conform to current offerings. In some cases, the rewriting was so extensive that only the title remained unchanged.

The New Syndicate

Adams died in 1982. Two years later, Simon & Schuster—the Syndicate's new publisher since 1979—purchased the Syndicate. Concerned that they were losing older readers, Simon & Schuster devised a strategy to reach young adults: they split each series, continuing the original in digest-sized paperbacks, and creating a new line of "smaller, adult-size" paperbacks for adolescents (the Nancy Drew Files and Hardy Boys Casefiles). Responsibility for acquiring manuscripts shifted to Mega-Books, a book packager. Freelance writers submitted one-page synopses of proposed stories, followed by detailed outlines and final drafts. The staff at Mega-Books worked in conjunction with an editor at Simon & Schuster to select, critique, and edit these submissions. Such methods were necessary because of the number of titles issued each year: early in the series, volumes appeared annually; later, the digest-sized series were published bimonthly and the young adult series monthly.

synopses condensed statements or outlines of narratives

Nancy and the Hardys in the 1980s and 1990s

Digest-sized Nancy has gone through several phases. As Betsy Caprio writes in *The Mystery of Nancy Drew,* books from the early 1980s sometimes turn her into "a quasi-Gothic novel heroine . . . beset by everything from flying saucers to vampires" (pp. 25–26). Those from the late 1980s and after restore much of the traditional Nancy, but often amid contemporary settings. The Nancy Drew Files offer a different, more adolescent Nancy, one interested in dating, fashions, and shopping, sometimes to the detriment of her cases. She inhabits a trendy world, almost entirely peopled by young, affluent Caucasians, and investigates cases at fashion magazines, ski resorts, spas, and similarly glamorous sites. Surprisingly, amid all her modernity, Nancy's methods of detection have changed little in fifty years: unlike the Hardy

Boys, who drive a van full of sophisticated surveillance and tracking equipment, Nancy rarely employs technology more advanced than her lock-picking kit (another indication, perhaps, of gender distinctions between the series).

The larger, digest-sized Hardy Boys continue the regular series, drawing on current events and concerns for many of their plots. Later volumes restore minor characters from early in the series and seem especially well written. One study of the books, Ian McMahan's "Today's Hardy Boys Adventures," notes that they (as well as the Casefiles) "map onto the psychological differences" between preteens and adolescents by giving the culprits simpler, "one-dimensional" motives (such as greed), rather than the more complex or morally ambiguous motives found in some Casefiles.

The Hardy Boys Casefiles initially differed from the digest paperbacks in other ways. The first volume makes a dramatic break with the past by killing Joe's girlfriend of many decades with a terrorist bomb (although she lives on in the digest series). The boys, now high school graduates, soon achieve a semiprofessional status, undertaking assignments for a top secret government organization. They jet about the globe tracking professional assassins, traitors, and saboteurs, moving through a dark, dangerous, and adult world. Volumes from the 1990s restore a more familiar environment: the Hardys are again in high school, but with freedom to investigate crimes that frequently deal with current trends or high technology, such as pirating computer software.

Recombinant Nancy Drew and The Hardy Boys

Simon & Schuster also capitalized on the characters' popularity by launching related series. Nancy and the Hardys, who had been paired in a television series from the 1970s, team up in the Nancy Drew and the Hardy Boys Be a Detective Mystery Stories, modeled on Choose Your Own Adventure books; in several volumes of short stories; and in the Nancy Drew & Hardy Boys Super Mysteries, using the characters from the Files and Casefiles. The Hardy Boys also join inventor Tom Swift for two science fiction adventures, while one of the Nancy Drew Files, *The Suspect Next Door,* introduces a new series, River Heights (Nancy's hometown).

A cross between Sweet Valley High and a soap opera, River Heights focuses on the romantic and social problems of students in a local high school, using stereotypically good (that is, generous, honest, kind) and bad (that is, conceited, conniving, deceitful) characters. Most volumes employ cliffhanger endings, resolving one character's problems but presenting another character's new dilemma to be addressed in the next book. In 1994, an eight-year-old Nancy begins investigating grade school mysteries in the Nancy Drew Notebooks. In 1995, a college-age Nancy, accompanied by Bess and George, enrolls in Wilder University in the Nancy Drew on Campus series; there she ends her sixty-five-year relationship with Ned Nickerson and chooses to divide her time between dating, socializing, sleuthing, and studying.

In the decades since their inception, the Hardy Boys and Nancy Drew have experienced many alterations and permutations. Although Stratemeyer's basic premise and ideas for the series still underlie much of the digest-sized Nancy Drew Mystery Stories and Hardy Boys Mystery Stories (and, to a lesser extent, the Files and Casefiles series), the spin-offs—especially the newer Nancy Drew offerings—reflect a different sensibility, one that alters Stratemeyer and his daughters' vision of the characters and concept.

The marketability and readability of the series stem from many factors: some talented writers, appealing protagonists, exciting stories, reader identification, wish fulfillment, and the series' continuing awareness of contemporary tastes and trends. This winning combination initially occurred through Stratemeyer's design and efforts: his daughters and, later, Simon & Schuster strove to maintain it with varying degrees of success. As with any successful commodity, the production methods, packaging, and composition of the series have changed over time—and will undoubtedly continue to evolve to reach further generations of consumers.

In the decades since their inception, the Hardy Boys and Nancy Drew have experienced many alterations and permutations (changes).

If you enjoy reading books from the Stratemeyer Syndicate series, you also may like books by Sir Arthur Conan Doyle, Jay Bennett, Lois Duncan, or Sue Ellen Bridgers.

Selected Bibliography

WORKS BY EDWARD STRATEMEYER

Series Published Under Stratemeyer's Name
Bound to Succeed, 3 vols. (1894–1899)
Ship and Shore, 3 vols. (1894–1900)

Old Glory, 6 vols. (1898–1901)

Colonial, 6 vols. (1901–1906)

Series Published Under the Pseudonym Captain Ralph Bonehill

Young Sportsman, 5 vols. (1897–ca. 1902)

Mexican War, 3 vols. (1900–1902)

Boy Hunters, 4 vols. (1906–1910)

Series Published Under the Pseudonym Arthur M. Winfield

Rover Boys, 30 vols. (1899–1926)

Putnam Hall, 6 vols. (1901–1911)

SELECTED SERIES PRODUCED BY THE STRATEMEYER SYNDICATE

Series Published Under the Pseudonym Franklin W. Dixon

Ted Scott Flying Series, 20 vols. (1927–1943)

Hardy Boys Mystery Series (1927–)

Hardy Boys Casefiles (1987–)

Tom Swift and Hardy Boys Ultra Thriller, 2 vols. (1992–1993)

Series Published Under the Pseudonym Carolyn Keene

Nancy Drew Mystery Stories (1930–)

Dana Girls, 34 vols. (1934–1979)

Nancy Drew Picture Books, 2 vols. (1977)

Nancy Drew Ghost Stories, 2 vols. (1983–1985)

Nancy Drew Files (1986–)

River Heights, 17 vols. (1989–1992)

Nancy Drew Notebooks (1994–)

Nancy Drew on Campus (1995–)

Series Published Under the Joint Pseudonyms Carolyn Keene and Franklin W. Dixon

Nancy Drew and the Hardy Boys Super Sleuths, 2 vols. (1981–1984)

Nancy Drew & the Hardy Boys Be a Detective Mystery Stories, 6 vols. (1984–1985)

Other Selected Stratemeyer Syndicate Series

Bobbsey Twins, by Laura Lee Hope. 115 vols. (1904–1992)

Tom Swift, by Victor Appleton. 40 vols. (1910–1941)

Bomba the Jungle Boy, by Roy Rockwood. 20 vols. (1926–1938)

Kay Tracey Mystery Stories, by Frances K. Judd. 18 vols. (1934–1942)

Mel Martin Baseball Stories, by John R. Cooper. 6 vols. (1947–1953)

Happy Hollisters, by Jerry West. 33 vols. (1953–1970)

Tom Swift, Jr., by Victor Appleton, II. 33 vols. (1954–1971)

Honey Bunch and Norman, by Helen Louise Thorndyke. 12 vols. (1957–1963)

Linda Craig, by Ann Sheldon. 23 vols. (1962–1964; 1981–1990)

Tom Swift (III), by Victor Appleton. 11 vols. (1981–1984)

Tom Swift, Jr., by Victor Appleton. 13 vols. (1991–1993)

WORKS ABOUT EDWARD STRATEMEYER

Billman, Carol. *The Secret of the Stratemeyer Syndicate: Nancy Drew, The Hardy Boys, and the Million Dollar Fiction Factory.* New York: Ungar, 1986.

Caprio, Betsy. *The Mystery of Nancy Drew: Girl Sleuth on the Couch.* Trabuco Canyon, Cal.: Source Books, 1992.

Chamberlain, Kathleen. "The Secrets of Nancy Drew: Having Their Cake and Eating It Too." *The Lion and the Unicorn,* June 1994, pp. 1–12.

Craig, Patricia, and Mary Cadogan. *The Lady Investigates: Women Detectives and Spies in Fiction.* New York: St. Martin's Press, 1981.

Dizer, John T. *Tom Swift and Company.* Jefferson, N.C.: McFarland, 1982.

Dyer, Carolyn Stewart, and Nancy Tillman Romalov. *Rediscovering Nancy Drew.* Iowa City: University of Iowa Press, 1995.

"For It Was Indeed He." *Fortune,* April 1934, pp. 86–89.

Greenberg, Anne. "Fashioning the New Nancy Drews." In *Rediscovering Nancy Drew.* Edited by Carolyn Stewart Dyer and Nancy Tillman Romalov. Iowa City: Univ. of Iowa Press, 1995, pp. 66–72.

Johnson, Deidre. *Edward Stratemeyer and the Stratemeyer Syndicate.* New York: Twayne, 1993.

————. "From Paragraphs to Pages: The Writing and Development of Stratemeyer Syndicate Series." In *Rediscovering Nancy Drew*. Edited by Carolyn Stewart Dyer and Nancy Tillman Romalov. Iowa City: Univ. of Iowa Press, 1995, pp. 29–40.

————. *Stratemeyer Pseudonyms and Series Books: An Annotated Checklist of Stratemeyer and Stratemeyer Syndicate Publications*. Westport, Conn: Greenwood, 1982.

Keeline, James D. "The Secret of Box MSS 107; or, What the Nancy Axelrad Papers Revealed." 2 parts. *Newsboy,* January/February–March/April 1994, pp. 11–18; 11–16.

————. "Who Wrote the Hardy Boys? Secrets from the Syndicate Files Revealed." *Yellowback Library,* November 1994, pp. 13–16.

————. "Who Wrote Nancy Drew? Secrets from the Syndicate Files Revealed." *Yellowback Library,* January 1995, pp. 5–8.

Lapin, Geoff. "The Outline of a Ghost." *Lion and the Unicorn,* June 1994, pp. 60–69.

MacLeod Anne. "Nancy Drew and Her Rivals: No Contest." Part III. *Horn Book,* July/August 1987, pp. 422–450.

Mason, Bobbie Ann. *The Girl Sleuth: A Feminist Guide.* Old Westbury, N.Y.: Feminist Press, 1976.

McFarlane, Leslie. *Ghost of the Hardy Boys.* New York: Two Continents, 1976.

McMahan, Ian. "Today's Hardy Boys Adventures: A Social-Developmental Analysis." *Dime Novel Round-Up,* October 1994, pp. 83–89.

Phillips, Louis. "Me and the Hardy Boys." *The Armchair Detective,* vol. 15, no. 2, 1982, pp. 174–77.

Prager, Arthur. *Rascals at Large; or, The Clue in the Old Nostalgia.* Garden City, N.Y.: Doubleday, 1971.

Seebeck, John. "The Great Hardys." In 3 parts. *Yellowback Library,* February/April 1991, pp. 5–9 (Feb.), 14–17 (Mar.), and 11–14 (Apr.).

Wirt Benson, Mildred. "The Ghost of Ladora." *Books at Iowa,* November 1973, pp. 24–29.

Rosemary Sutcliff

(1920–1992)

by Bea Naff

It is a dreary day. The library seems like you—practically empty. You think, *I'll check out by checking out some scribbles.* So you comb the stacks, hoping for a thriller, but instead you hit upon your first Rosemary Sutcliff book, *The Lantern Bearers* (1959). You flip the yellowing cover page as you stumble upon an antiquated map with place names like *Brigantes, Ordovices, Aquae Sulie, Londinium, Calleva Atrebatum, Rutupiae,* and *Segontium.*

You look further for some translation key. To your relief, you see "Britain at the time of this story." But then you think, Did the Rolling Stones tour these places? Is this book for me? You flip further. . . .

For you who flip further, the books of Rosemary Sutcliff may provide a temporary exit from the shopping malls and fast-food chains that glut your modern days. She takes you back through British history via imaginative re-creations that are uniquely hers. She shares her versions of Arthurian legends, charioteers, Roman rule, and Bronze Age lore. Like

glut   fill and crowd

251

Like many of you, Sutcliff enjoyed imagining alternate worlds that are partially based on historical legend or fact.

many of you, Sutcliff liked imagining alternate worlds that are partially supported by historical legend or fact. In a way, she was a "dungeons and dragons" type from the 1950s, sustaining her historical fantasies with blank pages instead. As an author, she drew from childhood stories, her artistic sensibilities, and her own historical research as she imaginatively configured Britain in bygone days.

Rosemary's Start as Writer

At an early age Rosemary Sutcliff was forced to spend many hours alone without much youthful activity. Throughout her life in Devonshire, England, she suffered from an arthritic condition that confined her to a wheelchair. In fact, she suffered so much that it barred her from a traditional school setting. When loved ones would visit, she wanted to tell them stories. Her mother shared classic fairy tales along with stories by Kenneth Grahame and Rudyard Kipling. Her dad, a naval officer, regaled her with fantastic stories about his voyages to distant seas.

tenacious determined

Rosemary could have let her condition cripple her, but she was tenacious. She devised ways to release herself from her paralyzing condition, finding freedom in artistic expression. Instead of sharpening her tennis serves, she would sharpen her observational skills. As a teenager, she became an expert miniaturist painter and won several awards for her work, making it all the way to the Royal Academy by the time she had just turned twenty.

At twenty-five, Rosemary was ready to begin writing, since her painting "was becoming more of an exercise than an art." In *Rosemary Sutcliff: A Walck Monograph*, by Margaret Meek, Rosemary describes her composing process as a highly creative one that involves both inspiration and sheer labor:

For me the whole thing starts with the basic idea, which has nothing to do with the plot—that comes later . . . I have to wait and eventually an idea comes sometimes from outside, from having read something perhaps, or from going to an old house and wondering what the people were like who lived in it . . . .

I [then] invest in a large red notebook and get to work collecting my notes. I always start off with the encyclopedia. Not only does it help with a bit of something about everything: it also provides a list of books. So I emerge with a long list of books and then tackle the County Library. Of course, all have bibliographies at the back, so the thing goes on like a snowball. Little by little. . . the picture begins to emerge. (P. 12)

After engaging in elaborate brainstorming and fact-finding, she then begins to compose:

I get down to what I enjoy much more, recreating the daily life of the people: the sort of houses they lived in, how they were furnished, what food they ate and how it was cooked, what they grew in their gardens, how they travelled, their clothes and weapons, and, very important from my point of view, what songs they sang and what stories they told round the fire at nights.

I do not put much of the plot into my red exercise book because it changes so much. . . . I make a draft outline, two or three thousand words, and then start writing. It takes four drafts—or rather three and a fair copy—to get the story properly into shape. That means about eight months' work and usually a couple of months' research beforehand. (*Rosemary Sutcliff: A Walck Monograph*, pp. 12–13)

Sutcliff's life history and explanation of her composing process do much to help readers appreciate her unique style and central theme.

Rosemary Sutcliff's Style and Central Theme

Sutcliff's description of her writing process is apt because a review of her work suggests that her stylistic specialty is setting and scenery. She does an excellent job of capturing diverse communities and geographies in specific detail. Cadwan, the harpist who serves as narrator in *Song for a Dark Queen* (1978), captures the flow of life around A.D. 30 in the northeastern part of England, where the Iceni flourished prior to Roman invasion. Sutcliff fills his descriptive reverie with insights about the terrain, weapons, social caste, and mood of the day:

caste   class

> A day in hawthorn time came when the Lady Boudicca was six years old, and the King her father had moved down to his summer steading with all his household, as he often did at that time of year, to see how the foals on the southern runs were shaping. And in the lag end of the night, a man on a sweating horse brought word of raiders within our borders, loose in the grazing land between the forest and the fens. Then the king and his sword-companions came out from sleep, calling for spears and horses, there were flaring torches and the trampling of war-ponies brought from the stables, and a yelping of horns to summon the fighting men from round about, just as I had known it all a score and a score of times before.

Likewise, in *The Capricorn Bracelet* (1973), the Roman wine merchant's son describes Londinium (London) prior to Boudicca's attack as if he wants the reader to love it as passionately and as particularly as he:

wharves and jetties piers and breakwaters of a port

basilica   official government building in the ancient world

> It was a rich and busy merchant town already, with shipping coming and going up and down the broad river or lying alongside the crowded wharves and jetties; and a great forum where the markets were held and the people gathered on all kinds of public occasions; a basilica along one side of it, where the Magistrates met to govern the city; and temples and bathhouses, and long straight streets where the noise of carts and hooves and chariots and feet went on all day and most of the night. It was a very new city, mind you, in fact in places it was still something of a shanty town, because we—the Romans, that is—had been less than twenty years in Britain.

Setting descriptions like these abound throughout all Sutcliff's books.

Rosemary Sutcliff's life struggles are also evident in her work. Most of her books have a heroic theme and plot structure that suggest that the hero or heroine must sacrifice self to a larger social purpose before they find acceptance and a sense of self within cherished communities. In addition, these young heroes must struggle with their identities as they come to terms with their potentially crippling conditions, be they emotional, political, or physical. As Margaret Meek has aptly noted in her biographical monograph (1962), Sutcliff constantly crafts "maimed heros" (p. 61). The maimed find their "true" identities by forgetting about their petty ailments as they fully participate in the struggles of their day. For example, in the Bronze Age (3000–1000 B.C.) *Warrior Scarlet,* Drem has to prove himself a man and worthy of his warrior scarlet, a finely woven cloth made by his mother. To do this, he must slay a wolf with his spear, but Drem's right arm is withered, so he must learn to use a throwing spear with his left arm. He finds support for his challenge through Talore, the great one-armed warrior. After proper training at the Boys' House, he is more than ready for the challenge, surpassing boys with healthy arms. Yet when the wolf appears, Drem is caught off guard. He panics and ends up slaying a beautiful white swan. He is banished to the shepherd people, who stress virtues such as caring and patience. With them he becomes a fine shepherd, eventually slaying the wolf that would destroy their sheep. Because of his self-sacrifice, Drem eventually gets his warrior scarlet. Sutcliff suggests that the hero will gain entry into his cherished community as he loses himself in its struggles.

Other maimed heroes face similar challenges. In *The Dark Queen,* the suppressed Iceni Queen Boudicca (A.D. 62) fights back for her people instead of submitting to Roman rule. She leads her men in battle, knowing that the odds are against her both as a woman and leader of a suppressed clan, knowing that she may well suffer defeat. She dies heroically instead of submitting to a conquering army, but her name and valor are remembered.

Sutcliff's heroic theme is fully present in *The Lantern Bearers,* the 1959 Carnegie Medal winner, the book with the British map full of strange-sounding names. In this story, Aquila, a scholarly type, is unable to develop rich relationships with others since he is wrapped up in his own personal pains and feelings of injustice and outrage. As the last of the Roman legions are pulling out from Britain around A.D. 450, Aquila feels that he has become attached to his homeland and cannot leave, although his allegiance has always been to Roman ways. Consequently, he deserts on the last night, holding a flaming torch on the shores of Rutupiae on the eastern coast of Britain, suggesting his hope for some light in this newly darkened land.

Then, only five days after his defection, Aquila sees the brutal slaying of his valiant Roman-British father at the hands of what he calls the barbarian Jutes and Saxons. His farm is destroyed and his family members are either killed or imprisoned. He becomes a thrall, a slave, to the Jute invaders and returns with them to what is present-day Denmark for several years of harsh labor. His only light during that time is his copy of Homer's *Odysseus* and the hope he has in daily prayer. After three years, the Saxons and Jutes, in need of more food and resources, return to Rutupiae, letting Aquila row their boats despite the imprisoning heavy iron ring that bedecks his neck. Upon reaching land, coincidentally, he finds his long-lost sister, who helps him plan a means of escape but who also reveals that she has married a Saxon and blessed him with a child. She refuses to leave with her brother, so Aquila moves forward, bitter and alone. How could his sister marry a Saxon, a member of a murdering band that killed her own father?

With a monk's help, Aquila moves on, seeking to find the young Prince Ambrosius in the northern mountains, hoping to fight at his side as the last of the Roman Britons hold on. Ambrosius befriends him, lets him fight by his side, and eventually helps him with a marriage contract. Yet Aquila's bitterness makes it impossible for him to love his wife or share his past with his fighting buddies. He fights valiantly but in a lonely way for over twelve years before he finds his young Saxon nephew wounded in battle. Only at this point is he able to fully forgive his sister for marrying a Saxon. After all, he realizes that his estranged wife left her people to marry him and that eventually all the various peoples on the big island would have to learn to live and work together. He is finally able to open up to his wife and fighting friends, even his own son, only after he is able to accept that he is part of a much larger and diverse community.

Suggestions for the Reader

If you have decided to flip through Sutcliff's work, you may want to prepare yourself for the trip. A British map and a copy of a beginner's history of England will help you through your travels. The *Cambridge Introduction to the History of Mankind* (1971) is especially useful because it is loaded with color pictures and easy-to-use historical maps. An unabridged English dictionary might also help with the pronunciations of obscure place names, since the author assumes that British youth would readily understand her allusions.

allusion reference

Sutcliff also tends to be pro-Roman in her narrative accounts. The reader should be critically minded and realize that Sutcliff is providing one version of a possible historical situation. Ask yourself such questions as "Were the Saxons really savages?" How would the Saxons write *The Lantern Bearers*?

If you are interested in the Arthurian legends, you may wish to start with *The Sword and the Circle: King Arthur and the Knights of the Round Table* (1981), *The Road to Camlann: The Death of King Arthur* (1982), or *The Light Beyond the Forest: The Quest for the Holy Grail* (1980). Sutcliff also has a series related to England during and after the Roman occupation that includes *The Eagle of the Ninth* (1961), *The Silver Branch* (1959), and *The Lantern Bearers* (1959). At the end of *The Capricorn Bracelet* (1973) is a helpful Roman-British background and chronology section. *The Shield Ring* (1956) and *Knight's Fee* (1960) are related to the Norman influence in England.

Sutcliff was sometimes inspired by something she had seen. *Sun Horse, Moon Horse* (1978) gives an explanation of how the chalk horses in the Berkshire Downs, still visible today, came to be carved into the high downs. She suggests that a young Iceni artist agreed to sculpt the horses if his people can go free.

If you really start to flip through Sutcliff's pages, you may want to start a list of possible places to visit when you travel to the United Kingdom. Sutcliff could be a wonderful tour guide, since her books take you into the heart and historical sweep of her cherished homeland.

If you like the works of Rosemary Sutcliff, you might also like the works of Leon Garfield, Anne McCaffrey, and Ann Rinaldi.

Selected Bibliography

WORKS BY ROSEMARY SUTCLIFF

The Chronicles of Robin Hood (1978)

The Queen Elizabeth Story (1950)

The Armouer's House (1951)

Brother Dusty-Feet (1952)

Simon (1953)

The Eagle on the Ninth (1954)

Outcast (1955)

Lady in Waiting (1956)

The Shield Ring (1956, 1962)

The Sliver Branch (1957, 1959)

Warrior Scarlet (1958, 1966)

The Bridge-Builders (1959)

The Lantern Bearers (1959, 1965)

The Rider of the White Horse (1959), also published as *Rider on a White Horse* (1960)

Knight's Fee (1960)

Houses and History (1960)

Dragon Slayer (1961, 1980), also published as *Beowulf* (1962)

Dawn Wind (1961, 1962)

Rudyard Kipling (1960, 1961)

The Hound of Ulster (1963)

Heroes and History (1965)

The Mark of the Horse Lord (1965)

A Saxon Settler (1965)

The Chief's Daughter (1967)

The High Deeds of Finn MacCool (1967)

A Circlet of Oak Leaves (1968)

The Witch's Brat (1970)

Tristan and Iseult (1971)

The Truce of the Games (1971)

Heather, Oak, and Olive: Three Stories (1972)

The Capricorn Bracelet (1973)

The Changeling (1974)

We Lived in Drumfyvie (1975)

Blood Feud (1976, 1977)

Shifting Sands (1977)

Sun Horse, Moon Horse (1977, 1978)

Is Anyone There?, editor, with Monica Dickens (1978)

Song for a Dark Queen (1978, 1979)

The Light Beyond the Forest: The Quest for the Holy Grail (1979, 1980)

Eagle's Egg (1981)

Frontier Wolf (1980, 1981)

The Sword and the Circle: King Arthur and the Knights of the Round Table (1981)

The Road to Camlann: The Death of King Arthur (1982)

Blue Remembered Hills: A Recollection (1983, 1984)

Bonnie Dundee (1983, 1984)

The Roundabout Horse (1986)

Flame-Colored Taffeta (1985, 1986)

Little Hound Found (1989)

A Little Dog Like You (1990)

WORKS ABOUT ROSEMARY SUTCLIFF

Books

Arbuthnot, Mary Hill, and Zena Sutherland. *Children and Books*. Glenview, Ill.: Scott, Foresman, 1972.

Block, Ann, and Carolyn Riley, eds. "Rosemary Sutcliff." In *Children's Literature Review*. Detroit: Gale Research, vol. 1, 1976.

Butts, Dennis, ed. *Good Writers for Young Readers*. St. Albans: Hart-Davis Educational, 1977.

Cameron, Eleanor. *The Green and Burning Tree: On the Writing and Enjoyment of Children's Books*. Boston: Little, Brown, 1969.

Crouch, Marcus. *Treasure Seekers and Borrowers: Children's Books in Britain, 1900–1960*. London: Library Association, 1962.

———. 1972 *The Nesbit Tradition: The Children's Novel in England 1945–1970*. Benn.

Egoff, Sheila A. *Thursday's Child: Trends and Patterns in Contemporary Children's Literature*. Chicago: American Library Association, 1981.

Field, Elinor Whitney, ed. *Horn Book Reflections: On Children's Books and Reading; Selected from Eighteen Years of the Horn Book Magazine—1949–1966*. Boston: Horn Book, 1969.

Georgiu, Constantine.*Children and Their Literature*. Englewood Cliffs: Prentice-Hall, 1969.

Green, Roger Lancelyn. *Teller of Tales: British Authors of Children's Books from 1800 to 1964*. London: E. Ward, 1965.

Inglis, Fred. "Reading Children's Novels: Notes of the Politics of Literature." In *Writers, Critics, and Children: Articles from Children's Literature in Education*. Edited by Geoff Fox et al. New York: Agathon Press, London Heineman Educational Books, 1976.

Meek, Margaret. *Rosemary Sutcliff: A Walck Monograph*. New York: Henry Z. Walck, Inc., 1962.

Norton, Donna. *Through the Eyes of a Child: An Introduction to Children's Literature*. 2d ed. Columbus, Ohio: Merrill Publishing Company, 1987.

Riley, Carolyn, ed. "Rosemary Sutcliff." In *Contemporary Literary Criticism*. Detroit: Gale Research, vol. 26, 1983.

Townsend, John Rowe. 1971. *A Sense of Story: Essays on Contemporary Writing for Children*. Lippincott.

———. *Written for Children: An Outline of English Language Children's Literature*. Lippincott.

Periodicals

Best Sellers. 15 February 1970.

Booklist. 1 February 1955.

Book Week. 15 March 1964.

Horn Book. June 1958; February 1968; April 1970; December 1971; August 1980; February 1982.

Junior Bookshelf. December 1981.

Junior Libraries. January 1955.

New Statesman. 2 October 1954; 16 November 1957; 12 November 1960.

New Yorker. 22 October 1984.

New York Herald Tribune Book Review. 14 February 1960.

New York Times Book Review. 26 October 1952; 9 January 1955; 17 March 1957; 29 June 1958; 4 January 1959; 22 April 1962; 11 November 1962; 26 May 1963; 3 May 1964; 7 November 1965; 30 January 1966; 15 February 1970; 30 September 1973; 5 April 1987.

Observer. 6 February 1983.

Publishers Weekly. 1 December 1969; 1 November 1971; 7 January 1983; 6 October 1989; 8 June 1990.

Saturday Review. 11 May 1957; 1 November 1958; 12 November 1960.

School Library Journal. August 1980; July 1990.

Times (London). 26 January 1983; 9 June 1990.

Times Educational Supplement. 23 October 1981; 19 February 1982; 14 January 1983; 13 January 1984.

Times Literary Supplement. 27 November 1953; 19 November 1954; 21 November 1958; 4 December 1959; 25 November 1960; 14 June 1963; 17 June 1965; 9 December 1965; 25 May 1967; 30 October 1970; 2 July 1971; 28 September 1973; 4 April 1975; 10 December 1976; 15 July 1977; 2 December 1977; 7 July 1978; 21 November 1980; 27 March 1981; 22 April 1983; 30 September 1983; 19 September 1986.

Tribune Books Chicago. 8 March 1987.

Voices of Youth Advocates. February 1987.

Washington Post Book World. 5 November 1967. 9 September 1990.

Marc Talbert

(1953-)

by Bonnie O. Ericson

The following scene occurs near the beginning of Marc Talbert's first book, *Dead Birds Singing* (1985). It is an exciting and terrible scene that keeps the reader turning the pages to see what will happen next. It is also a scene that gives some clues about Talbert's books.

Matt stretched out and snuggled into the length of the back seat of the car and listened to the tires on the pavement. It sounded like a continuous strip of Velcro ripping apart—only muffled. . . .

His mother gasped and slammed on the brakes. Matt was jerked farther into the folds of the back seat. "Oh my God!" The car slid sideways, and Matt's mother frantically turned the steering wheel, first left and then right, shoving him feet-first toward one door and then headfirst toward the other. His mother's voice rose in a scream. "No! NO!"

Matt tried to scramble up onto his hands and knees to see what was happening. A violent explosion of crunching metal, shattering glass, and Matt was hurled, shoulder-first, into the back of the front seat. (Pp. 12–14)

In this story, Matt will have to come to terms with the tragic death of his mother and his sister after the accident. Talbert's characters in other books face a number of equally difficult situations. Family and friends play important roles, eventually allowing a character to better understand, and begin to come to terms with, his or her situation. While there are no easy answers, really, there can at least be hope for the future.

Such a novel might lead you to think that Talbert is simply an author of "problem" novels for boys. In fact, most of his books deal with a variety of difficult problems that young people may face: sexual molestation, the divorce of parents, a family member with a fatal or life-altering disease. But Talbert's books are also very much books of place, most of them set in either Iowa, the state in which Talbert grew up, or in New Mexico, the state in which Talbert has spent much of his adult life. Exploring these different elements of Talbert's writing may give you additional insights into a book or books of his that you have already read, or it may pique your interest in one of the books you have not yet read.

pique to arouse or provoke

Some Main Characters and Their Problems

Most of Talbert's books feature characters who are of middle school age, from ten to fourteen. These protagonists, such as Matt in *Dead Birds Singing*, Martin in *Thin Ice* (1986), Toby in *Toby* (1987), Jeremy in *The Paper Knife* (1988), or Luke in *The Purple Heart* (1992), are not the most popular boys, but they are not the bullies either. They are normal kids in many ways. They love their parents, although they can also find a parent—or sibling—annoying or embarrassing or disappointing. They may live with a single parent, as is so often true in real life. They are acutely aware of the changes that are beginning to occur in their bodies. They usually have a single best friend who will be important in the book, either as a giver of support or as a complication.

These traits of the characters in Talbert's books make them easy to relate to, and it is this combination of "normal" characters dealing with very serious problems that makes Talbert's books compelling. Discussing a few books more specifically will give you a better idea of the characters, the kinds of problems they face, and the ways in which they cope.

From the earlier opening quotation, you have already learned a little about Matt in *Dead Birds Singing*. Here is more detail. A seventh-grader, Matt wins a race in a swim meet, but on the way home a drunk driver swerves into the car his mother is driving, killing Matt's mother instantly and seriously injuring his sister. After the amputation of one of her legs, the sister slips into a coma and dies. Having lost his father in the Vietnam War, Matt is left completely without a family. Understandably, he is traumatized by the deaths and holds tremendous anger toward the driver of the other car.

Most of the book is about how Matt comes to terms with his anger and his loss, and how he picks up the pieces of his life as he attends funerals and returns to school. It is a struggle, but readers are given the feeling that he will make it, largely because of the love and understanding of longtime family friends who adopt him.

In *Thin Ice*, Martin has a bundle of issues to deal with. His parents have separated, and his father has moved far away, to Alaska. His sister is diabetic, he is fighting with his best friend, Barney, and to top it all off, his mother starts dating his teacher! This book is a good example of one of Talbert's strengths as a writer: his depiction of life as tough and complex. The story is told in a straightforward manner, but the events and details convincingly show these problems and just how interrelated they can be.

In another of Talbert's books, *The Paper Knife*, Jeremy and his mother have run away from her physically abusive boyfriend, George. As the book begins, they go to live with George's parents in a small town, where Jeremy soon finds a friend in his classmate Jennifer. He is also befriended by his teacher, Mr. Williams. What is unknown for much of the book—except to Jeremy and the reader—is that George had

diabetes a disorder in which the body produces insufficient insulin, causing an excess of sugar in the blood that must be moderated through diet and insulin injections

sexually molested Jeremy. Much of the tension of the first part of the story comes from wondering how and when this fact will become known to the other characters. At first, Jeremy carries a small pocketknife, which he feels will keep him safe if George should return. After the knife is taken away from him at school, he writes a note about the abuse, what he calls his "paper knife."

When the note is discovered, Mr. Williams is wrongfully accused of the molestation, although eventually he is cleared. With the help of his friends Harriet and Mr. Williams, Jeremy is able to begin to make sense of his complicated feelings and stand up to his mother so that they do not run away from trouble again. Even following the devastating experience of molestation, Jeremy achieves a tempered hope for the future. Once again, not all the problems are solved, but readers will feel comfortable about Jeremy's prospects when they finish reading the book.

tempered adjusted; moderated

In *The Purple Heart,* Luke's father returns from the Vietnam War a badly shaken man, prone to nightmares and fits of crying. Luke and his friend Mike, both ten years old, have always glorified war in their play, and Luke is embarrassed and confused by the differences in his father. Things get even worse when Luke loses his father's Purple Heart while he and Mike play a prank on an elderly neighborhood woman. Then his friend ignores him because of the trouble. (A helpful and interesting author's note at the end of the novel explains the history of this medal.)

It is with the perseverance and support, even in difficult times, of his mother and father that Luke begins to understand more about courage, war, and family relationships. In this book, support also comes from a completely unexpected source, the neighborhood woman, showing that the complexities of life include all the people involved.

Examining these protagonists, their problems, and the ways in which they learn to better understand themselves and others is one important way of looking at Talbert's books. It is apparent that Talbert understands and can convey the complexity of his characters. They are unique and realistic persons, and not even supporting characters are flatly portrayed as all good or bad. A second way of looking at the writing of Talbert, which may yield additional insights, is to consider how the setting, or time and place, of his books is connected to the characters.

Some Settings and Why They Are Significant

In all Talbert's books there is a strong sense of place, of the time and physical surroundings. *The Purple Heart,* for example, takes place in 1967, a more innocent time for kids, yet a time when the Vietnam War was splitting the country in two, into supporters and protestors of the war. In other books, the setting takes on even greater significance.

In *Pillow of Clouds* (1991), the parents of thirteen-year-old Chester have split up. According to their divorce settlement, it is up to him to decide where he would like to live: with his father in New Mexico or with his mother in Iowa. The New Mexico setting is bright, open, warm, and filled with sun—as is Chester's life with his father, his dad's girlfriend, Florence, and Chester's friend José. When we are with Chester in Iowa, on the other hand, outside it is oppressively humid and hot, while indoors the air conditioning makes for a sterile, cool indoor environment, one removed from the reality outside. The Iowa streets are laid out in rigid grids, so that they run north and south, east and west. Both the weather and the streets are confining and stifling—like Chester's life with his alcohol-abusing and manipulative mother.

Still, the characters in *Pillow of Clouds* are drawn realistically and with complexity. For example, there is no doubt that Chester's mother loves him or that he loves her. Ultimately, she is even able to tell Chester that he is not responsible for her suicide attempt, and he is able to let go of his guilt and live in New Mexico. In this book, the two settings are much more than just two places. They mirror the two relationships Chester has with his parents.

In *A Sunburned Prayer* (1995), the setting is again New Mexico. Eleven-year-old Eloy is determined to complete a seventeen-mile pilgrimage on Good Friday to Santuario de Chimayo, which he believes could save the life of his grandmother. She is seriously ill with cancer, and Eloy is terrified at the thought of her death because he believes his *abuela* (grandmother) is the only person who truly understands and unconditionally loves him. Eloy's journey on the hot desert highway is so physically challenging that he must overcome the setting itself. But the physical journey parallels the personal pilgrimage that Eloy is completing, a journey that will lead him to the acceptance of the rhythm of life and death.

pilgrimage a journey to a shrine or sacred place

Eloy's faithful friend on both journeys is a dog he names Magdalena; others who provide support are the grandmother and his brother.

Heart of a Jaguar (1995) takes place in the ancient Maya civilization. This setting was a marked departure for Talbert, whose previous works are set in the present (or at least in the late 1960s) and in the United States. And yet while this book is in many ways very different, it bears many similarities to Talbert's earlier works. In *Heart of a Jaguar,* fourteen-year-old Balam struggles with situations that are not much different from those that confront Talbert's other protagonists: coming of age and family relationships. Overshadowing all Balam's individual concerns, however, is a drought that is slowly leading to the starvation of the people in his village.

conquistadors the leaders in the Spanish conquest of America and especially of Mexico and Peru in the 1500s

The culture of the time period, around A.D.1200, three centuries before the arrival of the Spanish conquistadors, is fascinating and sometimes terrible. (A glossary of Maya terms and their pronunciations at the end of the book is extremely useful.) Talbert interweaves various aspects of this culture—the calendar, the foods and daily activities, the coming-of-age and sacrificial rituals—into this story, which would not have been possible outside this culture. Readers may find certain scenes shocking and distressing, but they are in keeping with the historical reality of the Maya culture and give the story credibility.

Marc Talbert's Life

An overview of Talbert's life may give readers additional insights into his writing and especially into his stories' characters, their problems, and the importance of their settings. Talbert certainly seems to embody the old saying that authors have the most success when they write about the things they know. He was born on 21 July 1953 in Boulder, Colorado, the son of Willard and Mary Talbert. He grew up in Iowa and attended Grinnell College in Grinnell, Iowa, (1971–1973) and Iowa State University in Ames, Iowa, where he earned a bachelor of science degree in 1976. He worked as a newspaper columnist for newspapers in several Iowa towns and at Iowa State University. After graduating from college, he taught the fifth and sixth grades in Marshalltown, Iowa, from 1976 to 1977, and the fifth grade in Ames from 1977 to 1981.

The influence of his childhood and teaching experiences in Iowa are obvious in Talbert's fiction. The overwhelming majority of his books take place in the fictional town of Clifton, Iowa, or in an unnamed town very much like it. The characters in these books are most likely based on students whom Talbert knew during his years of teaching. And the problems that his characters face are similar to those of his former students. Talbert has said, for example, that *Dead Birds Singing* resulted from the death of one of his students in a car accident. When he looked to find books that his students might read with a similar topic, he found few that addressed such a senseless death. So Talbert's first book was written in response to a real-life situation, and many of his books concern characters, situations, and places with which he is familiar. That familiarity has allowed him to give the types of detail that make his stories seem poignantly real.

In 1981, Talbert moved to New Mexico. He and his wife, Moo Thorpe (look for his mention of her in dedications), along with their two daughters, Molly and Jessie, reside in Tesuque, New Mexico, near Sante Fe. While spending much of his time in New Mexico writing books for young adults and children, Talbert has also held a number of interesting jobs there. He has been a writer, editor, or speechwriter for Los Alamos National Laboratory in Los Alamos and for the National Science Foundation. He has also taught children's literature courses at the University of New Mexico.

The influence of his move to New Mexico is obvious in Talbert's later writing. *The Rabbit in the Rock* (1989), a book aimed at older readers and Talbert's only story with a female protagonist, takes place on a cattle-turned-dude ranch in New Mexico. *Pillow of Clouds* and *A Sunburned Prayer* are also set in New Mexico, and these books feature Talbert's first non-Caucasian characters: José and his family in *Pillow of Clouds,* and Eloy in *A Sunburned Prayer.* That these Hispanic characters ring true and are portrayed with sensitivity should not be surprising, given Talbert's years in New Mexico.

Talbert's familiarity with the Mexican American culture of New Mexico probably led to his interest in the culture of the ancient Maya civilization, an interest that resulted in *Heart of a Jaguar.* What will Talbert's next books be like? Given that he has two daughters, perhaps he will write a book featuring a main character who is female. Whatever his future

Talbert's first book was written in response to a real-life situation, and many of his books concern characters, situations, and places with which he is familiar.

directions, readers can be assured that Talbert will draw on his own experiences to develop realistic and honest characters and stories.

What the Critics Have Said

Talbert has won a number of awards for his books, including the highly prestigious American Library Association's Best Books for Young Adults award for *Dead Birds Singing. Toby,* a book about a boy of normal intelligence whose mother is mentally retarded and whose father is regarded as "slow," was named a Notable Children's Book by the National Council of Social Studies. Many of Talbert's books have been widely and positively reviewed in a variety of journals read by public librarians, school librarians, and teachers. Reviewers praise Talbert for two main reasons: First, he deals with adolescents' problems realistically, yet hopefully. Second, he respects his characters and his audience.

The reviews of Talbert's first book demonstrate how well he has been received. Writing about *Dead Birds Singing* in the August 1985 issue of *School Library Journal,* Jack Forman compared him with Katherine Paterson, stating, "With humor and compassion this uncommon story evokes the same sparks of hope and endurance in the midst of tragedy as *Bridge to Terabithia*." Jim Trelease, the well-known author of *The New Read-Aloud Handbook* (1989), called *Dead Birds Singing* "one of the most powerful books I've ever read. I was literally shaken by it. . . . It's been months since I read it, but I can still close my eyes and picture whole scenes from the book."

There is an article about Katherine Paterson in volume 2.

Other books by Talbert also have received praise. In the January 1987 issue of *School Library Journal,* Todd Morning commended *Thin Ice* for dealing not only with important issues faced by young people, but for recognizing "that the problems of growing up don't come in single file." The reviewer Susan Oliver, in the March 1991 issue of the same publication, called *Pillow of Clouds* "a moving, thought-provoking novel." Of *The Paper Knife,* the children's literature expert Zena Sutherland commented in *The Best in Children's Books, 1985–1990* (1991) that Talbert "sees children as people, avoiding either condescension or evasion in depicting them." Karen Hunt also focused on Talbert's characters in her December 1991 *Booklist* review of *The Purple Heart,* noting that "the characters have integrity and depth, especially Luke, who is particularly convincing and well developed."

A few reviews have been less complimentary. Roger Sutton, for example, complained in the January 1992 issue of the *Bulletin of the Center for Children's Books* that Talbert's plot in *The Purple Heart* is "predictable and the theme told as much as shown." This same reviewer called *Thin Ice* a story "burdened by overwriting and heavy doses of bibliotherapy, and Talbert's attempt to convey how kids really talk and feel is sincere but too apparently deliberate." The word *bibliotherapy* refers to counseling or giving direct advice to readers through what the novel's characters say and do, or through the narrator's comments. Nevertheless, these critics still found admirable qualities in Talbert's writing. For example, Sutton also commended *Thin Ice*: "The raucous classroom scenes do ring true, as does Martin's stormy relationship with Barney—Talbert understands well the difficulties that pride and embarrassment present in repairing a damaged friendship."

raucous loud and disorderly

As a reader, you will have to decide whether you think Talbert is "heavy-handed" or whether you agree with the critics who appreciate the way that he depicts his characters and the situations that they encounter. Although Talbert has not yet achieved the tremendous success of a Katherine Paterson or a Robert Cormier, since 1985 he has been steadily writing books for middle school readers, and these books have received mostly positive responses. That is an admirable track record.

There is an article about Robert Cormier in volume 1.

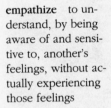

Conclusion

If you are the kind of reader who enjoys books that focus on serious issues and that let you empathize with characters who must make difficult choices, then it is likely that you will enjoy Marc Talbert's books. Maybe you will count your blessings at the end of a story, maybe you will approve or disapprove of how a particular character acts, or maybe you will feel less alone knowing that others have similarly serious problems. However you respond, most readers will appreciate the honesty of this writer's unique characters and their stories.

empathize to understand, by being aware of and sensitive to, another's feelings, without actually experiencing those feelings

As a writer for children and adolescents, Talbert sees it as his responsibility to portray real kids and real problems. As he explains on the *Dead Birds Singing* book jacket, "In some ways, life *is* like a bed of roses. The job of the novelist is not to invent a bed of roses without thorns. A novelist should leave the thorns on the roses—not downplay the scratches and cuts—but then balance the hurt with the beauty of the flowers, the way they smell and look and feel." It is Talbert's accomplishment that the lives of his characters have thorns and roses both.

Selected Bibliography

WORKS BY MARC TALBERT

Dead Birds Singing (1985)

Thin Ice (1986) —

Toby (1987)

The Paper Knife (1988)

The Rabbit in the Rock (1989)

Double or Nothing, illustrated by Toby Gowing (1990)

Pillow of Clouds (1991)

The Purple Heart (1992)

Heart of a Jaguar (1995)

A Sunburned Prayer (1995)

WORKS ABOUT MARC TALBERT

Chinn, Sharon. "Modern Fairy Tales: Archetypal Structure in the Novels of Marc Talbert." In *ALAN Review,* spring 1990, vol. 17, pp. 35–37.

If you like Marc Talbert's books, you might also like those by Isabelle Holland, Katherine Paterson, or T. Ernesto Bethancourt. If you liked Marc Talbert's books a year or two ago and are ready to read books for older students, you may like works by Chris Crutcher, Harry Mazer, Todd Strasser, or Julian Thompson.

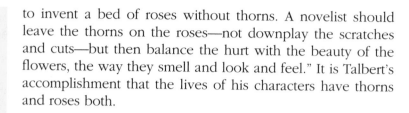

How to Write to the Author

Marc Talbert

Route 4, Box 1B

Santa Fe, NM 87501

Mildred Delois Taylor

(1943-   )

by Susanne Porter Kirk

As a schoolgirl, Mildred Delois Taylor always wondered why her textbooks did not include stories about African Americans. The illustrations showed girls and boys with blond hair and blue eyes, not characters that resembled Taylor and her family. She was also troubled about the lack of information about African Americans in history books. The limited coverage of the African American experience often seemed distorted. The African Americans mentioned in the books bore little resemblance to the proud people Taylor knew through stories passed down from her parents, aunts and uncles, and grandparents.

Oral History

When she was growing up, family stories of ordinary African Americans captured Taylor's imagination. She savored the experience of listening to her family pass to another generation real accounts of their ancestors and African American history. This tradition has been practiced by many ethnic and cultural minority groups in America as a way of keeping their cultural history alive. In the days before radio and television, storytelling was a primary art form, polished to perfection by many retellings and acting performances designed to entertain as well as inform. The act of storytelling was another link in the legacy of African Americans to their beginnings in Africa. At the many gatherings she attended when she was a child, Taylor says in the August 1977 *Horn Book,*

> there was always time for talk, and when we children had finished all the games we could think to play, we would join the adults, soon becoming enraptured by their talk, for it would often turn to a history which we heard only at home, a history of Black people told through stories.

> Those stories about the small and often dangerous triumphs of Black people, those stories about human pride and survival in a cruelly racist society were like nothing I read in the history books or the books I devoured at the local library. There were no Black heroes or heroines in those books; no beautiful Black ladies, no handsome Black men; no people filled with pride, strength, or endurance. There was, of course, always mention of Booker T. Washington and George Washington Carver, Marian Anderson, and occasionally even Dr. Ralph Bunche. But that hardly compensated for the lackluster history of Black people painted by those books, a history of a docile, subservient people happy with their fate who did little or nothing to shatter the chains that bound them, both before and after slavery. There was obviously a terrible contradiction between what the books said and what I had learned from my family, and at no time did I feel the contradiction more than when I had to sit in a class which, without me, would have been all white, and relive that prideless history year after year. (Pp. 404–405)

"There was obviously a terrible contradiction between what the books said and what I had learned from my family."

Master Storyteller

Taylor considered her father, David, a master storyteller. He could make a story come alive, so much so that Taylor could see his characters, hear them talk, and feel their pain. She often imagined herself as the storyteller as she listened. Her gift of story was developing as she heard the crafting of settings, vivid characters brought to life through dialogue, and captivating plots that were action-packed from beginning to end. In her author's note to *Roll of Thunder, Hear My Cry* (1976), Taylor says:

dialogue conversation between characters

> My father was a master storyteller. He could tell a fine old story that made me hold my sides with rolling laughter and sent happy tears down my cheeks, or a story of stark reality that made me shiver and be grateful for my own warm, secure surroundings. He could tell stories of beauty and grace, stories of gentle dreams, and paint them as vividly as any picture with splashes of character and dialogue. His memory detailed every event of ten or forty years or more before, just as if it had happened yesterday.

Taylor's father was her guiding light in becoming a writer. Although he was not formally well educated, his intelligence and courage were reflected in high moral principles. Growing up during the Great Depression in Mississippi, Taylor's father did not have opportunities for schooling. Instead of enduring the discrimination and prejudice prevalent in the South, he went North and found work in Toledo, Ohio. Her father's steadfast support convinced Taylor that she could accomplish any goals. David and Stacey Logan—two characters Taylor later created—bear a strong resemblance to her father. Her father's strong sense of right and wrong is evident throughout Taylor's works.

The **Great Depression** was a severe recession that began when the stock market crashed in 1929 and that lasted almost ten years. By the winter of 1932–1933, 14 to 16 million Americans were unemployed. Many died from a lack of food and inadequate living conditions.

Profession: Storyteller

Taylor first considered becoming a writer when she was nine or ten. She was intrigued by the idea of making "her people" come alive through literature so that others could understand the "true" African American experience. During high school Taylor realized that the gift of storytelling was alive in her as well as in her father. She realized that her storytelling would not be through the traditional oral form but through the written word. Her gift of story could be shared around the world, evoking the strength and sound of her ancestral characters. All through her childhood, Taylor had nurtured stories of proud African Americans who withstood dreadful hardships but still struggled for a better life.

Taylor, usually the only African American student in her classes, worked hard to prove herself. She was successful in school—an honor student, a class officer, and the editor of the school newspaper. (However, she admits to really wanting to be a cheerleader!)

In addition to wanting to become a writer, Taylor had a dream of joining the Peace Corps and traveling to Ethiopia. After earning a bachelor's degree in education from the University of Toledo, Taylor's two dreams were realized through her Peace Corps assignment to Ethiopia. While teaching English and history in Ethiopia, she traveled and explored her African roots. She enjoyed the proud and friendly people who reminded her of her own family and their stories.

The **Peace Corps,** established in 1961, is a volunteer program of the United States government. Volunteers work in developing countries. They work to improve living conditions and train the native people to carry out this work.

After earning a master's degree in journalism at the University of Colorado and working with the Black Studies Program there, Taylor decided to focus seriously on her writing. The manuscript for her first book, *Song of the Trees,* won first prize in the African American category of the Council on Interracial Books for Children competition and was published in 1975. Six books later, she continued to write about the Logan family, which she introduced in *Song of the Trees,* and other strong African American families in the South.

Song of the Trees was also named Outstanding Book of the Year by the *New York Times* in 1975. Taylor's other books include: *Roll of Thunder, Hear My Cry,* a 1977 John Newbery Medal winner and *Boston Globe–Horn Book* Honor book; *Let the Circle Be Unbroken* (1981), the winner of the 1983 Coretta Scott King Award and a nominee for the American Book Award in 1982; *The Friendship* (1987), the winner of the 1984 Coretta Scott King Award, and *The Gold Cadillac* (1987), the winner of the Christopher Award in 1988; *The Road to Memphis* (1990), the 1991 Coretta Scott King Award winner; and *Mississippi Bridge* (1990).

The Logans

Taylor's novels revolve around the Logan family of rural Mississippi during the Depression and the pre–World War II era. The characters—David and Mary Logan, the parents; Big Ma, the grandmother; Uncle Hammer of Chicago; and the Logan children, Stacey, Cassie, Christopher-John, and Little Man—interact with other African American farm families and whites struggling to make a living during the hard times of the Depression. Harlan Granger, a powerful white landowner who covets the Logans' land, and Wade Jamison, a white lawyer who is the Logans' friend, also play important roles.

Family and community life near the small town of Strawberry serves as the primary setting in Taylor's novels, except for *Road to Memphis,* which also take place in Jackson and Memphis. Taylor's many childhood trips to the South enable her to create the mood of that time and place, complete with appropriate sounds, smells, and sights. Her description in *Roll of Thunder, Hear My Cry* of the preparations for Christmas is a good example of her style and tone:

style a distinctive manner of expression

> The day before Christmas I awoke to the soft murmuring of quiet voices gathered in the midnight blackness of morning. . . .

tone style or manner of expression in speaking or writing

> By the dawn, the house smelled of Sunday: chicken frying, bacon sizzling, and smoke sausages baking. By evening, it reeked of Christmas. In the kitchen sweet-potato pies, egg-custard pies, and rich butter pound cakes cooled; a gigantic coon which Mr. Morrison, Uncle Hammer, and Stacey had secured in a night's hunt baked in a sea of onions, garlic, and fat orange-yellow yams; and a choice sugar-cured ham brought from the smokehouse awaited its turn in the oven. In the heart of the house, where we had gathered after supper, freshly cut branches of long-needled pines lay over the fireplace mantle adorned by winding vines of winter holly and bright red Christmas berries. (P. 110)

Through the Logans' daily activities of going to school, to the market on Saturday, or for a ride in a new car, the tight-knit family members come to life. In Taylor's first book, eight-year-old Cassie Logan tells the story of her family. In the sequels, Cassie also narrates the Logans' story as she grows into adolescence. Through Cassie, a composite of Taylor's aunt and several relatives, Taylor seems to speak. She expertly creates multidimensional and lifelike characters through compelling dialogue and vivid description.

The Logans and their African American neighbors become the African American heroines and heroes whom Taylor so desperately craved during her youth. Each of the Logans reveals a strong inner core, despite situations fraught with adversity and temptation. They act on principle, believing in their self-worth and God-given abilities and rights. However, Taylor's characters sometimes commit simple human errors. Often, the children act like children, following their strong-willed ideas. Sometimes these schemes lead to outrageous fun, such as the disabling of the white children's school bus in *Roll of Thunder, Hear My Cry* or to deep trouble such as cousin Bud's skirmish with Stuart Walker in *Let the Circle Be Unbroken*. Regardless of the circumstances, the Logans try to do the right thing. Nevertheless, they attract resentment and hostility.

The Logans own 400 acres of land and a comfortable home—a rarity for African Americans at that time. The land, a symbol of the Logans' success, and Mary Logan's education as a schoolteacher give the family self-reliance and strength. David Logan is considered a leader of the African American community. Therefore, the Logans serve as a lightning rod whenever the white sharecroppers or landowners wish to express their displeasure. Representing the independence that African Americans can achieve, the Logans are a definite threat to the status quo of the South.

> *Each of the Logans reveals a strong inner core, despite situations fraught with adversity and temptation. They act on principle, believing in their self-worth and God-given abilities and rights.*

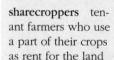

sharecroppers tenant farmers who use a part of their crops as rent for the land

Racial Confrontations

Before the 1970s, trouble for African Americans in the South could have serious consequences. Too often, such trouble came in varied forms of harassment or retaliation by hateful whites. The economic ruin of families, public humiliation, beatings, hangings, and burnings, all stemming from racism among white people, were regular occurrences for African Americans.

The Logans, living so close to resentful whites, seem too proud and too self-sufficient for their white neighbors. Consequently, the Logans are careful to respond to racially charged situations as judiciously as possible. They are aware of their expected "place"; however, they rarely allow whites the luxury of intimidation. Taylor employs humor and timeless themes to avoid the pitfall of overmoralizing the oppression. The Logans experience more than their share of confrontations with angry whites over seemingly trivial events. These unpleasant encounters give readers opportunities to see these disturbing times through Cassie's eyes in *The Friendship* or through the resignation of weary sixty-five-year-old Mrs. Lee Annie, who would like to vote once in her lifetime, in *Let the Circle Be Unbroken.* The Logans are ordinary people acting in an extraordinarily brave and heroic way, considering the threats to their safety and existence.

> **themes** central messages about life in literary works

Heroines and Heroes

The Logans usually triumph over wrong, yet sometimes they must learn life's lessons the hard way. Taylor's plots twist and turn, revealing the ups and downs of actual life journeys. Trite happy endings rarely occur. T. J., in *Roll Of Thunder, Hear My Cry,* and *Let the Circle Be Unbroken,* serves a prison sentence, while his white accomplices in crime, the Simms Boys, unfairly escape punishment.

In *Let the Circle Be Unbroken,* Stacey runs away to work in the cane fields to help with the family land payment. Taylor deftly communicates the Logan family's anguish. Consumed with worry, they are unable to celebrate the Christmas holidays without their son. They are forced to simply go through the motions of normalcy as humans do in times of trauma. It would be so predictable, such a relief for Taylor to bring Stacey home, but she remains true to real life, which seldom works perfectly.

Taylor creates powerful events that move the novels and escalate the tension. For example, *Roll of Thunder, Hear My Cry* gains momentum throughout, captivating readers until the stunning climax. Taylor's easy-to-read poetic style transports readers to another time and place in the rural South. Her comfortable southern dialect deepens the characters, showing their humanness.

> *Taylor creates powerful events that move the novels and escalate the tension.*
>
>

The heroism of Taylor's characters often comes through in situations related to race and discrimination. Instead of surrendering to injustice, her characters stand their ground, which sometimes results in violent disputes. In *The Road to Memphis,* Stacey and Cassie confront the white Aames Brothers, who are chasing down their friend as if he were an animal. Characters find creative solutions to problems, such as David Logan's burning of cotton fields to forestall a hanging in *Roll of Thunder, Hear My Cry.*

Taylor's characters reveal human emotions common to subordinated people: anger, frustration, fear, contempt, resentment, and hopelessness. They often experience disappointment, as Harris does in *Road to Memphis,* when his white friend Jeremy does not protect him. However, Jeremy's actions are understandable given the tightrope he must constantly walk as a white boy who befriends African Americans. Later, Jeremy gets the chance to redeem himself as he hides Moe from the lynch mob, thereby jeopardizing his own safety.

lynch mob a mob that unlawfully puts someone to death— usually by hanging

Taylor's characters, always cognizant of their unjust treatment, do not surrender to despair. Instead, the Logans attempt to live a full life, not consumed by their plight but confident in their love and respect for each other. They are determined to keep hope alive and work for justice. The strength of the African American extended family, depicted by Big Ma, Uncle Hammer, and the Logans' neighbors and friends, enables the characters to sustain rough times. Building on the loving support of her own extended family, Taylor deftly portrays the anchor of the Logans' success.

Through her characterizations, Taylor examines motivations, showing the rich complexity of human beings, who are seldom one-dimensional. For example, Cassie's obvious jealousy toward Suzella in *Let the Circle Be Unbroken* sharply contrasts with her usual intelligence and caring.

Taylor's Contributions

Through the eyes of children, Taylor depicts unlawful, immoral acts inflicted on African Americans. Initially, the Logan children cannot understand the unenforced laws, the lack of rights for African Americans, or hostility from most whites. Forced to confront harsh realities, they realize that white children have privileges not even bestowed on African American adults.

The absurdity of prejudice and discrimination grips readers. For example, Cassie, in *Roll of Thunder, Hear My Cry,* cannot understand the logic of addressing a white girl of her same age as "Miss." Cassie says:

> "Yes'm," I murmured, then flared, "But mama, that Lillian Jean ain't got the brains of a flea! How come I gotta go 'round calling her Miz' like she grown or something?"

> Mama's voice grew hard. "Because that's the way of things, Cassie."

> "The way of what things?" I asked warily.

> "Baby, you had to grow up a little today. I wish . . . well no matter what I wish. It happened and you have to accept the fact that in the world outside this house, things are not always as we would have them to be."

> "But, mama, it ain't fair. I didn't do nothin' to that confounded Lillian Jean. How come Mr. Simms went and pushed me like he did?" (P. 95)

A love of the land and humans' attachment to the land for food, financial well-being, and independence are woven throughout Taylor's works. The Logans revel in the beauty and peace of their farm, while struggling to keep the land in their family. This legacy serves as the foundation for a sense of place and home to the Logans. The universality of home and appreciation of nature connect Taylor's novels to the present. Although her writings illuminate the past, their relevance shines brightly on contemporary issues.

Taylor's novels offer a view of American history that gives readers more in-depth understanding of the times than would merely reading history textbook facts. The migration of African Americans to northern urban centers in search of work and the beginnings of unionization undergird some of the plots.

Taylor's works rival Mark Twain's *Huckleberry Finn* (1884) and Harper Lee's *To Kill a Mockingbird* (1960) in en-

undergird to form the foundation of

There is an article about Harper Lee in volume 2.

abling readers to experience the sociopolitical mood of an era. Through Taylor's works, readers come to understand the bonds of the African American family and its message of love, moral courage, and African American pride. One of Taylor's greatest contributions to literature may be her unique ability to lay open the African American experience to all readers.

Living in Boulder, Colorado, in 1996, Taylor continues to use her gifts to pass on her family's values and heritage through story. Her father would have been justifiably proud.

If you like the works of Mildred Delois Taylor, you might also enjoy The Mouse Rap, Fast Sam, Cool Clyde, and Stuff by Walter Dean Myers or Words by Heart by Ouida Sebestyen.

Selected Bibliography

WORKS BY MILDRED TAYLOR

Song of the Trees (1975)
Roll of Thunder, Hear My Cry (1976)
Let the Circle Be Unbroken (1981)
The Friendship (1987)
The Gold Cadillac (1987)
Mississippi Bridge (1990)
The Road to Memphis (1990)

WORKS ABOUT MILDRED TAYLOR

Fogelman, Phyllis J. "Mildred D. Taylor." *Horn Book,* August 1977, pp. 410–414.

Olendorf, Donna, and Diane Telgren, eds. *Something About the Author.* Detroit: Gale Research, 1993, vol. 70, pp. 222–226.

Sarkissian, Adele, ed. *Something About the Author Autobiography Series.* Detroit: Gale Research, 1988, vol. 5, pp. 267–286.

Taylor, Mildred. "Newbery Award Acceptance Speech." In *Horn Book,* August 1977, pp. 401–409.

———. "Boston Globe–Horn Book Award Acceptance Speech." In *Horn Book,* March/April 1989, pp. 179–182.

How to Write to the Author
Mildred Delois Taylor
c/o The Dial Press
1540 Broadway
New York, NY 10036

Theodore Taylor

(1921-)

by Donna J. Camp

" V ariously, I've been a sports reporter, crime writer, merchant seaman, naval officer, prizefighter manager, movie press agent, and production assistant, not to mention earlier, less exciting endeavors—delivery boy and chicken plucker" (Gallo, *Speaking for Ourselves, Too,* pp. 209–210).

Perhaps best known as the author of *The Cay* (1969), Ted Taylor has been publishing books at the rate of about one per year since the early 1950s. Taylor works from 8:30 in the morning to 4:30 or 5:00 in the evening, seven days a week— except during football season. Taylor is an avid football fan. From September to Super Bowl Sunday, Taylor cuts his work week to Monday through Friday.

When he is not traveling, writing, or watching football, Taylor enjoys walking on the beach near his home in Laguna Beach, California, where he lives with his wife, Flora.

Taylor uses his extensive travels and other varied life experiences as the basis for his novels as well as for his many

> *About his writing, Taylor says, "Every story I have written is about real people and stems from real-life events. They include kids who have figured out things for themselves because kids like that really exist."*
>
>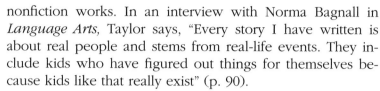

nonfiction works. In an interview with Norma Bagnall in *Language Arts,* Taylor says, "Every story I have written is about real people and stems from real-life events. They include kids who have figured out things for themselves because kids like that really exist" (p. 90).

A good example of Taylor's use of real-life people and places is in *The Cay,* his most famous novel. The background and setting for this book came from his years of living in the Caribbean and sailing on merchant marine ships. Taylor based Phillip, his protagonist in *The Cay,* on a young boy he knew while growing up in the Piedmont area of North Carolina. This childhood playmate of Taylor's had a deep-seated, irrational hatred and distrust of all African Americans. These racist views had been taught to this boy by his mother. Taylor used his friend's racist mother as the model for Phillip's mother in *The Cay.*

Originally, the idea for *The Cay* came to Taylor while he was researching one of his nonfiction books, *Fire on the Beaches.* During this research, Taylor came across a report that described the rescue of an eleven-year-old Dutch boy in 1942 who had been found floating on a raft in the Caribbean. The boy had been aboard a ship that had been torpedoed by a German submarine. That story stayed in the back of Taylor's mind for almost ten years before he wrote the award-winning novel.

The Cay

For most readers, *The Cay* is the best known of Taylor's books. Published in 1969, it sold more than 2.5 million copies and was responsible for establishing Ted Taylor as a major writer for young adults. *The Cay* was extremely popular in Japan as well as in the United States. According to Taylor, the universal themes of survival and interdependence are what make *The Cay* appealing to so many readers.

The Cay is set in the Caribbean Sea during World War II. Phillip Enright is a twelve-year-old boy who lives on the island of Curaçao off the coast of Venezuela. When German submarines begin sinking oil tankers and threaten the refinery on Curaçao, Phillip's mother insists upon returning to their home in Philadelphia. She and Phillip are aboard the

SS *Hato,* afloat somewhere on the Caribbean Sea, when the ship is struck by torpedoes. The ship sinks, and Phillip is injured when he jumps overboard. Timothy, an old black man, rescues Phillip by pulling him onto one of the rafts. Phillip's injuries soon cause him to lose his sight. With only a few supplies and the ship's cat for company, Timothy and Phillip finally find a small cay, or low island.

Initially, Phillip blames Timothy for all his troubles. His hatred and distrust of the black man make the relationship between the two of them difficult. As Timothy strives to teach Phillip how to survive on his own, Phillip's resentment and racism gradually disappear.

The Cay has won more than eleven literary awards, including the Jane Addams Book Award. However, it is also Taylor's most controversial book. The Council on Children's Books labeled *The Cay* racist, and it was banned in many public libraries. In 1975, five years after winning the Jane Addams Book Award, Taylor was asked to return it. He did. Taylor denies the charge of racism in *Something About the Author:* "*The Cay* is *not* racist, in my firm belief, and the character of Timothy, the old black man, modeled after a real person and several composites, is 'heroic' and not a stereotype" (Commire, p. 145).

> *In 1975, five years after winning the Jane Addams Book Award, Taylor was asked to return it. He did.*

stereotype a character that lacks originality or individuality because it conforms to preconceived notions

Timothy of the Cay

For years, readers (including Taylor's own children) wanted to know what happened to Phillip after he was rescued. They begged Taylor to write a sequel. Finally, he responded with that story and more. *Timothy of the Cay* (1993), which is both the prequel-sequel to *The Cay,* was named a Best Book for Young Adults in 1993 by the American Library Association (ALA). The story begins in 1942 with Phillip in the sick bay of the ship that rescued him. The plot then backtracks to 1884 as twelve-year-old Timothy is seeking work on a sailing ship. The story continues to alternate between Phillip's long struggle to regain his sight and the West Indian sailor's life on the sea as it leads up to Timothy's fateful meeting with Phillip. The book ends with Phillip finally returning to the cay where his friend Timothy lost his life.

The Outer Banks Trilogy

Taylor was thirteen when he first encountered the Atlantic Ocean. On a trip to the beach with a friend, he watched a Coast Guard crew practicing rescues in the surf. Later in life, Taylor used the memory of that scene to write about the surf-boat crews practicing in the stories he set on the Hatteras Banks of North Carolina in The Outer Banks Trilogy: *Teetoncey* (1974), *Teetoncey and Ben O'Neal* (1975), and *The Odyssey of Ben O'Neal* (1977).

trilogy a series of three literary works that are closely related and share a single theme

The three Outer Banks stories concern the adventures of Taylor's young hero, Ben O'Neal, and the young girl he rescues and calls Teetoncey. The trilogy won the 1980 Recognition of Merit Award of the George S. Stone Center for Children's Books, an award in recognition of both the quality of the books and their popularity with young adult readers.

Taylor researched these books at the University of North Carolina, where he examined old diaries and documents from the Outer Banks. Teetoncey was the first young female character Taylor attempted to create. He says that he was afraid to write about a girl because he did not have a good imagination. Teetoncey, like Taylor's male characters, is drawn from real life. Lacking firsthand experience in being a young girl, Taylor used his daughter Wendy as the model for the character Teetoncey.

Stranger from the Sea: *Teetoncey*

Teetoncey is the first of three adventure stories set on the Outer Banks. The protagonist for these three stories is young Ben O'Neal. During one of the fierce storms that frequently rip the Outer Banks, Ben and his dog rescue a young girl from a wrecked ship. She is suffering from the shock of her experience and is unable to speak. Ben and his mother take her to live with them while she is recuperating and she soon wins a place in their hearts.

Box of Treasures: *Teetoncey and Ben O'Neal*

treacherous marked by hidden dangers and hazards

In the second book of the trilogy, Teetoncey regains her speech and tells of treasure she saw slide into the sea just before her ship, the *Malta Express*, sank. Risking death in the treacherous seas, Ben and his friends try to find the treasure box and claim the treasure for themselves. Ben's mother grows closer to Teetoncey as she realizes that Ben's strong desire to follow in his father's footsteps and go to sea will soon take him away from home.

Facing the Wind: *The Odyssey of Ben O'Neal*

The final book of the trilogy begins with Ben saying good-bye to Teetoncey as she begins her long journey home to England. Ben, the son of a drowned sailor, is about to realize his dream of following his father's career on the high seas. He lands a berth aboard a sailing ship bound for Barbados. Before his ship sails, Ben receives an urgent message that Teetoncey is in trouble and needs his help. Ben's plans are interrupted once again when he goes to the aid of Teetoncey and her dog.

The Tuck Tales

Dogs play an important role in many of Taylor's stories. During the early 1930s, Taylor was given a small mongrel puppy whom he named Napoleon but called Nappy for short. Of the many dog stories Taylor has written, his most popular are *The Trouble with Tuck* (1981) and its sequel, *Tuck Triumphant* (1991). These are the tales of Friar Tuck, a golden Labrador retriever, and Helen, his fourteen-year-old owner.

The Trouble with Tuck

Friar Tuck has been Helen's faithful companion for many years. When Tuck begins to lose his sight, Helen embarks on a campaign to give him back as much as possible of the life he had known before. Based on a true story, *The Trouble with Tuck* tells how Helen trains Tuck to work with a guide dog.

Tuck Triumphant

This sequel to *The Trouble with Tuck* is set one year later. Helen's parents decide to adopt a Korean baby, but the baby, Chok Do, turns out to be a six-year-old boy with a handicap. Helen, with the help of her faithful Labrador retriever Friar Tuck, finds a way to make it possible for her parents to keep their new son.

> *Taylor met his current wife, Flora, while walking his dogs on the beach one morning. One of Taylor's dogs attacked Flora's dog, beginning a friendship that led to their owners' marriage.*

sniper a person who shoots at exposed individuals, often from a hidden vantage point

Dogs remain important in Taylor's life. Taylor met his current wife, Flora, while walking his dogs on the beach one morning. One of Taylor's dogs attacked Flora's dog, beginning a friendship that led to their owners' marriage.

Sniper

Some of Taylor's adventure stories, like *Sniper* (1989), may appeal more to older readers. *Sniper* is the story of young Benjamin Jepson who lives with his family on Los Coyotes Preserve in southern California. Benjamin's father established the preserve to study big cats, such as leopards, jaguars, lions and tigers. This exciting Taylor novel begins with peacocks squalling in the early hours of the morning, warning of a sniper who shoots one of the big cats.

Ben's parents are on one of their frequent trips to Africa, and they left Alfredo Garcia to run the preserve. However, Alfredo is in intensive care following a head-on collision with another vehicle and fifteen-year-old Ben is now on his own at the preserve. A sniper is killing their treasured cats and Ben must decide what to do.

Taylor got the idea and setting for *Sniper* while on an animal preserve doing his research for an adult book. *Sniper* was named an ALA Best Book for Young Adults in 1990.

Sweet Friday Island

Sweet Friday Island (1984) is a father-daughter adventure story set in Mexico. Fifteen-year-old Peg Toland has been looking forward to a trip with her father for months. Their long-planned camping vacation takes them to Friday Island, a remote site between the west coast of mainland Mexico and the Baja California peninsula. The island is supposed to be uninhabited, but Peg and her father soon find they are not alone on the island. *Sweet Friday Island* is a frightening story that celebrates Peg's courage and resourcefulness as she struggles to save herself and her father.

The Weirdo

Another Taylor novel with a female protagonist is the award-winning *The Weirdo* (1991). Samantha Sanders is still having bad dreams about the murdered man whose body she uncovered near her home seven years ago. Then, it happens again. Samantha witnesses someone dumping a body in the swamp near her home.

The swamp is also home to Chip Clewt and his father. No one knows much about Chip. Samantha and her friends refer to him as "The Weirdo." Horribly scarred in a fire, Chip tries to avoid all contact with people, including Samantha and the others who live near the swamp. When Samantha finally meets Chip face-to-face, she learns to appreciate him as a human being. Their friendship grows, and soon Chip joins Samantha to search for a killer in the swamp.

The Weirdo was a winner of the Edgar Award and was named an ALA 1992 Best Book for Young Adults.

Walking Up a Rainbow

Taylor dedicated *Walking Up a Rainbow* (1986) to his wife, Flora, who asked, "Write me a tall tale about an adventuresome girl." He did. The full, rather enticing title of this book is *Walking Up a Rainbow: Being the True Version of the Long and Hazardous Journey of Susan D. Carlisle, Mrs. Myrtle Dessery, Drover Bert Pettit, and Cowboy Clay Carmer and Others.*

Susan Carlisle is a teenage orphan with a huge debt. She has just thirteen months to earn enough money to save her Iowa home. To pay off her parents' debt and save her home, Susan hatches a plan to sell sheep in the gold mines of California. She joins a wagon train and begins driving 2,000 sheep to California. Susan's hazardous journey is complicated when she meets cowboy Clay Carmer and falls in love.

Taylor is also well known for his nonfiction works. His early days in the merchant marine, and later in the U.S. Navy, provided him with background material and ideas for his World War II nonfiction stories. According to Taylor, the most popular of these books is *Air Raid: Pearl Harbor!* (1971). This book is still popular with twelve-year-old boys who have been writing to Taylor for many years telling of their enjoyment of this nonfiction work.

Air Raid: Pearl Harbor!

Air Raid: Pearl Harbor! is the story of the Japanese air assault on Pearl Harbor, which marked America's entrance into World War II. What is unique about this book is that the story is told alternately from the American and Japanese points of view. Taylor brings the story alive for readers by sharing first-hand accounts of both Japanese and American participants in this historic event. Taylor based this book directly on research for *Tora! Tora! Tora!* The text for *Air Raid: Pearl Harbor!* is accompanied by excellent illustrations and maps.

Battle in the Arctic Seas

Battle in the Arctic Seas: The Story of Convoy PQ17 (1976) is the story of the voyage of the *Troubadour* and other ships in a convoy that sets out from Iceland and heads for Russia during 1942. Taylor drew some of the information for this book, as he does for many of his other books, from his personal experience serving on convoys during World War II. He also used information from the diary of the main character, Howard Carraway. Like *Air Raid: Pearl Harbor!,* this book also provides excellent maps, diagrams, and illustrations.

Ted Taylor continues to write his adventure stories in his home at Laguna Beach. He lives in a house surrounded by trees that is only three blocks from the Pacific Ocean. Still addicted to travel, Taylor and his wife try to take at least one foreign trip each year. When he is not traveling, he writes seven days a week—except during football season.

If you like the works of Theodore Taylor, you might also enjoy the works of Gary Paulsen and Scott O'Dell.

Selected Bibliography

WORKS BY THEODORE TAYLOR

Novels for Young Adults

The Cay (1969)

The Children's War (1971)

The Maldonado Miracle (1973)

Teetoncey, illustrated by Richard Cuffari (1974; 1991)

Teetoncey and Ben O'Neal, illustrated by Richard Cuffari (1975; 1991)

The Odyssey of Ben O'Neal, illustrated by Richard Cuffari (1977; 1991)

The Trouble with Tuck (1981; 1989; 1993)

Sweet Friday Island (1984; 1994)

The Cats of Shambala, with Tipi Hedron (1985; 1992)

Rocket Island (1985)

Walking Up a Rainbow: Being the True Version of the Long and Hazardous Journey of Susan D. Carlisle, Mrs. Myrtle Dessery, Drover Bert Pettit, and Cowboy Clay Carmer and Others (1986; 1994)

The Hostage, illustrated by Darrell Sweet (1987; 1991)

Sniper (1989)

Tuck Triumphant (1991)

The Weirdo (1991)

Maria, A Christmas Story (1992)

The Ox and the Hinny, A Christmas Story (1992)

To Kill the Leopard (1993)

Timothy of the Cay (1993)

Nonfiction

People Who Make Movies (1967)

Air Raid: Pearl Harbor!, illustrated by W. T. Mars (1971)

Rebellion Town: Williamsburg, 1776, illustrated by Robert Cuffari (1973)

Battle in the Arctic Seas: The Story of Convoy PQ17, illustrated by Robert Andrew Parker (1976)

A Shepherd Watches, A Shepherd Sings, with Louis Irigaray (1977)

Battle Off Midway Island, illustrated by Andrew Glass (1981)

HMS Hood vs. Bismarck: The Battleship Battle, illustrated by Andrew Glass (1982)

The Battle in the English Channel, illustrated by Andrew Glass (1983)

Works About Theodore Taylor

Bagnall, Norma. "Theodore Taylor: His Models of Self-Reliance." *Language Arts,* January 1980, vol. 57, pp. 86–91.

Commire, Anne, ed. *Something About the Author.* Detroit: Gale Research, 1989, vol. 54, pp. 135–146.

De Montreville, Doris, and Elizabeth D. Crawford, eds. *Fourth Book of Junior Authors & Illustrators.* New York: H. W. Wilson, 1978, pp. 325–327.

Gallo, Donald R., ed.. *Speaking for Ourselves, Too: More Autobiographical Sketches by Notable Authors of Books for*

How to Write to the Author
Theodore Taylor
c/o Harcourt Brace & Co.
1250 Sixth Avenue
San Diego, CA 92101

Young Adults. Urbana, Ill.: National Council of Teachers of English, 1993, pp. 209–211.

Lesniak, James G., and Susan M. Trosky, eds. *Contemporary Authors, New Revision Series.* Detroit: Gale Research, 1993, vol. 38, pp. 424–427.

"The Best, the Notable, and the Recommended." *Emergency Librarian,* vol. 17, March-April 1990, pp. 9–22.

Joyce Carol Thomas

(1938-)

by Leslie S. Cook

The author of six adolescent novels, seven books of poetry, six plays, and the editor of a collection of short stories for young people, Joyce Carol Thomas exudes her own unique musical style. Born on 25 May 1938 in Ponca City, Oklahoma, Ms. Thomas spent her childhood as a migrant farm worker within a large family. Moving to Tracy, California at the age of ten, Thomas mentally collected characters that would later appear in her writing. She put herself through college while supporting her children as a telephone operator, eventually going on to become an English and French teacher in a public high school. After teaching and writing at several universities in California, Ms. Thomas has been teaching creative writing at the University of Tennessee in Knoxville, Tennessee since 1989.

migrant one who moves regularly from one place to another to find work

steep to thoroughly
soak with something

Thomas is about style, childhood memories, and being a Black woman. Her six novels for adolescents are steeped in the themes of mysticism that surround her characters, nature's indiscriminate power, and conflict leading to growth. Her work, admittedly influenced by the gospel music of her childhood, sings praise to the elements that make up both her personality and her writing.

Childhood Memories

evoke to call to
mind

Ms. Thomas shows she knows how to evoke memories of childhood with her words. Drawing on her life as a pre-adolescent in Ponca City, she talks of a tall hill she used to roll down as a child:

> What I thought was a hill was just a bump. The memory was accurate, but it's the memory of a child, the sights and sounds and smells and tastes were much more sharp. Poetic license allows imagination to pick up colors in the vivid way we looked at things when we were much younger. (Pearlman, p. 126)

Poetic license certainly was present when Thomas composed the poem "Sisters" found in *Brown Honey and Broomwheat Tea*. Based on an incident during her childhood in Ponca City, Oklahoma, she remembers the townspeople calling her and her sister "the gold dust twins." Thinking it sounded beautiful,

> And all the time I'm thinking
> It's the dust from the yellow flowers
> sequining the Moroline, Vasiline
> on our shiny legs

she was disheartened when her mother told her she was being mocked because of her skin color. Relying on the voices of her childhood as a source of inspiration lends a sincere tone to Thomas' writing, and the beauty of her language never belies the fact that the voice of experience is writing about days passed.

Role of Women

Though writing from her perspective as a Black woman growing up in a large, poor agricultural family, Thomas writes for all people. When asked in an interview to tell of a time when her worked evoked a strong reaction from a young person, she told about an incident when her book, *Marked by Fire*, was used as a peace maker between a public and a private school known to have a longstanding rivalry. Ms. Thomas noted twice that the response she received about this novel "was mainly from young women" wanting to know more about the main character Abyssinia (Interview).

Women are an integral part of Thomas's work, from the matriarchy of *Marked by Fire* to the reign of Queen Mother Rhythm in *When the Nightingale Sings*. Women are not only the main support for Abbysinia and Marigold, but also their worst enemies. In *Journey, Water Girl,* and *Bright Shadows* the main characters are on personal quests. Meggie is trying to save her friends from death at the hands of a villain, Amber is searching for a sense of belonging, and Abbysinia is trying to expose evil. Thomas' female characters are participating in activities that have usually appeared in male-dominated stories, and the young women are filled with courage and inner strength that help them overcome all obstacles.

> *Thomas's female characters are participating in activities that have usually appeared in male-dominated stories, and the young women are filled with courage and inner strength that help them overcome all obstacles.*

Mysticism and Symbolism

Spiders don't whisper in babies' ears, rivers don't tell tales of Indians, and dead people don't come back to life unless you heed the mysticism and symbolism in the world around you. Dreams are vehicles through which most all of Thomas' characters find the answers to their problems. Abbysinia is known at birth to be a highly intuitive child, and as she grows, her dreams serve to inform and enrich her daily life. In *Marked by Fire*, Abby's dream of Trembling Sally coming to her in the form of a tornado presents an intricate analysis of the mind and spirit of the woman who "had no choice but to harness the wind" (p. 120). Dreams also help Abby to see that she will sing again and give her warning of Mother Barker's death. It is a dream of the song of a nightingale that leads Marigold to Queen Mother Rhythm, and Amber's

symbolism the use of **symbols,** or things that stand for or represent something else

mysticism the experience of communion with spiritual reality

dream of the dancing deer gives her vision to see the truth around her.

Thomas will not deny that she likes happy endings: "If a happy ending is what I want, I write one" (SAAAS, p. 306). Often her desire for a happy ending results in a *deus ex machina,* but rather than detract from the story, her mystical endings remind us of the magic in the world. In *Golden Pasture* there is a noticeable lack of the fantastic. Carl Lee does not have visions like Amber, dreams like Abby, or fateful findings like Marigold, yet in the end the ultimate in magic happens as a flash of lightning streaks from the sky to stop the evil Hellhound from killing both Carl Lee and his horse Thunderfoot.

Several scenes in Thomas' books are of church revivals or gospel conventions. When talking about her upbringing Thomas says that she was brought up almost literally under the wing of the church. The reality of the intense spiritual occurrences in her writing is a part of Thomas' mystical childhood that is not a widely accepted part of Western tradition. Her weaving of the fantastic throughout her novels reminds young people of the possibilities of the mind and the magic that exists in everyday life. Even as Thomas describes her own creative processes she talks of being in a trance, at the mercy of the muses, with characters "walking into [her] space" (Interview) announcing their names and telling their stories.

The Power of Nature

Nature is respected in Thomas' novels. Her first four book titles encompass the four elements: *Marked by Fire, Bright Shadows, Water Girl,* and *Golden Pastures.* Young readers may seek to learn the mystery of the golden alfalfa fields through Carl Lee's eyes, or strain to hear the lesson of the aroma of the lilies and gardenias with Marigold's ears. Nature with its many heads, is a key player whose presence can never be forgotten. In a time when environmental consciousness is a must, Thomas gives meaning to environmentalism by bringing her readers back to a time when we lived closer to our source.

Growing up in an agricultural community, Thomas was also a participant in and witness to the random power of nature. Her books are filled with the messengers of the earth.

deus ex machina in fiction or drama, a character, device, or event that is introduced suddenly and provides a contrived solution to a problem that does not appear to have one

muse In Greek mythology, the nine Muses are goddesses who preside over the arts, sciences, song and poetry. Today, the muse is considered a source of inspiration.

four elements the four substances formerly believed to make up the physical universe: fire, air, water, and earth

Thomas values the fact that we share this planet not only with people of races and nationalities, but also the animals that make their homes beside us (SAAAS, p. 305). All of her books have animal friends that play integral roles in the main characters' lives. Memory of *Journey* is born with a tarantula whispering in her ear, a dancing deer leads Amber to enlightenment in *Water Girl,* and a horse unites father and son in *Golden Pasture*. Still, nature is not always kind, and the wasps that sting young Abbysinia in *Marked by Fire* have their place in its scheme too.

The tornado plains of Oklahoma and the earthquake zones of California provide Thomas the material to explore the destructive side of Mother Nature. Her memories of the power of the storms and tremors pervade the lives of her fictional young friends. In *Marked by Fire,* Abby was born in the middle of a cotton field as a tornado raged around her mother's head. The threat of the devastating twisters hangs in the shadows of Ponca City and shapes the lives of its people. Both Abby's father, Strong Jackson, and her nemesis, Trembling Sally, are broken when a tornado destroys their lives. *Water Girl's* Amber is haunted by California earthquakes that have been rumored to have swallowed whole towns. Amber's respect for this natural phenomenon grows upon hearing the story of the earthquake; once a friend of the Indians, the earthquake became angry when he saw his friends being cut down by a savage tribe, so he vowed to reap destruction for their deaths. In *When the Nightingale Sings,* Marigold discovers the peaceful side of the hurricane when she is caught in its path. Though the storm ravages the Swamp, its eye brings her peaceful visions that lead her to her destiny.

nemesis a formidable and usually victorious rival or opponent

Using the fruits of the earth to heal is Mother Barker's way of transferring her respect for nature to Abbysinia. In *Marked By Fire,* Mother Barker is the town healer who teaches her art to Abby before she dies because "these educated doctors'll be running out of medicine . . . medicine'll stop working because they're moving away from mother nature" (p. 141). Abby shows mutual respect by opting to stay home after high school to continue her godmother's practice; though she returns to college in *Bright Shadows,* she is still dedicated to the healing gifts of the earth. Thomas, herself, attests to the healing properties of broomwheat tea. "Good for what ails you," her mother would say as she poured them a cup for their sore throats. When Thomas writes it "gives

elixir a liquid that heals illness or enhances one's powers

[her] comfort to see this elixir steeped in an imaginary cup and drunk by one of [her] characters" (SAAS, p. 301).

Conflict Leading to Growth

Joyce Carol Thomas sees conflicts as her "principle quest" (SAAS 209). Her belief that conflict leads to growth is a theme from which everyone can most certainly learn. Her characters deal with true-to-life problems such as rape, murder, and abuse; yet the fact that they surmount these obstacles only to come out the stronger makes Abby, Carl Lee, Marigold, Memory, and Amber excellent role models.

No longer must adolescent novels be candy coated versions of life, and Ms. Thomas makes no apologies for the often graphic depiction of life in her own work. Both *Marked by Fire* and its sequel, *Bright Shadows,* contain emotionally charged scenes. In *Marked by Fire,* the main character, Abbysinia, is raped by a trusted member of her church. At ten years of age, this child must learn to overcome the horror. Though it takes months of silence and the loving support of the women of Ponca City, Abby finally comes to the realization that God has not singled her out for hate, an admirable lesson for any age. In *Bright Shadows,* Abby is again confronted by the evils of the world when she discovers her aunt grotesquely murdered in her room by her own husband. Abby's deeper questioning of the existence of God's benevolence leads her to triumph over the dark and embrace the shadows.

Conflict leading to growth is present in a different way in *Journey.* The heroine, Memory, is confronted by the monstrosities of the outside world when her friends are being dismembered in the park. Her inner voice speaks to her in a soothing tone, a spidery voice, that keeps her calm. Outside of her guitar playing mind, the world is screaming for her to become a part of its anger. Confronting her fears while keeping herself enclosed in her calm inner world, Memory is able to escape from a certain death at the hands of her villainous neighbors.

The struggle for identity is an educational adventure that all of Thomas' characters undertake. *Water Girl* involves a twist of fate that leads the protagonist, Amber, out of her comfort zone. After discovering one afternoon that she does not really belong to the family she has called her own for fifteen years, Amber runs away in search of her real parents, Abbysinia and Carl Lee. In the woods she discovers that she is "the daughter of many mothers" (p. 118), a title that she relishes. Tangled roots also play a role in the growth of Marigold in *When the Nightingale Sings*. Displaced in the Cinderella world of the Swamp, Marigold accepts the painful teasing of her stepsisters and bitter Aunt Ruby, and lives her life in naiveté until love strikes her eyes. In her search for her self, her talent brings two worlds and two sisters together, and in turn, finds her own family ties in the language of music. *Golden Pasture*, Thomas' only book to date almost entirely absent of women, chronicles a summer of growing in thirteen-year-old Carl Lee's life. His anger and distrust of his abusive father is tempered by his grandfather who points out the father and son's mystical bond of a horse.

naiveté lack of wisdom about the world

Conclusion

True to her name, Joyce Carol Thomas shapes words so that they read like a song, yet the song is not always joyful. Maybe it's the rhythm of the music that comes through her words like a gospel convention; or maybe it's the tornado-like way she whips her stories around you, leaving you with the back cover of a book and enough mind food for a week. Thomas strives to "evoke in the readers some kind of response. It doesn't have to be laughter. It can be anger; it can be crying; a whole range of emotions" (Interview). Her readers are very important to her, and with them she shares the secrets of her success through her novels for young people. Her pride in her identity translates into a style that resonates with memories of childhood. The result of Thomas' own introspection is a magical set of books which convey her wisdom in using obstacles to grow and her respect for the powerful force of nature. Admittedly somewhat autobiographical, Joyce Carol Thomas' novels provide their readers a glimpse into the mind of a child with all its mysticism that evades the harnessing of words. Perhaps the fountain of youth is found by remaining a child at heart. Joyce Carol Thomas' books can teach young people how to grow outside while forever remaining true to the child within.

> *Thomas strives to "evoke in the readers some kind of response. It doesn't have to be laughter. It can be anger; it can be crying; a whole range of emotions."*

If you like books by Joyce Carol Thomas, consider reading works by Maya Angelou, Langston Hughes, Virginia Hamilton, Walter Dean Myers, Gary Soto, Mildred Delois Taylor, and Virginia Euwer Wolf.

Selected Bibliography

WORKS BY JOYCE CAROL THOMAS

Novels for Young Adults

Marked by Fire (1982)

Bright Shadows (1983)

The Golden Pasture (1986)

Water Girl (1986)

Journey (1988)

When the Nightingale Sings (1992)

Poetry

Bittersweet (1973)

Crystal Breezes (1974)

Blessing (1975)

Black Child (1981)

Inside the Rainbow (1982)

Brown Honey in Broomwheat Tea (1993)

Gingerbread Days (1994)

Plays

A Song in the Sky (1976)

Look! What a Wonder! (1976)

Magnolia (1977)

Gospel Roots (1981)

I Have Heard of a Land (1989)

When the Nightingale Sings (1991)

Editor

A Gathering of Flowers: Stories About Being Young in America (1990)

WORKS ABOUT JOYCE CAROL THOMAS

Commire, Anne, ed. "Joyce Carol Thomas." In *Something About the Author*. Detroit: Gale Research, vol. 40, 1985, pp. 208–209.

Nakamura, Joyce, ed. "Joyce Carol Thomas." In *Something About the Author Autobiographical Series*. Detroit: Gale Research, vol. 7., 1990, pp. 299–311.

Pearlman, Mickey and Katherine U. Henderson. *Inter/Views*. Lexington, Kentucky: University of Kentucky Press, 1990, pp. 125–131.

Thomas, Joyce Carol. Personal interview. 9 November 1993.

How to Write to the Author
Joyce Carol Thomas
c/o HarperCollins Publishers
10 East 53d Street
New York, NY 10022

Julian F. Thompson

(1927-   )

by Daniel J. Cox

Julian Thompson writes about,
What if . . . ?
Huh?
You know, What If? Like, what if your parents paid to have you killed? Or your mother and older brother were murdered in a car bombing? Or the father you did not know died and left you millions of dollars—with which you bought a town just for teenagers? Or you lived in a world in which people lived under domes? Or you could experiment with different career choices before you really had to decide? Or you were abducted by gypsies and taken to another Earth? Or you suddenly found yourself facing trial for *witchcraft!*

And how about: what if you could spend all your time talking with your friends about all the weird stuff: sex and drugs and nuclear war and diseases and death and parents? Maybe you would even find an adult now and then who really listened to your questions—and your answers. Would that be great or what?

Julian Thompson seems to be one of those adults who listen to young people. His novels give them the chance to look at how they feel and the (sometimes) outrageous things they think. His books help readers see some possible answers to the questions they just cannot seem to ask anyone but a best friend. These are the reasons that readers want to know more about this writer. (Can you believe that some guy who has been a teacher and who has even graduated from college long before you were born can write about what is in your head? And you like it? And lots of adults do not like it?)

Who is Julian Thompson?

Julian Francis Thompson, born on 16 November 1927 in New York City, was much like some of his characters when he was growing up. His dad, also named Julian Francis Thompson, was a businessman and sometime playwright. His mother was Amalita (Stagg) Thompson. Thompson's father died when Julian was eleven. That pretty much ended the "easy life" of spending summers on a farm in Fairfield, New York, and winters in a Park Avenue apartment in New York City. Thompson's mother had to sell the family's farm and change their lifestyle.

Thompson was attending a private day school (elementary school) and might have had to quit, but his grades were good enough that he got a scholarship. He even earned a scholarship to the Lawrenceville School, a special preparatory school (high school) in New Jersey. He liked school, for the most part, but he considered sports to be the best part, even though he was not especially good at any of them. These interests helped Thompson to cope with his father's death as well as with his worries about his mother and his own future.

After high school Thompson went to Princeton University for his bachelor's degree (1949) and then to Columbia University for his master's degree (1955). His education and his work as a coach in summer camps and college prepared him to return to Lawrenceville School as a coach and teacher of Greek and Roman history (from 1949 to 1962 and from 1965 to 1967). Later he became interested in working with students in "alternative" schools and was asked to be the director of Changes, Inc., an alternative high school in East Orange, New Jersey, from 1971 to 1977.

When Did He Start Writing?

The writing bug had bitten Thompson, however, and he started writing during school vacations. He spent some time at the Bread Loaf Writer's Conference at Middlebury, Vermont, in 1963 and could not shake the need to see if he could write full time. In 1978 he married Polly Nichy, an artist, and they moved to Vermont, where many of his novels are set, to write and work. Most of Thompson's novels deal with issues that teenagers spend time thinking about. They elaborate on or derive plots from characteristics of some of the students he knew as a teacher and as a teenager himself.

The writing itself is a long process for Thompson. He does not use a word processor. The handwritten notes he sends to people are readable, but he says his handwriting is so bad that he relies on his old Royal portable typewriter for anything he writes that others need to be able to read. When he is writing a book, he writes rough drafts in longhand and later types them to be sent to his publishers.

Thompson has been writing since 1963 and successfully publishing his work since 1983. The ideas keep coming as he remembers events in his life and reads about what is happening in today's schools. All his novels feature teenagers facing big questions. Sometimes they present quite a stretch from reality, but reality does not always seem real to teens, does it? The situations might be far-fetched, but they are always based on those questions and situations that all teenagers know about. If they did not deal with the touchy subjects that teens have to face, Thompson's books would not be so controversial for parent groups and librarians, would they?

Since his first novel, *The Grounding of Group 6* (1983), Thompson has faced a good deal of criticism from book reviewers. They do not like that he writes so openly about teenagers thinking about (and sometimes even having) sex. They do not like the negative way in which he usually portrays adults (even though each novel seems to have at least one adult whom the teenage protagonists can admire). And they do not like that he writes with so many parenthetical expressions (as if it were hard to read these asides). But Thompson does not write for critics or adults. He writes for teenagers. And with these readers in mind, he keeps asking, "What if . . . ?"

> *The writing itself is a long process for Thompson. He does not use a word processor.*

Will There Be More?

How many more novels can we expect? What if Julian Thompson made so much money that he did not need to keep writing? In a telephone conversation on 9 May 1995 he answered that question: "I love doing this, and, if I were a millionaire, I'd still do it."

That philosophy is a good thing. Someone needs to keep shaking things up. What if there were no books like his, books that show their readers what would happen if . . . ? You can read Thompson's own description of his life in the *Something About the Author Autobiography Series.*

What Are His Novels About?

The Grounding of Group 6 is probably the best known of Thompson's novels. It is the one that launched his writing career. It includes a really big What If: What if your parents thought you were such a loser that everyone would be better off without you? That's just what happens to five sixteen-year-old youths, three girls and two boys, whose parents send them to a private school in Vermont where Nat Rittenhouse, their "guide," is supposed to have them killed! What happens when the teens find out? How do they escape death and what do they do with themselves, knowing they cannot go home again? This first novel is a good introduction to many of the themes to which the author returns many times in later works.

Facing It (1983) adds Thompson's love of sports and coaching to his story line. This novel draws on the author's own life experiences—not that he ever had the chance to play professional baseball, but his love of sports focused on coaching kids. The youngsters at camp and the other counselors all have their own problems to overcome and learn to rely on one another to deal with them and become successful.

A Question of Survival (1984) picks up the survival-in-the-wilderness theme again. Toby and Zack are a couple sent to the Frances Marion Institute to learn self-sufficiency. They end up at the mercy of some extremely sadistic characters and become the hunted instead of the hunters. Similarities to *The Grounding of Group 6* are a bit obvious, but Thompson

theme central message about life in a literary work

sadistic excessively cruel

always has enough other answers to "What if . . ." to make each plot intriguing.

Discontinued (1985) has high school basketball star Duncan Bannigan searching for clues to the bombing deaths of his mother and brother. Another popular theme for Thompson— the threat of nuclear war and how people might go off the deep end preparing for it—appears again here after first coming up in *A Question of Survival.* The role of drugs in society is also important to the plot. As usual, there are lots of twists and turns as Dunc goes off on his own. He meets a very beautiful and friendly "older woman" who just happens to be the daughter of the leader of a kind of cult preparing for the war. When Dunc accidentally finds out how their operations are financed, he gets too many answers for his own good!

cult a religious group that follows a living leader who promotes unusual teachings or practices

A Band of Angels (1986) includes many of the devices that Thompson likes to use in his novels: a teen forced to depend on himself after the death of a caretaker adult, threatening authority figures, cross-country odysseys, and couples searching for answers about relationships. There are hints of other well-known plots, too: scientists who create a terrible virus and defy the government, and the federal witness protection program (sort of). The main character Jordan/Amos lives many lives in a very short time!

Simon Pure (1987) is about fifteen-year-old Simon Storm, a freshman at fictional Riddle University in Vermont. This time the protagonist is grouped with Grebe, a psychology professor, Amanda, a college sophomore, and Kate, the university president's daughter. They try to keep the economics fraternity from taking over the university. It is not as hair-raising as the death-defying plots of previous novels, but it is funny and fun and includes lighter versions of some of the events in *Discontinued.* It offers different answers to "What if . . . ?"

protagonist the main character of a literary work

In *The Taking of Mariasburg* (1988) Maria (pronounced Muh-rye-ah) has taken some of the millions her unknown father left her and dedicated the place to teenagers. Naturally, this means that the local adults are more than a little uneasy and want it "investigated" (which means shut down or controlled by them). Talk about a "What if . . . "! Think of what it would be like to live in a town run *by* teenagers just *for* teenagers. Thompson sees the results as much different from those envisioned by William Golding in *The Lord of the Flies.*

William Golding wrote ***Lord of the Flies*** in 1954. The novel deals with a group of boys stranded on an is-land. After losing all moral purpose, they resort to violence.

Thompson's teenagers are usually good, especially when adults leave them alone.

Goofbang Value Daze (1989) moves from the green hills of Vermont to a futuristic Texas town under a weather dome. The dome might represent the control that Authorities of all shapes and sizes want to impose on people's thinking. Thompson seems to have anticipated today's debates over teaching values in the schools and provides an example of what might result when some rather extreme values are made part of the curriculum. The teenage protagonists, of course, resist these impositions and fight for the values of parental wisdom, common decency, acceptance of all people and ideas.

Herb Seasoning (1990) is even more fantasy than *Goofbang Value Daze*. Herbie Hertzman finds himself able to try out a variety of lives or careers. The characters and their wacky names, the in-one-episode-and-then-another plot, and the situations in which Herbie finds himself are like career guidance in Alice's Wonderland. It would be nice to find a place like the counseling firm Castles in Air and get a real feel for all the possibilities life has to offer before deciding what to do with the rest of it. Many graduating high school (or even college) seniors might like a glimpse inside Thompson's crystal ball.

Gypsyworld (1992) is off-world adventure. An ancient fear of European parents has been that their children would be kidnapped by gypsies and never seen again. In this novel, Josip and Marina, the king and queen of Gypsyworld, abduct the five teenage protagonists to their parallel Earth. The five are supposed to be part of an experiment to see if they can adapt to the gypsy ways on this planet where everyone lives in harmony and peace with the universe. The teens try their own hand at kidnapping in order to get back home. Of course, in the process they face all sorts of problems together—problems that are typical of Thompson's stories.

Shepherd (1993) takes a close look at relationships, particularly among graduating seniors Shep Catlett and his life-long friend Tara Garza, and freshman Mary Sutherland. Shep and Tara are two great kids full of hope and promise. Mary wants to grow up too fast and cannot help noticing that Shep and Tara are already where she wants to be and have what she wants to have. Thompson weaves these three together in order to deal once more with some of those themes and questions that possibly have filled the lives of teenagers.

Julian Thompson himself described the plots of his last three novels in a letter of 17 May 1995:

The Fling (1994): Felicia wants to be a writer. She starts a story that contains the very elements she feels her life is lacking: romance, mystery and adventure. And soon, to her amazement, it appears that she, and certain of her friends, are taking part in a peculiar version of her story, in real life.

Philo Fortune's Awesome Journey to His Comfort Zone (1995): Philo Fortune takes off in his parents' old VW [Volkswagen]. On his trip he hopes to figure out how he can make a lot of money. Along the way he's joined by Thea and by Genie, a peculiar girl and giant dog, respectively. And is very nearly killed, finds love, and learns he's really different than he'd thought.

The Trials of Molly Sheldon (1995): From the time that Eben Wheeler comes to Saphouse Junction, Vermont, and into Molly Sheldon's high school and her life, unexpected things begin to happen. First, she discovers she has psychic healing powers, then The Happy Hunting Ground (her father's eclectic general store) becomes the target of a group of self-appointed moralists. And finally, Molly finds herself accused in a modern day witch trial.

eclectic composed of elements from various sources

Selected Bibliography

WORKS BY JULIAN F. THOMPSON

The Grounding of Group 6 (1983)

Facing It (1983)

A Question of Survival (1984)

Discontinued (1985)

A Band of Angels (1986)

Simon Pure (1987)

If you like the works of Julian F. Thompson, you might also like the works of Jay Bennett.

The Taking of Mariasburg (1988)

Goofbang Value Daze (1989)

Herb Seasoning (1990)

Gypsyworld (1992)

Shepherd (1993)

The Fling (1994)

Philo Fortune's Awesome Journey to His Comfort Zone (1995)

The Trials of Molly Sheldon (1995)

WORKS ABOUT JULIAN F. THOMPSON

Commire, Anne, ed. "Julian F. Thompson." In *Something About the Author.* Detroit: Gale Research, 1989, vol. 55, pp. 152–153.

Senick, Gerard J., ed. "Julian F. Thompson." In *Children's Literature Review.* Detroit: Gale Research, 1991, vol. 24, pp. 226–233.

Nakamura, Joyce, ed. "Julian F. Thompson." In *Major Authors and Illustrators for Children and Young Adults: A Selection of Sketches from "Something About the Author."* Detroit: Gale Research, 1993, vol. 6, pp. 2298–2299.

Thompson, Julian. "Defending YA Literature Against the Pharisees and Censors: Is It Worth the Trouble?" *The ALAN Review,* winter 1991, pp. 2–5.

Thompson, Julian F. "Julian F. Thompson." In *Something About the Author Autobiography Series.* Edited by Joyce Nakamura. Detroit: Gale Research, 1991, vol. 13, pp. 231–246.

Tjogas, Stella. "Julian Thompson: An Interview." In *The Voya Reader.* Edited by Dorothy M. Broderick. Metuchen, N.J.: Scarecrow, 1990, p. xii.

How to Write to the Author
Julian F. Thompson
P.O. Box 138
West Rupert, VT 05776

J. R. R. Tolkien

(1892–1973)

by Deborah Webster Rogers

"Home" was a place the boy had never seen. John Ronald Reuel Tolkien (called Ronald), age three, was sailing for England with his mother and baby brother, Hilary, leaving South Africa behind. His father had planned to follow when his banking business allowed. But instead, Arthur Tolkien died, leaving Mabel Suffield Tolkien to fend for herself and for their two little sons in the midlands of England, where their relatives lived.

A Boy Needing Roots

Ronald's health, which had been weak in the South African climate, dictated the move, and this change at a young age did him good, physically. But too many other changes and losses followed too soon, beginning with the loss of his father.

When Ronald was eight, his mother and her boys became Roman Catholics. As an adult, Tolkien held his faith passionately and regarded it as positive gain, but at the time, Mabel's conversion resulted in a loss of goodwill from the Suffield and Tolkien families. This tension, Tolkien believed, brought on the failure of his mother's health. She died of diabetes when Ronald was twelve and Hilary ten. At sixteen, Tolkien met Edith Bratt and they fell in love, but his guardian, Father Francis Xavier Morgan, standing faithfully by the orphans, not only forbade the teenager to marry but also prohibited him from seeing or even writing to his love. So for a period Tolkien nearly lost Edith, too.

Tolkien threw himself into school activities and friendships, especially "the Tea Club," which included his friends Christopher Wiseman, Rob Gilson, and Geoffrey Smith. Tolkien said, "By 1918 all but one of my close friends were dead."

Tolkien's many personal losses are often reflected in his writing, with its tone of sadness for the passing of time and of people.

Tolkien's many personal losses are often reflected in his writing, with its tone of sadness for the passing of time and of people. The author loved a sense of rootedness, wherever he could find it. The family made its home around Birmingham, near both of his grandfathers, and he felt connected to that place. The years Tolkien spent in a country village, where seasons and plants were constant in their cycles, gave him joy.

Once Tolkien was twenty-one and out of guardianship, he married Edith (after wresting her from her fiancé), and they remained husband and wife for fifty-eight years. They had three sons and a daughter, to whom Tolkien was a loving father. Throughout his life he formed and joined groups of friends, successors to the Tea Club. As an undergraduate, a young teacher, and a professor, he kept on with clubs: with tea, beer, pipes, skits, Norse sagas, their own writings, and discussions of God and everything else. The most famous such group was the Inklings. From the 1930s to the 1950s, this unorganized bunch of cronies at Oxford University included C. S. ("Jack") Lewis.

And Tolkien struck root in Oxford, which he had loved since the start of his undergraduate days in 1911. He became a professor there in 1925 and lived in Oxford for forty-three years. Perhaps the surplus of change in his early life was connected with the external quietness of his adulthood, which in turn contrasts with his sweeping, adventurous fiction.

A Student of Philology

Tolkien also felt rooted in language. In South Africa the Zulus spoke a Bantu language, the Dutch settlers spoke Afrikaans, and the English spoke English; so he must have had some feeling of linguistic pluralism, even as a baby. His mother taught him Latin, French, and German. In school he learned more Latin, and also Greek. Father Morgan loaned him Spanish books. In one house, Tolkien's window overlooked the train tracks, where he saw words such as "Penrhiwceiber" on the cars: Welsh names. Some words gave him goosebumps. Besides liking words, as a boy Tolkien was interested in how words were used. Why could he not say, "a green great dragon," he wondered; why would it have to be "great green"?

> **linguistic pluralism** familiarity with more than one langugage

He learned not only foreign languages but two that were no longer spoken, the older forms of English: Middle English and Old English (also called Anglo-Saxon). Tolkien liked the story-poems he read, and he learned to translate from these tongues. A particular thrill for Tolkien was learning that *Sir Gawain and the Green Knight* was written in the West Midland dialect of Middle English. It would have been the language that his Suffield ancestors used! So he realized that he had a personal connection to this magnificent poem. In fact, one of his first scholarly works was to edit it; he also made a translation into modern English, striving to reproduce both the story and the poetry.

Tolkien started his undergraduate work as a classics major but did better in his philology course. (Philology, a Greek word meaning "love of words," is the study of language and its relationship to literature.) So he changed his major to philology and Anglo-Saxon. After he had graduated from Oxford and served in World War I, Tolkien was hired to work on the *Oxford English Dictionary*, where the older philologists were impressed by his abilities. After five years of teaching at the University of Leeds, he was hired by Oxford University as a professor of Anglo-Saxon.

Tolkien knew a great deal about living languages, which made him happy—but not completely. To satisfy his creative urges, he invented new languages. When he had visited his cousins as a child, they would talk in a coded language that the grown-ups did not understand. But Tolkien kept working on other languages, not just coded English, and each was

> *When Tolkien had visited his cousins as a child, they would talk in a coded language that the grown-ups did not understand.*

better developed than the last. He used Father Morgan's Spanish books. He used a Finnish grammar. He used his imagination and every factual rule he knew about how words are used and how sounds change. Tolkien possessed the passion of a teenager with a hobby and the precision of a philologist. His combination of wide invention with deeply detailed consistency is one reason that his fantasy stories possess so much realism and conviction.

conviction persuasive force

Stories and Histories

Besides words and languages, Tolkien loved stories. As a boy, he was especially impressed by the tale in which Sigurd kills the dragon Fafnir. His own mind created dreams of a great wave overwhelming the land. The Bible was full of stories, including a flood and the verse about "giants in the Earth in those days" (Genesis 6:4). He read classical myths about Zeus, Aphrodite, and Herakles (Hercules); Norse myths about Odin, Brynhild, and Sigurd; and he found the *Kalevala,* a collection of Finnish myths, whose material and language were like none he had known. They included the story of Kullervo, who inadvertently married his sister.

Norse myths were mainly created by Norsemen who lived in Scandinavia during the Middle Ages.

But England had no such body of myths. Its nearest equivalent, the legends of King Arthur, seemed too near to known history. Feeling the need to account for England's mythic past, Tolkien would not be daunted. In fact, his private language prodded him in that direction, for a developing language demands speakers and a history. The loss of his friends in the war impelled Tolkien to write. His young wife, who enjoyed his stories and poems, urged him on. But he did not compose a detailed mythology from beginning to end (nor had he planned to). He developed certain tales and rewrote them. Then his direction changed.

He began writing about an island with a towered city that was pulled back and forth between Middle-earth and the land of the gods. The island was to be England, and the city was to be the origin of Warwick, where once he had visited Edith. A Catholic writing about plural gods? Yes. Tolkien held faith in one Creator, but he could easily envision gods like those in other mythologies as angelic powers under the One. They, the Valar, remain in his mythic history. Earlier references to present-day geography were eventually shed.

Stories that especially occupied Tolkien were the star-messenger (Earendil), the sunken land (Numenor), the accursed hero (Turin), and the heroic couple (Beren and Luthien). He wrote them in prose, in rhyme, and in the style of Anglo-Saxon alliterative verse. Turin is perhaps the person Tolkien could have become in the wake of his own personal misfortunes. Beren is what he became with Edith: BEREN and LUTHIEN are engraved on the Tolkiens' headstones, names of a couple who brave all threats.

The mythology developed by fits and starts. The Tolkiens had four children who loved stories, although they wanted something shorter and plainer than mythology. Their father's yarns came to include the adventures of the unadventurous, namely that of a hobbit named Bilbo Baggins. The word "hobbit" popped into Tolkien's mind once when he saw a blank sheet of paper. On reflection he "found out" that hobbits were like the villagers of his boyhood: *not* heroic, nothing like the powerful elves of his mythology. But the question occurred to him, "What is heroic?" Even before the war, he had thought about that. Tolkien knew that his family name translates as "foolhardy," and that a family legend told of an ancestor who captured the Sultan's standard in 1529. And he knew that dashing deeds are admirable. But in Anglo-Saxon poetry, Tolkien found the true story of the Battle of Maldon, in which the Saxon Beorhtnoth imprisons a band of invading Vikings on an island. When he decides to allow them ashore for a battle, they kill Beorhtnoth and all his loyal troops. Then the Vikings go raid other Saxon towns. Beorhtnoth acts the hero but it does not work. Tolkien wrote a sequel to *Maldon* reflecting on the question. And his children's book *The Hobbit* surprises us with its main character, Bilbo Baggins. This reluctant little hobbit becomes a hero. He proves able to sneak, fight, and scheme, but more important, he can give up a coveted possession—for Tolkien, a vital point.

The Hobbit, or There and Back Again, published in 1937, was a hit. The publisher wanted sequels. Tolkien stalled. To him the mythology was more important. But as he worked, read his work to the Inklings, and sent chapters to his son Christopher during World War II, it turned out that Tolkien's stodgy hobbits were a pivot-point of his history. Their destruction of the Ring of Power ended the Third Age and brought the age of humankind to Middle-earth. He had seen

There is an animated movie version of *The Hobbit* which was released in 1978.

coveted strongly desired

stodgy boring, dull

unpretentious modest, not showy

in World War I what he says in *The Fellowship of the Ring:* "Such is oft the course of deeds that move the wheels of the world: small hands do them because they must, while the eyes of the great are elsewhere." Hobbits are Tolkien's tribute to unpretentious people.

Tolkien, Foolhardy?

Tolkien's own life was unpretentious. He published little scholarly work, scarcely traveled, never cut a great figure. He loved his family, his job, and his writing, but can we see him as foolhardy, embodying his name? He would probably say no.

voluminous lengthy; winding or convoluted

But look at his actions another way and you could hardly imagine a more foolhardy move than offering a voluminous fairy tale for publication in 1954. Fantasy was *out*. It was regarded as unwholesome, even for children. Literature was supposed to be realistic, and "realistic" meant literally reproducing everyday experience. Furthermore, much literature of the mid-twentieth century was short on hope. Wars, influenza epidemics, and economic depression had appalled many of the best writers.

The image of humankind in the fashionable literature of Tolkien's day showed people as poor and needy, often unpleasant and often doing bad things. Reading such works can affect one like the eyes and discourse of Glaurung, the dragon in *The Silmarillion* (1977). Turin "hearkened to his words, and he saw himself as in a mirror misshapen by malice, and he loathed that which he saw." Even fantasy could carry such a view; take, for example, the disturbing works of Franz Kafka.

Franz Kafka (1883–1924) was a Czech novelist and short-story writer. His works include "The Metamorphosis," a short story in which a man turns into an insect.

Tolkien's work, on the other hand, especially *The Lord of the Rings,* contradicted that literary establishment in every way. Fantasy it was, yet minutely realistic too, first in the story's underlying languages, which Tolkien crafted with such care, and second in his portrayal of Middle-earth, our planet. The phases of the moon, the weather, rocks, and landforms, the plants, the distances marched, all win the credulity, or belief, of knowledgeable readers. Tolkien checked his facts as carefully as any writer professing realism in the ordinary sense.

Yet whereas the common realism of Tolkien's time seemed drawn to the unpleasant (like Mordor or Sharkey's

Shire), Tolkien had more good places, cultures, and characters. Instead of the poor humanity of mainstream literature, he shows us people of various races becoming heroes and friends. This is one source of hope in *The Lord of the Rings,* and no wonder that young readers in 1965 grabbed the paperback hungrily.

Two more hopeful ideas in Tolkien's work are the reality of the world and the power of action. The philosophy that everything arises from one's own mind has made some writers and readers queasy. Tolkien's love and respect for a creation independent of us is reassuring. And, in his tales, the individual's choices make a difference. It can be for ill, like Fëanor's decision to fight for the Silmarils forever. But more strikingly and more often we see good decisions having better consequences, as with the choices of Bilbo, Frodo, and Sam to spare Gollum.

Tolkien lectured on the importance of fairy tales in providing fantasy, recovery, escape, and consolation. More important, he wrote tales that provide these elements for many readers. Although when he began, he had no more idea than Frodo of what he was getting into, the orphaned philologist became a kind of quest-hero bringing riches to his culture.

> *Instead of the poor humanity of mainstream literature, he shows us people of various races becoming heroes and friends.*

Selected Bibliography

WORKS BY J. R. R. TOLKIEN

> If you like Tolkien's works, other authors in this collection to try are his friend C. S. Lewis, as well as Madeleine L'Engle, Ursula K. Le Guin, and Lloyd Alexander.

Sir Gawain and the Green Knight (1925)

The Hobbit, or There and Back Again (1937)

Preface to Beowulf and the Finnesburg Fragment, translated by John R. Clark Hall (1940)

Farmer Giles of Ham (1949)

The Fellowship of the Ring: Being the First Part of The Lord of the Rings and *The Two Towers: Being the Second Part of The Lord of the Rings* (1954)

The Return of the King: Being the Third Part of The Lord of the Rings (1955)

The Adventures of Tom Bombadil and Other Verses from the Red Book (1962)

"Once Upon a Time" and "The Dragon's Visit," published in *Winter's Tales for Children* (1965)

The Tolkien Reader, collection of earlier material (1966)

Smith of Wootton Major (1967)
The Road Goes Ever On: A Song Cycle (1967)
Poems and Songs of Middle Earth, recording (1967)

WORKS BY J. R. R. TOLKIEN PUBLISHED POSTHUMOUSLY

Bilbo's Last Song (1974), published in book form in 1990.
"Guide to the Names in The Lord of the Rings," in *A Tolkien Compass,* edited by Jared Lobdell (1975)
Sir Gawain and the Green Knight, Pearl and Sir Sorfeo, modern English translation (1975)
J. R. R. Tolkien Reads and Sings . . . ., two Caedmon recordings (1975)
The Father Christmas Letters (1976)
The Silmarillion (1977)
Pictures by J. R. R. Tolkien (1979)
Unfinished Tales of Numenor and Middle-Earth (1980)
The Letters of J. R. R. Tolkien (1981)
The Monsters and the Critics and Other Essays (1984)
The Book of Lost Tales, Part I (1984)
The Book of Lost Tales, Part II (1984)
The Lays of Beleriand (1985)
The Shaping of Middle-earth (1986)
The Lost Road and Other Writings (1987)
The Return of the Shadow (1988)
The Treason of Isengard (1989)
The War of the Ring (1990)
Sauron Defeated (1992)
Morgoth's Ring (1993)
The War of the Jewels (1994)
Poems and Stories (1994)

WORKS ABOUT J. R. R. TOLKIEN

Anonymous. *J. R. R. Tolkien: Life and Legend.* Oxford: Bodleian Library, 1992.
Becker, Alida, ed. *The Tolkien Scrapbook.* New York: Grosset & Dunlap, 1978.

Carpenter, Humphrey. *Tolkien: A Biography.* Boston: Houghton Mifflin, 1977.

———. *The Inklings.* Boston: Houghton Mifflin, 1979.

Crabbe, Katharyn W. *J. R. R. Tolkien.* Rev. ed. New York: Ungar, 1988.

Day, David. *A Tolkien Bestiary.* New York: Ballantine, 1979.

De Camp, L. Sprague. "Merlin in Tweeds." In *Literary Swordsmen and Sorcerers.* Sauck City, Wis.: Arkham House, 1976.

Flieger, Verlyn. *Splintered Light.* Grand Rapids: Eerdmans, 1983.

Foster, Robert. *The Complete Guide to Middle-earth.* New York: Ballantine, 1981.

Green, William H. *The Hobbit.* New York: Simon & Schuster, 1995.

Helms, Randel. *Tolkien's World.* Boston: Houghton Mifflin, 1974.

———. *Tolkien and the Silmarils.* Boston: Houghton Mifflin, 1981.

Hillegas, Mark R., ed. *Shadows of Imagination.* Rev. ed. Carbondale: Southern Illinois Univ. Press, 1979.

Isaacs, Neil D., and Rose A. Zimbardo, eds. *Tolkien and the Critics.* Notre Dame, Ind.: Univ. of Notre Dame, 1968.

———. *Tolkien: New Critical Perspectives.* Lexington: University Press of Kentucky, 1981.

Johnson, Judith A. *J. R. R. Tolkien: Six Decades of Criticism.* Westport, Conn.: Greenwood, 1986. Bibliography.

Kocher, Paul. *Master of Middle-earth.* Boston: Houghton Mifflin, 1972.

Mathews, Richard. *Lightning from a Clear Sky.* San Bernardino: Borgo, 1978.

Rogers, Deborah, and Ivor Rogers. *J. R. R. Tolkien.* Twayne English Author Series. Boston: G. K. Hall, 1980.

Rosebury, Brian. *Tolkien: A Critical Assessment.* New York: St. Martin's, 1992.

Salu, Mary, and Robert T. Farrell, eds. *J. R. R. Tolkien, Scholar and Storyteller.* Ithaca, N.Y.: Cornell Univ. Press, 1979.

Tolkien, John, and Priscilla Tolkien, eds. *The Tolkien Family Album*. Boston: Houghton Mifflin, 1992.

Tyler, J. E. A. *The New Tolkien Companion*. New York: St. Martin's, 1979.

West, Richard C. *Tolkien Criticism: An Annotated Checklist*. Kent, Ohio: Kent State University, 1981.

Mark Twain

(1835-1910)

by Allison Ensor

ew American writers are so well known as Samuel
Langhorne Clemens, whose pseudonym "Mark Twain"
is one of the most famous in literature. Two of his novels, *The Adventures of Tom Sawyer* and *The Adventures of Huckleberry Finn,* long ago established themselves as American classics, and Tom and Huck, the boy heroes of those books, are among the best-known fictional characters of the nineteenth century. The scene in which Tom Sawyer whitewashes the fence—or persuades other boys to whitewash it for him—is as well known as any in American literature.

    Mark Twain's novels and stories have been made into stage plays, films, television programs, Broadway musicals, and even operas. Others have written sequels to his novels, and Twain himself appears as a character in several recent novels and television programs. His life has served as the inspiration for at least one film, several television specials, and a summer musical drama. Hal Holbrook is only one of several men who regularly impersonate Twain in platform per-

pseudonym fictitious or pen name

321

formances. New books about Mark Twain and his work appear every year, and he is the subject of several journals and newsletters.

In the field of American humor Mark Twain stands alone, the only major humorist who was also one of the country's most outstanding writers. Such quips as "The reports of my death are greatly exaggerated" are constantly quoted and imitated.

quip a witty or funny observation, usually made on the spur of the moment

Life and Writings

Sam Clemens was born in the village of Florida, Missouri, on 30 November 1835, a few months after his father and mother—John Marshall and Jane Lampton Clemens—arrived from Fentress County, Tennessee. A few years later the family moved to the town of Hannibal, on the Mississippi River. It is Hannibal (called "St. Petersburg" in the novels) that serves as the setting for all of *Tom Sawyer* and the first part of *Huckleberry Finn*.

Sam Clemens had very little schooling. His father died when he was eleven, and young Sam dropped out of school at that time. Much of his informal education came in the print shops of Hannibal and other midwestern towns.

According to Mark Twain's *Life on the Mississippi,* the "one permanent ambition" of the boys of Hannibal was to get some kind of position on the steamboats, which were the most glamorous means of river transportation in those days. Young Sam succeeded in doing so and was taught the river in the late 1850s by Captain Horace Bixby, a process that Twain recorded amusingly in *Life on the Mississippi*. He later claimed that he loved steamboating better than any other profession he followed, that he expected to follow it for the rest of his life, but the outbreak of the Civil War in 1861 brought this aspect of Sam's life to a close.

After two weeks' service with a little band of Confederate soldiers, Sam joined his brother Orion in traveling to the Territory of Nevada, where Orion had been appointed territorial secretary. While the war was being fought in the eastern part of the country, Sam spent his time in Nevada and California and did not return to the East until after the war was over. While in the West, he wrote for several newspapers, including the Virginia City, Nevada, *Territorial Enterprise,* in which

Confederate soldiers fought on behalf of the Confederacy, the Southern states that broke away from the United States during the Civil War (1861–1865).

he first used the name "Mark Twain," a river term indicating that the depth of the water was two ("twain" is an old-fashioned word for "two") fathoms, or twelve feet.

While in the West, Twain heard a story about a stranger and a man who owned a frog, which he worked up into a piece for an eastern paper, calling it "Jim Smiley and His Jumping Frog." Published in New York in 1865, it was widely circulated and much admired. Two years later Twain used it as the title story for his first book, a collection of pieces he had already published in newspapers, calling it "The Celebrated Jumping Frog of Calaveras County."

After a trip to Hawaii during which he sent back a series of letters to be published in California, he returned to the eastern part of the country via Central America and was soon making plans to join a group of Americans in a kind of pilgrimage to Europe and the Holy Land. The trip lasted several months, during which Twain dispatched regular letters for publication in New York and San Francisco. These letters formed the basis for his humorous travel book, a piece of fictionalized autobiography, *The Innocents Abroad; or, The New Pilgrim's Progress* (1869). Though greatly impressed by a few sights in Europe (the gardens of Versailles, the cathedral at Milan), Twain was more often disappointed by what he found, and his cynical attitude proved popular with home-loving American readers.

With the success of *The Innocents Abroad*, Mark Twain began to dig further back into his past to find material for books. His western experiences and the journey to Hawaii were treated in *Roughing It* (1872). In an 1875 series, "Old Times on the Mississippi," later a part of *Life on the Mississippi* (1883), he told of his experiences on the river. *The Adventures of Tom Sawyer* (1876) took him still further back in time, to childhood, for many of the happenings and characters were based on actual persons and events. A less fictional treatment of his days in Hannibal and on the farm of his Uncle John Quarles near Florida, was eventually given in his autobiography, parts of which were published in 1906–1907, near the end of his life.

After his first three books, Twain turned to writing a novel in collaboration with his Hartford, Connecticut, neighbor Charles Dudley Warner. *The Gilded Age: A Tale of Today* (1873) begins with chapters set in Tennessee, based on the real-life experiences of Twain's father. From Tennessee the

---

Israel and the West Bank of the Jordan River make up most of the biblical **Holy Land,** where the religious and national identity of the Jews developed between 1800 B.C. and A.D. 100 and where Christianity had its origins.

collaboration working together, especially in the creation of an intellectual work

gilded coated with
a thin layer of gold

action moves on to Missouri and then to Washington for an exposure of corruption in government during the post–Civil War years, a time that has come to be called the Gilded Age, taking its name from the novel. The phrase suggests a greater concern with outward appearance than with inner substance—a gilded, rather than a golden age.

Far better remembered by the American people have been the novels that followed: *The Adventures of Tom Sawyer*; *The Prince and the Pauper* (1881); *Adventures of Huckleberry Finn* (1884); and *A Connecticut Yankee in King Arthur's Court* (1889). Other novels, particularly *The Tragedy of Pudd'nhead Wilson and the Comedy of Those Extraordinary Twins* (1894) and *The Mysterious Stranger: A Romance* (1916), have attracted interest but have never been as widely read or as frequently adapted for movies and television.

Mark Twain traveled and lectured around the United States and in many parts of the world, visiting such places as Great Britain, France, Italy, Germany, Austria, Switzerland, Spain, Sweden, Russia, Hawaii, Australia, India, South Africa, the Holy Land, and Egypt. He described many of his travels, often with humorous exaggeration, in three books: *The Innocents Abroad, A Tramp Abroad* (1880), and *Following the Equator* (1897).

In 1870, Mark Twain married Olivia "Livy" Langdon of Elmira, New York, a young woman whose brother he had met while on his 1867 journey to Europe and the Holy Land. The couple had four children: Langdon, Susy, Clara, and Jean. Of these, only Clara outlived her father, and there are no descendants of Mark Twain living today. For many years the Clemens family lived in a large Victorian house built for them in Hartford, Connecticut. During the summers of the 1870s and 1880s, they usually lived with Livy's relatives at Quarry Farm, near Elmira, where the greatest part of Twain's work on his most celebrated books was completed.

Halley's Comet is a
brilliant comet that
appears approxi-
mately every 77
years as its orbit ap-
proaches the sun.
Named after the Eng-
lish astronomer Ed-
mund Halley, the
comet's last appear-
ance was in 1986.

Besides his famous novels, Mark Twain wrote short stories and tales, humorous sketches, essays, speeches, his autobiography, and a great many letters. Many of these, along with his notebooks and journals, have been published, though others still remain unpublished.

Halley's Comet, which had been in the sky at his birth in 1835, returned in 1910 as he died at his house, "Stormfield," near Redding, Connecticut. After a funeral in New York City, he was buried in Elmira beside his wife, who had died in Italy a few years earlier.

What the Critics Have Said

The greatest amount of critical attention has been given to what is usually regarded as Twain's masterpiece, certainly his most controversial work, *The Adventures of Huckleberry Finn*. This story details a journey down the Mississippi by a runaway slave named Jim and a boy, Huck Finn, who is trying to get away from his father and from all "sivilizing" influences. The time is the 1840s, about fifteen years before the Civil War. Although Mark Twain had narrated Tom Sawyer's adventures, in the sequel he lets Huck step forth as the narrator, and it is Huck's voice that we hear throughout the story.

Though widely praised for its realism, its depiction of the various levels of life in the Mississippi River valley, its treatment of slavery and race relations, and its use of dialect, the novel has also been sharply criticized. Most of the discussion focuses on two points: the ending and the treatment of race.

Many readers have found the last part, the Phelps farm section, too coincidental (how does Huck happen to find the one house where Tom Sawyer's relatives live and where Tom is expected at that moment?), and they have objected to Tom's extravagant schemes for freeing Jim, who Tom knows has already been set free by his owner—an act of kindness one would hardly expect from her. Readers have also criticized Huck's willingness to stand aside, making only minimal objections to the ordeal through which Tom puts Jim, largely to satisfy his own romantic notions. To some it seems that Huck forgets much of what he has learned about Jim's humanity.

While some readers have found the novel an attack on racism and have admired the way in which Huck rejects the teachings of the white society of that day, others see the book as racist and object to its frequent use of the word "nigger" and to what they see as the presentation of Jim as a stereotyped figure of the kind often seen in the minstrel shows of Twain's day.

Professor Shelley Fisher Fishkin introduced an element into the question of race in the novel. She suggested that Twain modeled Huck's speech on that of a young black boy he met while on a lecture tour in Illinois in the early 1870s—an incident Twain recorded in a piece called "Sociable Jimmy," published in the *New York Times* in 1874. Fishkin's theory was readily accepted by some critics, while others were unconvinced.

stereotype a character that is not original or individual because it conforms to a preconceived category

Minstrel shows were a form of American entertainment that began in the 1840s and lasted until 1900. The shows featured white performers who blackened their faces to impersonate blacks, reinforcing lasting negative images of blacks.

A musical film adaptation of *The Adventures of Tom Sawyer* was released in 1973 and featured Jodie Foster as Becky Thatcher. Another version, *Tom and Huck*, was released in 1995 and starred Jonathan Taylor Thomas and Brad Renfro.

inevitable unable to be avoided

If you like the works of Mark Twain, you might also like the works of Robert Louis Stevenson.

The Adventures of Tom Sawyer, with its tales of boys playing pirate, of Tom and Huck witnessing a midnight murder in the graveyard, of Tom and Becky Thatcher being lost in the cave, and of Tom and Huck's finding a hidden treasure, has attracted far less criticism. Despite the threat posed by Injun Joe in *Tom Sawyer, Huck Finn* is obviously a much darker book.

In recent years critics have faulted Mark Twain for his failure to present adult females as well-rounded characters. The only Twain book in which a woman is the central character is *Personal Recollections of Joan of Arc* (1896), and the Maid of Orléans is so idealized as not to be entirely real. In portraits of African American women Twain succeeded best with "Aunt Rachel" (based on Mary Ann Cord, who was well known to Twain) in "A True Story" and with Roxana ("Roxy") in *Pudd'nhead Wilson.*

Criticism of *A Connecticut Yankee in King Arthur's Court,* Twain's time-travel novel in which a man of the nineteenth century goes back to the days of Camelot, has mostly focused on the title character. Some have seen the Yankee as a good, well-intentioned man who brings modern technology to sixth-century England in an attempt to help that society; others view him as representing the frightening consequences of American interference in an underdeveloped country. Film versions of the novel, in which such beloved actors as Will Rogers and Bing Crosby have starred, inevitably portray the Yankee in a more favorable light and omit the violence and sadness of Twain's ending.

Whatever praise and condemnation may come from the critics, one thing seems abundantly clear: Mark Twain will continue to be read and discussed for years to come. Whether one sees him as the nostalgic recaller of boyhood days, as the teller of tall tales and funny stories, as a master of the stinging one-liner, or as a critic of America, human beings, and God, he will remain one of the country's most fascinating literary figures.

Selected Bibliography

WORKS BY MARK TWAIN

Travel Books

> *The Innocents Abroad; or, The New Pilgrim's Progress* (1869)

Roughing It (1872)

A Tramp Abroad (1880)

Life on the Mississippi (1883)

Following the Equator (1897)

Novels

The Gilded Age: A Tale of Today (1873)

The Adventures of Tom Sawyer (1876)

The Prince and the Pauper (1881)

The Adventures of Huckleberry Finn (1884)

A Connecticut Yankee in King Arthur's Court (1889)

Tom Sawyer Abroad (1894)

The Tragedy of Pudd'nhead Wilson, and the Comedy of Those Extraordinary Twins (1894)

Personal Recollections of Joan of Arc (1896)

Short Stories

Tom Sawyer, Detective (1886)

Autobiography

The Autobiography of Mark Twain, edited by Charles Neider (1959)

Modern Editions of Collected Works

The Complete Short Stories of Mark Twain, edited by Charles Neider (1957)

The Complete Novels of Mark Twain, edited by Charles Neider (1964)

The Mark Twain Papers. Berkeley: Univ. of California Press, (1966–). In progress; primarily material not previously published.

The Works of Mark Twain. Iowa-California edition. Berkeley: Univ. of California Press, (1972–). In progress; includes *Tom Sawyer, Huckleberry Finn, The Prince and the Pauper,* and *A Connecticut Yankee in King Arthur's Court.* Extensive annotations and original illustrations.

The Library of America: Mississippi Writings (1982)

The Mark Twain Library. Berkeley: Univ. of California Press, (1982–). Available in paperback; includes *Tom Sawyer, Huckleberry Finn, The Prince and the Pauper, A Connecticut Yankee in King Arthur's Court.* Annotations and original illustrations.

The Innocents Abroad and Roughing It (1984)

Collected Tales, Sketches, Speeches, and Essays (2 vols., 1992)

Historical Romances (1994)

WORKS ABOUT MARK TWAIN

Principal Biographical and Critical Studies

Emerson, Everett. *The Authentic Mark Twain: A Literary Biography of Samuel L. Clemens*. Philadelphia: Univ. of Pennsylvania Press, 1984.

Fishkin, Shelley Fisher. *Was Huck Black? Mark Twain and African American Voices*. New York: Oxford Univ. Press, 1993.

Hearn, Michael Patrick. "Mark Twain." In *Writers for Children: Critical Studies of Major Authors Since the Seventeenth Century*. Edited by Jane M. Bingham. New York: Scribners, 1988, pp. 573–582.

Inge, M. Thomas, ed. *Huck Finn Among the Critics: A Centennial Selection*. Frederick, Md.: University Publications of America, 1985.

Kaplan, Justin. *Mr. Clemens and Mark Twain*. New York: Simon & Schuster, 1966.

Leonard, James S., Thomas A. Tenney, and Thadious Davis, eds. *Black Perspectives on Huckleberry Finn*. Durham, N.C.: Duke Univ. Press, 1992.

Paine, Albert Bigelow. *Mark Twain: A Biography*. 4 vols. New York: Harper, 1912.

Smith, Henry Nash. *Mark Twain: The Development of a Writer*. Cambridge: Harvard Univ. Press, 1962.

Sundquist, Eric, ed. *Mark Twain: A Collection of Critical Essays*. New Century Views. Englewood Cliffs, N.J.: Prentice Hall, 1994.

Wecter, Dixon. *Sam Clemens of Hannibal*. Boston: Houghton Mifflin, 1952.

Wilson, James D. *A Reader's Guide to the Short Stories of Mark Twain*. Boston: G. K. Hall, 1987.

There are several historic sites associated with Mark Twain, including:

Mark Twain Birthplace Historic Site
Route 1, Box 54
Stoutsville, MO 65283

Mark Twain Home and Museum
208 Hill Street
Hannibal, MO 63401

Mark Twain Memorial
351 Farmington Avenue
Hartford, CT 06105-4498

(1942-   )

by Suzanne Elizabeth Reid

Cynthia Voigt loves to sail, to eat, and, especially, to write. Although anchored to the traditional family and literary values she learned early in life, she ventures widely, catching winds from the world of rock and roll to the early Middle Ages of northern Europe, from the forested shore of rural Maine to the glamour of New York City. Her books teem with sophisticated references to literature, music, and art, and her characters, style, and plots change from novel to novel, but the themes of loyalty to family, friends, and self remain constant.

teem overflow, swell

Early Life

Born in Boston on 25 February 1942 to Frederick Irving, a corporate executive, and Elise Keeney Irving, Voigt remembers her childhood as happy, full of family fun with her two sisters and younger twin brothers, and full of books. She

There is an article about William Shakespeare earlier in this volume. Leo **Tolstoy** (1828–1910) was a Russian realist novelist. His novels include *Anna Karenina* and *War and Peace*.

read the Nancy Drew and Cherry Ames series and books such as Frances Hodgson Burnett's *The Secret Garden* and Walter Farley's *The Black Stallion* before moving on to adult authors such as Shakespeare and Tolstoy. While in the ninth grade, she decided to become a writer and submitted several short stories and poems to publishers who rejected them but failed to discourage her.

After attending Dana Hall School, a boarding school in Wellesley, Massachusetts, Voigt entered Smith College in Northampton, Massachusetts; she studied creative writing but still did not publish. After graduation in 1963, she worked one year for a public-relations firm in New York City, where she met fascinating characters, and one year in Santa Fe, New Mexico, where she became accredited to teach. Then she moved to Maryland and taught English at the Key School in Annapolis. While there, she learned about the kinds of stories young people like to read and the questions they want to ask.

In 1974 she married Walter Voigt, a fellow teacher who shares her love of sailing and who composes some of the music she enjoys hearing. Three years later, while caring for her young children, Jessica and Peter, Cynthia Voigt began to write regularly. In 1987, the family moved to Deer Isle, Maine, where she writes full-time in a rooftop study full of windows. There, her mind, like the ocean she loves, ranges far and deep.

Early Novels

gothic a style of fiction characterized by remote and mysterious settings

In *The Callender Papers* (1983), a gothic mystery set in the early twentieth century in western Massachusetts, the prim, studious orphan Jean is torn between the stern logic of the artist Mr. Thiel, for whom she organizes family papers, and the heartwarming, glamorous Enoch Callender. How did Mr. Thiel's wife die, and what happened to their young child? In an exciting climax, Jean discovers answers that reunite her with her family and extend her sense of self. The novel's style mirrors the era it portrays.

There is an article about Carl Sandburg earlier in this volume.

The title of *Tell Me If the Lovers Are Losers* (1982), from Carl Sandburg's poem "Cool Tombs," refers to passion for life rather than romance. The novel, about three roommates at a small New England college in the early 1960s, reflects Voigt's

own college experience, but it originated with a friend's remark about playing sports terribly after he got glasses. In this intellectually stimulating novel, the mental brilliance of Niki and the spiritual gentleness of Hildy are balanced by Ann, a conventional and scholarly girl from a middle-class family, who struggles to understand and complement the best strengths of both her friends. Niki's restless competitiveness and Hildy's stubborn faith are tested in volleyball tournaments and also in their academic work, especially after Hildy's vision is corrected when Ann insists she wear glasses. A tragic death clears Ann's own moral vision.

The Tillerman Series

Voigt's first publishing success was *Homecoming* (1981), selected as a Notable Children's Trade Book in the Field of Social Studies by the joint committee of the National Council for Social Studies and Children's Book Council; it also was nominated for the American Book Award. Its sequel, *Dicey's Song* (1982), won the prestigious John Newbery Medal in 1983. Voigt then created five other novels about the Tillermans and their friends. It all began when Voigt saw a car full of kids left alone in a parking lot and wondered what would happen if the adult in charge failed to return.

Homecoming opens with four children abandoned by their mother in a car at a shopping mall: thirteen-year-old Dicey is practical and responsible; intellectual James is ten; nine-year-old Maybeth, pretty and blonde, seems slow-witted yet instinctively senses how to reach out to people's needs with her music; and six-year-old Sammy, sunny and stubborn by turns, grows to be sturdy and dependable. The four set out walking on a dangerous journey toward the seaside village of Crisfield, Maryland, where their feisty grandmother reluctantly welcomes them into her lonely life. *Dicey's Song* tells how the Tillermans adjust to their new life and to the death of their mother. Alternately heartwrenching and heartwarming, the two books have attracted many devoted fans to Voigt's work.

A Solitary Blue (1983) traces the development of Dicey's friend Jeff, who must define himself in relation to his fun-loving, activist mother, who abandons him, and to his uncommunicative professor father, who ignores him. The portrait of

Jeff's mother, Melody, as shallow and immature yet irresistibly attractive to Jeff and his father, is unforgettable. In this highly regarded novel, Jeff's desperate loneliness almost destroys him until he learns the quiet self-respect of a solitary blue heron.

The Runner (1985) explains Gram's reluctance to care for her grandchildren by describing her relationship with her youngest son, Bullet, a long-distance runner at Crisfield High School during the 1960s. Bullet struggles with his own racial prejudices toward Tamer, an African American teammate, and toward the facile rebelliousness of his friends. Pushed into self-destructive anger by his stern and silent father and by the passive resistance of Gram, Bullet finally escapes by joining the army and going to Vietnam.

Set ten years later, *Come A Stranger* (1986) also examines the pain and confusion caused by racial prejudice, this time from the viewpoint of Mina, an African American girl who later befriends Dicey. At first scornful of her roots in rural Chrisfield, she realizes the cruel snobbishness of the exclusive world of classical ballet. Her friendship with Tamer, now a minister whose own painful experiences have deepened his sympathetic nature, helps her realize her family's strengths.

Sons from Afar (1987) traces the personal development of James and Sammy, now teenagers, who wonder about their missing father. Their quest to define his identity, and then their own, results in a dangerous bar fight before each settles into a job that develops his individual strength. In the end, they become responsible young men who focus on helping their younger sister, Maybeth, rather than brooding on their own inadequacies.

The last novel of the Tillerman series, *Seventeen Against the Dealer* (1989), returns to Dicey, who has started a business of building sailboats. Stubbornly independent, she refuses help, trusting hard work, instinct, and chance. After several incidents that endanger even her relationship with her fiancé, Jeff, she realizes independence is not enough; she needs others.

The Tillerman books are related thematically. Characters learn to reach out beyond themselves and what they know to other people and new experiences. They hold on to what is valuable from their past, and they let go of harmful memories and prejudices. These themes are represented by images of music and songs that enable these characters to reach

facile easily accomplished; lacking in sincerity

Characters learn to reach out beyond themselves and what they know to other people and new experiences. They hold on to what is valuable from their past, and they let go of harmful memories and prejudices.

out, images involving wood that help them hold on, and images of sailing that allow them to let go. Like most lasting relationships, the connections among these novels are complex and full of profound implications.

Shifting Viewpoints

Four of Voigt's novels reveal how different perspectives on familiar situations can broaden understanding and solve problems. In *Izzy, Willy-Nilly* (1986), teenager Isobel ("Izzy") Lingard loses a leg in an automobile accident. She must shift her image of herself from that of a pretty, popular cheerleader to the image that her family and friends now see: an accident victim who does not fit neatly into their pattern of a "nice," normal life. Her new friendship with the socially awkward Rosamunde helps Izzy emerge as a stronger person who can claim her individuality. Accurate in portraying how many people react to disfigurement, this novel also explores the structure of middle-class high school popularity.

In *Building Blocks* (1984), seven-year-old Brann, upset by bickering between his assertive mother, who likes change, and his more passive father, who leaves circumstances to fate, falls asleep among his blocks. In what appears to be a dream, Brann recreates his father's boyhood family in the Great Depression of the 1930s, a family made harsh and rough by poverty. There, Brann learns the source and the value of his father's cautious nature. Back in the present, he uses his newfound understanding to convince his parents to compromise in a new life that is satisfying for both of them.

Tree by Leaf (1988), set on the forested Maine seashore just after World War I, also contains a supernatural, or imaginary, viewpoint. Thirteen-year-old Clothilde is resentful after her father, disfigured by a war accident, isolates himself, and after her mother, confused, ceases to care for the household. Clothilde hears a mysterious voice that helps her to understand the adults' motivations and to insist that each member of the family accept responsibilities. The striking imagery of a fog-shrouded land evokes the mystical quality of Clothilde's insight, and the diction reflects the differences in social class of that historical period. The themes of reaching out as well as holding on are evident in this novel.

mystical mysterious

The Vandemark Mummy (1991), a modern mystery in Maine, pits the scholarly intellect of fifteen-year-old Althea Hall against the common sense of her twelve-year-old brother, Phineas. They have just moved to a small college town with their father, a professor of classics; their mother has moved to Portland, Oregon, to pursue her own career. During their first week, a lovely mummy from a new shipment of artifacts is savagely disfigured, threatening Dr. Hall's reputation. Phineas is able to save his sister from danger when he sees that his own kind of sensitive intelligence is as valid as scholarly knowledge. Will Professor Hall's wife return to live with the family? The question remains realistically unresolved.

Medieval Heroic Adventures: A Trilogy

Jackaroo (1985) describes the misery of peasants whose lives are controlled by fear of hunger, cold, thieves, and the power of the lords under whose rule they live. Because reading and learning are denied to them, these peasants are also ruled by laws of tradition. The innkeeper's daughter, Gwyn—sturdy, capable, and independent—is unwilling to conform to the customary woman's role. Instead, she dons the robe of Jackaroo, a mythical figure like Robin Hood, hoping to alleviate the injustices of her poverty-stricken society. After many dangerous adventures, she discovers, like Dicey, that courage and a kind heart are not enough to succeed.

dons wears

A generation later, Gwyn's granddaughter, Birle, tries to escape mundane reality by running away with the lordly prince Orien. An inverted fairy tale, *On Fortune's Wheel* (1990) describes their journey toward self-discovery as they are stranded on an island, kidnapped by pirates, and enslaved, until they finally return to a luxurious life in the Kingdom. Is this Birle's dream come true? Feeling useless and awkward, Birle returns to her home, now eager for the daily round of work she had previously scorned.

mundane ordinary, common

These two novels graphically describe the limited choices for peasants in preindustrial times and the constant, heavy burden of work necessary to survive, especially for servants and slaves. They also depict the burden of responsibility for those in power, who are also limited in their choices. But if work and responsibility can be hard and challenging, they also provide deep satisfaction that, for Voigt's characters, is as important as the power to make choices.

Third in the series, *The Wings of a Falcon* (1993), explores social cruelties that are still part of human history. The island on which Birle and Orien had been stranded has become the domain of the cruel Damall, who buys young boys and raises them to be slaves. But he fails to break the nameless lad who hides his fear and wins the loyal friendship of Griff. The two escape, and the nameless boy takes the name Oriel. Captured by savage marauders, fittingly named Wolfers and similar to the tribes who swept through Europe during the Dark Ages, Oriel and Griff finally escape into the Kingdom, where they meet Birle and Orien's descendant, Beryl. The imagery of stone and hardness recurs, reflecting both Oriel's ability to survive and his difficulty with love; only his friend Griff's loyalty keeps him from hardening completely. The tragic ending of this long and horrific adventure is softened by the promise of a new age.

Living with Modern Evils

David and Jonathan (1992) explores the impact of war and cruelty on individuals. David, a survivor of the Holocaust, comes to live with his distant cousins the Nafiches on Cape Cod in the 1950s, disrupting their warm family life and the friendship between fifteen-year-old Jonathan and Henry, the cautious narrator of this story.

The novel begins in Vietnam, where Jonathan has just entered the hospital with life-threatening injuries and where his old friend Henry is a doctor. The action flashes back to their teen years when David, just arrived, both fascinates and repulses the boys—first with his sly implications and half-truths, then as a symbol to their consciences, especially after his suicide. The novel uses frequent biblical references to grapple with the difficult philosophical issue of individual responsibility in the face of guilt for social evils. Henry and Jonathan agree that, while no individual can stop social evils, it is possible to limit the damage.

Glass Mountain (1992) is a lighthearted version of the folk tale by the same name. Glittering with references to art, music, and the glamorous life of upper-class Manhattan, it imitates Shakespeare's *Twelfth Night* in its comedic handling of mistaken identities. Gregor poses as a butler on the prowl for a rich wife. His employer, the playboy Theo Mondleigh, resigns himself to marrying "Pruny" Rawlings, a social "catch." To tell the ending would spoil the pleasure of surprise heaped on surprise in this funny, clever novel that, nonetheless, explores the serious problems of fabricating an identity, especially in love.

In *Orfe* (1992), Voigt reverses the myth of Orpheus and Eurydice and alludes to the fairy tale "The Frog Prince" as she examines the issue of assertiveness in the world of rock music. Here, people can feel successful, even while hiding from life with drugs or riding passively on the noise and show of a few gifted performers. The structure of this novel is a collection of vignettes, unfolding as Enny remembers it, more by free association than by strict chronology. With its conversational tone and rhythmic poetic language, this novel is intuitively felt as much as it is understood on a rational level.

When She Hollers (1994) is a powerful scream of protest against incest, a story of the day when seventeen-year-old Tish decides to fight back against her stepfather, who is sexually abusing her. When Tish finally finds an adult who is willing to recognize the danger of her situation, she discovers that, as long as she is a minor, she has little protection against such abuse. Voigt tells this story from inside Tish's mind, mirroring the voices of high school gossip, faithfully recording her fears, her doubts, and, finally, her hope. Tish's story is judged psychologically accurate by professionals and a literary triumph by critics. Voigt's inverted use of Shakespeare's *The Tempest* adds a deep irony for those who know the play.

Most critics of young adult literature recognize Voigt as an extraordinarily thought-provoking writer who explores a wide variety of profound questions about young people's development into individuals. Her characters are as complex as real-life people. They learn to think about their lives and have the courage to make their own decisions. Besides the importance of intelligence and independence, Voigt also portrays the comfort of caring relationships; the friendships and families she describes are deeply warming. Even when treating the most horrible circumstances, Voigt's books glow with faith in human strengths. Reflective readers who welcome the challenging questions she poses learn to treasure her work.

In Greek mythology, **Orpheus** is a poet and musician. He is given the chance to lead his dead wife, **Euridice**, back from the underworld, provided that he does not look at her. When he does, she disappears forever.

Even when treating the most horrible circumstances, Voigt's books glow with faith in human strengths.

Selected Bibliography

WORKS BY CYNTHIA VOIGT

Novels

Homecoming (1981)

Dicey's Song (1982)

Tell Me If the Lovers Are Losers (1982)

The Callender Papers (1983)

A Solitary Blue (1983)

Building Blocks (1984)

Jackaroo (1985)

The Runner (1985)

Come a Stranger (1986)

Izzy, Willy-Nilly (1986)

Sons from Afar (1987)

Tree by Leaf (1988)

Seventeen Against the Dealer (1989)

On Fortune's Wheel (1990)

David and Jonathan (1991)

The Vandemark Mummy (1991)

Glass Mountain (1992)

Orfe (1992)

The Wings of a Falcon (1993)

When She Hollers (1994)

Children's Book:

Stories About Rosie (1986)

Speech

Newbery Acceptance Speech. *Horn Book,* August 1983, p. 401.

WORKS ABOUT CYNTHIA VOIGT

Commire, Anne, ed. *Something About the Author.* Detroit: Gale Research, 1987.

Dresang, Eliza T. "A Newbery Song for Gifted Readers." In *School Library Journal,* 3 November 1983, pp. 33–37.

Gallo, Donald R., ed. *Speaking for Ourselves.* Urbana, Ill.: National Council of Teachers of English, 1990.

Readers who enjoy Cynthia Voigt's works might also enjoy reading works by Katherine Paterson and Harper Lee among modern writers, as well as exploring Voigt's allusions to the plays of William Shakespeare.

Henke, James. "Dicey, Odysseus, and Hansel and Gretel: The Lost Children in Voigt's *Homecoming*." In *Children's Literature in Education,* Spring 1985, pp. 45–52.

Jameson, Gloria. "The Triumphs of the Spirit in Cynthia Voigt's *Homecoming, Dicey's Song,* and *A Solitary Blue*." In *Triumphs of the Spirit in Children's Literature.* Edited by Francelia Butler and Richard Rotert. New York: Library Professional Publications, 1986.

Kauffman, Dorothy. "Profile: Cynthia Voigt." In *Language Arts,* December 1985, pp. 876–880.

Metzger, L., and D. Straub, eds. *Contemporary Authors: New Revision Series.* Detroit: Gale Research, 1986.

Reid, Suzanne Elizabeth. *Presenting Cynthia Voigt.* New York: Twayne, 1995.

Senick, Gerard J., and Melissa Reiff Hug, eds. "Cynthia Voigt." In *Children's Literature Review.* Detroit: Gale Research, 1987.

Voigt, Cynthia. "Writing of *A Solitary Blue*." *Language Arts,* November 1983, p. 1026.

How to Write to the Author
Cynthia Voigt
c/o Scholastic, Inc.
555 Broadway
New York, NY 10012

Jill Paton Walsh

(1937-)

by Aileen Pace Nilsen

Jill Paton Walsh was born in a suburb of London just before
the outbreak of World War II. She was two years old when
the Soviets signed a pact with Nazi Germany and the Nazis
invaded Poland. She was three when Norway and Denmark
fell to Germany, followed by German invasions of the Nether-
lands, Belgium, and Luxembourg. Then came the Fall of
France, the evacuation of Dunkirk, and the Battle of Britain,
which for the English began five long, bitter years of war.

Although the defeat of the Nazis in 1945 meant that Lon-
doners no longer had to live in fear of the massive bombing
commonly referred to as the Blitz, recovery from the war
took several more years, and Walsh ruefully gives Hitler   ruefully regretfully
credit for making her first a reader and then a writer. She explains that during long periods of her childhood, spent
mostly in London but sometimes in Cornwall, she was in and
out of air-raid shelters or confined in houses where there
was nothing to do but read. The only available books were
bound sets of Victorian classics, so as a child she read books

written for adults. And then as an adult, when she went to Oxford—the same university where Lewis Carroll and J. R. R. Tolkien had been on the faculty—she found herself fascinated by the strong story lines and the dragons and the magic in medieval tales such as *Beowulf, Sir Gawain and the Green Knight,* and Chaucer's *Canterbury Tales,* and she decided that she wanted to write for children (Gallo, *Speaking for Ourselves,* p. 219).

Her development of literary appreciation in the reverse order from that of most of us may be a contributing factor to the unusualness of her books, which various reviewers have praised for their immediacy and intensity, cheerful and plucky characters, historically authentic settings, subtle construction, vivid and sometimes terrifying word pictures, and, most importantly, their ability to make readers ask questions.

Stories of War

Fireweed is the book that most closely relates to Walsh's World War II experiences. The title comes from a flowering weed that grows up after an area has been burned. It is now rare in England, but after the war, London was filled with such flowers, which in Walsh's story represent the bittersweet memories of a boy known only as Bill. As the adult narrator of the story, Bill looks back to when he was fifteen years old. He had met a girl named Julie during the Blitz. Their families had sent them out of London for safety, but they both had returned and were trying to keep away from the authorities and make it on their own. Not until the end of the story does Bill realize that Julie is from an upper-class family; had the Blitz not taken place, they never would have spoken to each other.

Walsh's other World War II story, *The Dolphin Crossing,* also uses the war to explore friendships across social classes. It is the story of the evacuation of 300,000 British soldiers from the French port of Dunkirk. They had been fighting in France, and when the country fell to the Germans, the soldiers were rescued and transported back to England across the straits of Dover, many of them in small boats by fishermen and other civilians. The story is told from the perspective of two boys: one is the upper-class, well-educated, but fearful John, and the other is the brash but resourceful Pat, a Cockney evacuee.

Remembering that Walsh was only three years old when these events occurred helps readers recognize the books as historical fiction, rather than as memoir. But her inventiveness makes the stories no less real. Walsh wrote in an article for *Horn Book* that

> to be a historical novelist you have to be as good at history as any historian. You have to do the work; you have to have the right attitude; you have to have a historian's allegiance to history. You have to want to write what did happen and what it felt like, and not what would have been romantic had it happened, or what you wish it had been like, or what would make a much better story if only it had been true. You have to believe, I think, that what really happened is bound to make the best story of all. (Pp. 17–23)

A Slightly Antique Mood

Even when Walsh sets her stories in the present or the future, they seem to have a historical ring to them, what Phyllis Theroux in the *New York Times* called a "slightly antique mood." Theroux was writing about *Gaffer Samson's Luck,* a book about a young Yorkshire boy being forced to change his lifestyle and to make new friends when his family moves to the Fens. But her description is even more apt for *Torch,* a futuristic post-Holocaust story.

Torch begins on a primitive Greek Island, where a group of people live in a manner reminiscent of the time of Christ. The protagonists are young Cal and Dio, whose parents have arranged their marriage. As is the custom, they are sent to get a blessing and instructions from an old man, the Guardian, who lives among marble ruins. When Cal and Dio arrive, they find the Guardian injured and dying. They stay the night with him, and when they follow his instructions about his burial, they find a special "Olympic" torch. This they understand must be taken to "the games." Their search for "the games" and the structure of the torch, which is an interesting combination of high technology from the "ago" days and almost primitive magic, are the symbols through which Walsh explores questions of competition, greed, friendship, and loyalty, as well as the importance of memory and knowledge of the past.

A Chance Child is a contemporary story with a definite "antique mood." In it, a mistreated, illegitimate child, whose family calls him "Creep" and has kept him hidden in a nook under the stairs, escapes when a hole is accidentally knocked into the wall of his family's home. Creep wanders into the outside world, finding himself in a grim industrial area's garbage dump that abuts an oily canal. He finds a small abandoned canal boat, which at first he does not recognize as anything more than a hut. He breaks its rusted lock, climbs inside to escape the pelting rain, and falls asleep. When he wakes up, a man on a working canal boat shows him how to walk along the canal bank, pulling his boat along.

In a plot that is unusual even for Walsh, the boy rides the canal boat not only through space but also through time. In the England of more than a hundred years ago, Creep aligns with two other waifs trying to support themselves by working the kinds of dangerous jobs reserved for children in mines, foundries, factories, and mills. A companion story told through alternating chapters is the search made for Creep by his half brother.

waif homeless or lost person, especially a small child

In *A Parcel of Patterns,* Walsh does not use fantasy but instead relies on the spare but gentle prose of a young woman, Mall Percival, to acquaint readers with the horrors of an earlier historical period. While Mall is a fictional character created by Walsh, the situation is true. In 1665, a tailor in the village of Eyam received a bundle of burlap dress patterns sent from London. The patterns were infested with the bacterium that causes bubonic plague. We now know that the usual way the disease was spread was from rats to humans through insects. All that the villagers knew, however, was that the tailor was the first to die, followed over the next thirteen months by 267 people out of a total population of 350.

Unusual about the village is that in June of 1666, at the urging of their minister, the townspeople decided to quarantine themselves to save neighboring villages from suffering the same plight. In vowing to have no outside contacts, Mall is making an extraordinary sacrifice because she is in love with Thomas, who lives in a neighboring village. When he has no word from Mall, Thomas is frantic and makes his way into the village, realizing full well that he will not be able to leave. He and Mall are married by the minister, but Thomas soon succumbs to the plague. Mall begins writing her story in hopes of lessening her grief.

In *Grace,* Walsh tells the story of Grace Darling, a real-life English heroine born in 1816. She lived with her family in a lighthouse off England's northeast coast. One stormy morning just at dawn, Grace spots a shipwreck. She and her father set out in their small boat and rescue the nine survivors (many others have already drowned) just before the official lifeboat arrives. The men on the lifeboat have risked their lives as much as have Grace and her father, but they get neither the fame nor the pay that is the usual reward for such a rescue. Although Grace is resented by the wives of these men, to people a little farther removed she is an instant celebrity. She experiences all the good and the bad that came with such anointing, even though the story takes place long before this century, when the artist Andy Warhol made the observation that each of us is allotted fifteen minutes of fame.

Andy Warhol (1928–1987) was an American Pop artist and cultural figure in the 1960s and 1970s.

Walsh dedicates the book to the memory of "a good girl about whom a great deal of nonsense was talked." It is interesting to compare this story of a young woman's response to fame in the 1830s with that of today's celebrities. And as Roger Sutton wrote when he reviewed the book for the *New York Times Book Review,* Walsh doesn't allow "her heroine the contemporary comforts of self-help jargon. Grace doesn't have an 'identity crisis' or a 'stress reaction' to the considerable torments visited upon her. Instead, she is thoughtful, scared, sometimes naive and poignantly alone in her fears."

The Ever-Present Sea

It is obvious that Walsh has a deep affinity for the sea and for the men and women who risk their lives to rescue others. Lighthouses, lifeboats, shipwrecks, and what one reviewer called "the constant presence of the sea" are motifs running through several of Walsh's books.

motifs situations or themes that recur throughout an artistic work

The Emperor's Winding Sheet, set in the mid-1400s, is about a young teenager from Bristol, England, who is the lone survivor of a shipwrecked merchant vessel. He is picked up by pirates but manages to escape to a monastery garden. There he is found by Constantine, who is about to be crowned emperor. Constantine takes the boy, renames him Vrethiki, meaning "lucky find," and vows to keep him as a talisman because of a prophecy: if even one person who is at his side when he takes the crown stays with him always, the city named after the first emperor Constantine will not perish.

The boy is at first resentful of the role thrust upon him, but eventually he comes to love and respect Constantine. Even when offered his freedom, he chooses to stay, and he is present in 1453 when his city, Constantinople, falls to the Turks and the emperor is killed. Only then does the boy make his way back to England.

The sea plays a much more constant role in Walsh's two books that are best known to North American readers: *Goldengrove* and its sequel, *Unleaving*. At the center of the action is "Gran's cottage," actually a good-sized house, set back from a beach in Cornwall and sheltered by a small orchard from which the house gets its name. But Walsh had a deeper purpose in choosing *Goldengrove* and *Unleaving* as the titles for the two books. The names come from a line in the poem "Spring and Fall: To a Young Child," by Gerard Manley Hopkins:

> Margaret, are you grieving
> Over Goldengrove unleaving
>
> . . .
>
> It is the blight man was born for,
> It is Margaret you mourn for.

The first book opens with Madge and her younger "cousin" Paul arriving for their annual visit with their grandmother. In many ways, the book is a quiet, coming-of-age story about Madge, not at all like the more action-oriented coming-of-age stories about young men. Walsh explores the emotions of the two young people as they observe the changes in each other and in their grandmother, as well as in the ways they relate to each other, and especially in the way Madge is attracted to the blind professor who has rented Gran's cottage. Near the end of *Goldengrove,* Gran decides that it is time to let Madge and Paul know that they are really brother and sister, kept apart by the bitterness of their divorced parents.

The second book is harder to follow, in that it tells Madge's story both from her youth and from her own days as a grandmother. To the surprise of the family, Gran leaves her house to the girl, Madge, instead of to the boy, Paul, as was expected. Madge does not know what to do with the house, but in the first summer of her ownership she gets an opportunity to rent it to a philosophy professor. He brings a group of students to Cornwall for "a reading party," a kind of summer seminar. The professor's family comes with the group, and Madge finds herself attracted to their son, who, like Madge, responds to life emotionally rather than in the cold, intellectual manner of his father. The family has a five-year-old daughter who has Down's syndrome. Much of the drama centers on this child and the varying reactions of the family to what they all view as a tragedy.

The story is too complicated for a succinct summary, but its message is fairly simple. It is what Madge as a grandmother advises her grandson about taking life "two-handed and in full measure." She tells him to clap his hands and sing, and when he asks her, "What about?" she replies:

> What shall we clap?
> The lifeboat in the storm.
> What shall we sing?
> The wonders of the world.

Down's syndrome a congenital condition (acquired during development before birth but not through heredity), characterized by moderate to severe mental retardation and physical deformities

Walsh's Ongoing Career

This has been only a partial introduction to the books of Jill Paton Walsh. Anyone looking for a complete collection will be frustrated because many of them are out of print; however, the Kerlan Collection at the University of Minnesota owns several manuscripts. And because she is a prolific writer, chances are that book stores and libraries will have new books to make up for the ones no longer available.

A minor inconvenience relates to this author's name. In 1961, she married Antony Edmund Paton Walsh, a man whose surname would be more typically British if it were hyphenated. In recent years, as the traditional way married women list their surnames has begun to change, some librarians and some editors have begun to alphabetize Walsh under *P* as if Paton Walsh were hyphenated, while others view Paton as her birth name or a middle name and alphabetize her under *W* for Walsh. This latter form seems most fitting because it is the one used most often.

For the future, Walsh plans to follow her own advice, continuing to grasp life with two hands and "in full measure." She entices her family to share her enthusiasm for knowledge. She laughs at herself for being interested in so many things, for having what she calls a "butterfly mind." Yet such a description is more modest than accurate, because while Walsh's curiosity may take her across a wide range of topics and from prehistorical to post-Holocaust settings, she stays with her topics much longer and works with more depth than is implied by the flitting of a butterfly. No butterfly has ever become fluent in French, "adequate" in Latin, and able to read Old English, Icelandic, Italian, and Greek—accomplishments that Walsh casually mentions as a sidenote to her many other interests (Commire, p. 164).

Selected Bibliography

WORKS BY JILL PATON WALSH

Novels for Young Adults
  Hengest's Tale (1966)
  The Dolphin Crossing (1967)
  Fireweed (1967)
  Wordhoard: Anglo-Saxon Stories, with Kevin Crossley-Holland (1969)
  Goldengrove (1972)
  The Dawnstone (1973; 1974)
  The Emperor's Winding Sheet (1974)
  The Butty Boy, also known as *The Hustler* (1975)
  The Island Sunrise: Prehistoric Britain, nonfiction (1975; 1976)
  Unleaving (1976)
  Crossing to Salamis (1977)
  Children of the Fox (1978)
  A Chance Child (1978)
  The Green Book (1982)
  A Parcel of Patterns (1983; 1987; 1992)
  Gaffer Samson's Luck (1984; 1985)
  Torch (1987; 1988)
  Grace (1991; 1992)

Short Story Collection
  Five Tides (1987)

Works About Jill Paton Walsh
  Atkinson, Judith. "Paton Walsh, Jill." In *Twentieth Century Young Adult Writers.* Detroit: St. James, 1994.

Readers who have enjoyed Walsh's historical books will probably also enjoy the historical novels of Rosemary Sutcliff, while those who enjoy her realistic and her imaginative stories about young people growing up may want to go on to read Madeleine L'Engle's and Katherine Paterson's books.

Bach, Alice. Review of *Unleaving* in *New York Times Book Review,* 8 August 1976, p. 18.

Commire, Anne. "Paton Walsh, Gillian." In *Something About the Author Autobiography Series,* vol. 3, Detroit: Gale Research, 1987.

Gallo, Donald R., ed. "Jill Paton Walsh." In *Speaking for Ourselves: Autobiographical Sketches by Notable Authors of Books for Young Adults.* Urbana, Ill.: National Council of Teachers of English, 1990.

Heinz, Paul. Review of *A Chance Child* in *Horn Book,* vol. 55, February, 1979, p. 64.

Moss, Elaine. "A Wondrous World: Review of *Unleaving.*" In *Times Literary Supplement,* 2 April 1976, p. 375.

Stanek, Lou Willett. *Avon Books Study Guide: Jill Paton Walsh.* New York: The Hearst Corporations, no date (late 1970s).

Sutton, Roger. Review of *Grace* in *New York Times Book Review,* 14 June 1992, p. 31.

Theroux, Phyllis. Review of *Gaffer Samson's Luck* in *New York Times Book Review,* 16 June 1985, p. 30.

Walsh, Jill Paton. "History Is Fiction." In *The Horn Book Magazine,* February 1972, pp. 17–23.

How to Write to the Author
Jill Paton Walsh
c/o Farrar, Straus & Giroux, Inc.
19 Union Square West
New York, NY 10003

Barbara Wersba

(1932-   )

by Elizabeth A. Poe

Have you ever felt out of place, perhaps like a loner, a misfit, or even a loser? Did you ever think your parents did not understand you? Have your parents disapproved of your friends? Do you love animals? Do you have artistic dreams? Many of the characters in Barbara Wersba's young adult novels, and even Wersba herself, would answer yes to all these questions.

The Author's Life

As an only child raised in the small California town of San Mateo, Wersba, who was born on 19 August 1932, in Chicago, spent many solitary hours creating stories and imagining places she would rather be. Her mother and father, a businessman who was frequently away from home, had an unhappy marriage. A sad child who perceived herself as somehow different, Wersba was generally uncomfortable

> *Because she understands what it is like to be a loner, Wersba writes sensitive stories about teens who are alienated from their peers and who approach life in unusual ways.*
>
>

> *Arnold loves Rita, who is five foot three and weighs two hundred pounds, and he helps her see herself as something other than a fat girl who eats to soothe her feelings of loneliness.*
>
>

with other children, and this feeling of being a misfit continued in her teenage years. Because she understands what it is like to be a loner, Wersba writes sensitive stories about teens who are alienated from their peers and who approach life in unusual ways.

Residents of Sag Harbor and Water Mill

Take Rita Formica, for example. Rita is sixteen years old when she falls in love with Arnold Bromberg, a man twice her age. Arnold loves Rita, who is five foot three and weighs two hundred pounds, and he helps her see herself as something other than a fat girl who eats to soothe her feelings of loneliness. Wersba begins Rita and Arnold's story in *Fat: A Love Story* (1987). In *Love Is the Crooked Thing* (1987), Rita's parents are alarmed to learn she is having sex with a thirty-two-year-old loser. Agreeing he is not good for Rita, Arnold leaves town. Ten months later, Arnold returns and *Beautiful Losers* (1988) begins. Rita, by now eighteen, has decided to skip college and become a writer. Arnold wants to get married, but Rita thinks they should live together first. As Rita and Arnold work out their problems, Rita's parents come to appreciate Arnold for the talented, if unusual, man he is. The story ends as Rita and Arnold are married aboard the ferry that regularly crosses Sag Harbor.

Rita and Arnold, both misfits or losers who see value in one another that others do not, are the type of characters Wersba often writes about. Wersba likes to place her characters in settings familiar to her. Like Rita and Arnold, Wersba lives in Sag Harbor, New York. She can point out the abandoned cottage where she envisions that Rita and Arnold lived, the church where Arnold played the organ, and the ferry on which they got married. When she describes Sag Harbor—a whaling port turned factory town, which is now one of the summer resorts near the ocean on the east end of Long Island called the Hamptons—she is talking about the little town in which she lives.

In the Rita Formica trilogy, Wersba primarily portrays Sag Harbor's working class. In *Crazy Vanilla* (1986), she focuses on the affluent residents of the Hamptons through fourteen-year-old Tyler Woodruff, who is socially isolated because he loves bird photography. Fortunately, he meets Mitzi Gerrard, another loner who shares his interest in bird photography and helps him deal with his difficult family. The pond where Tyler and Mitzi go to photograph birds is well known to Wersba because it lies directly beyond her yard. She is a wildlife photographer herself, and, just as Tyler confesses to liking birds better than people, Wersba freely admits that she has always loved animals better than humans.

Wersba is devoted to her writing. She rises at five o'clock every morning and writes for about six hours in her spacious, book-lined attic studio. She writes every day, holidays included, whether she feels like it or not. In the afternoons, she generally reads, does errands, walks on the beach, visits friends, or teaches writing classes. Sometimes she returns to her typewriter in the evening. Besides the wild creatures that dwell in the nearby marshes and woods, Wersba always has at least one cat or dog around; a Norfolk terrier named Willie is now her primary companion.

Wersba's 1994 book, *Life's What Happens While You're Making Other Plans,* takes place in Water Mill, the town next to Sag Harbor, where the class oddball Justin Weinberg is struggling with how to tell his father he wants to attend acting school instead of college. With the help of the New Zealand film actress Kerry Brown, Justin's artistic Aunt Theo, and his mixed-up friend Bruno, Justin succeeds in taking the first step toward realizing his dream.

Habitants of Manhattan and the East Village

Artistic loners are central to all Wersba's novels, but not all her misfits live in Sag Harbor. Many of them live in New York City, where Wersba lived for many years. Although she lived in California throughout elementary school, Wersba moved to New York City when her parents divorced. She and her mother lived in a brownstone apartment and Wersba, who was twelve at the time, attended Miss Hewitt's, a private girl's school. Enthralled by the big city, Wersba, like many of the teenagers in her books, spent her after-school hours exploring museums, perusing bookstores, and attending theatrical performances. Many of her characters are misfits who live in Manhattan and attend prep schools.

For example, in *Tunes for a Small Harmonica* (1976), fifteen-year-old J.F. McAllister attends Miss Howlett's School for Girls. When not wearing the required school uniform, J.F.

Wersba freely admits that she has always loved animals better than humans.

brownstone faced with a reddish brown sandstone

dresses like a boy and looks like a teenage cab driver. She falls in love with her poetry teacher, Harold Murth, and believing him to be poverty stricken, plays her harmonica and panhandles in the theater district to raise money for him.

David Marks, in *Run Softly, Go Fast* (1970), attends the Spencer School because his father, Leo, a self-made business success, wants David to have advantages that he, as the son of Jewish immigrants, did not. Leo wants David to study business at Dartmouth. But David's passion is painting, and he refuses to attend college. When he can no longer endure his domineering father, David moves in with a friend in the East Village but continues to attend prep school.

Wersba's Acting Career

Wersba's own father was the son of Russian-Jewish immigrants. He wanted her to attend Vassar and was furious when she choose Bard College, a small liberal arts school that, as it turned out, would one day award her an honorary doctorate degree as one of its distinguished alumnae. Barbara ignored her father's rage because attending Bard was part of a goal she had set for herself as a child in California. Wanting to be an actress, she had performed at a community theater playhouse when she was eleven. When she moved to New York City and saw Laurette Taylor star in Tennessee Williams' *Glass Menagerie*, Barbara vowed to become a great stage actress like the famous Eva Le Gallienne.

Toward this end, Wersba studied acting at the Neighborhood Playhouse while she attended prep school and then majored in drama and studied dance with Martha Graham at Bard College. Immediately after college graduation in 1954, she played the leads in all the productions of a Princeton, New Jersey, summer-stock company. But even though she was a successful professional actress, Wersba constantly suffered severe stage fright. As she was shy and solitary by nature, making the rounds and attending open auditions for performers was painful for Wersba, and such experiences showed her the cruel side of the theater.

Although she had grown up in affluent circumstances, Wersba struggled to support herself after college. Like many aspiring performers, she lived humbly in the Manhattan neighborhood known as the East Village and took an assort-

Tennessee Williams (1911–1983) was an American playwright. He is best known for two plays, *The Glass Menagerie* and *A Streetcar Named Desire*. In *The Glass Menagerie*, Tom Wingfield recreates his memories of his crippled sister, Laura, and his mother, Amanda.

> *Although she had grown up in affluent circumstances, Wersba struggled to support herself after college.*

ment of part-time jobs. She worked in bookstores, department stores, restaurants, government offices, film studios, radio stations, television stations, and art studios while she studied acting at the Paul Mann Actors Workshop and sought work as an actress. Just as experiences and people from Wersba's prep-school days later inspired her writing, so did her experiences making the rounds and meeting people while she was living in the East Village. Chandler Brown, the aspiring actress in *The Carnival in My Mind* (1982), is such a character.

Chandler infatuates Harvey Beaumont, who is unhappy both at prep school, where he is constantly hazed, and at home where his aristocratic mother pays more attention to her Irish setters than she does to him. Harvey leaves their Fifth Avenue apartment and moves in with Chandler. Basking in Chandler's motherly kindness and her interest in his writing, Harvey begins to feel better about himself. When he sees Chandler act, however, he knows she will never make it as an actress. He is distressed when he learns she is a call girl.

The character of Chandler was inspired by a young actress with a stream of gentlemen callers who lived in the same East Village cold-water flat as Wersba when she was striving to break into the theater. Jeffrey Collins, in *Just Be Gorgeous* (1988), is also based on would-be artistic performers Wersba knew during this period of her life.

Jeffrey, twenty years old, gay, and homeless, tap-dances on the streets of New York, hoping to be discovered and become a Broadway star. Heidi Rosenbloom, sixteen, short, and affluent (although she dresses in thrift-shop garb), is a loner at her prep school and she welcomes Jeffrey's friendship. Eternally optimistic, Jeffrey helps Heidi see the importance of being herself and following her dream, which in Heidi's case is caring for dogs. In *Wonderful Me* (1989), the sequel to *Just Be Gorgeous,* Heidi's English teacher, Lionel Moss, falls in love with her. Their relationship ends abruptly when Heidi learns that Lionel is quite mad and believes himself to be the World War I English poet Rupert Brooke. Heidi swears off men but confirms her devotion to dogs.

Heidi is almost eighteen in *The Farewell Kid* (1989) and has graduated from the Spencer School. She must support herself because she declined to attend college, so she sets up housekeeping and a dog-rescue business in a defunct bar-

hazed subjected to ridicule and criticism

bershop. Harvey Beaumont, now eighteen, and Heidi become friends, then lovers. Harvey moves in with Heidi and they plan to marry. In addition to running the dog-rescue business, they will each pursue their own education, Harvey at the Manhattan Institute of Photography and Heidi, eventually, at Hunter College. Both Heidi and Harvey may be oddballs who have had some unusual relationships, but they are well suited for one another and will respect and protect each other's solitude.

Dreams

Some but not all of the aspiring artists in Wersba's stories achieve their dreams. And sometimes characters change artistic directions. Harvey, for instance, decides he wants to be a photographer rather than a writer. Similarly, Wersba redirected her artistic talents and turned from professional acting to professional writing. Although she could have continued her successful acting career, she chose not to follow up on a famous director's offer of a part on Broadway. After a three-month road trip with six other young actors, during which she contracted hepatitis, she decided to leave the theater.

hepatitis viral disease that affects the liver and is usually transmitted through contaminated water or food

Throughout the fifteen years Wersba devoted to acting, she had also been writing stories and poems in her free time. Like many of her characters, she did not like what she wrote and usually left her pieces unfinished. But while recovering from her bout with hepatitis, Wersba completed the first story she ever liked. This children's story, *The Boy Who Loved the Sea,* published in 1961, launched Wersba's new career as a writer. After writing several children's books, in 1968 Wersba wrote her first book in a newly recognized genre called young adult literature. Since then she has written fourteen more novels for young adults. Most of these books deal with teenage loners like Rita Formica, Tyler Woodruff, Harvey Beaumont, and Heidi Rosenbloom.

Those Who Live Elsewhere

Wersba's original social misfit, Albert Scully, did not live in Sag Harbor or New York City. *The Dream Watcher* (1968), her first young adult novel, takes place in a New Jersey housing development. A loner and failure at life, Albert gains faith in himself via Mrs. Orpha Woodfin, the eighty-year-old neighborhood eccentric. Mrs. Woodfin tells Albert about growing up in a titled British family and of her triumphs as a great actress. She encourages Albert to follow his dreams and to dance to a different drummer.

When Wersba left the theater and became an author of children's books, she did not expect to return to the theater. But life came full circle for her when the actress Eva Le Gallienne read *The Dream Watcher* and asked Barbara Wersba to write a play for her based on the book. Wersba spent five years working on the play, in which Le Gallienne played the part of Mrs. Woodfin. The play was a success at the White Barn in Connecticut, but bad casting, set design, and directing caused it to fail in Seattle, and it never made it to Broadway, as they had hoped it would. Nevertheless, Wersba was now a playwright, and she had the honor of working closely with the great actress who had so inspired her own acting career.

Another of Wersba's early works, *The Country of the Heart* (1975), was also adapted for television and film production. In this story, nineteen-year-old Steven Harper, an aspiring but misunderstood poet, attends the local community college in Cromwell, New York. Steven has a brief but passionate love affair with Hadley Norman, a forty-year-old award-winning poet who, although Steven does not know it, is dying from cancer. *The Country of the Heart* was made into a television movie called *Matters of the Heart,* starring Jane Seymour as Hadley Norman.

Many of Wersba's young adult novels capture the hopefulness that comes through improbable relationships, in which unlikely people touch each other's lives and change them for the better. Although the characters and story lines are similar in many of her novels, Wersba becomes less intense in her later books. Nevertheless, the voices of Rita Formica and Heidi Rosenbloom ring just as true as do those of Albert Scully, Steven Harper, and David Marks.

> *Many of Wersba's young adult novels capture the hopefulness that comes through improbable relationships, in which unlikely people touch each other's lives and change them for the better.*

More New York City Dwellers

Wersba becomes quite playful in her novels of the 1990s. In *The Best Place to Live Is the Ceiling* (1990), a spoof on action-adventure best-sellers, Archie Smith, a social outcast who is sixteen and lives in Queens, gets his wish for adventure when amazing circumstances make him part of an international diamond smuggling caper. This fast-paced hoax takes place in Zurich and Davos, two of Wersba's favorite Swiss towns. Continuing in this lighter vein, *You'll Never Guess the End* (1992) parodies mystery detective stories. In this story, Joel Greenberg and his dog, Sherlock, solve the mystery of the kidnapping of an heiress, Marilyn Schumacher. The character of Marilyn, like others created by Wersba, echoes the author's life. Marilyn attends Miss Howlett's School for Girls and at one time wants to be an actress, just as Wersba attended a prep school and planned to act professionally. Like many of Wersba's New York City teens, Joel has a weakness not only for animals but for taxicab rides.

Over the past twenty-five years, several generations of teenagers have read the novels of Barbara Wersba. Although she is pleased to touch the lives of these teens, Wersba's primary motivation for writing is an attempt to make sense of her own unhappy childhood. Fortunately, as she writes to come to terms with her own personal experiences, Wersba creates intriguing young adult fiction.

To find out why Joel Greenberg named his dog **Sherlock,** read the article about Sir Arthur Conan Doyle in volume 1.

If you like the works of Barbara Wersba, you might also like books by M. E. Kerr and Francesca Lia Block.

Selected Bibliography

WORKS BY BARBARA WERSBA

Young Adult Novels

The Dream Watcher (1968)

Run Softly, Go Fast (1970)

The Country of the Heart (1975)

Tunes for a Small Harmonica (1976)

The Carnival in My Mind (1982)

Crazy Vanilla (1986)

Fat: A Love Story (1987)

Love Is the Crooked Thing (1987)

Beautiful Losers (1988)

Just Be Gorgeous (1988)

The Farewell Kid (1989)

Wonderful Me (1989)

The Best Place to Live Is the Ceiling (1990)

You'll Never Guess the End (1992)

Life's What Happens While You're Making Other Plans (1994)

Adaptations

The Dream Watcher (1975)

Matters of the Heart (1990)

Children's Books

The Boy Who Loved the Sea (1961)

The Brave Balloon of Benjamin Buckley (1963)

The Land of Forgotten Beasts (1964)

A Song for Clowns (1965)

Let Me Fall Before I Fly (1971)

Amanda Dreaming (1973)

The Crystal Child (1982)

Poetry

Do Tigers Ever Bite Kings? (1966)

Twenty-Six Starlings Will Fly Through Your Mind (1980)

WORKS ABOUT BARBARA WERSBA

Commire, Anne, ed. *Something About the Author.* Detroit: Gale Research, 1990, vol. 58, pp. 179–187.

Eaglen, Audrey. "Barbara Wersba." In *Twentieth-Century Young Adult Writers.* Edited by Laura Standley Berber. Detroit: St. James, 1994, pp. 689–690.

Garrett, Agnus, and Helga P. McCue, eds. *Authors and Artists for Young Adults.* Detroit: Gale Research, 1989, vol. 2, pp. 235–243.

Janeczko, Paul. "An Interview with Barbara Wersba." *English Journal,* November 1976, pp. 20–21.

Mercier, Jean F. "Barbara Wersba." In *Twentieth Century Children's Writers,* 2d ed. Edited by D. L. Kirkpatrick. New York: St. Martins, 1983, pp. 810–812.

Sarkissian, Adele, ed. *Something About the Author.* Detroit: Gale Research, 1986, vol. 2, pp. 293–304.

Vandergrift, Kay. "Barbara Wersba." In *Dictionary of Literary Biography, American Writers for Children Since 1960: Fiction.* Edited by Glenn E. Estes. Detroit: Gale Research, 1986, pp. 374–380.

Wersba, Barbara. "Barbara Wersba—As a Writer." *Top of the News,* June 1975, pp. 427–428.

How to Write to the Author
Barbara Wersba
c/o Henry Holt & Co., Inc.
115 West 18th Street
New York, NY 10011

Robert Atkinson Westall

(1929-1993)

by Lanny van Allen

D o not even think of beginning a Robert Westall book the night before you have a test. Although you would read a thoroughly satisfying, action-packed, well-written piece of literature, you would not want to put it down, and you would not have time to study for the test. As Wes Adams, one of Westall's American editors, wrote me, "He was a storyteller in the truest sense: his words hold you in a spell from the very first sentence."

Westall wrote more than thirty books. Some are about his experiences as a twelve- and thirteen-year-old boy growing up in England in the middle of World War II. Some are about the close relationship he always had with the sea. Some are about cats, and some deal with fantasy and the supernatural. Many of his books include all those elements and more. If you have not yet met Robert Westall in his books, many exciting hours of reading await you.

I knew I liked Robert Westall when I read that Tim Vaux in *Stormsearch* (1990) sticks his dinner into a padded envelope and addresses it to UNICEF (United Nations Children's Emergency Fund). Many of us who were children during World War II dreamed of doing this daring act every time we had to clean our plates but did not want to. Tim's dad, a professor of agriculture, and his mom, an assistant to his dad, travel to underdeveloped countries, where they encourage the governments to grow beneficial foods. When Tim or his sister asks for something like a tape recorder for Christmas, their parents give a lecture on how many poor children in Country X could be fed on the amount of money a tape recorder costs.

One night, when Tim—disliking the cottage pie his mom has prepared—does not finish his dinner, he gets the usual speech about starving orphans. He is so enraged that he takes his plate of food, stuffs it into a padded mailing envelope, addresses it in huge black letters to UNICEF, and hands it to his dad. After this incident, Tim's relationship with his parents is never quite as good as before.

Rocky Relationships?

Westall often points out family friction between adolescents and adults. Like Tim Vaux, Harry Baguely in *The Kingdom by the Sea* (1990), almost thirteen, realizes that after his experiences of the previous two months, his relationship with his dad will probably never be as good as before:

> **gannet** large seabird that feeds on fish and lives primarily on offshore islands

> Dad had never seen a gannet dive. He had never seen the dawn come up over the breaking waves of Druridge Bay. He would *never* understand . . . . Harry had grown too big for his family, as if he'd drunk from some magic bottle . . . . And Dad knew it. And hated it. (P.173)

But positive father-son relationships also are represented in Westall's books: by Artie and his son Keith, and by Mr. M and his son Freddy, in *The Kingdom by the Sea,* and by Joe Clarke and his son Kevin in *The Stones of Muncaster Cathedral* (1991). Westall himself enjoyed very close relationships with his father and his son, Christopher, who died tragically at eighteen in a motorcycle accident. In *The Kingdom by the Sea,* Harry lives for a time with Mr. M, who continues to grieve over his young son lost in the war. Harry believes Mr. M wants Harry around "to fill up a boy-sized hole inside himself" (p. 161).

Because Westall was a teacher for many years, he was familiar with many students and many family situations, and these naturally influenced his writing. Timothy and Jane only mention their dad in *Yaxley's Cat* (1991). They want to play Dirty Scrabble because Dad will not let them play at home; he did not come with them on their wild and crazy trip. Their mother, Rose, often thinks about her husband and her relationship with him before the trip; she tries to call him several times but always gets a recorded message. The family focus in this book is on Timothy and Jane's close and healthy relationship with Rose.

The families that Westall creates typically have a somewhat traditional structure, usually a mother, a father, and two children—a boy and a girl—such as Harry and Dulcie in *The Kingdom by the Sea*, Tim and Tracey in *Stormsearch,* and Timothy and Jane in *Yaxley's Cat.* Westall does not say that any of the families or family structures are ideal. He just draws them honestly (as he does everything), and deals with situations like divorce when necessary. He won an award for his book *The Scarecrows* (1981), about a divorce from the child's point of view, and he had written of divorce earlier in *The Watch-House* (1977). An obituary for Robert Westall indicates that he was divorced in 1987 from his wife, Jean. He did not remarry.

Even though Westall seldom gives girls or women important roles in his works, he does not demonstrate any particular animosity toward them. He develops the character of Rose, the mother in *Yaxley's Cat,* more than most mothers. He includes a girl, Audrey, in the title group in *The Machine-Gunners* (1975). Yet girls will enjoy reading Westall's books for many reasons. If they are looking for a girl in a *major* role, they may like Maggi in *Ghost Abbey* (1988), Anne in *Watch-House,* Valerie in *The Promise* (1990), and Rachel in *Rachel and the Angel* (1986).

animosity ill will or resentment

Resourceful Kids

While Westall shows a strong sense of family in his books, he also shows most of his youthful main characters moving toward independence. They find themselves in situations that

> *Westall frequently calls attention to phony, pious adults.*

plot the deliberate sequence of events in a literary work

require them to make clear decisions, and in dilemmas that require them to determine right from wrong. Westall frequently calls attention to phony, pious adults, such as the clergyman Morris in *The Stones of Muncaster Cathedral*. And he frequently builds his plots so that the young people outsmart the grown-ups. Harry Baguely, alone and very vulnerable, has to outsmart adults every step of his journey up the coast in order to survive: an old grocer, a mad farmer, and passersby who might report him to the police, as well as a mean and nasty gang. With only an old pistol and a flashlight, young Timothy plans and successfully defends his mom and sister against at least four adults in *The Machine-Gunners,* a glorious masterpiece showing a few young people outsmarting many adults.

Westall was also interested in portraying kids outsmarting other kids, from serious gang activities (as Harry encounters in his travels, and as Chas encounters in *The Machine-Gunners*) to lighter games such as Dirty Scrabble played by Timothy, Jane, and Rose. In reflecting on his own school days, Westall said he was the one who *advised* the leader of his gang, sort of "teacherly," even then. As a writer, he continued to be quite interested in gang structures and operations. To fight and win in life's battles, he believed, it is necessary to be fit: physically, of course, but also intellectually and morally. Chas McGill is such a "fit" character.

War, or the Morning After

To give his son Chris an idea of what it was like to grow up in the middle of a war, literally in his own backyard, Westall wrote *The Machine-Gunners*. He is quoted in Peter Hollindale's "Westall's Kingdom" as saying that the book's main character, Chas McGill, was "a mixture of me at twelve and my son Christopher" (p. 150). Chas at fourteen has the second-best collection of World War II souvenirs in Garmouth, a town modeled after Westall's hometown of Tyneside. Chas collects the souvenirs in a grocery-store cart every morning after the bombings. When he and his family come out of their air-raid shelter after an attack, Chas and other schoolboys race (before reporting to school) to see who can find the best pieces of enemy bullets, bombs, and such.

Boddser Brown, not a friend of Chas's, has the best collection in Garmouth because he has found the nose cone of a 3.7-inch antiaircraft projectile, and a nose cone is worth lots of points in this competition. But one morning Chas hits the jackpot: he finds in a nearby clearing most of a German bomber plane (Heinkel He III), its dead Nazi pilot, *and* a black, new type of machine gun. Chas and his best friends cut the machine gun away from the plane (no small task) and build a bunker around it, hiding it from adults and the Boddser Brown group. Westall's fascination with gang structures and operations is evident in this book through Chas's gutsy stand against the Boddser Brown bullies.

In *The Kingdom by the Sea,* written fifteen years after *The Machine-Gunners,* we find young Harry Baguely emerging from his backyard air-raid shelter after a night of bombing. Seeing his house burning, he thinks that his father, mother, and sister are all dead because they did not make it to the shelter with him. Rather than be picked up by police and taken to a war-orphans' home, Harry takes his blanket roll and runs away up the coast, fending off all sorts of enemies, including a mean gang.

air-raid shelter a building made of heavy material, such as concrete, in which people take shelter from bomb attacks

Blitzcat (1989) combines two of Westall's recurring subjects: the war and cats. Lord Gort (a cat) tries to find her way home (yes, he's a *she*) through England during the Blitz (the name for the campaign of air bombings of England by Nazi Germany). Readers see this bloody fire-bombing from the cat's point of view. We get to know the interesting characters she meets and reflect on the way the war affects them. It is another good journey story, a format Westall liked to use.

As in the case of Lord Gort, Westall's fictional journeys often take the reader by the sea. Westall was born "in a marvellous harbor," he wrote in *Speaking for Ourselves, Too* (Gallo, ed., 1993). He grew up with the sights, sounds, smells, and colorful variety of people that he generously shares in his books. In *Fathom Five* (1979), the sequel to *The Machine-Gunners,* he wrote of Chas again:

> **Fish Quay was the best place he knew. Dead herring flung all over the place . . . . Herring squashed to a pink pulp by wheels . . . . There were herring gulls on the quay, big as geese. Walking around your legs bold as brass. You let them alone; one snap of their**

trawling fishing by
the use of a cone-
shaped net, which is
dragged along the
ocean floor by a boat

beaks could take your hand off. Trawlermen were great, swearing nonstop. Mad generous . . . . Trawling all night, they took their sleep when they could. The way they talked, life was one big laugh. Trawling up German mines in their nets and firing rifles at them. Fighting off German bombers that tried to machine-gun them; calling them names like Horace the Heinkel. (Pp. 6–7)

Westall's vivid descriptions take us directly to the English seacoast where he lived.

All the Fish in the Sea

The seacoast is the setting for *Stormsearch,* and the wind and the tides are important to the people in the story, including young Tim Vaux and his sister, Tracey. So are the magnificent model sailing ships, probably inspired by Westall's personal experience: his father crafted many fine model sailing ships. An important element in the story is the *Ebenezer,* a sailing vessel four feet long, and four-and-a-half feet to the top of the mainmast. Tim and Tracey help others lift the *Ebenezer* into a cove, where she sails. This "seaworthy" model helps them sort out a solution to a romantic and mysterious sea tale.

But *The Kingdom by the Sea* is Harry Baguely's story of his extensive relationship with the sea—its gifts, its power, and its creatures. Joseph teaches Harry about gathering sea-coal and slank (a seaweed substitute for green vegetables) early in the mornings, and about bringing in loads of fish after bombers pass overhead. On up the coast, Artie, who grew up in the country, teaches Harry to set snares for rabbits:

Artie knew all about birds; and foxes and stoats and weasels. Artie knew all about the land, and Harry knew all about the sea, from Joseph. They told each other things . . . . (P. 88)

The boys watch an eider duck with her ducklings going into the sea. They watch gannets diving for fish, and they build sandcastles and watch the sunsets. Farther along up the coast, Harry is alone, trying to cross a sandbridge to an island, when he gets caught in heavy surf, feels the tug of strong waves, and understands the power of the sea:

> He felt dizzy, as the endless waves moved past him, with their burden of sand. The ground seemed to be moving under him, sucking his feet away. He nearly fell, and there was nothing to hang on to in the whole moving world. (Pp. 129–130)

> And the sea sent its messengers before it. The very air he breathed was full of salty spray, so that he breathed a mixture of air and water, half boy, half fish. And the bigness of the sea overwhelmed him; the bigness of the sound of it. The land seemed so far away, it was nowhere. Nothing but sea. The sound of the waves did not soothe him. The sea had tried to kill him. Might still kill him. Meanwhile, he watched it. (P. 133)

The sea seems to symbolize freedom and growth, especially Harry's growth toward being his own person, independent.

Yet the sea did not always play a major role in Westall's books. Sometimes its qualities were mentioned only in passing. For example, Rose, in *Yaxley's Cat,* thought Yaxley's house was too quiet, so she "decided she would go and walk by the sea; it would soothe her" (p. 61). It is interesting how the sea affects people in different ways; for Harry, the sound of the waves is not at all soothing!

Scared-y Cat, Scared-y Cat

Yaxley's Cat is completely unlike *Blitzcat* or the fantasy *The Cats of Seroster* (1984) or the two younger children's books, *Christmas Cat* (1991) and *If Cats Could Fly* (1990). Yaxley's cat is the type Westall used for his ghostly, supernatural, and scary stories—full of "enormous cruel strength and diabolical ferocity" (p. 89). This cat disappears when its master, Sepp Yaxley, disappears and comes back involved in something like witchcraft. It seems mad and throws itself at closed doors. Strange cats also play a part in *The Wind Eye* (1976), *The Devil on the Road* (1978), and *Urn Burial* (1987).

It is not cats but gargoyles that make things chilly, evil, and scary in *The Stones of Muncaster Cathedral*. There seems to be an awful curse on one especially grotesque gargoyle, so Joe Clarke, steeplejack, has to unravel the curse before he or his young son, Kevin, falls victim:

> Every time I hit the stone, the chisel made its ringing noise; and in the ringing noise, I could hear the crying of children. But it was even more than that . . . . I could feel the forces trapped inside the stone, wanting to break out. (P. 76)

Reading *The Stones of Muncaster Cathedral* is a very chilling experience. It reminded me of some stories by H. P. Love-craft (1890–1937), an American horror writer.

Other books in which Westall explores the supernatural are *The Wind Eye, The Devil on the Road* (both time-travel fantasies), and *Stormsearch*. He conjures up ghosts and demons in *The Scarecrows* and *The Promise*; the future in *Futuretrack Five* (1983) (futuristic science fiction) and *Urn Burial*; and a modern political fable in *Gulf* (1996).

The Mother Tongue?

Now that you have had a brief introduction to Westall's works, you may need to brush up on your *British* English! It is easy to catch most meanings from the context. Here are a few examples of "The Other English" from Westall's sto-ries: *petrol* for gasoline; *telly* for television; *lino* for linoleum (a floor covering); *fag* for cigarette; *bloke* (also *sod, chap*) for guy; *bairns* for babies or kids; the *loo* (or the *lav*) for bath-room; *nowt* for nothing; and *biscuits* for cookies. You may notice that the English stop to have tea and sweets like bis-cuits, no matter that war is going on all around, and no mat-ter where. In *The Kingdom by the Sea,* Harry goes for a swim:

> He jumped and splashed a lot, even after he'd had enough. When he finally did come out, shivering and goosefleshed, Mr. M was busy pumping up an old

brass Primus stove, on which a billy-can of water was boiling. "Tea," said Mr. M. "Nothing like a mug of hot tea after a swim. And cake. Plenty of cake." (P. 161)

Robert Westall was born on 27 October 1929. He earned a bachelor's degree in fine arts before serving in the Royal Signals, a branch of the British army. After his military service, Westall earned a doctoral degree in fine arts and went into teaching in a Northwich secondary school. There he remained for twenty-five years. Following his long career in teaching, Westall took up the antiques business. And then, after all these years of experiences, associations, ideas, and inspirations, Westall became a writer—a writer for the young adults he knew well and who, he said, had open minds.

The publication dates of Westall's books reveal that he lived a long time before he became a writer, and that he was very prolific once he started. He read drafts of his first three books to his son, Chris, mainly to give him an idea of what it was like to be twelve years old in the midst of World War II. Chris encouraged his dad to submit one of the drafts for publication. *The Machine-Gunners* was immediately recognized and won the British Library Association's Carnegie Medal, an unusual accomplishment for a first novel. Even more amazing, Westall won the Carnegie Medal again for *The Scarecrows*. Later he won the overall Smarties Award (in 1989) for *Blitzcat*. *The Kingdom by the Sea* was honored twice: it received the American Library Association Best Books for Young Adults award and the Guardian Award for Children's Fiction.

Westall's critics have said that his books were too violent and realistic. Westall responded that he would tell only the truth in his writing, that he would not pasteurize it or sanitize it. He wanted to be clear and truthful with the young adults for whom he wrote. We might say he "told it like it is." His texts are rich with little pieces of history, but included only when they are appropriate. The beauty and strength of nature is always a part of Westall's writing, and his characters are varied and colorful. He was influenced by Jack London's books, and he learned much about characters from Charles Dickens. Imagine how he enjoyed reading about little Oliver Twist outsmarting all those adults.

> *After all these years of experience, Westall became a writer—a writer for the young adults he knew well and who, he said, had open minds.*

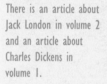

There is an article about Jack London in volume 2 and an article about Charles Dickens in volume 1.

The small room where Robert Westall wrote is close to the street. It is full of antique clocks from his years in the antiques business and jam-packed with cats! We would have expected that. You need to know all of these things because Robert Atkinson Westall may well become your favorite author very soon.

Selected Bibliography

WORKS BY ROBERT WESTALL

Novels for Young Adults

The Machine-Gunners (1975)
The Wind Eye (1976)
The Watch-House (1977)
The Devil on the Road (1978)
Fathom Five (1979)
The Scarecrows (1981)
Futuretrack 5 (1983)
The Cats of Seroster (1984)
Urn Burial (1987)
Ghost Abbey (1988)
Blitzcat (1989)
Old Man on a Horse (1989)
The Kingdom by the Sea (1990)
The Promise (1990)
Stormsearch (1990)
Yaxley's Cat (1991)
The Stones of Muncaster Cathedral, two novellas (1991)
The Ghost in the Tower (1992)
Falling into Glory (1993)
Gulf (1996)

Short Story Collections

Break of Dark (1982)
The Haunting of Chas McGill and Other Stories (1983)
Rachel and the Angel (1986)
Ghosts and Journeys (1988)
Ghost Story Anthology, edited by Robert Westall (1988)
The Call and Other Stories (1989)

If you like Robert Westall, you might also like the works of Gary Paulsen.

A Walk on the Wild Side (1989)

Echoes of War (1989)

The Fearful Lovers (1992)

Demons and Shadows—The Ghostly Best Stories, published posthumously (1994)

Books for Younger Readers

The Witness (1985)

Rosalie (1988)

If Cats Could Fly (1990)

Christmas Cat (1991)

Size Twelve (1992)

Nonfiction

"Jack London's White Fang." *Children's Literature in Education,* March 1993, pp. 31–42.

WORKS ABOUT ROBERT WESTALL

Eccleshare, Julia. "Robert Westall." *Independent Gazette,* 21 April 1993, p. 18.

Gallo, Donald R., ed. *Speaking for Ourselves, Too.* Urbana, Ill.: National Council of Teachers of English, 1993.

Grimes, William. "Robert Westall, 63, Art Teacher and Author of Children's Books." *New York Times,* 20 April 1993, p. B8.

Hollindale, Peter. "Westall's Kingdom." *Children's Literature in Education,* September 1994, pp. 147–157.

Nilsen, Alleen Pace. *Your Reading: A Booklist for Junior High and Middle School Students.* Urbana, Ill.: National Council of Teachers of English, 1991.

"Robert Westall." *London Times,* 23 April 1993.

Wurth, Shirley, ed. *Books for You, A Booklist for Senior High Students.* Urbana, Ill.: National Council of Teachers of English, 1992.

Laura Ingalls Wilder

(1867–1957)

by Janet Spaeth

Who was Laura Ingalls Wilder? That question is at the same time both easy and impossible to answer. Certainly she was the author of the Little House books. As a child who experienced the height of westward expansion in the United States, she realized that she was in a unique position: having seen the span of the homesteading movement, she said, "I understood that in my own life I represented a whole period of American history" (Bookweek Speech, 1937).

The Name's the Same

Readers usually feel that they know Wilder because they know Laura, the main character in eight of the nine books Wilder wrote. The character and author share the same name, so it is natural to assume that they are the same.

But are they?

When people write about their own lives, it is called autobiography. The Little House books are based upon events that actually happened to Wilder and her family, but they are not truly autobiographical. Wilder did try to make events as true as possible, but sixty years had intervened. Names became approximations (Nellie Oleson, Laura's rival in the series, is based upon a girl named Nellie Owens) and mentally recreating the town of De Smet required some mapping. As much as she relied upon her memory, Wilder also relied upon her skill as a writer.

In many cases the artistic effect that Wilder wanted had to be achieved by reworking the truth into fiction. She often left out facts or compressed time to give the story more appeal and impact. An example of this method occurs in the first book: the family lived in the Big Woods of Wisconsin twice but Wilder combined the two times into one in *Little House in the Big Woods* (1932).

The books are properly called historical fiction. Wilder was not the only author to have written this kind of book. *Little Women,* for instance, is based upon the life of the author Louisa May Alcott, but the book is not strictly true to Alcott's life.

There is an article about Louisa May Alcott in volume I.

Does recognizing that the Little House books are not one hundred percent factual make them less true? Those who have read the Little House books and felt Laura's joy in discovering the wonders of the sunlit prairie or shared her anger when the new teacher, Miss Wilder, chastises Carrie know that there is a truthfulness that goes beyond mere facts such as what happened when. It is the truthfulness of the human spirit, especially in childhood, and Laura Ingalls Wilder captures that.

The Little Houses

Laura Elizabeth Ingalls was born 6 February 1867 in the Big Woods of Wisconsin, but she did not stay there long. She was introduced at a very early age to the wanderlust that affected her father, Charles Ingalls (Pa). By the time Laura was just entering into her teens, the Ingalls family had moved seven times, finally settling in De Smet, a new town in what would become South Dakota.

wanderlust a strong longing to wander

For some children, moving that often would be unsettling. But Laura managed to turn it into something exciting. Always the pioneer, she knew life would "be better farther on" (*The First Four Years,* p. 134). It was this ability to keep herself looking forward that carried her through times of strife and allowed her to portray this prairie childhood as filled with joy and comforting love.

And it served her well when she was a grown-up, too. While she was in De Smet, she married Almanzo Wilder, whom she called "Manly." The beginning of their life together is told in *The First Four Years* (1971). They are four years of hardship: crop loss, the death of a son, failure to prove up on a claim, and a devastating house fire. But they are also four years of love, for not only did Laura and Almanzo have each other, they also had Rose, their daughter.

In 1890, the Wilders moved to Missouri and concentrated on developing the orchards at their new home, Rocky Ridge Farm near Mansfield. Laura's skill at getting her chickens to lay eggs became known around the region, and farm groups often asked her to speak. At one such gathering, a man named John Case heard her talk and asked her to write for his magazine, *The Missouri Ruralist.*

It was the start of a wonderful career.

The story of how *Little House in the Big Woods* came into existence is a convoluted one.

"Pioneer Girl" was the first draft, and it covered Laura Ingalls Wilder's childhood until she married Almanzo. Then Wilder—along with her daughter, Rose Wilder Lane, already a well-known writer and journalist, and her friends Elmer and Berta Hoerner Hader—decided to shorten the story and try to market it as a picture book. The manuscript was titled "When Grandma Was a Little Girl."

Marion Fiery, an editor at Alfred A. Knopf publishing house, liked the book but wanted it to be longer. She did not like "Pioneer Girl" and wanted the shortened scope of "When Grandma Was a Little Girl." Revisions were done, and an offer was made on "Little House in the Woods," as it was titled next.

Knopf decided to disband their children's books section, however, and Wilder searched for another publisher. The manuscript went to Virginia Kirkus at Harper and Brothers (now HarperCollins), who saw in it "the miracle book that no depression could stop," referring to publishing problems

pioneer one of the first to settle in a territory

convoluted intricate; involved

The **Great Depression** was a severe economic crisis that began when the stock market crashed in 1929 and that lasted almost ten years. By the winter of 1932–1933, 14 to 16 million Americans were unemployed. Many died from a lack of food and inadequate living conditions.

caused by the Great Depression. It was accepted on 26 November 1931 (appropriately, Thanksgiving Day) and published in an amazingly short time, on 6 April 1932, as *Little House in the Big Woods*.

It was the first of what was to become one of the most beloved series of all children's literature.

Growing Up with Laura

One of the most interesting elements of the Little House books is the way the reader "grows" along with Laura. With each successive book, the reading difficulty increases as Laura gets older. At the beginning of the first book of the series, *Little House in the Big Woods*, Laura is four years old, and the book is written at approximately a third-grade reading level. By the time Laura gets married at the end of *These Happy Golden Years* (1943), the reading level has risen to that of junior high. The writing style and reading level of the last book in the series, *The First Four Years*, however, do not quite fit with the rest of the series. Wilder once referred to trying her hand at writing a novel for adults, and the manuscript for *The First Four Years*, discovered after her death, may have been that attempt.

Another way in which Wilder shows Laura's growth to adulthood is the change in how Laura deals with her surroundings, whether it be her physical environment or the people around her. At first, Laura is unsure when faced with a strange setting. She and her family move from the comfortable neighborhood of the Big Woods—leaving behind her extended family of grandparents and aunts and uncles—to the seemingly threatening and empty world of the prairie. Because Laura is young, she reacts as a child would: with suspicion. As the prairie (and its inhabitants) become known to her, she is able to reconcile with them and accept them as part of her world.

prairie a large area of uncultivated land, usually with rich soil covered with grasses

Laura is met with one new experience after another. The unsettledness of the Ingalls family's lives as they move from one place to another is partially due to Pa's wanderlust. But life itself forces them to move. Pa's decision to leave Indian country in *Little House on the Prairie* (1935) is prompted by his hearing of the government's decision to remove white settlers from the land. Certainly he could have waited for official word from the government, but he chose not to. Removal seemed inevitable.

The grasshopper plague in *On the Banks of Plum Creek* (1937) nearly depleted the family's resources, but the bout of scarlet fever that affected Mary, Carrie, Grace, and Ma and left Mary blind (occurring in the interval between *On the Banks of Plum Creek* and *By the Shores of Silver Lake* (1939)) forced the family's final relocation to the Dakota Territory. They would move again, but always within the area of De Smet. Even the endless blizzards that later held the town captive in *The Long Winter* could not move them again. They had settled at last.

Why Readers Love the Little House Books

The Little House books are notable for their warmth, the quality that makes the reader identify with the main character and feel good about having met him or her. Laura is not just a character whom children wish they were. She *is* who they are. Readers feel a strong sense of familiarity, even though the stories are set in the past and the circumstances are different from today. Only the surroundings are different: the child inside has not changed.

Why Some Readers Do Not Like Them

Although the books have become beloved American classics, they also have been the subject of debate. Probably the most controversial element of the books is the racial insensitivity demonstrated by some of the characters. Most of the negative attention has been focused on the way Native Americans are portrayed, or the way the characters perceive them, especially Ma. She is either terrified or disdainful, depending upon how much distance there is between herself and the Indians.

There is, however, a questioning tone in several of the passages dealing with Native Americans that cannot be overlooked. When the issue of Indian removal comes up late one night in *Little House on the Prairie,* Laura asks why the Indians will be going west, as Ma predicts. Pa's brief answer tries to encompass the theories of both eminent domain (the government's right to take a person's land) and manifest destiny (the divinely endowed right and responsibility of white Americans to expand settlement westward). "The government makes them, Laura," Pa says. That falls short of satisfying Laura, who persists by asking a question that goes straight to the heart of these two political theories. She points out that they are in Indian Territory: "Won't it make the Indians mad to have to—" Pa, unable to defend or explain either concept, cuts off the conversation (*Little House on the Prairie,* pp. 236–237).

Later in the same book, the family sits on the porch and watches a long, solemn trail of Native Americans file past as they are removed from the area. It is an occasion filled with the Indians' sadness, dignity, and nameless sorrow. Pa salutes Soldat du Chene, a brave Osage who had tried to work for peace between the whites and the Native Americans. Laura cries out for a baby whose eyes capture her soul. For a reason she cannot explain, she wants that baby. It is a symbol of an irrevocable change in the pattern of her life. The entire Ingalls family stays in the doorway until the Native Americans are gone from view. Even Ma feels the impact of the occasion and is not happy. She comments that she does not want to get up because she is "so let down" (*Little House on the Prairie,* p. 310).

A concern that should arise about the racism of the books has to do with their time frames. A historical novel has two historical periods to deal with: the time in which it is written and the time it is written *about.* Clearly the time of western expansion in the United States was one of enforced racism. White Americans saw the land as unpopulated, unsettled, and wild, when in fact it was populated, settled, and well maintained by the native people. Wilder would have been remiss to have left out that aspect of pioneering.

It is also important to remember that Wilder wrote these novels in the 1930s and 1940s, a time in which people of color were often barred from living near or working with white people. This policy, called segregation, would soon be challenged by the civil rights movement, but the organized movement as we know it today had not yet become a major force. This may explain why Wilder did not always portray people of color or varying ethnic backgrounds with the sensitivity that modern readers like.

Farmer Boy: A Big Little House

Farmer Boy (1933) is the one book in the series that does not deal with Laura. It is, instead, the story of Almanzo Wilder's childhood on a prosperous upstate New York farm. It can be looked at in two ways: either as a free-standing novel, independent of the others, or as a part of the series because Almanzo Wilder does appear elsewhere in the series. In *The Long Winter,* Laura first meets him, the man who will become her husband.

Yet in *Farmer Boy,* Almanzo Wilder still has not thought of Laura Ingalls or even the Dakota Territory. Instead, he is eight-going-on-nine, and his concern is proving himself to be capable of owning a colt.

There are many parallels to be drawn here. As a child, Almanzo concentrates on "proving up" to own a colt; as an adult, he will try to "prove up" to own land. The comfort of the farm in this book does echo the coziness of Laura's childhood, but the Wilder prosperity and financial solidity contrasts sharply to the relatively little owned by the Ingalls family. The Wilders are settled and secure; the Ingalls family is transient and, at times, erratic.

Farmer Boy is a staunch pitch for awareness of the farmer's importance. In fact, James Wilder, Almanzo's father, almost seems to be making campaign speeches when he addresses the issue of farming, particularly during the Fourth of July celebration in the town of Malone. He speaks at length about the glorious history of the nation and how the farmers drew it together into the power it is. He concludes his speech with, "It was farmers who took all that country and made it America, son. Don't you ever forget that" (p. 189). Laura Ingalls Wilder was certainly aware as she was writing those lines how they were an expression of the framework of the pioneering saga.

erratic lacking in consistency and regularity

staunch faithful; loyal

Painting with Words

One of the characteristics of something done well—whether it be writing, gymnastics, or dance—is that it looks effortless. There is a gracefulness in the Little House books that might lead a reader to think that writing them was easy.

It was not.

> *Wilder once referred to writing as "painting with words." But, as she went on to explain, words are not perfect: "The only stupid thing about words is the spelling of them."*

The *Little House on the Prairie* television series starred the director, Michael Landon, as Charles Ingalls and Melissa Gilbert as Laura.

Wilder was lucky to have her daughter's help in shaping the Little House books. Although Rose Wilder Lane lived for a while in a house on Rocky Ridge Farm and was able to work in person with her mother, they also communicated through letters.

Through their correspondence, we can realize Wilder's frustration when the writing just did not work. In a letter dated 19 February 1938, Wilder told her daughter, "You see I know the music but I can't think of the words." Later that year, on 17 August 1938, she pointed out that balancing fiction and fact was a bit troublesome. She had started the story structure by basing it upon her life, but as she worked through the series, even figuring out how to deal with the family pets required more than she had reckoned.

Wilder once referred to writing as "painting with words." But, as she went on to explain, words were not perfect: "The only stupid thing about words is the spelling of them" (Donald Zochert, *Laura: The Life of Laura Ingalls Wilder,* p. 212).

But Is It Over?

Wilder died on 10 February 1957. Her story, however, did not. The books received a boost in popularity in 1974 when NBC aired the first episode of *Little House on the Prairie.* This television show took the basic story line of the books and greatly embellished them. The series (later called *Little House on the Prairie: A New Beginning*) ran until 1983 and still can be seen in reruns.

HarperCollins, in an attempt to expand the reading base of the Little House books, has selected some chapters of the books and released them as independent picture books. Roger Lea MacBride, who was the heir to the Wilder-Lane estate and its executor, also wrote some novels for young readers expanding on the experience. This series, called *Little House: The Rocky Ridge Years,* is based upon the life of Rose Wilder Lane. A collection of Christmas stories, *A Little House Christmas: Holiday Stories from the Little House Books,* was published in 1994. Related materials include a diary and a "memory" book designed for young readers to write in themselves, perhaps sparking a new generation of biographical fiction writers.

Selected Bibliography

THE LITTLE HOUSE BOOKS BY LAURA INGALLS WILDER

First Editions

Little House in the Big Woods, illustrated by Helen Sewell (1932)

Farmer Boy, illustrated by Helen Sewell (1933)

Little House on the Prairie, illustrated by Helen Sewell (1935)

On the Banks of Plum Creek, illustrated by Helen Sewell (1937)

By the Shores of Silver Lake, illustrated by Helen Sewell (1939)

The Long Winter, illustrated by Helen Sewell (1940)

Little Town on the Prairie, illustrated by Helen Sewell (1941)

These Happy Golden Years, illustrated by Helen Sewell (1943)

The First Four Years, illustrated by Garth Williams (1971)

Reissued Editions

The entire series of Little House books was reissued in 1953, with new illustrations by Garth Williams. These editions were reprinted in paperback in 1971.

OTHER WORKS BY LAURA INGALLS WILDER

On the Way Home: The Diary of a Trip from South Dakota to Mansfield, Missouri in 1894, with a setting by Rose Wilder (1962)

West from Home: Letters of Laura Ingalls Wilder, San Francisco, 1915, edited by Roger Lea MacBride (1974)

A Little House Sampler (1988)

Little House in the Ozarks, edited by Stephen W. Hines (1991)

If you like the works of Laura Ingalls Wilder, you might also like books by Louisa May Alcott and Lucy Maud Montgomery.

WORKS ABOUT LAURA INGALLS WILDER

Books

Anderson, William. *Laura Ingalls Wilder: A Biography.* New York: HarperCollins, 1992.

————. *Laura Ingalls Wilder: Pioneer and Author.* New York: Kipling Press, 1987.

Hines Stephen W. *I Remember Laura: Laura Ingalls Wilder.* Nashville, Thomas Nelson, 1994.

Holtz, William. *The Ghost in the Little House: A Life of Rose Wilder Lane.* Columbia: University of Missouri Press, 1993.

Spaeth, Jane. *Laura Ingalls Wilder.* Boston: Twayne, 1987.

Zochert, Donald. *The Life of Laura Ingalls Wilder.* New York: Avon Books.

Periodicals

Anderson, William. "The Literary Apprenticeship of Laura Ingalls Wilder." In *South Dakota History* 13, winter 1983, pp. 285–331.

Dorris, Michael. "Trusting the Words." In *Booklist* 89, 1 June and 15 June, pp. 1820–1822. Considers the racial bias of the books from the point of view of a Native American father.

Erisman, Fred. "Farmer Boy: The Forgotten 'Little House' Book." In *Western American Literature* 28, August 1993, pp. 123–130.

Erisman, Fred. *Laura Ingalls Wilder.* Boise State University Western Writers Series, Number 12. Boise, Idaho: Boise State University, 1994.

Fellman, Anita. "Laura Ingalls Wilder and Rose Wilder Lane: The Politics of a Mother-Daughter Relationship." In *Signs* 15, spring 1990, pp. 535–561.

Moore, Rosa Ann. "Laura Ingalls Wilder and Rose Wilder Lane: The Chemistry of Collaboration." In *Children's Literature in Education* 11, 1980, pp. 101–109.

————." Laura Ingalls Wilder's Orange Notebooks and the Art of the Little House Books." In *Children's Literature* 4, 1975, pp. 105–119. Traces the evolution of Wilder's prose from notes to final print copy.

————. "The Little House Books: Rose-Colored Classics." In *Children's Literature* 7, 1978, pp. 7–16.

In between the years described in *On the Banks of Plum Creek* and *By the Shores of Silver Lake,* the Ingalls family spent a year in Burr Oak, Iowa. You can visit or write to this home at:
Laura Ingalls Wilder Park and Museum
Box 354
3603 236th Avenue
Burr Oak, IA 52131

Brenda Wilkinson

(1946-   )

by Susan G. Bennett

B renda Wilkinson is best known for her three novels about an African American girl named Ludell: *Ludell* (1975), *Ludell and Willie* (1976), and *Ludell's New York Time* (1980). This trilogy begins during 1955 in rural Georgia, where Ludell is a ten-year-old fifth grader, and follows her to New York City, where she is a senior in high school. Another book for young adults, *Not Separate, Not Equal* (1987), is about the struggles of African American teenagers to survive and succeed during the racial integration of their school in the 1960s. *Definitely Cool* (1993), commended for its authentic use of rap and jive talk, concerns peer pressure in a Bronx junior high school.

Brenda Wilkinson's Novels

Besides reading four of her novels myself, I asked my daughters—a ten-year-old fifth grader and a fourteen-year-old eighth grader—to read *Ludell.* I wanted to see how their reactions and evaluations compared to those of professional critics. Both daughters agreed with critics that Wilkinson's books were appropriate for readers in grades five through nine. They were enthusiastic about her treatment of some facets of recent American history, which they believe are not addressed in enough of the fiction they read.

facets aspects

Wilkinson's Use of Dialect

Not everyone appreciates the way Wilkinson uses irregular spellings to portray African American dialect. Figuring out the dialogue can be part of the attraction of reading her books. Sometimes, though, the use of dialect is distracting, such as when she uses *ou-r* for "our" and *th-een* for "then" to illustrate a southern drawl. More than one critic has stated sentiments similar to this one by Cynthia King in the *New York Times Book Review:* "I had to reread passages to be sure of the meaning. There are overheard conversations that stretch credibility, [and] spelling conflicts within the same line of dialogue" (*Children's Literature Review,* p. 207).

At its worst Wilkinson's use of dialect sounds self-conscious. At its most successful the richness of Ludell's language and that of the other characters allows readers to enter a time and place that may be inaccessible to them otherwise. For example, in the following passage from *Ludell,* the dialect helps transport readers directly into the characters' world.

> "I thought they was gon start laffing, but Mattie she went to cussing and told him to turn roun and take me back! I was so mad! I started to tell mama bout how she was hugging and kissing on him on the way. You should 'ave been there. She was justa smacking all over him and he was going, 'Cool it bay-bee!' wit his ugly self. . . . Mattie say Alvin Jr.'s family don' wanna own the baby. They claim it aine his, but all anybody got to do is look at that lil rascal and rat away you

know he's a Green—they whole family got them bull-dog faces!"

"Where we going girl?" Ludell asked, laughing as they turned the corner. "You just running yo mouth and aine said a word bout where you heading." (P. 36)

Although younger readers might find reading southern African American dialect a challenge, they will be drawn to Ludell and the dilemmas she faces as a normal preadolescent. My ten-year-old daughter reported, "I like how it talks in dialect and it seems like it is real. Like when she had an accident in school. My teacher gets mad, too, when we ask to go to the bathroom after recess." Here is an excerpt from that scene in *Ludell* :

> "Why now?" she thought despairingly. "Well, I was gon have to get up to ask to be excused, so what I'll do is finish my diagraming and then ask her to go."
>
> Sliding from her desk, she walked up to the board, keeping her thighs pressed close together. She hadn't picked up the chalk good before she realized she wasn't going to make it. She could feel the pee warm, about to drop. It seemed she went crazy then. . . . She kept running until she reached the toilet but didn't know just why, cause she was through.
>
> She was standing near the sink, feeling shame and looking pitiful when Mis Rivers stomped in.
>
> "Why didn't you ask to be excused earlier?" she asked.
>
> "I-I was scared you was gon be mad for me not going at recess, and wouldn't let me go," she answered, tears rolling down her cheeks. (P.30)

Critical Reception

Wilkinson's readers have the opportunity to watch Ludell mature and to share her decisions like those facing any young person—about school, a career, and marriage. My teenage daughter, who also appreciated the previously cited

Although young readers might find reading a southern African American dialect a challenge, they will be drawn to Ludell and the dilemmas she faces as a normal preadolescent.

empathy   sincere concern and sensitivity

restroom episode, expressed her empathy for Ludell's overall circumstances. Wilkinson's story vividly reminded her of how difficult life can be for many children like Ludell and of the hurdles they have to face.

Critics agree that Ludell is an appealing character because she always remains true to herself. By the time *Ludell* ends, we care enough about the main characters in the book to look forward to reading *Ludell and Willie,* which jumps to high school and Ludell's romance with her next-door neighbor. Ludell and Willie have an unusually restrained relationship for the 1990s, and even for the time in which the novel takes place. For example, unlike some of her friends and many of today's teens—who have the freedom to go to parties, after-school programs, and evening sports events—Ludell rarely is able to participate in any social activities. Ludell's grandmother, with whom she lives and who has reared her, makes sure that Ludell places school, church, and chores before socializing and boys. Willie, a sports hero at his school, admires Ludell and sticks by her in spite of the temptations of more popular and available girls.

Yet the vivid details and sympathetic characters are not enough for some readers. One of my daughters found the book's quiet pace less than exciting. Similarly, some adult reviewers praise Wilkinson's strength in relating details with unparalleled balance and honesty, but they criticize her weakness in exploring characters' emotional territories. After long passages describing the small details of characters' lives, readers hunger for something more. What was Ludell's mother's story? We want to know. What happened to Willie's father and siblings? Did Ludell's upstairs neighbor in Harlem turn out all right? Readers want to know more about Stanley's future, Malene's development as an activist, and the fate of the Bowens. By focusing on descriptions of daily life, Wilkinson may have missed opportunities to evoke stronger responses from her readers, such as passion, incredulity, and moral outrage—especially in *Not Separate, Not Equal.* In her review of *Ludell,* Cynthia King writes: "I wished for an intensity of emotion that I never felt, but by the end of the book I liked Ludell. I was glad to have known her and her friends" (*Children's Literature Review,* p. 207).

incredulity   disbelief

Even with their weaknesses, Wilkinson's books will continue to have a wide appeal because they present universal stories. Although her best-known novels take place before today's adolescents were born, the books reflect a contemporary perspective. The decisions and dilemmas that Ludell confronts would be familiar to anyone her age. Wilkinson's themes—honesty, respect, and dependability—transcend any specific time, culture, gender, or place. She uses these themes to show the effects that circumstances and events have on the decisions individuals must make. None of her characters is entirely good or evil, guilty or innocent. Even though they make choices that the reader may not have made, Wil-kinson's characters have believable motivations that help us understand why few things in life are simple or one-dimensional.

Some critics, comparing Wilkinson to writers of the Harlem Renaissance, say that she is carrying on the tradition of telling the stories of the migration and adjustment of African Americans from the particular hardships of the South to the different but equally oppressive difficulties of the North. As Geraldine Wilson has written in a *New York Times Book Review*: "Many people think books for young people should not . . . convey explicit 'moral' messages. That might be OK if there weren't lots of teenage alcoholics. . . . But Brenda Wilkinson is a responsible writer who knows the African American story-telling tradition, . . . part of which has a direct teaching function" (*Interracial Books for Children Bulletin*, 1981, vol. 12, no. 2, pp. 18–19).

All her reviewers agree that each of Wilkinson's books is worth reading and has more strengths than weaknesses. They appreciate how she compares and contrasts rural and urban life, portraying neither the country nor the city as perfect or evil. Critics also praise the way Wilkinson provides insights into the clashes among various groups of African Americans. Her books show that divisions such as educational opportunities, economic advantages, and standards of beauty exist among all groups, regardless of color, culture, or religion. Characters in all her novels honestly contemplate the effects that hair texture, skin tone, dialect, neighborhood, occupation, and clothing have on their choices, opportunities, and status.

Reviewers admire Wilkinson's ability to illustrate values and morals through the telling of a good story and through character development. Readers feel the injustices of Ludell's life, understand the unfairness of segregation, and empathize with her difficulties.

> *Wilkinson's themes—honesty, respect, and dependability—transcend any specific time, culture, gender, or place.*
>

Personal Reactions

Of the three novels about Ludell, my least favorite was *Ludell's New York Time,* maybe because I was looking forward to this one the most. First I had read what previous reviewers had said about each of Wilkinson's books. Knowing that Wilkinson lived and worked in New York, I was expecting glimpses of the richness of Harlem life during the early 1960s and scenes of Harlem painted as vividly as pictures. I had been particularly impressed that *Ludell and Willie* had kept my interest as much as *Ludell* had. Too often, each succeeding book in a series is less compelling than the first. Since Wilkinson's second book maintained the standard set by the first one, I was anticipating that the third would do the same.

I had grown to like Ludell and her friends and was hoping for some kind of resolution by the end of the third book. Knowing that the first two novels had sequels, I was not bothered that they seemed to end abruptly with some "loose ends," but I hoped that *Ludell's New York Time* would tie various events together and tell the reader what happened to some of the characters introduced earlier. Unlike the first two books, in which I could see and feel Wilkinson's attachment to the rural Georgia of her youth, *Ludell's New York Time* focuses less on storytelling and more on teaching. This scene from the book is an example of her tendency to lecture:

adamantly in a fixed and unyielding manner

"I don't drink anything alcoholic!" I adamantly stated.

"Not even a little wine now and then?" he asked.

"Nooo Lord!" I shouted. "People say that'll drive you crazy! There were these fast girls in the twelfth grade at home who people say had started drinking wine! Everybody's saying it's going to make them crazy— course as I see it, they crazy to begin with for drinking the stuff!"

"You can't believe everything you hear, baby," he responded. "There's nothing wrong with a little wine. It's only the cheap kind that messes folk up—and then

only when somebody's drinking it day and night. Actually, too much of any of this stuff—liquor, beer,
wine—TOO MUCH OF ANY OF IT AINE NO GOOD
FOR YOU! Believe me. I know. Trying my best t'give
it up right now. . . . The bad feeling the next day is
one more reason this drinking can be such a dog! . . .

"Cause when it's all over you right back where you
started. You can't stay high forever—got to come
down sometime." (Pp.21-22)

The setting for this scene is Ludell's first meeting of her
mother's boyfriend. Ludell has never been to a big city before,
let alone New York, and she is still adjusting to the death
of her beloved grandmother who reared her. Her mother, almost a stranger since leaving the rural South when Ludell was
a toddler, has just plucked Ludell from her home, friends, and
high school sweetheart six weeks before she is to graduate
and then marry. How does she feel? What kinds of things
would be on her mind? When I read the preceding quoted
passage, I stopped and asked myself these questions because
the conversation Ludell has with her mother's boyfriend
the day she arrives in Harlem sounded unnatural and implausible to me. Not only did this discussion seem untimely,
but also the use of capital letters in Frank's speech made the
message too obvious. This kind of lecturing is found throughout the book.

Fact and Fiction

Brenda Wilkinson is the mother of two children and lives
in New York City. Many people who have commented on
Wilkinson's books say they are autobiographical, that Ludell
is really the author who was born and reared in a small town
in Georgia and then moved to New York and attended
Hunter College. But all effective writers write about what
they know, which usually includes events and people in
their lives. They then change or combine these facts with fictional elements to tell a compelling story. In an interview for
Something About the Author, Wilkinson says, "Like my protagonist Ludell, I am a product of the last of the segregated

school system in the South. What I've attempted in the trilogy I've written is to give a 'factional' account of this period" (Commire, 1978, p. 206).

Wilkinson and Today's Readers

Wilkinson's novels give young adult readers a better understanding of many contemporary issues that are debated in the press, the courts, and schools. Her books provide a human perspective on current issues such as affirmative action, prejudice, sexism, and the effects of poverty. The migration of southern African Americans to Harlem, the breakup of families to try to improve their living conditions, the lack of facilities and opportunities in all-black schools, the gains as well as losses endured by the African American community during and after integration: Wilkinson explores all these topics in her novels, not by telling but by showing the details of the lives of her characters.

The following scene from *Ludell,* for example, strikingly shows how hunger and poverty effect everyone in Ludell's school:

> Kids were playing tic-tac-toe, trying to draw paper dolls, planes, trains, or were playing hand games. That was about all you could do on the inside. Everybody had read about a thousand times the three or four books Mis Rivers kept on the shelf and had looked up and giggled over the one sex word listen in the big red Webster's. That dictionary had been messed with so much that the instant you opened it, it automatically fell to the I's. . . .
>
> As the bell rang ending recess, Mis Rivers was finishing up what appeared to be a piece of sweet bread. "Long as it took her to finish," Ludell thought, "she must have had enough lunch to share with everybody who didn't have nothing! Cause she sho wasn't eating slow!" She kept staring at Mis Rivers, thinking, "Look at her! Just chopping like somebody mad! If I was a teacher and had so many children in my class who didn't have no lunch, I'd buy a big loaf of light bread

everyday and keep a big thing of peanut butter in the room! It couldn't cost that much! I 'on see how she can sit there and enjoy . . . maybe that's it! Maybe that's why she always eat like she do—fast 'n face down." (Pp. 7-8)

Conclusion

Wilkinson and I were both born in 1946, and her books remind me of events from my life. When I was twelve years old, in 1958, my family spent a summer in a southern state. Having come from the North, I had never seen a sign that said "colored only" on a drinking fountain or a restroom. I did not know that I was not supposed to ride the horse of the farmer across the street from our apartment or feed his chickens because he was black and I was white. But even though thirty to forty years ago might seem like ancient history to readers in grades five through nine, Wilkinson's books bring readers right into the time in which the stories take place. They help today's adolescents experience and understand the history of racism in America and the difficult legacies of the past with which we are still coping today.

> *Wilkinson's books help today's adolescents experience and understand the history of racism in America and the difficult legacies of the past with which we are still coping today.*

If you like the works of Brenda Wilkinson, you might also enjoy the works of Maya Angelou.

Selected Bibliography

WORKS BY BRENDA WILKINSON

Ludell (1975)

Ludell and Willie (1976)

Ludell's New York Time (1980)

Not Separate, Not Equal (1987)

Definitely Cool (1993)

WORKS ABOUT BRENDA WILKINSON

Commire, Anne, ed. *Something About the Author.* Detroit: Gale Research, 1978, vol. 14, pp. 250–252.

Gillespie, John T. *Best Books for Junior High Readers.* New Providence, N.J.: R. R. Bowker, 1991, p. 21.

Halbig, Alethea, and Agnes R. Perkins. *This Land is Our Land: A Guide to Multicultural Literature for Children and*

Young Adults. Westport, Conn.: Greenwood Press, 1994, pp. 80–81.

May, Hal, and James G. Lesniak, eds. *Contemporary Authors*. Detroit: Gale Research, 1989, vol. 26, p. 470.

Miller-Lachmann, Lyn. *Our Family, Our Friends, Our World: An Annotated Guide to Significant Multicultural Books for Children and Teenagers*. New Providence, N.J.: R. R. Bowker, 1992, p. 77.

Senick, Gerard J., and Sharon R. Gunton, eds. In *Children's Literature Review*. Detroit: Gale Research, 1990, vol. 20, pp. 206–212.

How to Write to the Author
Brenda Wilkinson
c/o Scholastic, Inc.
555 Broadway
New York, NY 10012

Virginia Euwer Wolff

(1937-)

by Teri S. Lesesne

"I turned into a reader the summer of my sixteenth birthday when I read *The Catcher in the Rye*. *The Catcher in the Rye* changed my life . . . somebody spoke for me," writes Virginia Wolff in *Teaching Young Adult Literature: Sharing the Connection*. Virginia (Jinny) Wolff took up the banner from J. D. Salinger and carries it proudly for a new generation of adolescent readers.

There is an article about J. D. Salinger earlier in this volume.

Speaking Up and Speaking Out

Each of her three novels provides a powerful voice for young adults who are frequently *not* subjects of books. She gave voice to Nick Swansen, a developmentally disabled high school student who desperately wants to fit in, in *Probably Still Nick Swansen* (1988). Next Jinny Wolff gave voice to Allegra Shapiro, a talented athlete and gifted musician, in *The Mozart Season* (1991). Most recently, LaVaughn, a fourteen-year-old girl who attempts to rescue an unwed teenage mother from a life of failure and poverty, found her voice in *Make Lemonade* (1993). Although each voice is distinctive, all three characters have much in common, most notably their humanity. Wolff speaks for those who are not always afforded the opportunity to do so for themselves.

Losing, Growing, Playing

Many factors influenced Wolff during her childhood and adolescence. They continue to affect her writing today. The death of her father when she was quite young left her puzzled and confused. She gives what she calls her "sense of bewilderment" to the characters in her novels, she says in *Speaking for Ourselves, Too*. Through their confusion, Nick and Allegra and LaVaughn must struggle to arrive at some form of the truth, some kernel of knowledge that will propel them in the right direction. That powerful sense of loss, which Wolff experienced as a child, also serves to underscore her belief that childhood emotions are raw and, therefore, compelling. Each of her main characters allows us to see these painfully raw emotions. Perhaps this is one of the reasons that Wolff's books touch a responsive chord in her readers.

A second strong influence Wolff acknowledges is her own love of music. As a violinist, she believes music is very powerful. Music frequently plays in the background while she is writing. Wolff's musicianship also has made her appreciate the value of constructive criticism. Certainly this is beneficial whenever she reads what reviewers have to say about her writing. The uncertainty of playing and performance is yet another facet of music that affects Wolff's work. Never being quite sure what the next note will sound like is somewhat akin to the writing of a novel. What comes next, what will happen next to the characters in the story, is not always planned. Wolff, for example, notes that she was not sure whether Allegra from *The Mozart Season* would win the music competition; that not knowing kept her writing.

The final influence Wolff mentions (Gallo, p. 228) is living in the Pacific Northwest surrounded by nature. Her love for and appreciation of the outdoors is especially evident in *Make Lemonade*. LaVaughn, in an attempt to create some semblance of beauty and order in Jolly's littered apartment, brings a pot, some soil, and a handful of lemon seeds. This act of faith involved in growing things, especially a tree, serves as a wonderful metaphor for the novel. Keeping the faith through the tough times is a theme evident in all Wolff's writings.

metaphor a figure of speech in which one thing is referred to as something else, for example, "My love is a rose"

Comforting the Afflicted and Afflicting the Comfortable

In *Probably Still Nick Swansen,* sixteen-year-old Nick wants, like most adolescents, to fit in and be accepted by his peers. Being a member of Room 19 makes his goal a bit more difficult to reach, however. Room 19 is for the special education class. Its members are often the butt of jokes and taunts by the other students at school. Nick even overhears an adult calling the special education students "droolers." After some careful planning, Nick decides to ask someone to the prom. He chooses Shana, a former resident of Room 19 who has "gone up" (been mainstreamed). Nick rents his tuxedo, buys the prom tickets, and even delivers a gorgeous corsage to Shana's house. When Shana stands him up on Prom Night, Nick's self-confidence is shattered. He believes he is one of the "droolers" and begins to question whether he will ever be able to do anything correctly.

Nick's quest to be "normal," to be accepted, is a universal desire. In this way and through the various feelings Nick experiences, Wolff allows readers to see that people are more alike than they are different. Nick ultimately learns that even Shana shares his lack of confidence; it is then that Nick (and the reader) realizes how conscious we are of how we appear to others. Wolff wrote *Probably Still Nick Swansen* so that readers would be able to get inside a character who was developmentally disabled. Through her sympathetic characterization of Nick and the other members of Room 19, she ably demonstrates how one must deal with a disability.

> *Wolff allows readers to see that people are more alike than they are different.*

Using Nick as the narrator adds to the believability of the story and serves to make the connection even stronger between Nick and readers. Readers enter fully into Nick's world; they see his thought processes and emotions. This empathetic bond joins readers and characters together, allowing readers further insight into the trials and triumphs of Nick and others with learning disabilities.

empathetic having sincere concern and understanding

In this novel, as in her others, Wolff creates strong secondary characters, especially those of the adults. Nick's parents, Shana's mother, and Nick's special education teacher are all individuals. Readers learn a great deal about these adults and their importance in Nick's life. Nick's parents allow him to try things on his own, even though he may fail. They support and encourage him in all that he attempts. Nick's teacher, Mr. Norton, also fosters Nick's independence by allowing him to build on his strengths rather than pointing out his weaknesses. For contrast, Wolff shows other adults who are not understanding or supportive. Most notable are the parent chaperones at the prom, the ones who label the special education students as droolers. Shana's parents serve as another contrast to Nick's parents and teacher. Strong adult role models are a hallmark of Wolff's writing.

Stories That Become Teachers

Allegra Shapiro, the twelve-year-old protagonist of *The Mozart Season* (1991) is the youngest finalist in a prestigious violin competition. She plans to spend her summer practicing Mozart's Fourth Violin Concerto. Her music teacher, Mr. Kaplan, tells her that she must find the music inside herself; somehow she must imbue the piece with her own personality without allowing her own personality to take over the piece entirely. Other people offer unsolicited advice on how to perform the concerto. It is Allegra who must find her own way into and out of the music, however. An unexpected gift from her grandmother provides Allegra with the inspiration she needs to let the music flow from her to the audience.

Allegra Shapiro is an unlikely protagonist. A good kid who does not make headlines, she is one of the often overlooked character types in young adult literature. Why did Wolff choose such an unusual young girl? As a violinist herself, Wolff found writing about Allegra a bit easier than it had been to write about Nick Swansen. Although Allegra's music is an essential part of who she is as a person, Wolff allows readers to see Allegra as a complete young woman. She is a musician, but she is also a softball player, a younger sister, a daughter, and a granddaughter. She is, most importantly, an adolescent. These various facets of Allegra create a character who lives and breathes off the pages of a book as well as be-

imbue to fill or inspire

unsolicited not requested or desired

tween its covers. Allegra quarrels with her pesky older brother, rails against her parents when she feels they are being overprotective, and giggles with her friends about boys. Once again, Wolff permits Allegra to tell her own story by using first-person narration.

Sports serve as an important analogy in this story about music. The pairing of the two may seem odd at first, but the metaphor works beautifully. In the opening chapter, Allegra likens her music teacher, Mr. Kaplan, to her softball coach. Later, a friend of Allegra's mother tells her that performing is the same whether one is playing basketball in the NBA or singing operatic arias. For the basketball player, each free throw carries with it the history of all the shots that preceded it. The memory of the past shots is important, but the present shot is also a new and immediate experience. So it must be with music. When Allegra plays the concerto, she must make it her own, play it in the here and now; at the same time she must bring to the piece its history, the memory it creates for her. In essence, Allegra must find her own *voice* in her music in much the same way as Nick finds his voice in *Probably Still Nick Swansen*. Nick and Allegra share another similarity in that they both see beyond the surface of people and events and look at things closely. Each is a character outside of the mainstream as well.

This novel is remarkable because it shows Allegra growing in an environment that supports and nourishes her and her music. Here is a musician who possesses tremendous talent. Her talent, however, is not enough. Wolff depicts the effort and determination necessary for Allegra's success as a musician. This novel demonstrates the hard work and almost obsessive behavior necessary to become an accomplished performer. Allegra does not simply become a talent; she makes sacrifices for her music.

Once again, Wolff includes positive adult characters. Allegra's parents and her music teacher exhibit real caring and concern, yet they are human as well. Mr. Kaplan loses patience with Allegra; Mr. and Mrs. Shapiro set limits for Allegra in addition to encouraging her to develop her musical talents. This development of secondary characters is yet another quality that makes Wolff's novels shine. The characters are not stereotyped, nor is the plot predictable. Readers are kept in suspense during the competition. Allegra may not be the winner; life does not hold that kind of guarantee. The

stereotyped characters that are not original or individual because they conform to a preconceived category

suspense created by Wolff in the closing chapters is akin to an adventure or survival story. Anything can happen. In the case of *The Mozart Season,* what does happen is not always what is expected by the reader.

In Love with Language and Its Myriad Possibilities

In *Make Lemonade,* LaVaughn is just fourteen years old when she sees an ad for a mother's helper. Thinking about how a little extra money could assist her in her plans to go to college after high school, LaVaughn answers the ad. She is taken aback when she discovers that the mother who needs some assistance is also a teenager. Jolly is seventeen, unmarried, and the mother of two young children. Her apartment is filthy, something for which she offers no real apology. LaVaughn, sickened by the mess, is about to seek out other job opportunities, but Jolly's children win her over completely. She begins her job and a not-always-subtle campaign to get Jolly back in school. When Jolly loses her job because she reports her boss for sexual harassment, LaVaughn forgoes payment to continue baby-sitting. She is ultimately able to convince Jolly that education is the only way out of the poverty and helplessness in which she lives.

Once again, Wolff gives voice to those whose stories often go untold: the children of poverty. Once again she employs first-person point of view, allowing LaVaughn to tell her story and that of Jolly without rancor, judgment, or condescension. Although LaVaughn and Jolly come from impoverished backgrounds, the major problems they face are similar to those all adolescents understand and share: the need for acceptance by peers and love from parents, and the value of education.

rancor bad feeling or ill will

The importance of education is a theme underscored in this novel by several characters and events. Early in the story, LaVaughn describes the word *college* as something solid, like a piece of furniture. LaVaughn's mother has sunk her teeth into the idea of college and constantly tells LaVaughn that she will be the first in her family as well as the first in their apartment building to go to college. College is more than a goal: it is a lifeline for LaVaughn. She spends a great deal of time persuading Jolly that education is essential for herself as well as for her children. That essential nature of education is confirmed when Jolly uses the CPR technique she has learned in class to save the life of her own child. That critical aspect of learning is revealed frequently through the actions of LaVaughn and Jolly both.

Parental love is once again evident in Wolff's writing. LaVaughn is a strong young woman partly because her mother is strong. LaVaughn has a role model, something Jolly lacks. Secondary characters, especially LaVaughn's mother and Jolly's children, are fully realized. This ability of Wolff to make readers care about secondary characters is apparent in all her work. This may explain why her novels have met with positive critical reception. There is something in each of the stories to appeal to the adolescent and the adult reader alike.

What sets this novel apart from the other two, however, is Wolff's style of writing. It is a total departure from that in *Probably Still Nick Swansen* and *The Mozart Season*. The prose in this novel is rhythmic. The lines are arranged on the page as poetry. It is as if LaVaughn is simply thinking the story. This use of stream of consciousness gives a different beat to the language; thoughts and sentences are incomplete and choppy. The pattern more closely approximates the language of real teenagers, complete with ungrammatical construction. "Language reveals its meaning by surprise," Wolff says in *Speaking for Ourselves, Too* (Gallo, p. 229). This is most evident in the rhythmic pulse of this story.

At the Heart of the Story

Wolff confesses that she becomes the characters about whom she writes. Some part of her is Nick Swansen, the young person unsure of his own abilities, needing someone to show him his strengths and restore his confidence. Part of Allegra Shapiro is Jinny Wolff too. Not only is Wolff a musician, she shares other traits with Allegra, most notably her love of family. Even LaVaughn, born in poverty, is a part of Wolff. Although Wolff has never experienced the bleak poverty of LaVaughn and her family, she recognizes the value of education. Indeed, Wolff is quick to credit her writing career to the encouragement and influence of several teachers.

Virginia Euwer Wolff has provided readers with many hours of satisfying reading. Her books have managed to con-

If you enjoyed reading *Probably Still Nick Swansen*, you might also wish to read these two books featuring characters who are developmentally disabled: *Just One Friend* by Lynn Hall and *Daphne's Book* by Marion Dane Bauer. For another gifted musician protagonist similar to Allegra Shapiro in *The Mozart Season*, try reading Bruce Brooks's *Midnight Hour Encores*. Finally, if you appreciated the unusual style of *Make Lemonade*, you might want to read Avi's *Nothing but the Truth: A Documentary Novel* or *The Fling* by Julian F. Thompson. Of course, you will want to read the book Jinny Wolff credits as her inspiration, *The Catcher in the Rye* by J. D. Salinger.

How to Write to the Author
Virginia Euwer Wolff
c/o Holt, Rinehart & Winston, Inc.
1120 South Capital of Texas Highway
Austin, TX 78746

nect us to each other and to remind us that we have much in common.

Selected Bibliography

Works by Virginia Euwer Wolff
   Probably Still Nick Swansen (1988)
   The Mozart Season (1991)
   Make Lemonade (1993)

WORKS ABOUT VIRGINIA EUWER WOLFF

Brown, Jean and Elaine C. Stephens. *Teaching Young Adult Literature: Sharing the Connection.* Belmont, Calif.: Wadsworth Publishing, 1995, pp. 149–150.

Gallo, Donald R., ed. *Speaking for Ourselves, Too.* Urbana, Ill.: National Council of Teachers of English, 1993, pp. 228–229.

Laurence Yep

(1948-   )

by Dianne Johnson-Feelings
and Catherine Lewis

In recounting some of his memorable experiences as an author, Laurence Yep tells about one of his school visits to Minneapolis. A boy in the audience was reluctant to participate in the discussion. Yep explains that he often refers to Godzilla movies to engage young readers, and as he did so in this lecture, the formerly unresponsive boy began to show interest in Yep's presentation. It so happens that the boy had seen as many Godzilla movies as Yep had. When Yep asked him why he liked the movies, the boy responded that the monster was awkward because of his size and that he had not been told how to act; without guidance, the creature could not help his destructiveness.

Quotations from Laurence Yep that are not attributed to a published source are from a personal interview conducted by Dianne Johnson-Feelings on 3 May 1993 and are published here by permission of Laurence Yep.

> *Yep recalls that "as an eigth-grader, I was particularly sensitive to feeling like an alien myself".*

manifestation the way something reveals or shows itself

motif situation or theme

The Writer's Life

This anecdote embodies much of what distinguishes Laurence Yep as a writer. He is attuned to his young audiences and is aware that their emotional and external experiences, as well as the physical changes of adolescence, cause them to feel like outsiders, maybe a little like monsters, as they try to negotiate places for themselves in society. In his autobiography, *The Lost Garden* (1991), Yep recalls that "as an eighth-grader, I was particularly sensitive to feeling like an alien myself" (p. 82). From his own self-observations, to his Ph.D. work in literature and psychology at State University of New York at Buffalo (1975), to his creative writing, Yep's explorations of "alienness" and "otherness" have generated a canon of work for school-age readers that acknowledges and accepts the difficulties of youth. At the same time he offers suggestions for successfully navigating that adolescent turbulence.

For Yep, such otherness makes historical fiction, fantasy, and science fiction appropriate genres in which to work. His outsider may be a creation such as the dragon Civet in *Dragon of the Lost Sea* (1982), or an entire species. It may be a human being who must settle into a new locale, like Sean in *Liar, Liar* (1983) or Casey Young in *Child of the Owl* (1977). Yep examines his characters' otherness through common themes including alienation, isolation, class conflicts, gender conflicts, and cultural history. Despite the differences in their physical manifestations, his characters contend with the same problems as they seek self-identity and peace in their environments.

Much of Yep's writing advocates that commonalities such as these are what beings should consider when relating with one another, instead of allowing differences in appearance, language, and place of origin to dictate the course of their relationships. To exemplify this belief in comparable characteristics, Yep weaves similar motifs—such as family, the past, and imagination—throughout all his works, whether they are classified individually as fantasy, science fiction, historical fiction, or picture books.

Family Ties

In *The Lost Garden,* his autobiography, Laurence Yep writes movingly about his transition from childhood to adulthood. The figures foremost in his development were the various members of his family: parents, grandparents, brother, uncles, and aunts. Growing up Chinese American in San Francisco provided for Yep, as it did for his character Uncle Foxfire in *Dragon's Gate* (1993), a "double set of eyes."

Yep's father, Yep Gim Lew, known as Thomas, was born in Toisan district, Kwangtung province, China, in 1914 and moved to the United States at the age of ten to join his father. Franche Lee, Yep's mother, was born in Lima, Ohio, and grew up in Clarksburg, West Virginia; thus Laurence Yep is both first- and second-generation Chinese American with immediate ties to China. Although his family lived outside of Chinatown, above the grocery store they owned, they remained closely tied to that neighborhood by extended family, friends, and cultural alliances. In Yep's own neighborhood there lived working-class families of African Americans and Caucasians of various national origins. From his dual identity Yep has gained great insight into what it means to identify with two groups, neither of which can be experienced without the influence and pull of the other.

Because Yep was, as he calls himself, his "neighborhood's all-purpose Asian," he felt marginalized (*Lost Garden*, p. 38). He admits that, as a child, he "didn't want to be Chinese" (p. 43) and that he "associated being Chinese with the artificial and commercial 'Asian-ness' of [Chinatown's tourist-attracting store] windows" (p. 45). But Yep's family and community would not allow him to deny his ethnic background. He recalls being scolded by "old-timers" whom he barely knew. He remembers suffering in Chinese school because he did not speak Chinese and because he had American interests and American tastes in food. He gives his grandmother, Marie Lee, the most credit, however, for keeping him linked to his Chinese heritage. "She represented a 'Chineseness' in my life that was as unmovable and unwanted as a mountain in your living room," he says (p. 46).

Although Yep's Grandmother Lee often embarrassed him with her loud denunciations of her children's and grandchildren's American ways and interests—as well as the appearances and customs of non-Chinese people—Yep notes that she, too, "was an outsider and not like her other friends in Chinatown. . . . As a result, she had developed a kind of self-reliant toughness. In fact, she was actually an interesting blend of China and the Midwest," even though "she never budged from California again and rarely emerged even from Chinatown" (pp. 47–48).

marginalized excluded from or existing outside the mainstream of society

Yep gives his grandmother, Marie Lee, the most credit, however, for keeping him linked to his Chinese heritage. "She represented a 'Chineseness' in my life that was unmovable and unwanted as a mountain in your living room."

Yep is a sort of chemist, one who creates from the materials of his life—loved ones, experiences, questions, problems, wondering "what if"—to yield products of imagination and greater understanding of the world around him.

nostalgia a sentimental yearning to return to a past time

Yep's family and the area and time in which he grew up provided him with a world of complexity and the means by which to make sense of it. His feelings of otherness both in his family and in his community gave him the material he writes about; his interests and talent synthesize those resources into novels. Yep says in his autobiography that he struggled in college to choose between chemistry and writing as a career. Although he chose writing, he is nevertheless a sort of chemist, one who creates from the materials of his life—loved ones, experiences, questions, problems, wondering "what if"—to yield products of imagination and greater understanding of the world around him.

Laurence Yep acknowledges in *The Lost Garden* that his grandmother was the inspiration for Cassia Young in *The Serpent's Children* (1984) and its companion book *Mountain Light* (1985). But in *Child of the Owl* (1977), an American Library Association Notable Children's Book, he tells the story of twelve-year-old Casey Young. She wanders with her father, Barney, who is unemployed and who gambles. Casey is a descendent of Cassia and a representation of what Yep imagines his grandmother might have been like as a teenager.

When the novel begins, Barney is in the hospital, so Casey must go to live with an aunt and uncle. She stays with them only for a short time, however, because she does not fit in well with them. They are financially secure and concerned with their status in society, and Casey feels that they are controlled by their material concerns.

She is then sent to Chinatown to live with her maternal grandmother, who is "as superstitious and impossible to live with as anybody can be" (p. 23). In Chinatown, Casey learns how varied people of a single culture can be. Because she does not feel at ease in either of the worlds of her family, she must come to terms with her own identity. To help her, Yep uses animal mythology—which is common in Chinese culture—to draw an analogy to Casey. In the mythic frame, the owl/woman must learn to cope in two places, in the air and on the ground, just as Casey must learn to cope as a Chinese and as an American. Unlike Casey, though, the owl has little regard and respect for family. Casey learns from her grandmother to become better assimilated into both worlds by allowing space for each in her life.

Family, nostalgia, and curiosity are important themes in Yep's fiction. He confesses that, of his works, *Sea Glass*

(1979) is his favorite because it is about himself and his father. His brother (Thomas, in real life) and uncle appear in it also. Craig Chin, Yep's alter ego, must contend with being different from other American boys and even different from his family members; he is not interested in sports as they are. The uncle helps Craig to learn more about his father, such as his love of gardening. *Sea Glass,* like Yep's other novels, makes much of symbolism, such as the "lost garden" of Craig's father (hence the title of Yep's autobiography) and "sea glass" that, like Craig, has its rough edges smoothed by experience and time.

Symbols and a strong sense of the past pervade *The Star Fisher* (1991) as well. Modeled on Yep's maternal family's migration from Ohio to Clarksburg, West Virginia, the book tells the story of fifteen-year-old Joan Lee. Because Joan is patterned after Yep's mother, the book becomes a way for Yep to explore, appreciate, and celebrate his own family history. In the story, the girl and her family must confront social prejudice. People immediately assume that because the family does not look "American," they are immigrants, even though they are not. The family is subjected to racial epithets, and Joan must inform her teacher that she is a native-born American.

Trustworthy friends at school and at home help Joan face the narrow-mindedness of the community. In addition to her alienation in the town, Joan feels isolated by her parents, who prefer to keep themselves apart, even from the good neighbors, much like the farmer in the tale of the star fisher that gives the book its title. Like the legendary star fisher, Joan endures alienation and rejection. But also like the star fisher, she gains from perseverance and patience the freedom of spirit that allows her to hope as she reaches for the stars.

perseverance persistence in the pursuit of something, despite many obstacles

Into the Past

In addition to his family and youth, Laurence Yep looks to the past to provide him with stories. Because many of his ancestors and countless other Chinese people immigrated to the United States and struggled with assimilation while retaining their own rich culture, testaments of strength and ingenuity abound in their cultural history. From one of these stories comes Yep's most enduring and awarded story, *Dragonwings* (1975). It was designated a Newbery Honor Book in 1976, and in 1995 it won the Phoenix Award, given by the

assimilation absorption of a minority group into the culture of a population or dominant group

Children's Literature Association for a book of lasting importance twenty years after its publication.

Dragonwings was inspired by the story of Fung Joe Guey, a Chinese man who in 1909 built and flew a biplane in San Francisco. Windrider, the character who dreams of flying, is modeled not only on his actual historical counterpart but on Yep's father, also a kitemaker. By combining his imaginings of Fung Joe Guey's quest with the biographical influence of his father, Laurence Yep blends the actual past and the imaginary one to create the genre of historical fantasy, a mode of reconstruction that has become a common tool for him.

Yep says that *Dragonwings* grew out of his interest in science fiction, and particularly out of his first novel, *Sweetwater* (1973). The former work created whole new alien worlds. In this fabrication, Yep says, he learned that otherworldly aliens experience much of what the Chinese who came to America experienced in their quest for cultural integration. In writing *Dragonwings*, he says, he finally confronted his own Chinese-American identity. This identity is bound up in understanding what Chinese Americans endured after leaving their homeland to come to the United States. They hoped, loved, laughed, dreamed, and grieved, but, according to Yep in the afterword of *Dragonwings*, these details of their lives are commonly subordinated to statistics. As Yep peers into the stories and lives of these people, he gives them identities and, by doing so, better establishes for himself a sense of place.

subordinate to treat as of less value or importance

Similarly, *Dragon's Gate*, a Newbery Honor Book begun at the time of *Dragonwings*, explores the experiences of Chinese railroad laborers in the United States. Through the boy Otter and his father and uncles, Yep imagines the hardships, dangers, and prejudices that confronted the Chinese railroad workers as they helped build the America that exploited them. Yep gives the workers some of the attention due them; at the same time, he introduces them to today's young readers, helping them "remember," just as Shaky, usually silent in the story, pleads for someone to do (p. 248).

exploit to use something or someone unjustly for one's own advantage

The Power of Imagination

Besides finding inspiration in the past, Laurence Yep is equally capable of searching his own fancy for stories. Always an ardent fan of science fiction, he writes it well and brings to it a fondness for examining relationships and encounters between beings of various worlds. *Sweetwater* and the books of the *Dragon of the Lost Sea* fantasies—*Dragon of the Lost Sea* (1982), *Dragon Steel* (1985), *Dragon Cauldron* (1991), and *Dragon War* (1992)—all investigate alien worlds and magical creatures who, like humans, learn to face conflict among themselves and with others at home and abroad.

Because of Yep's extraordinary vision, he sees that beings have much in common and his works defy neat delineation as to type; for him, literary genres are not exclusive. He blends science fiction, fantasy, and history. *The Mark Twain Murders* (1982) and *The Tom Sawyer Fires* (1984) not only retell parts of Twain's stories but also integrate some of Twain's real-life experiences as a reporter in San Francisco. *The Rainbow People* (1989) and *Tongues of Jade* (1991) are Yep's retellings of Chinese myths. He also reworks myths and folktales in his picture books *The Shell Woman and the King* (1993), *The Butterfly Boy* (1993), and *The Boy who Swallowed Snakes* (1994).

Broad-ranged and prolific, Yep is not content to remain confined or cushioned by his former successes, although he has a well-established career and a solid understanding of successful types of books and plots. In addition to the various types of novels, essays, picture books, and anthologies in his canon, he continues to reach for more. He has contributed to the Star Trek series of novels with *Shadow Lord* (1985). He writes plays and edits anthologies. He has also written and continues to write for all audiences: adults, adolescents, and children.

With this dedication to his readership, the continued exploration of possibilities in his fiction, the candor and introspection of his autobiographical observations, and his drive to create, Laurence Yep has acquired the just reputation of excellence as a writer.

There is an article about Mark Twain earlier in this volume.

anthologies collections of selected literary pieces or passages

Selected Bibliography

WORKS BY LAURENCE YEP

Novels

Sweetwater, illustrated by Julia Noonan (1973)

Dragonwings (1975; 1977 [audiocassette]; 1979 [record, audiocassette, filmstrip with audiocassette])

Seademons (1977)

Readers who enjoy works by Laurence Yep might also like works by Mark Twain.

Child of the Owl (1977; 1978)

Sea Glass (1979)

The Mark Twain Murders (1981)

Dragon of the Lost Sea (1982)

Kind Hearts and Gentle Monsters (1982)

Liar, Liar (1983)

The Serpent's Children (1984)

The Tom Sawyer Fires (1984)

Dragon Steel (1985)

Mountain Light (1985)

Shadow Lord (1985)

Monster Makers, Inc. (1986)

The Curse of the Squirrel, illustrated by Dirk Zimmer (1987; 1989 [audiocassette])

The Rainbow People, Chinese myth retold by Yep, illustrated by David Weisner (1989)

Dragon Cauldron (1991)

Tongues of Jade, illustrated by David Weisner (1991)

The Star Fisher (1991; 1992)

Dragon War (1992)

The Butterfly Boy, illustrated by Jeanne M. Lee (1993)

Dragon's Gate (1993)

The Man Who Tricked a Ghost, illustrated by Isadore Seltzer (1993)

The Shell Woman and the King: A Chinese Folktale, retold by Yep, illustrated by Yang Ming-Yi (1993)

The Boy Who Swallowed Snakes, illustrated by Jean and Mou-Sien Tseng (1994)

The Ghost Fox, illustrated by Jean and Mou-Sien Tseng (1994)

The Junior Thunder Lord, illustrated by Robert Van Nutt (1994)

Hiroshima (1995)

Later, Gator (1995)

Thief of Hearts (1995)

Tiger Woman, illustrated by Robert Roth (1995)

Tree of Dreams (1995)

Autobiography

The Lost Garden (1991)

Short Stories

"The Eddystone Light." In *Demon Kind*. Edited by Roger Elwood. New York: Avon, 1973.

"The Electric Neon Mermaid." In *Quark 2*. Edited by Samuel R. Delany and Marilyn Hacker. New York: Paperback Library, 1971.

"In a Sky of Daemons." In *Protostars*. Edited by David Gerrold and Stephen Goldin. New York: Ballantine, 1971.

"The Looking-Glass Sea." In *Strange Bedfellows: Sex and Science Fiction*. Edited by Thomas N. Scortia. New York: Random House, 1972, pp. 165–177.

"The Selchey Kids." *Worlds of If,* February 1968, vol. 18, pp. 88–108. (Collected in *World's Best Science Fiction of 1969*. Edited by Donald A. Wolheim and Terry Carr. New York: Ace, 1969.)

Plays

"Dragonwings." *American Theatre Magazine,* September 1992, vol. 9, pp. 34–35.

"Pay the Chinaman." In *Between Worlds*. Edited by Misha Berson. New York: Theatre Communications Group, 1989.

Anthologies

American Dragons: Twenty-Five Asian American Voices, edited by Laurence Yep (1993)

Articles

"Author's Commentary." In *Children's Literature Review*. Edited by Gerard J. Senick. Detroit: Gale Research, 1989, vol. 17, pp. 201–202; *Literature for Today's Young Adults,* 2d ed. Edited by Alleen Pace Nilsen and Kenneth L. Donelson. New York: Scott, Foresman, 1985, pp. 426–427.

"A Cord to the Past." *CMLEA Journal,* fall 1991, vol. 15, pp. 8–10.

"Fantasy and Reality." *Horn Book,* April 1978, vol. 54, pp. 137–43.

"A Garden of Dragons." *ALAN Review,* spring 1992, vol. 19, pp. 6–8.

"The Green Cord." *Horn Book,* May/June 1989, vol. 19, pp. 318–322.

"The Ethnic Writer as Alien." *Interracial Books for Children Bulletin,* 1979, vol. 10, p. 5.

"Writing *Dragonwings*." *The Reading Teacher,* January 1977, vol. 30, pp. 359–363.

Forthcoming Publications
The Star Maker
When Dragons Weep

WORKS ABOUT LAURENCE YEP

Cai, Mingshui. "A Balanced View of Acculturation: Comments on Lawrence [*sic*] Yep's Three Novels." In *Children's Literature in Education*, 1992, vol. 23, pp. 107–118.

Dinchak, Marla. "Recommended: Laurence Yep." *English Journal*, March 1982, vol. 71, pp. 81–82.

Garrett, Agnes, and Hilda McCue, eds. "Laurence Yep." *Artists and Authors for Young Adults*. Detroit: Gale Research, 1990, vol. 5, pp. 245–252.

Khorana, Meena. "The Ethnic Family and Identity Formation in Adolescents." In *The Child and the Family: Selected Papers from the 1988 International Conference of the Children's Literature Association*. Edited by Susan R. Gannon. New York: Pace University, 1989.

Li, Leiwei. *Monkeying Tradition: Reconstructing Contemporary Chinese-American Literary Culture*. Ann Arbor: University Microfilms, 1991.

Lin, Mao-Chu. *Identity and Chinese-American Experience: A Study of Chinatown American Literature Since World War II*. Ann Arbor: University Microfilms, 1988.

Norton, Donna E. "Multiethnic Literature." In *Through the Eyes of a Child: An Introduction to Children's Literature*, 2d ed. New York: Merrill, 1987, pp. 500–561.

Schirmer, John. "Cognitive Development Assignment: Building Bridges Between Chinese-Americans and Elementary School Classrooms." ERIC ED353162, 1991.

Stanek, Lou Willet. "A Teacher's Resource Guide to Laurence Yep." New York: HarperCollins, 1991.

How to Write to the Author
Laurence Yep
c/o HarperCollins Publishers
10 East 53rd Street
New York, NY 10022

Jane Yolen

(1939-)

by Margaret T. Sacco

Jane Hyatt Yolen, America's Hans Christian Andersen, is a distinguished storyteller, scholar, poet, editor, critic, teacher, folksinger, and award-winning author of over 125 books for children, young adults, and adults. Jane is best known for her literary folktales and fairy tales. She writes science fiction and fantasy, realistic novels, books with outrageous puns, picture books, songbooks, biographies, poetry, mysteries, humor, adventure stories, and nonfiction. Married since 1962, Yolen lives with her husband, David Stemple, a computer professor at the University of Massachusetts. Yolen and Stemple live on Phoenix Farm in western Massachusetts. They met during a wild party, when Stemple crawled through her apartment window. He kissed Yolen on the nape of her neck and introduced himself.

Yolen, a recent grandmother, is the proud mother of three grown children: Heidi, Jason, and Adam. Heidi is a writer. Jason is a freelance photographer. Adam is a record producer and the lead guitarist in a world beat band. Yolen has a B.A.

(Smith College), an M.Ed. (University of Massachusetts), and an honorary LL.D. (College of Our Lady of the Elms). She is also a member of many professional organizations such as the Society of Children's Books Writers, Science Fiction and Fantasy Writers of America, and the National Association for the Preservation and Perpetuation of Storytelling.

Her work has received many awards, including: the Caldecott Medal for *Owl Moon;* the Kerlan and Regina medals and the Keene State Award for the entire body of her work; the Jewish Book Award for *The Devil's Arithmetic* and the World Fantasy Award; and twice the Mythopoeic Society Award for best fantasy novel (*Cards of Grief* and *Briar Rose*).

Background

In New York City on 11 February 1939, Jane Yolen was born into a family that honored, respected, and practiced the storytelling tradition. Her great-grandfather in Finno-Russia was the *Reb,* the "storyteller," who told stories at his inn. Her mother, Isabelle, was a writer who created crossword puzzles. William Hyatt Yolen, her father, was a famous journalist, author, and kite flier. He shared his passions for folk literature, folk songs, and kites with his daughter.

Jane Yolen attended public and private schools where teachers encouraged her to read and write. She received many gold stars and thought she was very intelligent until she attended a school for gifted students.

In high school she was a marginally popular nondrinker known for her funny stories, wisecracks, and flirtations with boys. At Smith College, Yolen won poetry prizes and was published. This success helped her to obtain various jobs at publishing firms, but she learned to avoid the mistakes that writers often make by working in editorial positions. Eventually she quit her job and traveled abroad with her husband for nine months. An olive grove in Greece became the setting for *The Girl Who Cried Flowers* and the tableland in Thessaly inspired *The Boy Who Had Wings.* She and her husband returned to the United States where Jane started her family and began writing full-time.

As an oral storyteller and author, Yolen strives to write wise and honest books. She writes for the child within her and not for an audience, for Yolen believes that if a book is "wise" it will appeal to all ages. Adults and children should

tableland a broad, level, elevated area; plateau

be able to enjoy the honesty in her books. Stories do not exist on a page or in someone's mouth. Readers can make her stories their own because the story exists between the writer and reader, or between the teller and listener.

Jane Yolen refers to herself as an empress of thieves. She borrows familiar folklores and combines them with psychological insight. She then weaves her stories into a rich tapestry. Sometimes she creates original stories from classic tales. These literary folktales or folk-tale collections (such as *The Girl Who Cried Flowers, Dream Weaver, Neptune Rising,* and *The Faerie Flag*) are famous for their beautiful poetic language, imagery, and ethereal qualities. These tales often deal with good versus evil, yet they do not preach. Possessing magical powers carries responsibility in Yolen's stories. Beasts are transformed into humans, or humans are changed into beasts. In *The Moon Ribbon and Other Tales,* stories of familial love and devotion, a ribbon becomes a silver river and eventually leads to a sliver-haired woman.

Yolen writes short prose and poems, using her words economically. Thus most of her stories are brief. Yolen has edited and contributed to many short-story collections (*Visions, Xanadu, Vampires, Werewolves, Things That Go Bump in the Night, Dragons and Dreams, Shape Shifters, Zoo 2000,* and others). She admits that her strengths lie in inventiveness, style, and story. She displays her genius through richly woven stories of folklore and high fantasy. However, Yolen, as well as her critics, thinks her characters are not well developed. In her folk literature the characters tend to be archetypes (models from which copies are made). In her first novel for young adults (*The Gift of Sarah Barker*), however, and her novels that followed, the plots, settings, and characters are all well developed.

Yolen wishes she could plot more intricately when she writes mysteries and tries to think two or three moves ahead. Her love of British mysteries influenced the witty and hilarious *Piggins* series and *Shirlick Holmes and the Case of the Wandering Wardrobe.*

Themes That Run So True

Jane Yolen is a member of the International Kite Fliers Association and the American Kite Fliers Association. Her father, William Yolen, was cited in the *Guinness Book of World*

imagery words or phrases that appeal to one or more of the five senses in order to create a mental picture

ethereal relating to regions beyond the earth; unworldly, spiritual

Records and *Ripley's Believe It or Not.* He once kept a kite in the air for 179 hours and on another occasion held 178 kites in the air at one time. William Yolen inspired his daughter's interest in kites and flying, which resulted in such books as *The Seventh Mandarin, The Boy Who Had Wings, The Girl Who Loved the Wind, Rainbow Rider,* and *Wings.* Yolen also wrote a fascinating history of kites, *World on a String: The Story of Kites.* While doing research for this book, Yolen came across a reference to a Chinese emperor who was rescued from a tower prison with a kite. This inspired her 1968 Caldecott Honor book, *The Emperor and the Kite,* the story of a daughter who pleases her father when she saves him with a kite.

The theme of pleasing one's father runs throughout many of Yolen's stories (*The Dragon's Boy*). William Yolen never read any of his daughter's books. He felt that his daughter was not a real author because she wrote for children. Yolen admits that she tried to pleased her father and often failed. Their relationship became easier when he was dying and she saw him sleeping with his mouth open and realized that "the dragon had no teeth," as she says in her collection of short stories and poems *Here There Be Dragons.* The novel for young adults *The Stone Silenus* is based on their relationship.

symbol anything that stands for or represents something else, for example, "The dove is a symbol of peace"

Dragons frequently serve as symbols and metaphors in Yolen's stories. This is true in her critically acclaimed Pit Dragon fantasy trilogy (*Dragon's Blood, Heart's Blood,* and *A Sending of Dragons*) for young adults. The fighting abilities of the mighty dragon Heart's Blood grant bond boy Jakkin his freedom in *Dragon's Blood.* Heart's Blood's slain carcass saves Jakkin and Akki from freezing to death in the sequel, *Heart's Blood.* Inside the dragon they are transformed and emerge the next day stronger and with new gifts that allow them, whether close by or far away, to hear intruders and to communicate telepathically. Thus, as the critic William Kreuger explains, the dragon becomes a symbol of human potential and the inner strength necessary to overcome woe. Likewise, "merfolk," wizards, unicorns, and other mythical characters are used as symbols. Readers who enjoy Yolen's fantasy novels should also enjoy the fantasy novels of Helen Hoover and Roger Zelazny, who also combine science fiction and fantasy.

metaphor a figure of speech in which one thing is referred to as something else, for example, "My love is a rose"

bond boy a boy bound to service without wages; slave

Death and dying are features of Yolen's stories, too. She does not always give her readers happy endings. *Cards of Grief,* the story of a society that values grieving as its highest art, was inspired by her father's death. Yolen's mourning of her mother's death resulted in *The Bird of Time* and "The Boy Who Sang for Death" from *Dream Weaver*. In *Writing Books for Children,* Yolen insists that when one writes for young people, one must write better than for adults because books change young lives and have the power to heal. A nurse who read to a dying child *The Girl Who Loved the Wind,* a story about a young girl who is protected from life by her father, helped ease her through her final pain.

Religion, Music, and Other Themes

Growing up in New York City, Yolen thought everyone was Jewish until she moved to Westport, Connecticut. She dealt with her feelings about being Jewish in two Holocaust stories. One, *The Devil's Arithmetic,* is a realistic, graphic depiction of Holocaust horrors. Hannah, the protagonist, travels back in time to a death camp during Passover seder. In her other Holocaust story, *Briar Rose,* Yolen reminds readers that no women were known to have survived the concentration camp at Chelmo.

Religion, music, and independent females are other prominent themes in Yolen's work. Quaker beliefs of pacifism and the equal treatment of women appeal to her; she converted to the religion after she attended, and later volunteered at, a Quaker camp. A Quaker cousin-in-law who was a pacifist and active in musical festivals known as hootenannies influenced many books. This relative introduced Yolen to George Fox, the founder of Quakerism. Yolen's biography of him, *Friend: The Story of George Fox and the Quakers,* led to *Simple Gifts,* a story about Mother Ann Lee and the founding of the Shakers. Her interest in Shakers led her to write *The Gift of Sarah Barker.* This story is about Sarah and Abel, who become forbidden lovers in a celibate Shaker community. Shaker communities segregate men and women, who are given strict rules and roles. A similar community exists in her Pit Dragon trilogy.

Yolen's knowledge of Catholicism was used in her stories about Arthurian legends (*The Dragon's Boy, Merlin's Booke, The Acorn Quest*). Stories of quests are among her favorite themes. In the Pit Dragon trilogy, self-discovery is Jakkin's holy grail. A bar mitzvah from Judaism is crossed with a Quaker silent meeting to form the ceremony of Thrittem in *The Magic Three of Solatia.*

The **Holocaust** was the mass murder of at least 11 million people, especially Jews, by the Nazis during World War II. The word "holocaust" means thorough destruction by fire.

Maria Tallchief (1925–) became the first ballerina trained in America to achieve international importance. She founded the Chicago City Ballet in 1980.

Jane Yolen's love of music is evident in her prose, poetry, and music books. As a teen Yolen wanted to become a ballet dancer. Her teacher was the famous ballerina Maria Tallchief. Yolen's sense of rhythm and love of movement is evident in such poetry collections as *Dinosaur Dances*. She is known for witty metaphors, among which are "over the mirror the noble swan slides while under the surface she bicycle rides" (*Bird Watch*). Her music books are attributed to her participation in hootenannies.

In Yolen's first book, *Pirates in Petticoats* (1963), independent women are portrayed in nontraditional roles. Yolen write about females who do not wait around to be rescued by men. Her females are warriors and power brokers (*Sister Light, Sister Dark* and *White Jenna*). They attempt to save men ("The Lady in the Dark" in *The Wizard Islands, Tam Lin, Dove Isabeau, The Emperor and the Kite,* and *The Ballad of the Pirate Queens*) and usually succeed.

Another theme is muteness and language. In *A Sending of Dragons,* the dragon hatchlings develop their own language. The Austarian dragons communicate by telepathic colored patterns. Melusina in *The Mermaid's Three Wisdoms* helps a twelve-year-old deaf girl learn wisdom. In the tragedy *Children of the Wolf,* the girls raised by a wolf do not learn language in an orphanage. This novel is based on a true discovery of feral (wild) children.

Writing Process Rituals

In *A Letter from Phoenix Farm,* Yolen described her life as a writer. The book uses beautiful color photographs by her son Jason. She begins each day at 6:00 A.M. by either writing or editing. In the editing room she works to help others turn their books into stories. In the writing room she works on her own books.

Writing requires thinking and reading and Yolen thinks about her writing and reads whenever she gets a chance. She read thousands of books for her 1986 book *Favorite Folktales from Around the World,* which took one and a half years of research to complete. She culled 500 stories and had to cut back to just 170 in order for the book to be published.

Sometimes Yolen feels that stories leak through her fingers while her fingers are on the keys of her typewriter. Yolen has to have the feel of running a draft through the typewriter again and again. When she works with her daughter, Yolen uses a computer. She cannot listen to music while she is writing, because it forces a rhythm different from the rhythm of her writing. When at home, Yolen takes walks along the Connecticut River. This activity helps her to get ideas, plots, and characters. Yolen reads her work aloud because it has to sing. She gives her work to her husband, who is her very best first reader. Finally, she shares her manuscript with a group of fellow writers before sending it off to her agent. Her work usually goes through many revisions, and since publishing is a buyer's market, not all her manuscripts have been published. Over the years, she says, her rejection letters could "paper a room."

Readers frequently ask Yolen where she gets her ideas. She generally responds that ideas come from everywhere. Her stories spring from her life. Yolen's family members often become characters in her stories. She depends on serendipity for ideas, which now come like a spigot that she can turn on at will. Yolen usually works on ten or twelve stories at a time. She keeps an idea file. To feed the file she carries a notebook, into which she frequently jots a snippet or a verse that catches her fancy. One hour's work writing down a list of titles in 1962 yielded over twenty years of inspiration.

The Owl Moon, her continuously best-selling book that won the prestigious Caldecott Medal for John Schoenherr's illustrations, came from her husband taking her daughter out owling. Yolen's prose—for example, "When you go owling you don't need words or warm or anything but hope"—and the harmony of parent and child have made the book an instant classic.

serendipity the phenomenon of finding things when one is not seeking them

Touching the Magic and Passing It On

In her book *Touch Magic,* Yolen reminds us that "storytelling is our oldest form of remembering the promises we have made to one another and to our various gods, and the promises given in return." Storytelling is a way of recording our human emotions, desires, and taboos. Stories are an essential part of our humanity. To last, a story must be engrossing and well told, and Yolen's books are both. Many of her fiction and nonfiction works contain maps and illustrations to guide the reader. Yolen strives to write stories that will provide readers with a "star map" for the future. She believes fiction should stress values, and that stories should become a rehearsal for life as it should be lived.

Yolen feels strongly that established writers need to touch the magic of a story and pass on this magic to help beginning authors. She has helped aspiring authors, therefore, by conducting workshops on writing for children. She has taught college courses on children's literature. The author Patricia MacLachlan, who won the John Newbery Medal for *Sarah, Plain and Tall,* cites Yolen's course for influencing her to become a writer.

Yolen continues to share her great gifts by continuing to write. She is also an editor of her own imprint, Jane Yolen Books, for Harcourt Brace Jovanovich. This position gives her an opportunity to teach authors to become better writers. In *Authors and Artists for Young Adults,* Jane advised young people who want to become writers to read and write and "read and read. It's the only way you will discover what great stories you want to tell better. Write every day because writing is like a muscle that needs to be flexed."

Teens who want to become authors or comedians could benefit by studying Yolen's diverse, imaginative books and her articles and books on writing.

Yolen's correspondence on the Internet has created a great deal of excitement. Additionally, she loves to get letters from her fans and answers every one. Her address is Phoenix Farm, 31 School Street, Hatfield, Massachusetts, 01038, and if you ever come to the farm, you will see her collection of unicorns, selchies, (seal-men), wizards, mermaids, and, of course, dragons.

> Yolen's advice to young people who want to write is "to read and read. It's the only way you will discover what great stories you want to tell better. Write every day because writing is like a muscle that needs to be flexed."

Readers who enjoy Jane Hyatt Yolen's works might also enjoy Mollie Hunter, Ursula K. Le Guin, and Anne McCaffrey.

Selected Bibliography

WORKS BY JANE YOLEN

Fiction

The Emperor and the Kite (1968)

The Seventh Mandarin (1970)

The Bird of Time (1971)

The Girl Who Loved the Wind (1972)

The Boy Who Had Wings (1974)

Rainbow Rider (1975)

The Magic Three of Solatia (1974)

The Transfigured Hart (1975)

The Moon Ribbon and Other Tales (1976)

The Hundredth Dove and Other Tales (1977)

The Seeing Stick (1977)

The Mermaid's Three Wisdoms (1978)

Dream Weaver and Other Tales (1979)

The Acorn Quest (1981)

Shirlick Holmes and the Case of the Wandering Wardrobe (1981)

The Gift of Sarah Barker (1981)

Sleeping Ugly (1981)

Dragon's Blood: A Fantasy (1982)

Neptune Rising: Songs and Tales of the Undersea Folk (1982)

Tales of Wonder (1983)

Cards of Grief (1984)

Children of the Wolf (19840

Heart's Blood (1984)

The Stone Silenus (1984)

Dragonfield and Other Stories (1985)

Merlin's Booke (1986)

Owl Moon (197)

Piggins (1987)

A Sending of Dragons (1987)

"Words of Power." In *Visions: Nineteen Short Stories by Outstanding Writers for Young Adults*. Edited by Donald R. Gallo (1987)

The Devil's Arithmetic (1988)

Picnic with Piggins (1988)

Sister Light, Sister Dark (1988)

The Faerie Flag: Stories and Poems of Fantasy and the Supernatural (1989)

Piggins and the Royal Wedding (1989)

White Jenna (1989)

The Dragon's Boy (1990)

Tam Lin (1990)

Hark! A Christmas Sampler (1991)

Wizard's Hall (1991)

Wings (1991)

Briar Rose (1992)

Encounter (1992)

Here There Be Dragons (1993)

The Ballad of the Pirate Queens (1994)

Beneath the Ghost Moon (1994)

The Girl in the Golden Bower (1994)

Good Griselle (1994)

Here There Be Unicorns (1994)

Sacred Places (1994)

The Wild Hunt (1995)

Here There Be Witches (1995)

Merlin and the Dragons (1995)

Nonfiction

Pirates in Petticoats (1963)

World on a String: The Story of Kites (1968)

Friend: The Story of George Fox and the Quakers (1972)

The Wizard Islands (1973)

Ring Out! A Book of Bells (1974)

Simple Gifts: The Story of the Shakers (1976)

Touch Magic: Fantasy, Faerie, and Folktale in the Literature of Childhood (1981)

Writing Books for Children (1982)

Guide to Writing for Children (1989)

A Letter from Phoenix Farm (1991)

Poetry

How Beastly! A Menagerie of Nonsense Poems (1980)

Best Wishes: Poems for Halloween (1989)

Bird Watch (1990)

Dinosaur Dances (1990)

Weather Report: Poems (1993)

Animal Fare: Zoological Nonsense Poems (1994)

WORKS EDITED BY JANE YOLEN

Zoo 2000: Twelve Stories of Science Fiction and Fantasy Beasts (1973)

Shape Shifters: Fantasy and Science Fiction Tales about Humans Who Can Change Their Shape (1978)

Favorite Folktales from around the World (1986)

2041: Twelve Short Stories about the Future by Top Science Fiction Writers (1991)

Xanadu (1993)

Xanadu 2 (1994)

Xanadu 3 (1995)

Dragons and Dreams: A Collection of New Fantasy and Science Fiction Stories, with Martin Greenberg and Charles Waugh (1986)

Spaceships and Spells: A Collection of New Fantasy and Science Fiction Stories, with Martin Greenberg and Charles Waugh (1987)

Werewolves: A Collection of Original Stories, with Martin Greenberg (1989)

Things That Go Bump in the Night: A Collection of Original Stories, with Martin Greenberg (1989)

Vampires: A Collection of Original Stories, with Martin Greenberg (1991)

WORKS ABOUT JANE YOLEN

Commire, Ann, ed. *Something About the Author.* Detroit: Gale Research, 1973, vol. 4, pp. 237–239.

Copperman, Paul. *Taking Books to Heart.* Reading, Mass.: Addison-Wesley, 1982.

de Montreville, Doris, and Elizabeth D. Crawford, eds. *Fourth Book of Junior Authors and Illustrators.* New York: H. W. Wilson, pp. 356–358.

Fuchs, Marcia G. *Twentieth-Century Writers,* 3d ed. Edited by Tracy Chevalier. Chicago: St. James, 1989, pp. 1075–1078.

Gallo, Donald R., ed. *Speaking for Ourselves: Autobiographical Sketches by Notable Authors of Books for Young Adults.* Urbana, Ill.: National Council of Teachers of English, 1990, pp. 225–227.

Garrett, Agnes, and Helga P. McCue, eds. *Authors and Artists for Young Adults.* Detroit: Gale Research, 1990, vol. 4, pp. 229–241.

Kilpatrick, William, et al. *Books That Build Character: A Guide to Teaching Your Child Moral Values Through Stories.* New York: Simon & Schuster, 1994.

Kreuger, William E. "Jane Yolen." In *American Writers for Children Since 1960: Fiction. Vol. 52 of Dictionary of Literary Biography.* Edited by Glen Estes. Detroit: Gale Research, 1986, vol. 52, pp. 398–404.

Roginski, Jim. "An Interview with Jane Yolen: Author of Fantasy and Fairy Tale." *The ALAN Review,* Spring 1985, vol. 12, pp. 37–42.

Ross, Jean W. *Contemporary Authors, New Revisions Series.* Detroit: Gale Research, 1990, vol. 29, pp. 463–469.

Rudman, Kabakow Marsha, ed. *People Behind the Books: Writers in Children's Literature: Resource for the Classroom.* Norwood, Mass.: Christopher-Gordon, 1989, pp. 51–55.

Sarkissian, Adele, ed. *Something About the Author Autobiography Series.* Detroit: Gale Research, 1985, vol. 1, pp. 327–346.

Senick, Gerald J., ed. *Children's Literature Review.* Detroit: Gale Research, 1994, vol. 4, 255–269.

Stevenson, Jean Myers. "The Writing Processes of Theodore Taylor and Jane Yolen." Ph.D. dissertation, University of North Dakota, 1989.

Telgen, Diane, ed. *Something About the Author.* Detroit: Gale Research, 1994, vol. 75, pp. 223–221.

How to Write to the Author
Jane Yolen
31 School Street
Hatfield, MA 01038
or JaneYolen@aol.com

Paul Zindel

(1936-)

by Jack Forman

M arsh Mellow, Schizoid Suzy, and Edna Shinglebox—
these are only some of the bizarrely named characters who appear in Paul Zindel's novels for young
adults. The titles—including *Pardon Me, You're Stepping on
My Eyeball* (1976); *Confessions of a Teenage Baboon* (1977);
The Undertaker's Gone Bananas (1978); and *Harry and
Hortense at Hormone High* (1984)—are also hilariously
strange. As you might expect, the characters are eccentric,
and the stories are unconventional. Where did these exaggerated devices come from? The answer might become clear
if we take a look at Zindel's life and at why he writes young
adult novels.

Early Experiences

When Zindel was two years old, his father—a policeman in
New York City—abandoned his family for a woman he met
in a bar. The author remembers that his mother, a traveling

nurse (and sometime hatcheck girl and shipyard riveter), moved almost every year after that, making Zindel and his older sister feel rootless and confused. In addition, Zindel believed that his mother—who died an extremely painful death from cancer in 1968—passed on her low self-esteem and social awkwardness to him. Zindel had another traumatic experience at age fifteen, when he won an eighteen-month battle with tuberculosis in a sanatorium.

A couple of years after graduating from college with a major in chemistry and a keen interest in theater, Zindel accepted a job as a high school science teacher. During his ten years as a teacher, he took a two-year sabbatical to write and produce a play called *The Effect of Gamma Rays on Man-in-the-Moon Marigolds* (1971), which won the Pulitzer Prize in 1971. In 1969, he quit teaching because he became disillusioned with his suburban students, who he thought were "spaced-out" on drugs and did not want to learn, and because he wanted to devote himself to playwriting full-time.

About two years before leaving the teaching profession, Zindel received a call from Charlotte Zolotow, a writer and editor for Harper & Row Childrens Books. She had seen a television adaptation of *Gamma Rays* and was so impressed with Zindel's characterization of the teenagers in the play that she invited him to write a novel for this age group. The result was Zindel's first and most influential novel—*The Pigman* (1966), which helped launch a "revolution" in young adult literature and a successful career for Zindel as an author of young adult novels.

The Pigman Books

The Pigman is considered one of the three books that created the genre now known as the "young adult realistic novel." In 1967, S. E. Hinton's *The Outsiders* and Robert Lipsyte's *The Contender* were published. These two books about imperfect teens living in an imperfect society present conflicts—among teenagers themselves and between teenagers and adults—resulting from socioeconomic stratification and ethnic and racial distrust in the community. Before these three books, novels for teenagers were mostly about the problems teenagers faced in their immediate environments—the home and school—and dealt almost exclusively with middle-class, gender-typed concerns (such as

sabbatical time off from a job, often with pay, for rest, travel, or research

There are articles about S. E. Hinton and Robert Lipsyte in volume 2.

stratification division into classes or ranks

sports for boys and school dances for girls). The "realistic novel" attempted to tell the story of teenagers as they lived rather than how adults perceived them.

The Pigman, published the year after *The Contender* and *The Outsiders,* explores the subject of individual responsibility for one's actions. John and Lorraine, sensitive but immature young teenagers alienated from their unhappy and overbearing parents, randomly telephone people to see how long they can keep them talking. During one of these games, John reaches a lonely old man named Mr. Pignati, who invites the pair over to his house. When they arrive, they find a strange house filled with the old man's impressive collection of pigs made of glass, marble, and clay. He claims that his wife lives in California, but when the two inquisitive teenagers uncover papers in his attic revealing that his wife is dead, they realize that their new friend cannot accept the reality of her death.

As John and Lorraine's lives become more closely entwined with the Pigman's (their name for Mr. Pignati), the old man suffers a near-fatal heart attack. While the Pigman recuperates in the hospital, John and Lorraine throw a party for their boorish classmates at the Pigman's home. A riot ensues, and the Pigman's prized collection is smashed. Mr. Pignati never recovers from the shock and suffers a fatal heart attack soon after. John and Lorraine are left to ponder their responsibility for his death.

boorish crude and insensitive

In *The Pigman's Legacy*—a sequel written in 1980—the guilt-ridden characters John and Lorraine return to Pigman's house, only to find a homeless, sick old man reliving his past. The two young people take the man on a wild gambling spree to Atlantic City before he dies. John and Lorraine feel that they have redeemed themselves by making this Pigman substitute gloriously happy in his final hours of life. As the novel ends, the two declare their love for one another.

In *The Pigman and Me,* Zindel's autobiographical memoir about one year of his childhood, he describes the person on whom he based the Pigman. When Zindel was growing up, his mother was a close friend of an Italian-American woman whose twins Zindel baby-sat and whose father was an inspiration for the Pigman character. An eccentric man who liked to tell jokes and talk nonsense, he was the person who made Zindel confront his destiny as a writer. Because he did not have a father when he was growing up, Zindel created the Pigman as a father figure. In addition, he enriched the character with elements of these autobiographical experiences: Zindel once bought a car from a woman whose brother could not accept the fact that his wife had died, and a friend of Zindel told him about a strange old man who collected pig figurines.

composite combination of distinct parts

To one extent or another, the characters and plots of Zindel's young adult novels are composites from his own experiences. The stories all portray teenage characters who try to build their identities while struggling with a dysfunctional family environment similar to the one the author grew up in. Zindel creates characters who seek self-esteem and the love of someone else at the same time they learn the importance of responsibility for their actions. It is no accident that Zindel writes most of his novels as first-person narratives. As Zindel said in his telephone interview, "You end up writing about yourself, but you don't know it."

first-person narrative a story told from the position or perspective of someone inside the story, using the pronoun "I"

Variations on a Theme

In his second novel, *My Darling, My Hamburger* (1969), Zindel applies his message about personal responsibility to sexual behavior. But the story's most important message concerns the role of parents in influencing teenagers to act responsibly. Supported by their communicative and caring parents, Maggie and Dennis are close friends who date each other while imposing sexual limits on their relationship. Sean and Liz, on the other hand, are deeply alienated from their overprotective, suspicious, and hypocritical parents; to escape their difficult home lives, they become sexually involved with each other. When Liz becomes pregnant, Sean wants to marry her, but his materialistic, hard-nosed father convinces him that Liz should get an abortion. Liz then turns to Maggie for help. When the illegal operation fails, Maggie gets help to save Liz's life. Sean and Liz are left with lifetime scars from their experience, while Maggie and Dennis remain friends even though they have different plans for their lives after graduation. *My Darling, My Hamburger* is one of the few of Zindel's novels that portray a set of parents who are not dysfunctional; Zindel credits Maggie's and Dennis' parents with transmitting moral values to their children, while he severely indicts Liz's and Sean's parents for the irresponsible behavior that they pass on to their children.

indict to charge with a fault or offense, such as a crime

One reason Zindel stopped teaching high school in the sixties was that he thought his students were too distracted to learn. This experience caused him to examine the negative aspects of that exciting decade, which he does in *I Never Loved Your Mind* (1970). In this novel, a self-involved but innocent young high school dropout named Dewey Daniels falls in love with Yvette Goethals, a young nurse who is also a vegetarian and rock band groupie. Dewey notices, with clinical precision, that Yvette has "a commendable frontal insulation for the respiratory cage" (p. 14). When she is through playing with Dewey, she drops him as if he ceased to exist. Dewey then sees the light, rejects her lifestyle—and plans to go to medical school.

Another book that pokes fun at the sixties is *Pardon Me, You're Stepping on My Eyeball* (1976). It is the story of fifteen-year-old Marsh Mellow, who cannot come to terms with his father's death in a car accident for which Marsh was partly responsible. He keeps his father's ashes under his bed and tells preposterous lies about him to Edna Shinglebox, a classmate in his special education class. Edna's two parents push her to do things she does not want to. Unable to cope with their lives, the two run away together. Eventually, in an action-packed climax, Edna helps Marsh confront his father's death, and Marsh helps her to break her dependence on smothering parents. After they have developed their self-esteem, the two teenage outcasts fall in love with one another. The story is also a savage—and funny—indictment of pop psychology, and the touchy-feely games that Marsh and Edna were forced to play in their special education classes and that Zindel believed were taking over American education.

Zindel believes his most autobiographical story is *Confessions of a Teenage Baboon*. The "baboon" of the title is sixteen-year-old Chris, whose domineering mother is a traveling nurse hired by the shiploader Lloyd Dipardi to care for his own mother, who is terminally ill. Lloyd spends most of his time throwing parties for troubled teens in his neighborhood and giving them advice. He successfully helps Chris wean himself from his mother and find his way into the loving arms of a member of Lloyd's teen entourage. Despite his ability to help others with similar problems, Lloyd cannot resolve his love-hate relationship with his own strict and manipulative mother. Chris gets his girl, but Lloyd commits suicide just after his mother dies. Chris and Lloyd appear to

neurotic affected
with a **neurosis,** a
mental and emo-
tional disorder that
affects only part of
the personality, and
is accompanied by
various physical, psy-
chological, or mental
disturbances, such as
irrational fears or
anxieties

be two sides of Zindel's younger self; the author has created Lloyd to show his teen readers just how important it is to free yourself from unhealthy dependence on neurotic parents and attain self-esteem and fall in love.

With more humor and suspense, Zindel writes about the same themes in *The Undertaker's Gone Bananas* (1978). Rebellious Bobby and his dependable, insecure girlfriend, Laurie, persist in following a suspicious undertaker until they catch him in the act of a crime. In doing so, they put themselves in great danger. Zindel says the story is based on a very strange neighbor he and his wife met just after they got married. In addition to wanting to promote the importance of self-esteem and love to his young readers, Zindel says that using this undertaker in the story is his attempt to get rid of his memory of that man.

The Girl Who Wanted a Boy is a story similar to *I Never Loved Your Mind,* but it is told from a girl's point of view. In *I Never Loved Your Mind,* Dewey Daniels first idealizes the girl of his dreams and then discovers who she really is. In *The Girl Who Wanted a Boy* (1981), Sibella idealizes the boy of her dreams—who makes loves to her, takes the van she bought him with all her savings, and then abandons her. What Zindel calls the "secret of love" eludes both Dewey and Sibella, but both carry away from their experiences a measure of self-esteem that neither had before.

For his novel *Harry and Hortense at Hormone High,* Zindel uses characters similar to John and Lorraine in *The Pigman,* but changes their names to Harry and Hortense. They are an enlightened and sensitive boy and girl attending a high school ruled by peer pressure and permeated by boring classes. In their quest for a hero, Harry and Hortense discover Jason Rohr—a strange new student who claims he is a Greek god and who, the two discover, has been traumatized by having witnessed his father kill his mother and then commit suicide. Harry and Hortense help Jason escape the wrath of their yahoo classmates, only to seem him plunge to his death after trying to fly (like the Greek mythological character Icarus as he attempted to reach the sun). Their dream of a hero has died a hard death, but Zindel implies that Harry and Hortense's grandiose leap of faith was a justified rebellion against the unthinking materialism of our culture.

In Greek mythology,
Daedalus and his son
Icarus tried to es-
cape the labyrinth
with wings fashioned
from wax and feath-
ers. The wax in
Icarus's wings melted
when he disobeyed
his father's cautions
not to fly too high
(near the sun). He
fell to his death.

The Amazing and Death-Defying Diary of Eugene Dingman (1987) follows Zindel's alter ego as he emerges from an innocent, powerless childhood willing to confront an arch-enemy who is threatening his relationship with a girl he thinks he loves. He takes on this Goliath by catching him off guard and beating him at his own game. The fact that his girlfriend leaves him—as Yvette did to Dewey in *I Never Loved Your Mind*—shocks him into reality and forces him to take control of his life once and for all.

One of Zindel's unresolved conflicts is his failure to come to terms with his mother's painful death from cancer. In *A Begonia for Miss Applebaum* (1989), Zindel addresses this issue by using the high school students Henry and Zelda as stand-ins for himself and by having them provide support for Miss Applebaum, their beloved biology teacher who is dying of cancer. We also learn what Zindel wants his readers to learn: that "death is not a foe, but an inevitable adventure" (*The Undertaker's Gone Bananas,* p. 178). This book shows, too, that it is important to affirm life in the presence of those who are dying.

Henry and Zelda become David (the name of Zindel's son) and Della in Zindel's 1993 novel *David and Della*. It is the story about a would-be playwright (like the younger Zindel) who is emotionally repressed, and his relationship to Della, an alcoholic and severely disturbed young actress. It is not always clear what is happening in this offbeat novel, but David and Della (like their previous counterparts) end up helping one another overcome their neuroses.

Zindel's novel *Loch* (1994) veers off in a different direction but ends up teaching the same lessons Zindel's teenage characters always learn. Loch, his younger sister Zaidee, and Loch's girlfriend, Sarah, try to save a baby version of the Loch Ness Monster, whom they have befriended and named Wee Beastie. The novel has similarities to a play Zindel wrote in 1973 called *Let Me Hear You Whisper,* in which an anthropomorphized dolphin is exploited by military scientists. With the exception of Loch and Zaidee's recently widowed father, the adults are the villains, who are trying to kill the "monster" for glory and profit. Loch's father has been hired by Sarah's father to join a team trying to hunt down the monster, but gradually Sarah and Loch convince him to quit his job and help save the Wee Beastie (and most of Wee Beastie's "family"). In the end, Loch and Zaidee are able to keep their family intact as well.

A monster also plays a central role in *The Doom Stone,* but in this story the creature is not a benevolent Wee Beastie;

The **Loch Ness Monster** is a monster said to inhabit Loch Ness, a lake in Scotland. The loch is a popular tourist attraction for people trying to catch a glimpse of "Nessie."

anthropomorphized (something not human) given a human form or personality

he is an ugly and violent life form who attacks humans without warning or cause. Fifteen-year-old Jackson, while visiting his Aunt Sarah—an archaeologist conducting a dig in Stonehenge, England—witnesses the monster attacking and biting his aunt. The creature, named "Skull Face" by Jackson, soon gains control of Aunt Sarah's mine and absorbs her knowledge.

Jackson and a new female friend, Alma, follow one clue after another to uncover the secret of Skull Face's demonic power. They risk their lives repeatedly looking for the underground home of this scary and wily creature. Eventually, with Aunt Sarah's help, they kill the monster. But . . . deep beneath the ground, a whole new generation of monsters is evolving, waiting for the right time to return.

What the Critics Say

There are two basic criticisms that are sometimes made about Zindel's young adult novels. One is that Zindel is writing the same story again and again—a view shared by the author himself. The reason is that he writes about the unresolved conflicts left over from his own adolescence. The other criticism is that Zindel panders to the stereotypical outlook of his reading audience. As Lillian Gerhardt wrote about Zindel's work in the April 1976 *School Library Journal:* "Other kids (besides the protagonists) are criminoid or kooks. Parents are psychotic pains. Teachers are at least half-etched. The government is grimy. All realities are wretched" (p. 45). Others agree with Zindel's own characterization of his stories, as he explained it to Audrey Eaglen in her interview with him in the Winter 1978 issue of *Top of the News:* "I tell [readers] that tomorrow becomes today through self-inspection and action and belief, that their minds come equipped by God or Nature with the spirit and means to be joyful and intimate with their fellow human beings" (p. 182). Zindel believes that the farcical humor he uses and the exaggerated caricatures he creates are literary devices to keep teenage readers interested in reading his novels. Regardless of which view you take, it is clear that Zindel's novels have played a large part in shaping the young adult "realistic novel." In addition, his stories have entertained and guided a whole generation of teenagers, who have been exposed over and over again to Zindel's lessons of life.

pander to provide gratification for someone's desires

farcical resembling **farce,** a light dramatic composition characterized by broad satirical comedy and a highly improbable plot

Selected Bibliography

WORKS BY PAUL ZINDEL

Novels for Young Adults
The Pigman (1968)

My Darling, My Hamburger (1969)

I Never Loved Your Mind (1970)

Pardon Me, You're Stepping On My Eyeball (1976)

Confessions of a Teenage Baboon (1977)

The Undertaker's Gone Bananas (1978)

Pigman's Legacy (1980)

A Star for the Latecomer, co-authored by Bonnie Zindel, his wife (1982)

Harry and Hortense at Hormone High (1984)

The Amazing and Death-Defying Diary of Eugene Dingman (1987)

A Begonia For Miss Applebaum (1989)

David and Della (1993)

Loch (1994)

The Doom Stone (1995)

Plays for Young Adults
The Effect of Gamma Rays on Man-in-the-Moon Marigolds (1971)

Let Me Hear You Whisper (1974, 1970)

Autobiography
The Pigman and Me (1992)

WORKS ABOUT PAUL ZINDEL

Books
Donelson, Kenneth, and Alleen Pace Nilsen. *Literature for Today's Young Adults.* Glenview, Ill.: Scott Foresman & Co., 1988.

Forman, Jack. "Paul Zindel." In *Twentieth Century Young Adult Writers.* Edited by Laura Standley Berger. Detroit: St. James, 1994, pp. 731–733.

Forman, Jacob Jack. *Presenting Paul Zindel.* Boston: Twayne, 1988.

Henke, James T. "Six Characters in Search of the Family: The Novels of Paul Zindel." In *Children's Literature.* Philadelphia: Temple University, 1976, vol. 5, pp. 130–140.

Articles

Gerhardt, Lillian. "Finn Pinn Award." In *School Library Journal,* April 1976, p. 45.

Haley, Beverly A., and Kenneth Donelson. "Pigs and Hamburgers, Cadavers and Gamma Rays: Paul Zindel's Adolescents." In *Elementary English,* October 1974, pp. 941–945.

Hoffman, Stanley. "Winning, Losing, but Above All Taking Risks: A Look at the Novels of Paul Zindel." In *Lion and the Unicorn,* Fall 1978, pp. 78–88.

Stanek, Lou Willet. "The Junior Novel: A Stylistic Study." In *Elementary English,* October 1974, pp. 947–953.

Interviews

Chambers, Aidan. "An Interview with Paul Zindel." In *Times Literary Supplement* (London), September 1973, pp. 55ff.

Eaglen, Audrey. "Of Life, Love, Death, Kids and Inhalation Therapy: An Interview with Paul Zindel." In *Top of the News,* Winter 1978, pp. 178–185.

Forman, Jack. Telephone Interviews with Paul Zindel, May 1987.

How to Write to the Author
Paul Zindel
c/o Bill Morris
HarperCollins Children's Books
10 East 53rd Street
New York, NY 10022

Contributors

Professor Richard F. Abrahamson
University of Houston
RUSSELL FREEDMAN

Professor Hugh Agee
University of Georgia
VERA AND BILL CLEAVER

Dr. Jane M. Agee
State University of New York at Albany
OLIVE ANN BURNS

Professor Suellen Alfred
Cookeville, Tennessee
SCOTT O'DELL

Professor Lynne B. Alvine
Indiana University of Pennsylvania
BETTE GREENE

Professor Michael Angelotti
University of Oklahoma, Norman
CARL SANDBURG

Professor Bruce Appleby
Southern Illinois University at Carbondale,
    Professor Emeritus
T. ERNESTO BETHANCOURT

Dr. Kylene Beers
Sam Houston State University, Huntsville, Texas
SUSAN BETH PFEFFER

Professor Susan G. Bennett
Humboldt State University, Arcata, California
BRENDA WILKINSON

Dr. Rudine Sims Bishop
Ohio State University
WALTER DEAN MYERS

Ms. Susan P. Bloom
Simmons College, Boston, Massachusetts
ZIBBY ONEAL

Ms. Joni Bodart
University of Denver
NORMA FOX MAZER

Ms. Jeannie Borsch
Tampa, Florida
BROCK COLE

Professor James Brewbaker
Columbus College, Columbus, Georgia
LARRY BOGRAD, CHRIS LYNCH

Professor Jean E. Brown
Saginaw Valley State University,
    University Center, Michigan
JOAN BAUER, TERRY DAVIS

Ms. Lois Buckman
Moorhead Junior High School, Conroe, Texas
NICHOLASA MOHR

Professor John H. Bushman
University of Kansas, Lawrence, Kansas
SANDY ASHER

Professor Donna J. Camp
University of Central Florida, Orlando, Florida
THEODORE TAYLOR

Ms. Patricia J. Campbell
Columnist, *Horn Book*
FRANCESCA LIA BLOCK, ROBERT CORMIER

Professor Pamela S. Carroll
Florida State University, Tallahassee, Florida
SUE ELLEN BRIDGERS

Mr. Michael Cart
Booklist, Los Angeles Times Book Review
ROBERT LIPSYTE

Professor Betty Carter
Texas Woman's University, Denton, Texas
PETER DICKINSON

Dr. Michaeline K. V. Chance-Reay
Kansas State University, Manhattan, Kansas
STELLA PEVSNER

Professor Leila Christenbury
Virginia Commonwealth University,
    Richmond, Virginia
WILLIAM SHAKESPEARE

Professor Patricia J. Cianciolo
Michigan State University,
    East Lansing, Michigan
CHRISTOPHER COLLIER AND JAMES LINCOLN COLLIER

Professor Linda Miller Cleary
University of Minnesota, Duluth
ALICE CHILDRESS

Dr. Pam B. Cole
Kennesaw State College, Kennesaw, Georgia
STEPHEN CRANE, MICHAEL FRENCH

Ms. Melissa Reese Comer
University of Tennessee, Knoxville
L. M. MONTGOMERY, COLBY RODOWSKY

Ms. Leslie S. Cook
University of Tennessee, Chattanooga
JOYCE THOMAS CAROL

Professor Daniel J. Cox
Peru State College, Peru, Nebraska
JULIAN F. THOMPSON

Professor Chris Crowe
Brigham Young University, Provo, Utah
BRUCE BROOKS, GRAHAM SALISBURY

Mr. Allan O'Grady Cuseo
Greece Arcadia High School,
    Greece, New York
SANDRA SCOPPETTONE

Dr. Patricia L. Daniel
University of South Florida, Tampa, Florida
HILA COLMAN

Ms. Hazel K. Davis
Athens, Ohio
WILLIAM SLEATOR

Professor James E. Davis
Ohio University, Athens, Ohio
ROBIN F. BRANCATO

Mr. Terry Davis
Mankato State University, Mankato, Minnesota
CHRIS CRUTCHER

Dr. Kenneth Donelson
Arizona State University, Tempe, Arizona
LEON GARFIELD

Professor Charles R. Duke
Appalachian State University,
    Boone, North Carolina
GLORIA D. MIKLOWITZ

Mr. Daniel Dyer
Harmon School, Aurora City Schools,
    Aurora, Ohio
JACK LONDON

Professor Ira Elliot
City College of New York
ERNEST HEMINGWAY

Dr. Allison Ensor
University of Tennessee, Knoxville
MARK TWAIN

Professor Bonnie O. Ericson
California State University, Northridge
MARC TALBERT

Mr. Theodore F. Fabiano
Blue Valley Northwest High School,
    Overland Park, Kansas
GARY SOTO, TODD STRASSER

Professor Jack Forman
Mesa College Library, San Diego, California
PAUL ZINDEL

Professor Harold M. Foster
University of Akron
NAT HENTOFF

Ms. Melinda Franklin
University of Tennessee, Knoxville
LOIS LOWRY

Professor Warren French
University of Wales, Swansea
J. D. SALINGER, JOHN STEINBECK

Professor Donald R. Gallo
Central Connecticut State University,
    New Britain, Connecticut
CAROLINE B. COONEY, RICHARD PECK

Professor Philip Gerber
State University of New York, Brockport
ROBERT FROST

Professor Jeanne Marcum Gerlach
West Virginia University,
    Morgantown, West Virginia
K. M. PEYTON

Professor Colleen P. Gilrane
University of Tennessee, Knoxville
BETSY BYARS, C. S. LEWIS

Professor Esther W. Glass
Patchogue, New York
JOAN AIKEN

Ms. Beth Goza
Enumclaw High School,
    Enumclaw, Washington
ANNE FRANK

Professor Joyce Graham
Radford University, Radford, Virginia
MAYA ANGELOU

Professor M. Jean Greenlaw
University of North Texas, Denton, Texas
EVE BUNTING

Professor Betty Greenway
Bishopton, Swansea, United Kingdom
MOLLIE HUNTER

Professor Donald R. Hettinga
Calvin College, Grand Rapids, Michigan
MADELEINE L'ENGLE

Dr. Marjorie Hipple
University of Tennessee, Knoxville
S. E. HINTON

Dr. Ted Hipple
University of Tennessee, Knoxville
AIDAN CHAMBERS, SIR ARTHUR CONAN DOYLE

Professor Rosemary Oliphant Ingham
Belmont University, Nashville, Tennessee
LOUISA MAY ALCOTT

Professor Claudia Durst Johnson
University of Alabama, Tuscaloosa
HARPER LEE

Ms. Deidre A. Johnson
West Chester University of Pennsylvania
EDWARD STRATEMEYER

Professor Dianne Johnson-Feelings
University of South Carolina,
Columbia, South Carolina
LAURENCE YEP

Dr. Marjorie M. Kaiser
University of Louisville
ROBBIE BRANSCUM

Professor Jeffrey S. Kaplan
University of Central Florida, Orlando, Florida
JAY BENNETT

Professor Marilyn H. Karrenbrock Stauffer
University of South Florida, Tampa, Florida
MARILYN SACHS

Dr. Joan Kaywell
University of South Florida, Tampa, Florida
HADLEY IRWIN

Professor Patricia P. Kelly
Virginia Polytechnic Institute
and State University
MARGARET (MAY) MAHY, JOAN LOWERY NIXON

Dr. Cosette Kies
Northern Illinois University, De Kalb, Illinois
LOIS DUNCAN

Professor Susanne Porter Kirk
Xavier University, Cincinnati, Ohio
MILDRED DELOIS TAYLOR

Ms. Kathleen Krull
San Diego, California
PAULA DANZIGER

Professor Karen Kutiper
Harris County Department of Education,
Houston, Texas
ANNE MCCAFFREY

Ms. Lorraine Mary Leidholdt
College of Saint Benedict,
Saint Joseph, Minnesota
Saint John's University, Collegeville, Minnesota
JEAN CRAIGHEAD GEORGE

Professor Teri S. Lesesne
Sam Houston State University, Huntsville, Texas
GORDON KORMAN, VIRGINIA EUWER WOLFF

Professor Catherine Lewis
University of South Carolina,
Columbia, South Carolina
LAURENCE YEP

Professor Terry C. Ley
Auburn University
ALDEN R. CARTER

Professor Hollis Lowery-Moore
Sam Houston State University, Huntsville, Texas
JUDIE ANGELL

Ms. Nancy Lund
Duluth Public Schools, Duluth, Minnesota
AVI

Professor Catherine Mairs
University of Maryland, Baltimore County
MILTON MELTZER

Professor Jill P. May
Purdue University, West Lafayette, Indiana
LLOYD ALEXANDER

Professor Joy H. McGregor
Texas Woman's University, Denton, Texas
ANN RINALDI

Professor Alan M. McLeod
Virginia Commonwealth University,
Richmond, Virginia
EDGAR ALLAN POE

Professor Nina Mikkelsen
Indiana, Pennsylvania
VIRGINIA HAMILTON

Dr. Diana Mitchell
Williamston, Michigan
NORMA JOHNSTON

Professor Virginia Monseau
Youngstown State University,
Youngstown, Ohio
OUIDA SEBESTYEN

Dr. Beatrice Naff
Clemson University, Clemson, South Carolina
ROSEMARY SUTCLIFF

Professor Alleen Pace Nilsen
Arizona State University, Tempe, Arizona
M. E. KERR, JILL PATON WALSH

Professor Allene Phy-Olsen
Austin Peay State University,
Clarksville, Tennessee
NORMA KLEIN

Dr. Elizabeth Poe
Radford University, Radford, Virginia
BARBARA WERSBA

Professor Carol A. Pope
North Carolina State University,
Raleigh, North Carolina
JEANNETTE EYERLY

Ms. Laura Pritchard
Suffolk, Virginia
CHARLES DICKENS

Professor Heidi M. Quintana
University of South Florida, Tampa, Florida
HADLEY IRWIN

Professor Arthea (Charlie) Reed
University of North Carolina at Asheville
HARRY MAZER

Professor Suzanne Reid
Emory, Virginia
URSULA K. LE GUIN, CYNTHIA VOIGT

Ms. Deborah Webster Rogers
Des Moines, Iowa
J. R. R. TOLKIEN

Professor Lucy Rollin
Clemson University, Clemson, South Carolina
ISABELLE HOLLAND

Professor Margaret T. Sacco
Miami University of Ohio
JANE YOLEN

Professor Gary M. Salvner
Youngstown State University,
Youngstown, Ohio
GARY PAULSEN

Professor Barbara G. Samuels
University of Houston, Clear Lake
KATHRYN LASKY

Professor E. Wendy Saul
University of Maryland, Baltimore County
MILTON MELTZER

Professor Gary D. Schmidt
Calvin College, Grand Rapids, Michigan
KATHERINE PATERSON

Professor William H. Shurr
University of Tennessee, Knoxville
EMILY DICKINSON

Professor John S. Simmons
Florida State University
ROBERT NEWTON PECK

Dean Robert C. Small, Jr.
Radford University, Radford, Virginia
JERRY SPINELLI

Professor Marilou Sorenson
University of Utah, Professor Emeritus
MONICA HUGHES

Professor Janet Spaeth
University of North Dakota,
Grand Forks, North Dakota
LAURA INGALLS WILDER

Ms. Susan Stan
Editor, *The Five Owls*
LYNN HALL

Dr. Elaine C. Stephens
Saginaw Valley State University,
University Center, Michigan
MARION DANE BAUER, TODD STRASSER

Professor Lois Thomas Stover
St. Mary's College of Maryland
PHYLLIS REYNOLDS NAYLOR

Professor Wendy Sutton
University of British Columbia
KEVIN MAJOR

Professor Edgar H. Thompson
Emory and Henry College, Emory, Virginia
WILL HOBBS

Dr. Lilyanne (Lanny) van Allen
Texas Education Agency, Austin, Texas
ROBERT ATKINSON WESTALL

Professor Nancy Vogel
Fort Hays State University, Hays, Kansas
MAUREEN DALY

Professor Maryann Weidt
Duluth, Minnesota
JUDY BLUME

Professor M. Jerry Weiss
Jersey City State College, Professor Emeritus
KIN PLATT

Professor Linda J. Wilson
Radford University, Radford, Virginia
ROBERT LOUIS STEVENSON

Professor Connie Zitlow
Ohio Wesleyan University, Delaware, Ohio
PAULA FOX

Category Index

Page numbers in boldface refer to the main discussion of the subject.

Index

Page numbers in boldface refer to the main discussion of the subject.

One Hundred Summers

A Kiowa Calendar Record

Candace S. Greene

Foreword by

Ellen Censky

Preface by

Daniel C. Swan

Glossary by

Gus Palmer Jr.

UNIVERSITY OF NEBRASKA PRESS | LINCOLN & LONDON

Publication of this volume was assisted by
a grant from the Institute for Museum and
Library Services, Washington DC

© 2009 by the Board of Regents of
the University of Oklahoma

♾

Library of Congress Cataloging-
in-Publication Data

Greene, Candace S.
One hundred summers : a Kiowa calendar
record / Candace S. Greene ; foreword by
Ellen Censky ; preface by Daniel C. Swan.
        p. cm.
Includes bibliographical references and index.
ISBN 978-0-8032-1940-3 (cloth : alk. paper)
1. Kiowa calendar. 2. Kiowa art. 3. Silver Horn,
1860–1940. I. Title.
E99.K5G73 2009
299′.78—dc22
2008031318

Typeset in Galliard.

Printed in China

Contents

Illustrations

Foreword

Ellen Censky

Among the greatest pleasures that accompany my work as director of the Sam Noble Oklahoma Museum of Natural History is the opportunity gain a bird's eye view of the museum's work fostering understanding of "the natural and cultural world through collection-based discovery, interpretation, and education," as the museum's mission statement puts it. The story of the *One Hundred Summers* project symbolizes this mission perfectly and in multiple ways. As an artist and historian of his people, the Kiowa, Silver Horn was an acute observer and documenter of the world around him—cultural, social, historical, geographic. In crafting his calendar history he was preserving a record of his people's story, and of their wider perspective on the world, for future generations. He was a native of the region now centered on Oklahoma. The visual documents that he left us, including this calendar history, provide a distinctive and unparalleled resource for understanding Oklahoma and its place in global history. Silver Horn's life's work thus parallels the museum's mission, both promoting understanding of the world in general and exploring Oklahoma's place within it. The book before you holds something for almost every interest, contributing in its own special way to fields as diverse as military and aviation history, geography, and meteorology, to say nothing of the obvious disciplines of history, art history, anthropology, and Native American studies. The museum shares many of Silver

Horn's interests and my colleagues and I easily find inspiration from his remarkable efforts.

The museum's work is about building and using collections to pursue discovery, interpretation, and education. It is a serious responsibility and a distinct honor to steward the Silver Horn calendar in the collections of the Sam Noble Oklahoma Museum of Natural History. Museum scholars often make discoveries outside the museum walls, bringing back with them objects and specimens that help document and bring these discoveries to life in tangible form. In the case of the Silver Horn calendar, the discovery was actually a rediscovery, and responsibility for it was not the museum's doing. Marcia Bassity discovered the brown paper bundle in which the drawings had long been hidden underneath a safe, all part of the Roberts Indian Store collection that Mrs. Bassity was organizing after the passing of her aunt, Nelia Mae Roberts. Recognizing the historical and cultural importance of the drawings, Mrs. Bassity contacted the museum and began the process of donating them, and other items from the Roberts collection, to the university. The family was concerned to see to it that these priceless works would be preserved and would become accessible to the native communities of Southwest Oklahoma from which they came as well as to scholars and the general public. The University of Oklahoma was honored to receive the gift, and the museum staff looks forward to preserving and interpreting the collection for generations to come.

After the Roberts-Bassity family rediscovered the drawings, Candace Greene of the National Museum of Natural History at the Smithsonian Institution played a part. First, she confirmed that Silver Horn was the artist/scholar responsible for them. Having already completed a study of Silver Horn's life and work, Dr. Greene was the ideal collaborator for this project. Beyond her scholarly credentials and firsthand acquaintance with many Kiowa people, she possessed the added benefit of knowing the Sam Noble Oklahoma Museum of Natural

History (SNOMNH) and its collections well, having long served on its staff as a curator of collections. The project's discovery phase provided the basis for ongoing work of interpretation and education. This volume is aimed at both of these goals, as are the exhibition and curriculum projects that have been developed to accompany it.

There is also the prospect of further discovery. Our hope is that publishing the calendar in full will enable Kiowa community members and scholars of Kiowa culture and history to draw upon it in new ways, both to strengthen educational and historical initiatives and to promote better understandings of Kiowa artistic, cultural, and social history. Publication of the calendar also makes it available to audiences interested in Native American art, Oklahoma history, and other topics that it touches. Most important, publication of the calendar, and especially the educational materials that the museum has prepared to accompany it, are intended to make it useful to younger audiences and their teachers, to enrich their studies both inside and outside the classroom.

On behalf of the museum and the university, a number of other people deserve thanks for their work on this project behind the scenes. Evelyena D. Honeymon provided the University of Oklahoma Foundation with key financial support that enabled the Roberts Indian Store collection to come to the university. Ron Burton and the staff of the OU Foundation worked hard to facilitate and promote this significant addition to the museum's collections. Michael Mares, former SNOMNH director, provided additional funding to ensure the collection's stabilization and its safe delivery to the museum.

Once it came to the university, conservation of the Silver Horn calendar was made possible by a valuable grant from the program Save America's Treasures. This work was undertaken by paper conservator Ellen Livesay-Holligan and directed by SNOMNH conservator Victoria Book. While the central goals of the *One Hundred Summers* project are educational and interpretive, publication also helps preserve the original document, making it available to many who would otherwise require hands-on study of the newly conserved, but still quite fragile, original document.

This project was the brainchild of Jason Jackson, associate professor of folklore at Indiana University and former assistant curator of ethnology at SNOMNH. Without his dedication to preserving and sharing Oklahoma's unique history, you would not be reading this book. A grant from the Institute of Museum and Library Services supported publication in a collaboration between the museum and the University of Nebraska Press and also funded development of educational materials to support its use in K–12 classrooms. Thanks go to the curriculum and book development consultants—Jim Anquoe, Sandranel Behan, John Chiodo, Wendy Gram, Delores Harragarra, Gus Palmer Jr., Barbara Schindler—as well as to Gary Dunham, former director of the University of Nebraska Press, and his staff.

It is my hope that Silver Horn's legacy can be an inspiration to all who read and enjoy this book. It is a moving illustration of how one person's record of cultural and natural occurrences can impact many generations to come.

Preface

Daniel C. Swan

The publication of *One Hundred Summers: A Kiowa Calendar Record* is an important event for the Department of Ethnology of the Sam Noble Oklahoma Museum of Natural History. The book represents the institutional strengths of ethnology at SNOMNH—collections stewardship, engaged scholarship, and public education. A spring 2009 exhibition of the Silver Horn calendar at SNOMNH is one step highlighting the historical and cultural insights gained from this important historical document and describing our efforts to conserve it. A second step is a website for teachers and students to facilitate use of the calendar to support curricula in geography, American history, and cultural studies.

Museums preserve and utilize their collections to stimulate the human experiences of exploration, discovery, contemplation, and discussion. The ethnology collections of SNOMNH are well positioned to address this mission on a global basis. In addition to the outstanding collection of Native North American objects in its worldwide ethnology holdings, the Department of Ethnology also curates important collections of fine art (including Native American painting and sculpture) and classical archaeology. The ethnology collections of the former Stovall Museum, and its successor, SNOMNH, have expanded through a variety of mechanisms and activities. Many of our core holdings are the result of generous gifts and donations by individuals and organizations. Two prominent examples are the Fred and Enid Brown Collection of Native American Art and the Dorothy Dunn–Santa Fe Indian School Painting Collection, which together provide important resources to explore the intersection between American Indian ethnography and art history. The department has also benefited from the systematic collecting and field research of numerous anthropologists, including Robert E. Bell, William Bittle, S. F. Borhegyi, A. F. Ricciardelli, Morris E. Opler, Karl Schmitt, and Willard Z. Park. As faculty members and affiliates in the Department of Anthropology at the University of Oklahoma they helped build the museum's ethnology collections and advanced our knowledge about them.

The Department of Ethnology has worked for many years to develop mutually beneficial partnerships with Native American communities in North America and especially within Oklahoma. A key objective is to provide broad access to collections and to encourage scholarly and community discourse on their historical and contemporary contextualization. The department is exploring a variety of projects to continue this legacy of engaged scholarship and community partnerships through electronic dissemination of collections and their associated documentation. Current efforts are focused on developing open-access publications, online access to the collections database, weblogs, and online exhibitions.

Two other social science sections at SNOMNH are the Department of Archaeology and the Department of Native American Languages. Together the three social science departments pursue a holistic approach to the study of cultural history and provide an important foundation for museum anthropology at the University of Oklahoma. Each department engages in a robust program of undergraduate and graduate instruction that incorporates research, service, and professional training opportunities.

Currently we are examining options regarding the reinstallation of the Hall of the People of Oklahoma, opened in conjunction with the completion of the new museum facility in 2000. The early twenty-first century has been a vital time for interpretation of Native American culture and heritage within museum settings. Evidence of the changing scene includes the opening of the National Museum of the American Indian in Washington DC; the increasing importance of tribal museums and cultural centers in Oklahoma; and construction of new and expanded facilities for several of the state's public museums, among them the National Cowboy and Western Heritage Museum, SNOMNH, Fred Jones Jr. Museum of Art, and the Oklahoma History Center. Development of the American Indian Cultural Center in Oklahoma City is another component in the evolving paradigm for interpretation of Native American culture and heritage in Oklahoma museums.

The Silver Horn calendar record is one important holding among the seven thousand objects curated in the Ethnology Department of the SNOMNH. These collections provide the cultural and intellectual capital for future programs stimulating discourse among scholars and the larger community.

Acknowledgments

This book owes its existence to the clear vision of the Sam Noble Oklahoma Museum of Natural History. Under the leadership of Dr. Ellen Censky, SNOMNH has been a model of museum practice in all things relating to the Silver Horn calendar. As soon as the staff received this book of drawings, they recognized that it would be of enormous interest to Kiowa people and to scholars but also realized that it was too fragile to survive repeated examination. The museum resolved this dilemma by securing support for publication to make the material widely available for reference, and then went on to find support for conservation to ensure continued preservation of the drawings. I deeply appreciate then curator Jason Jackson's invitation to prepare the book for publication, as well as the enormous support that his successor Daniel Swan has provided in moving the publication along, while developing plans for an accompanying exhibition. It was a pleasure to work with conservator Victoria Book, who was introduced to Plains art through an internship at the Smithsonian, and with graduate assistant Michael Jordan, a devoted student of Kiowa art and also a former intern. Many thanks to Wendy Gram, head of the museum's education department, who organized a workshop to develop supporting curriculum materials and brought in OU Professor of Education John Chiodo to create teaching resources based on the Kiowa calendar for use in secondary schools. My thanks to the whole museum—a great team to work with!

The book benefited enormously from collaboration with OU Professor of Anthropology Gus Palmer Jr., who prepared the Kiowa glossary. A native speaker as well as a trained linguist, he labored heroically (and cheerfully) to make sense of the mangled versions of Kiowa names recorded long ago by James Mooney, a brilliant ethnologist although evidently possessed of a tin ear. Thanks to Gus, Kiowa people will be able to connect more of these entries to their family history. I also thank him for his insights on the deeper meaning of some entries and his thoughts on the best way to present them to readers.

I am deeply indebted to the wider Kiowa community, where I have invariably found a welcome as well as a strong interest in both preserving and sharing their culture history, so beautifully embodied in distinctive pictorial calendars. The Silverhorn family stands first among these connections; I have been honored to meet and work with many of them on this and previous projects. Conversations with many other Kiowa people informed my readings of the pictures. Special thanks for assistance on this project to Jacob Ahtone, Jim Anquoe, Dorothy Whitehorse Delaun, Delores Harragarra, Kenny Harragarra, Vanessa Jennings and her husband Paul, Gus Palmer Sr., and Florene Whitehorse Taylor.

Marcia and CB Bassity generously shared their memories of Marcia's Great Aunt Nelia, just as they generously placed her collection with the SNOMNH. All of us are indebted to them for ensuring that the Kiowa calendar was preserved where it could be enjoyed by many people.

Consultation with several archival repositories was involved in pinning down specific dates and places for entries in the calendar, tying them together with Kiowa memories. Towana Spivey of the Fort Sill Museum has been of immense assistance on this and other projects over the years, sharing both collection resources and personal knowledge relating to the historic post. The staff of the Oklahoma Historical Society guided me to many useful sources. Thanks particularly to Jeff Briley, Mary

Jane Ward, and Bill Wehlge. Betty Layton made my work at the American Baptist Historical Society, poring over the Reverend Treat's papers, particularly rewarding.

Colleagues Mike Jordan, Tom Kavanagh, Bill Meadows, and Doug Parks generously shared their knowledge to help me sort out various details, while the expert reviewers of the manuscript saved me from several errors. I would like to thank Smithsonian colleagues Jake Homiak, director of the Anthropology Collections and Archives Program, for his continued support; Marcia Bakry, anthropology illustrator, for production of the map of Kiowa territory; and Robert Leopold and Stephanie Ogeneski of the National Anthropological Archives for numerous images from that collection.

Endless thanks for personal and logistical support go to Julie and Farrel Droke for providing an Oklahoma home away from home and to Will Greene and Emily Greene for their love and support, not to mention digital editing and graphics production.

Note on Language

The Kiowa language contains many sounds that cannot be represented accurately using the standard English alphabet. Linguists have developed a system of special phonetic notation that can be used to represent the sounds of any language. However, the Kiowa have their own system for writing their language. It was developed in about the 1930s by Parker McKenzie, a Kiowa who was fascinated with the study of his native language. He was familiar with existing systems of linguistic notation, but he wanted something simpler that could be produced on the standard manual typewriter of the time. He taught this system both to Kiowas interested in writing their language and to non-Kiowa linguists and scholars who were studying it. The Parker McKenzie orthography has been adopted by the Kiowa Tribe as the official form of the written language and is used in language retention programs.

In order to make this book more easily readable by people not familiar with Kiowa, most names and terms are presented here translated into English or with commonly used Anglicized spellings. Some of these spellings are so far from their Kiowa origins that the original form has been lost. Most, however, can be recognized by contemporary Kiowa speakers. In order to capture some of the original meanings of those terms as well as their correct sounds, we invited Dr. Gus Palmer Jr., a Kiowa anthropologist and linguist, to prepare a Kiowa glossary with a pronunciation guide, which appears at the end of the volume.

One Hundred Summers

I

The Kiowa Calendar Tradition

Much of the history of the Native people of North America as taught in schools is based on written records—government documents and observations passed on by literate travelers, traders, missionaries, and military men who came into contact with American Indians for brief or lengthy periods of time. Native peoples' own records of their history were long carried primarily in oral form, stories about the past that were handed on from generation to generation. Among some tribes of the Great Plains, these oral traditions were supplemented with pictorial records. This book presents one of those pictorial records, a calendar kept by the Kiowa artist Silver Horn covering one hundred years of his tribe's history from the summer of 1828 to the winter of 1928–29.

Pictorial Calendars

The Kiowa called their calendar *sai-guat*, which can be translated as winter marks or winter pictures. The calendar was a document that recorded a series of years by means of pictures standing for events that occurred over time. The Kiowa calendar recorded two events each year, one for the summer season and one for the winter. Although both seasons were marked, the calendars were called "winter marks" as the word for year is the same as the word for winter, and years were counted by winters. Each entry in the calendar represented a half a year, and these were named after a memorable event rather than given a sequential number as in the Western calendar system. Instead of 1861, the entry was known as the summer that they tied the spotted horse, followed by the smallpox winter (1861–62). These chronological entries were standardized and widely known, serving as a shared reference system for all of the Kiowa. It was the responsibility of an individual designated as a calendar keeper to maintain this shared reference work, remembering the stories associated with each entry, keeping the entries in proper order, and adding new ones as time passed. In order to keep all this information in proper order, calendar keepers drew pictorial charts with simple mnemonic images suggesting a key element of the seasonal designation that would serve to bring to mind the associated event. The word *guat*, which comes from the act of marking or painting, has continued in use to designate writing, and the charts must have served the calendar keepers much like written notes.

The events recorded in the calendar entries were not necessarily ones of great importance. It was more important that they be distinctive or memorable. Kiowa history was carried primarily in people's memories, transmitted through oral tradition. The calendar was used to position such memories in time. Events would be remembered as having taken place in the summer or winter of a named event. Reference to the calendar could establish the relative sequence of other events, which one came first, and how much time there was between the two. Some were the stuff of communal history, events that affected the whole tribe or band, but people commonly used the calendars to reference their personal history as well—births, deaths, first war expeditions, or buffalo hunts. Silver Horn reported that he was born in the summer that Bird Appearing was killed, which we know as 1860. His brother Hauvahte was born in the winter that the woman was frozen (1851–52), which the calendar records as occurring nine years earlier.

The Kiowa were not the only North American tribe who

kept pictorial calendars.[1] A few other Plains Indian tribes also kept such pictorial records, generally known as "winter counts." Those of the Lakota, or Western Sioux, are the best known, but counts have been recorded from the Blackfoot, Mandan, Hidatsa, and Cheyenne as well as the Plains Apache, close affiliates of the Kiowa.[2] Other tribes may well have kept some sort of calendric records as well. Some of these records reach back much farther in time than the Kiowa calendar, some beginning in the eighteenth century, and it seems likely that the Kiowa did not originate the idea. The Kiowa calendar system is unique, however, in recording two events for each year, offering a finer grained record of the passage of time and twice as many entries for any given period.

Much of our knowledge about the origins and history of Kiowa calendars comes from the work of the Smithsonian anthropologist James Mooney. Mooney began intensive work with the Kiowa in Indian Territory in 1892, and he published his *Calendar History of the Kiowa Indians* in the 17th Annual Report of the Bureau of American Ethnology, which appeared in 1898. Kiowa people told him that the first calendar keeper in their tribe was Little Bluff, or Tohausan, who was the principal chief of the tribe from 1833 to 1866.[3] Some of Mooney's information came from Little Bluff's nephew, also called Little Bluff, who took over responsibility for maintaining the calendar after his uncle's death, but Mooney also worked with two other calendar keepers, Settan, or Little Bear, and Ankopaingyadete, In the Middle of Many Tracks, commonly known as Anko. Throughout his wide-ranging research on Kiowa culture, Mooney found that many of the men he interviewed had a keen sense of history.[4] They were interested in their tribal past, and they commonly placed events in time by referring to the calendar. Following their lead, he used the calendar as the central device around which to organize all of the historical information he assembled about the Kiowa. Using it as a framework, he drew together historical narratives from many Kiowa men, which he supplemented with information from various non-Kiowa sources, including government documents and correspondence with former Indian agents.

The calendars that Mooney acquired from Little Bear and Anko consisted of very simple pictures drawn on paper, although Mooney had some copied onto a deerskin to make a more impressive-looking specimen.[5] Little Bluff's calendar, which was acquired by the scholarly warrior Lt. Hugh Scott around the same time, consists of similarly simple figures drawn in pencil on a sheet of brown paper. Clearly the calendar keepers viewed these as utilitarian mnemonic devices intended to keep events in the proper sequence. Calendars were copied over when they became worn, or when more space was needed for new entries, and the old versions were discarded. Readily available materials were used, originally buffalo hides but later manufactured trade materials when they became available.[6]

Calendars were not the major form of pictorial art on the Plains, however, and the Kiowa had a number of highly gifted artists who lavished attention to produce beautiful and highly detailed drawings. Representational art—pictures of things one can recognize—was the exclusive domain of men, and most drawings represented men's personal accomplishments, especially their military honors. Women had their own art forms, painting geometric designs on buffalo robes or rawhide cases as well as executing them in beadwork. Early Kiowa paintings on hide have not been preserved, but a wealth of works on paper survive from the last quarter of the nineteenth century, most on the pages of blank ledger books or on the leaves of artists' sketchbooks.[7] Unlike the simple calendar pictures, those drawings include many details of the events they illustrate.

We see figures on horseback charging the enemy, fully illustrated with details of war gear, weaponry, and wounds given and received. Although we usually are not able to recognize the hero by name, surely a knowledgeable Kiowa viewer of the time could. And with only a little study, we can begin to

FIGURE 1-1. Kiowa drawing (detail) showing White Horse capturing a Navajo boy. By Koba or Etahleuh, 1875–78. MS 39c. Courtesy of the National Anthropological Archives, Smithsonian Institution.

reconstruct the entire encounter from the drawing alone. These pictures were intended to narrate an event, not merely to allude to it through the spare mnemonic figures of the calendars. Unlike the calendars, however, these pictures are not arranged in careful chronological order but are more random in their placement, following idiosyncratic patterns of association. Detailed as they are about "what" and "who," Plains drawings seldom provide information about "where" and "when." Such information was transmitted in oral rather than visual form. James Mooney found that old Kiowa warriors often dated such events by reference to the calendar.

Silver Horn, or Haungooah, was a rare individual who both kept a calendar and made other types of drawings. He was an enormously prolific and gifted artist, and his skill in drawing as well as his impulse to convey information in graphic form have resulted in a calendar that is unique in the power of its images and the amount of information that they convey. His pictures are much more elaborate than those made by any other calendar keeper, and one often can guess what a picture represents even without an accompanying text, though some background on Kiowa history and culture is helpful.

The Kiowa

The Kiowa are a Southern Plains people, many of whom still live in southwestern Oklahoma on lands that were once part of the Kiowa reservation. The reservation, shared with the Comanche and Apache, was established in the mid-nineteenth century, its boundaries defined by the 1867 Medicine Lodge Treaty with the U.S. government. The reservation was part of a much wider territory that the Kiowa previously claimed as their own. Their earliest oral traditions record that they once lived near the headwaters of the Yellowstone River, in the foothills of the Rocky Mountains in what is now Montana. Sometime during the eighteenth century they moved eastward onto the open plains. No doubt they were attracted by new hunting strategies made possible by the introduction of horses, which had been brought to North America by the Spanish when they colonized Mexico and the greater Southwest. Bison, or buffaloes as they are usually called, were abundant on the Plains and provided not only meat for food but also hides to make tipi covers and warm bedding. People had been hunting bison since ancient times, but horses made it possible to travel farther to locate the moving herds, to hunt these huge animals more efficiently, and to transport quantities of preserved meat and hides.

Other tribes were also moving onto the Plains around this time, attracted by the same opportunities, and it was an era of conflict as different groups sought to stake their claims to hunting territories. The Kiowa jostled their way south, fighting for territory when they needed to, forming alliances with neighboring groups when they could. By the time that this pictorial calendar history begins in 1828, they were well established in an area that takes in lands now part of Oklahoma, Texas, Kansas,

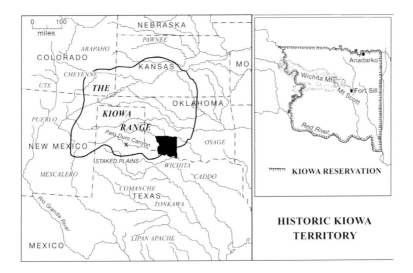

FIGURE 1-2. Nineteenth-century Kiowa territory and subsequent reservation boundaries. Map created by Marcia Bakry, Smithsonian Institution.

and Colorado. They had for decades been allied with the Comanche, another powerful people of the southern Plains, but as we shall see in the calendar, they were enemies of the Cheyenne and Arapaho, who were moving into this territory. This large region was their hunting territory and their home base, but the Kiowa looked beyond it for other resources. Mexican and American settlements to their south and west maintained huge herds of horses, and the Kiowa expanded their hunting economy to include raiding for horses that could profitably be exchanged with traders and settlers as well as with other tribes to the north and east. This pattern of long distance raiding and trading is reflected in the calendar, with entries referring to encounters far south into Mexico and north as far as the villages of the Upper Missouri River. Summer encampments, however, where tribal members gathered to celebrate the Medicine Lodge ceremony, the Kiowa form of the Sun Dance, cluster in a rough circle about three hundred miles in diameter centered on the Oklahoma panhandle.

American expansion into this region brought a new player into the struggle for territory. American traders were welcomed at first. They were a good alternative to the Comancheros, as the itinerant Spanish traders from Santa Fe were known. They offered a different source of manufactured goods that could be obtained in exchange for buffalo robes and dried meat—or horses. Once Charles Bent's trading post was permanently established in what is now southeastern Colorado, the Kiowa were glad to travel there rather than to the trading villages of the Missouri River. The calendar records amicable encounters with a number of other traders who established posts briefly within Kiowa territory. Aside from bright lengths of cloth and durable metal kettles, firearms and associated ammunition had become indispensable to the Kiowa, as to other tribes on the Plains. Although bow and arrows (now tipped with iron) remained the preferred weapon for buffalo hunting, a tribe without firearms could not hold their hunting territory against intruders who were better armed. Traders were critical to maintaining access to now essential trade goods.

The commercial buffalo hunters who followed the traders were bitterly resented, however. They constituted direct competition for resources. Even before their numbers were sufficient to reduce the bison population significantly, commercial hunters scattered the herds and reduced the efficiency of the great summer hunt on which Native people relied for a major supply of dried meat. Among the Kiowa as in other tribes, the communal hunt was carefully policed to ensure that no one started out ahead of the others and spooked the selected herd into dispersing. Anyone who violated the rules would be punished, perhaps whipped, his weapons broken, even his horse killed. But the white buffalo hunters followed no such rules, and the Kiowa sought to check them, just as they challenged anyone who threatened their territorial resources.

Horse raiding became an increasingly essential part of the Kiowa economy. As long as the horses came from Mexican territory or from the Republic of Texas, the U.S. government had no objections to this pattern of activity. Once New Mexico and Texas were incorporated within the United States, Kiowa raiding in the same areas they had always exploited was redefined as an attack upon U.S. citizens and their property. Horse raiding and attacks on commercial hunters provoked retaliation by the U.S. Army. To reduce conflict, the government sought to draw lines separating the Kiowa (and other raiding tribes) from American citizens, using a series of treaties that defined territories and established forts to maintain them, but these divisions made little difference to anyone. Hide hunters and settlers continued to drift into Kiowa lands, and Kiowa raiders continued to strike where they chose. The American Civil War brought the Kiowa some respite from these pressures as military attention was occupied elsewhere, but it was a brief pause in the process of American expansion. After the war, railroad lines expanded across the West, solving a major problem that commercial buffalo hunters had always faced—how to transport the heavy hides to eastern markets. The hide hunters descended like a plague of locusts, and in the mid-1870s the Southern Plains herds were destroyed, converted into rotting carcasses and heaps of hides rapidly being transformed into belts for industrial machinery. Only small and widely scattered groups of animals survived.[8]

The Kiowa joined with other Southern Plains tribes in resisting this onslaught upon their territory and way of life. U.S. Army troops were dispatched to force the Kiowa into the confines of the reservation as defined by the Medicine Lodge Treaty of 1867, which land they were to share with the Comanche and Apache. Some band leaders saw this as inevitable, while others actively resisted. By early 1875 all of the Kiowa had been forced to surrender and were confined to the reservation.

The first half of the calendar published here records the years prior to settlement on the reservation; the second half deals with the reservation period and what came after. It was a period of hunger and hardship, of graft and corruption, of cultural and religious oppression. But as the calendar reveals, it was also a period of resistance and resiliency, of cultural creativity and religious revitalization.

The reservation economy was based on resources issued by the government rather than on hunting or raiding. The Medicine Lodge Treaty had promised various resources in exchange for land—rations of food, clothing, and canvas for tipi covers to be issued annually for thirty years. The government further agreed to expend some $25,000 each year to provide for other needs. None of this was expected to yield an adequate living, but it would serve as a supplement while the Kiowa learned to use their remaining land base for agriculture. The treaty anticipated that the Kiowa would make a ready transition to farming, adapting themselves to the basic economic model of rural America. It anticipated that the Kiowa would eventually give up communal, tribally held land and welcome title to individually owned farms, and it included a provision that further land cessions could be made with the consent of three quarters of the adult male population.[9]

In fact this transition was fraught with problems. First, the government proved to be a poor partner. Resources were all funneled through the Department of Indian Affairs, which was notoriously corrupt. Contracts were awarded on the basis of bribes, and the rations issued were often underweight and of poor quality. Second, the Kiowa did not embrace the idea of farming with any enthusiasm. It was not a part of their heritage and was considered a demeaning form of labor. Stock raising might have had greater likelihood of success, but it did not fit the economic model the government had chosen. Stock required substantial tracts of land for grazing, and Indian policy was committed to individual ownership of small tracts. American cattlemen, however, were able to arrange leases that permitted them to graze their herds on reservation lands. Payments from the lease of grazing rights, which the Indians called "grass money," became another modest source of income to the Kiowa during the reservation period.[10]

This precarious economy was overturned for a second time within twenty years when Congress passed the General Allotment

Act. As arable land in the West filled up, there was growing political pressure on Congress to open Indian reservations to general settlement. If members of each tribe could be allotted individual pieces of land as homesteads, the remainder of their territory could be similarly platted and opened to non-Indian settlers. The terms of the Medicine Lodge Treaty required tribal approval to dissolve the reservation, and a government commission under the leadership of David H. Jerome was dispatched to Indian Territory to secure such agreement—by any means necessary. The commission soon returned to Washington, proclaiming that they had secured the signatures necessary to indicate tribal approval. Under the terms of the Jerome Agreement the land was platted into parcels of 160 acres each. Tribal members were required to select individual parcels, or allotments, and the remainder of the reservation was to be purchased by the government and opened to claim by homesteaders.[11] However, the Kiowa under the leadership of Chief Lone Wolf protested that "tribal approval" had been obtained by fraud. They asserted that people had been tricked into agreeing through false translation of what the commissioners said at meetings as well as through direct misrepresentation. In any case, the number of signatures obtained was not adequate. Further, it had been their understanding that the terms of the Medicine Lodge Treaty were to stand without revision for a period of thirty years, which the calendar made clear had not yet elapsed. Such tribal protests, vigorously supported by a number of independent observers, slowed but could not prevent congressional approval. The Kiowa-Comanche-Apache Reservation was opened to settlement in 1901. Ration issues stopped, and the Kiowa were expected to function as self-sufficient farmers, their meager incomes supplemented by annuities on interest from land sales and periodic grass money.

From the beginning of the reservation, the U.S. government was committed to transforming not only the Kiowa economy but many aspects of people's lives. Native religious practices, such as the Medicine Lodge, or Kado, were suppressed by the government, and various Christian denominations were encouraged to establish missions on the reservation. Children were required to attend school where Native hair styles and clothing were not allowed and English was the only language permitted. In addition to lessons in reading and writing, they received vocational instruction in farming and housewifery. The agency employed field matrons and resident farmers to visit people's homes and camps and instruct them in the new economy as well as to report on disapproved practices. Agents freely used their power to withhold rations as a means of forcing compliance with government programs. Even in the post-reservation period, agents exercised enormous authority over annuity payments and other economic resources.

Silver Horn's calendar illuminates much about Kiowa life during this period of intense pressure for assimilation. It reveals that the Kiowa continued to maintain a distinct cultural life, continuing old traditions as well developing new ones.

Although the Kiowa certainly did not invite these new institutions that were being forced upon them, they found some to be compatible with traditional values, and these they embraced as their own. As a warrior society, they understood and respected military service. A number of men, including Silver Horn, enlisted in Troop L, an all-Indian unit of the Seventh Cavalry based at Fort Sill. Others joined the agency police force. A variety of Christian denominations attracted members, although not necessarily to the exclusion of other forms of worship, as we shall see. A spiritual people, the Kiowa acknowledged that there might be many routes to spiritual power.[12] Surprisingly, even the boarding schools where children were separated from their families and sternly forced into new patterns were often viewed favorably by Kiowa people, who believed that such education was essential to cope with the new world in which they lived.[13]

Other changes arose from within Kiowa society and were purely Native in origin, although often drawing upon intertribal sources as had always been the case. The reservation years were an era of intense religious activity as people prayed for spiritual inspiration to cope with the cycle of hunger and disease that had descended upon them. The Medicine Lodge ceremony, with its close associations with bison hunting, faltered and died. The government claimed credit for crushing it, citing military disruption of the 1890 ceremony, which appears in the calendar as the "unfinished Kado." The Kiowa say rather that they "put it away" because the disappearance of the bison meant that the ceremony could no longer be performed properly, and indeed the erratic performance of the ceremony in the preceding years supports this.[14] Twice in the 1880s men received visions revealing ceremonies to restore the buffalo to the land, and twice people were cruelly disappointed by their failure. The 1881–82 event is noted in this calendar, but the effort of 1888 is not. The Ghost Dance, a messianic movement sweeping the Plains, had a longer impact on the Kiowa. As initially received from the Arapaho in 1892, the ceremony sought to restore the buffalo and expel the white intruders, and it received only a brief acceptance among the Kiowa. Within a few years it was reinterpreted by Kiowa prophets with a new goal of assisting people to reestablish connection with their lost loved ones through dancing and trance. Called the Feather Dance, it continued as an active spiritual practice until well into the 1920s; Silver Horn's calendar notes many participants, identified by a single feather marked with a cross.[15] Dances built on the model of the warrior societies also grew during the reservation period. Notable was the Ohoma Society, led by White Horse, which the calendar shows in 1917. The Peyote religion, incorporated today as the Native American Church, developed into its modern form during the reservation years on the Kiowa-Comanche-Apache Reservation. Although Silver Horn was a Peyote man and produced a rich series of images of the ceremony elsewhere, this religious movement is almost invisible in his calendar. The only entries related to it mark the deaths of Peyote participants (see 1888 and 1910–11).

Technological innovations in transportation that linked the Kiowa into a wider world appear often in the calendar. Trains are depicted in a number of entries, often the railroad that carried Lone Wolf to Washington on his numerous trips to oppose the Jerome Agreement. With the establishment of the army air corps at Fort Sill in 1914, the Kiowa became among the first people in the United States to see airplanes circling high above on a regular basis. Automobiles made their entrance in due time, though the only one that Silver Horn included in his calendar (1921–22) is shown upside down, its driver an early traffic fatality.

Social life had always revolved around a series of culturally defined units—from family, band, and tribe to wider affiliations with Indian and non-Indian communities. The calendar shows that these all continued to remain vital although they might find expression through new outlets. Intertribal visiting was an active part of reservation life in Indian Territory, in which formerly distant tribes were brought into closer proximity. Silver Horn recorded visits in 1882 and 1883 of some Nez Perce, a tribe recently exiled from their Idaho homeland. While most tribal gatherings were discouraged by the government agents in charge, summer "picnics" to celebrate the Fourth of July were permitted, and a large Kiowa camp came together for a period of days, much like the old Kado encampments. Christian church camp meetings were actively encouraged, and Silver Horn marked tent revivals for the summers of 1922 and 1925. Although prohibited, the Feather Dance continued to unite communities in gatherings that combined social and spiritual elements. The calendar marks one such summer gathering in 1911.

Then as now, family was the essential foundation of Kiowa society. Kiowa people today speak of the numerous calendars that began to be kept in the late nineteenth and early twentieth century as "family calendars," viewing them as distinct from the tribal record maintained by Little Bluff. While most of the early entries are drawn directly from that tribal record, the later years are oriented toward events that occurred within the local community, linked together by complex networks of kinship and containing many records of family births and deaths.

Silver Horn and a Family of Calendar Keepers

Silver Horn, or Haungooah, was the most highly esteemed artist of the Kiowa tribe in the late nineteenth and early twentieth century and a respected religious leader in his later years. While many people changed their names throughout their lives, he did not, retaining the powerful name he had been given in a special ceremony when a child. Haungooah, translated variously as either Silver or Iron Horn, was the name of the spirit buffalo with horns of metal that the Kiowa culture heroes, the Split Boys, had to overcome in ancient times.[16]

He was born in the Summer that Bird Appearing was Killed, recorded as 1860 in the Western calendar, during the era when the Kiowa lived a nomadic life based on buffalo hunting and horse raiding. He died in December 1940, a winter without a name, for his was the last generation to maintain the calendars marking years by name rather than number.[17] He was born into an important family. His father Agiati, or Gathering Feathers, a distinguished war chief and band leader, was the nephew (sister's son) of Little Bluff (Tohausan), who was the principal chief of the Kiowa for over thirty years. Silver Horn's mother, one of Agiati's three wives, was named Seipote, which can be translates as Traveling in Rain. Her brother Patadal, Poor Buffalo, was a noted war chief before the Kiowa were confined to the reservation and became a powerful spiritual leader of the Ghost Dance in later years.

Silver Horn was in his mid-teens when the Kiowa finally were forced to surrender and accept the confines of the reservation. Agiati established his camp in the Mount Scott area, and many of the people and events referenced in the calendar during the reservation years are from that region. It was here that he was registered as allottee number 94, duly receiving a rocky patch of 160 acres adjacent to that of other family and band members,

FIGURE 1-3. Silver Horn. Photograph by Gilbert McAllister, 1932. Courtesy of the Sam Noble Oklahoma Museum of Natural History, Norman, Oklahoma.

who continued to camp together. Some time after his marriage to Tanguma, Bending Knee Woman, in the summer of 1901, he and his growing family relocated to his wife's allotment on the eastern edge of the reservation near the town of Stecker. This brought him closer to the Red Stone community, where a number of relatives lived, including his brothers Lean Elk, White Buffalo Konad, and Oheltoint or Charlie Buffalo. Many of the twentieth-century entries in the calendar relate to local events in Red Stone and the surrounding area, so much so that many were also reported in a newsletter published during that time by the minister of the Red Stone Baptist Mission.[18]

Silver Horn lived until 1940, and older Kiowa people today remember him as an artist who produced many types of objects for use within their own community. He was a silversmith, working both in sterling silver, often made from coins, and in German silver, an alloy that can be purchased in sheet form. He did beadwork and featherwork, crafting ritual objects to be used in ceremonies, both the Ghost Dance and the Peyote church. Few people outside his immediate family realized that he was also a graphic artist, for although he produced hundreds of drawings, he sold most of these outside the Kiowa community. For a few years he worked intermittently as an illustrator for the Smithsonian anthropologist James Mooney, producing drawings on paper and paintings on hides as well as models of tipi covers and war shields painted with traditional designs. Mooney arranged for old warriors and other knowledgeable people to describe the designs on these important items to Silver Horn, who drew them on paper and later painted buckskin models of many.

Silver Horn also applied his graphic skills to one type of object that he kept for himself—calendars. He produced at least three different calendar records. The book illustrated here seems to be one that he kept over a period of years, adding new entries over time. His grandchildren remembered that he had a calendar in a "big book" that he would sometimes let them look at, and this may be it. Measuring about six inches by fifteen inches, this book is not especially large, but it may have seemed so to small children. In 1904 Silver Horn drew a calendar for the anthropologist James Mooney, working in a field notebook that Mooney brought with him from Washington. That calendar, which is in the Smithsonian's National Anthropological Archives (NAA), is more elaborately illustrated than the one published here.[19] The figures in it are smaller and more crowded, and he included illustrations not only of the main event from which the season took its name but often of several other things that occurred in each year as well. Silver Horn's youngest son, Max Silverhorn Sr., remembered yet another form of calendar that his father kept. This third calendar was drawn on a long strip of cloth with the entries following each other in a long line. The location of this strip calendar is not known, but several other Kiowa calendars used this same format (see appendix C).

The calendar published here, which I refer to as the OU calendar to distinguish it from Silver Horn's record in the NAA, has pictures but no accompanying written text. Silver Horn, like other calendar keepers, did not need one, and indeed he was not literate. He would have known what event each picture stood for, as well as the stories that went with them, and the fixed marks in the book ensured that each was kept in the proper sequence. For those of us not trained as calendar keepers, however, the pictures are enigmatic. Silver Horn's skilled graphic details provide clues to recognition but are not sufficient for us to understand fully the events that they depict. Fortunately there are several other calendars available with explanations of entries provided by the calendar keepers, capturing at least the name of the season and sometimes more discursive information. A number of these calendars were made by members of Silver Horn's own family.

The calendar most closely related to the OU one is of course the calendar that Silver Horn made for James Mooney, now in the NAA. It begins the same year as the OU calendar and ends in 1904. The drawings in the NAA book are much more elaborate and detailed than those in the OU calendar, but both cover the same basic events for the years they share. At the time the NAA book was produced, Mooney was deeply involved in a study of Kiowa shield and tipi designs and was regularly employing Silver Horn as an artist. Mooney had already published his calendar study by this time, and he did not record anything in his notes about how or why Silver Horn made this calendar.

FIGURE 1-4. Page from the calendar that Silver Horn produced for James Mooney, covering the period from summer 1840 to winter 1842–43. MS 2531, vol. 7. Courtesy of the National Anthropological Archives, Smithsonian Institution.

Probably Mooney learned that Silver Horn had a calendar of his own and asked him to make a copy of it as a part of his regular employment. It is drawn in the same type of government notebook that Mooney was using himself that year.

Once the new calendar was completed, Silver Horn and other men must have explained the meaning of each of the pictures while Mooney quickly jotted abbreviated notes directly on the face of the drawings. Unfortunately Mooney's writing is difficult to decipher. His handwriting was terrible under the best of circumstances, and it is especially so in these tiny notes, which were written partly in English and partly in Kiowa, with many abbreviations. Perhaps he intended to transcribe them in a more organized form at a later date, but that evidently never happened. While it is not possible to craft an organized text from these fragmentary bits, they are nevertheless useful in interpreting the OU calendar, as are Silver Horn's lovely pictures themselves.

A second useful reference is a calendar kept by Silver Horn's brother Hauvahte, whose name translates something like Hill Slope. Silver Horn and Hauvahte had the same father, Agiati

(Gathering Feathers), but different mothers. Hauvahte was nine years older than Silver Horn, but the two brothers had an especially close relationship. According to Silver Horn's son James, Hauvahte taught his younger brother many things, including calendar keeping.[20] The two calendars themselves support this, as they are almost identical in coverage, including missing entries for the same years.

In 1909 Mark Harrington, a collector for the newly founded Museum of the American Indian, purchased a pictorial calendar that Hauvahte had drawn on the pages of a notebook. Working through an interpreter, Hauvahte explained to Harrington what each entry represented. The picture calendar itself has been lost but the accompanying text that Harrington wrote down is still preserved in the archives of what is now the National Museum of the American Indian. While it is not possible to compare the pictures, the text fits well with the pictorial entries in Silver Horn's OU calendar. Hauvahte's explanations help to clarify and expand upon information in the NAA calendar, and they provide information for five additional years. A transcription of Harrington's handwritten text appears at the end of this volume as appendix B.

Silver Horn and Hauvahte were continuing a family tradition of calendar keeping. Their great-uncle Little Bluff, the famous principal chief, was also a calendar keeper, probably the first of the Kiowa to keep such a record.[21] Some time before his death in 1866 he had given his name as well as the responsibility for maintaining the calendar to his nephew Agiati, Silver Horn's father. The nephew accepted this responsibility for maintaining the calendar, continuing to add a new entry each season up until the time of his death in 1892.

Shortly before his death this second Little Bluff made a copy of the calendar for Lt. Hugh L. Scott, a cavalry officer and avocational anthropologist who served at Fort Sill in Indian Territory for several years. The calendar, still preserved in the collection of the Phoebe Apperson Hearst Museum of Anthropology at the University of California at Berkeley, is roughly drawn on a large sheet of brown paper. Scott interviewed Little Bluff as opportunity permitted over several weeks and recorded the meaning of each entry. They had reached the winter of 1867–68 at the time of the old man's death. Scott was able to fill in information on the rest of the years working with a Kiowa scout named Iseeo, or Plenty Fires. Scott's handwritten notes are in the archives of the Fort Sill Museum in Oklahoma. A transcription of them appears at the end of this book as appendix A.

James Mooney was working on his *Calendar History of the Kiowa Indians* at this time, and Scott loaned him these notes to use in that research.[22] Acknowledging the primacy of the Little Bluff calendar, Mooney presented it as the central reference point of his study of calendar history, though he incorporated information from many other sources. He worked with two additional calendar keepers, Little Bear (Settan) and Anko, and a number of respected older men gave him more details about each entry as well as about other events that could be tied to the calendars. The publication was actually illustrated with pictures from the Little Bear calendar, which Mooney had acquired for the Smithsonian.[23] Mooney added further information from government documents and other written sources. These diverse sources provide a rich and detailed account, respecting both Kiowa and Euroamerican historical perspectives in a way that was unique at the time. Mooney's study remains the primary source for understanding the Kiowa calendars and the events that they record up to 1892.

Mooney's effective integration of these diverse sources can make it difficult to trace the independent lines of each calendar to compare them. However, the discovery of Scott's original notes on the Little Bluff calendar (appendix A) makes much clearer the distinction between that calendar and the one maintained by Anko. Surprisingly, Silver Horn's and Hauvahte's calendars match the entries in the Anko record more closely than they do the Little Bluff record maintained by their father and his uncle before him.

Another calendar that corresponds closely to the events recorded by Silver Horn and Hauvahte is one that belonged to Jimmy Quitone, or Wolf Tail.[24] It was studied and recorded by Wilbur Nye in the 1930s, with the help of George Hunt, one of Quitone's sons, who often assisted Nye as an interpreter.[25] Quitone told Nye that it had been drawn by Hauvahte. Another son, Guy Quoetone, later explained that the family turned it over to his father when Hauvahte died.[26] The calendar continues until 1922, Quitone evidently having taken on the responsibility for adding entries for these later years, perhaps in consultation with others. The location of the original calendar, which appears to have been drawn on a long strip of cloth, is not known. Nye believed that it was probably destroyed when Quitone's house burned in 1937. Fortunately Nye had made a tracing-paper copy of the calendar, which is preserved together with his notes in the archives of the Fort Sill Museum.[27] Quitone, Hunt, and Nye worked together to record the meaning of each entry, jotting notes on the tracing as well as recording a more organized text in a notebook. Sadly, this enterprise was never finished; the text ends at the entry for 1864.

In 2002 the National Anthropological Archives acquired another calendar that is almost identical to the Quitone calendar as recorded by Nye. It covers the same period of years and marks them with the same images, although in this version the pictures are drawn on sheets of heavy card stock, first in pencil then reinforced with ink with watercolor additions. The pictures replicate the basic outlines of figures in the Nye tracing, but with less precision and detail, appearing to have been slavishly copied from that source by someone with limited graphic experience. Nothing is known about the origin of this calendar other than that it was acquired in Oklahoma some years previously. It could have been copied either from the now lost Quitone calendar or from Nye's replica of it.[28]

Quitone's son George Hunt also had a calendar of some sort. Its location is not known, but Alice Marriott included the text

FIGURE 1-5. Sheet from the NAA copy of the Quitone calendar, showing the winter of 1845–46 and the following summer. MS 2002-27. Courtesy of the National Anthropological Archives, Smithsonian Institution.

from it in her book *The Ten Grandmothers*, although without any information on the physical form of the calendar or its history. Marriott worked closely with the Hunt family for several years, but her original notes on the calendar, unfortunately incomplete, are dated 1935.[29] The entries correlate closely with those recorded up to 1864 for the Quitone calendar and match with the Quitone pictures for the remaining years available for comparison. For some reason, Marriott used 1900–1901 as the cutoff for all the calendars she published in her appendix. The Hunt record can be considered yet another version of the

Quitone calendar, itself a continuation of the calendar kept by Silver Horn's brother Hauvahte.

A number of other Kiowa calendars are preserved in public and family collections, with more coming to light over time. All of them have many entries in common, especially for the years prior to 1892. Jake Ahtone, nephew of Jimmy Quitone, suggested to me that this was because many more people began keeping calendars after Mooney published his *Calendar History of the Kiowa Indians.* They used Mooney's book and its entries up to 1892 as a starting reference, choosing their own events to mark the subsequent years. After that date, the calendars are more variable as different keepers choose different events to memorialize, many of them family centered. These other calendars, listed in appendix C, were particularly useful to me in deciphering the meaning of the entries in the final twenty years of the OU calendar. While none correlates closely in these years with Silver Horn's calendar, keepers sometimes did choose events that can be recognized in his pictures.

Kiowa pictorial calendars were created primarily as mnemonic devices, reference works intended to organize tribal history rather than to record it in full. Silver Horn's record is unique in the level of artistry and the amount of visual detail he was able to pack into each tiny image. A close reading of his pictures allows us to move beyond tracking specific events to tracing the texture of Kiowa life during a period of great change.

The Silver Horn Calendar

A New Discovery

The Silver Horn calendar now at the University of Oklahoma is from the estate of Nelia Mae Roberts, who died
in 2001. For decades she and her husband E. M. Roberts operated Roberts Indian Crafts and Supplies, one of several "Indian stores" in Anadarko, Oklahoma. The Robertses bought and
sold craftwork as well as carrying a stock of craft supplies, which
they sold for cash or exchanged for finished goods. In addition
to newly made items, Indian people sometimes brought in older pieces that they offered for sale or placed in pawn. Some of
these were eventually resold, but E. M. and Nelia Roberts kept
many of the older items as well as new material that they particularly liked. Over time their collection grew in a haphazard
fashion in the back room of the store, with favorite paintings
hung on the walls of their home. Details on the sources of most
items were recorded with a brief description, the name of seller
and sometimes the maker, and the pawn value.

Mrs. Roberts's great niece, Marcia Bassity, took responsibility for dealing with her aunt's collection after Nelia Mae's
death, cleaning out the long-closed store as well as the house
where her aunt had lived for years. There was a rich assortment
of beadwork, buckskin garments, and paintings that her aunt
had assembled during her long association with Indian people
in western Oklahoma. While sorting and packing all this, it occurred to Marcia to make a final check under the big iron safe

where her aunt had kept business papers, just in case anything had slipped beneath it. To her surprise she found a flat parcel wrapped in brown paper and tied up with string. It contained the tattered Kiowa calendar published here.

Marcia Bassity had never really seen all of her aunt's things before, although she remembered some pieces from her childhood. Most of the treasures had been packed away in boxes and trunks for years. As she went through it all systematically, she became convinced that the collection should be placed where many people could see and enjoy it. Acting on that idea, she donated her aunt's collection, including this calendar, to the Sam Noble Oklahoma Museum of Natural History at the University of Oklahoma, thus ensuring that it would always be available for public study and enjoyment.

Among the many items in the collection, this book stood out as one of the most intriguing in spite of its damaged condition. The name Silver Horn written on the paper wrapped around the book caught the attention of the museum's curator, Dr. Jason Jackson. He knew I had recently published a book on the Kiowa artist Silver Horn, and he asked me to look at it. I was delighted to verify that the drawings were by this noted artist, and I was eager to compare them to the calendar by Silver Horn at the Smithsonian Institution where I work. We agreed that it was important to publish the book so that many people could see this newly discovered record.

Reconstructing the Calendar

Silver Horn drew this calendar on the long, narrow pages of a bound ledger book, measuring six by fifteen inches in size. Such volumes with ruled columns and numbered pages were designed to facilitate the toting up and cross referencing of accounts, but they were often used as drawing books by Plains artists during the nineteenth century, particularly after trade goods had become more readily available than buffalo hides.[1] A wide range of manufactured materials was easily available by the time that

Silver Horn became active as an artist, and most of his other known drawings are on the unlined pages of drawing books or journals. This volume has seen hard use and is now badly damaged. The binding has disintegrated and the covers are long since lost. Parts of some pages have been torn away, and all are crumbling around the edges.

All of the pages are now loose, and their original placement had to be reconstructed. The original page numbers stamped in blue in the upper outside corner of each page were a natural point of reference, but a great many of these have been lost as the corners crumbled. Some former owner seems to have been concerned about maintaining the order of the pages and added various numbers in pencil. On several damaged pages, the original number provided by the manufacturer of the book has been written in. Presumably at a later date someone marked the pages with a separate sequential series of numbers running up to 62, although the first two pages of the calendar are too stained and damaged for these numbers to be read any longer. A few page fragments (discussed later) show no numbers. As I did not know what condition the book was in when these numbers were added to it, I was not prepared to rely on them without independent verification. Correlating the content of the calendar with other sources, however, has convinced me that the numbers mark the correct sequence for the pages. Some half a dozen pages are annotated with year designations in a small neat hand. With the exception of 1833, Stars Fall Winter, these are not correct.

The calendar covers the period from the summer of 1828 to the winter of 1928–29. But when were the drawings in this book actually made? Like all histories, much of it must have been as-sembled after the fact, drawing upon earlier records. I believe that the majority of the entries in the calendar were produced in the winter of 1905–6. The first forty-nine pages of the book, up through that winter, appear to have been drawn at the same time, presumably copied from an existing calendar. Each page is evenly divided by ruled lines into three sections with one seasonal entry in each section. Entries alternate between summers and winters (except for the first few entries), so that each page covers a year and a half. Beginning with the summer of 1906, however, the organization of each page becomes less regular, with anywhere between two and five entries. The drawing media that Silver Horn used also change at the same point in the calendar. The earlier pictures are consistently drawn with pen and ink with additional color provided by delicately applied watercolor wash. The entries after 1906 are varied but are mostly drawn in graphite pencil. They make less use of color and it is either colored pencil or crayon rather than watercolor. These later entries were probably added periodically over the course of more than twenty years, perhaps seasonally, perhaps letting a few seasons go by before bringing the calendar up to date.

Silver Horn used only one face of each page, the recto as envisioned by the manufacturer of the book, but a few pages have pictures on the backs as well. Six are tiny sketches no more than one inch high, which might have been made by Silver Horn, but two page backs are covered with crude images drawn in thick pencil in an entirely different style. Although they echo the form of calendar entries, they do not fit within the summer/winter sequence and seem extraneous. I would speculate that they were added at some point by a mischievous child. Reminiscing about calendars in their own families, two elderly Kiowa people, Jake Ahtone and Betty Nixon, told me that they had gotten in trouble as children for adding pictures of their own.

In addition to these drawings on the backs of pages, one full page and fragments of another do not fit into the reconstructed sequence of pages. The use of purple crayon in these pictures, a medium that appears no where else in the calendar, links them together. Significantly, they are not marked with the sequential numbers that the former owner applied to the other pages, suggesting that he or she did not consider them a proper part of the record.

The calendar ends a little over ten years before Silver Horn's death in 1940. It is remarkable that he was able to continue to add to it for so long. For many years Silver Horn suffered from trachoma, a painful infection of the surface of the eye, now readily treated with antibiotics. He was afflicted with the condition at least as early as 1903–4, for the calendar entry for that winter is a self-portrait of the artist with a patch over one eye. Hugh Scott visited him in 1920 and reported that he was nearly blind.[2] The varying quality of the later drawings in the calendar provides a graphic chart of the ups and downs in the course of the disease, which eventually led to complete blindness.

We do not know exactly how this calendar came to Mrs. Roberts. Many of Silver Horn's possessions were passed on to his oldest son James and were lost when James's home burned in the 1970s. Probably this book went instead to Silver Horn's son George, or Dutch, who was also an artist. The only written documentation is a slip of paper found with the calendar on which was written the name Lizzie Cat and a note of $14.55. Lizzie Cat was married to Dutch Silverhorn. Some years previously I had heard that Mrs. Roberts had a book of drawings by Silver Horn, and I visited her to ask about it. Most of her collection was packed away at that time, and I did not see the book. However, she told me that the book she owned had belonged to Dutch Silverhorn. This may well be the book to which she was referring.

Reading the Pictures

Silver Horn's calendar is remarkable in its visual richness. Most Kiowa calendars, like other Plains winter counts, employ spare, abbreviated figures that served to remind their keepers of the associated event but were too limited to be read independently. The pictures in the Silver Horn calendar are also much simpler than his other drawings, suggesting events rather than depicting them in full. He was so committed to detail, however, and so skilled in graphic communication that a great deal can

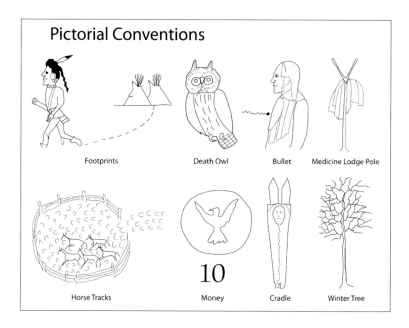

Pictorial Conventions

Footprints   Death Owl   Bullet   Medicine Lodge Pole

Horse Tracks   Money   Cradle   Winter Tree

FIGURE 2-1. Pictorial conventions from the Silver Horn calendar. Redrawn by Emily L. Greene, for the author.

be read from his pictorial calendar. His son Max Silverhorn Sr. impressed upon me that every element his father included in a picture was there to convey information, rather than for decorative effect.

"Reading" the entries in Silver Horn's calendar is a two-step process. First, it is necessary to recognize what each element represents. Some are direct representations while others are a sort of pictorial shorthand. Some of the shorthand conventions he employed were widely used in Kiowa or wider Plains art; others were distinctive to Silver Horn. After deducing what is illustrated, one can proceed to consider what these elements might have meant within Kiowa culture of the time.

The most frequent figures appearing in the calendar are the ones that Silver Horn used to designate the summer and winter seasons. Summer was denoted by an upright forked pole. This is the great central pole that supported the roof poles of the Kado, or Medicine Lodge, the structure in which the central ceremony of the summer was held. Silver Horn showed the center pole adorned with strips of red cloth and feathers, and across the crotch is draped the "buffalo effigy," a bundle of willow branches tied with a strip of buffalo hide and hung with numerous offering cloths. The picture of the pole meant that a Kado, generally known in English as the Sun Dance, was held that year. Since the ceremony took place only in summer, the pole appropriately denoted the season. By extension, it also represented the summer Medicine Lodge encampment, the social high point of the year when the whole tribe came together for the ceremony. In years when the Kado was not held, Silver Horn marked the summer season with a picture of a leafy tree. Winters were always designated simply by a bare tree. Other Kiowa calendar keepers also used the Medicine Lodge to mark summers, showing either the whole lodge or, like Silver Horn, just the center pole, but I have not encountered any other calendars that use a tree to mark the winters. Most have no particular associated symbol, the winter events being placed in time by their position between summer ceremonials, or they are marked by a simple device such as a black bar or a diamond shape.

A convention that Silver Horn adopted from Plains pictorial art was the use of a line of footprints to show a course of action. A simple dashed line represented human footprints, showing where a person had been, while horse tracks consisted of a series of U-shaped marks. The hoof prints were so clearly an indication of a horse that it was not necessary to include a picture of the animal itself to show that one had passed, and even in a tiny space he could economically suggest numerous horses by showing several rows of tracks.

Many entries in the calendar record people's deaths, and Silver Horn conveyed that idea in various ways. Sometimes he showed the cause of death, such as a bullet (a dot followed by a wavy line) coming toward the person who was killed. Often the wound itself was not shown, but in other instances blood is gushing from a wound or from the victim's mouth. One of Silver Horn's unique conventions, used by no other artist I have seen, is the picture of an owl in association with the person who died. Kiowa people explained to me that owls carry off the spirits of the dead. This bird of ill omen, the two crests of feathers on its head suggesting the great horned owl, seems to have been used most often in association with individuals who died from natural causes. Silver Horn's grandchildren, who were quite young when they last saw his calendar, vividly remember these chilling symbols of death scattered through the pages, and is was they who told me what the owl meant.

Births, happier events, were also noted in the calendar, particularly in the later years. In another unique innovation, Silver Horn represented them by a drawing of a cradleboard, the tiny face of a child peeking out from the beaded sack attached to double wooden slats.

Like births and deaths, many of the calendar entries record events associated with specific people, and Silver Horn, like other calendar keepers, sought to identify them accurately. Plains Indian artists did not produce portraits of individuals by working to capture a facial likeness. Instead, they relied on other devices to provide identification—a shield, a tipi, or a distinctive war headdress. In the calendars the most common means was to include a name glyph, a picture that was a literal representation of the person's name. Among all his drawings, it is only in the calendars that Silver Horn used name glyphs. Some names were easy to represent in picture form—for example, Black Bear (1853–54) or Wolf Lying Down (1858–59). Names that involved action were a little harder, but Silver Horn came up with creative solutions. Bird Appearing (1860) is represented by a bird on top of a hill with a series of tracks behind it, suggesting that it has just emerged into view.

Names were important to the Kiowa. The extent to which they were an integral part of an individual's identity is reflected in the calendar. Glyphs were often drawn above the person they identified, connected to the head by a wavy line, but in other instances the glyph itself stands for the person. The connection

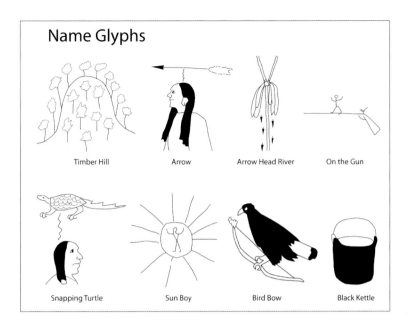

Name Glyphs

Timber Hill   Arrow   Arrow Head River   On the Gun

Snapping Turtle   Sun Boy   Bird Bow   Black Kettle

FIGURE 2-2. Name glyphs from the Silver Horn calendar. Redrawn by Emily L. Greene, for the author.

between person and name was so close that blood might be shown dripping from the glyph of a man who had been shot, and if a person died, the death owl was associated with the name glyph more often than with the human figure.

Although one can usually get the gist of the name from looking at a glyph, it is not always possible to tie it to a specific person without additional information. A person might have several names over the course of a lifetime—informal nicknames, perhaps based on some physical characteristic; one or more formal names; and after the reservation was established, an "agency name" by which the individual was listed in government records. Agency names might or might not derive from a Kiowa name, but they did not supplant the continuing usage of native naming practices. Names circulated as valuable possessions. Children did not automatically have the same name as their parents, but a name was often given away to a relative, or occasionally a close comrade, as a mark of honor, as is still done today. In this way a single name might belong to a series of individuals. Another problem is that the accuracy of names written in various historical documents depended on the linguistic ability of the person who recorded them. The Kiowa language has sounds and tonal inflections that are difficult for people who do not know the language well to distinguish clearly or record effectively in the standard Roman alphabet. Their translation into English was equally idiosyncratic.

The calendar entry for the winter of 1842–43 (pl. 7) illustrates these problems. A glyph of many bear tracks, paw prints with distinct claws, identifies the man known in Kiowa as Set-daya-ite, variously translated into English as Many Bears, Plenty Bears, or Heap of Bears. Several different men had that name during the mid-nineteenth century. There was the one recorded in this calendar entry; another Plenty Bears was killed by the Utes in 1868; and a third Plenty Bears was the chief priest of the Medicine Lodge from 1876 to 1883.[3]

It is surprising that the calendars have so many entries marking the deaths of well-known individuals, since the Kiowa had a prohibition against speaking the name of a person who had died recently.[4] Calendar keepers employed various strategies for getting around this problem. One was the use of indirect reference—the person who died was identified by connection to a kinsman rather than by his or her own name. For example, the entry for winter 1886–87 marks the death of Quiver Carrier's son, and the entry for winter 1901–2 uses the name glyph of Many Poles to refer to the death of his wife. Without accompanying information it would be easy to read the glyphs incorrectly as indicating the death of the person whose name is given. Another type of circumlocution was to identify the deceased by reference to a distinctive object with which the individual was closely associated. For example, Silver Horn marked the death of Stumbling Bear's son in summer 1889 with a picture of his father's shield. The image would read something like, "the son of the one who carried the bear shield died this winter." After a period of a few years, the prohibition expired and names came back into general use. Since calendars were recopied periodically, calendar keepers probably had the option to change the picture in later years to reference the actual name of the person whose death was noted, but some circumlocutions seem to have stuck.

Silver Horn used pictorial glyphs to represent the names of places as well as of people. Many drawings in the calendar represent the place where the Kado or other event took place. Just as he did not identify people through portraiture, he did not try to represent these places through realistic landscape drawings. Instead he drew a picture of the place name. Rainy Mountain is a steep hill with rain and clouds (1893, 1895–96), Timber Hill is a similar hill, but covered with trees (1867–68, 1927), and the Arrow Head River is a stream flanked with a row of arrow points (1848, 1863).

A Document of History and Culture

Silver Horn's calendar was not intended to be a comprehensive history of the Kiowa people. Like other primary documents, however, it reveals much about Kiowa history and the culture of the people who produced it. During the years covered in the first half of the calendar, the Kiowa were nomadic bison hunters. Many entries are concerned with a shifting political landscape of enmities and alliances with other nations, both indigenous and non-native. During the second half of the calendar, the Kiowa were restricted to the territory defined for their reservation, and many aspects of their lives were subject to external control. Entries in this section often record the impact of government policy on religion, the economic base, and interactions with other tribes. Other pictures document Kiowa resistance to this control, both through direct political action, like lobbying Congress, and through communal cultural expressions, such as religious revitalization movements. As the twentieth century progressed, Kiowa and non-Kiowa history were increasingly intertwined, and Silver Horn recorded events that were part of the experience of the wider Oklahoma population.

The entry for 1918–19 records that several Kiowa men were honored for their service in the armed forces during World War I. Events such as the establishment of the army air corps at Fort Sill in 1914–15 and the devastating Snyder cyclone of 1905 are sprinkled among records of Kiowa dances and deaths.

Place is an important feature throughout the calendar. Summers were often named for the place where the Kado was held. Even when entries are named for an event, the texts recorded with other Kiowa calendars make it clear that information on place was often included in the oral narratives accompanying them. This is especially so in the earliest recorded text for the Little Bluff calendar, appearing here as appendix A. If James Mooney had used this source of information alone, he might easily have titled his book a calendar geography rather than a calendar history. The calendars clearly were concerned with space as well as time—with what in modern terms can be recognized as historical geography. Even after the Kiowa were restricted to the much smaller territory of the reservation, Agiati and Hauvahte and Silver Horn after him continued to record where events took place, although it might be "on the Washita below Poor Buffalo's cornfield."

A distinctive feature of the Kiowa calendars is their focus on summers. The calendars of other Plains tribes marked only one event for each year, while the Kiowa recorded two. This allowed a more precise record of when events occurred, but the difference goes deeper than that. The nature of summer and winter entries is somewhat different, with summers primarily focused on the Kado—its location and events that took place within the Kado encampment—while winter entries are more diverse in their coverage. They record events that took place over a wider period of months, often in remote locations, frequently involving only a small group of people, such as a war party on a distant raid.

The winter entries in the Kiowa calendars are analogous to those marked by the Lakotas, for example, in their winter counts, although recording a distinct set of events. Since Kiowa calendars do not stretch as far back in time as those of the Lakota or the Blackfoot, it is reasonable to assume that the Kiowa borrowed the idea for a pictorial calendar from another tribe and adapted it to their own use, fitting their existing oral traditions to this convenient framework.[5] However, the Kiowa originator, probably Little Bluff, made a significant alteration in form. He chose to note two events, incorporating a series of distinct summer entries into a record of yearly markers.

Silver Horn's calendar suggests that the Kiowa maintained oral traditions of the sequence of summer gatherings even before they began to mark them in pictorial form. Silver Horn's calendar record begins in 1828, including five entries prior to the Little Bluff record, which begins in the winter of 1832–33. Silver Horn's father, the last keeper of that calendar, explained to Hugh Scott that "he remembered nothing of note" prior to that time. However, other men of the tribe did have longer memories, or perhaps a keener interest in recording the past. James Mooney noted in the NAA calendar, which Silver Horn drew for him in 1904, that Gaapiatan, or Crow Lance, had provided information on these earlier years, together with some input from Tebodal. Significantly, these early entries consist only of summers.

Summer was the time when the dispersed bands of the Kiowa came together. It was in summer that each group took its designated place in the great circle of the Medicine Lodge encampment, and the Kiowa tribe constituted itself upon the landscape. The Big Shield band was in the north, the Kogui or Elk to the south, and the Kata or Ree on the east next to the entrance to the camp. The closely allied Plains Apache camped as a band in the northeast. In the very center stood the Kado, the Medicine Lodge itself. Here the priests held ceremonies to ensure the success of the communal buffalo hunt that would follow the encampment. It was in summer that the Kiowa came together as a people and staked their claim to a hunting territory, sanctifying that claim through ritual. Long after the buffalo were gone, when the Kiowa could claim no more land than individual allotments scattered among new white neighbors, the importance of summer remains visible in the calendar. The importance of this union, and often the territory within which it took place, were commemorated and made manifest in the Kiowa calendar. This distinctive feature inspired the title *One Hundred Summers*.

3

The University of Oklahoma Calendar

Silver Horn's calendar can be seen in the following pages. Although now tattered and torn, all of the pages seem to have survived in at least partial form. There are a few fragments for which the original position could not be determined; in the interest of completeness pictures of them appear at the end of the book. A number of rough drawings from the backs of pages that do not seem to be a part of the original calendar are also illustrated at the end (plate 64).

Each page contains a series of entries alternating between summer and winter events, except for a few anomalies in the early years. The calendar starts out with only summers marked for the first few years, and the first winter (1832–33) records no accompanying event. The calendar settles into the regular pattern of alternating seasons beginning in the winter of 1833. Even then, a comparison with other Kiowa calendars reveals that a few years have been skipped in this first decade. The same omissions appear in another calendar copy that Silver Horn made as well as in the closely related calendars kept by Hauvahte, Quitone, and Hunt. I have filled in information for these missing seasons using detail from the calendar kept by Silver Horn's father, Little Bluff (Tohausan). In a few places, parts of a page are torn and missing so that whole entries have been lost. Reproduction of corresponding sections from Silver Horn's calendar in the National Anthropological Archives helps to fill these voids in the pictorial record.

This calendar was received with no accompanying written text. Silver Horn's pictures are full of amazing detail, much richer than that of other calendar keepers, but I would not have been able to interpret them without other points of reference. The explanations of pictures that I offer here are based on many sources: published and unpublished written records, comparison with other pictorial sources, and discussion with a number of Kiowa people and others familiar with Kiowa history. The primary source of information for the years between 1832 and 1892 was James Mooney's *Calendar History of the Kiowa Indians*. All information that is not otherwise cited is from the corresponding seasonal entry or from the Kiowa-English glossary in that publication. Other Kiowa calendars and the texts recorded from their keepers have been another important set of sources, especially useful for the years after 1892; these are referred to by the names of their keepers. Appendixes to the volume provide complete transcripts of the original texts recorded from Silver Horn's father, Little Bluff, and from Silver Horn's brother, Hauvahte, as well as a list of other Kiowa calendars consulted. The calendar copy Silver Horn made in 1904, now in the Smithsonian's National Anthropological Archives, was also a key source. It provides pictures that can be compared to the OU calendar, and its collector James Mooney scribbled many cryptic explanatory notes directly on the calendar pages. I refer to it as the NAA calendar, to distinguish it from the calendar reproduced here. Much information on twentieth-century events came from Kiowa people and from others who have studied Kiowa history.

I have not attempted to reiterate fully the rich fund of Kiowa history covered by Mooney and several fine sources published since, nor to note all of the events referenced in the other calendars. Instead I have tried to stay close to the events Silver Horn chose as markers, providing only enough additional information to place them in historical and cultural context.

The last twenty years of the calendar when texts of other family calendars were not available for comparison were the most difficult to decipher. Some other Kiowa calendars cover the same decades, but their keepers often did not select the same events as points of reference. Extensive Bureau of Indian Affairs records exist for this period, as the Kiowa were deeply enmeshed in governmental bureaucracy, but again the events that Silver Horn selected were not necessarily recorded by such officials. Equally significant, people's "agency names"—the names under which they were tracked by agency officials—were not always the meaningful, often hereditary, personal names recorded by Silver Horn in the form of tiny, evocative name glyphs.

The significance of some of the pictures has eluded my research and remains enigmatic, waiting for some Kiowa elder to view them and say, "Ah, yes. I know what that must stand for. That was my grandfather's name. I remember that story."

The University of Oklahoma Calendar

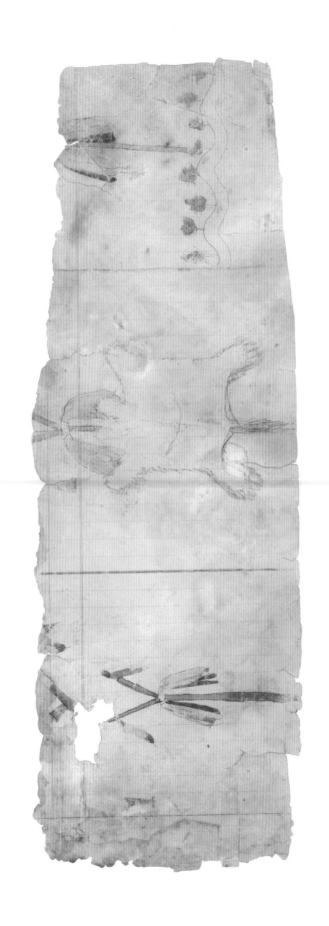

1828 Pipe Dance Kado

The calendar opens with a picture of an upright forked pole draped with offering cloths. It represents the great center pole of the Medicine Lodge in which the Kiowa held the Kado, or Sun Dance ceremony, each summer, as discussed in chapter 2. The fragmentary picture above it shows parts of a pipe with a black bowl and feathers hanging from the stem. According to the NAA calendar it indicates a Pipe Dance, an adoption ceremony in which the Wichita adopted the son of Wolf Teat (Gui-aza). Quitone said it was his grandfather Buffalo Udder (An-zah-te) who was honored on this occasion and that Buffalo Udder made rich gifts to his new "relatives" in return. Ritualized adoption of adults was a mechanism to establish formal bonds of friendship between tribes or communities. Records of Pipe Dances occur several times in the Silver Horn calendar, marking personal alliances with members of various other tribes.

1829 Buffalo Hide Kado

The picture shows a full buffalo hide, tanned with the hair on to make a warm robe. The NAA calendar is captioned "Ka-tode-a Pa Gado." Mooney translates this as "creek where the buffalo robe was returned" and notes its location near Fort Elliott in the Texas Panhandle. Many summer entries in the calendar are named for the place where the Kado was held, rather than for an event that occurred that year. Conversely, many regular camping places were named for events that had once happened there. Quitone did not remember this event for certain, but he thought a man who had had trouble with his wife had demanded a robe from her relatives.

1830 Dry Creek Kado

Any identification for this summer that may have been along the top edge of this drawing has been lost. The NAA entry is captioned "Ton-hen Gado, possibly Tonhen

Pa, Sand Creek of Colorado." This was a northern tributary of the Arkansas River, notable as the site of a Cheyenne camp that was massacred by Col. Chivington and a troop of Colorado volunteers in 1864.[1]

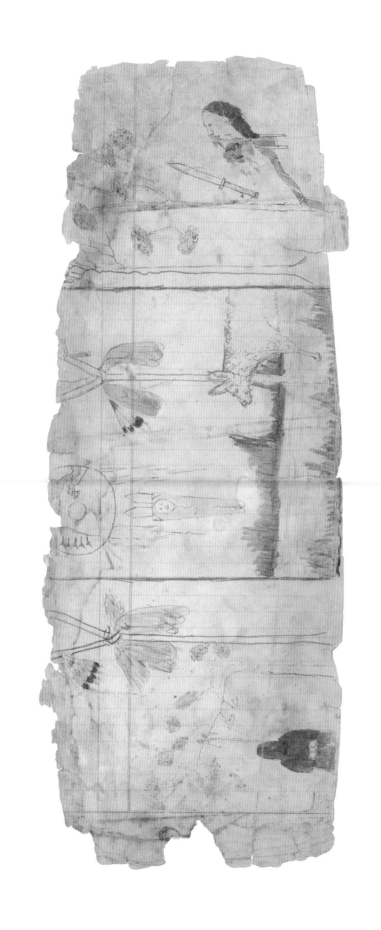

1833–34 Stars Fall Winter

The Leonid meteor storm of November 1833 is noted in the calendars of all the Plains tribes. This meteor shower is an impressive display recurring on a thirty-three-year cycle, and the showing of this year was spectacular all over North America. Coming on the heels of the disaster of the previous summer, it must have been particularly impressive to the Kiowa. From this point in the calendar, Silver Horn consistently marked winter events with the image of a leafless tree.

1834 no entry

Silver Horn did not make an entry for this summer, nor did his brother Hauvahte.

The Little Bluff calendar records this as "When the Kiowa girl was brought back by the soldiers." Mooney provided a detailed account of this event, as did the artist George Catlin, who was present. In an effort to encourage peace between the two tribes, an expedition of the U.S. Dragoons returned a young Kiowa girl who had been taken captive by the Osage the previous year. The overture was successful. Both tribes agreed to peace, and the Osage returned the precious Taime to the Kiowa.

1834–35 no entry

This season was also omitted by both Silver Horn and his brother. It is identified in the Little Bluff calendar as the winter that Bull Tail was killed by Mexicans. This was during the Texas war for independence from Mexico and took place in territory that is now part of either Texas or New Mexico.

1835 Water Plant Kado

This was the first Kado held since the return of the Taime. The ceremony was under the direction of a new Taime keeper, Long Foot, and perhaps the picture on the left represents him. The dancers were not allowed to drink but were given water plants to chew on to relieve their thirst. Both Mooney and Quitone identified the plant as the cattail.

1835–36 Unnamed winter

Silver Horn shows the bare winter tree without further identification in either calendar. Hauvahte's calendar had no entry for this or the following two seasons. The Little Bluff calendar recorded that Wolf Hair was killed while on the warpath in Mexico.

6

1836 no entry

Silver Horn omits this summer. The Little Bluff calendar records that the Kado was held on Wolf Creek, the North Fork of the Canadian River, as it had been in 1832.

1836–37 no entry

Silver Horn omits this winter, while the Little Bluff calendar records that someone named Man was killed on the warpath in Mexico.

1837 Wailing Kado

This summer was a battle in which the Kiowa surrounded a group of Cheyenne and killed them. The circle represents the surrounded enemies with many arrows pointed toward them. Several Kiowa warriors were killed as well, and the news of their deaths arrived during the Kado. Although the battle was a Kiowa victory, many people mourned for lost relatives during the celebration. This picture shows a woman weeping, while Silver Horn's other calendar shows a man shedding tears. The figure on the left with a bullet coming toward him may represent one of the Kiowa warriors who were killed.

1837–38 Buffalo's Son died winter

This fragmentary picture shows a partial drawing of a buffalo. The NAA entry shows the shooting of a buffalo followed by a calf, and is captioned "Pa-yia killed by Cheyenne." Hauvahte's record gives the name as Buffalo's Son, while Quitone called him Buffalo Calf.

1838 entry missing

The part of the page containing this entry has been torn away. Silver Horn's other calendar shows a camp on Wolf Creek, and a figure in a warbonnet that Mooney identifies as a Cheyenne. The Cheyenne

attacked in revenge for the massacre of their people the previous summer, but the Kiowa successfully defended their camps and drove off the Cheyenne. A leafy tree indicates that no Kado was held, as many Kiowa had been killed.

FIGURE 3-2. NAA calendar entry for 1838, by Silver Horn. MS 2531, vol. 7. Courtesy of the National Anthropological Archives, Smithsonian Institution.

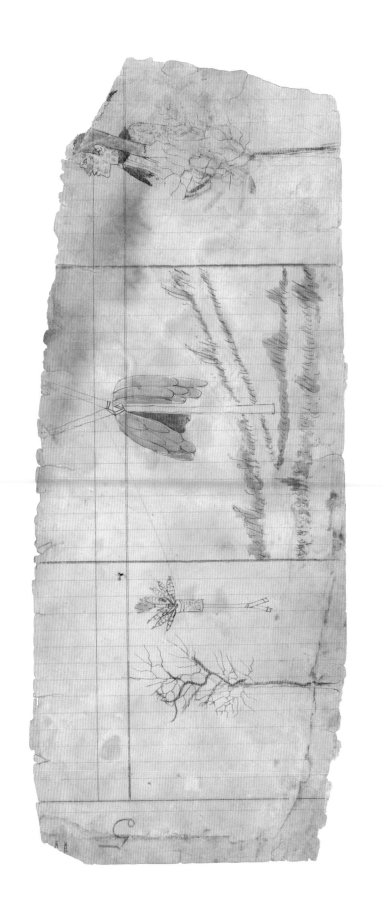

1838–39 Taimpego organized winter

The picture shows a rattle with a cylindrical head trimmed with feathers, representing the regalia of the Taimpego society, which was organized during this winter. Hauvahte identifies the winter as "Dog Soldier society started." The term Dog Soldier has often been used as a generic designation for any of the *yapahe*, or warrior societies of the Kiowa.[2]

1839 Peninsula Kado

The Kado was held a number of times on a large bend in the Washita River, referred to by the Kiowa as Piho, "peninsula." Silver Horn consistently represents this location as a projection of land in the V of a stream. Little Bluff described it as below Poor Buffalo's place, which Mooney said was a short distance below Walnut Creek and the line of the Wichita reservation. Quitone said it was northeast of the present town of Carnegie, Oklahoma, where the Kiowa Tribe now has their offices.

1839–40 Smallpox winter

All of the calendars record the smallpox epidemic of this year.

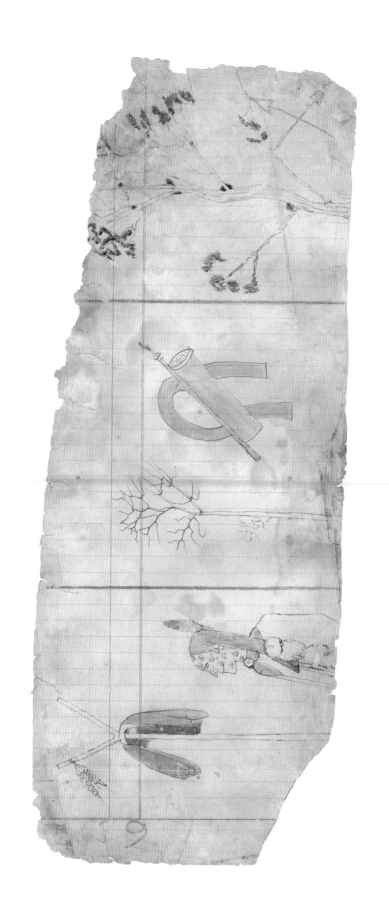

1840 Smallpox Kado

The calendar records that many were still suffering from smallpox by the summer. The NAA calendar not only includes the smallpox-spotted figure but also records that the Kado was held at Guadal Doha, or Red Bluff (see fig. 1-4).

1840–41 Hide quiver winter

A simple quiver is shown, unlike the highly decorated ones favored by young men. Mooney explains that it represents a war party of old men who no longer had such fancy gear.

1841 Unnamed summer

No dance was held this summer. The meaning of the crossed arrows is not known, but they also appear in the Quitone calendar. Mooney notes that this was the year the Kiowa established peace with the Arapaho.

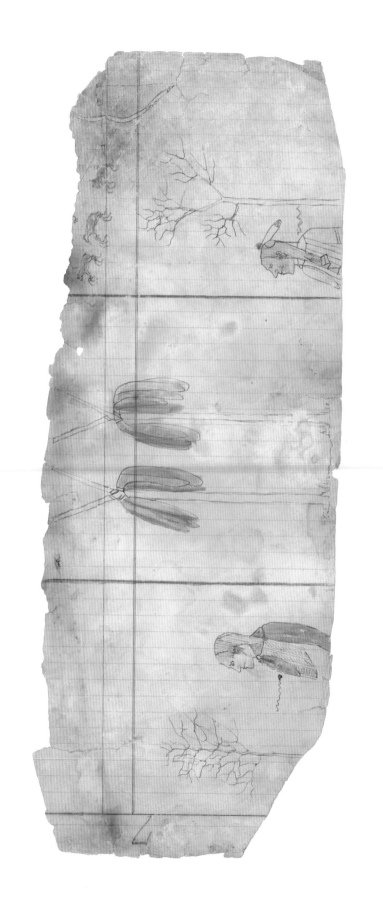

1841–42 Sloping Hair killed winter

This noted chief was killed during a horse raid into Texas. He is distinguished in the picture by his hair, worn with some short and some long. All the calendars record this event, but each interpreter provided a different translation for the man's name. Mooney reported that his name was Adalhabakia in Kiowa, which he translated as Sloping Hair. The interpreter of the Hauvahte calendar called him Cut Hair, while the interpreter for the Little Bluff calendar rendered the name as Long Hair.

1842 Repeated Kado

The double set of poles indicates that two dances were held, as two men had independently vowed to sponsor the ceremony. Men must usually have made their intentions of sponsorship widely known, as this was a rare event, recorded only twice in the calendar, this summer and again in 1878.

1842–43 Heap of Bears killed winter

The death of Heap of Bears is indicated by an arrow pointing toward his name glyph. According to both the NAA inscription and Hauvahte's account, he was killed by Kiowa Apaches. This refers to a group of Plains Apaches who had long been closely allied with the Kiowas, forming one of the recognized bands of the tribe, although retaining their own language and beliefs. It appears that his death was the result of a quarrel among members of a war party.

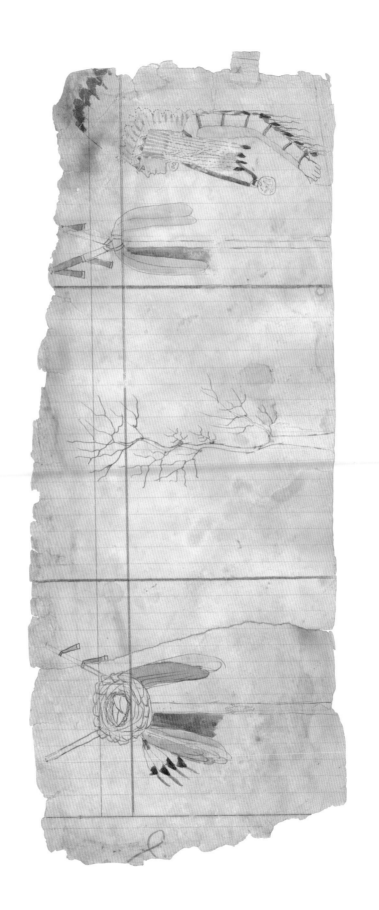

1843 Nest Building Kado

A bird's nest is shown in the fork of the Medicine Lodge center pole. Hauvahte identifies it as a crow's nest. According to Mooney's sources, a bird built a nest there after the dance was concluded.

1843–44 Unnamed winter

Both of Silver Horn's calendars show a tree without any further identifying picture. Hauvahte's calendar has no entry for this winter. Little Bluff recorded two events: the death of his brother on a raid into Mexico, and a friendly visit by the Sioux, which Silver Horn placed in the following summer.

1844 Sioux Kado

A visit by a Lakota, or Western Sioux, is noted by depicting a finely dressed man with a full feather warbonnet and a circular shell ornament at his throat. According to the Little Bluff calendar, the Sioux were known as Shell Necklace People. The man also has what is probably a peace medal suspended around his neck by a red strap. The U.S. government issued such medals to noted leaders as tokens of respect.

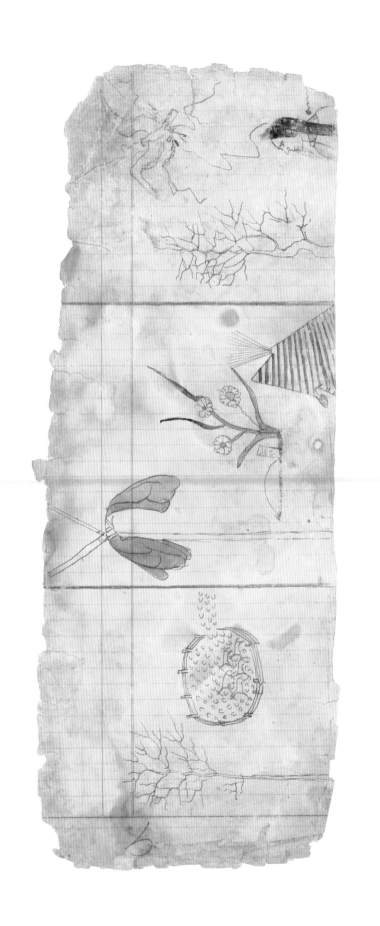

1847–48 Windbreak winter

Lightly sketched lines over a row of tipis represent a brush windbreak built around the winter camp, which Little Bluff says was on the White River, an upper branch of the South Canadian. Such an elaborate construction was unusual among the Kiowa, who moved their camps often. Quitone reported that they kept their camp in the same place for so long during this winter that the grass was worn away down to the sandy soil. The dark band in the foreground may represent bare earth around the camp.

1848 Koitsenko initiated Kado

The red painted figure is a member of the Koitsenko warrior society, dressed in the dance regalia of the society: fluffy feather headdress, eagle bone whistle worn as a pendant, and a long red sash slipped over one shoulder and trailing down on the other side. The Koitsenko was the most prestigious of all the Kiowa warrior societies, consisting of only ten members, who were considered the bravest of the brave. The badge of office was the "no retreat" sash known throughout the Plains. It had a slit in the trailing end through which a wearer might stake himself to the ground during a fight, swearing not to retreat. Other than through death (perhaps not uncommon), a Koitsenko could leave the society only when a new member was initiated. Such an installation would be a notable event of the summer encampment.

This Kado was held on the Arkansas River, widely known on the Plains as the Flint River. Among the Kiowa it was Se-se Pa, or Arrowhead River, indicated here by a series of arrowheads, in this case metal points rather than the stone ones that became obsolete as soon as metal was available through trade.

1848–49 Ice rising winter

This ambiguous drawing is explained by a caption in the NAA calendar, "Ice Rising, so called when ice breaks up and piles in gorge." This entry suggests an unusually cold winter.

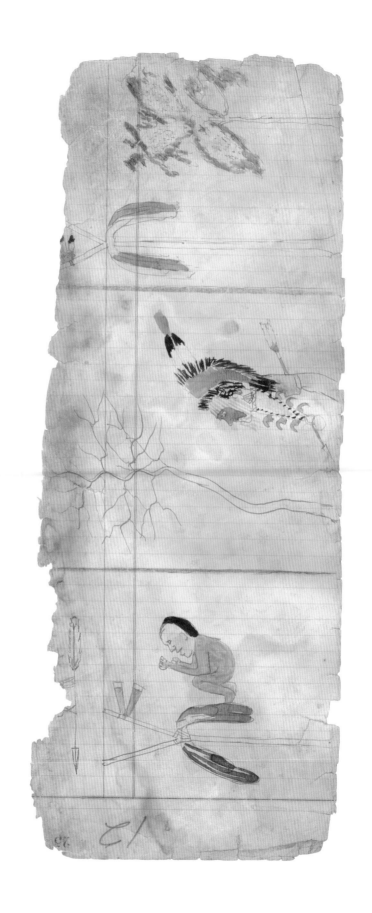

FIGURE 3-4. NAA calendar entry for 1849, by Silver Horn. MS 2531, vol. 7. Courtesy of the National Anthropological Archives, Smithsonian Institution.

1849 Cramp Kado

The cramped figure represents the terrible cholera epidemic that swept the Plains in 1849. The fragmentary name glyph at the top of the page appears more fully in the NAA calendar. Hauvahte recorded that On the Arrow was the first victim of the disease.

1849–50 Pawnee killed winter

Silver Horn carefully delineated the dress and ornament of this Pawnee enemy, including a roach headdress made of deer hair, bear claw necklace, ball and cone earrings, silver armband, and peace medal as well as elaborate face paint. Hauvahte calls him "a very brave Pawnee," clearly an enemy worthy of note.

1850 Chinaberry Kado

This year was named for the trees that grew plentifully around the camp, which was at the junction of Beaver Creek and Wolf Creek, near present-day Fort Supply, Oklahoma. Mooney's notes in the NAA calendar say it should be called Bonha Gado, referring to berries that are not eaten. This is an instance in which Kiowa speakers and interpreters struggled to find common language to discuss Kiowa plant knowledge. In American usage, chinaberry commonly designates an invasive oriental tree (*Melia azedarach*), while it seems more likely that the calendar refers to a native species for which they did not know a word in English.

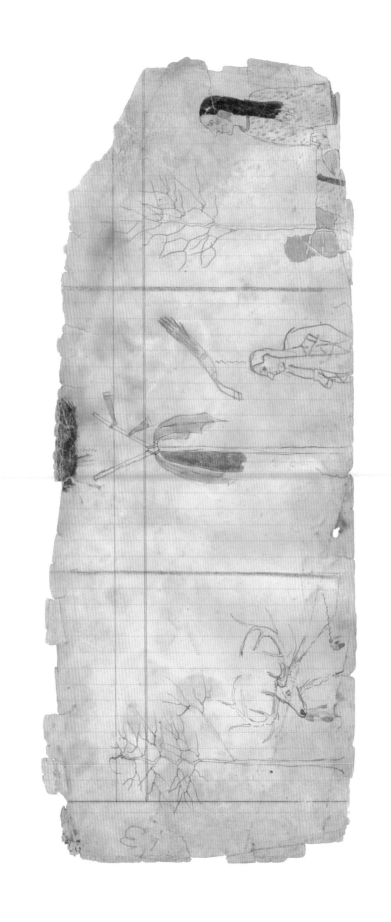

1850–51 Deer killed winter

The bleeding buck is not a picture of an actual deer but a name glyph representing the death of a man named Deer (Tangiapa). He was killed on a war expedition across the Rio Grande River.

1851 Dusty Kado

The dark smudge above the forked pole of the Medicine Lodge is a cloud of dust. The significance of the man with a fan for a name glyph is not recorded. Hauvahte records the capture of a Pawnee boy this summer.

1851–52 Woman frozen winter

This woman, identified by Little Bluff as Pretty Girl, was eloping with Big Bow while her husband was away on a war expedition. Big Bow left her concealed out of doors while he went home to gather his gear. Knowing the trouble this escapade would cause, his father foiled their plans by detaining him, leaving the waiting woman exposed to the cold so long that her feet were frostbitten. By including this event in the tribal calendar, Little Bluff made certain that other women considering such action would remember her fate and think again.

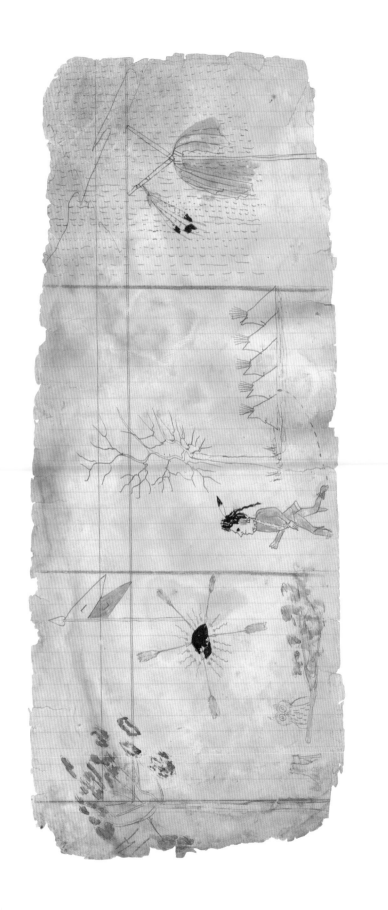

1852 Surround fight summer

There was no dance this summer. The calendar suggests a group surrounded in a fight, attacked by enemies with both guns and arrows. Silver Horn has added a flag to suggest that the engagement involved regular army troops. Curiously, the flag is the swallow-tailed guidon, twice blazoned with the letter *L*, the same insignia he used in the entry for 1891–92 to mark his enlistment in Troop L of the Seventh Cavalry. A similar picture in the NAA calendar is captioned "Mexican soldiers killed," suggesting that in Silver Horn's view the symbolism of the guidon transcended nationality as well as dates in which specific equipment was issued.

Hauvahte explains that the death owl next to a felled tree represents Lone Bear, who fell dead while cutting tipi poles. The event was memorable as it was a disgrace for a man to cut poles, which was considered women's work.

1852–53 Pawnee boy ran away winter

The figure running away from a tipi camp is a young Pawnee. Silver Horn has included a number of elements to indicate his tribal identification: the roached hairstyle, the high-topped black moccasins, and the forked tab at the knee of his buckskin leggings. The boy was a captive, taken prisoner the previous summer. According to the Little Bluff calendar, the boy not only escaped but took with him a highly valued racehorse. The Kiowa must have admired his courage, but perhaps they also vowed to stick to capturing only younger, less troublesome children in future.

1853 Showery Kado

Streaks of rain pour down on the center pole of the Medicine Lodge. Quitone reported it being was so wet that they had to put covers over the Taime to protect it.

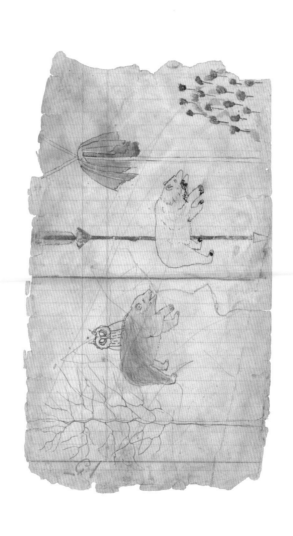

1853–54 Black Bear died winter

The name sign for Black Bear appears with the ominous owl of death. According to Quitone, Black Bear was a keeper of one of the tribal medicine bundles known as the Ten Medicines, and died in a sweat lodge. Small hide-covered structures filled with steam by pouring water on heated rocks, sweat lodges were used for purification. Proper maintenance of the bundle would have required periodic rituals of purification, but Black Bear might also have undertaken a "sweat" for more personal healing.

1854 Timber Mountain Kado

The Kado was held at Timber Mountain this year. The most notable event was that White Bear received a large arrow-shaped lance, known as a *zebat*. The NAA inscription reports that it was given to him by Black Bear, who had died just months before. Some time previously Black Bear had transferred to White Bear the right to the lance, but this was the first time White Bear exercised that right by making and displaying it. As with many other medicine objects, the transfer focused on the right to make and use a ritual item and its associated powers. The physical object itself was only a token of the underlying power. The original object might be discarded or buried with its previous owner, while the new owner made a new version for use.

1854–55 Likes Enemies killed winter

This section of the OU calendar is missing. The NAA calendar shows a man called Likes Enemies being shot from ambush. Silver Horn identified the enemy as a Pawnee, although his brother and father said the man was an Osage. The confusion may be due to translation of the Kiowa word Alaho, which is sometimes used for the Osage but also for another nearby tribe, possibly the Omaha. Silver Horn further

noted the birth of twins this year. These were his brothers White Buffalo and Oheltoint, also known as Charlie Buffalo, who were full brothers to Silver Horn and half-brothers to Hauvahte.

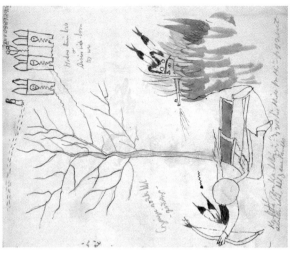

FIGURE 3-5. NAA calendar entry for 1854–55, by Silver Horn. MS 2531, vol. 7. Courtesy of the National Anthropological Archives, Smithsonian Institution.

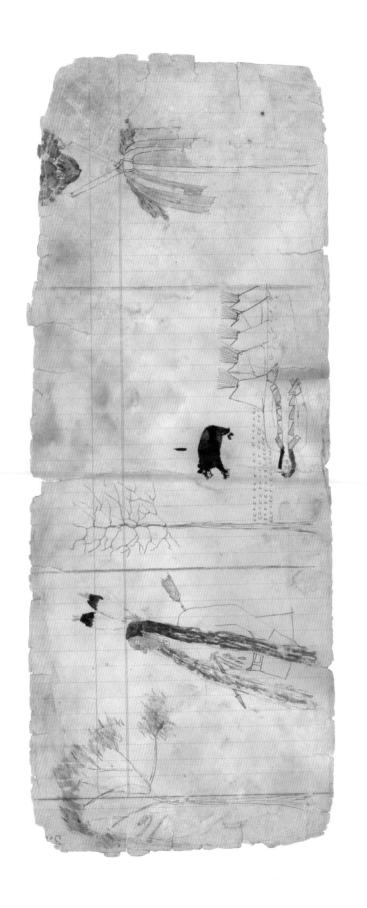

1855 Long-haired Pawnee killed summer

The calendar shows a man pierced by an arrow who is distinguished by his very long hair. Hauvahte identifies him as a Pawnee. Silver Horn usually represented the Pawnee with their heads shaved except for a strip of hair, called a roach, on top. This enemy was particularly remembered for his unusual appearance. No Medicine Lodge was held in the summer of 1855.

1855–56 Going on the Road killed winter

The row of tracks leaving camp and the prostrate figure indicate the death of a man identified by Little Bluff as Going on the Road, who was killed on a war party into Mexico. The single figure of a bear stands for Lone Bear. The NAA calendar says he was "pipe bearer," the leader of the expedition, and that he took a scalp; Hauvahte says he captured a Ute boy. Both events could have occurred on the same expedition on which Going on the Road was killed.

1856 Prickly Pear Kado

The partial image at the top of the page is a prickly pear cactus in blossom. Little Bluff describes the dance as held "when plums were ripe" and places it on the Arkansas River below Bent's Fort in present-day Colorado.

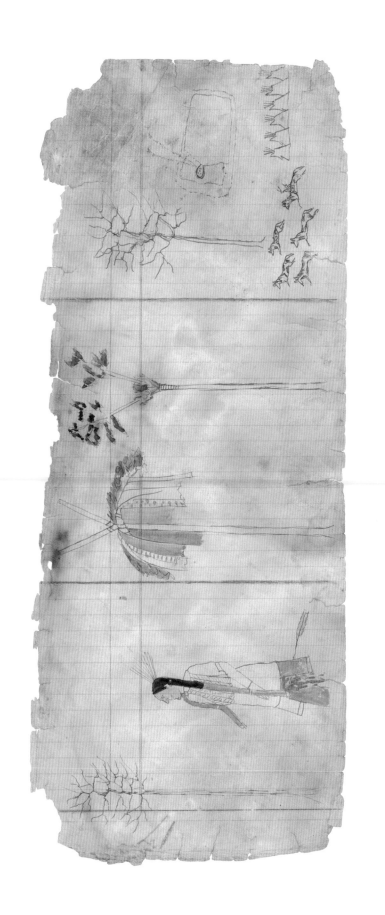

1856–57 Loud Talker shot winter

The man shot with an arrow is identified in the NAA calendar as Loud Talker. He is shown there with the same distinctive spiked headdress he wears here. The inscription reports that he was shot in a quarrel by a man named Wolf Lying Down. According to Quitone, Loud Talker had been involved with Wolf Lying Down's wife and the angry husband shot him, although not fatally.

1857 Forked stick sprouted Kado

New growth is shown sprouting from a forked stick tied with blue sage. According to Mooney's sources this depicts a medicine staff that belonged to a man named Falls Over a Bank. At the end of the Medicine Lodge ceremony he left it thrust into the ground, and the next year it was found to have sprouted miraculously, although the wood was old.

1857–58 Pawnees stole horses winter

The scene at the bottom of the page is a Pawnee driving off a group of spotted horses from a tipi camp. The NAA inscription says the horses belonged to Tebodal, whose name translates as One Who Carries a Pack of Meat from the Buffalo's Lower Leg. (His name, difficult to convey in English, is represented in a simple glyph for the year 1885–86.) The upper figure of a man lying in bed with wavy lines coming from his mouth represents an attack of whooping cough, one of many new diseases attacking the Kiowa.

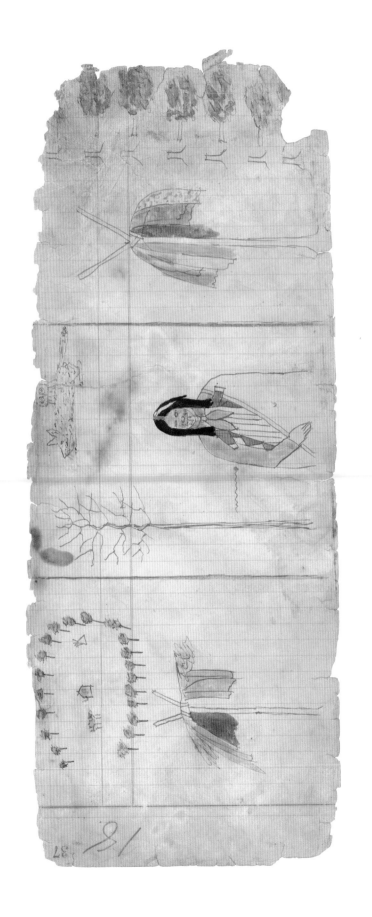

1858 Timber Circle Kado

The Medicine Lodge camp was set up in a natural clearing. The lodge itself and the lone tipi of the Taime keeper are shown within the circle of trees.

1858–59 Wolf Lying Down killed winter

The death of Wolf Lying Down is graphically represented with blood gushing from the mouths of both the man and his name glyph. In both of Silver Horn's calendars, the man's right eye is squinted, suggesting an identifying feature. Little Bluff says he was killed on a war party into Old Mexico.

1859 Timber Clearing Kado

According to Hauvahte, this dance was held north of the Arkansas River in an area where timber was scarce. They had to cut down all the available trees to construct the Medicine Lodge arbor.

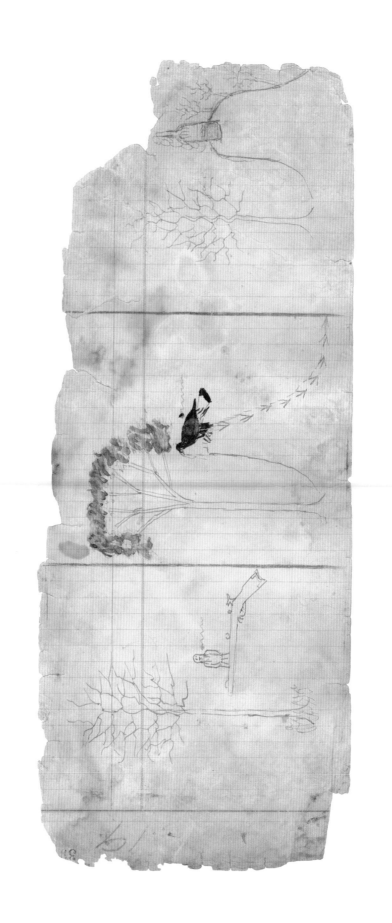

1859–60 On the Gun killed winter

The name sign of On the Gun is shown with a bullet coming toward it.

1860 Bird Appearing killed summer

There was no dance this summer. The calendar shows a golden eagle appearing over the brow of a hill, a bullet coming toward it. The NAA inscription reads "Tenebati killed." The word *tene* can be applied to any bird, and Mooney translates the name as Bird Appearing. The name glyph fits better with the translation for Hauvahte's calendar, which calls him Eagle Peeping Out, or the Quitone calendar, which calls him Appearing Eagle. According to Mooney's sources he was shot by a Caddo who was a scout for the army. Mooney was unable to find any military record of this engagement or to establish exactly why troops would have been pursuing the Kiowa at this time.

This was the summer that Silver Horn was born.

1860–61 Crazy Bluff winter

The picture of a liquor bottle on top of a hill represents a celebration when many people behaved wildly. According to the Little Bluff and Hauvahte calendars the Kiowas had led a successful revenge raid against the Caddo and acted "like drunk or crazy at the scalp dance." It is not clear whether they were actually crazy with drink or whether liquor is used here to symbolize craziness from any cause. Mooney describes the place name as coming from "rejoicing on this occasion."

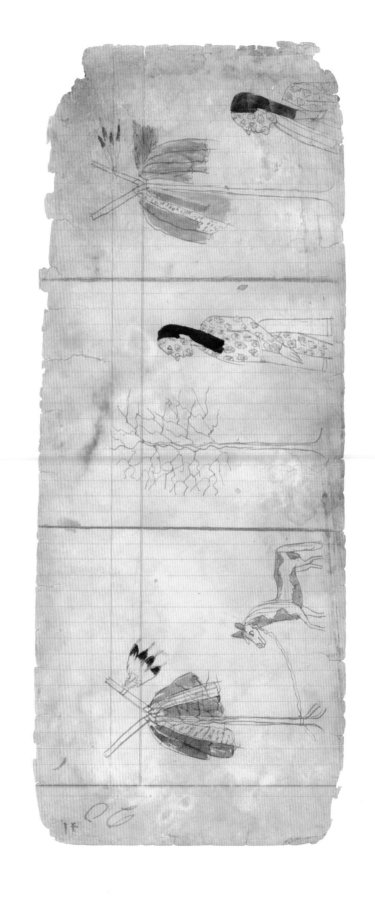

1861 Spotted horse tied Kado

This red-spotted pinto was tied to the center pole of the Medicine Lodge by its owner. It was left there to die as a sacrifice. The owner of the pony must have prayed to the Taime for assistance sometime during the year and vowed that he would make such a sacrifice if help were granted.

1861–62 Smallpox winter

The figure with spots represents smallpox. The NAA calendar is captioned "Tadalkop," the Kiowa term for the disease, which Mooney translates literally as "hole sickness." Quitone recorded that he suffered smallpox himself but survived. Many did not. The Little Bluff calendar reports that half of the Kiowa died. This epidemic was widespread on the Plains and is reported in many of the Lakota winter counts as well.

1862 Smallpox Kado

This summer is noted merely as a continuation of the smallpox time.

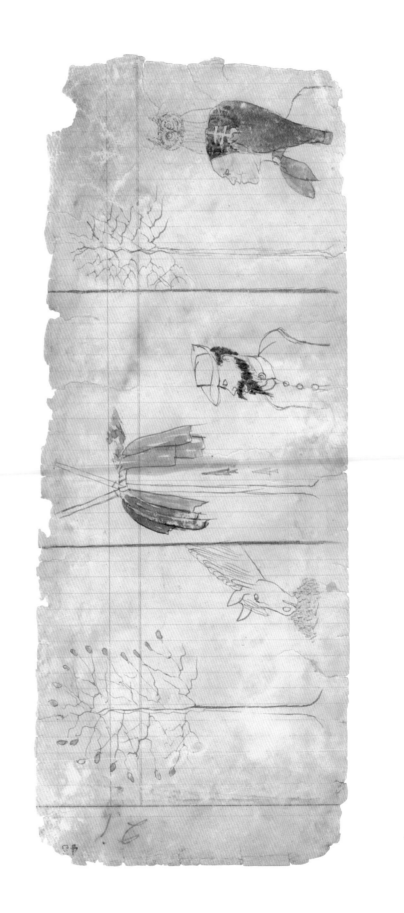

1862–63 Horses ate ashes winter

The stooping horse is eating ashes, as the horses could not reach the grass through the deep snow. Such conditions were rare on the Southern Plains, where snowfall was generally light and strong winds soon swept open areas clear. While northern tribes found it difficult to keep horses in good condition over the winter, herds flourished on the southern grasslands. Trade in surplus horses ranked along with buffalo hunting as a mainstay of the Kiowa economy.

1863 No Arm's Kado

The armless man represents a white man whom the Kiowa called Tsodalhente, or No Arm. Mooney says his name translated literally as "without wing"; Hauvahte termed him One Wing. The man, who was missing one arm, operated a trading post near the confluence of Walnut Creek and the Arkansas or Arrowhead River, where the 1863 dance was held. The location is indicated by the arrowheads next to the pole, a device Silver Horn also used for the Kado of 1848.

1863–64 Big Head died winter

The death owl appears with a large figure representing Big Head, a Kiowa warrior. According to Mooney's sources, he died while the Kiowa were in their winter camp on the North Canadian River. His nephew, who had the same name, was a chief during the time that Mooney was writing his *Calendar History*.

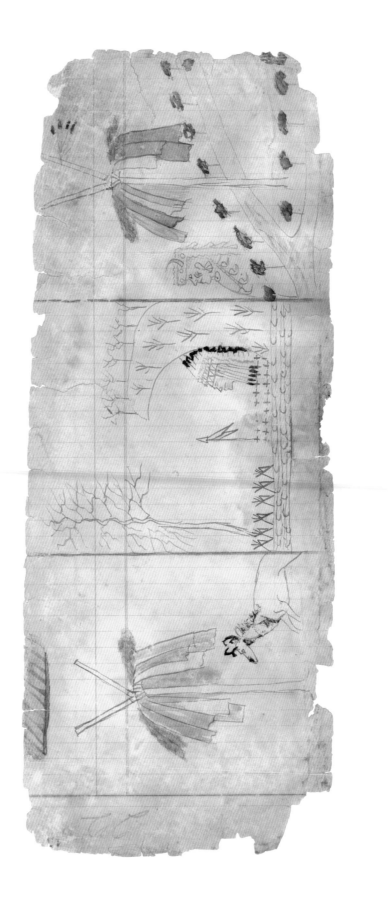

1864 Ragweed Kado

The calendar records two events for this summer. The patch of green above the center pole of the Medicine Lodge represents a plant that grew in abundance around the camp. Mooney gives the word for the plant as *asabe*, literally "green plant," which he identifies as ragweed. Other sources offer different translations of the term; it is called "screw worm medicine" in Hauvahte's record and "flowers" in the Little Bluff account.

The other picture is of a pronghorn antelope. Hauvahte explains its significance: "They roped an antelope to make a new inner sack for the Taime. They cannot shoot an animal for this purpose." Activities associated with the Taime and Kado ceremony generally avoided any shedding of blood, even by accident. Dancers in the Kado did not pierce their flesh as other tribes did during their related sun dances.

The prohibition extended as far as the buffalo bull that was killed to make the central effigy, which was supposed to be downed with a single arrow placed so as cause as little bleeding as possible.

1864–65 Fight with Ute at Red Bluff winter

This calendar graphically illustrates the different perspectives that Kiowa and Western historians often bring to the same event, such as this November 1864 attack on a Kiowa camp by army troops under the leadership of Captain Kit Carson. All the Kiowa calendars refer to it as a fight with the Utes, and Silver Horn represents the Ute enemies by a figure wearing a full feather warbonnet. The Kiowas were in their winter camp on the upper Canadian River in the Texas Panhandle at a place known as Red Bluff when they were attacked. The camp is suggested by a row of lodges, one colored red, perhaps indicating White

Bear's red tipi. Silver Horn's great uncle Little Bluff played a prominent role in successfully defending the camp, although he was by then an old man. In the NAA calendar, his striped tipi is shown in the row of lodges. The Utes, longtime enemies of the Kiowa, were serving as scouts for the U.S. Army and were in the forefront of the attack on the village. They were the combatants that Silver Horn chose to present most prominently. He acknowledges the regular army troops with a flag (similar to that shown for 1891–92) and a neat double row of crosses, presumably representing the white soldiers.

In Western historical sources this event is known as the first battle of Adobe Walls. It is named for the nearby ruins of an abandoned trading post rather than for the engagement riverside bluff that the Kiowa chose as a point of reference. To Western writers it was an engagement between the Kiowa and army troops. The seventy-two scouts, who included both Utes and Jicarilla Apaches, are barely mentioned.[4] The army recruited many Native men to serve as scouts against tribes that were their traditional enemies—and even at times against other bands of their own tribes. Scouts not only located the enemy but also often served as shock troops who led the attack. Many Plains drawings that appear to represent intertribal warfare may in fact depict combat with such advance forces for the U.S. Army.

1865 Peninsula Kado

In addition to the tree-lined bend of the river, the calendar shows a large figure of an eastern Plains tribe, possibly an Osage or Pawnee. He is not further identified here and none of the other calendar texts sheds light on his identity.

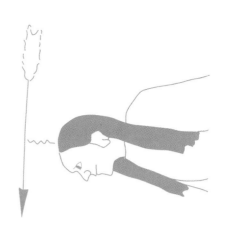

1865–66 Old Man Wagon died winter

Old Man Wagon was another appellation for the great chief and calendar keeper Little Bluff, the first of that name, who died of natural causes this winter and was buried on the Cimarron River near where it crosses the Kansas line. For decades the Kiowa had seen traders, explorers, and the military using wagons to transport goods, but very few Kiowas were attracted to the idea of wheeled transport. Little Bluff was the exception. He owned a light wagon he had been given by friendly army officers in 1859, and both a wagon and a buggy belonging to him were among the property destroyed in the Ute attack the previous winter.[5] By the time of his death he had given his name as well as the responsibility for maintaining the calendar to his nephew, Silver Horn's father, and was known by the nickname Old Man Wagon based on his unusual possession.

1866 Flat Metal Kado

This summer was named for the quantities of German silver ornaments acquired at the time. This metal, actually an alloy of tin and brass containing no silver, is cut and hammered from flat sheets rather than melted and cast like true silver, which is softer. The picture shows a set of hair plates, a series of metal disks attached to a long piece of cloth and worn by men suspended from the back of the head as an ornament. In earlier times hair plates were fashioned by hammering out silver coins into large, thin disks. Catlin's 1834 portrait of Little Bluff shows him wearing a set of hair plates, although such a valuable trade item was probably available only to the wealthy members of the tribe at that date. German silver became available through traders probably as early as the late eighteenth century, but evidently it was still a scarce and valued commodity.

The calendar also includes the figure of an eastern Plains warrior, similar to the unexplained one shown the previous summer.

1866–67 Struck His Head Against a Tree killed winter

The usual bare tree indicating the winter season has been incorporated into the image to suggest the name of the man who died this winter. According to Little Bluff, he was a Mexican captive and was killed in Texas while on a war party led by Big Bow and Plenty Bears.

1867 Koitsenko initiated again Kado

The notable event of the summer was the initiation of new members of the Koitsenko warrior society (see summer 1848 for a previous initiation). The figure wears a feather headdress and is holding a society rattle made of dew claws attached to a stick, called a hoof rattle. An eagle bone whistle projects from his mouth. His no-retreat sash is black. While most members of this small, elite society wore red sashes, the leader wore a black one.[6] Hauvahte's name for this calendar event is given as the Choking Dance, referring to the sash that was worn around the neck like a choker collar. The dance was held in Kansas at a place known to the Kiowa as Timber Hill.

1867–68 Treaty winter

This winter the Kiowas together with members of other Southern Plains tribes gathered on Timber Hill Creek to meet with U.S. treaty commissioners. The resulting agreement, known to the whites as the Medicine Lodge Treaty after the Cheyenne name for the site where they met, is represented by a pile of trade goods placed between a white man and a Kiowa. This treaty was intended to secure peace on the Southern Plains, opening the area to construction of roads and railroads and to increased settlement. Among other things, the U.S. government now sought to protect the citizens of Texas from Indian raids—a switch from actually encouraging raids during the recent Civil War, when Texas was part of the Confederacy. Through this treaty the Kiowa ceded control of their territory to the U.S. government except for a specific reservation within Indian Territory. They reserved hunting rights to a portion of the ceded land and were to receive annual payments in goods and services for thirty years.[7] Regrettably, corruption was deeply seated in the Indian Service, and few provisions of the treaty were fairly administered.

A small detail in the picture of the Kiowa man relates to the tribe's continued horse raiding. His nose is dark colored, a detail explained by Hauvahte's calendar: he called this black mucus winter because Kiowas went to Texas and it was "so cold their 'snot' froze."

1868 Without Horn killed Kado

The figure with a headdress of a single horn represents the name of the man killed this summer. Hauvahte calls him Lost One Horn, while the NAA inscription identifies him as Without Horn, who was killed by the Utes. Mooney provides an extended account of this disastrous battle, in which many warriors were killed and one of the sacred Taime figures was captured by the Utes. Silver Horn produced a powerful and detailed drawing of this event, showing Plenty Bears in battle with the Taime exposed and hanging upon his chest.[8]

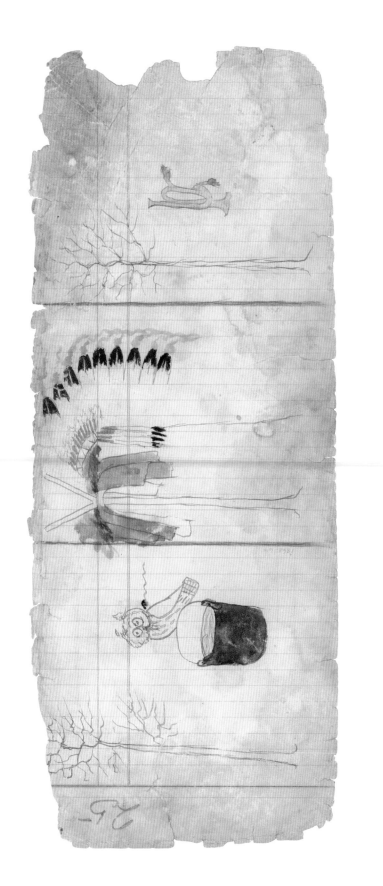

25-

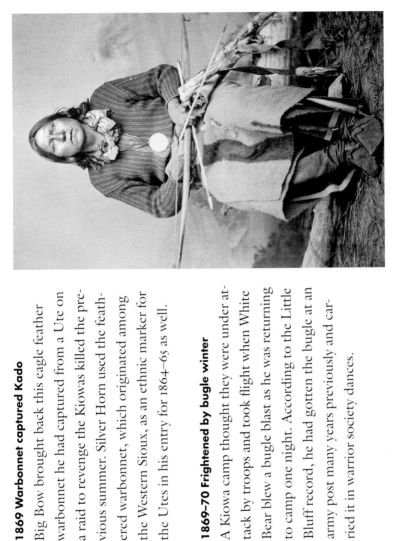

FIGURE 3-6. Set-taintè, or White Bear. Photograph by William S. Soule, ca. 1867. GN 01380a. Courtesy of the National Anthropological Archives, Smithsonian Institution.

1868–69 Black Kettle killed winter

The death owl perched on the handle of a bucket indicates the death of Black Kettle, the Cheyenne chief killed by Custer's troops in the Battle of the Washita. While this event is remembered primarily as a tragedy affecting the Cheyennes, some Kiowas who were camped with their Cheyenne allies were also directly involved. For all the tribes of the region, it was a particularly ominous event, as even Black Kettle's efforts to abide by the terms of the Medicine Lodge Treaty and cooperate with the whites did not bring safety to his people.

1869 Warbonnet captured Kado

Big Bow brought back this eagle feather warbonnet he had captured from a Ute on a raid to revenge the Kiowas killed the previous summer. Silver Horn used the feathered warbonnet, which originated among the Western Sioux, as an ethnic marker for the Utes in his entry for 1864–65 as well.

1869–70 Frightened by bugle winter

A Kiowa camp thought they were under attack by troops and took flight when White Bear blew a bugle blast as he was returning to camp one night. According to the Little Bluff record, he had gotten the bugle at an army post many years previously and carried it in warrior society dances.

1870 Plant growing Kado

The growing plant represents a stalk of corn. On returning to the site of the Kado encampment a few months after the ceremony, people found that some seeds they had dropped from corn obtained in trade had sprouted into new plants. The picture of a foot refers to Long Foot, the keeper of the Taime and leader of the Medicine Lodge ceremony. This was the last Kado that Long Foot led before his death the following winter. He had kept the Taime since it was returned by the Osage in 1834.

1870–71 Kill on the Mountain killed winter

The upper picture represents the name of the man killed this winter, Kill on the Mountain. He died pierced by an arrow in a drunken fight with another Kiowa.

1871 White Buffalo given a pipe summer

There was no Kado this summer as no one had been named to the position of Taime keeper following the recent death of Long Foot. White Buffalo received a pipe from the Wichitas, perhaps in an adoption ceremony like that indicated in the first entry of the calendar. This was probably Silver Horn's brother, although at least one other Kiowa man was known by the same name. The lower figure of a man riding away from a camp carrying a scalp on a pole is not explained.

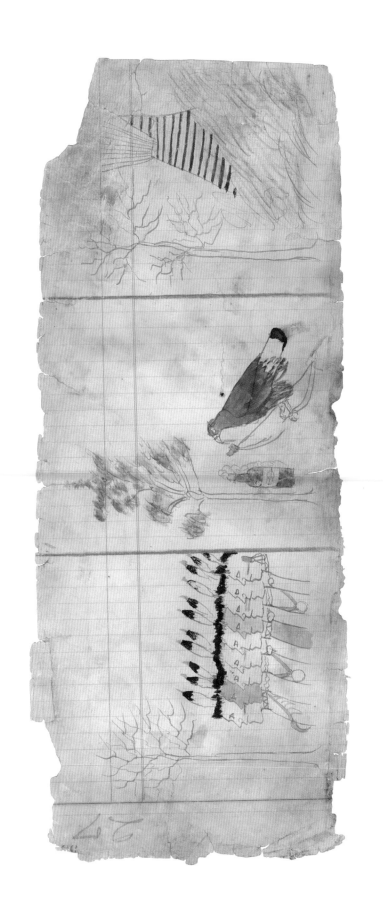

1871–72 Pawnee visit winter

A delegation of Pawnees, longtime enemies of the Kiowas, came seeking peace this winter. Silver Horn carefully detailed their roached hair, dangling earrings, and various necklaces. All the tribes of the Southern Plains were increasingly aware of the common threat of the advancing white frontier, and the Pawnee were exploring the option of relocating to a reservation within Indian Territory. As this would place them close to traditional enemies, they began with a trial visit to the neighboring Wichita, a tribe to whom they were distantly related. Mooney felt the calendars placed this event in the wrong year, as various government sources recorded a major Pawnee delegation the following year. Such delicate negotiations, however, might well have required several visits, and the calendars may record a visit that escaped the notice of agency officials.

1872 Bird Bow killed summer

There was no dance in 1872 as no Taime keeper had yet been named. Bird Bow was killed in a drunken fight, the second such event noted in as many years. According to Mooney's sources, he was killed by Sun Boy. The onus of this event clung to Sun Boy for many years. Although he was still acknowledged as a chief, many people considered him unlucky and chose to avoid living in his camp.[9]

1872–73 Battle tipi burned winter

The calendar shows a striped tipi burning. This was the Tipi with Battle Pictures that Little Bluff had received in the summer of 1845; it was passed down in the family along the same lines as the calendar itself. The NAA inscription identifies it as "Hauvahte's striped tipi," although his father would have been the owner in the 1870s. This tipi appears again in the entry for 1912.

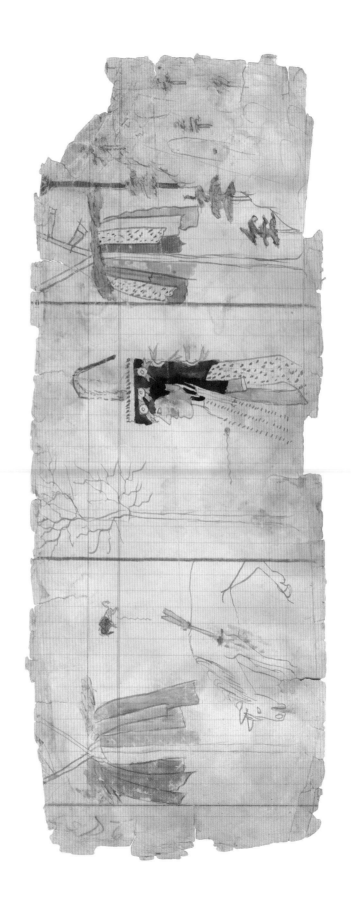

FIGURE 3-7. Lone Wolf's son, Tau-ankia. Photograph by William S. Soule, ca. 1872. BAE Neg. 1432a. Courtesy of the National Anthropological Archives, Smithsonian Institution.

1873 Black Buffalo's horses killed Kado

The drama of the Kado camp this summer was the shooting of Black Buffalo's horses. They were killed by Wolf Appearing (Hauvahte calls him Peeping Coyote) in retaliation for Black Buffalo stealing one of his wives. Such destruction of property was the customary prerogative of the wronged party and was expected to settle the matter.

The Kado resumed in 1873 under the direction of the new Taime keeper, No Moccasins.

1873–74 Lone Wolf's son killed winter

Lone Wolf's son was killed this winter while on a raid into Texas. He is shown elegantly dressed, with otter fur turban, hairpipe breastplate, and spotted calico shirt. The calendar entry is strikingly similar to a photograph of him taken by Will Soule, probably in 1872. Prints of Soule's images were widely circulated, and it is possible that Silver Horn based his drawing on the photograph. This is probably the event that Mary Buffalo's calendar refers to as "Otter Head Gear died." The death of this favored son deeply affected Lone Wolf. Mooney attributed the old warrior's participation in later attacks on whites to his bitterness over this loss.

1874 End of Mountains Kado

The Kado was held at a place in what is now Greer County, Oklahoma, known as Last Mountain, meaning the end of a series of hills or mountains. White Bear, who had been released from prison the previous winter, gave his famous zebat, an arrow-shaped lance represented here by the red shaft next to the mountain, to White Cowbird. The zebat is noted also in entries for 1854 and 1878–79.

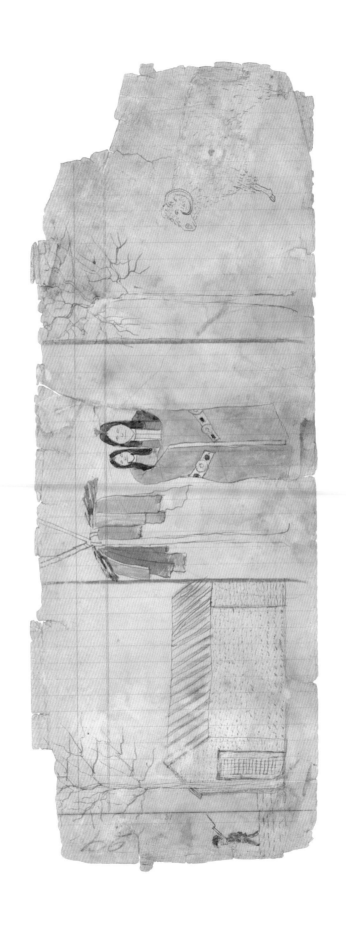

1874–75 Kiowa prisoners to jail

A number of Kiowa men were arrested following an attack on the Wichita Agency at Anadarko, which occurred while U.S. troops were trying to disarm the visiting bands. The men were held at Fort Sill this winter, as represented by many footprints going into a windowless building. The ice house was one of the few solid buildings completed at the new fort, and it was used as a temporary jail for the warriors arrested.

Most of the men were ultimately released, but twenty-seven were selected for continued imprisonment without benefit of trial. Together with individuals from other Southern Plains tribes, they were sent to Saint Augustine, Florida, where they were held at Fort Marion for three years. One of Silver Horn's brothers, Charlie Buffalo, was among the Kiowa prisoners.

1875 Love Making Spring Kado

The picture of a couple wrapped together in a single blanket represents a courting custom originating among the Lakota and widely adopted on the Plains. Hauvahte called it the Sweetheart Sun Dance as many young people were "sparking." The pleasant image conjured by Silver Horn's picture is welcome among the dark events surrounding the Kiowa at this time. However, according to the Little Bluff record, the Kado camp was named for the place where it was held on the north fork of the Red River rather than for immediate events: "This place has from very ancient times been called 'the place where the man was killed for interfering with another man's wife.'" Mooney's sources told him that the spring where they camped was so named because some young Kiowa men once "stole" two girls who had come to the spring for water.

1875–76 Given sheep winter

The government issued sheep to the Kiowa, who were now closely confined within reservation boundaries. The intent was to convert the Kiowas from buffalo hunters to sheep herders, an unlikely scenario with predictable results.

1876 Sun Boy's horses stolen Kado

The theft of Sun Boy's horses is indicated by many tracks in association with a rayed figure representing his name. Indian Territory had by this time become a no-man's-land, a haven for white horse thieves. The Kiowas were never able to establish the identity of the thieves.

No Moccasins had died the previous winter, and this was the first Kado led by another new Taime keeper, Plenty Bears or Heap of Bears, a relative of the man killed by the Utes in 1842–43.

1876–77 Rode a buffalo winter

As in the previous year, a mass of horse tracks lead to Sun Boy's name glyph, drawn somewhat differently this time. Hauvahte reports that Sun Boy had received permission to lead a group of hunters off-reservation to hunt buffalo, which had become

exceedingly scarce. The NAA inscription explains that a man fell from his horse and rode a buffalo, perhaps to avoid being trampled. The row of tipis is unexplained and may represent the camp of the hunting party. The Porcupine Tipi, reported to have been the last buffalo hide tipi used by the Kiowa, is clearly depicted.[10]

1877 Measles Kado

The measles epidemic of 1877 was particularly severe. Mooney reported that it killed even more children than the devastating epidemic of 1892.

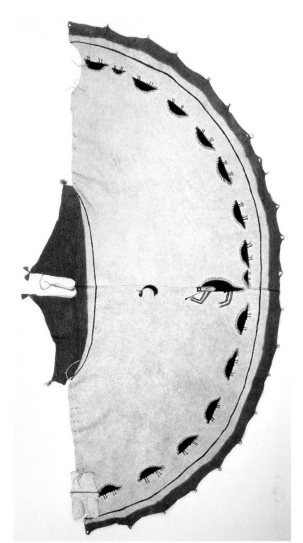

FIGURE 3-8. Painted buckskin model of the Porcupine Tipi. Cat. no. 229,904. Courtesy of the Department of Anthropology, Smithsonian Institution.

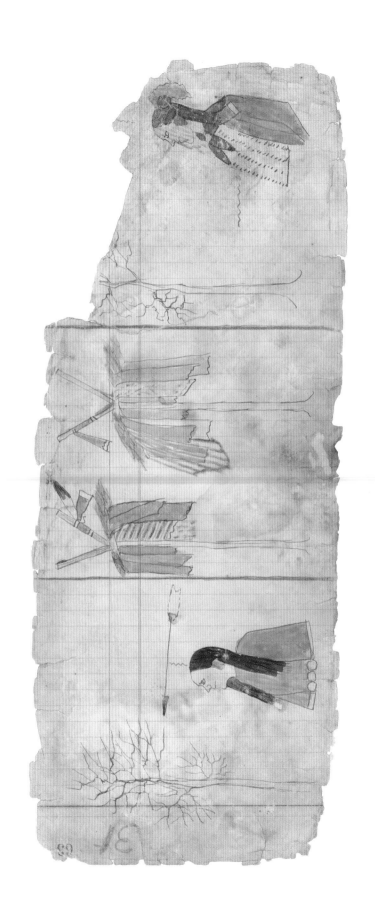

1877–78 Arrow woman winter

A woman named Arrow went crazy this winter, according to Hauvahte's account as well as Mooney's notes on Silver Horn's other calendar. No other information about the event is recorded in the calendars.

1878 Repeated Kado

The double set of poles represents two Medicine Lodge ceremonies held this summer, in recognition of vows made by two separate men. Another repeated Kado was noted for 1842.

1878–79 White Cowbird killed winter

White Cowbird, who had received the *zebat* arrow lance at the Kado of 1874, was killed this winter. Mooney reported that he was killed by Texans while hunting in what is now Greer County, Oklahoma. The hunting party was accompanied by troops intended to protect the Indians and ensure their peaceful conduct, but the party had scattered in search of the now scarce bison. Local officials refused to pursue White Cowbird's killer. Hauvahte refers to him as Arrow Owner, identifying him with his *zebat*. The lance does not show in this picture, although it might have been on the part of the page that is now lost. Instead, White Cowbird is distinguished by his headdress, a red spray similar to that shown for Koitsenko members in the entry for 1848.

1879 Horse eating Kado

With the failure of the hunt, the Kiowas were reduced to eating their own horses this summer. The man with drum and drumstick is participating in a victory dance, with a short-haired enemy scalp displayed on a pole. Hauvahte's record explains that a Texan was killed and his was scalp taken to avenge the death of Arrow Owner.

1879–80 Red Buffalo died winter

Red Buffalo died of consumption. According to Hauvahte, he was the first Kiowa to die of tuberculosis, a disease that ravaged the tribe throughout the reservation period and well into the twentieth century. He is graphically depicted coughing up blood from disease-ravaged lungs.

1880 Big Bow died

There was no dance in 1880. Big Bow's death is marked by the death owl in association with this name glyph. The NAA inscription notes that he was the brother of the man later known by that name.

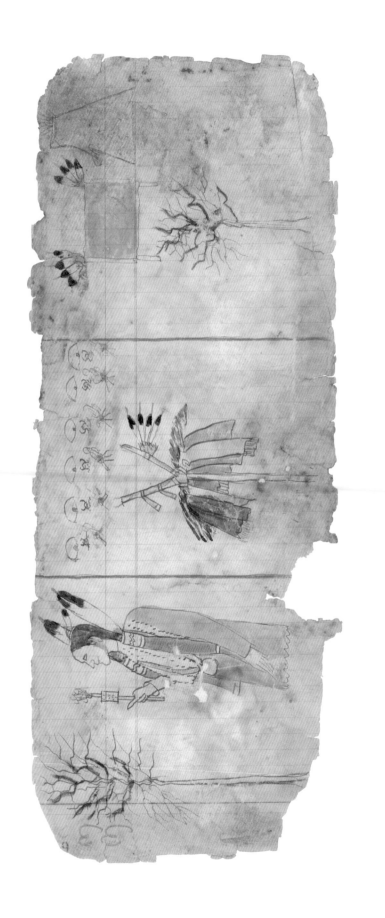

1880–81 Dance winter

This entry shows an unidentified man with a cylindrical rattle similar to that shown for 1838–39 to represent the organization of the Taimpego society. Silver Horn's other calendar shows an enigmatic horned anthropomorphic figure quite unlike the conventionally dressed man shown here, although both display two large eagle feathers. In the NAA calendar the picture is captioned as Tonaka's (Turtle's) dance, with a glyph of a snapping turtle, and it may represent a dance performed by this medicine man.

1881 Sweat lodge Kado

Many sweat lodges were built this year, as shown by the domed structures with buffalo skulls and fires in front of each. According to George Hunt's calendar, the number of lodges was ten times seven. During this period of starvation and illness, the Kiowa desperately sought to purify themselves and gain spiritual assistance through many sweat lodge ceremonies. The Kado ceremony itself was long delayed as it was very difficult to find a buffalo bull to sacrifice for the central effigy.

1881–82 Red blanket winter

A medicine man claimed to have received power to bring the buffalo back, taking a new name of Buffalo Coming Out. He carried out the ceremony of restoration screened behind a red blanket set up before his tipi. Silver Horn's other calendar shows him playing the hand game against another medicine man as a test of power. This was the first of three efforts by Kiowa medicine men to restore the natural order through public ceremonial action. Commonly referred to as messianic movements, ceremonies of revitalization were widespread among Western tribes during the last quarter of the nineteenth century, with the Lakota Ghost Dance probably best known because of its tragic outcome at Wounded Knee. Most such movements dwindled and declined quietly as followers lost faith when medicine men like Buffalo Coming Out were unsuccessful.[11]

1882 Nez Perces visited summer

There was no Kado this summer. This figure, identified in the NAA calendar as a Nez Perce, is distinguished principally by his hairstyle. Men of the Nez Perce tribe, like some other Columbia Plateau people, cut their hair short in front and coated it with clay or other pomade so that it would stand upright. As ethnic markers Silver Horn colored the man's pompadour red and added a shell gorget at his neck, a breastplate, and a tufted wand. The stuffed ermine skin behind his head likely represents his personal medicine.

Following their defeat in the Nez Perce war, Chief Joseph and his band were exiled to Indian Territory in 1879, far from their Idaho home. They were assigned a small territory in the Cherokee Outlet in what is now north-central Oklahoma until 1885, when they were relocated to the Colville Reservation in Washington state.[12]

1882–83 Bag shot himself winter

The gun grasped by this figure with blood gushing from his mouth suggests that he shot himself, though whether this was accidental is not indicated. His name is given in Hauvahte's calendar as Bag, represented in the NAA calendar by a glyph of a painted rawhide container used to carry meat and other goods.

1883 Nez Perces came again Kado

Silver Horn shows a Nez Perce joining the Kiowa at the Medicine Lodge ceremony, perhaps following up on an invitation issued the previous year. The Little Bluff record notes the visit of a tribe who had their hair cut short in front but says they were from a tribe other than Nez Perce.

A second image shows a shell necklace dripping blood from a bullet wound. According to Hauvahte's record, a man named Green Necklace was killed by Little Bow. The NAA inscription calls him Blue Necklace and says Little Bow acted out of jealousy. The Kiowa word *sahe* can be translated as either blue or green.

The 1883 Kado was held under the direction of the new keeper named Taimete, or Taime Man, who took over the responsibility following the death of Plenty Bears in the spring.

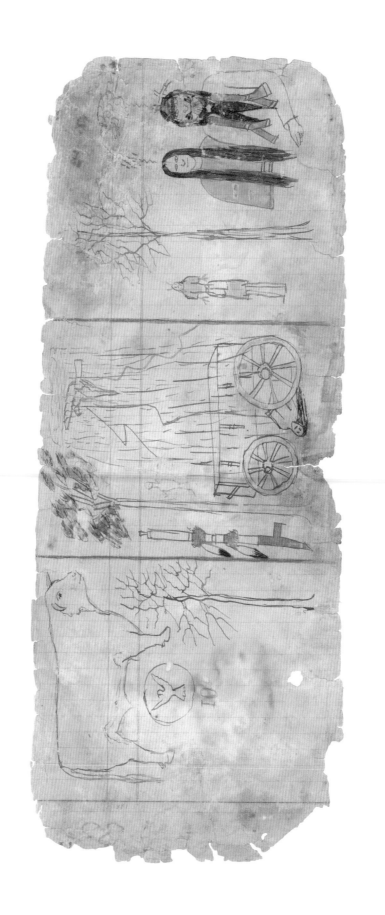

1883-84 Grass money winter

Cattlemen in surrounding states were anxious to gain access to the rich grasslands of the Kiowa and Comanche reservations, and it was nearly impossible to keep their stock out. The Indian Department ultimately resolved the situation by leasing out grazing rights in return for payment of "grass money" to the tribes involved. In an effort to engage Indians themselves in stock raising, Indians were sometimes paid in cattle to be used for breeding, and a few men built up large herds, most notably the Comanche Quanah Parker. According to Hauvahte, this was the winter when chiefs were issued both cattle and a cash payment, as indicated by the coin with the flying eagle, representing the silver dollars in which payment was issued. Mooney reported that the Kiowas did not receive money for grass leases until 1886, although the Comanche had received such payment the previous year.[13] The calendar suggests earlier experiments with this economic arrangement.

1884 Woman killed by lightning summer

There was no dance this year because the Kiowa could not locate a buffalo, as required to make the central effigy. The remarkable occurrence of the summer was that a woman was struck and killed by lightning while seeking shelter under a wagon. Mary Buffalo gives her name as Charged Through the Line. The thunderstorm is dramatically illustrated with dark cloud, pelting rain, and the powerful thunderbird with lightning bolts shooting from it.

The second picture of a pipe with red bowl and wrappings is explained by Hauvahte's calendar as a peace pipe the Kiowas gave to a Comanche named Dry Shoulder, perhaps another instance of the Pipe Dance or adoption ceremony.

1884-85 Snapping Turtle stole a woman winter

Snapping Turtle, shown here with a black handkerchief around his neck and an elaborately painted face, stole a woman this winter. George Hunt gives her name as Konma, but provides no translation; Mary Buffalo says she was the wife of Otter Tail. Her name glyph suggests something like Many Tracks. According to Mooney's sources, her aggrieved husband whipped her and killed a number of Turtle's horses. Snapping Turtle, or Tonaka, was a powerful medicine man, and his name figures in several stories of community trouble during the reservation era. Black handkerchiefs were used by medicine men in conjuring.

The second picture of a tall, emaciated woman also appears in Silver Horn's other calendar, representing a woman who died. In both pictures she has small horns or projections on her head.

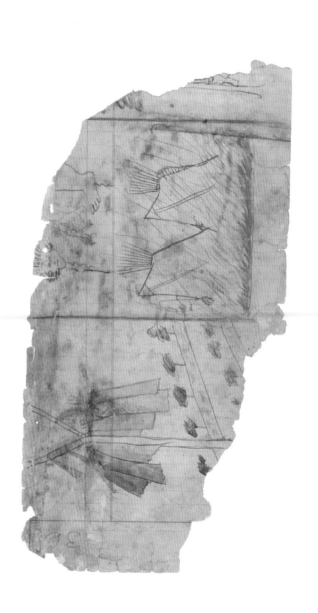

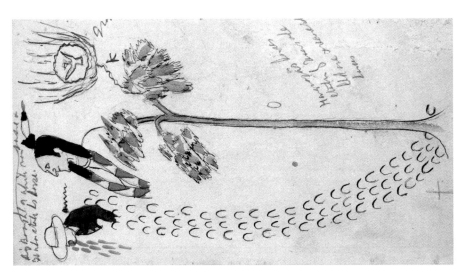

1885 Peninsula Kado

The fragmentary image on this damaged page can be recognized as the forked stream indicating the peninsula on the Washita River where dances were held in 1839 and 1865. A buffalo for the central effigy of the Medicine Lodge was found far out on the Staked Plains in the Texas Panhandle.

1885–86 Tipis burned winter

A row of name glyphs identifies the owners of tipis lost in this fire. The one on the left is surely Frizzle Head, while the one on the right represents Tebodal. Hauvahte translates the name Tebodal as Calf of the Leg, corresponding well with this picture of a man's lower leg. Mooney gives a fuller translation of the name as One Who Carries a Pack of Meat from the Buffalo's Lower Leg. The glyph used here, while not an accurate representation of the full

sense of the name, serves effectively as an identification.

1886 Big Bow killed a horse thief summer

This section of the calendar is missing. No Kado was held this year because the Kiowa could not locate a buffalo. The NAA calendar records that Big Bow pursued and shot a white man who had stolen his horses. Hauvahte's calendar records that Loud Talk's son was also involved.

FIGURE 3-9. NAA calendar entry for 1886, by Silver Horn. MS 2531, vol. 7. Courtesy of the National Anthropological Archives, Smithsonian Institution.

1886–87 Quiver Carrier's son killed himself winter

This fragmentary image records the shooting death of a man identified by a glyph of a quiver and bowcase. The NAA inscription says the young man committed suicide. According to Mooney's sources, he killed himself because he had been rebuked by relatives for taking someone's horse without permission.

While Mooney was eventually able to obtain the young man's name, Sand Son, people at first would identify him only as the son of a woman named Quiver Carrier. This is one of many examples in the calendar where Silver Horn identified someone who had died by reference to a relative or through other circumlocution, honoring the custom of avoiding the name of the recently dead.

1887 Oak Creek Kado

The upper edge of this entry is missing, but it appears to have contained an image similar to that of the NAA calendar, an acorn-laden tree, representing the Oak Creek Kado. This is the last Medicine Lodge ceremony referenced in the calendar for many years. The Little Bluff record agrees that the Oak Creek Kado was the last one but places it in the following summer. Buffalo had been exterminated from the region, but a captive animal was purchased for one hundred dollars from Charles Goodnight, a rancher in the Texas Panhandle, to construct the central effigy.

1887–88 Cattle issued winter

The figure of Sun Boy, identified by a prominent name glyph, is drawn together with the head of a steer. Formal leasing of grazing rights began this year, establishing "grass money" as a new part of the Kiowa economy (see 1883–84). Mooney reported that there was disagreement among the

Kiowa as to whether stock should be accepted in lieu of cash payment. Both Hauvahte and Silver Horn associate Sun Boy with this event, suggesting that he was an advocate for the livestock option, and Hauvahte's notes for the following winter confirm this.

FIGURE 3-10. NAA calendar entry for 1887, by Silver Horn. MS 2531, vol. 7. Courtesy of the National Anthropological Archives, Smithsonian Institution.

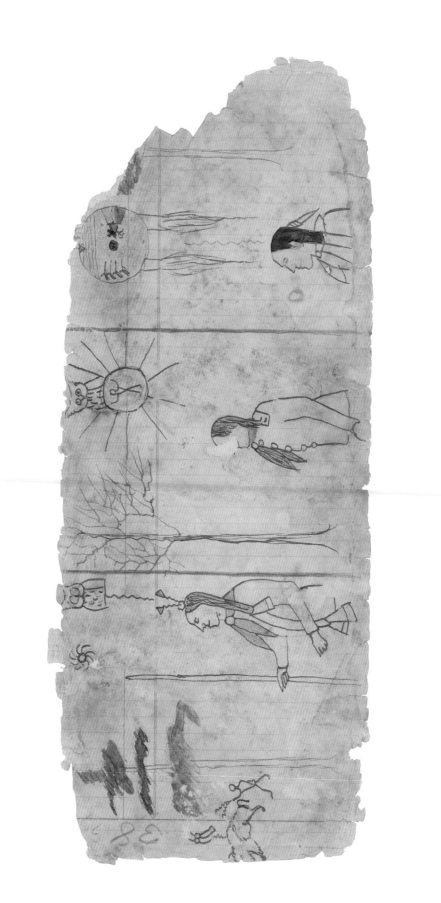

1888 Peyote Man died summer

The death of Peyote Man is represented by a whorl and a death owl. Silver Horn regularly used the whorled design representing the top of the peyote button to refer to the mildly hallucinogenic cactus that is the central sacrament of the Peyote religion to which he belonged. This use of the symbol may have been unique to Silver Horn. It was not incorporated into the rich visual iconography of the Peyote religion developed by Kiowa artists of the following generation. Silver Horn's other calendar places Peyote Man's death in the following winter, and Hauvahte's calendar may also—he notes the death of a man named Stick, perhaps referring to the tall staff shown in this man's hand. According to the Domebo calendar (see appendix C), the man was Sun Boy's brother.

Summer entries in both Hauvahte's record and Silver Horn's other calendar focus on the activities of the messianic medicine man In the Middle, who claimed that all the white people would be swept from the earth by a strong wind, and he would himself then bring back the buffalo and make possible the old ways of life. He summoned all the Kiowas to come to his camp on Elk Creek to await these events under his protection. A tiny figure in the NAA calendar (fig. 3-11) shows many hoof prints converging on a tipi camp along a tree-lined creek. (The rectangle to the left is intended as a man's legging marked with the medicine man's personal symbolism.) As had happened with the efforts of Buffalo Coming Out in 1881–82, many people came, but they were soon disillusioned about his power.[14] The small picture on the left of a

FIGURE 3-11. NAA calendar entry for 1888, by Silver Horn. MS 2531, vol. 7. Courtesy of the National Anthropological Archives, Smithsonian Institution.

buffalo and a man, identified by Mary Buffalo as "Running Calf died," may have some association with this event.

For some reason the drawings on this page were originally sketched in pencil and then gone over in ink, obscuring the original delicate drawing and resulting in a coarser outline with less internal detail than in other parts of the calendar.

1888-89 Sun Boy died winter

The death owl and name glyph mark the death of Sun Boy, whose activities are noted several times in the calendar (see entries for 1872, 1876, and 1887–88). As with the previous entry, both Hauvahte's and Silver Horn's other calendar record a somewhat different sequence of events, placing Sun Boy's death in the following winter.

1889 Stumbling Bear's son died summer

Continuing the practice of indirect reference to the dead, the young man who died is identified only by reference to his father. Stumbling Bear's well-known shield is used here in place of the usual name glyph, just as it was used to mark Stumbling Bear's birth in 1832. A death owl may have been drawn on a part of the page that is now missing. According to the Ananti calendar (see appendix C) he died of a spider bite.

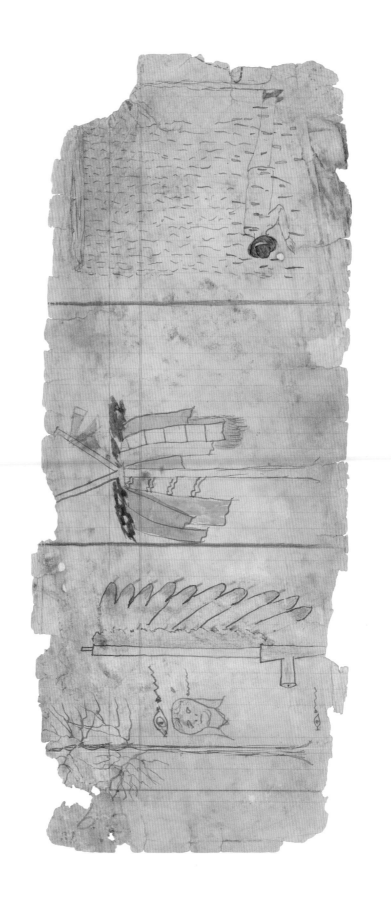

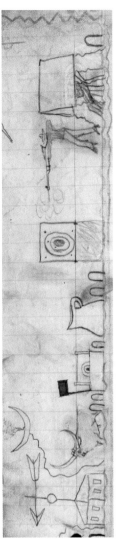

1891 Snapping Turtle shot a man summer

Snapping Turtle, whose wife stealing escapade was noted for the winter of 1884–85, is shown here shooting a man. The name of the victim is not indicated.

1891–92 Scouts enlisted winter

During this winter Silver Horn and a number of other Kiowa men enlisted in Troop L of the Seventh Cavalry, serving at Fort Sill. This entry may be a self-portrait, showing him in uniform beside the troop guidon. (See 1852 for earlier discussion of the guidon.) Unlike that of previous Indian scouts, who were hired as needed by the quartermaster for a period of a few months, their enlistment was for a five-year period of regular military service. Troop L was commanded by Lt. Hugh L. Scott, an avid amateur ethnologist interested in Kiowa culture. He learned to communicate in the Plains sign language used by many tribes, and he gathered extensive information on Kiowa

FIGURE 3-13. Entry from pictorial diary by Silver Horn. MS 4252. Courtesy of the National Anthropological Archives, Smithsonian Institution.

history and culture from tribal elders. He purchased the Little Bluff calendar from Silver Horn's father and recorded the notes on it that are published as appendix A to this volume.

Silver Horn maintained a pictorial diary for several years while he was serving in Troop L, noting such troop activities as target practice, guard duty, and escort service for pay wagons. Many drawings show the guardhouse with its elaborate weathervane, now part of the historic section of Fort Sill, which is still an active military post.

1892 Measles summer

The figure covered with red spots represents the tragic measles epidemic of this year that killed many tribal members, particularly young children. It spread rapidly among the camps as the agency boarding school closed when many students fell ill, and the infected children were dispersed to their homes throughout the reservation, carrying the disease with them. According to James Mooney, 15 percent of the young children died as a result of the inept management of this disease outbreak.[16]

Rows of circles represent silver dollars. A particularly large payment of grass money was made to the tribe at this time.

1892–93 White Horse died winter

The prominent warrior White Horse died this winter. White Horse was one of the warriors who had been sent to Fort Marion, Florida, in the 1870s, as noted in the entry for 1874–75. Before his death he had passed his name on to his nephew. This may be why Silver Horn felt free to use it here, since it no longer belonged to him. Rather than naming the man who died, this entry could be read along the lines of "White Horse's uncle died" or "the man once known as White Horse died."

1893 Big boy summer

The most remarkable event of the summer was a boy whom the Kiowas saw on display at a circus or show that came to Anadarko. The NAA calendar is inscribed, "Big fat boy here on Fourth and we look at him." Although the agent discouraged most tribal gatherings, "picnics" were allowed on the Fourth of July, and dispersed families and bands could come together to camp for a few days. These events filled the place of some of the social aspects of the former Medicine Lodge encampments.

The military jacket shown at the top of the page correlates with the picture in Silver Horn's other calendar, showing a cavalry officer identified there as Lt. Nichols. From November 1893 to October 1894 Lt. Maury Nichols, of the Seventh Cavalry, served as temporary agent for the Kiowa reservation.[17]

Small figures faintly sketched on either side of the tree trunk are probably later additions by some other member of the family.

1893–94 Little Bluff died winter

The name Little Bluff is graphically identified by the death owl, now partially missing, perched on top of a small bluff or hill. During this decade this name was held by two men, both descendants of the original Little Bluff whose death was marked for 1865–66. The two descendants, who were cousins, died around the same time, and the oral text connected to the calendar may have noted both deaths.[18] Harrington understood Hauvahte to say that the calendar marked the death of his (and Silver Horn's) father, the second Little Bluff, who had been given the name as well as the role of calendar keeper by the great chief of that name. However, Mooney's inscription in the NAA calendar identifies the dead man as Badai's brother. This would be the third Little Bluff, the cousin to whom Silver Horn's father had given the name some time previously. Details in the picture support this identification. This third Little Bluff was noted for his war shirt ornamented with ermine strips and hair from enemy scalps (see fig. 3-14). Mary Buffalo called the year "Scalps on Sleeves died."

The other picture is Rainy Mountain School, a substantial brick building

FIGURE 3-14. Little Bluff, the third member of the family to carry that name, with his wife Ankima. GN 01308. Courtesy of the National Anthropological Archives, Smithsonian Institution.

with multiple chimneys. The accompanying hill and cloud are a name glyph for the place rather than an illustration of the landscape. The NAA calendar inscription records, "Schoolboys taken" and "Camp near there." When their children went off to boarding schools, Kiowa families were apt to abandon their new frame houses and cornfields and set up camp near the school.

When the Rainy Mountain School opened for its first term in 1893, it had no problem in recruiting students. Kiowa parents seem to have been supportive of the idea of formal education, while also recognizing that the school would provide their children with basic food, clothing, and shelter, things that not all parents could themselves guarantee in these difficult times.[19]

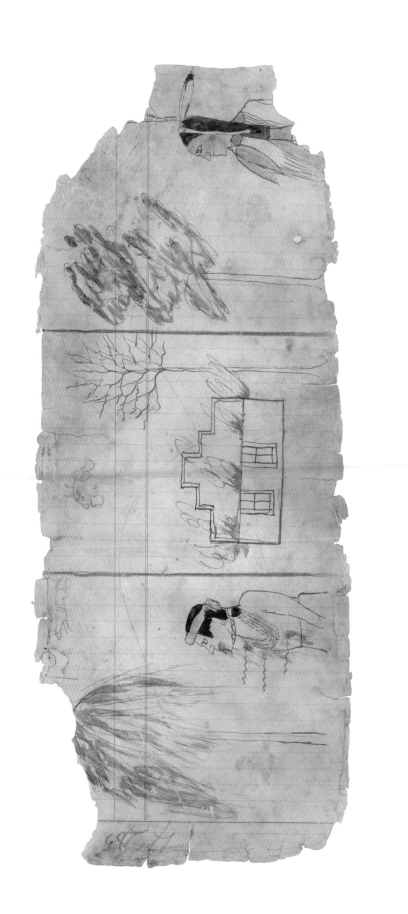

1894 Caddo man killed

The man with a head band and many necklaces is identified by Hauvahte as a Caddo named Inkinish. The NAA calendar inscription elaborates on Hauvahte's identification, reporting that he was killed by robbers. The Caddo reservation was adjacent to Kiowa lands, and both areas were constantly troubled by outlaws who viewed Indian Territory as a lawless no-man's-land.

1894–95 Quinette's store burned winter

The flaming building is identified by Hauvahte as Quinette's store, which was the official post trader store at Fort Sill. William H. Quinette had begun working for the post trader in 1878 and was proprietor of the establishment by this time. The building with its frontier-classic stepped facade was vacant but still standing in 1915, when it was purchased for use by the School of Fire, Fort Sill's Artillery School.[20]

1895 White Bear's brother died summer

The identifying name glyph has been lost from this torn page. The NAA calendar notes the death of a young man named Talo-ti, the brother of White Bear, while Hauvahte's calendar refers to two deaths: Low Bowels and Snapping Turtle.

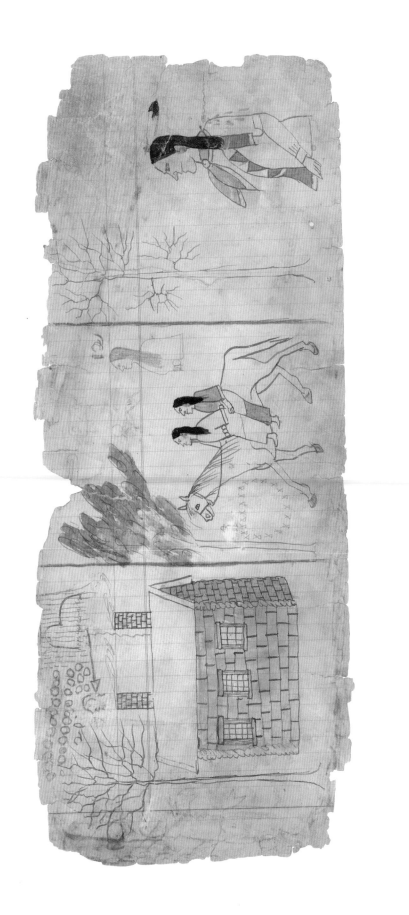

1895–96 Payment at Rainy Mountain

Rainy Mountain School appears again, two years after its opening was marked. It was occasionally used as a meeting place for agency affairs as it was more centrally located than Anadarko, which was on the far eastern edge of the reservation. The number 20 is surrounded by many circles representing dollars. The NAA calendar also shows twenty circles in two neat rows, which Mooney inscribed as a twenty-dollar payment made at Rainy Mountain. The picture of a lance probably refers to involvement by Ahpeahtone, or Wooden Lance.

1896 Kiowa girls ran away summer

These two Kiowa women are running away to the Comanches, according to information provided by Hauvahte. Mooney recorded their names in the NAA calendar, Ooti and Gets Down and Dies with Him, but was unable to solicit any further information. The Domebo calendar also notes this event, giving one woman's name as Oh-oh-da. This entry is unusual, as women and their doings are seldom noted in the calendars. The upper figure of a woman may be a name sign for one of them.

A small, faint sketch of a longhorn steer correlates with Hauvahte's reference to young cattle being issued this summer. It is branded ID, for Indian Department.

1896–97 White Feather shot winter

The portion of the page that would contain the man's name glyph is missing. The Hauvahte and other Silver Horn calendars identify him as White Feather and say he was shot in the shoulder during a scuffle with a white man.

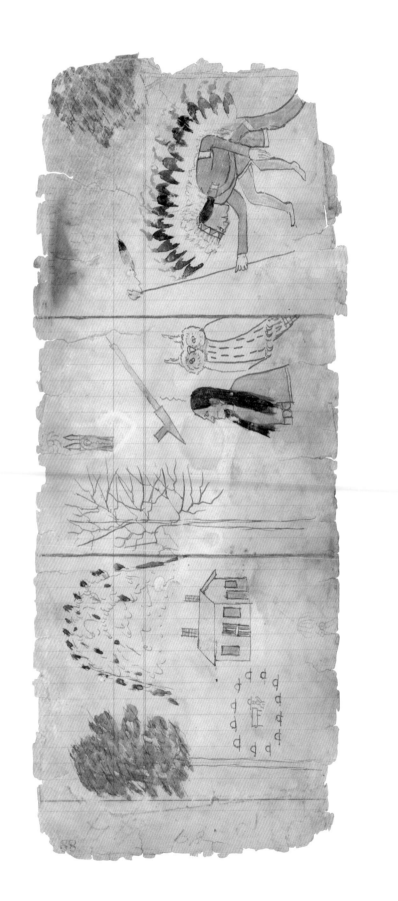

88

1897 Council at Mount Scott summer

This council is identified in the NAA calendar as taking place at Mount Scott in the Wichita Mountains, shown as a wooded hill. In that version Silver Horn shows the participants seated in a circle, all wearing broad-brimmed hats. Here the hats alone represent the participants. Hauvahte reported that the council was regarding a rock quarry, which the Kiowa ceded to the government; he noted that after the council, the hats were put away. Kiowa men traditionally put on headdresses only for ceremonies or formal occasions and did not wear anything on their heads as part of everyday dress. At this date it appears that store-bought hats, like earlier types of headdresses, marked a formal occasion.

The faint sketch at the bottom of the page of a dome with the death owl corresponds to Hauvahte's note of the death of Standing on Sweat House. According to Wilbur Nye, he was a medicine man with owl power.[21]

1897–98 Leader died winter

A woman named Leader died this winter. Hauvahte said she was Sankadote's wife. The pipe is an appropriate name glyph as it was the sign of the leader of a war party. The calendar also notes the birth of Hauvahte's daughter Old Peyote, shown by a cradle board and a peyote whorl. Hauvahte's own calendar places her birth in the previous summer.

1898 Poncas visit and dance summer

The dancing man in a full feather bonnet represents the visit of another tribe during the Kiowas' Fourth of July dance gathering in 1898. The NAA inscription identifies them as Poncas, although the style of dress is more consistent with Hauvahte's identification of the visitors as Arapahos.

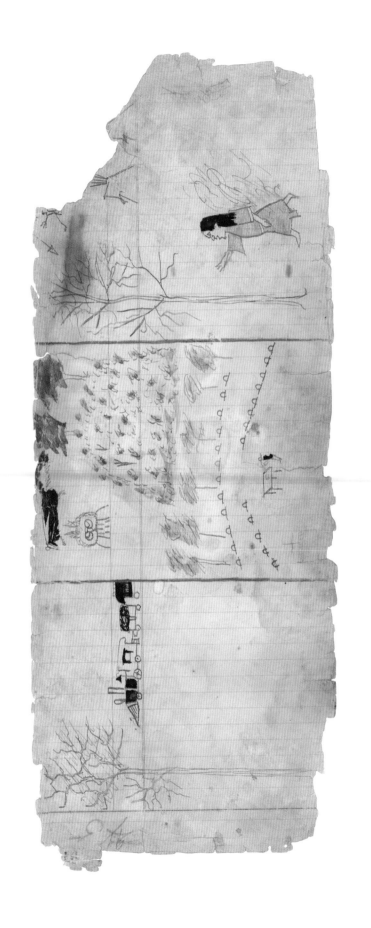

1898–99 First train winter

The steam locomotive is identified in the NAA inscription as the first railroad to cross the Washita River at Chickasha. This was an era of rapid railroad expansion throughout the region, further connecting Kiowa people to wider American society.

1899 Second Council at Mount Scott summer

A gathering of hats again indicates a council at Mount Scott. The topic of concern was undoubtedly resistance to the infamous Jerome Agreement, under which the reservation was broken up and opened to settlement (see The Kiowa, chapter 1). The death of White Skunk, or White Polecat, as Hauvahte calls him, is also noted.

1899–1900 Woman burned winter

This woman with her dress on fire does not appear in either the NAA or the Hauvahte calendar.

Both those calendars record that Wooden Lance was whipped by a man whose son had fallen ill while attending the council the previous summer; the man blamed Wooden Lance for the son's death. The same event may have appeared on the torn upper edge of this page, which has a fragmentary image of a running man with a lance above his head, possibly Wooden Lance's name glyph. According to Mary Buffalo, White Fox whipped him for "meddling in his affairs."

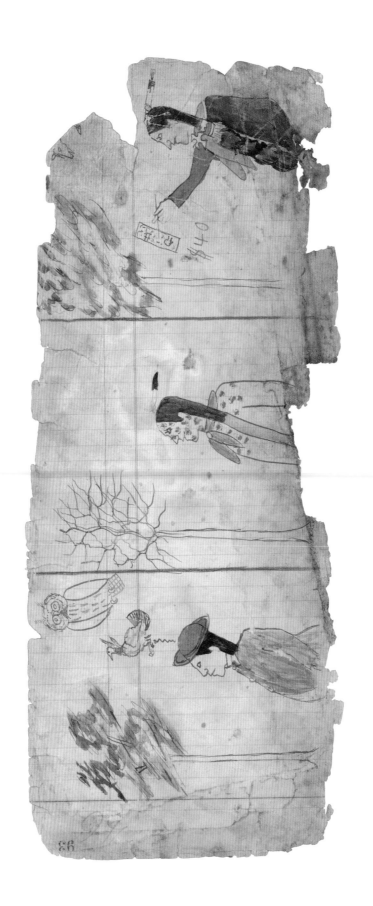

1900 Prairie Chicken died summer

This entry records the death of a man with a name glyph representing a prairie chicken. He is presumably an Indian although he is dressed in a store-bought jacket and hat. Other Kiowa calendars record the death of a medicine man and of a peyote man, neither of whom clearly relates to this image.

1900–1901 Measles winter

A figure with spots records another outbreak of disease. The NAA inscription identifies it as measles, while Hauvahte says the Comanches had smallpox.

1901 Check fraud summer

This elegantly dressed figure is shown in the act of changing the amount on a check he had received. Hauvahte gives a full explanation: "Old Buffalo Bull added to check more summer; a young Indian man raised a small government check for $40.00 to $640.00 and was sent to pen." All in all, things were simpler when heavy wagons brought loads of silver dollars to the reservation, and payments for treaty obligations and leasing were made in cash.

A fragmentary image of a horse appears at the top of the page. The NAA calendar shows a wounded horse, and Hauvahte says a horse was found shot. Killing a man's horse was a conventional way for a person who felt his rights had been violated to settle the score with the person he held responsible. Incarceration in a penitentiary was not a traditional part of the Kiowa justice system.[22]

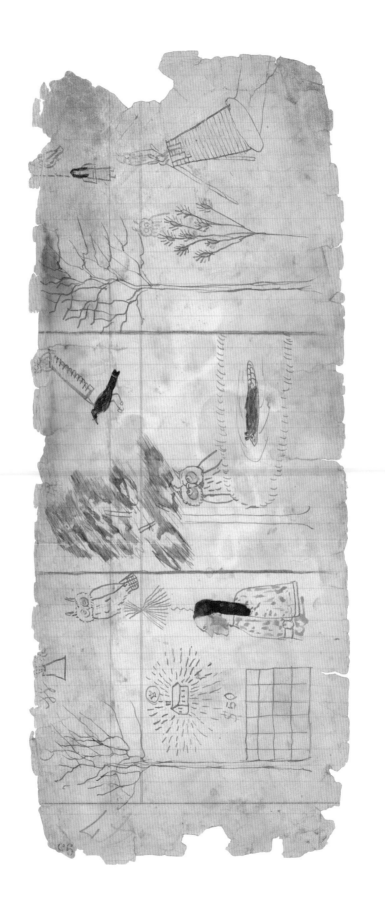

1901–2 Land allotted winter

The grid at the bottom of the page represents allotment, the end of the Kiowa reservation. Kiowa people were required to choose individual plots, which were called "allotments." Some land was set aside for common pasturage, and all the remaining territory was opened to settlement by homesteaders. The federal government paid two million dollars for the land ceded, holding some in trust and paying some out in cash.[23] This payment is shown by many tracks converging on a building with a silver dollar drawn above it and $50 written below. Communal ownership of the reservation was terminated by the Jerome Agreement, by which the Kiowa people purportedly agreed that the government could break the terms of the Medicine Lodge Treaty of 1867, which had established the reservation. In spite of many claims of fraud and misrepresentation on the part of the Jerome Commission, all the land was platted into individual parcels of 160 acres. The legal history of Kiowa challenges to allotment is well covered in the book *Lone Wolf vs. Hitchcock* by Blue Clark. The calendar provides a Kiowa perspective, with numerous entries recording trips by Chief Lone Wolf to lobby Congress for relief.

The calendar also notes the death of a woman identified by Hauvahte as the wife of Many Poles.

The crumbled edge of the page shows a fragment of Silver Horn's Kiowa signature. While Silver Horn never became literate, he did learn to sign his name using various spellings over time. He had been listed in army records as Hawgone and he used that spelling for a time, eventually shifting to Haungooah, the spelling adopted by the agency. Many names were inconsistently or inaccurately recorded in government files, as the sounds of the Kiowa language are quite different from English and cannot be easily distinguished or readily reproduced by those who do not know the language.

1902 Crow Lance and Beaver died summer

Two deaths mark this summer: Crow Lance and Beaver, each effectively indicated by name glyphs. Crow Lance, or Gaapiatan, had worked closely with James Mooney, and Mooney lived in Crow Lance's camp during the years when he was assembling information on the Kiowa calendars. In June 1902 Mooney wrote to the Smithsonian noting the recent death of the old chief, who was eighty-five years old.[24]

Silver Horn began working for Mooney in the spring of 1902, and he notes this association in his other calendar.

1902–3 Bed died winter

Further deaths are marked this winter. One was a woman named Oga-ti (Bed or Bed Hanger). The picture shows a trapezoidal panel hanging from a tripod, which was an essential part of a well-furnished tipi. Made of willow rods strung together, such back rests or "head boards" could be easily rolled up and packed when moving camp.

Other deaths are marked as well, one with a glyph of a plant with red buds and the other with the small figure of a woman.

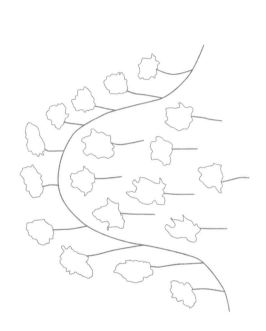

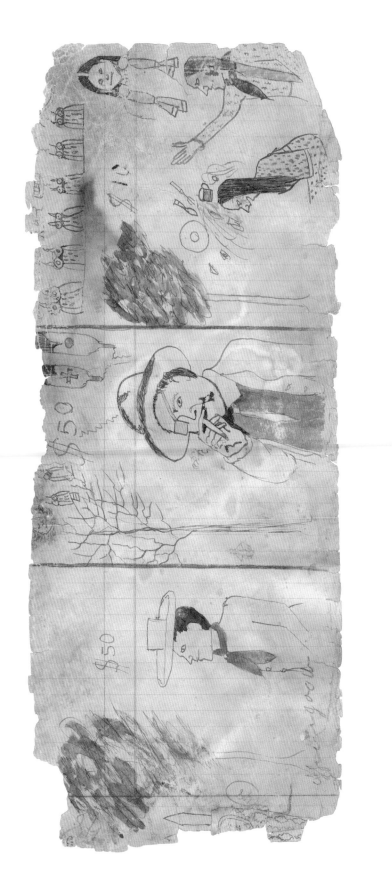

1903 Payment winter

The identity of the figure wearing a broad-brimmed hat is not clear, although the red neckerchief suggests that it is a Kiowa or at least an Indian man. The NAA calendar shows a representative from Washington with a high collar, identified as Mr. Leupp. Francis E. Leupp, once a lobbyist for the Indian Rights Association and later Commissioner for Indian Affairs, had come to the reservation in early 1903 on behalf of the Indian Office. He investigated accusations of graft made against Agent Randlett's administration and arranged for Kiowas and Comanches to witness and verify the distribution of funds paid for yet further losses of commonly held pasture land.[25] Silver Horn notes a payment of $50.

The partial image on the left of a cradle board records a birth. According to the NAA inscription, Silver Horn's son was born this summer. This was his oldest son, recorded by the agency as Billy but known

throughout his life as James Silverhorn. Silver Horn's signature appears at the bottom of the page, somewhere in transition from Hawgone to Haungooah.

1903–4 Eye sore winter

This is a self-portrait of the artist, with hat, cigarette, and eye patch. The NAA calendar is inscribed "Eye sore," referring to the painful trachoma that eventually blinded Silver Horn. (In the following winter, Hauvahte noted that Silver Horn went away to seek treatment for his eyes.) Another $50 payment is noted, which Hauvahte says came from Colonel Randlett, who was the Kiowa agent at this time.

The two decorated feathers in the upper right are the type worn by members of the Ghost Dance, or Feather Dance, as the ceremony was known among the Kiowa. This is the first reference in this calendar to the religious movement, although in his other calendar Silver Horn noted its introduction

to the tribe in 1890. After an initial period of skepticism, the ceremony was widely accepted by the Kiowa, and the Feather Dance continued into the mid-1910s. Silver Horn was one of the men who prepared the feathers worn by dancers, according to his son Max. Mary Buffalo's calendar records this year as "Agent tried to abolish the Ghost Dance." Such efforts at suppression continued over the next decade and a half.[26]

Two deaths are marked with owls in the upper left corner. One resembles the name glyph for Frizzle Head, but his death is more clearly noted for 1906–7. This might be another example of indirect reference, intended to identify a relative of his. The picture associated with the other death owl has been lost.

Silver Horn's NAA calendar ends in this winter, which was when he made and explained it to James Mooney. For subsequent years Hauvahte's is the only closely related calendar available for comparison.

1904 Many died summer

The main image for this year is a man throwing dishes at a woman's head, suggesting a domestic dispute. A $70 payment is noted; Hauvahte recorded receiving $75. A row of six owls along the top of the page indicates many deaths, but the page is too damaged to be able to decipher the name glyphs.

Cyclone at Snyder–1906

1904–5 Red Stone church built winter

This church, identified by Hauvahte as Red Rock, was named for the Red Stone area west of Anadarko where many family members took allotments. Silver Horn was buried in the Red Stone cemetery years later. The church still maintains an active congregation.

1905 Great cyclone summer

The major event recorded this season was the Snyder cyclone of May 10, 1905, in which more than one hundred people were killed. According to Hauvahte's calendar, a marshal was killed, his head torn off by the force of the storm, as Silver Horn graphically illustrates. Many storm victims were mutilated by flying debris. The National Weather Service ranks this as one of the most deadly tornadoes in U.S. history.[27]

The fragmentary figure in this damaged drawing represents the storm-maker Red Horse, shown more clearly in the next entry. This supernatural being has the upper body of a horse and a long sinuous tail like a snake, which it whips around to stir up tornadoes.[28]

Silver Horn's signature appears again at the bottom of the page together with a roughly sketched cradleboard. This could represent the birth of another of Silver

Horn's children. The crude drawing appears to be an afterthought and may have been added by another hand.

1905–6 Red Horse winter

Red Horse is more fully visible in this drawing. According to Hauvahte, this second destructive tornado was in Mountain View. The *Daily Oklahoman* reported that the storm hit on November 4, and the following day the paper carried a detailed account of the event, which it described as "second only to the great Snyder disaster last spring."[29]

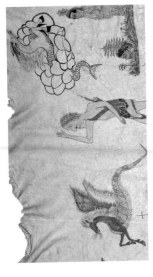

FIGURE 3-17. Two views of Red Horse. Detail of hide painting by Silver Horn, ca. 1904. Cat. no. 229,900. Courtesy of the Department of Anthropology, Smithsonian Institution.

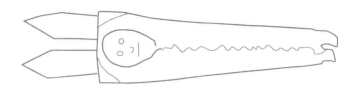

1906 Killed by train summer

Silver Horn provides no identification for the man killed by a train. Hauvahte's calendar notes that Red Tail died this summer, but as he does not indicate the manner of death, the two events cannot be linked. Kiowa Agency records report that an unnamed Kiowa man who lived near Cache was killed on the night of September 6 by a southbound Rock Island train on the stretch of track between Lawton and the Fort Sill school.[30]

This is the first page of Silver Horn's calendar that is not neatly divided into thirds. This entry is probably the first "new" picture in the calendar, with previous entries copied from an earlier source.

1906–7 Frizzle Head died winter

Silver Horn paid special attention to detail in this frontal portrait of Frizzle Head, wearing a jacket with epaulets and a large peace medal. The death of this old warrior was also noted by Hauvahte.

1907 Rainy summer

This fragmentary page indicates a rainy summer and the death of an unidentified man. Silver Horn has again written the name Haungooah across the drawing and notes a $40 payment, while Hauvahte records one for $30. The meaning of the fragmentary figure in the upper right corner is unknown.

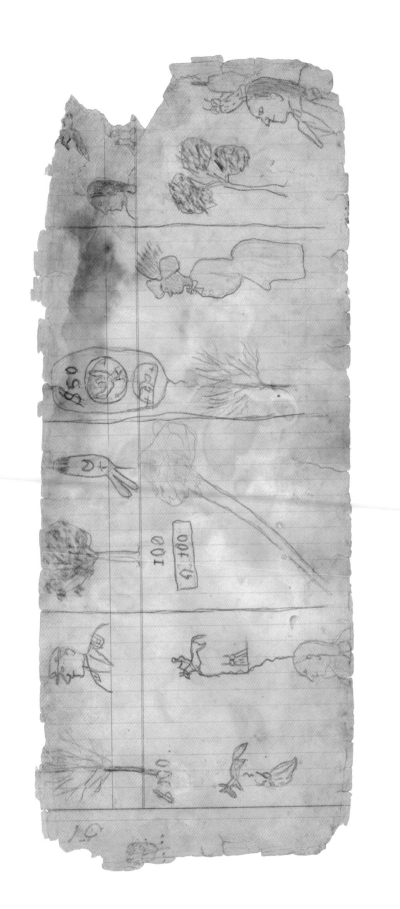

1909 Visited Crow summer

The upright feather worn by the lower figure appears to represent the death of a Ghost Dancer, although any name glyph that might have been along the edge of the page has been lost. The partial upper figure shows a man, a black bird, and the front of a steam locomotive. Hauvahte's calendar records that Kumate took a train to visit the Crow tribe on their reservation in Montana.

This is the final entry in Hauvahte's calendar. From this point on, no other family calendars are available for comparison.

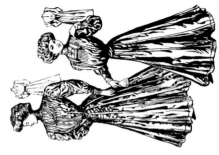

FIGURE 3-18. Ladies fashion, adapted from the 1908 Sears, Roebuck Catalogue. Redrawn by Debbie Kaspari for the Sam Noble Oklahoma Museum of Natural History, Norman, Oklahoma.

1907–8 Two died winter

Several small pictures were used to mark this winter. Two deaths are marked by owls. The associated glyphs indicate that one name referred to a wolf or fox, while the other related to a rider. The figure $100 is written just below the winter tree, probably recording a payment. At the top of the page is an army officer with shoulder bars and a forage cap, but the meaning of the figure is unknown. The Quitone calendar at Fort Sill records that Kiowa Sam died this year.

The drawings on this page mark a period when Silver Horn's vision must have been seriously affected by the trachoma.

1908 $100 payment summer

This summer shows another $100 payment, which the Domebo calendar says was made at Mount Scott in the Wichita Mountains. A Ghost Dance feather with two attachments may stand for the deaths of Ghost Dancers, which Hauvahte recorded in his calendar. The cloud with a long tail looks like a tornado but is quite different from the images of Red Horse that Silver Horn showed in entries for 1905 and 1905–6.

1908–9 $50 payment winter

This winter records a $50 payment. The woman shown on the right is fashionably dressed in American style of the time, with high-necked blouse, flaring bustle, and a highly decorated hat. The Sears and Roebuck mail order catalog for 1908 includes many illustrations of women in such dress, similarly posed to emphasize the curious reshaping of their figures. Oklahoma had become a state by this time, and Kiowa interactions with white settlers and American clothing fashions continued to increase.

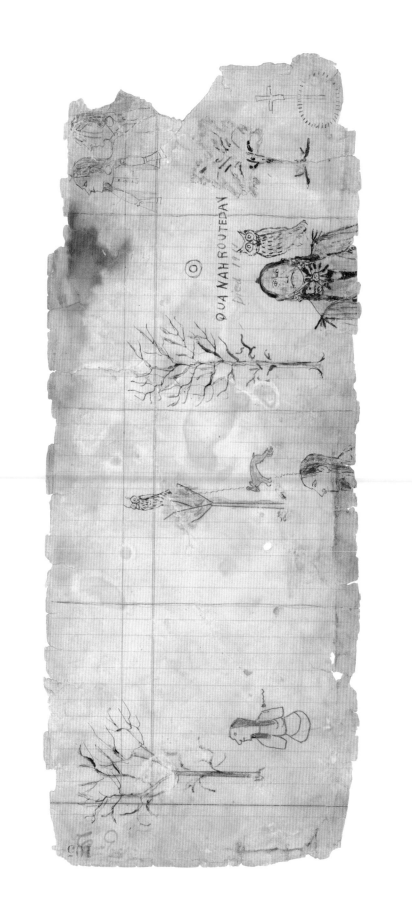

1909–10 Woman shot winter

Silver Horn included no identifying elements in this roughly drawn figure of a woman with a bullet coming toward her. The Domebo calendar says a girl was shot at Rainy Mountain by accident.

1910 Poor Bear died summer

This summer was marked by the death of a man whose name glyph is a bear. The Kiowas recognized bears as an important source of spiritual power, and many men's names referred to bears. Although the coloring of the glyph might suggest the name Black Bear, the picture fits well with the Ananti calendar, which records the death this summer of Poor Bear. The name could alternately be translated as Lean Bear, and Silver Horn's drawing emphasizes the shrunken belly of a thin, or poor, bear. Poor Bear, Patadal, was Silver Horn's uncle.

1910–11 Quanah died winter

Quanah Parker was a Comanche leader who died in 1911. He was a prominent chief during the reservation period, whose actions influenced the Kiowa in many ways. A shrewd businessman, he was a key figure in negotiations with cattlemen that led to grazing leases for both the Kiowa and the Comanche. On a more personal note, he was the Peyote leader whom Silver Horn followed when he first entered the religion. He is shown here dressed for a Peyote meeting in a buckskin shirt with flicker feathers, valued for their healing powers, on the shoulders and at the neck. It is not clear what the second word in the inscription means.[31]

1911 Feather Dance Circle summer

The dashed lines around a pole topped with a cross represent a circle of dancers participating in one of the large summer Feather Dances, the Kiowa form of Ghost Dance that continued well into the twentieth century. Around this same year Silver Horn painted a beautifully detailed picture of the dance circle on a deer skin, which is now in the collection of Brown University's Haffenreffer Museum of Anthropology. Silver Horn's vision must have improved for a time, as the entries in the calendar for this period are delicately drawn and the hide painting of the Feather Dance is among his finest works.

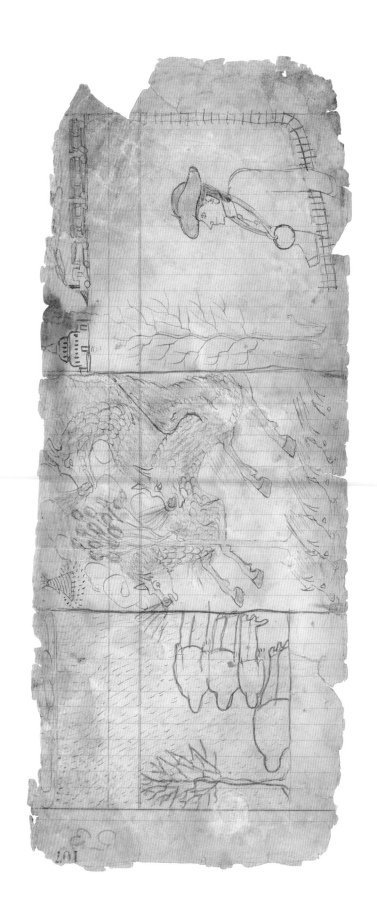

1911–12 Overtaken by a storm winter

This picture of four men lying face down, pelted by precipitation, is eerily reminiscent of the entry for the winter of 1890–91 when the schoolboys were frozen, but this event has not yet been identified.

1912 Many storms summer

The winged horses breathing flame are another representation of Red Horse, the creator of tornadoes, illustrated more fully in the entry for 1905–6. Evidently Red Horse visited Kiowa territory repeatedly this summer. In a 1935 interview Mary Buffalo explained that a small cyclone is Red Horse shaking his ears, while a big cyclone is many horses running.[32]

A small picture in the upper corner shows a striped tipi, representing the Tipi with Battle Pictures, which at this time belonged to Mary Buffalo's husband Charlie Buffalo, Silver Horn and Hauvahte's brother. Numerous small marks surrounding the tipi indicate many people gathering there. Mary Buffalo's granddaughter Betty Nixon told me that during her childhood in the 1930s people would gather around Grandpa Buffalo when there was a storm, as he had the power to make it pass safely by.

This tipi, which belonged to Little Bluff, has a lengthy history. It has been made and remade in various contexts from the 1840s up to the present.[33] Although it, like other painted tipis, fell out of use in the 1890s, this calendar entry demonstrates that was once again in use by 1912.

1912–13 Went to Washington winter

This entry shows a man with a large peace medal on his chest traveling to the national capital by train. The calendar records a number of trips to Washington over the next few years, always represented by the domed Capitol building. Most record trips by Chief Lone Wolf, as indicated by his name glyph. He was always accompanied

FIGURE 3-19. Delos K. Lonewolf with his wife and son. Photographed while visiting Washington DC in 1913. GN 04756. Courtesy of the National Anthropological Archives, Smithsonian Institution.

by his nephew Delos K. Lonewolf.[34] This picture may represent the younger Lone Wolf, who was photographed together with his wife at the Smithsonian wearing such a medal in 1913.

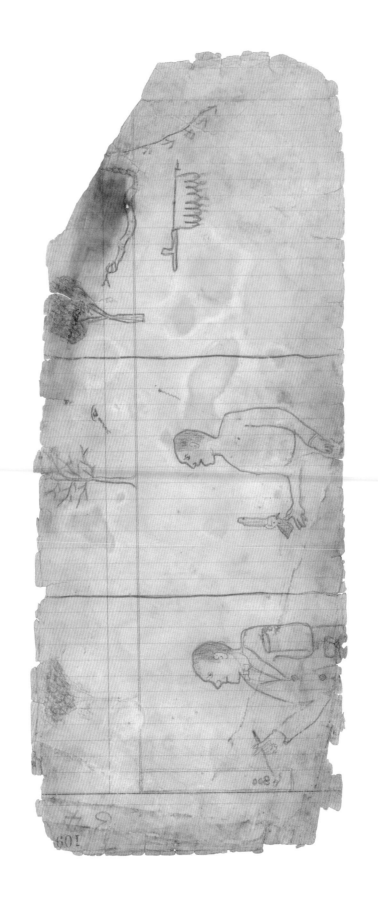

1913 One Arm came summer

A man who is missing his left arm is shown writing out the amount of $800. The Quitone calendar in the NAA also shows a one-armed man, who is captioned there as "Guy Tucker," while the Ananti calendar records "paid debts." In an interview with Charley Apekaum in the 1930s, he remembered that the government had sent a one-armed man to resolve issues arising from merchants extending credit to Indian people who had no means of repayment.[35]

1913–14 Boy was shot winter

A figure is shown holding a pistol, two discharged bullets in the air. This may refer to a Kiowa man who took his six-shooter to the barn and shot himself when he was unable to resolve his debts. Such anguish was probably the result of family conflict over the situation rather than financial despair. His creditor had tried to seize horses and other stock he had put up as security, only to discover that they belonged to other people. Fortunately the bullet missed his heart and lodged behind his shoulder blade, a painful but not fatal wound. In reporting this event in the local church newsletter, the Reverend Harry Treat warned, "May all Indians remember that creditors are not always friends—they often make trouble."[36]

1914 Pipe Dance summer

The feathered pipe stem suggests a Pipe Dance, or adoption ceremony, as recorded periodically throughout the calendar. Pictures of a snake and bird tracks going up a hill probably relate to the names of the people involved.

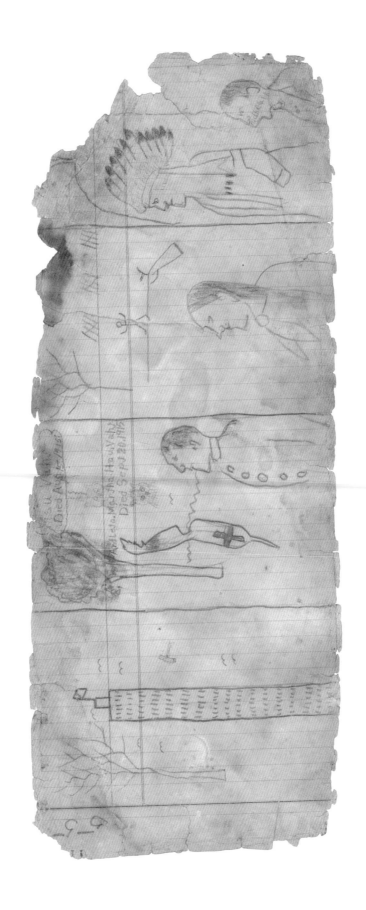

1914–15 First flight winter

A tiny biplane appears in the sky to the right of a tall structure topped by a flag. This was the year that the army air corps was formed at Fort Sill.[37] The structure may be a navigational tower. The Ananti calendar entry is: "First airplane made its journey and people were scared of it."

1915 Broke the Feather Dance summer

The short-haired man shown here probably represents C. V. Stinchecum, who became the superintendent of the Kiowa Agency in April 1915. Stinchecum was adamantly opposed to Kiowa dancing and to other displays of communal culture. Within months of taking office he was able to disrupt the large Feather Dance gathering planned for midsummer by threatening to withhold annuity payments from those who participated.[38] The broken dance feather shown in front of him records this.

The inscription above this picture reads, "Hauvaut died Aug. 15, 1915 . . . and Leto Martha Hauvaut died Sept. 20, 1915." This was Silver Horn's elder brother Hauvahte, also recorded as Haba, and Hauvahte's daughter Martha. There is no indication who added the inscription, but it would not have been Silver Horn, who was not literate and did not speak English. It is possible

that the inscription together with the associated owl pictures may have been added in later years. Hauvahte would have been sixty-three or sixty-four years old at this time. According to agency records Martha died suddenly, shortly after bearing her third child.[39]

1915–16 On the Gun elected winter

The name glyph represents the man On the Gun, or Hawzipta, also known as Charlie Jackson. He was one of five Kiowa men elected in January 1916 to serve as a business committee for the tribe.[40]

FIGURE 3-20. Early aviation at Fort Sill. Photographer unknown, 1916. Wayne P. Campbell Coll. #22243;27423. Courtesy of the Research Division of the Oklahoma Historical Society.

1916 Dance summer

White Buffalo Konad sponsored a large dance around the Fourth of July, probably an Ohoma dance, and a number of Cheyennes and Arapahos visited for another big dance in mid-August.[41] The full feather bonnet that the figure wears was more typical of the Cheyennes and Arapahos than the Kiowa, so the entry may represent that August dance. The second figure may be Agent Stinchecum, although with mutton-chop whiskers not shown in the entry for the summer before. Stinchecum was determined to suppress dance gatherings, such as the Ohoma. He assembled a list of participants, whom he termed the "dance crowd," and withheld their annuity payments that fall, seeking to crush this dance as he had the Feather Dance in the previous year.[42]

1918–19 Veterans Honored winter

Many dances were held to honor the Kiowa men who served in the U.S. military during World War I.[47] Even Ahpeahtone, or Wooden Lance, the principal chief of the Kiowa and a devout Christian who was opposed to dancing, sponsored a dance to honor his son Lon, who had served overseas. That dance is recorded in the Ananti calendar for the summer of 1919.

Silver Horn's calendar entry records a celebration in which ten men were honored, each identified by a name glyph. Three are marked with small owls behind their heads. Government records list only the government or agency names of the men who served, while these glyphs represent their traditional Kiowa names, and I have not been able to correlate these two sources.[48]

1919 Summer

The edge of the page containing the entry for this summer is missing.

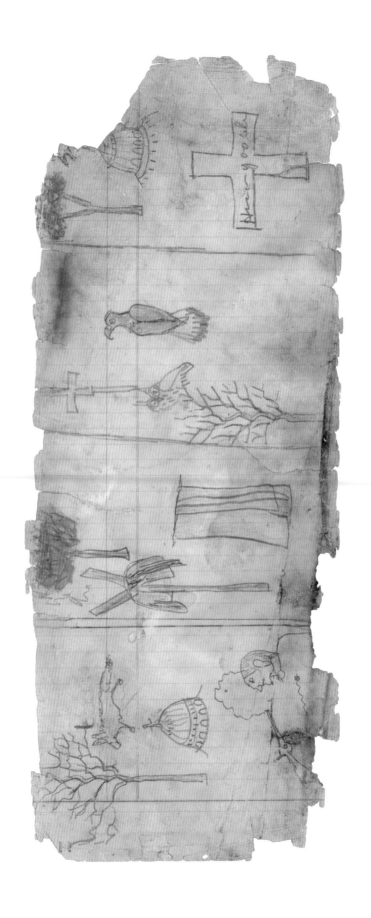

1919–20 Delegation to Washington winter

This records another year in which Lone Wolf, indicated by his name glyph, visited the Capitol in Washington DC. The March 20 issue of *Home and School* newsletter reported that Lone Wolf and Kiowa Bill had left for Washington the week before with Lewis Ware as interpreter.[49]

The lower figure represents an unidentified man who was shot. The Ananti calendar refers to a family member named Robert who accidentally shot himself in the ear this winter. As the usual wavy line connecting the figure to a name glyph leads to the gun pointed toward him, this may represent that same incident.

1920 Medicine Lodge held again summer

As in 1918, Silver Horn has included the center pole of the Medicine Lodge, suggesting that a ceremony was held, perhaps in thanks for the safe return of a warrior. The blue rectangle with red stripe might represent the leg of a military uniform, as a similar image for the summer of 1927 almost certainly does. In the 1890s when Silver Horn served with Troop L of the Seventh Cavalry, a red stripe on the outer leg indicated the artillery corps.

1920–21 Ghost Dance leader died winter

The equal-armed cross on a pole is the same figure that Silver Horn used in the summer of 1911 to represent the Ghost Dance. The figure of an eagle may represent the name of the person who died. The Ananti calendar records the death of Father Isadore of the Saint Patrick Mission in Anadarko.

1921 Ceremony in Washington summer

The Capitol dome and the partial name glyph indicate another trip to Washington by Lone Wolf. This time he went to participate in the Armistice Day celebration and the dedication of the Tomb of the Unknown Soldier held at Arlington National Cemetery on November 11.[50] The Ananti calendar records that Jasper Saunkeah took Lone Wolf to Washington for a parade. The warbonnet that the Crow chief Plenty Coups presented on the same occasion is displayed at the visitor center in the cemetery.[51]

The significance of the cross with Silver Horn's Kiowa name Haungooah written on it is not known.

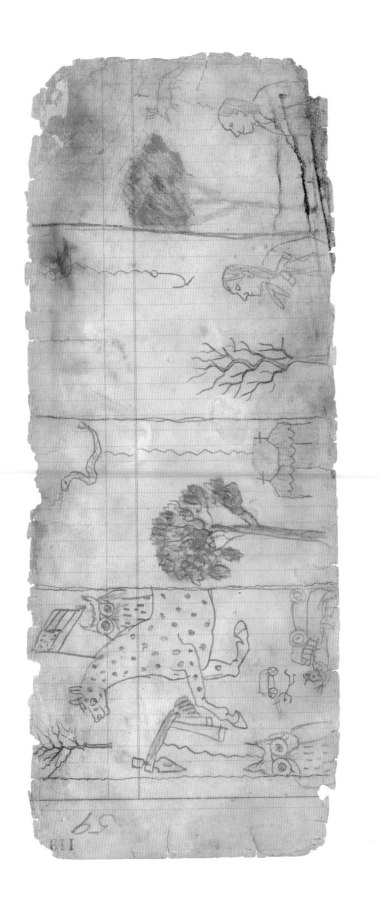

1921–22 Spotted Horse died winter

Silver Horn marked this winter with three events. The largest picture records the death of a man named Spotted Horse. He was one of the first deacons of the Saddle Mountain Mission and the son of Sergeant Iseeo, who was still serving in the army at Fort Sill. Spotted Horse was at Fort Sill when he died of double pneumonia on February 11, according to Rev. Harry Treat's newsletter.[52] Another owl with a tomahawk glyph marks the death of Joshua Kaulaity, or Two Hatchet, whose passing was noted in the same newsletter issue.

A tiny but complicated scene in the lower right shows a car flipped upside down and a man sprawled beside it. The NAA Quitone calendar notes this event for the preceding summer with a picture of a speeding roadster. The inscription there avoids naming the dead man, identifying the picture as the "Boake's future son-in-law was killed in a race." The Ananti

calendar identifies the man killed as Robert Poolaw, and the *Home and School* newsletter provides additional details of the accident, which took place on November 6.[53] This incident was long remembered in the Kiowa community. When I showed Jake

FIGURE 3-22. Entry for 1921–22, from the Quitone calendar. MS 2002-27. Courtesy of the National Anthropological Archives, Smithsonian Institution.

Ahtone this calendar picture more than eighty years after the event, he immediately suggested that it might be the Poolaw car wreck, remembering people pointing out the location where it had occurred.

1922 Prayer meeting summer

The tent topped with crosses suggests an evangelical revival. Treat reported several Christian camp meetings this summer. The Methodists held a camp meeting in July, which many Red Stone people attended, the Indian Christians association met at Saddle Mountain around the same time, and in August the Western Oklahoma Indian Baptist Association met at Post Oak Mission near Indiahoma, setting up arbors and tents.[54]

The picture of a snake is evidently a name glyph for someone who was associated with the event. An early Christian Kiowa called Paul Zotom, whose name translated as Biter and who appears as a snake glyph in other records, had died several years before, but his name may have been passed on by this time.[55]

1922–23 Hook died winter

Hook, or Fish Hook, whose name in Kiowa was Haunpo, was a keeper of one the Ten Medicines of the tribe. After his death his widow took responsibility for the bundle, the first Kiowa woman to hold such a role.[56] Kiowa Agency files record a hearing regarding the settlement of his estate in June of 1923, probably a few months after his death.[57]

1923 Lone Wolf summer

The figure is identified by the name glyph for Lone Wolf, but no particular activity is shown in this entry. According to the Ananti calendar, Old Lone Wolf, the adoptive father of Delos Lonewolf, died this summer. It was also in this year that Delos was licensed as a Methodist preacher, among the first Kiowas to receive such authority.[58]

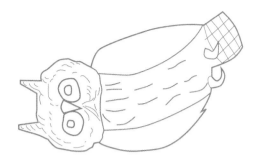

1923–24 Big Nose died winter

Two deaths are marked for this winter. A man is shown with an exaggerated nose, probably indicating his name, which might be translated into English as Roman Nose. The second figure appears to be a woman with a bird for a name glyph.

Some sort of vehicular incident appears as a tiny image in the upper corner.

1924 Many died summer

This summer is marked with three deaths. The figure at the top must be the woman that Rev. Harry Treat reported was shot in the neck by her husband, a rare instance of one Kiowa killing another.

Silver Horn's brother White Buffalo also died this summer.[59] The identity of the man with the snake name glyph remains uncertain.

1924–25 Big fire winter

The notable event of this year was a tragic fire in the small community of Babbs Switch, in which thirty-six people were killed. More than two hundred people were crowded into the small local school building, which also served as community center and Sunday school facility. The fire took place at a Christmas eve party, started from candles on the Christmas tree. Many people were unable to escape from the overcrowded building as the windows were covered with strong wire screening.[60] I learned from Delores Harragarra that two young Kiowa children were among those fortunate to make their way out, although one was badly burned. They were Max and Hattie Cizek, whose Kiowa mother was married to William J. Cizek, a non-Indian. The Ananti calendar also records this event.

Silver Horn also recorded the death of a man whose name glyph is the same as

the one he used to mark the death of Poor Bear in 1910. Probably the name had been passed on.

1925 Six Moons was shot summer

The picture records the shooting death of a man. The six crescent or moons above him probably represent his name. The Ananti calendar records that two Pawnees fought during the Anadarko fair, and one was killed. The drawing of a double-peaked tent might represent a fair, although the crosses on top suggest a revival tent. A name suggesting six moons is not known among either the Kiowa or the Pawnee.[61]

1925–26 Unmarked winter

No event is shown in association with this winter.

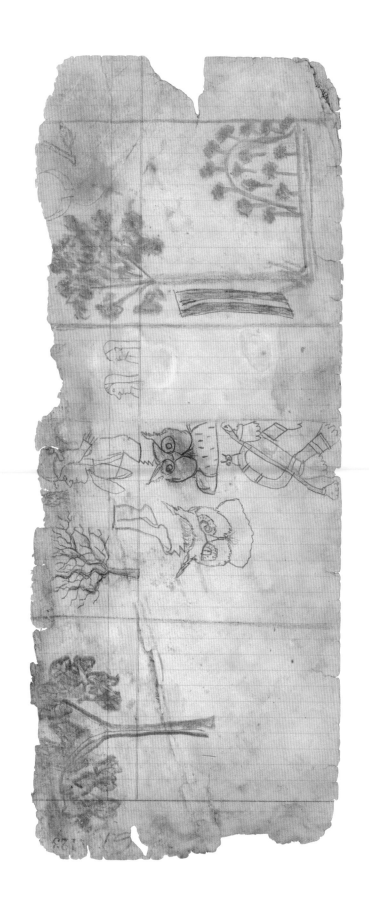

1926 Unmarked summer

As during the previous season, no event is shown in association with this summer. Silver Horn's vision may have deteriorated further at this time.

1926–27 Three died winter

This winter marks the deaths of three individuals. The name glyph for the figure at the top is partially destroyed, but he wears a distinctive headdress mounted with buffalo horns. This is probably the man commonly known as Gotebo, after whom the town in Kiowa County is named. His name is more accurately rendered as Kotebohon, referring to a cap or hat made of fur. The name of the figure on the left is probably Barefeet, recorded in agency records as Bat-chaddle.[62] The glyph at the bottom of a bow case and attached quiver has not been

identified. The two figures on the right appear to be part of an unfinished picture.

1927 Medicine Lodge anniversary summer

A celebration was held in October of this year at the site of the 1867 Medicine Lodge Treaty to mark the sixtieth anniversary of that event. Cavalry troops participated, as indicated by the yellow stripe on the blue pants leg, and so did representatives from the Kiowa, Comanche, Plains Apache, Cheyenne, and Arapaho tribes. Hugh Scott, who had commanded Troop L when Silver Horn was enlisted, was among those attending the event, and he made many photographs of the site and participants.[63] Government records regarding the exact location of the original council grounds seem to have been inadequate, and the old Kiowa scout Iseeo was asked to

define the location of the council, which he had attended as a teenager. Conveniently, it turned out to be close to the small town of Medicine Lodge, Kansas, which was sponsoring the event.[64] Silver Horn identifies the locale with a timbered hill, identical to the place symbol he used for 1867.

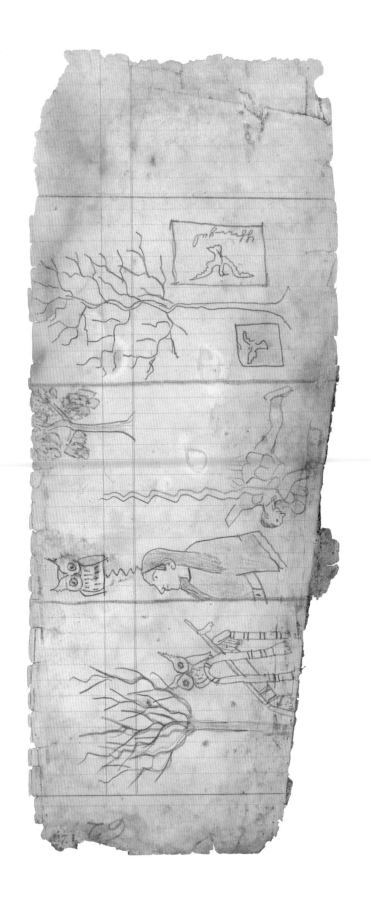

1927–28 Quiver died winter

This entry mirrors one for the previous winter, marking the death of someone identified by a glyph of a bowcase and quiver.

1928 Struck by lightning summer

According to the Ananti calendar Harold Dupoint was struck by lightning at his home south of Mountain View in July of 1928. The woman on the left with the death owl is distinguished by the blue wool dress she is wearing, but her name is not otherwise indicated.

1928–29 Eagle Flies winter

It is not clear what the square and rectangle drawn here denote. Silver Horn has inscribed his Kiowa name Haungooah within the larger figure. Both contain pictures of flying birds, which are similar to the birds he used in the pictorial diary he kept while he was in the army to record paydays, which in military slang were known as "when the eagle flies."[65] The picture may record some form of payment received.

This appears to be the final entry that Silver Horn drew in the calendar.

The book contains a few other pictures that I do not believe were produced by Silver Horn. The original position of these pages is unknown, but they were probably located at the end of the book and may represent someone's intention to continue the calendar where Silver Horn left off.

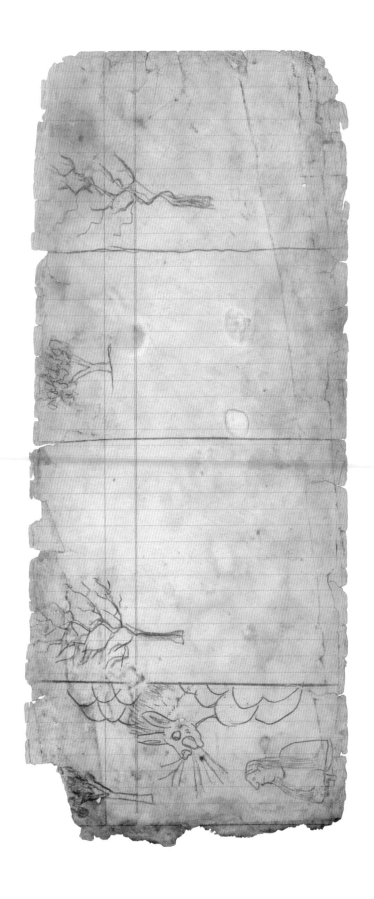

These drawings do not form part of the calendar sequence and their authorship is unknown.

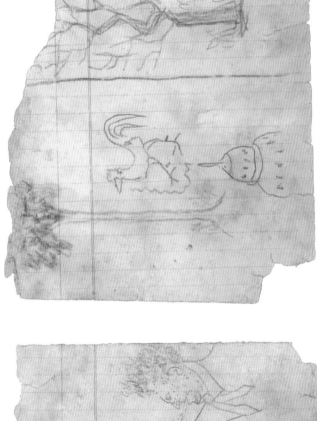

Kiowa Glossary and Guide to Pronunciation

Gus Palmer Jr.

Kiowa Word Entries

The bold-faced entries are those that appear in the text. The phonemic words appear in parentheses and are followed by English translation or definition.

Explanatory Notes on Kiowa Nouns

It is hard to determine whether many of the Kiowa words are singular, dual, or plural forms. Kiowa regularly employs singular (s), dual (d), and plural (p) forms for nouns. It appears that Mooney and others did not understand the Kiowa nominal system clearly to determine noun number (s/d/pl). The entry *yapahe* (yáfáhé:) would indicate singular (s) or dual (d) Kiowa warrior(s), making *yáfáhé:gàu* the plural (pl) form "Kiowa warriors." *Taimpego* (*Jái:fègàu*) (Kiowa Gourd Clan members) indicates plural (pl). There is no singular or dual for *Jái:fègàu*. To indicate such numbers would require suffixing *qí* (male) to *Jái:fè*, as in *Jái:fèqì* to indicate (Kiowa Gourd Clan member) singular or dual (s/d). *Koitsenko* (Qáuichè:gáu) (Wild Horses/Mustangs) is also a plural (pl) noun entry.

Kiowa-English

Entries are alphabetized by the common English rendering of the Kiowa word, followed by a guide to pronunciation (in parentheses) and translation. Proper names are capitalized here as in

English, although the Kiowa writing system does not use capitalized letters.

Adalhabakia (Áulhà:bàqì). Sloping Hair (ʔ); possibly Man with Hanging Hair (qí is a male gender marker, essentially, "man").

Agiati (Á:gîà). Probably Gathering Feathers/Picking Up Feathers. Silver Horn's father.

Ahpeahtone (Á:fîtàun). Wooden Lance. Given in some sources as Apiatan.

Alaho (possibly Àlàhógàu, pl.). Quapaw tribe of Indians.

Ankopaingyadete (Àunkóv*a̱*ui:gàdè:jè). Standing in the Middle of the Path.

An-zah-te (Àu:zâjè). Buffalo Udder.

asahe (á:sàuihyè: or á:sàuhyè:). Green plant or tree.

Gaapiatan (Càuáu:fîtàun). Crow Lance.

Guadal Doha (Gúljòhàu: or Jòháu:gùl). Red Bluff.

guat (cút). Book/drawing/writing.

Gui-aza (Cûiàu:zà:). Wolf Teat.

Haba or **Hauvahte** (H*a̱*u:fâjè). Sharp Iron or Metal.

Haungooah (H*a̱*u:g*ù̱*à:). Silver Horn or Silver Horns.

Haunpo (H*a̱*u:pò). Metal hook.

Hawzipta (H*a̱*uzèptài:). On Top of the Rifle, name of Charlie Jackson; a kind of early carbine.

Iseeo (Ái:s*é̱ó̱*:). Much Fire Smoke; is translated Plenty Fires.

Kado (qáu:jó). Ceremonial Sun Dance lodge; lodge where the Sun Dance ceremony occurred (also qáu:jócùngà, ceremonial Sun Dance; ceremonial lodge dance).

Ka-tode-a Pa Gado (Káu: tó:déà: fàqàu:jò). Creek Where the Buffalo Robe was Left Sun Dance.

Kodalta (qóltà). Beheading; probably refers to Qóltà:qòp, Cut Throat Mountain, site of the massacre of a Kiowa encampment in 1833, near the present town of Cooperton, Oklahoma.

Kogui (qócáui). Elk; a Kiowa band name.

Koitsenko (Qáuiché:gáu, pl.). Wild Horses/Mustangs; a Kiowa warrior society.

Kotebohon (Qó:débòhòn). Refers to a kind of fur hat; a Kiowa known by that name after whom the town of Gotebo, Oklahoma, is named.

Oheltoint (Ó:èljòi). Speaks with Big Voice, (?) name of Charlie Buffalo.

Ohoma (Óhòmàu). The Kiowa Óhòmàu Society, which holds an annual celebration dance in June.

Patadal (Páu: tául). Poor Buffalo or Lean Buffalo.

Pa-yia (Páuí:). Buffalo's son.

Piho (ví:òi). About or near the rear of, as part of a river or waterway; could be vernacular for river bend or peninsula.

Pohd-lohk (Fóláu: or Fóláu:jè). Aged or Old Male Wolf.

Quitone (Cûitòn). Wolf Tail, name of Jimmy Quitone.

sahe (sáuihé:/sáuhyé:). Can be translated as green or blue.

sai-guat (sái: cùt). Winter/year book; also annual or yearly drawing; can be translated as winter marks or winter pictures.

Seipote (Séphò:jè). Traveling in Rain or Rain Darkening or Darkness.

Se-se Pa (Sé:sévàu). Arrowhead River (Arkansas River).

Setangya (Sétá:gà). Sitting Bear. Given in some sources as Satank.

Set-daya-ite (Sétjáuáuidè). Many Bears or Plenty Bears.

Settan (Sétsyàn/Sétsàn). Little Bear.

Tadalkop (tálkòp). "Hole sickness" or wasting away illness, smallpox; referring to pock marks or round scars left by the disease.

Taime (Tái:mê). Translation unknown; central medicine object of the Kado.

Taimete (Tái:mé:jè). Keeper of the Tái:mê Sun Dance medicine; One Who Keeps Tái:mê

Taimpego (Jái:fègàu, pl.). Translation unknown; now known as the Kiowa Gourd Clan members.

Talo-ti (Tàló:jè). Term of affection of Kiowa grandmother for oldest grandson; name of the brother of Sétth*á*i:dé, White Bear.

Tau-ankia (Tàu*á*:gà). Sitting in the Saddle.

Tebodal (Thébòljè). Refers to an incident where someone was transporting a deer or antelope rump that became putrefied, after which the name was given teasingly by the Kiowas; could also be a rotted buffalo rump being transported by horseback.

Tenebati (Th*è*:nébàu:jè). Bird Appearing or Eagle Emerging. Given in some calendars as Eagle Peeping Out or Appearing Eagle.

Tohausan (Jòháu:sàn). Little Bluff, a famous Kiowa chief (1833–66). The name was subsequently transferred to his nephew Agiati and later to the original Little Bluff's son.

Tonaka (Tónàu:qàut). Rough or Gnarled Tail; describes the common snapping turtle, common translation Snapping Turtle.

Ton-hen Gado (T*ó*:h*é*:qàu:jò). Without Water Sun Dance; possibly T*ó*:h*é*:vàu (Sand Creek in Colorado).

Tsodalhente (Xólh*è*:jè). Wingless/No Wing/ Without Wings; alt. Without Arms (due to amputation), possibly Empty Sleeves.

yapahe (yáfáhé:). Kiowa warrior.

zebat (zèbàut). Arrow.

Kiowa Terms for Names Appearing in English

Arrowhead River. Se-se Pa (Sé:sévàu), Arkansas River.

Bird Appearing. Tenebati (Th*è*:nébàu:jè), alt: Eagle Emerging.

Black Bear. Sétk*ó*:gá.

Buffalo, Charlie. Oheltoint (Ó:èlj*ò*i), Speaks with Big Voice, (ʔ)name of Charlie Buffalo.

Crow Lance. Gaapiatan (Càuáu:fìtàun).

Feather Dance. Á:mâdècùngà, feather dance; popularly known as Ghost Dance.

Gathering Feathers. Agiati (Á:gîà), probably Gathering Feathers/Picking Up Feathers.

Hook. Haunpo (H*á*u:pò), Metal hook.

Lean Elk. Q̇ócáuitàul, alt. Poor Elk, Thin Elk.

Little Bear. Settan (Sétsyàn/Sétsàn).

Little Bluff. Tohausan (Jòháu:sàn).

Lone Wolf. Cûifá:gàu.

Many Tipi Poles. Gúnááui:, Many Tipi Poles.

On Top of the Gun. Hawzipta (H*á*uzèptài); alt. On Top of the Rifle, referring to an early type of carbine; name of Charlie Jackson.

Plenty Bears. Set-daya-ite (Sétjáuáuidè), alt. Many Bears, Heap of Bears.

Plenty Fires. Iseeo (Ái:s*é*ó:), Much Fire Smoke; commonly translated Plenty Fires.

Poor Buffalo. Patadal (Páutául), alt. Lean Buffalo.

Red Bluff. Guadal Doha (Gúljòhàu or Jòháu:gùl).

Red Horse. Ch*é*gùl, name given to the Storm Spirit or tornado, fashioned by the Kiowas in mythical times; also Màunkáuí:.

Silver Horn. Haungooah (H*á*u:g*ù*à:), alt. Silver Horns.

Sitting Bear. Setangya (Sét*á*:gà).

Snapping Turtle. Tonaka (Tónàu:qàut), Rough or Gnarled Tail; describes the common snapping turtle, commonly translated Snapping Turtle.

Standing in the Middle of the Path. Ankopaingyadete (Àunkóv*à*ui:gàdè:jè).

Sun Dance/Sun Dance Lodge. Kado (qáu:jó), medicine lodge/Sun Dance lodge where the ceremonial takes place; also qáu:jócùngà, ceremonial Sun Dance; ceremonial lodge dance.

White Buffalo. Konad (Páu:th*á*i:dê).

Wolf Appearing. Cûibàu:dè, alt. Wolf Emerging.

Wolf Lying Down. Cûiqáu:jè.

Wolf Tail. Quitone (Cûitòn), name of Jimmy Quitone.

Kiowa Phonemic Writing System*

CONSONANTS

There are thirty-two consonantal sounds in Kiowa. Fourteen are the same as they are in English, and eight are variations of /p/, /k/, /t/, and /c/, what Parker McKenzie called the "distinctive" Kiowa sounds. The first group are unaspirated /p/ /t/ /k/. McKenzie lists (in bold face) these so-called soft consonantal sounds as f /p/, c /k/, and j /t/, respectively. The "soft" sounds occur as the p sound in "spot," the k in "Scot," and the t in "stop." These "soft" or unaspirated sounds are generally unnoticed in English because they do not occur in word-initial position as they do in Kiowa.

Kiowa also has so-called hard or ejective consonant sounds. They are listed in the McKenzie system as v /p'/, q /k'/, th /t'/, ch /c/, and x /c'/. Like the "soft" consonants, these sounds can be easily pronounced with practice just like their consonantal counterparts in the Kiowa alphabet.

All the remaining Kiowa consonants are equivalent to English sounds.

THE PALATAL GLIDE /Y/

In Kiowa when consonants /c/, /g/, /k/, and /q/ proceed vowels /a/ and /ai/, there is a /y/ sound, making /ca/ pronounced *cya*, /ga/ pronounced *gya*, /ka/ pronounced *kya*, and /qa/ pronounced *qya*, respectively. Although the McKenzie system does not include the glide marking in the environment where it occurs, it is understood to be there nonetheless.

The palatal glide occurs in the following Kiowa:

Kiowa word	*Pronounced*	*English*
qá:hį̀	k'yá:hį̀	man
kâi:gùn	kʰyáy:gùn	jump
Câigù	kyâygù	Comanche
cúngà	kúngyà	dance

VOWELS

There are ten vowel elements in Kiowa. Six are vowels; four are diphthongs and are sounds made like those in English. When they are combined with consonants and given the qualities of tone, length, and nasal, the vowels and diphthongs become sounds that are characteristically Kiowa.

The ten vowel inventory comprise the following symbols and sounds:

i	pronounced	(ee) as in feet
e	prounounced	(ay) as in day
a	pronounced	(ah) as in father
u	pronounced	(oo) as in boot
o	pronounced	(oh) as in boat
au	pronounced	(aw) as in caught
ai	pronounced	(ahy) as in write
ui	pronounced	(ooy) as in phooey
oi	pronounced	(owy) as in toy
aui	pronounced	(awy)

TONE

All Kiowa vowels contain tones. Tones can be high, low, or high-low. Tones are indicated by tone markers over the vowel. High tones are found in the words fái (sun), són (grass), and fígá (food). Low tones are found in hàu: (yes), gàu (and), and nàu (but, I, me, my, our). High-low tones are found in the words chḗ (horse) and zêbàut (arrow).

LENGTH

Vowels may also have length as a contrasting element in pronunciation and meaning. In the McKenzie system, length is noted by a colon (:) after the vowel. Length indicates a drawn out vowel pronunciation. Words such as xó: (stone) and já: (star) have a high tone and length. There are many Kiowa words where length is a critical factor in denoting the meaning.

NASAL

Many Kiowa vowels are nasalized. The nasal marker is indicated by a line (_) drawn underneath the nasalized vowel, as in chȩ (horse), fi̱gá (food), há̱utò̱ (axe), pá̱ò̱ (three), pá̱i (dirt), kó̱:gí (grandfather), tá̱:cí (maternal grandmother), and jó̱:gá (speak, word(s), language). In diphthongs, the first vowel is underscored although the entire diphthong is sounded as a nasal.

Pronunciation Table

STOPS	unaspir	aspir	glottal	voiced
Labial	p	pʰ	p'	b
Kiowa	**f**	**p**	**v**	**b**
Dental	t	tʰ	t'	d
Kiowa	**j**	**t**	**th**	**d**
Velar	k	kʰ	k'	g
Kiowa	**c**	**k**	**q**	**g**
AFFRICATIVES				
Dental	c		c'	
Kiowa	**ch**		**x**	

The remaining consonants are the same as they are in English and include

h, l, m, n, s, w, y, z

VOWELS	i	u	
	e	o	
	a	au [ɔ]	
DIPHTHONGS	ai	ui	
	oi	aui	
Tone	high (á)	low (à)	high/low (â)
Length colon	(:)		
Nasalization	underscore (a̱)		

*Based on the Parker McKenzie Kiowa Orthography

Appendix A

Little Bluff Calendar Text

Papers of Hugh L. Scott, Fort Sill Museum Archives

This thirty-one-page handwritten manuscript was produced by Lt. Hugh L. Scott while he was serving at Fort Sill in Indian Territory. He recorded the entries numerically, beginning with number 16. Western calendar designations for some years appear to have been inserted in the margin at a later time. For convenience of reference, two changes have been made in the manuscript. The letters S and W are used to indicate summers and winters, and year designations provided by Scott follow in parentheses. Some punctuation has been added.

Translation of the chart obtained from Tohausen (nephew of Old Tohausen) at Fort Sill O.T. August 1892—Tohausen stated that this chart had been kept from his youth up—at one time upon hides and as fast as one wore out another [illegible] from it—its [illegible].

"I" represent the winters and the middle of the space between, the summers—Tohausen was born in 1817 and died in the winter of 1892–3 at Anadarko O.T. Tohausen means "Little Mountain" in the Kiowa Tongue—Old Tohausen was one of the greatest chiefs the Kiowas ever had—he was their head chief before they split up into small factions—he died on N[orth] F[ork] Canadian about 1868 a very old man—his nephew was said to resemble him very much—(called Quahada Tohausen because he lived for a long time with the Quahada Comanches). He always wore a silver cross on his chest with his name engraved on it; there was still another Tohausen son of the old one who died at Anadarko in the winter of 1893–4.

The first fifteen years of his boyhood he remembered nothing of note and consequently had nothing to record.

16W (1832) Black Wolf was killed in Mexico while on the warpath

16S The Kiowas were camped near Stumbling Bear's north of Mt. Scott—most of their able bodied men were away on the warpath—one day a young man discovered a buffalo that had been killed by an Osage arrow. He immediately reported at the Camp that an Osage war party was lurking around them. The camp broke up in terror one party going south of the mountains by the pass at Mt. Sheridan—one northwest toward mouth of Rainy Mtn Ck & one past Saddle Mtn, going through a pass now called "Cut Off Head" pass south of Timedays—where they camped at a spring on west side of the range (a cottonwood tree is marked at that place now H.L.S.) Before daylight the next morning the Osage party that had followed the last division struck them and destroyed the village killing many old men, women, and children. Some of the survivors got away & carried the news to the other villages & when help arrived they found the village destroyed and all the heads of the dead bodies were missing. They had been cut off by the Osages and put up in the mountains near the Pass & these mountains are called "Cut Off Head Mountains" yet by the Kiowas.

17W (1833) "A great many stars fell". This year 1833 is remembered by all the tribes on the Plains as well as by white people.

17S "When the Kiowa girl was brought back by soldiers—" This circumstance is related by Catlin in his "N. American Indians" and agrees with the Indian account in every particular—the girl had been stolen by the Osages from the village destroyed at "Cut off Head" Mountain & was purchased (with her brother & the Kiowa Medicine captured at the same time) by the 1st Dragoons—and delivered to the Kiowas at the Wichita Village on the North Fork Red River about two miles west of the cattle trail. The boy was killed by a goat near Fort Gibson. The medicine was delivered with the girl. This was the first time the Kiowas and Comanches ever saw a U.S. soldier, the initial trip of the 1st Dragoons.

18W (1834) "Buffalo Tail" was killed on warpath in Mexico.

18S Tonanti made a Sun dance at the Red Hills on the S. Canadian; "Tonanti" was a Kiowa half breed part Arapahoe. He held the Kiowa medicine for many years. This medicine was originally obtained from the Crows of Montana by an Arapahoe & those who have held it since and managed it had Arapahoe blood—Timeday now (1892) has it. The word "Tonanti" is Arapahoe and the Kiowas cannot give its meaning. At this dance the Kiowas used the medicine recovered from the Osages who had captured it at "Cutoff head" mountains—for the first time since its recovery. The drawing represents the medicine.

19W (1835) "Wolf Hair" (a Kiowa) was killed on warpath in Mexico.

19S Tonanti (same man) made the Sundance on North Fork of Canadian.

20W A Kiowa man named "Man" was killed on the warpath in Mexico.

20S Kiowas besieged a lot of Cheyennes in fort at mouth of Turkey Creek on Salt Fork—40 Cheyennes were killed, none escaped.

21W Kiowas camped near the head of Red River went out to war against the Arapahoes who were higher up—at place called "Lots of oak [?]timber". Kiowa man "Stone Head" killed an Arapahoe & took his head home.

21S "Mourners Dance"—The Cheyennes coming after revenge found all the Kiowas & Comanches camped together on North Fork and a great many were killed on both sides, a Kiowa Chief "Wolf Lying Down" was killed.

22W (1838) Kiowas discovered an Arapahoe war party and fought them. A Kiowa man "Heart Eater" was shot in the leg by an Arapahoe arrow.

22S Tonanti made Sundance on Washita below Poor Buffalo's place—where the big bend with bluff on north side is.

23W (1839) The Kiowas had the small pox on Little Wichita, a great many died.

23S Tonanti made Sundance at Red Hill Canadian River.

24W (1840) A war party composed only of old men went to war in Old Mexico carrying quivers of buffalo hide—they got a great many horses and mules.

24S Arapahoes came to make peace with the Kiowas above canyon of Red River at White Hills—Pawnee skulls killed by Arapahoes same place.

25W (1841) Kiowas fought with Texans at "White Hills," Long Hair a Kiowa was killed—got many horses from the Texans

25S Tonanti made two sundances on head of North Fork Canadian

26W (1842) "Crow Neck" a big Kiowa chief died at "Windy canyon" on White River

26S Tonanti made sun dance on North Fork Canadian at mouth of Beaver Creek

27W (1843) Warparty left last sundance the leader Tohausens brother was killed (holding red pipe) a great many Mexicans were killed and their houses burned—The Sioux made them (Kiowa's) a visit—represented by Sioux necklace S. called by the Kiowas Odlepansa or people who wear necklaces (probably Sioux sign originates from this, HLS)

27S Tonanti made Sun dance at the same place (26 S). There were a great many fine cottonwood trees there.

28W (1844) Went to war to Old Mexico "Bear Neck" a Kiowa chief was killed there.

28S Tonanti made sun dance at same place as before (26–7 S). A woman by the name of "Stone Neck" died there. [marginal note] Name of Sun dance = Where Found Tree had a crows nest in the fork (before it was cut down)

29W (1845) A white trader by the name of "Red Neck" came on the Canadian at mouth of Elk Ck & built a dirt house Adobe Walls—he came from Arkansas River—traded 2 years & went back & house was abandoned

29S Tonanti made sundance at same place (26–7–8 S). A Kiowa chief by the name of "Hornless Buffalo" died there.

30W (1846) Satanke was shot in the moustache by Pawnee arrow on North Fork Canadian.

30S Kiowas fought with white soldiers north of the Arkansas below Bents Fort & got the Soldiers mules. A Kiowa man "Red Arm" was killed.

31W (1847) Camped on "White River" all winter

31S Tonanti made Sundance near Bents Fort. Elk horse Indian soldiers (a band) instituted for the first time.

32W (1848) The Kiowas killed an unusual number of antelope on the Arkansas.

32S Tonanti made sundance near Bents Fort—a great many Kiowas died of cramps after the dance—Cholera

33W (1849) Kiowas met a Pawnee w. party on Salt Fork & killed one Osage & 3 Pawnees.

33S Tonanti made Sundance at junction of Wolf & Beaver Cks (near present site of Fort Supply). An elm tree stood by the Medicine Lodge.

34W (1850) "Deer" a big Kiowa chief was killed on the war-path by Mexicans.

34S Tonanti made a sundance at (26 S). The Kiowas killed a Pawnee there.

35W (1851) "Big Bow" stole "Pretty girl" and ran away with her in the winter time. Pretty Girl froze her nose, fingers, & toes.

35S Kiowas in summer (leaves shown on trees) being camped all together at Big Timber Ck (runs into the Arkansas from the North) sent out a war party which killed a Pawnee shooting him in the eye. [N.B. above Pawnee is written "Cheyenne" in James Mooney's hand]

36W (1852) When on war party (35 S) they captured a Pawnee boy—who got away (in 36 W) stealing a bay race horse—he made good his escape after a long chase

36S Tonanti made sundance (26 S) it rained [illegible] day while the sundance [illegible] built

37W (1853) Went to Old Mexico on warparty. "The man who makes Offerings to the Sun" was killed (Pan-giat-an-eke)[?]

37S Tonanti made sundance at same place that Medicine Lodge council was afterwards held—while house was being built, Ioway Indians killed "Black Horse" a Kiowa chief.

38W (1854) Osages killed Ko-mal-ty's uncle who was trying to steal horses from them at night-("Likes to fight any other tribes") was the name of this man.

38S The Cheyennes came to the Kiowas to dance ponies at Black Hill which is four sleeps beyond the Arkansas (N). The Cheyennes got a great many horses from the Kiowas.

39W (1855) A Kiowa man "Going on the Road" was killed on warparty in Old Mexico—Tohausen (leader) & Poor Buffalo went on warpath at same time against the Osages at the Osage old village on Arkansas & killed one Osage. [marginal note] "Long winter"

39S Tonanti made sundance when plums were ripe on Arkansas River near Bents Fort—"Bent was an Eagle nosed white man with a Cheyenne wife."

40W (1856) A few Kiowas camped with the Cheyennes at Bents Fort for the winter—A Cheyenne man got mad at the Kiowas who ran away & left their lodges standing. The Cheyennes kept their lodges & horses.

40S Tonanti made a sun dance on Salt Fork—a forked stick was growing by the Medicine Lodge. "Forked Stick Sundance"

41W (1857) Tay-bolt (Buffalo calf of leg/ Calf of Buffalo's leg) had a great many horses stolen by Pawnees on "No Timber" Creek. This runs into the Arkansas from the S. on the Kiowa trail going from the S. towards the North.

41S Tonanti made a sundance on "Elk horse soldier Ck"—surrounded by trees. This ck is a tributary of Medicine Lodge Ck Kans. [marginal note] Made in a horseshoe bend.

42W (1858) "Lying Down Wolf" was killed on war party [in] Old Mexico. The Kiowas fought with Arapahoes on Red River a little below Palo Duro Canyon.

42S Tonanti made a sundance at "Cedar tree standing on hill" Ck on the north side of Arkansas River. "Cedar Tree on bluff."

43W (1859) Tohausen's Grandfather "Wide Back" died and was buried with a cross over his grave.

43S White soldiers with Caddos, Delawares, Wichitas, & Tonkaways fought the Kiowas at "Black Hill" Creek. Eagle Heart's son-in-law "Eagle coming up the hill" was killed also a Comanche good man named Silver Knife was killed.

44W (1860) The Kiowas in revenge for 43 S went to war against the Caddos & killed one near where Arapahoes village near Cloud Chief stands on Washita and brought back his scalp.

44S Tonanti made sundance on "Cedar Hill" creek. A Kiowa young man "gave a red spotted pony to the sun", i.e. he tied it to the Medicine Lodge & went off and left it.

45W (1861) The Kiowas had smallpox, some were camped on Arkansas & some on the little creeks on this side. Half died.

45S "Small pox dance" Tonanti made a sundance on "Elk horse soldier" creek

46W (1862) Nothing to remember this year by (trees)

[marginal note] Tahbone after taking the chart away for about a month and consulting with some old men translates this by saying that at the forks of Beaver Ck (near "Piedras Parada" Miley map) where Kiowa war parties were accustomed to stop—a K. warparty heard singing going over the tops of the trees. Believe it was an echo now—but the warparty did not know what to make of it. It has been heard since. The line represents the voice going over the trees.

46S Tonanti made sundance on S. side of Arkansas opposite to the house of a white man (trader) with one arm. "one armed white man dance"

47W (1863) "Big Head" Comalty's uncle died.

47S "Flowers" dance—Tonanti made sundance where there was no grass but the lodge was surrounded by flowers on "Elk horse Soldier" Creek

48W (1864) All Kiowas were together on Canadian at Red Hills & the Utes attacked them—White soldiers were with the Utes. Stumbling Bear was a great chief at this fight. He killed a Mexican soldier & a Ute. The Kiowas ran away & abandoned their lodges which were burned by the Utes & soldiers. An old Kiowa man & woman were killed, also a good Apache & a good Comanche man.

48S "High bluff" d. Tonanti made sundance below Poor Buffalos cornfield on Washita opposite high bluffs.

49W (1865) "Black War Bonnet" died on little ck running into the Canadian from the South.

49S "Many silver headdresses" Tonanti made Sundance at mouth of Beaver Ck—While Medicine Lodge was being made every young man had German silver headdress & every young woman G. silver ornaments on belt & leggings for the first time. German silver had been purchased from white traders who came from the Arkansas during the previous winter it was purchased in sheets.

50W (1866) "Big Bow" & "Plenty Bears" were leading a war-party to Mexico. "Man struck on head by a Tree" a Mexican captive was killed at "Sun Water Springs" Texas.

50S Tonanti made sundance on Washita due south of the Antelope Hills. The Navajo stole a fine spotted horse during the dance from the Kiowas. [marginal note] Sign = Black Eared Pony" dance = Spotted.

51W "Medicine Lodge" Treaty was made, or as called by the Kiowas the treaty made at "Timbered Hill"

51S (1867) The following summer a sundance was made by Tonanti on Medicine Lodge ck and a few days afterward "Poor Buffalo" & "Plenty Bears" gave a pipe to every young man to go on warpath against the Utes". The Ute village was found beyond the headwaters of the Canadian at a salt lake and attacked. The Kiowas were repulsed with the loss of seven men killed one of whom was "Plenty Bears". The Kiowas were camped on the Arkansas at a "soldier house", probably Fort Dodge when they got the news. That fall they left the Arkansas for good and never as a people went back. They moved down to the Washita below Black Kettle's village & camped. That fall they gathered a war party which went to Texas (Tahbone was on that & the Ute expedition also).

52W (1868) "Tangoodle" was killed on warpath in Texas. He had a custom of having larger arrow than other Kiowas.

52S A sun dance was made by Tonanti near the site of Fort El-liott, Tex. on the North Fork Red River. While the dance was in progress "Big Bow" arrived with a warbonnet he had captured from the Utes. He had killed the owner a Ute chief beyond the Grand Canyon of the Arkansas.

53W (1869) A great many Kiowas were camped on beaver Creek above present site of Fort Supply. Satanta (who was coming down from a visit to the Arkansas with his family) blew a trumpet just at break of day near the village in order to locate it. The Kiowas thought that soldiers were about to charge on them which caused such a stampede that they abandoned the village and ran away getting out about four miles before the trick was discovered. Satanta carried this trumpet (which he had gotten at some Army Post) for many years using it in the sun dance and in the dance of the "Rattle soldiers" of which he was the chief.

53S Tonanti made a sundance at the "End of the Mountains" on North Fork Red River. Here traders brought a good many watermelons & corn. The Kiowas left here & later they came back & found that corn & watermelons had grown up from the seed dropped earlier in the village by accident.

54W (1870) Satanke's son was killed in Texas. He had the same name = "Sitting Bear"

54S There was no sundance this year because Tonanti had died the winter before. He had made the first dance when they got the "medicine" back from the Osages (30 dances in all) and no one was sufficiently versed in the sundance road to give the dance. The season was notable however for the capture of "Big Tree" (see hand cuffs & shackles)

55W (1871) This year the Pawnees came to visit the Kiowas for the first time and made peace with them. The Pawnee is shown by the head being shaved all but the single scalp lock. The Kiowas were then camped on the Washita near the mouth of Deadman's Creek.

55S There was no sundance this year for the same reason as before. A Kiowa man by the name of "Strong Bird" was shot while on the W. part southwest of Fort Sill by a white man but was not killed. He reached the Kiowa camp at the "End of the Mountains."

56W (1872) The Kiowas were camped on Rainy Mountain Creek and the Pueblo Indians came to trade with them for horses and buffalo robes, giving in exchange sugar, corn, clothing, eagle feathers and a large round cracker or hard bread biscuit. The Pueblos tie their hair behind the head.

56S "Got no Moccasins" (other name Plenty Stars) look up the sundance medicine. Sundance was on North Fork Red River at mouth of ck coming down from Elliott called "Battle Ck" by the Kiowas. "Rising Wolfs" wife was stolen by "Black Buffalo Bull". Rising Wolf, or better "Wolf Coming Up Over a Hill", got angry and killed a number of ponies belonging to "Black Bull"

57W (1873) Satanta's lodge was painted red. This winter he came back to it having been released from prison. The Kiowa camp was then close to Eagle Heart's place on Cache Creek.

57S Satanta had had an arrow for a long time. He gave this arrow to Sun Boys brother (thereby giving him a chiefs road) Sun Boys brother was called "Ap-to-dan". Sun dance was made by "No Moccasins" on NF Red River beyond cattle trail.

58W (1874) After the last sundance the Kiowas had a fight with White soldiers at Anadarko and ran off to the Staked Plains. They joined with the Comanches & Cheyennes and traveled about on the Plains pursued by white soldiers. They had a fight on the head of Red River at a canyon where a Kiowa chief "Horns on his warbonnet" was killed. This winter the Kiowas were all driven in to Fort Sill and put in the guardhouse. "This time poverty came and the white man punished us."

58S The Kiowas escorted by white soldiers made a sundance on N. Fork Red River at the mouth of Salt Fork. This place has from very ancient times been called the place where "the man was killed for interfering with another man's wife & this sundance has the same name.

59W (1875) This winter Agent Hayward sent to the mountains of Mexico and had a big band of sheep driven up and issued to the Kiowas, Comanches, & Apaches.

"No Moccasins" died in the Fall and the sundance medicine was taken up by "Plenty Bears a brother of Timeday and a relative of the "Plenty Bears" killed by the Utes (ante)—

59S Sundance was made by "Plenty Bears" on N. F. Red River near End of the Mountains (i.e. where the mountains running up the North Fork run out). During the dance "Sun Boy's" horses were driven off by somebody possibly Utes or Navajos or white men.

60W (1876) "Eapah" (now a soldier in Troop L 7 Cav 1893–4) killed his wife in the Kiowa camp on Cache Ck below Comanche schoolhouse. Her name was "Au-so-ly" = "Smooth Ridge"

60S Sundance was made near Dans Store on Red River. Lt. Crews 4th Cavy was escorting the Kiowas to prevent collisions with white people from Texas. The picture represents four trees. Long ago some women put down stakes here which afterwards grew up to be four trees.

61W (1877) Picture represents a white man's house. This year the Govt built white man's houses for some of the prominent chiefs. Stumbling Bear, Heidsick, Sun Boy, Cat, White Man, Toha, etc.

61S Made two sundances at End of Mountains were two nights at each dance.

62W (1878) Kiowas were with soldiers hunting buffalo south of Red River and the Texans killed Sun Boys brother—to whom Satanta had presented the arrow (ante)

63W (1879) The picture represents "Little Robe" holding a stick with a human eye to it. Little Robe went out on North Fork Red River to hunt for deer. Eapah's brother went with them. He told Little Robe one night that he had better not go to bed but to round up the horses and watch them for an owl (sap-oodle) had told him that the Navajo would try and steal the horses that night. During the night Eapah's brother fired at something and next morning the trail of a man was found & some drops of blood. This trail was followed by the Kiowas for a long distance but was finally given up. That night the owl told Eapah's brother that the Navajo who had been wounded was lying dead beyond where his pursuers had turned back and that he (the owl) would go and fetch him. The next morning upon rising Eapah's brother saw something strange in the lodge and upon examination by everybody, it proved to be a human eye (belonging to the dead Navajo sic) and Eapah's brother told Little Robe that they had better stop hunting and go home which they did, Little Robe carrying the stick to which the Navajo's eye was attached. [marginal note] Eapah's brother's name was Pado— "Pulls Branches off Trees"

63S No sundance was held but all planted corn and cultivated it during the summer. No one was well enough versed in the sundance medicine road to take it up & make a dance.

64W (1880) Paul Tsait-komp-te's house was built this winter near side of the Tonkaway village on Washita destroyed by Shawnees during the Civil War—represents a white man's house.

64S Had a sun dance on North Fork Red River at Salt Spring near End of Mountains. One lone buffalo bull was found for it near the head of Red River after a long search by the proper persons.

Pau-a-tane had a medicine to bring back the buffalo. Pau-a-tane was Woman's Heart's sons. Pau-a-tane is represented having a pipe (symbol of leadership) in one hand and some eagle feathers around wrist of the other hand (medicine). He wore a medicine shirt garnished with blue beads.

65W (1881) Figure represents two Pueblos and the year is the one Big Bow went to Santa Fe to visit the Pueblos.

65S Had no sundance this year, but planted corn. Sometimes the Sun Dance chief says we will have dance this year & sometimes he says it will not be good to have it. This year no buffalo could be found for it so they had none.

66W (1882) A great many children died this year of some unknown disease (not small pox or measles) Plenty Bears died in spring & Timeday took up his sundance road (still has it Feby 1894 HLS)

66S Timeday made a Sun dance where an Arapahoe village was three years ago, above present town of Cloud Chief on Washita. Some tribe of Indians who cut their hair off square above the eyes leaving it long on the sides but whose name is unknown were present at this dance. These people had been driven away from their early homes by white people & were not Nez Perce's, but were possibly Poncas. A lone buffalo bull was killed for this dance on this side of the head of Red River. Tohausen, Honameatah's brother (died Feby '94) had the pipe for killing the buffalo for sun dances.

67W (1883) Lone Wolfs brother built a house on the Washita close to the mouth of Cobb Creek on the south side.

67S Had no sundance. Timeday said not to have it because after a long search Tohausen failed to find a buffalo.

68W (1884) Picture represents a white man's house. Quite a number of Kiowas began to get them. One on the upper Elliott crossing of Rainy Mountain Creek.

68S Timeday made a sundance on the Washita below Poor Buffalo's cornfield. Ti-eh has a cornfield near there now. Tohausen found a buffalo on the Staked Plains beyond where the water of Red River is "wiped out". The line underneath the sundance lodge represents the steep bluffs at this place which skirt the north side of the Washita around a big bend.

69W (1885) The greater part of the Kiowas wintered together on the Washita above the mouth of Sulphur Creek.

69S No buffalo could be found so the sundance was not held.

70W (1886) On the head of Elk Creek "Middleman" did something crazy. He told the Kiowas that he was going to give a medicine to ten men (himself the 11th) to kill all the soldiers when they should come out after them. And everybody that wanted to fight must come to his camp on Elk Creek and he would fix it so that the soldiers bullets would fail to penetrate & the lightning would strike the soldiers and they would all be wiped out. A great number of Kiowas conger[g]ated at his camp on Elk Creek to await the outcome.

Capt. Lee Hall of the Texas Rangers was Agent at Anadarko. He advised Stumbling Bear and Sun Boy to hold themselves aloof from the main Kiowa camp. They had a council at Sun Boys house & among other reasons for obeying the agent it was stated by Stumbling Bear that if one body of Troops should be wiped out by Middleman another would be immediately sent out & still another & larger body until the Kiowas were all killed so they held their people out of this trouble & kept them near the mountains. Capt. Hall with some white soldiers went up the Washita & camped on Oak Ck—where the Cheyenne line south boundary struck the river. Capt. Hall sent for Sun Boy & Stumbling Bear & had them bring some Apache chiefs over from the camp on Elk Ck & after a council the Kiowas agreed to drop the whole thing, which was done & the trouble was all over.

70S No buffalo could be found so there was no sundance held.

71W (1887) The Agent turned the (grass money) from leases to cattle men into cattle (almost 2500) & issued them.

71S A sundance (Timeday) was held on Terrace on north side of Oak Creek where S. Cheyenne line crosses the Washita. A Buffalo was bought from Goodnight a cattleman in Panhandle of Texas for about $100.00. This was the last medicine dance held by the Kiowas.

72W (1888) Picture a tipi & a white mans house. By this is meant that a great many Kiowas are getting white mens houses but they still live in the tipis.

72S No buffalo could be gotten so no medicine dance was held.

73W (1889) Do not know what the lodge is intended to recall. Iseeo or Tahbone enlisted for a scout this winter.

73S The Commissioner forbid the holding of the sundance but the Kiowas were going to hold it anyhow. Cut & planted the pole and put a buffalo robe (in lieu of a buffalo) in the forks of the pole when the Agent (Adams) called on Fort Sill for Troops to stop it. The soldiers went to Anadarko & sent up word to the dance where the big bluffs are below Poor Buffalo's cornfield & the Kiowas stopped it & separated.

74W (1890) This winter the Kiowas danced the Messiah dance, where Tahbone, Wm. Jones, & Lt. Scott 7 Cav'y went to see the dance on Sulphur Creek. The feather represents the feather given by the Arapahoe John the Baptist Sitting Bull. When he brings the new religion to a tribe, he institutes leaders by giving them feathers.

74S Do not know what is meant by this figure except that the Messiah dance ceased

75W (1891) Nothing is recorded for this winter.

75S Lieut. Scott 7 Cavy had a council with Tahbone with the Kiowa chiefs on the Washita at which they got a great many soldiers for the first time, i.e. when the opposition to enlistment was broken down. This is recalled by the square top of head of the figure which is said to look like a soldiers cap.

15S.   A Kato
       Mourning Sun Dance. Women cried for people killed;
       news received at dance
16W.   Pai-yi-a (Buffalo's Son) died this winter
17S.   No Sun Dance. Camped on Canadian River for Sun
       Dance, but Cheyennes attacked and killed a number.
       No dance. Ka-kia (Ten) born
18W.   Dog Soldier society started
19S.   Pia Kato 1839
       Sun Dance in a bend of Washita, [later insertion]
       Peninsula Sun Dance
20W.   1839–40
       Smallpox this winter
21S.   Godl- to-ha Kato 1840
       Red Bluff Sun Dance on Canadian near a red bluff
22W.   Kaiso bi-em sai
       Made light quivers to go on the war path
23S.   No sun dance
24W.   1841
       A-la-ba-kia (Cut Hair) killed
25S.   Adl-ta Kato 1842
       Double sun dance
26W.   "Heap of Bears" nephew killed this winter by an
       Kiowa Apache who wanted to come back home, while
       his Kiowa companions did not
27S.   Man-so an-sem kodl-te Kato 1843
       Crow nest sun dance. A crow built a nest on sun
       dance pole
28W.
29S.   Godl pan kia Kato 1844
       Osage sun dance. Fight with Osage (?)
       [later insertion] Sioux visit, wrong interpretation
30W.   Kiowas and Comanches found a corral in Mexico and
       put their captured horses in it. Kie ka godl te (Crow
       Neck) killed.

31S. Tso kodl te Kato 1845
       (Rock Neck sun dance) Rock Neck's daughter died.
       Toha-e-te built a striped teepee because of a dream,
       he was the first to deal with the government

32W. A-so-ta-li (Thunder) killed this winter

33S. A-ka- to-dl Kato
       Measles sun dance

34W. 1846–47
       Setanpia "Moustache" an Indian shot this winter

35S. 1847
       No dance, Man ka-godl-te (Red Sleeve) a Comanche
       was killed

36W. Hon-ze-pan (Gun or Shot) a woman was born who
       took care of Martinez, winter camp shown with brush
       around

37S. A-pan Kato 1848
       Choking Sun Dance, on Se-se-pa (Arkansas Riv-
       er, Arrowpoint River), "Brave" dog soldiers started,
       initiated

38W. Ice jam on river; Old White Horse was killed (Tsein-
       tai-inte)

39S. Man-yia-kia Kato 1849
       Cramp sun dance (cholera), Ze-ba-tai (On the Arrow)
       died first

40W. Killed a very brave Pawnee this winter

41S. Pun-wa Kato 1850
       China berry sun dance; china berry trees around sun
       dance arbor

42W. Tan-kia pa (Deer, old name) killed this winter

43S. Pan Kato
       (Dusty Sun Dance) killed all Pawnees in one place
       after surrounding them, boy captured

44W. Woman ran away with a young man who left her;
       when she came back her feet were frozen

45S.   No dance. Killed a lot of Mexican soldiers. Set pa-koi (Lone Bear) died, fell dead while cutting tipi poles (it was disgrace for man to cut poles)

46W.   1852–53
Pawnee captive ran away

47S.   Bien-so Kato
Raining sun dance, rained all the time

48W.   Set-kon-kia (Black bear) killed. Somebody died. Also Tan yoin-te (Coffee Maker) once called Kaa-bo-hon (Crow Bonnet) was shot and his arm broken so it always hung loose

49S.   A-yadl-ta Kato 1854
High hill with trees sun dance. The "long arrow" given to White Bear, a very "honorable arrow"

50W.   Kyai-gua-on-te (Enemy Lover, Like to Fight) killed from ambush by Osages

51S.   Odl-kin-ni-a-hodl
Summer they killed long hair Pawnee. No dance. Kiowa killed a long haired Pawnee Indian

52W.   Captured a Ute boy, under Set-pa-ko (was leader)

53S.   Sin-a-lo Kato 1856
Prickly pear sun dance

54W.   "Loud Talk" was killed. Somebody got jealous of him and killed him. Hai-ka-yodl (a woman) was born

55S.   A-po-ta-e-kia-de Kato 1857
Stake green [?] sun dance

56W.   1857–58
Whooping cough winter, Pawnees stole a lot of Kiowa horses

57S.   A- to-bi-en Kato 1858
Surrounded by trees sun dance

58W.   1858–59
Gue-ka-te (Lying Coyote) killed by soldiers

59S. Aan- ton-te Kato 1859
Cut down all the trees to make the arbor, trees scarce,
up in Arkansas somewhere

60W. Honze-tai de hodl de sai
Killed On the Gun winter

61S. No dance—Te-ne-ba-de e hodl, killed Eagle Peeping
Out this summer

62W. Adl-kai- to-ha sai 1860–1
Crazy hill winter, killed Caddo Indians and were like
drunk or crazy at scalp dance

63S. Toe-kua a-pan tse-de Kato 1861
Tied a spotted horse sun dance; horse tied to a dance
pole. Had a fight with Utes, killed a number with war
bonnets

64W. Tadl ko sai
Smallpox winter; owners father's tipi, Utes stole his
fathers stock

65S. Tadl-ko Kato 1862
Smallpox sun dance

66W. Tsen-ko tsa-pan e-pa- to
Winter when the horses had to eat ashes, a bad winter.
Ema-a (Bear lying down and getting [up] continually)
born this winter

67S. Tsoodlen-te Kato 1863
"One wing sun dance" on Arkansas. White man
whom the Indians called "one wing" had house near
by

68W. Adl- to-m-wedl-hem de sai—
Big Head dead winter Honza-po- to (Gun Killer) also
died

69S. A-sa-he Kato 1864
Screw worm medicine weed sun dance (which I do
not know, this describes the weed, ragweed?) They
roped an antelope to make a new inner sack for the
Tai-me. They cannot shoot an animal for this purpose.

70W. Godl- to-ha sai, Yia- to-go em- to-hodl
Red Bluff winter. Utes and soldiers struck Kiowas at a
camp near Red Bluff on the Canadian. Tipis
destroyed.

71S. A-pio Kato 1865
Big bend sun dance (peninsula on Washita River)

72W. To-ha-a-san hem de sai
Small distant peak dead winter. He was the first man
to get a wagon.

73S. Atlan Kato 1866
Silver ornament sun dance, got a lot of these

74W. A-pa-modl-te e-hodl de sai
Leaning-his-head-against-a-tree killed winter, by Texas
people. In the spring of this year, about April, Martinez
came to the Kiowas.

75S. O-pan Kato 1867
Choking Sun Dance; new clothes (Opan) made for
dog soldiers. (owner) Hovate (owner) put up his first
tipi

76W. Tsen ya-tai-en-te a-va-ho-ka adlta e-ta-ta-ka.
Owner-of-a-white-horse had his head shot off by
Navajoes. They killed a Navajo with one ear off.
Sen-ko sai (black mucus winter, another name)
Kiowas went to Texas and it was so cold their "snot"
froze. Medicine Lodge treaty; govt. gave Indians 30
more years

77S. Yia- to-do-hodl te Kato 1868
Utes killed us (Kiowas) sun dance. Pa-gun-a-han
(Lost One Horn) was killed this summer. Heap-of-
Bears killed by Utes. 7 Kiowas were also killed.

78W. Cheyenne Chief "Black Bucket" killed by Gen. Custer
at scalp dance. Martinez was in this fight.

79S. A-ta-hoi kya-kon-de Kato 1869
      War bonnet brought sun dance. At this time Big Bow
      brought in the war bonnet of a Ute who had been
      previously scalped but not killed by other Kiowas.

80.   Tom-bo-de-pe de sai
      Scared by trumpet winter. Set-an-kya (Sitting Bear)
      killed. They heard a trumpet in the night and were
      scared.

81S. Pa- to a-tan-hodl de Kato 1870
      "Possessing" whipped sun dance (by Kia-tai-sonte or
      Little Chief with a war club. Indians found melons
      among some corn to eat at sun dance).

82W. Ko-pa-hodl-te a- ton-adl koi-hodl
      Kill-on-the-Mountain, they killed him drunk

83S. No sun dance. Pa-tai-en-te (White Buffalo) was given
      a peace pipe by the Wichitas

84W. Ku-we-ki-ya-ko ete-te-a-m
      First peace with Pawnees made this winter.

85S. Te-ne-ze-te a ton-adl-koi 1872
      No dance. Eagle bow killed drunk by San-bo, young
      man.

86W. Owner's tipi burned this winter. Killed Kwahada
      (antelope), Comanches

87S. Kue-be-te tsen-ka-yodl de Kato 1873
      Kuebate (Peeping Coyote) killed horses sun dance. A
      young man took one of his wives and he killed all that
      young man's horses.

88W. Gu-i-pa-go i-ya e-hodl de ha ni ko
      Killed Lone Wolf's son this winter, by Texas people

89   Tso-ka-kan Kato 1874
      Last-mountain sun dance, held at the edge of the
      Wichitas. Long arrow given to another man, owner's
      girl born.

90W. Em- ton-pan adl he bo
Put in jail with feet shackled. General McKenzie
captured a lot of Indians and put them in jail at Fort
Sill. Someone died, name lost.

91S. Ka-i- ton Kato 1875
Sweetheart sun dance, many young people were
sparking at this time

92W. Government gave sheep to the Indians. A woman
born

93S. Pai-ta-li tsin ko da sim ko de Kato 1876
Some tribe—no one knows who—stole Sun Boy's
horses

94W. Pe tai pa a sa i kya
Petai rode buffalo. Sunboy got permit to go on
buffalo hunt. On this hunt Petai rode a buffalo.
Somebody born.

95S. Kadl-godl sa-um ha pa de Kato 1877
Red buffalo blood sun dance. Just time a Kiowa had
consumption hemorrhage (also measles)

96W. A-ko-ate adl ka yam kia de sai
Went crazy winter. Woman (Akoate-Arrow) went
crazy on buffalo hunt

97S. Adl-ka Kato 1878
Double sun dance; eclipse of the sun

98W. Akotakia e hodl de sai
Arrow Owner killed winter. Sun Boy's brother
(A-ko-ta-kia) was killed by Texas people on a buffalo
hunt. Texas people scalped him and cut finger off
to get ring

99S. Tsen-pia Kato 1879
Eat Horse meat sun dance. Took a Texas scalp to pay
for arrow owners death

100W. Kadl godl hem de sai
Red Buffalo dead winter. Died of consumption, first
one.

101S. Ze-koi-ye-de hem de pai
       Big Bow dead summer. Big Bow died this summer.
       No dance.

102W. Ze-ko-ye-te te gun toi ba 1880–81
       Big Bow (another one) visit Pueblos winter. Built a
       school house at Anadarko, gone now

103S. Sadl-ko-a-ya de Kato
       Plenty sweat houses sun dance. They built a lot here,
       buffalo skulls shown. Ze-ba-tain (White Arrow) died.

104W. Godl-ka- to-e pain de sai 1881–82
       Tied red blanket winter. A man tried to make
       medicine to bring buffalo back. A baby born.

105S. A-doi kan kia hem 1882
       No dance. Man who tried to make buffalo medicine
       died. He was one of the leaders who hoped to
       bring the buffalo from under the ground.

106W. Odl-te-em ta-ga de sai
       Odl-te (Bag) shot himself winter

107S. Godl-pan sa he a hodl de Kato
       Green necktie killed medicine dance. Little Bow killed
       him.

108W. Kya-tai e-an-a-wa-koi ko sai
       Winter when they issued a cow apiece to the chiefs,
       also five dollars apiece

109S. (Don-ta-te) a i o me de pai
       No dance. Dry shoulder (a Comanche) given a peace
       pipe summer. This pipe was given by Kiowas.
       Lightning struck a woman under a wagon this
       summer.

110W. Tonakao yo koi po ha po de sai 1884–85
       Tonakao (Snapping Turtle) stole a girl winter

111S. Pi-ho Kato 1885
       Big Bend, a sun dance on Washita. Govt payment
       20.00

112W. Te-bodl-te to gua tlan de sai 1885–86
"Calf of the Leg" lost everything winter (his tipis
burned)

113S. Ta-ka-i-ke a hodl de pai
No dance. White man killed summer. They stole
Indian horses and Big Bow and Loud Talks son
followed and killed one.

114W. Sa-bin-odl-de-yia em-hodl de sai 1886–87
Quiver Carriers her son killed himself winter

115S. To-ka-ta Kato 1887
Oak sun dance at Oak Creek

116W. Tato-wa-koi-gua-e-on de sai 1887–88
Issued bulls to chiefs winter. Govt issued a bull apiece
to chiefs. Sun Boy chief at that time.

117S. Kia-gum-ka-i-tai de pai 1888
No dance. Run away from strong wind summer. They
had a strong wind and the Kiowas traveled around
fearing a storm. Pain-kiai, a medicine man, told the
Indians that they were to have a big wind and that
they should come to his place to be saved. Leggings,
feather, and staff of the medicine man's order are
shown.

118W. Pai-ta-li kadl ha kia de sai
Sun Boy took cattle winter. Govt tried to give Indians cattle but all afraid except Sun Boy who took all of
his. Sun Boys brother Toten (Stick) died at this time.

119S. Em-kia te-i hem de pai 1889
No dance. Stumbling Bear's son dead summer His
father's shield is shown.

120W. Pai-ta-li hem de sai
Sun Boy dead winter

121S. Kato a koi to-ta 1890
Run away and left sun dance. Put pole but did not
complete dance, government soldiers stopped it.

122W. Talio-e ka hem de sai 1890–91
       School boys froze dead winter. Three boys from
       government school ran away and were frozen this
       winter

123S. To-na-ka to godl adl ten a tak de pai
       Turtle shot another young man's head summer

124W. Koi-gu-e sodle a me de sai 1891–92
       Kiowa soldiers they made winter. Govt enlisted Kiowa
       soldiers, soldiers hat shown. Owners child born in Te-
       ka moon (geese go out moon) (month sign)

125S. Tadlio a ka todl hem de pai 1892
       Children dead of measles summer, all got measles,
       very sick

126W. Tsen-tai-inte hem de sai
       White Horse dead winter

127S. Ta-li-edl a somta de pai 1893?
       Looking at Big Boy summer. Big boy at white mans
       show at Anadarko

128W. To-ha-e-te hem de sai
       Small distant hill dead winter (owners father)

?129S. Set-ai-inte hem oyate pai 1894
       White Bear dead summer. Robbers killed Ekanish, a
       Caddo, this summer

130W. Ko ne to gudlan de sai
       Quinette's store burned winter

?131S. Set-tai-inte pa vi hem de pai 1895
       Low Bowels brother dead summer. Tonaka (a medi-
       cine man) died also.
       [n.b. (different) is inserted below the name Set-tain-te]

132W. Se-ya-dl-ta ton gua-tadli to a o me
       Rainy Mt. school built winter

133S. Tsa dla oyi e-on de pai 1896
       Young cattle issued summer; Ooete, a woman, ran
       away to Comanches

134W. Tsonte ka tone e ta ke de sai
White Feather shot in shoulder by white man winter

135S. Tongua ta ton e tem de pai 1897
Signed for rock quarry summer, ceded quarry to govt.
Sen-tsohina (Old Peyote) owner's daughter born. Te-
de-a, Standing-on-sweat-house, dead. Hats put away
after council.

136W. Hoa-kan de ta hem de sai
Sankadote's wife dead winter. Her name = Ton-yo-ma
= Leader (shown by pipe)

137S. A-hi-ya- to tsu lai tsan o ya te pai 1898
Arapahoes July came this summer, a fourth of July
dance

138W. Han-kin-ko e tse de sai
Railroad put here winter. Railroad first put through.

139S. A- ton-kia ko bedl kia de pai 1899
Hold a council Mt. Scott summer, big council at Mt.
Scott. Tadla him oya te har, White Pole-cat dead this
summer

140W. A-pia- ton a-tan hodl de sai
Apiaton whipped winter, by Kon-bonhon (Hat)
whose sick boy had died as a result of being taken to
Apiaton's council

141S. Pa-in-ki-ai hem de pai 1900
(medicine man) P—dead this summer. He holds meat
in picture. He used to hold meat up and pray before
eating.

142W. K-ai-a-giva tadl ko him de sai
Comanches dead of smallpox winter

143S. Pa-kiap a-dlan kia tai gua de pai 1901
Old-buffalo-bull added to check more summer. A
young Indian man raised a small govt check for $40
to $640, was sent to pen; a horse found shot this
summer.

144W. Guna oa a de ta him de sai
Many Poles his wife dead winter. Land allotted and opened.

145S. Ga-a-pia- ton hem oya-te pai 1902
Crow Spear dead summer. Poton (Beaver Tail) dead also.

146. O-ka-te hem de sai
"Bed" dead winter

147. On-ta kina taun de pai 1903
Fifty dollar payment summer. Leupp came to settle claims, had yellow clothes, fifty dollars payment.

148W. Randalet an-ta kina a-dla kia
Col. Randelet made 50.00 payment winter

149S. Pan-sen-kin an-ta-tain an de pai 1904
Seventy five dollar payment summer.
Tsenhi guaya-tsuna de hem oyate pai
Dog-running-behind dead summer. Koi-yan-an-te (Coyote Bark) dead; Odl-ka-ete (Bag's son dead)

150W. Ta-bi-en to da yam be oyate sai
Big Eye went away to cure eyes winter. Red Rock church built.

151S. Man-ka-yia e-a-tan de pai 1905
Cyclone kill a lot summer. This was the Snyder cyclone; a marshal was killed and his head cut off. Houses thrown down, blood. The cyclone maker has a snake's tail which destroys everything. The other half is some another animal. Once the Kiowas made a horse and put wings on it. All at once it began to move and become a cyclone maker.

152W. Man-ka yia ki-ai Mountain View kia
Cyclone went on Mountain View de sai winter. Mt. View cyclone. Houses destroyed, blood.

153S. A-ome ko bedl kia de pai 1906
Church Mt. Scott summer. Church built at Mt. Scott. Ton-kia godl (Red Tail) dead

154W. Po-bo-hon hem oyate sai

Beaver Bonnet dead winter. A-kon-bai (Last One) dead. Senodeta (Snot's wife dead); Adlpete (Frizzly Head dead).

155S. Pano-kian-an de pai 1907

30 dollar payment summer; owner's son broke leg; 3 little girls died.

156W. A-man ko ya sen a hen de sai

A lot of feathered ghost dancers dead winter (8)

157S. Kia-yadl-te hem oyate pai 1908

Run After Enemy dead summer. A-ma-tse-a (Carried on Back) dead, both women were feathered ghost dancers; 100 dollar payment

158W. Podl-kan-mai hem oyate sai

Woman Crinkled-forked-sticks dead this winter. Ton-kia-hodl-te (kill in water) a ghost dancer dead; Ko-ke-ki (Body paralyzed) dead, has a ghost dance bell in his hand

159S. Kumate ka-a-kia- to-wi ba de pai 1909

Kumate visits Crow Indians summer (This summer)

[The following letter is filed with the notebook.]

Anadarko, Okla, July 8, 1907 [sic]

Dear Mr. Heye:-

I enclose a calendar of the Kiowas with Mss. explanation. Each winter and summer are numbered consequetively [sic] and the explanations for each will be found opposite the corresponding number in the manuscript. The calendar would be a fine one if it had been painted on a hide instead of in a book. It was bought from Habate, an old Kiowa.

Today I am shipping you two boxes containing results since last shipment. The number is not as great, as Wm. Skye had to go home on account of his daughter's illness and Fullbright had to start in making hay.

I was disappointed in the shield and scalp dress I told you I expected. Both turned out to be nothing but clever modern imitations which I refused to buy.

In the shipment is a war medicine robe which, altho made of cotton sheeting I was told I was very lucky to get. I hope to get more of the "strong powers" before I leave and when I come back later. I fear I can not finish the Kiowa until I come back in September. The heat now is deadly which makes work difficult; moreover very few of the Kiowas are at home just now, but are roving about, hard to catch.

Yours faithfully, M. R. Harrington
I am glad the last shipment pleased you.

Appendix C

Other Kiowa Calendars

Calendars Published or in Public Repositories

Ananti

    Fort Sill Museum, D1049. Multiple pages in bound volume.

    Fort Sill Museum, D83.1.1. Multiple pages in bound volume.

    Fort Sill Museum, 66.28.31. Cloth strip.

    Fort Sill Museum, 83.1.449. Cloth strip.

Anko

    National Anthropological Archives, MS 2538. Multiple pages in bound volume.

    National Anthropological Archives Negative 46856. Photographic copy of painted hide.

Big Tree

    Published in Boyd, *Kiowa Voices*, vol. 2. Original form not described.

Buffalo, Mary

    Published in Marriott, *The Ten Grandmothers*. Original form not described.

Domebo

    Western History Collection, University of Oklahoma, Doris Duke Oral History Project files. Photographs of original cloth strip.

Gaukein

> Fort Sill Museum, 65.153.1. Cloth strip.
>
> Panhandle-Plains Historical Society, 1510/130. Cloth strip.

Hauvahte

> National Museum of the American Indian (see appendix B for transcription of text). Original reportedly in bound volume.

Hill, Bobby (White Buffalo)

> Southern Plains Indian Museum, Anadarko, Oklahoma. Painted hide.

Hunt, George

> Published in Marriott, *The Ten Grandmothers*. Original form not described.

Little Bluff

> Phoebe Apperson Hearst Museum of Anthropology, 2-4933
>
> (see appendix A for transcription of text). Single sheet of paper.

Poolaw, George

> Published in Marriott, *The Ten Grandmothers*. Original reportedly multiple pages in bound volume.

Poolaw, Moses

> Fort Sill Museum, D69.31.2. Multiple pages in bound volume.

Rowell, Charles

> Capitol Children's Museum, Washington DC. Painted hide.
>
> Haffenreffer Museum of Anthropology, Brown University. Painted hide.
>
> Southern Plains Indian Museum, Anadarko, Oklahoma. Painted hide.
>
> Square House Museum, Panhandle, Texas. Painted hide.

Quitone

> Fort Sill Museum, 68.39.1-4. Tracings of original cloth strip.

National Anthropological Archives, MS 2002-27. Multiple loose sheets.

Settan
National Anthropological Archives, BAE GN 01464A. Photograph of original on single sheet of paper.

Silver Horn
National Anthropological Archives, MS 2531, vol. 7. Multiple pages in bound volume.
National Anthropological Archives, MS 4252. Multiple pages in bound volume.

Ware, Harry (?)
National Anthropological Archives, MS 7268. Photographs of original cloth strip.

Unknown keepers
Gilcrease Museum, Tulsa, 4527.12.1. Multiple pages in bound volume.
Gilcrease Museum, Tulsa, 4527.18. Multiple pages in bound volume.
National Anthropological Archives, MS 2002-28. Cloth strip.
Oklahoma History Center, Oklahoma City, 2005.076.005. Cloth strip.

Related Records

Black Bear (Plains Apache)
American Museum of Natural History, 50.1/6208. Multiple pages in bound volume.

Big Bow (?) drawings, possibly calendric in nature
Fort Sill Museum, D62.99.2. Multiple loose sheets.
Gilcrease Museum, Tulsa, 4526.20-65. Multiple loose sheets.
Museum of the Great Plains, Lawton, Oklahoma, 88.13. Multiple loose sheets.

Notes

1. The Kiowa Calendar Tradition

1. In the Americas, only the Aztec and Maya civilizations of Mexico created numerical calendars.

2. To explore some of the Lakota winter counts, log onto http://wintercounts.si.edu. For more extensive background about their history, see Greene and Thornton, eds., *Year the Stars Fell*.

3. See Greene, "Exploring the Three 'Little Bluffs,'" for biographical information on the original Little Bluff and others of the same name.

4. As with other scholars of the time, almost all of James Mooney's information on Kiowa culture and history came from interviews with men.

5. See Greene and Thornton, eds., *Year the Stars Fell*, for illustrations of these calendars.

6. This late nineteenth-century attitude contrasts with the reverence that Kiowa writer N. Scott Momaday attributes to his great-grandfather Pohd-lohk, who preserved a calendar as a near-sacred heirloom. For him, the calendar, drawn on the pages of a ledger book, represented a tangible link with the past, both personal and tribal, amid the many changes of the twentieth century (Momaday, *The Names*, 47–52).

7. See Greene, "Southern Plains Graphic Art," for a discussion of early Kiowa art.

8. "A spasm of industrial expansion was the primary cause of the bison's near extinction" (Isenberg, *Destruction of the Bison*, 130). Although some hides were tanned with the hair on to serve as warm carriage robes, after 1870 the majority were converted into drive belts for industrial machinery. Development of new tanning methods suitable for raw hides coincided with expansion of railroad lines, which

provided transportation for the heavy hides. Together, these two factors made large-scale bison hunting commercially viable.

9. Blue Clark provides a detailed treatment of the Medicine Lodge treaty, together with a transcription of the original treaty in full (Clark, *Lone Wolf vs. Hitchcock*, 115–22).

10. For a discussion of leasing, see Buntin, "Beginning of the Leasing"; Foreman, "Historical Background"; Cooper, "The Big Pasture."

11. Politically influential Texas cattlemen who had negotiated favorable grazing rights on reservation land were not pleased with this populist approach, which favored small farmers. They were able to bring pressure to bear that preserved four pieces of land under tribal ownership, and these continued to be leased out for grazing. Over time, these also were lost. See Buntin, "Beginning of the Leasing"; Foreman, "Historical Background"; Cooper, "The Big Pasture."

12. See Kracht, "Kiowa Religion," for a broad overview of the topic. Lassiter and colleagues, in *The Jesus Road*, specifically address the integration of Christianity.

13. The primary author who has explored the Kiowa boarding school experience is Clyde Ellis; see especially Ellis, *To Change Them Forever*, 93.

14. The reasons for the end of this ceremony were a subject of wide discussion in the Kiowa community in 1997 during an unsuccessful effort to revive the sun dance.

15. Kracht, "Kiowa Ghost Dance."

16. See Greene, *Silver Horn*, for detailed biographical information on Silver Horn.

17. The only Kiowa calendar I have seen that continues as late as this is the one kept by Ananti, which includes only sporadic entries during the 1940s; see appendix C.

18. Rev. Harry H. Treat, pastor of the Red Stone Baptist Indian Mission, published the newsletter *Home and School* for over twenty years, from 1913 until 1935. A chatty local report, it served to maintain communication between Kiowa families and children away at boarding schools. I learned of the newsletter from a Kiowa friend, Kenny Harragarra, whose family still has a few issues from the 1920s. A full series is available in the archives of the American Baptist Historical Society.

19. Mooney, MS 2531, vol. 7.

20. Silver Horn and Hauvahte were actually biologically closer than half-brothers, since their mothers were related. As was proper for a man of prominence, their father Agiati had three wives to keep his household in order and provide hospitality to anyone who came to

visit. As a man of good sense, he chose to marry sisters, who were more likely to work together happily than women who were unrelated. Information on their personal relationship comes from Silver Horn's eldest son, James Silverhorn, "Doris Duke Oral History Project," Tape 18.

21. The late tribal historian Linn Pauahty believed that the Kiowa had learned calendar keeping from the Plains Apache people, a closely affiliated tribe, historically known as the Kiowa-Apache but now incorporated as the Apache Tribe of Oklahoma (Pauahty, MS 7268).

22. Handwritten notes by Mooney appear on some of the sheets.

23. Sadly, the Little Bear calendar was lost when it was sent out for photography during production of Mooney's book (Mooney, Letter to Alfred Kroeber, February 10, 1903).

24. For biographical information on Quitone, see Nye, *Bad Medicine*, 32–34, 278, and Corwin, *Kiowa Indians*, 203–5.

25. Wilbur Sturtevant Nye (1898–1970) was a West Point graduate, army officer, and military historian, retiring from the army in 1954 with the rank of colonel. While posted at Fort Sill in the 1930s, he began research on southern Plains history, which he continued after his retirement, eventually publishing a series of books and articles about the fort and the Indians of the region. I have been unable to find any record that he published anything relating to the Quitone calendar. Brief additional information on George Hunt is published in Moffitt, "Notes on Indian History," 283.

26. Quoetone, "Doris Duke Oral History Project," Tape 245b, 1–2.

27. Quitone and Nye, Cat. no. 68.39.1–68.39.4.

28. Images of this calendar are available in SIRIS, the online database for the National Anthropological Archives, under the entry for Manuscript 2002-27.

29. Alice Marriott's papers are preserved in the Western History Collection of the University of Oklahoma library system. They contain very limited information on the three calendars that she published in *The Ten Grandmothers* (1945). The anecdotal information she includes in *Greener Fields* (1962) is more illuminating.

2. The Silver Horn Calendar

1. See Berlo, *Plains Indian Drawings*, for an overview of Plains drawings.

2. Scott, MS 2932, box 2.

3. Mooney, *Calendar History of the Kiowa Indians*, 421.

4. While many sources note name avoidance, they are vague as to how

long it extended. The clearest statement comes from a 1935 interview with Kintadl, Silver Horn's sister. According to her, ten years should elapse following a death before a name was used again (LaBarre et al., Students' Notes, 392).

5. A number of Lakota calendars and at least one Blackfoot record begin in the eighteenth century; see Greene and Thornton, eds., *Year the Stars Fell*.

3. The University of Oklahoma Calendar

1. Mooney, *Calendar History of the Kiowa Indians*, 426.

2. See Meadows, *Kiowa, Apache, and Comanche*, for a detailed history of the Kiowa warrior societies.

3. For a discussion of the tipi, a valued family heirloom that makes several appearances in the calendar, see Greene, "Tepee with Battle Pictures" and "Exploring the Three 'Little Bluffs,'" and Greene and Drescher, "Tipi with Battle Pictures."

4. Nye, *Carbine and Lance*, 36; Mayhall, *The Kiowa*, 200–202.

5. Greene, "Exploring the Three 'Little Bluffs,'" 228.

6. Mooney, *Calendar History of the Kiowa Indians*, 285.

7. For details of this treaty see Mooney, *Calendar History of the Kiowa Indians*, 181–86, and Clark, *Lone Wolf vs. Hitchcock*, 115–22.

8. The drawing is illustrated in Greene, *Silver Horn*, pl. 1b.

9. Nye, *Bad Medicine*, 228.

10. Ewers, *Murals in the Round*, 21.

11. Mooney, *Calendar History of the Kiowa Indians*, 163; Greene, *Silver Horn*, 129–31.

12. Wright, *Guide to Indian Tribes*, 189.

13. Mooney, *Calendar History of the Kiowa Indians*, 354; see also Buntin, "Beginning of the Leasing."

14. See Greene, *Silver Horn*, 132.

15. Kracht, "Kiowa Ghost Dance."

16. Mooney, *Calendar History of the Kiowa Indians*, 235.

17. Mooney, *Calendar History of the Kiowa Indians*, 226.

18. See Greene, "Exploring the Three 'Little Bluffs.'"

19. Ellis, *To Change Them Forever*, 93.

20. Nye, *Carbine and Lance*, 292–321.

21. Nye, *Bad Medicine*, 281.

22. See Richardson, *Law and Status*, for an extended discussion of Kiowa law.

23. Foreman, "Historical Background," 140.

24. Mooney, Letter to W. J. McGee, June 25, 1902.

25. Clark, *Lone Wolf vs. Hitchcock*, 89.

26. On feather decoration, see Greene, *Silver Horn*, 134; on agency opposition to the dance, see Kracht, "Kiowa Ghost Dance."

27. See NWS-NOAA, "Snyder, Oklahoma Tornado," for an online exhibit about the storm.

28. Mooney, MS 2531, vol. 2.

29. Quoted in Anonymous, *Mountain View*, 21.

30. Kiowa Agency Records [KA–IA], "Deaths," entry for September 8, 1906.

31. On Quanah's relationship to Silver Horn, see Silverhorn, "Doris Duke Oral History Project," Tape 18, 5–6. For a general biography of Quanah, see Hagan, *Quanah Parker*.

32. LaBarre et al., Students' Notes, 1026.

33. See Greene, "Tepee with Battle Pictures."

34. Corwin, "Delos K. Lonewolf, Kiowa."

35. Apekaum, "Autobiography of a Kiowa," 145. The Kiowa were caught in a debt system similar to that which Berthrong describes for neighboring tribes in *The Cheyenne and Arapaho Ordeal*.

36. Treat, *Home and School* 1, no. 5.

37. Meador, "Birth of Aviation."

38. Kracht, "Kiowa Religion," 833.

39. Kiowa Agency Records [KA–IA], "Deaths," entry for October 6, 1915.

40. Treat, *Home and School* 3, no. 9.

41. Treat, *Home and School* 3, no. 18.

42. Kracht, "Kiowa Religion," 844.

43. Treat, *Home and School* 4, no. 10.

44. Goodnight, *Old Texas, 1916*.

45. Treat, *Home and School* 4, no. 18.

46. Kracht, "Kiowa Religion," 854–56.

47. Apekaum, "Autobiography of a Kiowa," 5.

48. See Meadows, *Kiowa, Apache, and Comanche*, 122–23, on Kiowas serving during World War I.

49. Treat, *Home and School* 7, no. 12.

50. Treat, *Home and School* 9, no. 4.

51. Ewers, "A Crow Chief's Tribute," 30.

52. Treat, *Home and School* 9, no. 10.

53. Treat, *Home and School* 9, no. 4.

54. Treat, *Home and School* 9, nos. 21, 22.

55. Petersen, *Plains Indian Art*, 172.

56. Kracht, "Kiowa Religion," 857.

57. Kiowa Agency Records [KA–NARA], Heirship Dockets.

58. Corwin, "Delos K. Lonewolf, Kiowa," 436.

59. Treat, *Home and School* II, nos. 17, 20.

60. Anonymous, *Pioneering in Kiowa County*, 252–54.

61. Parks, pers. comm., 2007.

62. Kiowa Agency Records [KA–NARA], Heirship Dockets.

63. Scott, MS 2932.

64. Thoburn, "Peace Celebration"; Swett, "Sergeant I-See-O, Kiowa Indian Scout."

65. See Greene, *Silver Horn*, 178.

Bibliography

Anonymous. *Mountain View: 1899–1999, The First 100 Years.* Mountain View OK: Main Street Association, 1998.

———. *Pioneering in Kiowa County*, vol. 6. Hobart OK: Kiowa County Historical Society, 1982.

Berlo, Janet C. *Plains Indian Drawings, 1865–1935: Pages from a Visual History.* New York: Harry N. Abrams, 1996.

Berthrong, Donald J. *The Cheyenne and Arapaho Ordeal: Reservation and Agency Life in the Indian Territory, 1875–1907.* Norman: University of Oklahoma Press, 1976.

Boyd, Maurice. *Kiowa Voices*, vol. 1: *Ceremonial Dance, Ritual, and Song.* Fort Worth: Texas Christian University Press, 1981.

———. *Kiowa Voices*, vol. 2: *Myths, Legends, and Folktales.* Fort Worth: Texas Christian University Press, 1983.

Buntin, Martha. "Beginning of the Leasing of the Surplus Grazing Lands on the Kiowa and Comanche Reservation." *Chronicles of Oklahoma* 10, no. 3 (1932): 369–82.

Clark, Blue. *Lone Wolf vs. Hitchcock: Treaty Rights and Indian Law at the End of the Nineteenth Century.* Lincoln: University of Nebraska Press, 1999.

Cooper, Charles M. "The Big Pasture." *Chronicles of Oklahoma* 35, no. 2 (1957): 138–46.

Corwin, Hugh. "Delos K. Lonewolf, Kiowa." *Chronicles of Oklahoma* 39, no. 4 (1961): 433–36.

———. *The Kiowa Indians: Their History and Life Stories.* Lawton OK: Hugh Corwin, 1958.

Crawford, Isabel. *Kiowa: Story of a Blanket Indian Mission.* New York: Fleming H. Revell, 1915.

Donnelley, Robert G., ed. *Transforming Images: The Art of Silver Horn and*

His Successors. Chicago: David and Alfred Smart Museum of Art, University of Chicago, 2000.

Ellis, Clyde. *A Dancing People: Powwow Culture on the Southern Plains*. Lawrence: University of Kansas Press, 2003.

———. *To Change Them Forever: Indian Education at the Rainy Mountain Boarding School, 1893–1920*. Norman: University of Oklahoma Press, 1996.

Ewers, John C. "A Crow Chief's Tribute to the Unknown Soldier." *American West* 8, no. 6 (1971):30–35.

———. *Murals in the Round: Painted Tipis of the Kiowa and Kiowa-Apache Indians*. Washington: Smithsonian Institution, 1978.

Foreman, Grant. "Historical Background on the Kiowa-Comanche Reservation." *Chronicles of Oklahoma* 19, no. 2 (1941): 129–40.

Goodnight, Charles (producer). *Old Texas, 1916* (Motion picture DVD). United States: Lindley-Ockander International Television, 2004.

Greene, Candace S. "Changing Times, Changing Views: Silver Horn as a Bridge to Nineteenth- and Twentieth Century Kiowa Art." In *Transforming Images: The Art of Silver Horn and His Successors*, ed. Robert G. Donnelley (Chicago: David and Alfred Smart Museum of Art, University of Chicago, 2000), 15–25.

———. "Exploring the Three 'Little Bluffs' of the Kiowa." *Plains Anthropologist* 41, no. 157 (1996): 221–42.

———. "From Bison Robes to Ledgers: Changing Contexts in Plains Drawings." *European Review of Native American Studies* 18, no. 1 (2004): 21–29.

———. *Silver Horn: Master Illustrator of the Kiowas*. Norman: University of Oklahoma Press, 2001.

———. "Southern Plains Graphic Art before the Reservation." *American Indian Art Magazine* 22, no. 3 (1997): 44–53.

———. "The Tepee with Battle Pictures." *Natural History Magazine* 102, no. 10 (1993): 68–76.

Greene, Candace S., and Thomas Drescher. "The Tipi with Battle Pictures: The Kiowa Tradition of Intangible Property Rights." *Trademark Reporter* 84, no. 4 (1994): 418–33.

Greene, Candace S., and Russell Thornton, eds. *The Year the Stars Fell: Lakota Winter Counts at the Smithsonian*. Lincoln: University of Nebraska Press, 2007.

Hagan, William T. *Quanah Parker, Comanche Chief*. Norman: University of Oklahoma Press, 1993.

Hodge, Frederick, ed. *Handbook of American Indians North of Mexico*. 2 vols. Bureau of American Ethnology Bulletin 30. Washington: Smithsonian Institution, 1907.

Hume, C. Ross. "Historic Sites around Anadarko." *Chronicles of Oklahoma* 16, no. 4 (1938): 410–24.

Kavanagh, Thomas W. *Comanche Political History: An Ethnohistorical Perspective, 1706–1875.* Lincoln: University of Nebraska Press, 1996.

Isenberg, Andrew C. *The Destruction of the Bison: An Environmental History, 1750–1920.* Cambridge: Cambridge University Press, 2000.

Kracht, Benjamin. "The Kiowa Ghost Dance, 1894–1916: An Unheralded Revitalization Movement." *Ethnohistory* 39, no. 4 (1992): 452–77.

Lassiter, Luke Eric, Clyde Ellis, and Ralph Kotay. *The Jesus Road: Kiowas, Christianity, and Indian Hymns.* Lincoln: University of Nebraska Press, 2002.

Loughlin, Patricia. *Hidden Treasures of the American West: Muriel H. Wright, Angie Debo, and Alice Marriott.* Albuquerque: University of New Mexico Press, 2005.

Marriott, Alice. *Greener Fields.* Garden City NJ: Dolphin Books, Doubleday, 1962.

———. *The Ten Grandmothers: Epic of the Kiowas.* Norman: University of Oklahoma Press, 1945.

Maurer, Evan, ed. *Visions of the People: A Pictorial History of Plains Indian Life.* Minneapolis: Minneapolis Institute of Arts, 1992.

Mayhall, Mildred P. *The Kiowa.* Norman: University of Oklahoma Press, 1962.

Meador, Mitch. "Birth of Aviation: Air Squadron Arrived at Sill 90 Years Ago." *Lawton Constitution*, July 28, 2005, section B, p. 4.

Meadows, William C. *Kiowa, Apache, and Comanche Military Societies: Enduring Veterans, 1800 to the Present.* Austin: University of Texas Press, 1999.

Merrill, William, Marian K. Hannson, Candace S. Greene, and Frederick J. Reuss. *A Guide to the Kiowa Collections at the Smithsonian Institution.* Washington: Smithsonian Institution Press, 1997.

Methvin, J. J. "Reminiscences of Life among the Indians." *Chronicles of Oklahoma* 5, no. 2 (1927): 166–79.

Moffitt, James. "Notes on Indian History." *Chronicles of Oklahoma* 20, no. 3 (1942): 278–84.

Momaday, N. Scott. *The Names: A Memoir by N. Scott Momaday.* New York: Harper and Row, 1976.

Mooney, James. *Calendar History of the Kiowa Indians.* Bureau of American Ethnology, 17th Annual Report, 1895–96. Washington DC: Government Printing Office, 1898; reprint, Whitefish MT: Kessinger, 2007.

———. *The Ghost-Dance Religion and the Sioux Outbreak of 1890.* Bureau of American Ethnology, 14th Annual Report, 1892–93. Washington DC:

Government Printing Office, 1896; reprint, Lincoln: University of Nebraska Press, 1991.

Nye, Wilbur S. "The Annual Sundance of the Kiowa Indians." *Chronicles of Oklahoma* 12, no. 3 (1934): 340–58.

———. *Bad Medicine and Good: Tales of the Kiowa*. Norman: University of Oklahoma Press, 1962.

———. *Carbine and Lance: The Story of Old Fort Sill*. Norman: University of Oklahoma Press, 1943.

———. *Plains Indian Raiders: The Final Phases of Warfare from the Arkansas to the Red River*. Norman: University of Oklahoma Press, 1968.

Petersen, Karen D. *Plains Indian Art from Fort Marion*. Norman: University of Oklahoma Press, 1971.

Richardson, Jane. *Law and Status among the Kiowa Indians*. New York: J. J. Augustin Publisher, 1940; reprint, Seattle: University of Washington Press, 1966.

Swanton, John R. "Names and Naming." In *Handbook of American Indians North of Mexico.*, ed. Frederick Webb Hodge, 2 vols., Bureau of American Ethnology Bulletin 30 (Washington: Smithsonian Institution, 1907), 2: 16–18.

Swett, Morris. "Sergeant I-See-O, Kiowa Indian Scout." *Chronicles of Oklahoma* 13, no. 3 (1935): 341–54.

Thoburn, Joseph B. "The Peace Celebration at Medicine Lodge." *Chronicles of Oklahoma* 5, no. 4 (1927): 397–99.

Thomson, Louise. "A Cross-Section in the Life of a Missionary Teacher among the Indians." *Chronicles of Oklahoma* 17, no. 3 (1929): 328–32.

Treat, Harry H. *Home and School*, vols. 1–23. Papers of Rev. Harry H. Treat, MP 94. American Baptist Historical Society Archives, Valley Forge PA, 1913–35.

Wright, Muriel. *Guide to Indian Tribes of Oklahoma*. Norman: University of Oklahoma Press, 1977.

Unpublished Sources

Apekaum, Charley. "Autobiography of a Kiowa." Recorded by Weston LaBarre, Anadarko OK. Papers of Weston LaBarre, National Anthropological Archives, Smithsonian Institution, 1936.

Kiowa Agency Records [KA–IA]. "Deaths." Microfilm roll 52, entry for September 8, 1906. Indian Archives, Oklahoma Historical Society, n.d.

———. "Deaths." Microfilm roll 52, entry for October 6, 1915. Indian Archives. Oklahoma Historical Society, n.d.

Kiowa Agency Records [KA–NARA]. Heirship Dockets, 1918–1933. Kiowa #20. Record Group 75: Records of the Bureau of Indian Affairs,

1793–1989, Kiowa Indian Agency. National Archives and Records Administration, Southwest Region, Fort Worth TX, n.d.

Kracht, Benjamin R. "Kiowa Religion: An Ethnohistorical Analysis of Ritual Symbolism, 1832–1987." PhD diss., Southern Methodist University, 1989.

LaBarre, Weston, et al. Typescript of Students' Notes. [Combined notes of Wm. Bascom, Donald Collier, W. LaBarre, Bernard Mishkin, and Jane Richardson of the 1935 Laboratory of Anthropology Field School, led by A. Lesser.] Papers of Weston LaBarre, National Anthropological Archives, Smithsonian Institution, 1935.

Mooney, James. Letter to W. J. McGee, June 25, 1902. BAE LR. National Anthropological Archives, Smithsonian Institution, 1902.

———. Letter to Alfred Kroeber, February 10, 1903. Papers of Alfred L. Kroeber, Correspondence Incoming. Bancroft Library, University of California, Berkeley, 1903.

———. Manuscript 2531, vol. 2. James Mooney notebooks principally regarding Kiowa, Cheyenne, and Arapaho shield and tipi designs. National Anthropological Archives, Smithsonian Institution, n.d.

———. Manuscript 2531, vol. 7. James Mooney notebooks principally regarding Kiowa, Cheyenne, and Arapaho shield and tipi designs. National Anthropological Archives, Smithsonian Institution, n.d.

NWS-NOAA. "The Snyder, Oklahoma Tornado of 10 May 1905." National Weather Service Forecast Office. http://www.srh.noaa.gov/oun/wxevents/19050510/ (accessed February 16, 2007).

Parks, Douglas. Personal communication, 2007.

Pauahty, Linn. Manuscript 7268. Calendar, with interpretation. National Anthropological Archives, Smithsonian Institution, 1977.

Quoetone, Guy. "Doris Duke Oral History Project," Tape 245b. University of Oklahoma, Western History Collection, 1968.

Quitone, Jimmy, and W. S. Nye. Cat. no. 68.39.1–68.39.4. Fort Sill Museum Archives, n.d.

Scott, Hugh L. Manuscript 2932, Papers of Hugh L. Scott. National Anthropological Archives, Smithsonian Institution, n.d.

Silverhorn, James. "Doris Duke Oral History Project," Tape 18. University of Oklahoma, Western History Collection, 1967.

Index

Page references in *italics* indicate a figure, illustration, or photograph.

Silver Horn's NAA calendar written for, 17
moons, *184*, 185
Mountain View OK, 156
Mount Scott, 15, *140*, 141, 143, 161, 233
Much Fire Smoke, Iseeo, 21, 181, 187, 196, 199
Museum of the American Indian, 20

NAA Calendar. *See* National Anthropological
    Archives (NAA) Silver Horn Calendar
names, avoidance, 34, 121
National Anthropological Archives (NAA), xvii
National Anthropological Archives (NAA)
    Silver Horn Calendar: 1828: Pipe Dance
    Kado, *45*; 1829: "Ton-he Gado, possibly
    Ton-hen Pa, Sand Creek of Colorado"
    summer, 45, 198; 1833: "Kodalta," 48, 196;
    1837–38: Pa-yia killed by Cheyenne winter,
    53; 1838: summer camp on Wolf Creek;
    Cheyenne revenge attack, 53, *53*; 1840:
    smallpox Kado at Guadal Doha/Red Bluff,
    19, 57; 1842–43: Heap of Bears killed winter,
    19, 59; 1844–45: first time corral used for
    horses, 63; 1845: Stone Neck/Necklace died
    Kado, 63; 1845–46: Thunder Boy killed
    winter, 63; 1846: measles Kado, 65; 1848–49:
    ice breaks up and piles in gorge winter,
    67; 1849: cholera epidemic Kado, 69; 1850:
    Bon-ha Gado, 69; 1852: Mexican soldiers
    killed, 73; 1854: White Bear receives lance
    from Black Bear, 75; 1854–55: Likes Enemies
    killed winter, 75, *75*; 1855–56: "pipe bearer"
    took a scalp, 77; 1857–58: spotted horses
    stolen from camp, 79; 1860: Tenebati killed,
    83; 1861–62: Tadalkop/sickness winter,
    85; 1868: Without Horn killed Kado, 95;
    1872–73: Hauvahte's striped tipi burned,
    101; 1876–77: man fell from horse and rode
    a buffalo, 107; 1880: Big Bow died, 111;
    1880–81: Tonaka's (Turtle's) dance, *112*, 113;
    1882–83: Bag shot himself winter, 115; 1883:
    Green Necklace killed by Little Bow, 115;
    1886: Big Bow killed white horse thief, 119,
    119; 1886–87: young man committed suicide,
    121; 1887: acorn-laden tree Kado, 121; 1888:
    medicine man bringing back buffalo,
    123, *123*; 1889–90: Kiowa friendship with
    Comanches, 127; 1890–91: Sitting Bull visits
    Kiowa, 128, *128*; 1891–92: Troop L activities,
    131, *131*; 1893: Big fat boy here on Fourth,
    132, 133; 1893–94: Badai's brother died (third
    Little Bluff), 133–34; 1894: Inkinish (Caddo)
    killed by robbers, 137; 1895: death of Talo-ti,
    137; 1896: Ooti and Gets down and Dies
    with Him ran away; payment at Rainy
    Mountain, 139; 1896–97: White Feather
    shot, 139; 1898: Poncas visit Kiowa, *140*,

141; 1898–99: First railroad to cross Washita
    River, 143; 1899–1900: Wooden Lance
    whipped, 143; 1901: horse wounded, 145;
    1903: payment at Rainy Mountain winter,
    151; 1903: Silver Horn's son born in summer,
    151; calendar Manuscript 2002-27, 22, *23*,
    243n28; elaborate drawings in, 18; Mooney's
    studies of, 17–18, 40
National Cowboy and Western Heritage
    Museum (Oklahoma City OK), xiii
National Museum of Natural History
    (Washington DC), viii
National Museum of the American Indian
    (Washington DC), xiii, 238
Native American art, publications on, ix
Native American Church, during reservation
    period, 13
Navajo, 211, 215
Nez Perce: hairstyle of, *114*, 115; shell gorgets
    worn by, *114*, 115; visits to Kiowa, 14, *114*, 115
Nichols, Lt. Maury, *132*, 133
Nixon, Betty, 165
No Arm, Tsodalhente, *86*, 87, 198
No Moccasins, 103, 107, 213
North Canadian River, 47, 87
Nye, Wilbur, 22, 141, 243n25

Oak Creek, 217
Ogeneski, Stephanie, xvii
Oheltoint, Charlie Buffalo, 16, 75, 105, 165,
    197, 198
Oh-oh-da, 139
Ohoma Dance, 170, *172*, 174
Ohoma Society, 13, 174, 197
Oklahoma: Anadarko, *7*, 105, 133, 139, 155;
    Babbs Switch fire, *184*, 185; Greer County,
    103, 109; Lawton, 159; mission churches in,
    155; nineteenth-century Kiowa territory, 6,
    7; Snyder cyclone in, *154*, 155, *155*, 245n27;
    Stecker, 16
Oklahoma History Center, xiii, 239
Oklahoma History Society, xvi
Old Male Wolf, 197
Old Man Wagon, *92*, 93
Omaha, as enemy of Kiowa, 75
On the Arrow, 69, *69*
One Who Carries a Pack of Meat from the
    Buffalo's Lower Leg, Tebodal, 79, 119, 198
One Wing, 87
On the Gun, On Top of the Rifle, Hawzipta,
    196, 199; death of, *82*, 83; elected to Kiowa
    business committee, *168*, 169; trip to
    Washington, *172*, 173
Ooti, 139
Opler, Morris E., xii
oral histories: of Great Plains, 1; of Kiowa, 1

Red Neck, 207

Red River, *7*, 105

Red Sleeve, *64*, 65

Red Stone: church, *154*, 155; community of, 16, 17, 174, 181

Red Stone Baptist Mission, 17, 242n18

red wool, *64*, 65

Ricciardelli, A. F., xii

Rio Grande River, 71

Rising Wolf, 213

Roberts, Nelia Mae, viii, xvi

Roberts Indian Store collection, viii, ix, xvi

Rocky Mountains, 6

Roman Nose, 185

Rough or Gnarled Tail, Snapping Turtle, 198, 199; as medicine man, *112*, 113; shot a man, *130*, 131; stole a woman, *116*, 117, *130*

Rowell, Charles, calendar keeping by, 238

Running Calf, 124

Saddle Mountain Mission, 181

sage, 79, *172*, 173

sahe, green or blue, 115, 197

sai-guat, winter marks, 1, 2, 197

Saint Augustine FL, 105

Saint Patrick Mission, 179

Sam Noble Oklahoma Museum of Natural History (SNOMNH) (Norman OK): Department of Archaeology, xii; Department of Ethnology, xi, xii, xiii; Department of Native American Languages, xii; Hall of the People of Oklahoma, xii–xiii; mission of, vii, viii–ix, xv; Roberts Indian Store collection, viii, ix, xvi

Sand Creek, massacre at, 45

Sand Son, 121

Sankadote, 141, 233

Satank, Setangya, Sitting Bear, *64*, 65, *65*, 197, 199

Saunkeah, Jasper, 179

Save America's Treasures, ix

scalp dance, 83

scalps, *98*, 99, *110*, 111, 133, *172*, 173

Scalps on Sleeves, 133

Schmitt, Karl, xii

Scott, Hugh L.: anthropological interests of, 4, 20–21; calendar studies by, 4; command of Troop L, 131, 187; purchase of Little Bluff calendar, 20–21, 131; text/notes on Little Bluff Calendar, 21, 203–19

screw worm medicine, 89

Seipote, Traveling in Rain, as Silver Horn's mother, 15, 197

Se-se Pa, Arrowhead River, Arkansas River, 67, 197, 224

Setangya, Satank, Sitting Bear, *64*, 65, *65*, 197, 198

Set-daya-ite, Plenty Bears, Many Bears, 197, 198; death of, 115; as Taime keeper, 95, 107; war party led by, 93

Settan, Little Bear, calendar keeping by, 3, 4, 21, 197, 199, 239

sheep, issued to Kiowa, *104*, 105, 214, 229

shell ornaments, 60, 61, *114*, 115

shields: capture of, 47; designs on, 18, 47, *122*, 124

silver dollars: compensation for stolen horses, *119*; as grass money payment, *116*, 117, *130*, 131; as treaty payment, *138*, 139, 145, *160*, 161

Silver Horn, 16; artistic skills of, 5–6; birth of, 2, 15, 83; calendar keeping by, vii, 1, 2, 5–6, 17, 239; dance circle painted on deer skin, 163; death of, 15, *154*, 155; enlistment in Troop L, 12, 73, 131, 179; "eye sore" trachoma of, *150*, 151, 161; on Feather Dance, 13; as Haungooah, 5–6, 15, 147, 151, *158*, 159, 179, *188*, 189, 196, 199; as Hawgone, 147, 151; Kiowa signatures of, *146*, 147, *150*, 151, *154*, 155, *188*, 189, 199; military service of, 12, 73, 131, 179; Mooney's employment of, 17, 147; as Peyote man, 13; as religious leader, 15; reservation experiences of, 15; silversmith works of, 17. *See also* National Anthropological Archives (NAA) Silver Horn Calendar

Silverhorn, James, 20, 151, 243n20

Silverhorn, Max, 18, 151

Sitting Bear, Setangya, Satank, *64*, 65, *65*, 197, 199, 228

Sitting Bull, 128, *128*, 218

Sitting in the Saddle, Tau-ankia, *102*, 103, *103*, 198

Six Moons, *184*, 185

sketchbooks, 4

Skye, William, 235

Sloping Hair, Adalhabakia, *58*, 59, 196

smallpox epidemics: in Hauvahte Calendar, 55, 145, 223; in Kiowa populations, 2; in Lakota winter counts, 85; in Little Bluff Calendar, 55, 85; in NAA Calendar, 55, 57, 85; in OU Calendar, *54*, 55, *56*, 57, *84*, 85; in Quitone Calendar, 55, 85; as Tadalkop, 85, 197

Smithsonian Institution, Anthropology Collections and Archives Program, xvii

snakes, *166*, 167, *180*, 181, *184*, 185

Snapping Turtle, Tonaka, 199; as medicine man, *112*, 113; shot a man, *130*, 131; stole a woman, *116*, 117, 131

Snyder cyclone, *154*, 155, *155*, 165, 245n27

Soule, William S., 65, *65*, 97, *103*

Southern Plains Museum (Anadarko OK), 238

Spivey, Towana, xvi

Split Boys, 15

Spotted Horse, *180*, 181

spotted horses, 2, *78*, 79, *84*, 85, 210, 211, 226

Utes: captured by Kiowa, 77, 225; Kiowa battles with, *88*, 89–90, 93, 95; Taime stolen by, 95; as U.S. Army scouts, 89, 90

Waldo, James, Kogaitadal, 173. *See also* Poor Elk.
Walnut Creek, 55
wand, tufted, *114*, 115
warbonnets. *See* feather bonnets/warbonnets
Ward, Mary Jane, xvi–xvii
Ware, Harry, 239
Ware, Lewis, 179
war gear, 4
warrior societies/*yapahe*, 195, 198; Dog Soldiers in, 55; Koitsenko, 67, *94*, 95, 195, 197; as source of dances, 13
Washita, Battle of the, 97
Washita River, *54*, 55, *118*, 119, 143, 227
Wehlge, Bill, xvii
Western Oklahoma Indian Baptist Association, 181
Western Sioux: calendar traditions of, 3; warbonnets of, 97
White Bear, *97*; brother of, *136*, 137; bugle frightening Kiowa camp, 97; lance/*zebat* of, *74*, 75, *102*, 103; red tipi of, *88*, *89*; release from prison, 103
White Buffalo, Bobby Hill, 238
White Buffalo, Konad, 199; death of, *184*, 185; Fourth of July dance sponsored by, 170; pipe received from Wichitas, *98*, 99, 228; in Red Stone community, 16; right to *zebat*/lance, 75; trip to Washington, *172*, 173
White Cowbird, 103, *108*, 109
White Feather, *138*, 139
White Fox, 143
White Horse: capturing Navajo boy, *5*; death of, *132*, 133, 232; imprisonment of, 133; as Ohoma Society leader, 13, *172*, 174

White Horse, Dorothy, 174
White Horse, Martha, 174
White Man, 214
White Polecat, 143
White Skunk, 143
whooping cough, *78*, 79, 225
Wichita: adoption ceremony, 45; Pawnee visit with, 101; pipe given to White Buffalo, *98*, 99; reservation territory of, 55, 105
Wichita Agency, 105
Wichita Mountains, *140*, 141
winter marks, *sai-guat*, 1, 2, 197, 199
Without Horn, *94*, 95
Wolf Appearing, 199
Wolf Coming Up Over a Hill, 213
Wolf Creek, 47, *52*, 53, 69
Wolf Emerging, 199
Wolf Hair, 51
Wolf Lying Down, 79, *80*, 81, 199, 206
Wolf Tail, Jimmy Quitone, calendar keeping by, 22, 24, 45, 197, 199, 238–39
Wolf Teat, Gui-aza, 45, 196
Wooden Lance, Ahpeahtone, *138*, 139, 143, 177, 196
Wooden Lance, Lon, 177
World War I, Kiowa soldiers serving in, 175, 245n48
Wounded Knee, 113

yapahe. See warrior societies/*yapahe*
Yellowstone River, 6

zebat/lance, *74*, 75, *102*, 103, 198
Zotom, Paul, 181–82